WITHDRAWN

HUMAN INQUIRY

PATRICK & BEATRICE HAGGERTY LIBRARY
MOUNT MARY COLLEGE
MILWAUKEE, WISCONSIN 53222

HUMAN INQUIRY

A Sourcebook of New Paradigm Research

Edited by

Peter Reason
Centre for the Study of Organizational Change and Development,
University of Bath

and

John Rowan
Independent Consultant, London

JOHN WILEY & SONS
Chichester · New York · Brisbane · Toronto

Copyright © 1981 by John Wiley & Sons Ltd.

Reprinted November 1985
Reprinted June 1987
Reprinted July 1988
Reprinted June 1989
Reprinted June 1990

All rights reserved.

No part of this book may be reproduced by any means,
nor transmitted, nor translated into a machine language
without the written permission of the publisher.

British Library Cataloguing in Publication Data:

Human inquiry.
1. Social psychology
I. Reason, Peter   II. Rowan, John
301.1   HM251   80-41585

ISBN 0 471 27935 8 (Cloth)
ISBN 0 471 27936 6 (Paper)

Photoset by Photo-Graphics, Yarcombe, Honiton, Devon.
Printed in Great Britain by
Courier International Ltd, Tiptree, Essex

00.11
918
981

Table of Contents

Foreword   xi

PHILOSOPHY

Chapter One   The positivist-empiricist approach and its
                   alternative
                   Rom Harré   3

Chapter Two   Philosophical basis for a new paradigm
                   John Heron   19

Chapter Three   *The Subjective Side of Science,* by Ian
                   Mitroff
                   Editorial appreciation   37

Chapter Four   *Methodological Approaches to Social
                   Science,* by Ian Mitroff and Ralph
                   Kilmann
                   Editorial appreciation   43

Chapter Five   The troubled fish: barriers to dialogue
                   John Southgate and *Rosemary Randall*   53

Chapter Six   The general and the unique in psycho-
                       logical science
                       G. W. Allport   63

Chapter Seven   *From Anxiety to Method in the
                       Behavioural Sciences,* by George Devereux
                       Editorial appreciation   77

Chapter Eight   *The Psychology of Science,* by Abraham
                       Maslow
                       Editorial appreciation   83

Chapter Nine   A dialectical paradigm for research
                       John Rowan   93

Chapter Ten   On making sense
                       John Rowan and *Peter Reason*   113

                       METHODOLOGY

Chapter Eleven   Why educational research has been so
                       uneducational: the case for a new model of
                       social science based on collaborative
                       inquiry
                       William R. Torbert   141

Chapter Twelve   Experiential research methodology
                       John Heron   153

Chapter Thirteen   *The Leaves of Spring,* by Aaron Esterson
                       Editorial appreciation   167

Chapter Fourteen   A model for action research
                       Nevitt Sanford   173

Chapter Fifteen   *Patterns of Discovery in the Social
                       Sciences,* by Paul Diesing
                       Editorial appreciation   183

Chapter Sixteen   Personal construct theory and research
                       method
                       Donald Bannister   191

Chapter Seventeen   The interviewing process re-examined
                        Fred Massarik   201

Chapter Eighteen   Heuristic research
                        Clark Moustakas   207

Chapter Nineteen   Illuminative evaluation
                        Malcolm Parlett   219

Chapter Twenty   Endogenous research: rationale
                        Magoroh Maruyama   227

Chapter Twenty-One   Issues of validity in new paradigm research
                        Peter Reason and *John Rowan*   239

EXAMPLES

Chapter Twenty-Two   Sharing the research work: participative
                        research and its role demands
                        Max Elden   253

Chapter Twenty-Three   Endogenous research: the prison project
                        Magoroh Maruyama   267

Chapter Twenty-Four   Culture and development in the Bagamoyo
                        District of Tanzania
                        Marja-Liisa Swantz   283

Chapter Twenty-Five   Dialogue as inquiry and intervention
                        Rajesh Tandon   293

Chapter Twenty-Six   Participative research in a factory
                        L. Dave Brown and *Robert E. Kaplan*   303

Chapter Twenty-Seven   *Personality Development in College*, by
                        Peter Madison
                        Editorial appreciation   315

Chapter Twenty-Eight   An exploration of the dialectics of two-
                        person relationships
                        Peter Reason   319

Chapter Twenty-Nine   A collaborative inquiry into voluntary
                           metropolitan desegregation
                           William R. Torbert   333

Chapter Thirty   Doing dialogical research
                           Rosemary Randall and *John Southgate*   349

Chapter Thirty-One   A practical example of a dialectical
                           approach to educational research
                           Jack Whitehead   363

Chapter Thirty-Two   From ethogeny to endogeny: how
                           participants in research projects can end up
                           doing action research on their own
                           awareness
                           David Sims   373

Chapter Thirty-Three   Mid-career change: reflections upon the
                           development of a piece of research and the
                           part it has played in the development of
                           the researcher
                           Audrey Collin   385

Chapter Thirty-Four   Making sense as a personal process
                           Judi Marshall   395

Chapter Thirty-Five   One researcher's self-questioning
                           Stephen I. Rosen   401

DIRECTIONS

Chapter Thirty-Six   Implementing new paradigm research: a
                           model for training and practice
                           Shulamit Reinharz   415

Chapter Thirty-Seven   Empirical, behavioural, theoretical, and
                           attentional skills necessary for collaborative
                           inquiry
                           William R. Torbert   437

Chapter Thirty-Eight   The democratization of research in adult
                           and non-formal education
                           Budd L. Hall   447

Chapter Thirty-Nine   Women's perspectives: research as re-vision
                         Helen Callaway   457

Chapter Forty   Funding research: practice and politics
                         Stephen Fineman   473

Afterword   485

References   493

Index   513

Foreword

This book is about human inquiry. It is about people exploring and making sense of human action and experience. It arose from discussions within the New Paradigm Research Group, which was formed in London in 1977 to discuss and develop ways of going about research which were *alternatives* to orthodox approaches, alternatives which would do justice to the humanness of all those involved in the research endeavour. As we discussed the theory of research, and as we looked at the actual research projects which group members were doing, we realized that while there were lots of ideas around about how to do research differently, and while there was lots of work actually going on, this was all scattered. It seemed to us that there *is* an emerging 'new paradigm' for research, which is being developed by all sorts of people in all sorts of fields all over the world, but there was no place where all these ideas and methods and actual examples were gathered; no place where a would-be new paradigm researcher could turn where all this was presented in some sort of systematic manner. Hence this volume, a *sourcebook* for new paradigm research, for psychologists, social psychologists, sociologists, economists, political scientists, anthropologists, psychiatrists, educationalists, for all those who engage in human inquiry.

Books about research tend to fall into three categories. There are those which spend a page or two on theory, ending with a statement that the experimental method is what it is all about really, and from that point on turn into books of applied statistics, or cookbooks for often-used methods. Then there are those which accept that the experimental method isn't everything, and discuss 'softer' methods such as survey research or participant observation; these often seem to regret that the experiment, the method of 'real science', cannot often be used in the behavioural sciences; they often accept, at least tacitly, the positivist assumptions and language of orthodox method. And then there is a third kind, which criticize orthodox methods, go into great philosophical discourse about what is wrong with them, tell you exactly how and why they are inadequate — but never tell you what to do instead.

This book is different: it *does* tell you what to do instead. The ideas and approaches which our contributors are offering are based on a careful consideration of the nature of human experience and action, and also on the nature of the inquiry process itself as a particular form of human endeavour. This book links the theory with the approach, and then goes on to show some examples of how this approach may actually work out in practice.

One of our central concerns in preparing this book has been to become clear about how the kind of work we are talking about here is situated in relation to orthodox research method. At first, we wanted to see our work as a total synthesis of research methodology, including traditional methods, but also including some important things which these left out. This view is particularly represented in John Rowan's thinking, as can be seen in his chapter in this book. But the trouble with this stance was that it was a bit flat, a bit low on energy, and overly diplomatic: if felt as though, in trying to be cool and calm and rational about research, we were denying something of ourselves. We certainly did not *feel* like exponents of a cool, balanced synthesis. When we came to examine what we were saying, and the way we were saying it, and how it came across to others (maybe *especially* how it came across to others), it became more and more obvious that we weren't merely being critical of the dominant place accorded to the standard textbook version of the scientific method — we were actively opposed to it. Through our balanced cool appraisal there comes an undercurrent of hatred and horror about what traditional research does to those it studies, those who do the research, and about the dreadful rubbish that is sometimes put forward as scientific knowledge.

So maybe our work must be seen as directly in *opposition* to orthodox work, a kind of antithesis, if that sort of language helps. But if this is true then we are in trouble, because as dialectical thinking shows, to be opposed to something is still to be bound to it. If we were simply *against* orthodox research, we would not be saying anything new, and we could easily be seen as simply 'anti-science'.

We can get some further illumination from the Hegelian thinking outlined later in this book (see Chapter 10). We can see *naive inquiry* as the starting point for the whole process. This is the kind of day-to-day thinking which we all start with, and which has been researched a lot in recent years: what information is looked for when decisions are made? how are data used to build up impressions of the world, and how to act in it? This kind of inquiry is of course very prone to error, the error of our biases and prejudices, of our anxieties, the error which arises from the pressures for group conformity, and so on. But it also has a lot of very good qualities, because it is involved, committed, relevant, intuitive; above all it is *alive*. So this kind of naive inquiry is a very important part of our humanity, it is what we all start with, and we lose a lot if we try to throw it out altogether.

But this is what so-called objective research does: in order to get away from the subjectivity and error of naive inquiry, the whole apparatus of experimental method, quasi-experimental method, statistical significance, dependent and independent variables, and so on, is set up. While this does counter some of the problems of naive inquiry, it also kills off everything it comes into contact with, so what we are left with is dead knowledge. What we are building in new paradigm research is an approach to inquiry which *is* a systematic, rigorous search for truth, but which does not kill off all it touches: we are looking for a way of inquiry which can be loosely called *objectively subjective* (see Figure 1). The new paradigm is a synthesis of naive inquiry and orthodox research, a synthesis which is very much opposed to the antithesis it supersedes.

There are some aspects of orthodoxy we would like to hold onto and even to urge more strongly. One is the idea of making clear where one is coming from in taking a particular view; the traditional way of doing this is to give references to previous work, but we think it is also desirable to give details of political standpoint, current work and relationships, general way of being in the world or whatever. Another one is the idea of acknowledging our intellectual debts; the traditional way of doing this is to give references to previous work again, but very often nothing that is more than 5 years old — we are happy to acknowledge people who were at work in the 1930s, or the early 1900s, or the seventeenth century, or in ancient times, if they had something to say that was relevant. A most important one is the basic idea of systematic checkable inquiry; and again we go further, and would want to include the earlier and later parts of the inquiry into the process, writing up these parts of the procedure with as much love and attention as normally given to the main central part of the investigation. Another one again is the idea of searching the literature and finding out what has already been done on a given topic area; but we would advocate a wider look than is usual, considering plays, novels, works of philosophy and theology, history books and so forth, as well as multidisciplinary searches within the social sciences.

But there is a great deal of orthodoxy which we do oppose, and which we believe is very open to criticism. Let us very briefly look at some of the things we object to.

Model of the person.   People are seen as isolable from their normal social contexts, as units to be moved into research designs, manipulated, and moved out again. People are seen as alienated and self-contained, stripped of all that gives their action meaning, and in this way they are trivialized.

Positivism.   The whole language of 'operational definitions', 'dependent and independent variables', and so forth is highly suspect. It assumes that people can be reduced to a set of variables which are somehow equivalent across persons and across situations, which doesn't make much sense to us.

Reductionism.   Studying variables rather than persons or groups or communities is a flight from understanding in depth, a flight from knowing human phenomena as wholes. It means that the person, group, community *as such* is never known.

Reification.   Processes are continually turned into things. Test results are continually turned into things. People are continually turned into things. None of this is philosophically defensible, and a lot of it is morally indefensible too.

Quantophrenia.   There is too much measurement going on. Some things which are numerically precise are not true; and some things which are not numerical are true. Orthodox research produces results which are statistically significant but humanly insignificant; in human inquiry it is much better to be deeply interesting than accurately boring.

Testing.   Intelligence tests and other tests of aptitude and personality are culturally biased and are used in unfair ways. There can be no fair tests within an unfair society.

Deception.   There is too much lying going on. Unnecessary withholding of information comes naturally to many orthodox researchers. There is an arrogance about this which does not commend itself. Research is a game which two or more can play.

Debriefing.   There is an assumption that a bad experience can somehow be wiped out by a brief and superficial explanation. But experience cannot be removed in that way. We should not inflict harm on people in the first place; good research means never having to say you are sorry.

Contamination.   Orthodox research tries to eliminate real life, but it cannot do so. Researchers give off all sorts of messages in all kinds of ways. They try to direct scenes on the research stage, but they are actually part of the play. The eye-blink reflex is natural, but measuring it is a social situation.

Sampling.   Large messages are extracted from small samples. Broad generalizations are made from unrepresentative bases. Old paradigm research often breaks its own rules in this area, quite regularly and shamelessly.

Detachment.   Researchers actually try to know as little as possible about the phenomenon under study — it might affect the results if they knew too much. This is exactly the opposite of an approach which could do justice to human action.

Conservatism.   Because of its lack of interest in the real social context, old paradigm research continually gets co-opted by those who want to prop up those who run the existing system. It studies those at the bottom while holding up its hands for money to those at the top. Thus in fact it serves to keep those at the bottom right there, and those at the top there.

Bigness.   Researchers in the old mode are continually asking for bigger and better instruments, bigger and better samples, bigger and better premises, bigger and better travelling expenses. This turns research into big business, and makes it more likely to be the servant of those who can afford to pay big money: it answers *their* questions.

Low utilization.   It is often remarked that large organizations pay for more research than they need, and then use only a tiny proportion of it. Sometimes questions are put to confirm decisions which have already been made. Because the whole process is alienated, there are few connections and very little commitment, and the people who receive the report may indeed be very different from those who commissioned it.

Language.   Research reports are written for the expert, and have heavy constraints on the way they have to be written up for journal publication. The effect is to mystify the public, hiding common sense notions actually being employed. Another effect is that conformity is rewarded more highly than creativity.

Pressures.   Journal publication policies and funding policies of grant-awarding bodies put severe pressure on for safe, respectable research. Fads come in from time to time and offer a band-waggon to climb upon. Researchers are continually short of time and funds, continually looking for projects which mean a minimum of disturbance to the even tenor of their ways. Research gets more and more specialized, less and less to do with anything real.

Determinism. Old paradigm research holds to a determinist model, where the independent variable coerces the dependent variable into performing correctly. Belief in determinism leads to the setting up of coercive (master-slave) relations in the laboratory, where there is an alienated relationship between the experimenter and the subject.

Scientific fairy-tale. Textbooks which have a chapter on the scientific method have various ideas about what this includes, but all of them are equally dogmatic about the three or four points they mention. What they put forward, however, is a storybook image, which does not correspond with the way in which science is actually carried on. In real science there are norms and counternorms: for example, in real science it is often considered highly praiseworthy to be unwilling to change one's opinions in the light of the latest piece of evidence; lack of humility is highly valued; bias is freely acknowledged; there is a lot of interest in how discoveries might be applied; there is a great deal of emphasis on the importance of intuitive judgement. So the textbook versions falsify science, and dominate education.

So much for the negative case. We are not going to elaborate it further because these arguments have been made many times and are easily available; all these separate points taken together add up to a powerful indictment (Israel and Tajfel, 1972; P. Brown, 1973; Joynson, 1974; Kamin, 1974; Heather, 1976; Argyris, 1968a; Friedlander, 1968; Bass, 1974).

What can we say more positively? if we are not coming from the old places, where are we coming from? The roots of the new paradigm lie widely within the behavioural sciences, and in every particular discipline there have been researchers who have been developing and using alternative approaches for many years. Thus while we are critical of orthodox psychology, we are strongly influenced by humanistic psychology, which offers a thought-out stance towards human beings, their experience and their actions, their origins and their potential, as exemplified in work of people like Maslow (Chapter 8). We are also influenced by the idea of the person as scientist which was the basis of George Kelly's work (Bannister and Fransella, 1980), although we are at times appalled at what orthodox research has done with this idea. And while research in psychology has usually been orthodox, we do see as valuable the vast array of ideas and knowledge which has come from the clinical work of people like Rogers (1968), Laing (1960, 1967), Jung (1964), Sullivan (1953, 1964), and Bion (1968), indeed going right back to Freud. This tradition of clinical exploration is clearly one of the forebears of the new paradigm. Particularly important for research method is the knowledge gained about the workings of the unconscious, and the way in which unconscious forces affect the investigator as well as the investigated (Devereux, Chapter 7).

Similarly in sociology and anthropology, approaches such as phenomenology, ethnomethodology, and participant observation, while not totally beyond reproach, at their best show that a researcher may get to grips with the messiness and confusion of everyday life with people and emerge with some reasonably valid understandings.

We have also been influenced by 'applied' behavioural science. Kurt Lewin was the first to coin the term 'action research', and interdisciplinary schools such as organizational behaviour and education have been using this term for many years under a number of different guises (see Sanford's chapter in this volume). There is also a huge body of research and experience in the area of group work and organization development, in which people like Argyris (1971), Bradford *et al.* (1964), and Bennis *et al.* (1969) have been involved, and which often uses an approach to process consultation (Schein, 1969) which can be seen as an informal research cycle. And experiential learning workshops such as T-groups were originally conceived as 'laboratory education' (Benne *et al.,* 1975) in which people could learn about their behaviour in groups through personal inquiry and experiment; certainly an enormous amount of our understanding of interpersonal and small-group behaviour has come from this approach. Charles Hampden-Turner (1970) has spelt out the way in which learning in the T-group and social research can be seen as examples of the same process.

Another important strand which must not be underestimated is Marxism. It is a strange fact that most of the American literature totally ignores Marxism, as though it didn't even exist. None of the contributors to this volume comes on with a straight Marxist line, but the impact of the critical philosophy can be felt at a number of points, and historical-materialist language and thinking occur at a number of points. Much of the material in this book, whether the people concerned know it or not, comes under Habermas' (1971) category of 'emancipatory interest', which seeks to free people not only from the domination of others, but also from their domination by forces which they themselves do not understand.

Another major strand is phenomenology (Filmer *et al.,* 1973). Like Marxism, this is also an attempt to somehow 'stand outside' the social phenomena it is studying, and achieve a point of view which is not taken in by the social lies which are being told. Phenomenology tends to be rather programmatic, and greater on promise than on performance, but it is clearly one of the major influences on our contributors.

Existentialism, too, comes through in a number of ways as a key to understanding what this book is about. There is an important concern running through many of the contributions about the authenticity of the researcher, and the need for the researcher to be involved as a whole person, not hiding behind a role. As Heidegger has said (in Friedman, 1964), 'The student is forced out into the uncertainty of all things, upon which the necessity for commitment then bases itself. *Study must again mean taking a risk....* '

A philosophical tradition which is both close to and distant from Marxism is the Hegelian dialectic. From this we learn to question in a very radical way the subject-object relation. And as Zelman (1979) has recently argued, dialectical logic involves an altered state of consciousness. This opens up the whole question of whether our ordinary object-oriented level of consciousnes, tied in with Aristotelean logic (or modern symbolic logic), is adequate to do justice to human subjects. Should we not have a logic which can also cope with the interdependence of people, the interpenetration of people, and the unity of people? And if this involves an altered state of consciousness (where we let go of our ordinary logic) then should we not learn more about the states and levels of consciousness which are involved in this? William Torbert (1972) is one of the few people who have ventured into this difficult and dangerous territory; the implications for the training of research investigators are very important (see Chapter 37).

However, quoting all these weighty precursors and forebears may obscure something extremely important about this book. It is not a record of people trying to apply philosophical purities to intractable daily-life problems. Much more it is a record of people being forced, by the logic of what works and what does not work with human beings, further and further in these directions. So Maruyama wants to find out what part violence plays in jails. He finds out that he can't ask the questions himself, because people don't trust him enough. He has to involve the prisoners themselves in the research, and learn from them and with them what works and what doesn't work in a prison. He has to get away from the alienation of the standard researcher-subject relationship in order to do the job at all, and in doing so he discovers what the erudite Giddens (1976) says: 'Sociology, unlike natural science, stands in subject-subject relation to its "field of study", not a subject-object relation...'.

Rajesh Tandon tries to research in rural villages in India, using structured questionnaires and unstructured diaries. He finds that the questionnaires don't tell him much (partly because fewer and fewer of them get filled in), whereas the diaries are enormously revealing, and even contradict some of the information emerging from the questionnaires. And in doing so he rediscovers some insights about psychology which Maslow wrote about: if you prod at people like things, they won't let you know them.

So although we can call on distinguished philosophical traditions if we wish, this book is really much more practical than theoretical. It is trying to say, 'Here is another way of doing research. Try it. Use it.' In doing so, you may find that you need the philosophical ideas to illuminate and inform your own actual experience, as you discover them for yourself. That is what human inquiry is all about.

Overview

The book is divided into four sections: PHILOSOPHY, METHODOLOGY, EXAMPLES, and DIRECTIONS. Obviously these sections intertwine and overlap: as Harré and Bannister point out, the theory we hold about persons, and about persons as inquirers, must have extended implications for the research method we choose, and also for how we carry it out in practice. So although these heads are broad indications as to content, the reader must expect to find practical considerations in the PHILOSOPHY section, philosophy in the METHODOLOGY section, examples in the DIRECTIONS section, and so on. It is just not possible or desirable to cut the field up into precise chunks. Some of the links are obvious, for example with John Heron, Magoroh Maruyama, and Bill Torbert, who have made more than one contribution to this book; in other cases we as editors have indicated the connections.

Within these four sections are three types of contribution. First, we have reprinted some pieces which we thought were important, such as Allport's classic discussion of the general and the unique in psychology, and Maruyama's account of endogenous research with prisoners. Second, we have written 'appreciations' of other important books which we want to draw to the readers' attention, and would like them to explore in more detail for themselves; most of these appreciations have been seen and approved by the original author. Third, we have included a lot of new articles specially written for this book, which indicate the many-sided development of the emerging new paradigm.

We are not going to review and critique all these contributions. Our own contributions are clearly labelled as such, and the field is far too new for us to editorially pull all the ends together. Rather, we invite the reader to apply her or his own critique: use the tools we offer in the PHILOSOPHY section — Heron's extended epistemology, Rowan's dialectical cycle, Mitroff and Kilmann's typology — to critique the contents of the METHODOLOGY section. Use both PHILOSOPHY and METHODOLOGY to critically examine the EXAMPLES. And use all three to develop your own sense of direction for your own research, and for the field generally. It is this capacity to critically relate philosophy to method, and both to practice, which has been so sadly lacking in human inquiry.

Rather than review what we have put in, we wish here to comment on some of the things we have left out, and which the reader might have expected to see in a book such as this one. The most notable exceptions are the qualitative methods such as phenomenology, participant observation, grounded theory, and ethnomethodology, which have been omitted partly because they are well represented in the literature already (e.g. Bogdan and Taylor, 1975; Lofland,

1976), but more importantly because although they are an important alternative to orthodox experimental and survey research, as they stand they are not in our view 'new paradigm' research.

For example, one of the most sophisticated and developed approaches to rigorous qualitative research is the *grounded theory* approach of Glaser and Strauss (1967; see also Glaser, 1978). Their argument is that theory must be generated from data by a 'constant comparison method', a series of 'double back steps' from entering the field through to publication of results, 'all guided and integrated by the *emerging* theory' (Glaser, 1978, p. 2), and they present in their methodological writings and in the substantive research (which is comprehensively referenced by Glaser) a systematic approach for doing this. Their approach includes useful ideas such as 'theoretical sampling' — in which the researcher decides what data to collect next and where to find them on the basis of emerging theory — and 'saturation' — which means that no new data are being found which add to understanding of the categories and their properties.

Many researchers claim to practise grounded theory, and the work of Glaser and Strauss has been enormously influential, although few researchers practise this method with the rigour which the originators advocate. But the main point is that although we think there is a lot in these two books, and would recommend the would-be researcher to read them carefully, we would also ask her to read them critically, because this is *not* new paradigm research. Grounded theory is an excellent example of a qualitative research approach which stays firmly within the old paradigm, and which stays, in terms of the Hegelian analysis, at the social 'objective' level. None of the questions which are emphasized in this book about research as a collaborative, experiential, reflexive, and action-oriented process are of primary concern to Glaser and Strauss. The questions they seek to answer are solely what Rowan calls efficiency questions (Chapter 9).

A similar criticism can be made of much work using the approach of participant observation, where the researcher essentially retains an 'objectivist' perspective and 'uses' his subject-matter to his own ends (Rowan, 1973; Reinharz, 1979a). This kind of research can be just as alienating, just as divorced from the experiential knowledge of those involved in the situation, and in the end just as suspect as experimental methods, as Maruyama points out in Chapter 20.

The problem with these methods is that they only move halfway towards a new paradigm: while seeming to offer an alternative they are in many ways stuck with the outmoded assumptions of positivism. Qualitative methods as they have been traditionally used are quite different from the notions of collaborative, experiential, heuristic, endogenous, and participatory research which are presented in this book.

Phenomenological research is a bit different in that it does rest on a set of different assumptions, and at its best offers us the possibility of a 'radical empiricism', returning to the phenomenon as it emerges, and moving beyond the presuppositions of the researcher. It is very clear that phenomenal mapping, 'noticing' as Heron puts it, is a central aspect of research, and the ability to sensitively and accurately describe what is going on is an essential starting point (the work of Grof, 1979, in mapping the 'realms of the human unconscious' is an excellent example of this, as also is Akin's, 1975, 'phenomenology of risk' and Richer's, 1978, study of illusions). But on the whole we are disappointed with the outcomes of phenomenological research, and have not found anything which is sufficiently different from established writings and which falls within our ideas of the new paradigm to include here.

Another area which we have not been moved to include is ethnomethodology. Again there are a number of varieties of this, but in the main it seems to represent a valiant attempt to question the old paradigm and substitute something better grounded. No one could fail to be impressed by the important work of Cicourel (1968, 1974), Daniels (1970), Garfinkel (1967), Wieder (1974) and so forth, which take very ordinary and taken-for-granted things, and throw a flood of new light on them.

But this always seems to be a very external kind of conclusion, which does not change what it observes. The information obtained seldom seems to be fed back to the informants, as an integral part of the research itself. Mostly it seems to be related to the reader with something of an 'isn't-it-fascinating-how-people-organize-their-weirdness' flavour about it. As Boughey (1978) has suggested, it is almost as if these researchers saw their task as one of creating a kind of art gallery or museum of exhibits held up for our wonderment; beside each picture or object there is an art critic's appreciation of it. To which our question is, 'So what?'

It is because of these major differences between new paradigm research and these other forms of research that we have written a chapter on issues of validity, which brings together philosophical issues with the methodological and practical, and we believe contributes to a new and coherent position.

The Feminism Issue

Two things are very obvious about this book, from a feminist standpoint. One is that the pronouns are often unreformed, so that unknown active subjects are male. The other is that there are very few women contributors. As editors, we don't feel too good about these two features of the book, and we feel we need to say something about this.

The question of pronouns is an important one. We totally reject the view of writers such as Glaser (1978) who uses the masculine gender throughout his book, baldly stating that it is 'trite and obvious to all but a few readers' that he is not referring only to men. We accept the objections of the Women's Movement to the practice of referring to persons of indeterminate gender as 'he' or 'him'; as Miller and Swift (1979) point out:

> The decisive argument against using masculine terms generically...
> is not that they are inadequate and sometimes ridiculous, but that
> they perpetuate the cultural assumption that the male is the norm,
> the female is the deviation.

There are a number of ways of responding to this issue. For a start, one can avoid pronouns and other sexist usage through better thought-out sentence structure. Other approaches are to use feminine pronouns throughout, or to use feminine and masculine alternately. Then there are the cross-gender neologisms such as 'te', 'tes', and 'tir' (Farrell, 1975) which are splendidly inelegant and thus serve as 'reality-violators and consciousness-raisers' (Miller and Swift, 1979). Probably the most common device is to use 'they', 'them', 'their' where necessary. This is strictly ungrammatical, but usage may make it acceptable in due course, because it is often quite acceptable in oral discourse. And an obvious answer is for women to use 'she' and men to use 'he'.

Quite clearly there is no 'right' answer to this question: the use of language is an unresolved political issue between men and women, a symptom of how language frames the world in male terms. If we had used 'she' throughout this book we would have been unclear as to whether we were being feminist, or just cute.

Nevertheless, this book is nowhere as clear as we would like in this respect. Of course, there is no way we could have been consistent, because we were reprinting some pieces and reviewing others which were written before feminist issues were raised so strongly. But with the new pieces, we really did not raise the issue either for ourselves or with our contributors until it was too late to do anything about it. This is what concerns us: we just didn't think about it. We believe we have the awareness, and have acted on it in other contexts, but we didn't apply it here: we failed to respond to our own questions about being aware and questioning the patriarchial patterns which surround us (see Chapter 9).

This leads on to a wider question about gender: when we sent a copy of an outline of the book to Helen Callaway, she remarked that it looked more like another version of *male* inquiry than human inquiry. At that stage we had included no explicit exploration of women in research, and very few women contributors. Obviously this was a mistake: we are just beginning to see the relationships between feminist scholarship and new paradigm research, and just beginning to learn about the wealth of research of a new paradigm character that has been carried out by women. Again, we just didn't look hard enough. And this is rather curious, because throughout this book are references to new paradigm research being a move away from 'male' towards a 'female' approach to inquiry.

So there seems to be a real danger that in new paradigm research men will take a 'female' way of looking at the world, and turn it into another 'male' way of seeing it: men may understand the words, but do they know the music? These dangers might materialize in things like manipulation (shining through a democratic facade), mystification (retaining an expert mystique, only this time a nicey-nicey one), and ownership (secretly retaining ownership and the right to define focus while overtly giving it away). Men need to find a way to explore and learn about these dangers, and one way to do this would be through dialogue between feminists and new paradigm researchers.

All this feels risky, and we both found this section difficult and unpleasant to write. We feel exposed in raising these issues so prominently at the beginning of our book; but they are important and we need to deal with them.

One Final Point

What we are contending for in this book is that you don't have to settle for second best. You don't have to accept projects you don't believe in and really don't want to do. You don't have to toe the line of an orthodoxy which is in many ways quite illusory. You can do research which is worth while for you yourself and for the other people involved in it. You can do research on questions which are genuinely important.

Thousands of researchers down the years have started on projects they really believed in, and which embodied ideas they really cared about. But too often these projects got pared down and chopped about and falsified in the process of getting approval, and the researchers got progressively more disillusioned and frustrated as they have gone on. Thousands of researchers have ended their research soured and disappointed and hurt or cynical. It doesn't have to be this way. Research doesn't have to be another brick in the wall. It is obscene to take a young researcher who actually wants to know more about people, and divert them into manipulating 'variables', counting 'behaviours', observing 'responses' and all the rest of the ways in which people are falsified and fragmented. If we want to know about people, we have to encourage them to be who they are, and to resist all attempts to make them — or ourselves — into something we are not, but which is more easily observable, or countable, or manipulable.

Someone has got to be the next generation of great social scientists — the women and men who are going to break the ground of new knowledge for human growth and development to the next stage. You, the reader, might be one of them — why not? But you will only be one of them if you care enough about what you are doing, and who you are, and who the people are who you are doing it with. That is what this book is all about.

England, July 1980   John Rowan

                                                                        Peter Reason

PHILOSOPHY

Human Inquiry
Edited by P. Reason and J. Rowan
© 1981 John Wiley & Sons Ltd.

CHAPTER ONE

The positivist-empiricist approach and its alternative

Rom Harré
Sub-faculty of Philosophy, Oxford University, UK

(1) Positivism and Realism

The positivist tradition in scientific methodology has been based upon the principle that the only reliable knowledge of any field of phenomena reduces to knowledge of particular instances of patterns of sensation. Laws are treated as probabilistic generalizations of descriptions of such patterns. The sole role of laws is to facilitate the prediction of future sensory experience. Theories are logically ordered sets of laws. In consequence theories are reduced to a logical apparatus necessary to the business of prediction. It follows that for a positivist, the task of understanding a theory is exhausted by two processes. Analysis of theoretical discourse is aimed at revealing its logical structure. The empirical content of the theory is supposed to be brought to light by identifying those logical consequences of the set of laws which purport to describe observations. There are, therefore, two sides of modern positivism: one logical and one empirical. Modern positivism is sometimes called 'logical empiricism'.

Realists, on the other hand, hold that scientific theories have a characteristic content. They are to be taken as descriptions of mechanisms which might be responsible for observable patterns of events and properties of things. Furthermore most realists would argue that facts and theories are not independent. Facts are revealed to a human observer who uses a theory to identify significant items from the complex flux of experience. It follows that a realist can admit that there may be real indeterminateness in the world. The

3

world may be made determinate to human experience by acts of observation and categorization which impose structures and boundaries on the deliverances of sense. There are suggestions of this in sub-atomic physics, but the point is of central importance to the human sciences and I shall return to it. Many human actions may be indeterminate, deliberately left vague and so remain open to various interpretations. An action may be made determinate only in the course of a social negotiation, in which what has been done is defended in the light of a folk theory of proper human activity. On the realist view, theories must be the central object of scientific concern in the human sciences. They purport to describe aspects of the world not available to direct experience but generative of it. They are actively involved in the schematizing of sensation into perceived fact and in the disambiguating of indeterminate events into socially meaningful actions. They are not a bare logical apparatus for prediction, so they must be judged not on their predictive power alone, but on the plausibility of the image of the world they help to create.

The relation between logical positivism, naive experimentalism, and behaviourism is very clear, and I shall not labour it. In this chapter I will be trying to demonstrate what a scientific psychology in the realist tradition would be like. We already know what a psychology in the positivist tradition is like.

An important preliminary observation has to do with the degree to which the explicit discourse of a science, what appears for example in textbooks or learned papers, represents the content of theories as they are actually held and used by scientists. Study of real cases shows that even in the natural sciences the content of a theory is not expressed fully in the explicit discourse of that science. There are tacit beliefs, principles and assumptions, which are essential both to the way in which the theory is understood by its users and to the analysis of that theory by those who wish to comment upon it. This fact has been one of the prime causes of the difficulties created for scientific practice by attempts to follow logical positivist analyses of theory as if they were prescriptions. As I have remarked, positivists paid attention only to logical structure and empirical consequences. The unverifiability, in their view, of the assertions that theories make about unobserved processes, was enough to eliminate them as unnecessary embellishments of the true formal core of theory. So positivistic analysis ignored content. Consequently, important metaphysical assumptions were overlooked since they were treated as a dispensable, almost rhetorical part of the way theories were used in practice and of only psychological importance. A scientist, adhering to the realist tradition, is obliged to take the content of his theories seriously since he believes that as possible descriptions of unobserved reality they are under the control of metaphysical assumptions which express his most general theories about man and nature, they provide a springboard for the inventive investigator to find ways of making that which when first conceived is unobservable, available for empirical scrutiny.

I have suggested that theory functions for a realist in two distinctive ways. It is involved in the creation and experiencing of facts, since it allows for the differentiation and separation from the experiential matrix of observable particulars of various kinds. And it functions to anticipate reality by carrying our conceptions beyond the empirically given. To exemplify how psychology might look if constructed according to the realist tradition, I must examine the role of theory in the genesis of fact through what I shall call analytic schemata, and the role of theory in the transcending of experience in what I shall call explanatory schemata.

Any science deploys two interrelated conceptual systems. There is an analytical scheme required to reveal, identify, partition, and classify the items which make up the field of interest. A biological taxonomy has this function. Then there is an explanatory scheme required to formulate theories descriptive of the mechanisms productive of the items revealed in analysis. In a mature and successful science the two systems are coordinate, the taxonomy finding a justification in the explanatory theories of a field. For instance, the electron theory of atomic structure has justified the periodic table of the elements. To propose an alternative to a positivistic psychology one must introduce both an analytical scheme and an explanatory scheme, and show how, in principle, they could be coordinate.

(a)   *The Analytic Schema*

Unless people ordinarily deploy an adequate conceptual system, both in producing their own actions and in understanding those of others, social life could not exist as a distinctive form of being overlaying the biological. It follows that elementary actions are revealed only by partitioning public episodes according to criteria such as meaning, which involve that very conceptual system. Let us call it a folk-psychology. Much of this system is available to scrutiny in the content of the accounts people offer to deal with infractions of social order and remedy its indeterminateness. But untutored study of people's public behaviour in some *milieu* may leave one still bewildered by its apparent formlessness. Common-sense concepts, like 'man', 'woman', 'shopping', 'waiting', help us to discern some texture in social life, but much activity remains mysterious and some goes unnoticed. Novel analytical concepts are required to supplement the folk-psychology. For example, if one adds Goffman's notion of a tie-sign to the repertoire of common-sense concepts, more of a texture of social life becomes available for empirical study. Tie-signs are used by people to show others that they are together or studiously not together. Such signs appear in ways of walking, exchange of glances, and so on. They include the signs used by someone waiting alone to show to others that she is not a 'single' but, though currently by herself, is socially 'half a with'. This little conceptual system allows new textures to reveal themselves in the otherwise seamless web of social reality. In this way we create a dialectic of understanding. In one phase we can make common-sense knowledge explicit by analysing the content and uses of accounts. In a complementary phase we can bring that level of understanding into interaction with a possible amplified analysis, by melding the products of the skilled observer's investigations with the actively employed ordinary scheme we know is actually creatively in use. The upshot of the dialectic is a growing analytical scheme.

(b)   *The Explanatory Process*

Analytical concepts help to reveal non-random structures, ordered patterns of actions interpreted as the performance of social acts. For instance, one may come to realize that each family tiff exemplifies a pattern very similar to those of its predecessors and that the social act performed on such occasions may be better understood as an affirmation of solidarity rather than a display of apparent discord. The first question to ask is 'how is such orderliness produced?'. The natural sciences proceed always in the same way in seeking to answer this kind of question. At first, an attempt is made to discover the mechanism which produces the pattern. But in most cases the equipment currently available, both experimental and conceptual, is incapable of revealing the required generative mechanisms. Mendel's monks could classify and count peas, but more than sharp eyes and a couple of baskets are needed to discern genes. Once it is realized that the generative mechanisms are hidden from observation, natural scientists try to find a simulacrum of the real but unknown pattern generator, which will produce patterns already revealed as observed regularities. So, Maxwell and Clausius imagine swarms of molecules whose behaviour would simulate the way real gases behave, as described in the gas law $PV = RT$. Imagined generative mechanisms are sometimes called explanatory models.

But the scientific creative imagination is constrained. Imagined mechanisms must conform to some general description of how the scientists of the period believe the world really is. We could call such beliefs, as concretely conceived, a source model; for example, the source model for Newtonian science was the belief that the world was made up of atoms in motion. To be plausible any explanatory model must be based on a source model, since we must be able to have some confidence that the mechanisms that we imagine to be in nature might be real. Natural selection, an explanatory model, is based upon domestic selection, a source model, and domestic selection is known to occur. Similarly, the concept of a native speaker producing grammatically orderly sentences by following rules is based upon the way a speaker of a language foreign to him may actually consult a rule to produce a correct formation. In this way the content of particular theories is controlled by the tacit but pervasive, scientific, metaphysical, and sometimes even social, assumptions of a historical period, since the source-models that seem plausible to a community are those that fit best with the rest of the culture.

The account of scientific method I have just laid out involves structural concepts for revealing and describing the patterns discerned by an 'educated' observer. It also involves a presumption that we can think beyond given experience to the imagined and hidden processes that could produce observed patterns, the presumption that we can think in depth. The analytical and explanatory aspects of a theory are linked in two important ways.

(i) Through the principle of structural explanation, that an observed structure is usually produced from some preformed template, one is justified in postulating a hidden structure forming some part of the generating mechanism and acting as a template controlling the form of action. For example, linguists postulate rules to explain the production of grammatically structured sentences by native speakers.

(ii) In an ideal science analytical concepts through which natural and social action reveal some of their structures, and explanatory concepts by which templates for the production of those structures are postulated, should be coordinate. A fluid model of the hidden nature of electricity is coordinate with our choice of pressure (voltage) and flow (current) to define observable patterns in the behaviour of electricity. The conception of a person as a rule-following agent is coordinate with a dramaturgical analytical model, in terms of which social episodes are analysed as if they were a dramatic performance, and the rules were a script.

While a scientific community has confidence in its cluster of analytic and explanatory models, scientists tend to take their models seriously as partial *representations* of reality. But sometimes panic and loss of confidence occur. When the schema I have described above is temporarily abandoned there begins a retreat to positivism. How does such a panic come about?

If we are to take an imagined mechanism seriously as a possible representation of reality there ought to be some way of deciding between rival candidates for the role of best explanation. Sometimes the ingenuity of theorists produces a multitude of seemingly possible mechanisms, all capable of being imagined to produce close analogues of the empirically observed patterned regularities. But at the other extreme, it sometimes happens that the most talented and imaginative thinkers can make no headway at all in imagining any mechanism capable of simulating the behaviour of the real world in the field they are investigating. The former situation brought on a positivist reaction among many astronomers in the sixteenth century, the latter among sub-atomic physicists in the twentieth. At the heart of a positivist reaction is a denial that theory could represent hidden realities. According to positivism a science should be taken to be no more than a well-attested body of rules for predicting the future course of observation. But these 'internal' historical conditions alone are not sufficient to account for the retreat to positivism. Historical studies clearly reveal an odd twist to this retreat. As scientists abandon the search for a deep knowledge of nature they tend to adopt a militant, even an arrogant posture, sometimes persecuting those who hope to continue on the path of scientific tradition. A kind of glorying in ignorance is displayed, like the Paduan professors who refused to look through Galileo's telescope. Positivist retreats seldom last beyond a single generation of scientists, though the damaging effect of widespread abandonment of realism can sometimes be felt for a long time after the dominant figures have departed.

(2) Structurism and Atomism

But the search for structure which I have assumed in the above discussion is sometimes abandoned in favour of a generally atomic way of conceiving and analysing the world. Atomism and structurism are the poles of a cycle of longer modulus than the ups and downs of realism and positivism. The high structurism of the Renaissance, crowned by Kepler's *Harmonices Mundi,* was followed by the extreme atomism of the eighteenth century, reaching its limit in Hume's *Treatise.* Structural ideas returned to chemistry in the late nineteenth century and have slowly gained ground in most sciences, penetrating in very recent times even to psychology, the very citadel of reactionary intellectual practices. When the search for structure and the struggle for depth are abandoned together then we have the kind of monumental reaction that all but destroyed psychology as a scientific discipline in the 1950s and 1960s. The natural sciences are less drastically affected by the coincidence of the cycles than the social and psychological sciences, since for them a positivistic reaction is, more often than not, a mere way of speaking, a rhetoric to censure over-optimistic speculation. Only in the recent history of quantum mechanics has there been in natural science anything like the Paduan stance taken up by the psychologists of the old-style experimentalist tradition.

(3) The Myth of Certainty

Positivism as a philosophy of science has two other more superficial features, that are often in practice the more obvious effects of adherence to the doctrine. There is a tendency to reduce meaning to a simple referential relation between a linguistic term and something actually experienced, usually in a single act of perception. In this way the imaginative underpinnings of science are swept away as meaningless, since most theoretical terms like 'action' or 'Complex' or 'dialectic' are related directly only to an *imagined* representation of the world. The only part of scientific discourse preserved under a positivist edict of expulsion are the descriptions of observed patterns, since they are actually experienced. So only the terms used to refer to observable properties and kinds can have meaning in positivist semantics. For Hume the test of the meaningfulness of a term (idea) was to find the experiential atom (impression) with which it corresponds. The logical positivists of our day identified the meaning of a term with the operations needed to assess the truth of a sentence in which it appeared. So meaning can be given to an expression only by finding the experiential 'atom' to which it refers. And for there to be public meaning there must be a public object to provide that meaning. So terms which seem to refer to a person's thoughts and feelings are either meaningless or actually mean something different from what we think they mean, e.g. their 'real' meaning is that of the behavioural correlate of what we have taken them to mean. 'Speech' becomes 'the emission of verbal behaviour'.

Behind the perennial urge to retreat from depth to surface lies another obsession — the strong urge to certainty. We have noticed the authoritarian and dogmatic character of many expositions of positivism. In philosophy the quest for the kind of certainty which would serve as a defence of absolutist claims to knowledge inevitably leads to an *impasse*. The more powerful and speculative, the deeper do our theories purport to go in the exploration of nature, the less can we be certain of their correctness. But by confining the world of scientific investigation to the mere appearances of things, to the behaviour of instruments arranged in certain configurations, and in the extreme case, to the sensations of an observer, one can accomplish a strategic retreat to certainty. However unsure I may be of the hypothetical entities and processes described in theories, at least I can be sure, it seems, of my present sensory experiences. The laws of nature are retrenched too, to become no more than rules for assessing the probability that future experiences will be of certain pre-identified kinds. On this view laws are just aids to prediction.

(4) An Example

Again, a kind of conspiratorial confluence appears, so that the principle for assignment of meaning confines the subject-matter of sciences to just the very surface elements of whose presence and properties we can be certain. So in a period of positivist reaction we have a science conceived as shallow, atomistic, observationalist, and certain. It is not hard to recognize in this list the presumptions for experimental psychology. Few psychologists would now be bold enough to publicly declare themselves behaviourists, but still, in *1980*, despite all that has been painstakingly pointed out about the unscientific character of their pursuits, psychologists continue to commit what they are pleased to call experiments. Let me describe a recent example, not untypical.

To exemplify the troubles infecting the naive 'experimental' methodology, one could choose almost any paper in the standard journals. To keep the analysis within reasonable compass, I shall discuss a simple and fairly transparent case, where the conceptual confusion and methodological errors are near the surface, so to speak. The study is reported in the *Journal of Personality and Social Psychology*. It is called 'Self-focus, felt responsibility and helping behaviour' and is by S. Duval, V.H. Duval and R. Neely (1979).

The events described by the authors as an 'experiment' went as follows: some young women, all psychology students, were first told a misleading tale about the episode they were to take part in. Then they were left for a full minute to contemplate an image of themselves in a television monitor. Afterwards they heard a television programme, a lecture on venereal disease. Some of them heard the lecture immediately after they had been watching themselves; some heard it four minutes later. They were all then asked to fill in a questionnaire inviting them to comment on their willingness to contribute in various ways to remedial programmes for venereal disease. There is clearly something bizarre about all this — but exactly what?

The first clue can be found in the title of the article, 'Self-focus, felt responsibility and helping behaviour'. Without as yet examining severally the viability of the three concepts here juxtaposed, it is clear that there is already a problematic conjunction between two conceptual systems with incompatible analytical models. The concepts of 'self-focus' and 'helping behaviour' are drawn from a system appropriate to describing human automatisms, while 'responsibility' — felt or otherwise — belongs to the representation of some moral order. The psychology of this would require judgement, decision, conscience, and so on. It is clear that there is supposed to be a causal relation between 'self-focus' and the onset or degree of 'helping behaviour'. The effect of the insertion of 'responsibility' into this conceptual framework and of the qualification of 'helping' by 'behaviour' is to propose that a form of conduct *(Handlung)* that is taken to be part of the moral order, should be subject to a putative psychological law. The idea that the moral order is part of a technology (in this case a psychological one) is a highly culturally-specific North American notion. The question of whether the North American mores which treats conduct as the behavioural output of trained automata is morally and politically acceptable, or generalizable to other cultures, is preempted by the way the 'experiment' is conceived. So we are presented with something as if it were empirical, which is heavily loaded with *unexamined* metaphysical and moral/political presuppositions.

Now to look more closely at the conceptual apparatus, in terms of which the phenomena are created as 'facts', and reminding ourselves of Eddington's remark '...it is also a good rule not to put overmuch confidence in the observational results until they have been confirmed by theory', I turn to examine the specific concepts of this paper in more detail.

The key notions are 'self-focus' and 'helping behaviour'. The overarching theory of which the experiment is supposed ultimately to be a test, is Heider's well-known idea that people are more likely to become engaged in something with distinguishable moral qualities when they conceive themselves to be personally involved. But there are several intermediate steps between that theory and the research programme of which the 'experiment' under discussion forms a part. The research programme began with some ideas of Duval and Wicklund (1972), which involved the forging of a dubious connection between Heider's general theory and the alleged state of consciousness called 'self-focus', by way of G. H. Mead's notion of the 'me'. To understand the basic confusion in the design of the 'experiment' we must go back to examine the original confusions involved in the 'operationalization' of Mead's theory of the 'I' and the 'me', via the notion of 'objective self-awareness'. In the original document one finds a confusion between the moral order and the causal order cross-multiplied with that between awareness of self and awareness of aspects of self. On pages 1 to 9 of their first chapter Duval and Wicklund claim to be defining a psychological condition corresponding in some way to G. H. Mead's 'me'. This they call 'objective self-awareness'. Its alleged importance lies in promoting self-evaluation; that is, it is supposed to introduce awareness of a proper subject of predication for concepts located in the moral order, such as 'responsibility'. Clearly, it can only be the self as person that is the proper subject of moral evaluation. But the self in that sense is just what can never be an object of objective self-awareness. Our authors themselves acknowledge this on page 14 of the same chapter. Contradicting their original definition of self-awareness they say that when someone focuses attention on themselves the intentional objects are e.g. 'his consciousness, personal history or body'. But none of these entities can be the subject of those categories of moral evaluation that include 'responsibility'. The conceptual confusions of the 1979 paper are already laid down in the book of 1972.

It is in this complex of confusions that automatization of the moral world of succour, aid, and assistance begins. I shall now turn to examine the concepts at work in glossing 'helping behaviour'.

There are three main ways in which concepts can present an appearance of generality. They may be generic, comprehending specific concepts taxonomically, e.g. 'ungulata' to 'sheep'. They may be determinable, comprehending determinants, e.g. 'colour' to 'red', or they may be equivocal, e.g. 'cohort' meaning a generation or 'cohort' meaning a military formation. Part of the source of our intuitions that there is something deeply wrong with this 'experiment' is that the scientistic terminology such as 'helping behaviour' is clearly equivocal in general and actually misapplied (outside any obvious equivocation) in this case. Taken *à pied de lettre* 'helping behaviour' might be thought to comprehend 'aid', 'succour', 'help', 'support', 'assistance', etc. Now assistance, and in one of its senses 'help', is rendered to someone who is trying but not succeeding, who has some, but not all, of the requisites for a task, etc. Here we have a determinable with a well-defined open class of determinates. But 'help' in the sense of 'succour' is an entirely distinct concept. Succour is rendered to someone already beyond trying, who is incapable of helping himself. The Samaritan gave both 'aid' (money) and 'succour' (medical attention) to the famous roadside victim. The moral order is involved in wholly distinct ways in assistance and in succour. Scarcely anyone, of whatever political pursuasion, would deny succour, but many, on moral grounds ('It is good for you to struggle') and political principle ('It is a waste of national resources') would refuse assistance.

To one's astonishment, in this 'experiment', the 'helping behaviour' turns out to be none of these, but something other — something one would be inclined precisely to *exclude* from helping behaviour. The young ladies involved (called oddly and significantly 'female subjects', a fairly clear indication of the taken-for-granted political stance of the experimenters) were not asked to render aid, succour, assistance, or even help, but to fill in a questionnaire about prospective actions of various kinds not actually committing themselves, but telling whether they would, under certain circumstances, commit themselves. They were not asked whether they would give immediate help to someone, in either sense of 'help', but only whether they would act indirectly, in a 'helping' programme.

So much for the 'effect' end of this study. What about the alleged cause? Again we find equivocation rather than either the determinable-determinate or generic-specific relation. 'Self-focus' is alleged to be a specific state of consciousness, being induced by looking at oneself in the television monitor. But states of consciousness are, if anything is, intentional. How could 'self' be the intentional object of a state of consciousness of the self? Taken literally, the idea is a self-contradiction. Clearly, the concept must be being interpreted not as focus on self, but focus on some aspect of self, as is clear from a consultation of the original text defining the research programme. There are large and diverse ranges of possibilities — general appearance, particular aspects of physical appearance, rings under eyes, skin cancer, expression, clothes and many more, even if we admit the constraints of the television monitor image as limiting the focus to what is being seen, a fairly static image of one's external appearance. None of these can be the proper subject of attributions of moral qualities such as 'responsibility'. Like 'helping behaviour', 'self-focus', taken now in 'aspect of self' sense, is radically equivocal. In particular, there can be no certainty that 'self-focus', whatever it may mean, has induced a state of consciousness that in Miss A is psychologically commensurate with 'self-focus' as induced in Miss B, since the conditions of the 'experiment' were such as to remove all hints as to the meaning given to these strange events and in particular to looking at oneself in a television monitor, so that the myriad aspects of self to which one might pay attention was underdetermined. Was the appropriate psychological concomitant embarrassment, interest, self-consciousness? The young ladies involved were given no clue as to what it was proper for them to feel, since they were provided with no way for resolving the equivocation. The self as moral agent is, of course, the one thing that cannot be focused on via a television monitor image, since it cannot be an intentional object of awareness at all.

But, someone might retort, despite all the conceptual confusion evident in the way the events in question were written up for publication, didn't *something* of significance happen? As A. J. Crowle has pointed out in a very penetrating study of the equivocations in much 'experimental' social psychology (Crowle, 1976), there are two dimensions to this. Perhaps something did happen that was essentially the same for every girl involved, but this, whatever it was, is susceptible of indefinitely many competing explanations, each of which could be true of a particular but different girl. On the other hand, since the terms in which these events were described are essentially and deeply equivocal, the statistical results are equally compatible with the hypothesis that something essentially different happened to each girl. The differences could be easily comprehended within the range of equivocation of both concepts, that used for describing the treatment ('self-focus') and that for describing its alleged effect ('helping behaviour'). Our conclusion must be that in the absence of conceptual clarification and more adequate definitions of the settings of the events in question, to constrain the interpretations of the participants within some more permanent conceptual framework, the results are worthless as psychology. However, they are of the greatest interest as manifestations of a particular moral and political attitude on the part of the experimenters.

In this discussion I have concentrated only on the metaphysics of man implicit in the treatment meted out to the 'subjects'. But buried deeper still in the procedures involved is a positivistic theory of causality.

(5) Theory of causality

A particular theory of causality is one of the important consequences that flow from following the positivist retreat in the face of epistemological difficulties. Traditionally associated with positivistic epistemology is a view of causality, the regularity theory of Hume. According to this doctrine, the only empirical content of a causal law is the set of actual concomitances of events that have been and will be observed. An event is identified as a cause by its temporal priority to a later event and by the statistical fact that events of that type regularly precede events of the type identified as effects. Neither the activity and productive power of an agent, nor implicit reference to the workings of a generative mechanism are admitted as part of the meaning of a causal law. To say that something caused something else, is only to say that an event of a certain sort regularly precedes an event of the kind to be explained.

It is easy to see how adherence to a degenerate Humean theory of causality leads directly to the mindless empiricism of much psychological experimentation. If there could be causation in the mere juxtaposition of events, no role is left for an agent or powerful particular in a theory of production of effects. As a positivist one is counselled to study the confidence levels of correlations between types of treatments and types of effects through examining numbers of cases. By adopting this advice, one can avoid the deep study of the internal processes and activities of agents which bring these effects about. But causal processes occur only in individual beings, since mechanisms of actions, even when we act as members of collectives, must be realized in particular persons. To study causal processes a psychologist would have to adopt an intensive design contrary to the traditional empiricist methodology.

The irony of the uncritical acceptance of the positivist methodology is emphasized most poignantly by the fact that the admired exemplar, physics, is based on a quite different conception of causation. Instead of a world of passive beings waiting quiescent, independent, and unchanging, to receive an external stimulus to action from another moving body, physicists conceive of a world of permanently interconnected, mutually interacting centres of energy, whose native activity is modulated and constrained by other such centres. The immediate cause of motion is the removal of a constraint from an active material being — for example, removal of a support from a body located in the gravitational or electromagnetic field, a body which has an active tendency to accelerate. Not even the mass of a body is a passive, independent property. According to Mach's principle, even the most intimate power, the power to resist acceleration, is an endowment from the system of bodies that make up the universe as a whole.

Even though psychology could benefit from a borrowing of the methodologies actually in use in physics and chemistry, which are based upon the need to get active agents to reveal their capabilities and to identify the invariants upon which the integrity of natural structures depends (Bhaskar, 1978), some cautions must still be entered. With an analytical model to reveal the texture of an experienced reality, an intelligent and active investigator sometimes discerns patterns of regularity in sequences of like phenomena. These can be at the level of acts, socially potent meanings, such as congratulations for a good performance and its deferential acknowledgement. Though patterns such as these are regularities among the most highly socially defined phenomena, they are likely to be found very widely, if not unversally, since however distinct a society may be in its practices there are likely to be public performances and critical audiences. But the orderly action-sequences with which act-patterns are realized on particular occasions and in particular places, are very local. For instances, even within the closed, closely related sub-cultures of Europe, there are radical differences in the actions conventionally used for certain acts. Eastern Europeans acknowledge applause from an audience by applauding back.

(6) Social Acts and Personal Actions

The act-action-movement distinction has become standard in social psychology and ethology (cf. von Cranach *et al.*, 1980). The distinction derives originally from J. L. Austin's differentiation between illocutionary and perlocutionary forces of utterances in his speech-act theory (cf. Searle, 1969), and more recently from Bruner's distinction of overt forms of an utterance from their role in a 'format'. For example, one may utter a question to make a request. The distinction can be illustrated in simple cases. Moving the hand up and down is a 'movement', moving the hand intentionally is an 'action', farewelling someone in moving one's hand up and down is an 'act'. The distinction functions in both taxonomic and explanatory contexts. Ethologists, for instance, have used it taxonomically to make 'top down' classifications of socially equivalent sets of behaviour units, and controversy still simmers over the intention implications of this use (cf. von Cranach and Harré, 1980). In an explanatory context, movements are related to other movements by physical and physiological mechanisms; actions are related to the intentions and projects of actors, while acts are embedded in a network of conventions, occasions, and consequences. Since acts are taxonomically more powerful than actions, and actions than movements, there has been a tendency to talk of action-structures and movement-structures as organizations of behaviour at different 'levels'.

For naive experimentalist psychology, the relative universality of act-patterns and the relative cultural specificity of the movements in which they are realized, must be a serious paradox.

The very items they study in the search for psychological laws, externally defined and identified behaviour, are the most culturally specific items of all. Acts, as the meanings of actions definable only in terms of actors' intentions and inter-actors' interpretations of this social world, i.e. 'internally', are the only likely relata of universal patterns. It is much more to be expected that in every culture a victor will triumph after winning a combat than that he will put his Spitfire into a Victory Roll. The paradox of 'levels', as we might call it, shows that there are unlikely to be laws of human social behaviour at the level of movements, the level of behavioural analysis, since actions involve movements which are conventionally related to the social acts they are used to perform. This distinction between act as social content and behaviour as realization has been found necessary in describing the social life of primates other than man. For instance, the choice by Mike, one of Jane Goodall's chimpanzees, of paraffin cans rather than of leafy branches, to perform his challenge of status within the chimpanzee hierarchy, illustrates they way in which the same social act can be realized in distinctive kinds of behaviour.

Allowing that there are likely to be at least local regularities at each 'level', how is one to study them empirically? Is there perhaps some place for properly designed experiments, or must we rely only on more powerful, but more difficult, empirical procedures, such as account analysis?

Recent work suggests that, like linguistic habits, most human regularities in thought, feeling, and behaviour are dependent on the existence of a common body of knowledge and so their psychological explanation involves a competence theory. The relevant body of knowledge includes preformed templates, the individual's access to which explains our ability as agents to generate structured or patterned actions, individually or coordinately. But account analysis cannot help to develop a performance theory. In most cases though, actors are aware of what they are doing (acts), but they are not aware of how they are bringing off a performance at the 'level' of action.

The understanding of how resources of competent actors are deployed in particular occasions to generate action — that is understanding the generative mechanisms of action — requires a different methodology. If one adopts as a general theory of action, that people are agents acting intentionally in accordance with socially grounded rules and conventions to realize projects, then the entities in need of empirical investigation are clearly defined. We would need to know about intentions and their modes of realization relative to more or less over-arching personal projects.

Novel techniques have recently been developed by Hacker and von Cranach (cf. von Cranach and Harré, 1980) to explore the existence and nature of these psychological entities empirically. The trick depends on the fact that when the smooth flow of action is interrupted, or breaks down, the cognitive machinery of means-end hierarchies is momentarily consciously represented. If we had to depend only on naturally occurring breakdowns, the chances of the moments of conscious representation covering the whole system between them, are remote. By engineering breakdowns systematically, both Brenner (1978) and von Cranach have been able to explore the cognitive machinery at work in some simple processes. Happily, the processual generators of actions as acts turn out to have within certain bounds, just the intention/convention/project structure the ethogenic theory predicted. They take the TOTE hierarchy form that Miller et al. (1960) hypothesized as the basic structure of cognitive processing.

Buried more deeply still in traditional psychology than the matters I have dealt with so far, is another positivistic assumption of the greatest moment that I referred to in section 1. One might call it the assumption of the stability and determinateness of fact. A psychology which seeks to formulate conditional laws with which it can predict the behavioural outcome of treatments must assume that the treatments are stable entities which once in existence are unchangeable by future contingencies. But in the social world one can change the past, not least by reinterpretation in successful use of rhetorical talk. One must also assume not only that facts are stable, but that social facts are determinate entities ultimately unambiguous and given as they come into existence. This is all resumed in the idea of data. But human social life is shot through with ambiguity and indeterminateness — not because life events cannot be made determinate, but because it is often injudicious so to clarify them. We need room for manoeuvre. Was what he said a reprimand, or merely a tasteless joke? Only time and the reactions of the others will tell. And much social activity passes into limbo unresolved in its essential ambiguity. Our actions are offered to others as open sets of possibilities to be more closely defined should the need arise. There are no data, and *a fortiori* to attempt to formulate the descriptions of regularities in the sequence of human action as data, is a folly.

Human Inquiry
Edited by P. Reason and J. Rowan
© 1981 John Wiley & Sons Ltd.

CHAPTER TWO

Philosophical basis for a new paradigm

John Heron
British Postgraduate Medical Federation, University of London, UK

Cooperative Inquiry

Research is a process of systematic (and not so systematic) inquiry that leads to knowledge stated in propositions. In social science research this inquiry involves an element of observation of, or interaction with, persons in order to offer empirical evidence for the research conclusions.

But there are two quite different ways of interacting with persons in research. One way is to interact with them so that they make no direct contribution to formulating the propositions that purport to be about them or to be based on their sayings and doings. This, of course, is the traditional social science experiment or study in which the subjects are kept naive about the research propositions and make no contribution at all to formulation at the stage of hypothesis-making, at the stage of final conclusions, or anywhere in between. In the extreme, and still popular form of this approach, the inquiry is all on the side of the researcher, and the action being inquired into is all on the side of the subject.

The other way — the way of cooperative inquiry — is for the researcher to interact with the subjects so that they do contribute directly both to hypothesis-making, to formulating the final conclusions, and to what goes on in between. This contribution may be strong, in the sense that the subject is co-researcher and *contributes* to creative thinking at all stages. Or it may be weak, in the sense that the subject is thoroughly *informed* of the research propositions

19

at all stages and is invited to assent or dissent, and if there is dissent, then the researcher and subject negotiate until agreement is reached. In the complete form of this approach, not only will the subject be fully fledged co-researcher, but the researcher will also be co-subject, participating fully in the action and experience to be researched.

My purpose in writing this chapter is to present a variety of arguments supporting the second of these two ways; that is, supporting a research paradigm in which the subject is also co-researcher, being actively and openly involved on the inquiry side of the research, as well as on the action side.

The Argument from the Nature of Research Behaviour

It is a presupposition of doing research of any kind that you have already committed yourself to some very general model of explanation with respect to the subjects or objects of your research. Most orthodox research takes absolute determinism as the general model of explanation; however difficult this is to achieve in practice, in principle human behaviour is regarded as part of a deterministic order, as the exclusive effects of prior antecedent conditions. This assumption is mistaken, I believe, because the presuppositional analysis is misplaced. It results from asking the wrong question first, which obscures a more radical question and one which is logically prior. The wrong question to ask first is, 'To what kind of explanation of the behaviour of my subjects am I committed?'. The prior and more radical question is, 'To what kind of explanation of my own research behaviour am I committed?'. This question is less obviously relevant in the physical sciences, but when the investigator is the same kind of being as the subjects of his investigation, then this reflexive question becomes of paramount importance.

Does it make sense to say that in principle research behaviour is precisely predictable and can be fully subsumed under causal laws? I think not. It is surely part of what we mean by 'research behaviour' that it is behaviour that is in particular detail unpredictable. We engage in it precisely because we cannot know in advance what particular form it will take. It is behaviour which in the nature of the case constitutes creative advance, surmounting and transcending the predictable. It depends on the generation of new ideas, new insights, fresh hypothesis, and innovative theoretical formulations; the notion that you could predict specifically the occurrence of the expression of new ideas on the basis of observations of what is already known is incomprehensible, for the ideas would not in any intelligible sense be new. There is no precise methodology for generating new ideas; new ideas are not the logical product of empirical observation, rather they arise unpredictably to direct it into ever more fruitful channels.

Research behaviour is, therefore, original creative activity which cannot in principle be contained within an explanatory model of absolute determinism; it is not the sort of event that could be predicted as the outcome of antecedent conditions. What explanatory model can be adopted for such behaviour? I suggest that central to any such model is the notion of intelligent agency, or to put it another way, the notion of a self-directing person. To give a full and sufficient explanation of research behaviour, some reference must be made to the notion of intelligent agency or self-direction, where this concept cannot be explained in terms of anything else.

To say that the researcher is an intelligent agent is to say that his behaviour is not fully subsumable under the causal laws of the natural order, but the expression of self-directed activity within that order. There are two fundamental statements here: (1) there is a causal order in nature; (2) there are creative acts of self-directing agents occurring within nature. But if the second statement cannot be included within, or reduced to, the first, how then can they be reconciled and made consistent while retaining their relative independence? One answer is provided by the thesis of relative determinism, which has been set out in detail in an earlier paper (Heron, 1971). This thesis holds that antecedent conditions delimit and determine a range of possible outcomes, and that the width of this range is a function of the position of an entity in the hierarchy of chemical and biological types from the atom to the human being: the human being, if not seriously damaged, has a significant degree of freedom and can bring intelligent, rational principles to bear on the direction of his or her activity within nature.

But human beings are social beings. Within the limits set by causal factors, members of a society make a tacit choice to relate to each other in accordance with certain norms and conventions. Thus for any piece of social behaviour there may be three distinct yet interrelated levels of explanation, none of which are necessarily mutually exclusive. There is a causal explanation in terms of relatively determining conditions of inner needs and environmental factors; there is a conventional explanation in terms of tacit commitment to prevailing social norms; and there is autonomous explanation in terms of a fully explicit self-directed commitment to certain purposes and principles. Research behaviour is a special case of social behaviour to which the level of autonomous explanation, *inter alia,* applies.

Thus the basic explanatory model for research behaviour is that of intelligent self-direction — commitment to purposes in the light of principles — combined with relative determinism. The next question is as follows: 'Given that I am committed to such a model to explain my own research behaviour, what explanatory model is relevant to my subjects' behaviour, and what method of inquiry is appropriate to apply to it?' I cannot without gross inconsistency apply to my subjects a model which is logically at odds with the one I apply to myself. I cannot responsibly argue that they are in principle to be seen as fully under the control of antecedent conditions within a scheme of absolute determinism, while it is a necessary condition of my researching them that I view myself as a self-directing intelligence within a scheme of relative determinism. I must surely see them in principle also as self-directing and intelligent agents. Hence my subjects become my co-researchers: together we decide what possibilities for intelligent self-determination are to be investigated through action. If the subjects are *not* privy to the research thinking, *they will not be functioning fully as intelligent agents.* For a self-determining person is one who generates, or takes up freely as his own, the thinking that determines his actions.

The Argument from Intentionality

Brentano (1973) and others have regarded intentionality as one of *the* defining features of the mental. Intentionality simply refers to the fact that when I am conscious I am always conscious *of* some content — whether perceptual, imaged, or other. Such content has some sort of meaning or significance for me: I *construe* it as content of this or that or the other sort. Furthermore, when I engage in choice and overt action, an important part of what I am conscious of is my *intent,* my purpose in doing what I am doing, my meaning in acting.

In my view, such construing-and-intending is original, creative human activity. It generates, and reference to it explains the origins of, any and every domain of inquiry. It is not susceptible of a reductive explanation in terms of the concepts of the domains it generates. Any attempt to do so necessarily presupposes its exemption from the attempt. It presents two polar and inter-dependent aspects of intelligent agency as a significant determinant and explanation of human behaviour: how persons construe their world, and the intentions with which they act within it. For whenever a person is functioning *as a person,* that person's construing-and-intending is a necessary irreducible part of the explanation of his or her behaviour. But it is not therefore a sufficient explanation of the behaviour. For, as we have seen in the previous section, explanation in terms of intelligent agency as an irreducible notion does not exclude further explanation in terms of relative determinism, that is, in terms of causal laws that delimit the range of options, the degrees of freedom, within which such intelligent agency can manifest itself.

On this analysis of intentionality, the wise researcher will at least consult his subjects to see whether *their* constructs and intentions concur with *his* conclusions based on their behaviour during the research. So as resarcher I may need to ask my subjects 'Did you in fact construe what was going on in the way that I have construed your reaction to it in my research conclusions?' And again: 'When you produced that piece of behaviour during the research, was your intention in doing it consonant with my interpretation in these conclusions?'

Asch's experiment on recency and primacy in impression formation (Asch, 1952) begs an important unanswered question about how the experimental subjects construed the experimental conditions. To one group he presented first nice adjectives, then nasty adjectives, about some imagined person; to the other group he presented the nasty adjectives first, followed by the nice. The first group saw the person as basically nice with some flaws, the second group saw the person as basically flawed with some redeeming features. Asch concluded that early information was more influential than later information in impression formation. But how did the subjects construe it all? We don't know, of course. They may have said: 'Look here, the way we construed it, it was not temporal order as such that counted. We took it on the basis of prior experience, that the temporal order signified a rank order of weighting or importance, and *that* was the crucial thing in determining our overall impression'. It would be interesting to re-run many experiments of this sort on the basis of cooperative inquiry.

When subjects are *acting* within the research arena, consulting them about the validity of the research conclusions depends on the level of behavioural analysis at which the conclusions are pitched. If it is simply overt physical movements I am reporting on where the limbs, trunk, head, fingers, etc. are moving in space — then my observations may be more reliable than the agent's. Again, if my description is simply at the level of what I will call basic actions — such as 'walks', 'talks', 'looks', 'points', and so on — it may well be quite unnecessary to check my account against the agent's account. But when I am interpreting such basic actions in terms of their more complex intentions and purposes, then I need to check my version against the agent's version of what he was about, for a person may walk, or talk, or look or point to fulfil many different higher-order intentions.

The general form of this argument is that human beings are symbolizing beings. They find meaning in and give meaning to their world, through symbolizing their experience in a variety of constructs and actions. This notion of symbolizing activity as an explanatory concept is irreducible to any other, since it is presupposed by and transcends any reductive argument. It points both to a determinant and to an explanation of human behaviour *sui generis*. To explain human behaviour you have, among other things, to understand this activity, and fully to understand it involves participating in it through overt dialogue and communication with those who are engaging in it.

Thus, if we want to explain the research behaviour of *researchers* we should not go and do some traditional non-consultative research *on* them, but to do some research *with* them. We should inquire through dialogue, interaction and cooperative endeavour, *how* they symbolize their experience of the world through scientific constructs and actions; and in the light of this understanding, to explain their behaviour. But the same model applies in any other domain of human symbolizing activity.

Another version of the same argument is to say that cultural explanations of human behaviour are irreducible to any other type of explanation. A cultural explanation is one that sees the values, norms, and beliefs of a person as significant determinants and explanations of his behaviour. Such values, norms, and beliefs may be autonomous: the person espouses them because he has really thought them through. Or they may be conventional: the person espouses them because others do. But autonomy and conventionality are themselves explanatory concepts that cannot be reduced back to some extra-cultural domain. To understand an autonomous or conventional culture, we need to participate in it through dialogue and interaction with those who exemplify it. Any cultural explanation needs to be checked with those within the culture.

Of course, a person may misconstrue his world, and may be deluded about his intentions in the sense that his stated purpose for an action is a rationalization of some process within him of which he is not fully aware. A person's construing and intending competence may go sadly awry. Human agency can lose its way. Each individual is not necessarily the best authority on the validity of his own constructs and intentions. Hence the importance of *cooperative inquiry* into what human agency is capable of. Co-researchers who are also co-subjects can give each other corrective feedback: they can illuminate and clarify the human process for each other.

The Argument from Language

The generation and use of language is the original, archetypal form of human inquiry. Language enables human beings to symbolize — that is, state propositions about — their particular experiences in terms of general concepts. I can use general terms to symbolize a particular experience, or I can use them to make a generalization about many particular experiences. In either case it is the generality of the terms of a language that gives it its peculiar symbolizing power.

When two people communicate in the same language, they necessarily agree in the use of the rules of that language. Agreement about these rules is, of course, agreement in use, it is not explicitly stated spoken agreement, since few people who know how to use a language can formulate its many rules. How can we explain such agreement in use?

Apart from the fact that in practice people who speak the same language don't use that language to agree about its rules, in principle agreement about the rules of language cannot ultimately be mediated by language. We cannot use words to agree about the use of *all* words: this is logically impossible. For language to get started at all, there must be some words agreement about the use of which is mediated non-verbally.

One might say, following Chomsky (1975) that human beings are genetically programmed with linguistic universals, deep structure rules that apply to any and every language. Apart from being a highly controversial theory, this doesn't help; for we still have to explain how persons agree in the use of a particular language, with all its idiosyncratic, surface structure rules.

Thomas Reid's thesis (Reid, 1764) was that agreement about the use of words is ultimately mediated by what he called the 'natural language' of eyes, facial expression, gesture, non-verbal sound; and indeed such non-verbal expressive signs would seem to be the only contenders for mediating agreement about language use. But unless human beings also agree in what *these* expressive signs mean, they cannot use them to agree about how to use words. So we now have to explain how people agree in the use of non-verbal expressive signs.

Reid dealt with this point by arguing that expressive signs have a meaning which every human being understands 'by the principle of his nature' and which is prior to all agreement. Wittgenstein (1953) made a related sort of point when he wrote: 'The common behaviour of mankind is the system of reference by means of which we interpret an unknown language.' What this kind of argument boils down to is the view that human beings can understand what at any rate some of their non-verbal signs to each other mean, without this understanding being mediated through any other set of signs. This view seems to be inescapable since (a) there appear to be no candidates for such a further set of signs, and (b) if there were, we would have launched ourselves on an endless regress of one set of signs mediating agreement about the use of another set of signs, agreement about the use of the former set being mediated by the use of a third set, and so on.

Our agreement about the use of the language we are both speaking, on this analysis, rests finally on a mutuality of understanding about some of the non-verbal expressive signs we make to each other. By 'mutuality of understanding' I mean that we each understand the same sort of sign produced by each other in the same sort of way, and moreover we know that we are so doing. One candidate for such a sign is eye contact; another is touch. When two persons look into each other's eyes, the mutual gazing combines both simultaneity and reciprocity. Each person is looking into the other's eyes and having his own eyes looked into; and all four phenomena are occurring simultaneously.

I suggest that there is a tacit dimension of mutual gazing (and associated signs) that enables us at a basic level of awareness to agree about the use of words; and that this dimension involves a pre-linguistic experiential knowing that is primarily relational. What we know is the relation between, the *interconnectedness* of: our presence to each other, our world, our eyes, and other signs. Such knowing is tacit, inchoate, unfocused. It does not of itself give us explicit propositonal knowledge of facts and truths about ourselves and our world, but it enables us to *agree how to use language to make such propositions*. Nor of course does it do so alone: there is also touch, and, tangential to the gaze, facial expression, gesture of head, arms and hands, sound, and so on. It mediates a tacit, experiential, primitive, Tao of knowing which constitutes a ground for the figure of explicit knowledge. The knowing is tacit in Polanyi's sense (Polanyi, 1967): we attend *from* the relational awareness implicit in this dimension of mutual gazing in order to attend *to* the meaning of what is being explicitly said and done in terms of our mastery of language and other social norms. But the significance of what we attend from is evident in the agreement in usage in what we attend to. Such tacit knowing is not immaculate: it needs the focusing provided by explicit propositional knowledge; and it is only one of three sorts of experiential knowledge of persons — a point which I shall develop in the next section.

What follows from this sort of analysis? If the use of language is validated by *interpersonal* experiential knowing, then language is primarily public and shared: it is a collective product whose primary locutions are relational — 'we', 'our world', 'our signs', 'our language'. Secondly, the original and archetypal paradigm of human inquiry is two persons who agree through face-to-face meaningful encounter about how to symbolize their experience in words. The propositions about persons in the world which they generate are a cooperative construct, a social artefact, whose use is validated for them by the touchstone of their direct encounter.

The use of language itself, then, contains within it the paradigm of cooperative inquiry; and since language is the primary tool whose use enables human construing and intending to occur, it is difficult to see how there can be any more fundamental model of inquiry for human beings into the human condition. For at its roots, language is used to mediate a *shared* vision.

Now, of course, I *can* use language to make statements about persons who have not contributed or assented to the formulation of those statements. And, of course, there is a strong case for so doing both in everyday life and certain sorts of more peripheral research on persons as beings who have reaction-times, psychophysical thresholds, and so on. But when we come to more central research on persons as intelligent agents in relation who construe, and have intentions within, their world, to use language in this way is to cut it off from its validating base in the realities of human encounter. For the researchers on the traditional research model encounter each other but generate out of *this* interpersonal experience no statements of a shared view about persons; and the researchers encounter their subjects but generate out of *this* interpersonal experience no statements of a shared view of persons. Rather the researchers encounter each other to generate statements not about themselves but about their subjects — who make no contribution to the formulation of those statements either out of their encounter with each other or with the researchers. The result is a set of alienated statements hanging in an interpersonal void: statements about persons not authorized by those persons in relation. For a science of persons as agents, my considered view of your reality without consulting you is a very different matter from our considered view of our reality.

Another way of putting this is to say that central research on persons cannot be separated from the revisionary use of language. Persons are language creators who in relation symbolize a shared vision and experience. In fundamental research on the human condition, persons in relation regenerate the use of language, revise and extend its protocols, through cooperative endeavour in symbolizing the ways in which they have extended the horizons of their shared vision and experience.

The Argument from an Extended Epistemology

Science, as product, is in the domain of propositional knowledge. The outcome of research is stated in propositions, which claim to be assertions of facts or truths, a contribution to the corpus of knowledge statements. A claimed fact or truth is a propositional entity, a construct, an artefact — it is a statement about the world. It does not constitute the world; is not part of, or found in, the world. Propositions may be latent in and inform our perception of the world, but perception is wider than and transcends its latent propositional content, as I shall argue below. Indeed, if this were not so, we could not use perception of the world as a check on the accuracy of our propositions about the world.

Science, as a process of inquiry, involves not only propositional knowledge, but also practical knowledge and experiential knowledge. Practical knowledge is evident in some skill, proficiency or knack, whether physical and/or mental. It is knowing how to do something. Knowing how to do research is a set of interrelated acquired skills which cannot be fully reduced to any set of written instructions. Understanding instructions about how to do research is not the same as having the actual practical knack of doing it.

Experiential knowledge is knowing an entity — person, place, thing, process, etc. — in face-to-face encounter and interaction. It is knowing a person or thing through sustained acquaintance. Empirical research, precisely because it is empirical, necessarily requires some degree of experiential knowledge of the persons or objects which the research is about. The researcher's conclusions are propositions about persons or things of which he or she has had experiential knowledge through direct encounter.

Experiential knowledge through encounter or acquaintance with what is before me involves more than just bare or minimal perception. It involvs familiarity with the encountered entity through sustained perception and interaction. It includes both construing and doing — with some degree of commitment to get to know what is in front of me. It is knowing the world present here and now before me, and cannot be fully reduced to a set of descriptive statements about that world. Reading a description of a place is never the same as getting to know that place through going there, exploring, and encountering it. But more than this, experiential knowledge of an entity always transcends any set of propositions about it, and any set of propositions that may be involved in the way we perceive it.

When I perceive an entity in front of me, there are at least two sorts of construing going on. I will call these propositional construing and presentational construing. *Propositional* construing in perception involves seeing the entity in terms of the concepts and identifying names that come with the acquisition of language. So I see it as an entity of some sort or kind, as a cat, house, tree, or my friend George; I see it as having certain describable qualities; and as being in certain describable relations with other entities. But this linguistic construing that informs perceptions is interwoven with a complementary, non-linguistic, spatio-temporal, *presentational* construing. At the physiological level, the former involves left hemisphere brain function, the latter right hemisphere brain function (Ornstein, 1977).

Presentational construing is at several levels. Firstly, it involves seeing the apparent, presented, perspectival form, colour, size as the whole, 'actual', or 'real' or 'constant' form, colour, and size. I imaginatively grasp the whole entity in and with this particular view of it. So I see that presented flattened little oval with a bluish hue as a white circular plate of regular size — and this spatial construing of total form and colour is not dependent on the propositional competence with which I here assert it. Secondly, it involves seeing or hearing a sequence of presentations, a seriatim display, as a total cycle process or metamorphosis. Thus I hear the serial sounds as a piece of music, I see the serial presentations of the form of a bird in the sky as a total arc or spiral of movement.

This construing of what is immediately presented as a spatio-temporal whole that transcends what is immediately presented, is not only a means of experiential knowing, it is also a fundamental kind of practical knowledge — knowing how to orientate oneself in space and time, knowing how to construe presentations or appearance in terms of spatial and temporal 'reality'. It is not language-dependent, it is extra-propositional, since it is evident in the spatio-temporal competence of animals, in their coordination of perception and action in their environment. It is also, of course, evident in children before the acquisition of language. Indeed, some significant degree of competence in presentational construing in perception can be argued as a necessary condition of language acquisition.

While I can make some translation of the process of presentational construing into propositional construing — as, for example, when I talk of the perceptual constancies and so on — yet I can never fully accommodate in language the perceptual achievement of construing these presentations as that spatio-temporal whole of which they are the presentations. This is a practical cognitive and perceptual skill operating essentially outside the domain of language. Such skill may indeed be enhanced by the acquisition and use of language; and for the adult, presentationally construed wholes may always at the same time be propositionally construed as wholes of certain sorts or named kinds. But the extra-linguistic right hemispherical nature of presentational construing remains irreducible, complementary to left hemispherical propositional construing. Furthermore, it enables us to make an empirical check on the validity of our propositional constructs about the world. My ability to discriminate between different presentations and different spatio-temporal wholes without this ability being dependent on language and proposition-making, provides a touchstone for the accuracy with which I symbolize such differences in propositions.

But there is a third level of presentational construing in perception: and that is construing a series of presentations or appearances not just as presentations of a spatio-temporal whole that transcends its immediate presentations, but also as the presentations of a *presence* in space and time. For the spatio-temporal whole is making a non-linguistic statement, it is 'saying' something in and through the gesture of its totality. I look at an owl on a perch in a cage. I construe the presented form and colour as the 'real' form and colour, the presented sequence of movements as a total gestalt of movement. But at the same time, I construe all these presentations as those of a unique and idiosyncratic presence in space and time. The spatio-temporal whole presented is the mark, the gesture, the signature, the 'speech', of a presence.

If you sceptically ask me to be more precise in defining a presence, then I can only repeat that it is what you extra-linguistically construe a spatio-temporal whole *as*. It is a matter, a basic and fundamental matter, of non-propositional, experiential knowledge of some entity here and now before you. Of course, the poet or artist is highly sensitive at this third level of presentational construing. He or she moves, in the creative act, swiftly from presentational construing of the unique spatio-temporal gesture of a presence either to linguistic construing, trying to find an analogue in words for that unique gesture, or to the generation of a presentational analogue in painting, sculpture, music, dance, and so on. In this domain of perception, the artist is concerned with the archetypal 'speech' of the encountered world, a 'speech' which finds only its remote echo in everyday language. It was, of course, a fundamental canon of classical Chinese art to catch in painting this rhythmic, vital, autonomous 'utterance' of things.

Now my fullest encounter with a presence in space and time is when that presence is encountering *me*. I can see a dog leaping up excitedly at someone else, and I am certainly having a passive, non-interactive, rather external encounter with a presence. The qualitative impact in construing that presence in space and time is very different when the dog leaps up excitedly at me. Similarly when an owl and I are looking at each other in face-to-face encounter, I construe the owl as presence more fully than when I see it going about other business from afar. No doubt both approaches, the onlooker and the face-to-face, are relevant to experiential knowledge; but the face-to-face approach is primary, for only then do I encounter a presence encountering me.

For persons, other persons are *the* pre-eminent presences in space and time. As with the dog and the owl, when I directly interact with a person, I construe and encounter him or her as present more fully than when I observe a person interacting with someone else. And the more fully I interact the more fully I construe him or her as a presence. I construe a person more fully as a presence when we are in a very aware committed, concerned, exploratory, inquiring relationship. Hence again the paradigm of cooperative inquiry.

On this sort of analysis the most complete empirical base for a science of persons is one in which my necessary experiential knowledge of my subjects is: (1) not dominated by propositional construing to the detriment of a really open presentational construing; (2) not simply restricted to observing them in interaction with others, but focuses centrally on their reciprocal interaction with myself, so that we become both co-researchers and co-subjects.

There would seem to be at least three sorts of presentational construing of a person as a presence. Firstly, there is the pre-linguistic, mutual and simultaneous, tacit construing of two persons as presences in relation in a shared spatio-temporal world — mutual gazing being central to this. I have already referred to this in the previous section as the primitive Tao of experiential knowing: a tacit knowing of the interconnectedness of human presences in and with their world, a knowing which provides a warrant for, and is evident in our agreement about, the use of language.

Secondly, I construe a person as a presence while talking and interacting with him or her. And this presentational construing is interwoven, of course, with propositional construing — that is, with seeing, hearing, acting towards, the person in terms of the concepts that come with language. But the presentational construing when fully exercised and opened up can include and transcend the propositional. For I can construe the whole spatio-temporal gestalt of a person, both non-verbal and verbal — including the sequence of gestures, postures, facial expressions, eye contacts, paralinguistic features of speech, together with the meaning of what is said and what is not said — as the idiosyncratic developing signature of a human presence. I am encountering and construing *how* such a presence is manifesting, and not manifesting, in space and time. I grasp this *how* presentationally, extra-propositionally, since it includes explicit speech and intention in a much more comprehensive 'speech' or 'statement' of a total way of being in a world. This kind of total presentational construing of a person is a skill, a competence, that can be cultivated. Its findings can be symbolized by propositions but never fully encompassed by propositions. It offers a fundamental empirical touchstone for any fully systematic enquiry into persons.

Thirdly, and in parentheses, there is perhaps a post-linguistic construing of a person as a presence: for example, when two people gaze into each other's eyes, suspend or bracket off the propositional elements in their perception and awareness of each other, and mutually apprehend each other as presences in relation. This can lead to experiences of dual unity and related altered states of consciousness.

What I am arguing in this section is that empirical research on persons involves a subtle, developing interdependence between propositional knowledge, practical knowledge, and experiential knowledge. The research conclusions, stated as propositions and laying claim to be part of the corpus of empirical knowledge about persons, necessarily rest on the researchers' experiential knowledge of the subjects of the inquiry. This knowledge of persons is most adequate as an empirical base when it involves the fullest sort of presentational construing; that is, when researcher and subject are fully present to each other in a relationship of reciprocal and open inquiry, and when each is open to construe how the other manifests as a presence in space and time. And knowing how to construe and encounter persons in this way is a skill, a knack, which is a critical sort of practical knowledge involved in doing effective research on persons.

So the propositional outcomes of the research depend critically on the practical and experiential components of the process of the research. But proposition-making is very much part of the process of the inquiry too. The co-researchers' practical competence in presentational construing in relation with each other can be enhanced or hindered by the sorts of propositional constructs used during the inquiry; and also, therefore, the co-researchers' openness or closure to what can be known experientially. If the inquiry is over-conceptualized and over-theorized, then the phenomenological noticing and awareness of the researchers will be inhibited and restricted. If the inquiry is under-conceptualized and under-theorized, then the researchers' pheno-menological noticing will be diffuse, unfocused, chaotic, ambiguous. Too much propositional construing blinds researchers to the gestures of being. Too much presentational construing keeps the archives of propositional knowledge empty, although it *may,* of course, fill up the vaults of presentational knowledge in the form of drawing, painting, sculpture, music, dance. Co-researchers who are also co-subjects need to find a mutually enhancing balance and interaction between left hemisphere and right hemisphere brain functions.

The Argument from Axiology

The products of research on persons are propositions (they could also be artistic presentations — but that possibility merits a separate paper). The hope and claim of effective research is to generate true propositions. The truth-value of a proposition is in part a function of its coherence with other and related propositions, and in part a function of its correspondence with extra-propositional dimensions of the world as encountered. Of these two criteria of truth, coherence and correspondence, the latter seems to me more fundamental, for however internally coherent any set of propositions, it remains but an unanchored set of possibilities until it corresponds in substantial part to the world as encountered. It is this that provides the basic touchstone for the truth value of propositions in empirical research. More precisely, it is the world as presentationally construed when encountered that provides the touchstone; for this provides the extra-propositional element in perception, and so provides a warp for the woof of propositions. I have argued this point in more detail in the previous section.

But the presentational or presented world is valued. And because we value it — for its charm, beauty, elegance, ineffability, or whatever other predicates we generate to convey our non-verbal delight in being — we seek to symbolize it adequately in propositions. The assertion of true propositions is a way of enhancing our appreciation of a world we already value in encountering it. Behind the truth-value of propositions lie the being values of the experienced, presented world. Between the two, mediating, lie the norms or rules of language, and of any other practical procedure that enables us to assert the truth about the world we value.

Because we value our encounter with what is there, we know how to symbolize it in words, and therefore our statement has the value of truth. Or to put it the other way round, our statement is true because we know how to formulate it to do justice to a valued experience. Out of our varied encounter with the world we generate norms of language and of related practices, to express true propositions about that world. There is an axiological hierarchy here: first the values of being, then the norms of language and of other practical procedures, then the truth-value of propositions, the facts or truths asserted in propositions.

More than this, language and the true propositions it is used to assert ultimately presuppose a *shared* community of value, a shared way of delighting in and valuing the world as encountered. This follows from the view that truth-values presuppose values of being, together with the view put forward earlier that agreement about the use of language presupposes a *shared* awareness of human presences in relation in their world. On this analysis, true propositions are asserted by those who know how properly to symbolize in words shared experiences of shared value: to learn a language and be able to state truths is *ipso facto* to acquire the norms and values of a shared culture — the immediate sub-culture and the wider culture of which it is part.

In general terms, truth is asserted through the application of norms of language and of other practical procedures by those who generate such norms out of a shared value system. The truths we assert are a function of our procedural norms which in turn are a function of our shared value system. The 'truths' researchers generate are a function of the researchers' procedural norms and underlying values. And if these 'truths' purport to be about persons other than the researchers then they have indeterminate validity, no secure status as truths, until we know whether those other persons assent to and regard as their own the norms and values of the researchers. For within the broad aegis of the culture of a whole society, there are manifold sub-cultures each with its own differential value system. Statements about you that do not take into account the values and norms of your sub-culture, but dress you up in the values and norms of my somewhat different sub-culture, are not really statements about you. Statements about persons as agents are true of those persons when the statements are reached by procedures that show cognizance of the values of those persons.

Thus, for example, questionnaires and all such instruments unilaterally designed by researchers will simply rest on their prior norms and values. And if the researchers make no attempt to determine whether those norms and values, and hence the design of the questionnaire, are acceptable to those who are invited to fill it in, then any statements about the respondents made by the researchers on the basis of the questionnaire results will have indeterminate validity. In some instances, of course, it may for all practical purposes be appropriate to *assume* consonance of the respondents' values with the researchers' values. In other instances, grossly distorted conclusions may emerge from so doing. For if the researchers are not themselves the respondents, then the conclusions will be 'truths' that hang in a curious void — alienated from the values of the researchers, and from the actual and different values of the respondents.

Finally, the idea that any science can be value-free is, in my view, a delusion. Persons in relation in their world symbolizing their experience of the value of the presented world constitutes a fundament of the human condition. Every science is just a special case of this symbolizing activity. When the subjects of a science are other persons, then the idea that the researchers' underlying value system can exclude, need not consult or consider or cooperate with the value system of the subjects, can only tend to generate alienated pseudo-truths about persons. For an authentic science of persons, true statements about persons rest on a value system explicitly shared by researchers and subjects, and on procedural research norms explicitly agreed by researchers and subjects on the basis of that value system. Hence, again, the model of cooperative inquiry.

The Political and Moral Argument

Traditional research on persons is also a way of exercising power over persons. The experimental subjects of course agree voluntarily to be subjects, but thereafter they do what they are asked to do in accordance with principles frequently not disclosed to them and in accordance with decisions made unilaterally by the researchers. At its very worst, researchers using this model get knowledge unilaterally from persons in order to be able to apply this knowledge unilaterally to other persons, with only token initial assent from these persons to initiate the research phase and the application phase. Research then becomes another agent of authoritarian social control. Knowledge and power are all on the side of the researchers and their political masters, and none is on the side of those who provide the data and are subject to its subsequent application.

Politics is essentially about power, and power is about who effectively makes decisions in what manner about what and about whom. In this sense, political issues are about the who, the what, and the how of decision-making, and pervade every arena of human life: the family, education, research, every organization and association of persons, as well as the state. Many researchers would probably assent to the moral case for political self-determination of citizens in the modern state. The moral principle of respect for personal autonomy requires that we give impartial consideration to the needs and interests of all, that we provide just conditions for the fulfilment of human well-being. Traditional and contemporary doctrines of human rights have spelt out some of the fundamental conditions required for such fulfilment: the right to freedom of speech and expression; the right to freedom of association and contract; the right to political membership of the community — to participate in the framing and the working of political institutions.

The last-named right — to political membership of the community — is in my view a special case of an all-pervasive right of persons to participate, through some appropriate arrangements, in decision-making that affects the fulfilment of their needs and interests. While acknowledging this right in the restricted political sense — that is, in the arena of local and national government — our society has been slow to acknowledge its relevance to industry and commerce, to organization structures generally, to the family, to education, and, of course, to research. But the same right must extend to the arena of research on persons. For persons, as autonomous beings, have a moral right to participate in decisions that claim to generate knowledge about them. Such a right does many things: (1) it honours the fulfilment of their need for autonomously acquired knowledge; (2) it protects them from becoming unwitting accessories to knowledge-claims that may be false and may be inappropriately or harmfully applied to others; (3) it protects them from being excluded from the formation of knowledge that purports to be about them and so from being managed and manipulated, both in the acquisition and in the application of the knowledge, in ways they do not understand and so cannot assent to or dissent from.

Knowledge fuels power: it increases the efficacy of decision-making. Knowledge about persons can fuel power *over* persons or fuel power *shared with* persons. And the moral principle of respect for persons is most fully honoured when power is shared not only in the application of knowledge about persons, but also in the generation of such knowledge. On this view researchers have a moral obligation to initiate subjects into the whole rationale of the research they are doing and to seek the free assent of subjects to this rationale so that, internalizing it as their own, the subjects can become autonomous inquirers alongside the researchers. Put in other words, doing research on persons involves an important educational commitment: to provide conditions under which subjects can enhance their capacity for self-determination in acquiring knowledge about the human condition.

Human Inquiry
Edited by P. Reason and J. Rowan
© 1981 John Wiley & Sons Ltd.

CHAPTER THREE

The subjective side of science
by Ian Mitroff: an appreciation

John Rowan
Independent Consultant, London, UK

This is really three books and an essay in one, and each of them is fascinating in itself.

The first book is about two contrasting versions of how scientists are supposed to work. The author gives a set of conventional norms, derived from orthodox texts and accounts of scientific method, and a set of counternorms derived partly from the work of Merton and partly from Mitroff's own work. These are shown in Table 3.1. The main point he makes is that both versions are used by scientists, and that the scientists who mainly use the counternorms are no less highly regarded than those who use the conventional norms. In fact, one of Mitroff's discoveries was that those scientists who were most highly regarded by their peers were those who adhered most to the counternorms, and who often dismissed the conventional norms as a 'storybook version' of science and scientists. And they looked down on those who did adhere to the conventional norms as mere journeymen or mere technicians.

So this first book, well supported by voluminous and precise data, is all about exploding the notion that science proceeds according to the storybook version. This means, of course, that Mitroff rejects the distinction put forward by Reichenbach between the context of discovery (where emotion and intuition are permitted) and the context of justification, where only sensation and thinking are allowed. Science, he says, has in actual practice learned how to make use of strong determinants of rationality (testing, evidence, etc.) plus strong emotional commitments.

37

Table 3.1 A dialectic between the conventional norms of science and a proposed set of counternorms

Conventional norms	Counternorms
1. *Faith in rationality*.	1. *Faith in rationality and non-rationality*.
2. *Emotional neutrality* as an instrumental condition for the achievement of rationality.	2. *Emotional commitment* as an instrumental condition for the achievement of rationality.
3. *Universalism*: in science all have morally equal claims to the discovery and possession of rational knowledge.	3. *Particularism*: in science some men have special claims to the discovery and possession of rational knowledge.
4. *Individualism* (which expresses itself in science particularly as anti-authoritarianism).	4. *Societalism* (which expresses itself in science in contrast to the lawlessness and chaos of anarchism).
5. *Community*: private property rights are reduced to credit for priority of discovery; secrecy thus becomes an immoral act.	5. *Solitariness*: private property rights are expanded to include control over the disposition of one's discoveries; secrecy thus becomes a necessary moral act.
6. *Disinterestedness*: men are expected to achieve their self-interest in work satisfaction and prestige through serving the community interest.	6. *Interestedness*: men are expected to achieve their self-interest in work satisfaction and prestige through serving their special community of interest.
7. *Impartiality*: a scientist concerns himself only with the production of new knowledge and not with the consequences of its use.	7. *Partiality*: a scientist must concern himself as much with the consequences of his discoveries as with their production; to do any less is to make the scientist into an immoral agent who has no concern for the moral consequences of his activities.
8. *Suspension of judgement*: scientific statements are made only on the basis of conclusive evidence.	8. *Exercise of judgement*: scientific statements are always made in the face of inconclusive evidence; to be a scientist is to exercise expert judgement in the face of incomplete evidence.
9. *Absence of bias*: the validity of scientific statement depends only on the operations by which evidence for it was obtained, and not upon the person who makes it.	9. *Presence of bias*: in reality the validity of a scientific statement depends both on the operations by which evidence for it was obtained and upon the person who makes it; the presence of bias forces the scientist to acknowledge the operation of bias and to attempt to control for it.
10. *Group loyalty*: production of new knowledge by research is the most important of all activities and is to be supported as such.	10. *Loyalty to humanity*: production of new knowledge by research in the general sustenance of man is the most important of all activities and is to be supported as such; elitism is to be frowned on.
11. *Freedom*: all restraint or control of scientific investigation is to be resisted.	11. *Management of research*: science is a scarce national resource and as such it is to be as carefully managed and planned for as any other scarce resource.

Reprinted by permission of the publisher from The Subjective Side of Science by Ian Mitroff, p. 79. Copyright 1974 by Elsevier North Holland Inc.

The second book is about setting up a typology of scientists. Mitroff found three main types of scientist:

Experimentalist. Markedly analytical and precise, this kind of scientist is very much of a specialist. He collects data and publishes them with little interpretation. He is a careful, good, thorough worker who often prides himself on not speculating at all.

Middle-of-the-road. A flexible scientist, who can get good data and interpret them in interesting ways. He is both an experimentalist and a theoretician. The majority of the scientists studied fell into this group.

Speculative theorist. Extremely brilliant, creative and aggressive, this kind of scientist is both biased and rigid in defence of his position. He excels at extrapolating from data, and relishes theorizing about them. Sometimes he will not even both to collect his own data, but will take other people's work, put it together, synthesize it and come out with a big picture.

It should be made clear that we are talking here about selenologists, and other types would appear in addition if we were considering social science. (See Chapter 4). But even as far as it goes, this is interesting, because it turns out that prestige in the field is lowest for the experimentalist, data-gathering type (sometimes dismissed as 'technicians with Ph.D.s'), and highest for the speculative theorists with all their defects of precision and orderliness.

In this book we get a rich picture of how real, living, breathing scientists talk and think about each other — and also how they fill in and think about psychological scales. For Mitroff not only administered semantic-differential scales to these scientists, but also recorded their detailed reactions to each scale — their objections, their confusions, and in some cases their refusals.

We get a lot of confirmation of the typology, by considering very specific controversies which were sorted out to some extent by the evidence of the moon rocks. The speculative scientists did indeed ignore evidence or reveal a highly selective approach to the evidence; they did indeed pay little attention to the scientific opinions of colleagues on the issues. With the experimentalist, on the contrary, it was hard even to identify his position in any polarized or contentious issue. He simply went with the evidence without any show of resistance.

Mitroff tries on some other ideas for size, like a Jungian typology and an Apollo/Dionysus contrast, but really these are not pushed very far, and the threefold typology remains dominant.

The third book is one about the philosophy of science. What is the epistemology of inquiring systems? Mitroff examines five such systems.

(1) *Formal-deductive* The interest here is in the construction and exploration of purely theoretical models. This is done by starting from a set of primitive truths, subjecting them to a set of formal operations or transformations, and

ending up with a network of formal propositions. This approach is best suited to well-structured problems, which have an optimal decision as a likely outcome. (Mitroff calls this a Leibnitzian system.)

(2) *Consensual-inductive* The approach here is to build up increasingly more universal inductive generalizations from the elementary sensory data of raw experience. This is subjected to a process of consensual validation, or intersubjective agreement. This again is an approach best suited to well-structured problems. (Mitroff calls this a Lockean system.)

(3) *Synthetic-representational* Here the approach is to produce at least two alternative models, so that the question of what underlying assumptions are made can be looked at. This approach attempts to reconcile the demands both of rationalism and of empiricism. It is particularly strong where a multi-disciplinary problem is in question, and is best suited to problems of moderate ill-structure. (This Mitroff calls a Kantian system.)

(4) *Dialectical-conflictual* As before, the approach is to produce at least two alternative models, but this time they must be in opposition. Each must be adversary to the other, in some way. It is hoped that out of a confrontation between contradictory interpretations, the underlying assumptions of both models will be brought up to the surface for conscious examination. This approach is best suited to wickedly ill-structured problems, which can involve intense debate over the true nature of the problem. (This one Mitroff calls a Hegelian system.)

(5) *Pragmatic-interdisciplinary* This is an approach which uses the language of commands. Instead of saying that something *has* a certain property, it says — 'Assume that it has that property!' This is to recognize that a decision only translates into reality if the inquirer can convince enough people to regard its conclusions as valid. As a computer programmer would say, the whole design is instructions, including the so-called data base. There is no problem of deducing an 'ought' from an 'is', because there is no reference at all to what is. Hence this version of science can be seen as ethical as much as scientific. It is best suited to problems having an ethical component which is important. (Mitroff calls this a Singerian-Churchmannian system.)

We can now see much more clearly that there are many inquiry systems, and hence many approaches to objectivity, validity, and truth. And this enables us to come full circle and see that the so-called counternorms of science which we looked at in the first book are in fact just a front for a whole range of different approaches which can justify them both logically and ethically. At first we saw them, perhaps, as just a curiosity of deviation; but now we see them as expressing deep insights about the pursuit of truth. Perhaps science advances through the process of scientists of widely different persuasions thrusting their opposing conceptions and commitments at each other, thus illuminating those who observe the process.

In the final essay, Mitroff suggests that science is a game. In the course of pursuing many interesting thoughts suggested by this metaphor, he puts forward the view that it is a peculiarly *masculine* game as now practised. The stereotypical scientist, as he discovered in his research, is seen as supporting traditional masculine values (aggressive, hard-driving, self-serving, power-oriented, authoritarian, sceptical, diligent, precise) and as unconcerned with feelings. And Mitroff suggests that the educational system underwrites and confirms this state of affairs, quoting Kubie with approval: 'I am unhappy at our complacency with a primitive educational process which to so large an extent reinforces everything neurotic in human nature.' Because the masculinity Mitroff found so highly stressed amongst scientists was of an exaggerated and peculiar kind. As Mitroff himself says — 'It is closer to the truth to say that it is their intense, raw and even brutal aggressiveness that stands out . . . As one of the respondents put it, "if you want to get anybody to believe your hypothesis, you've got to beat them down with numbers; you've got to hit them again and again over the head with hard data until they're stupefied into believing it". ' This masculinity perhaps makes it clearer why there are few women scientists.

Three books, then: one on the norms and counternorms of scientific method; one on a typology of physical scientists; and one on a typology of inquiring systems; and a final essay on science as a game. And it seems to me that they hang together well, and between them make some very powerful suggestions as to how we can think better about science and scientists.

In particular, the direct relevance to the present work is most obviously in the third of the three books: we can much more easily avoid falling into the traps of types 1 and 2 if we know about 3, 4, and 5. And perhaps more important from a practical point of view, we can avoid being pushed by supervisors, research committees, and funding bodies into Type 1, if we are able to argue in terms of types 2, 3, 4, and 5.

Human Inquiry
Edited by P. Reason and J. Rowan
© 1981 John Wiley & Sons Ltd.

CHAPTER FOUR

Methodological approaches to social science by Ian Mitroff and Ralph Kilmann: an appreciation

Peter Reason
Centre for the Study of Organizational Change and Development, University of Bath, UK

Starting from the view that there is a 'crisis in scientific belief', Mitroff and Kilmann aim to examine 'the underlying psychological and sociological reasons for different attitudes toward science'.

> Although we feel that some of the criticisms regarding science are misguided or wrong, we do feel the crisis is real. The critics are pointing to some serious defects, which are rooted in the structure of science. Our view is that science is in serious need of methodological and epistemological reform (p. 3).

The crisis is particularly serious in the social sciences:

> The main reason why the social sciences have given a fragmentary and incomplete account of the nature of man is that the social sciences have themselves been conceived of and practiced in a largely fragmentary and incomplete manner (p. 3)

Their view is that science has been largely created and practiced in terms of one particular psychological style, that it is the 'projection of one particular psyche'; their view is also that alternative forms of science based on alternative psychological styles are possible, and the major part of their book is a systematic mapping of some alternatives.

Their first step in this is to construct a typology of ways in which social scientists think about science — recognizing that while there are dangers in typology construction, they are nevertheless useful ways of helping us see and understand complex patterns. Having reviewed the writings of other authors who have attempted a similar task (Hudson, 1968; Gordon *et al.,* 1974; Mitroff, 1974; Maslow, 1966), they settle on the psychological types proposed by C. G. Jung (1971) as the basis for their own typology.

Jung's types are based on two dimensions: the first concerns the kind of input data the individual characteristically prefers (the informational dimension), and the second is about the preferred way of dealing with this information (the decision-making dimension). These two are independent and orthogonal. Individuals can take in information from the internal or external world either by sensation (S) or intuition (N); these are seen by Jung as antithetical psychological processes, that cannot occur simultaneously, so the individual develops a preference for one or the other. Those who prefer S take in information via the *senses,* are interested in details and the specifics of a situation, prefer hard, 'realistic' facts, and pay attention to the here and now, the practical. In contrast, those who prefer N take in information through their *imagination*, and are interested in the whole, in the gestalt; they are idealists, interested in hypothetical possibilities, in what might be, in the creation of novel, innovative viewpoints.

On the decision-making dimension, Jung again saw two antithetical possibilities: on the one hand thinking (T), and on the other, feeling (F). Individuals who prefer T use reasoning which is impersonal, formal, or theoretical; their thinking is independent of human needs and concerns, but seeks the 'truth'; they are interested in abstract generalizations. Thinking takes its highest forms in systems of logic. In contrast, those who prefer F as a decision-making mode are interested in reaching personalistic value-judgements which may be unique to the individual; they explain via empathy, and value things in human terms. While Thinking generalizes, Feeling individuates and is concerned with the unique worth of the phenomena or person. Feeling reaches its highest forms in the variety of ethical systems which have been developed.

Putting these two dimensions together suggests four 'psychological types': the sensing-thinking types, the sensing-feeling types, the intuition-feeling types, and the intuition-thinking types. Each type possesses and combines the characteristics of one pole of each dimension. These types are *not* necessarily fixed for life, but are rather pure types or extremes: an individual may switch between types, or may move from one type to another through her life-span. Also each type has an extreme opposite (e.g. the opposite of ST is NF) which represents the unconscious, blind, and undeveloped side of that type.

Mitroff and Kilmann argue that these four types also represent 'basic styles of thinking about and doing science': they map the work of the earlier authors

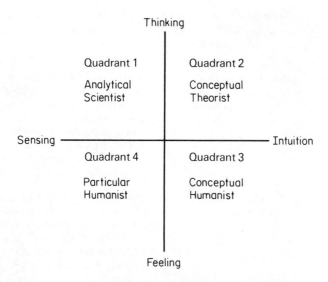

Figure 4.1   A typology of scientists (adapted from Mitroff
and Kilmann, 1978)

reviewed onto the Jungian typology (see Figure 4.1) and so develop their own
typology of scientists: The Analytical Scientist (S with T); the Conceptual
Theorist (N with T); the Conceptual Humanist (N with F); and the Particular
Humanist (S with F). The next four chapters of their book contain a detailed
analysis of these four types and their implications for social science
methodology.

There is obviously a lot to be said about each of these four types, and for a
detailed discussion the reader is referred to Mitroff and Kilmann's book. Here
we will simply indicate the central issue for each style, and reproduce Mitroff
and Kilmann's summary tables for each, so the reader may see the range of
their discussion (Tables 4.1-4.4).

The Analytical Scientist's basic drive is towards certainty; he or she is
concerned with precision, accuracy, and reliability:

> To know is to be certain about something. Certainty is defined by
> the ability to 'phrase' or enumerate the components of an object,
> event, person, or situation in a precise, accurate, and reliable
> fashion. Therefore knowledge is synonymous with precision,
> accuracy, and reliability. Any endeavour that cannot be subjected
> to this formula or line of reasoning is either suppressed, devalued,
> or set aside as not worth knowing or capable of being known (p.
> 33).

Table 4.1   Characteristics of the Analytical Scientist

	Evaluative categories	Attributed characteristics
External relations	Status of science as a special field of knowledge in relation to other fields	Occupies a privileged and a preferred position: value-free, apolitical, cumulative, progressive, disinterested, clearly separable from other fields, clear lines of demarcation, autonomous, independent, strict hierarchical ordering of scientific fields from precise to less precise fields.
Internal properties	A. Nature of scientific knowledge	Impersonal, value-free, disinterested, precise, reliable, accurate, valid, reductionistic, causal, apolitical, cumulative, progressive, clear standards for judgement, realistic, anti-mystical, unambiguous, exact.
	B. Guarantors of scientific knowledge	Consensus, agreement, reliability, external validity, rigour, controlled nature of inquiry, maintenance of distance between scientist and objects studied.
	C. Ultimate aims of science	Precise, unambiguous, theoretical and empirical knowledge for their own (disinterested) sake.
	D. Preferred logic	Aristotelean, strict classical logic, non-dialectical and indeterminate.
	E. Preferred sociological norms (ideology)	Classical norms of CUDOS*.
	F. Preferred mode of inquiry	Controlled inquiry as embodied in the classic concept of the experiment.
	G. Properties of the scientist	Disinterested, unbiased, impersonal, precise, expert, specialist, sceptical, exact, methodical.

* Communism, Universalism, Disinterestedness, Organised Scepticism.
From Mitroff and Kilmann, 1978.

The style of inquiry which the AS prefers may best be called controlled inquiry, of which the best representation is the controlled experiment, based on Mill's Canon of Induction (1872) and developed in modern form in Campbell and Stanley's (1966) treatise on experimental and quasi-experimental designs.

   The Conceptual Theorist shares the Thinking mode with the AS, and so shares the impersonal and theoretical orientation to science: where they differ

Table 4.2   Characteristics of the Conceptual Theorist

	Evaluative categories	Attributed characteristics
External relations	Status of science as a special field of knowledge in relation to other fields	Occupies a privileged and preferred position, but is not clearly separable from other fields; no clear lines of demarcation; not autonomous or independent, no strict hierarchical ordering of fields; all depend upon one another; science is, however, value-free and apolitical.
Internal properties	A. Nature of scientific knowledge	Impersonal, value-free, disinterested, holistic, valid, apolitical, imaginative, multiple-causation, purposeful ambiguity, uncertainty, problematic.
	B. Guarantors of scientific knowledge	Conflict between antithetical imaginative theories, comprehensive holistic theories, ever-expanding research.
	C. Ultimate aims of science	To construct the broadest possible conceptual schemes; multiple production of conflicting schemas.
	D. Preferred logic	Dialectical logics, indeterminate logics.
	E. Preferred sociological norms (ideology)	Norms are a function of one's theoretical perspective and cannot be separated from one's conceptual-theoretical interests.
	F. Preferred mode of inquiry	Conceptual inquiry; treatment of innovative concepts from multiple perspectives; invention of new schemas.
	G. Properties of the scientist	Disinterested, unbiased, impersonal, imaginative, speculative, generalist, holistic.

From Mitroff and Kilmann, 1978.

is on the information dimension: while AS is concerned with accuracy and certainty, in minimizing errors of hypothesis-testing and getting closer and closer to the 'truth', CT is concerned with imaginative and speculative theory building: he is interested in minimizing errors of hypothesis discovering. This viewpoint is best put over in an article by Davis (1971) entitled 'That's interesting . . .', in which the author argues that great scientists are great not because they produced 'true' theories but because they produced *interesting* ones, and goes on to classify and illustrate ways of being 'interesting'.

Table 4.3   Characteristics of the Conceptual Humanist

	Evaluative categories	Attributed characteristics
External relations	Status of science as a special field of knowledge in relation to other fields	Does not occupy a privileged and preferred position, is not clearly separable from other fields; no clear lines of demarcation; not autonomous and independent; all fields of knowledge depend upon one another. Science is not value-free; it is political.
Internal properties	A. Nature of scientific knowledge	Personal, value-constituted, interested activity; holistic; political; imaginative; multiple-causation; uncertain; problematic; concerned with humanity.
	B. Guarantors of scientific knowledge	Human conflict between knowing agent (E) and subject known (S); inquiry fosters human growth and development.
	C. Ultimate aims of science	To promote human development on the widest possible scale.
	D. Preferred logic	Dialectical behavioural logics.
	E. Preferred sociological norms (ideology)	Economic plenty, aesthetic beauty, human welfare.
	F. Preferred mode of inquiry	Conceptual inquiry; treatment of innovative concepts; maximal cooperation between E and S so that both may better know themselves and one another.
	G. Properties of the scientist	Interested; free to admit and know his biases; highly personal; imaginative, speculative, generalist; holistic.

From Mitroff and Kilmann, 1978.

So the CT's style of inquiry is 'conceptual exploration':

Whereas the AS attempts to find the single schema that best represents the world, the CT is interested in exploring, creating, and inventing multiple possible and hypothetical representations of the world — even hypothetical worlds themselves. Further, the CT's emphasis is on the large-scale differences between these different representations rather than the details of any single schema. A potential danger for the AS is getting bogged down in infinite details; a potential danger for the CT is ignoring them altogether for the sake of comprehensiveness. ASs tend to suffer

Table 4.4   Characteristics of the Particular Humanist

Evaluative categories		Attributed characteristics
External relations	Status of science as a special field of knowledge in relation to other fields	Does not occupy a privileged and special position; may be subordinate to poetry, literature, art, music, and mysticism as older, 'superior' ways of knowing.
Internal properties	A. Nature of scientific knowledge	Personal, value-constituted, interested; partisan activity; poetic, political, action-oriented; acausal, non-rational.
	B. Guarantors of scientific knowledge	Intense personal knowledge and experience.
	C. Ultimate aims of science	To help *this* person know himself or herself uniquely and to achieve his own self-determination.
	D. Preferred logic	The 'logic' of the unique and singular.
	E. Preferred sociological norms (ideology)	Counternorms to CUDOS.
	F. Preferred mode of inquiry	The case study; the in-depth detailed study of a particular individual.
	G. Properties of the scientist	Interested, 'all-too-human', biased, poetic, committed to the postulates of an action-oriented science.

From Mitroff and Kilmann, 1978.

from 'hardening of the categories'; CTs tend to suffer 'loosening of the wholes' (p. 68).

The Conceptual Humanist and the Particular Humanist are two styles of inquiry based on Feeling, and they are very different in style and outlook from the two previous styles: while AS and CT emphasize impersonal and dispassionate knowledge, CH and PH are about passionate and personal knowledge. They have developed — or rather are developing — in reaction to the inadequacy of AS and CT and to the distortion of understanding that they are seen to create. For CH and PH the goal is to produce a kind of social science which will further the development of human growth, awareness, and general welfare. Mitroff and Kilmann would probably see most of this book as falling within the style of the CH: indeed, they review in some detail John Rowan's research cycle (see Chapter 9) as an example of the CH style (we would disagree with this in some ways, since Rowan's intention is that the research cycle should encompass all modes of inquiry) particularly in its concern for questions beyond those about efficiency. Certainly the methodological approaches of Heron, Torbert, Esterson, Maruyama, and others in this book can be seen as broadly falling within the CH style.

But we are moving away from a traditional view of science here, and it is clearly important to map clearly what we are all about. At the end of their chapter on the CH style, the authors repeat C. West Churchman's question, 'Is storytelling science?', and rephrase it:

> The best stories are those which stir people's minds, hearts, and souls and by doing so give them new insights into themselves, their problems, and their human condition. The challenge is to develop a human science that more fully serves this aim.
>
> The question then is not, 'Is storytelling science?' but 'Can science learn to tell good stories?'

This challenge to traditional forms of science becomes most extreme in the style of the Particular Humanist, for whom 'Loving is a way of knowing, and for loving to know, it must personify' (Hillman, 1975). The PH has an

> intense concern with capturing and describing the uniqueness of particular human beings. The PH naturally treats every human being as though he or she were unique — not to be compared with anyone or anything else. Thus, the PH is not concerned in formulating general theories of human behaviour at all — not so much because this is impossible (although the PH argues it *is* impossible) but because it is not desirable. To study people in general, even from a humanistic perspective (like the CH's) is for the PH inevitably to lose sight of the unique humanity of an individual — to fail to capture precisely *this* person (p. 95).

Thus the preferred style of inquiry of the PH is the case study — 'the in-depth detailed rendering of the *life space* of a single individual or social group' — developed through participant observation with the added dimension of 'co-participant' interaction. And the preferred form of presentation is then the 'personalised descriptive account of real human characters' (the authors quote Torbert's account of a community of inquiry (1976a), as an example of this style). Thus we have in the PH a style of doing science which departs radically from the AS norms of detached rationality, but rather is based on a committed involvement:

> The challenge is to understand more fully what a Feeling science would look like by actively working to bring it about... Among

other things, a Feeling science would not be afraid to display an ever-present, underlying emotional basis beneath an apparently impersonal, logical, and rational surface structure of science, Science can no longer afford to deny its emotional foundations...

[C]onventional science is strongly masculine in its orientation, reflecting traditional stereotypical male values: it is 'hard-nosed', objective, value free; it eschews the ambiguous, the speculative, the vague, the beautiful, and the good. A feminine science in contrast is not afraid of the good, the speculative, the vague, or the unique; indeed, it openly courts them, openly confronts them, and makes positive virtues of them (pp. 103-4).

The authors suggest that it is the Particular Humanist who most enthusiastically adopts the counternorms outlined in the previous book, and who therefore makes the neatest antithesis to the Analytical Scientist. It is also antithetical in the sense that the Analytical Scientist is the most 'masculine' and the Particular Humanist the most 'feminine'.

Finally, in the last chapter of their book, Mitroff and Kilmann attempt to show that there is an interdependence between the four styles of doing science they have described, that they are interrelated aspects of a systemic view of knowledge, which must co-exist within the institution of science. Their final argument is that we must learn to see and appreciate the contributions of others working in different styles, and not get lost in the 'ethnocentrism' of our own particular approach and methodology. This final chapter attempts to tie all the ends together, but it fails quite signally to do so, and the reason is obvious. All this stuff is much too new, and it is too early to tie it all up with a neat bow.

Human Inquiry
Edited by P. Reason and J. Rowan
© 1981 John Wiley & Sons Ltd.

CHAPTER FIVE

The troubled fish: barriers to dialogue

John Southgate
Department of Applied Social Studies,
Polytechnic of North London, UK
and Rosemary Randall
Department of Community Education, Open University, UK

Much current research in the social sciences is concerned with being of some direct use to those who are normally considered to be the 'subjects' of the research process. Most of this goes under the name of 'action research' and one of the central problems facing its practitioners is the nature of the interactions between themselves and their 'clients', particularly where the research aspires to be a liberatory process for all concerned. In addition there is the problem of generalizing from research results that are often highly specific and of communicating them to other academics who may be critical of the methodology underlying action research and question its validity. At all levels the problem is one of communicating between groups who may hold widely differing assumptions about the nature and significance of what is being done.

We describe in another article how in some research we did we adapted the work of Paulo Freire (1976) to give ourselves a coherent methodological framework. One of Freire's key concepts is that of 'dialogue', a process of communication he counterposes to 'invasion' or 'cultural invasion'. Cultural invasion is the imposition of the values, belief systems, ideology, cultural norms and practices of an imperialist culture on those it has colonized and oppressed. Its basis is an unequal relationship. Its object is social, economic, and political control. The opposite process, dialogue, is based on equality in relationship (which has to have a real, material base), mutual respect, and understanding. Freire's concepts of dialogue and invasion are as applicable at the individual and small-group level as at the level of institutions and societies. In a culture based on invasion at all levels of relationship, dialogue can be hard to achieve even where the intentions of all parties are good. It is of course impossible where the intentions of one party, consciously or unconsciously, are to control the other. But there are many other situations, between individuals and groups of people, formal or informal, where dialogue is difficult or where it is hard to see whether or not it is really possible.

A contradiction we encountered in our research was that whereas we gradually became fairly sophisticated and effective in achieving dialogue with those we 'researched' it was another question altogether when we engaged in discussion with other academics. We felt invaded — misunderstood and misrepresented. We clearly had a similar effect on others. One could simply say that these somewhat explosive and unsatisfactory arguments were due to differing methodological and philosophical assumptions. Bourgeois scientists have never cared over-much for Marxist assumptions and have never tried over-hard to understand them. Political and ideological considerations, often unconscious, dictate such a state of affairs. We felt this to be a somewhat facile side-stepping of the issue, however. Although much that is good has been written on the philosophy and ideology of science, critiquing it from a Marxist perspective, it is not necessarily much use in practice. To simply accept the argument as confined to the ideological and political sphere consigned us forever to isolation as Marxists working in the area of group relations.

Our solution was a piece of what Freire calls 'problematizing', which we presented to the seminar we were participating in. It went as follows.

'A fish can have no understanding of the concept "wetness" since it has no idea of what it means to be dry.' A parable will help our exposition. Two Contractors arrive to work on a house. They have received instructions from the owner. The first is a Demolition Contractor with instructions to knock it down. The second is a Restorer of Ancient Buildings with instructions to restore it to its original condition. To solve their differences the Contractors call in four wise Consultants. Consultant A says 'You must each do your own thing. You are both right according to your own lights, your inner selves.' They don't find this information very satisfying. So they ask Consultant B for his opinion. He says 'There is a whole continuum of concepts and possibilities ranging from obliterating the house to restoring it. You should at least look at what part of this is common to you and vice-versa. Do a literature search. Be creative.' 'Oh', says the Demolition Contractor, 'I'll get the whole bloody lot down in 5 minutes with my ball and chain.' 'That'll destroy the building you fool', replies the Restorer. 'Let's ask Consultant C'. She says 'This building has a history and has grown like an organism. It can live or die but not both. Moreover, your two bodies of knowledge have also grown organically, one for destroying, the other for restoring buildings. You cannot sensibly communicate with each other. You have the problem the fish has with wetness.' 'Very true', they reply. 'But we have to do something.' 'Aha!', says Consultant D, 'There is some simple causal reason for your dilemma. I've phoned the Owner and he says he gave the wrong address to the Demolition Contractor who should be knocking down that slum across the road.' They all shake hands and live happily ever after.

This parable represents four methodological processes involved in problem-solving, and these are shown in Example 5.1.

A
Subjectivist
(Consultant A)

B
Eclectic-pluralist
(Consultant B)

C
Dialectical-organic
(Consultant C)

D
Causal-determinist
(Consultant D)

Example 5.1

From time to time almost everyone will switch from one method to another, depending upon the subject concerned. In the parable the most useful approach to solving the contractors' immediate problem was D — Causal-determinist. Typical positions for one of us are to be at C when solving social, political, and psychological problems; at B when trying to understand some unfamiliar area of knowledge; at A in judging the quality of a piece of music; and at D when playing billiards.

It is also useful to note (in Example 5.2) what kind of experimental and creative methods derive from each approach.

The immediate effect for us in presenting this was constructive. One person who had been particularly against what he saw as our dogmatic views responded with a paper where he was happy to see his position as (B) and recognize, but not agree with, our position (C). Instead of exchanging polemics we could subsequently continue the seminar, agreeing to differ on some aspects and collaborating upon others. The heat was taken out of the

A
Subjectivist
Introspection.
Reflection.
Developing analogues.
Creative fantasy.
Aims at making subjective
      experience manifest to others.

B
Eclectic-pluralist
Descriptions, comparisons,
correlations and generalizations.
Finding continuums.
Aims at breadth; the field of
investigation is totally open;
structures more than detailed
functions.

C
Dialectical-organic
Clinical and case-study
approach.
Action research.
Aims at depth, the field of
investigation is defined;
detailed functions more than
generalized structures.

D
Causal-determinist
Manuals.
Rules and formulae.
Experimental testing.
Deductive reasoning and logic.
Aims at objective, reproducible
knowledge.

Example 5.2

situation and we did not have to waste energy on fruitless argument which would in any case not have changed anybody's viewpoint.

It seemed to us that particular patterns of misunderstanding typically arose between the four positions. The ones we noted were these, although there may be others:

People at A (Subjectivist) perceive those at C (Dialectical-organic) to be at D (Causal-determinist). They usually accuse them of being mechanical, dogmatic, unimaginative. They generally perceive those who *are* at D correctly. They may identify those at B (Eclectic-pluralist) with themselves or with those at D. Thus in the extreme, their thinking is — everyone not at A (Subjectivist) must be at D (Causal-determinist).

People at D (Causal-determinist) perceive those at B (Eclectic-pluralist) to be at A (Subjectivist). They usually accuse them of being unscientific and

A
Subjectivist
Problem seen as an individual
variant in a totally variant world.
Entirely unpredictable.
Non-theoretical.

B
Eclectic-pluralist
Problem seen as a matter for
general exploration; a mainly
variant, plural structure;
theories arise on this basis.
Fairly unpredictable.

C
Dialectical-organic
Problem seen as part of a large
structure with fundamental
invariants giving rise via variant
factors to a complex organic
pattern. Theories arise on this
basis. Modestly predictable.

D
Causal-determinist
Problem seen as an invariant
cause-effect structure which is
translated into a strictly
determinable theory. Entirely
predictable.

Example 5.3

speculative. They generally identify those who *are* at A correctly. They may
identify those who are at C (Dialectical-organic) with themselves by
emphasizing the materialist aspect of their approach or identify them with
those at A by perceiving the dialectic in their arguments as fanciful. Thus, in
the extreme, they see everyone not at D as being at A.

People at B (Eclectic-pluralist) generally see those at C (Dialectical-organic)
to be at D (Causal-determinist). Like the Subjectivists they accuse them of
being mechanical, dogmatic, and deterministic. They usually perceive those at
D correctly. They may perceive those at A (Subjectivist) as being identical to
themselves or they may perceive them correctly. Thus in the extreme their view
is that everyone is either at B or D.

People at C (Dialectical-organic) usually see those at B (Eclectic-pluralist) as
being at A (Subjectivist). They accuse them of being fanciful, idealist, lacking
in rigour. They may correctly identify those at A. They may perceive those at
D as being identical to themselves or they may perceive them correctly. Thus in
the extreme their argument tends to be that everyone is either at C or at A.

The parable and its formulations proved a useful tool to us. They enabled us to establish sufficient dialogue to comprehend the real differences between people rather than conduct a polemical and point-scoring debate. We hope that they might prove similarly useful to others.

The question remains, however, as to what the four positions are. We imply that they are different approaches to problem-solving each of which is applicable to different situations — that is they represent different methodological approaches. Looking at them in this way it is possible to correlate them with points on a number of different continuums. For example one can take Piaget's (1953) double dimension of variant and invariant factors (see Example 5.3).

It is possible to illustrate this structure graphically (see Figure 5.1).

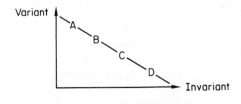

Figure 5.1

Similarly we can consider the distinction de Saussure (1966) makes between synchronic (structural relations independent of time) and diachronic (relations resulting from historical actions). The graph repeats as shown in Figure 5.2. In Position A (Subjectivist), time and history are of little importance. The Subject's immediate and changing reality is primary. In Position B (Eclectic-pluralist) the synchronic predominates over the diachronic. Connections can be made independently of various histories. At Position C (Dialectical-organic), there is a mutual balance between synchronic and diachronic. The historical factors are important but so are both the immediate and the deeper or underlying structures. At Position D (Causal-determinist) there is only the diachronic. Effects now were caused by preceding actions in time.

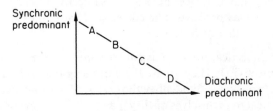

Figure 5.2

Koestler (1964) approaches the same ideas in regard to creative innovation. In his terms the 'new' arises where one suddenly switches from being within one set of matrices to another set. From this the new connection appears (or the point of the joke is clear). Again, if we take a continuum from (1) a high rate of change from one set of matrices to another, to (2) a low or nil rate of change from one set to another, we can plot the graph as shown in Figure 5.3.

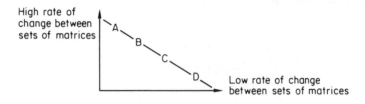

Figure 5.3

Another example can be taken from Matte Blanco (1975) who proposes a mathematical theory in regard to psychoanalysis. He postulates a Symmetrical mode, which operates only with infinite sets and where all propositions are reversible, i.e. the whole is the part and vice-versa. The deep, unrepressed Unconscious, he argues, operates only in the Symmetrical mode. The opposite mode is the Asymmetrical where divisions can be made and time and logic exist. Once more we can show this as a graph (see Figure 5.4). In Position A (Subjectivist) the Symmetrical mode is predominant with features like the lack of time and space dimensions, displacement, condensation, replacement of external by psychical reality, absence of negation and the lack of mutual contradiction. This is less so in Position B (Eclectic-pluralist) where the Asymmetrical (analysing and logical) mode is more significant. At Position C (Dialectical-organic) there is more of a balance and interaction. Position D (Causal-determinist) is almost totally in the Asymmetrical mode.

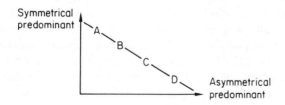

Figure 5.4

Finally we take two unlikely bedfellows — the psychoanalyst Anthony Storr (1976) and the Trotskyist Gerry Healy. They would both place the key factors as the Unity of Opposites and the Opposition of Opposites. This can be similarly graphed (see Figure 5.5). Storr argues that creativity in all its forms is dependent on the predominance of opposites. Gerry Healy argues in his lectures on Dialectical Materialism that (in our terms) the equivalents of the positions are that A represents Subjective idealism, B, Objective idealism, C, Dialectical materialism and D, Mechanical materialism.

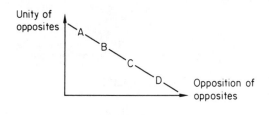

Figure 5.5

Thus one can also see the four positions as bases on which knowledge is accumulated and which reflect an underlying ideological tendency, philosophy, and political position. For example, a ruling class or elite has a vested interest as to which position is held under different circumstances. It is very important to a ruling class that questions are not asked which threaten the fundamental structure of the society. On the question of the dynamics of capitalism for example a ruling class ideology must resist the notion that its structure is inescapably leading to destruction, poverty, alienation, imperialism, and war. It requires that even the radical intelligentsia do not stray from an accumulation of knowledge (on this question) based upon Position B. This allows a liberal and eclectic-pluralist philosophy and method which in turn can justify utopian and optimistic speculations about the future while ignoring structural forces. It can also be functional for the status quo if people hold to Position A. Extreme individual subjectiveness is incompatible with collective action. Position D can also be functional. People with a 'left' orientation will not organize effectively on the basis of mechanistic formulae. Those on the 'right' will aid the status quo by mechanistically supporting it. Position C, however, implies a structural criticism and may well be the basis of challenging the system. If we look back to the period where the bourgeoisie were a revolutionary class we find a whole body of knowledge based upon Position C which accented the economic and social inefficiency of the feudal system. On a smaller scale we have observed similar dynamics in the development of groups and organizations.

What all this then gives is a picture of four very different ways of looking at the world, four different approaches to or methods of solving problems, with identifiable characteristics both conscious and unconscious, and different implications in relation to practice and action. The positions themselves, however, started out as descriptive categories which we used to explore the 'problem of wetness', a particular instance of the problem of dialogue. We used them then and have done since to gain an understanding of how people's differing ideas, values, and approaches to problems can prevent or facilitate dialogue. Sometimes the object of the exercise is to help dialogue to happen. Sometimes it is to show that dialogue is not in reality possible between the two opposing parties.

Sometimes dialogue is impossible because the two individuals or groups have differing interests — one desires to subjugate or control the other. Sometimes dialogue is possible, easy, creative, and fun with the exchanges flowing easily. In between these extremes lie a mass of complicated situations where dialogue is more or less difficult or complicated for numerous reasons. Dialogue may be possible at one level but not at another — for example we may be able to dialogue about physics but not about politics. It may be impeded by factors that can be overcome — for example a history and practice of invasive relating can split groups who have common interests. It can appear possible but turn out in the event not to be so. And so on.

It is clear that questions of creativity, ideology, method, philosophy, and politics will arise in considering whether and how one can achieve dialogue. We would not claim that our four positions are exhaustive or the only way of approaching the problem. The object of our parable is merely to help the fish put his head out of the water and still manage to breathe.

Human Inquiry
Edited by P. Reason and J. Rowan
© 1981 John Wiley & Sons Ltd.

CHAPTER SIX

The general and the unique in psychological science*

G.W. Allport (deceased)
formerly of Harvard University

Let me take my text from the opening sentence of *Ethical Standards of Psychologists,* the official code set forth by the American Psychological Association (1959). This sentence defines a psychologist as a person 'committed to increasing man's understanding of man'. The code itself makes it abundantly clear that both *man in general* and *man in particular* are the objects of our concern. Thus the psychologist, as psychologist, can properly make two sorts of statement; he can say:

(1) the problem of human personality concerns me deeply;
(2) the problem of Bill's personality concerns me deeply.

Although superficially similar the two statements are poles apart. In the second we are speaking of one and only one person; in the first we are abstracting elusive properties from all of the three billion inhabitants of the earth. Both statements are true; both appropriate; and both fall squarely within the domain of psychological science.

Some people, to be sure, object to this broad coverage. Artists, literati, some psychiatrists, perhaps a few clinical psychologists would say that to generalize about personality is to lose it. Bill, as an integral datum, we are told, cannot belong to scientific psychology. He can be represented only by the methods of biography, drama, or order artistic portraiture. Bill himself might say to the psychologist, 'If you think those pockmarks on your silly IBM card represent *me,* you have another guess coming.'

*This chapter first appeared in the *Journal of Personality,* XXX (1962), pp. 405-22. Copyright 1962 by Duke University Press.

Among scientific psychologists the objection takes a somewhat different form. Usually we repress one half of the APA definition, and say that our job is to reach only generalized formulae — propositions that hold across the board for all mankind, or at least for some identifiable section of the population. We recognize the single case as a useful source of hunches — and that is about all. We pursue our acquaintance with Bill long enough to derive some hypothesis, and then spring like a gazelle into the realm of abstraction, drawing from Bill a 'testable proposition' but carrying with us no coordinated knowledge of him as a structural unit. We tolerate the single case only as a take-off point. We forgive Ebbinghaus for performing 163 experiments on himself, since almost immediately his findings were confirmed on other subjects. Luckily these subjects, like him, displayed a logarithmic relationship between the percentage of material forgotten and the time elapsing after the original act of learning. We forgive Köhler and Wallach for intensive work on their own figural after-effects, for it was soon confirmed that others also show a displacement of the percept, after long stimulation, away from the retinal area stimulated.

But imagine the consternation if some deviant psychologist (perhaps I myself) were to say, 'Can't we linger longer with Ebbinghaus and discover in his life what relationships might exist between his memory functions and *his* motives and *his* cognitive style and *his* aspirations?' The objection would be: 'Of what use is that? Even if we find the relationship we'd have to generalize to other people or else we'd have nothing of any scientific value.'

Such is the prevailing 'response set' of our specialty. The intricacy of internal structure in concrete lives seldom challenges or detains us. Our concern is with commonalities and comparabilities across individuals.

This response set is undoubtedly derived from our submissiveness to the goals and procedures of natural science. And this submissiveness is not in itself a bad thing. Up to now it has taught us much. The question is whether we have become so enslaved that we overlook an important half of our particular professional assignment which is 'increasing man's understanding of man'.

It does no good to argue that every individual system in nature is unique; every rat, every porpoise, every worm; and that it is only the general laws of their functioning that lead to comprehension. No, we can't take this easy way out of the dilemma. The human system, unlike all others, possesses a degree of openness to the world, a degree of foresight and self-awareness, a flexibility and binding of functions and goals that present a unique structural challenge far more insistent than that presented by any other living system. It is because of their essential stereotypy and lack of variation that psychologists like to draw their generalizations from lower animals. But for my part I venture the opinion that all of the infrahuman vertebrates in the world differ less from one another in psychological functioning and in complexity of organization, than one human being does from any other.

And so I wonder whether the time has not come for students of personality to shake themselves loose from a too-rigid response set, and perhaps even to reverse it. Instead of growing impatient with the single case and hastening on to generalization, why should we not grow impatient with our generalizations and hasten to the internal pattern? For one thing we should ask, are our generalizations really relevant to the case we are studying? If so, do they need modification? And in what ways is this individual the asymptote of all our general laws?

Or to state the procedure more simply: Why should we not start with individual behaviour as a source of hunches (as we have in the past), and then seek our generalizations (also as we have in the past), but finally come back to the individual — not for the mechanical application of laws (as we do now), but for a fuller, supplementary, and more accurate assessment than we are now able to give? I suspect that the reason our present assessments are now so often feeble and sometimes even ridiculous, is because we do not take this final step. We stop with our wobbly laws of personality and seldom confront them with the concrete person.

The Dimensional and the Morphogenic

The issue before us is not new. More than a hundred years ago John Stuart Mill proposed that we distinguish sharply between psychology, the science of mind-in-general, and *ethology,* a science of character (having no relation to what is called ethology today). To his mind ethology should trace the operation of psychological laws in specifically individual combinations — such as the pattern of the single person or of a single culture or nation. Somewhat similar was Dilthey's proposal to distinguish between 'explanatory' and 'understanding' psychology. Said Dilthey, 'We explain nature, but we understand human beings.' Widelband too would recognize two classes of science: the nomothetic (seeking general laws) and the idiographic (dealing with structured pattern).

In confronting this same problem William James almost threw up his hands in despair. It is well known that after writing his textbook, he concluded that general psychological laws are poor stuff. He declared that psychology has not produced 'a single law in the sense in which physics shows us laws... This is no science, it is only the hope of a science' (1961 edn., p. 335). Perhaps the ensuing half-century of intensive research would have strengthened his faith in general laws; but I doubt it. At any rate he not only questioned the validity of general laws but, champion of the individual though he was, he seemed to feel that the concrete person must also inevitably elude psychology. In his *Memories and Studies* (1912) he wrote,

...in every concrete individual, there is a uniqueness that defies all formulation. We can feel the touch of it and recognize its taste, so to speak, relishing or disliking, as the case may be, but we can give no ultimate account of it, and have in the end simply to admire the Creator (pp. 109f.).

And so at the end of his career James seems to despair of psychology as a science of either the general or the concrete.

The problem has not yet been solved, but I for one detect signs of progress. For one thing it increasingly haunts us, in our dual roles as experimenter and clinician, as theorist and practitioner. Nearly a decade ago [this written in the early 1960s — Eds.] Meehl (1954) wrote a distinguished treatise on the subject entitled *Clinical vs. Statistical Prediction*. His own position he declared to be 'ambivalent'. Some called it middle-of-the-road (but only those, I think, whose own adaptation level was somewhere to the right of Sarbin and Lundberg).

Meehl's book draws an important distinction. It points out that in comparing so-called clinical with so-called statistical procedures we may be talking (a) about the methods we employ and the type of data we use, or (b) about the way we piece together these data and reach a final assessment. Thus the data, on the one hand, may be percentile scores or other quantifiable dimensional data; or they may be looser types of information, case records, free associations, and the like. Further, in reaching a conclusion from these data we may use statistical procedures with mechanical regularity, or we may — as Dilthey advises — simply try to 'understand' the pattern. Meehl's chief concern is with the latter issue. Does one handle the data (whatever they be) more successfully through using the statistical cookbook, or through global comprehension? While this issue is surely central, it is not the focus of my interest in the present chapter. Here I am concerned rather more with Meehl's first problem: the type of data that should go into our assessments.

More recently a German author (Graumann, 1960) put the problem this way: shall our units of analysis in the study of personality be derived from general psychological concepts, or from lives as actually lived? Another statement of the issue is found in the presidential address of L.S. Hearnshaw (1956) to the British Psychological Society. He first calls attention to the strain that exists between the demands of conventional scientific method and 'the appreciation of the richness of human individuality'. He pleads for 'a constant search for concepts which, while capable of scientific definition and employment, nevertheless possess humanistic implications' and reflect patterned structure accurately.

It would serve no good purpose here to review the long-standing debate between partisans of the nomothetic and idiographic methods, between champions of explanation and understanding. Indeed to insure more rapid progress I think it best to avoid traditional terms altogether. For the purposes of our present discussion I shall speak of 'dimensional' and 'morphogenic' procedures. Let me explain the latter term.

The science of molecular biology shows us that life-substances are identical across species. The building blocks of life — vegetable and animal — turn out to be strikingly uniform in terms of nucleic acids, protein molecules, and enzymatic reactions. Yet an antelope differs from an ash tree, a man from an antelope, and one man is very unlike another. The challenge of morphogenesis (accounting for pattern) grows more rather than less acute as we discover the commonalities of life. Yet biologists admit that morphogenic biology lags far behind molecular (or dimensional) biology. So too does morphogenic psychology lag far behind dimensional psychology.

The commonalities in personality are the horizontal dimensions that run through all individuals. We focus our attention chiefly upon these commonalities: for example, upon the common traits of achievement, anxiety, extraversion, dominance, creativity; or upon the common processes of learning, repression, identification, ageing. We spend scarcely one per cent of our research time discovering whether these common dimensions are in reality relevant to Bill's personality, and if so how they are patterned together to compose the Billian quality of Bill. Ideally research should explore both horizontal and vertical dimensions.

I have already rejected the easy solution that assigns the general to science and the unique to art. I should like also to dispose of another proposed solution. Some psychologists would say that Bill, our individual, is known primarily by his conformity to, or deviation from, universal norms or group norms. His private and unique qualities are only the residual peculiarities left over when we have accounted for most of his behaviour in terms of general norms. My colleagues, Professors Kluckhohn and Murray (1953, p. 53) have expressed the thought by saying

> ... every man is in certain respects:
> a. like all other men (universal norms)
> b. like some other men (group norms)
> c. like no other men (idiosyncratic norms).

Now it is certainly true that we often *wish* to use universal and group norms. We want to know whether Bill, relative to others, is high or low in intelligence, in dominance, in affiliativeness. But although Bill can be compared profitably on many dimensions with the average human being or with his cultural group, still he himself weaves all these attributes into a unique idiomatic system. His personality does not contain three systems, but only one. Whatever individuality is, it is not the residual ragbag left over after general dimensions have been exhausted. The *organization* of Bill's life is first, last, and all the time, the primary face of his human nature.

Since we cannot brush our problem aside we do well to ask how a truly morphogenic psychology (sadly neglected up to now) can become a scientific asset. To become such it will have to learn certain lessons from dimensional empiricism, and from positivism — most of all the lesson of observer reliability. It is not sufficient to 'intuit' the pattern of Bill or Betty. All of their friends do this much, with greater or less success. A science, even a morphogenic science, should be made of sterner stuff. The morphogenic interpretations we make should be testable, communicable, and have a high measure of predictive power.

My purpose is to suggest certain procedures that seem to me to be morphogenic in nature, or at least semimorphogenic, and yet to be at the same time controlled, repeatable, reliable. Before I do so, let us look more closely at the question of successful prediction, which, we are told, is the acid test of valid science.

Prediction: Dimensional and Morphogenic

Prediction based on general or dimensional information is called actuarial. For many purposes it is surprisingly accurate. One marvels, for example, at the correctness with which insurance companies predict the number of deaths that will occur by highway accidents, from cancer, or from suicide. The chances of a hypothetical average man for survival or death are all the insurance business wants to know. Whether Bill himself will be one of the fatal cases it cannot tell — and that is what Bill wants to know.

The situation is exactly the same in psychology. Actuarial prediction enables us, with fair success, to predict what proportion of boys, having a certain type of physique and family history, will become delinquent; what percentage of engaged couples, having various types of background, will enjoy successful marriage. Actuarial prediction can tell approximately what the average student's university record will be on the basis of his elementary school record or I.Q. It can advise industry concerning crucial cutting points on psychological tests by designating the score below which most applicants would probably fail on the job.

Note please that these actuarial predictions are far more useful to insurance companies, school authorities, police, and industrial management than to Bill himself. As a person he is frozen out, for although statistical generalizations hold with small error for large populations they do not hold for any given individual. And as practitioners we have fully as much responsibility to Bill as to his employers or the public. Nay, if we follow our own professional code of ethics, we have more.

Suppose we take John, a lad of 12 years, and suppose his family background is poor; his father was a criminal; his mother rejected him; his neighbourhood is marginal. Suppose that 70 per cent of the boys having a similar background become criminals. Does this mean that John himself has a 70 per cent chance of delinquency? Not at all. John is a unique being, with a genetic inheritance all his own; his life-experience is his own. His unique world contains influences unknown to the statistician: perhaps an affectionate relation with a certain teacher, or a wise word once spoken by a neighbour. Such factors may be decisive and may offset all average probabilties. There is no 70 per cent chance about John. He either will or will not become delinquent. Only a complete understanding of his personality, of his present and future circumstances, will give us a basis for sure prediction.

It was this line of argument, I believe, that led Meehl (1954) to say, 'Let us see what the research evidence is regarding the relative success of dimensional and morphogenic prediction.' Surveying such relevant studies as were available, Meehl concludes that morphogenic (what he calls 'clinical') prediction seems to be actually inferior. More successful are predictions made mechanically with the aid of a standard formula. Best to keep strictly to our Rorschach diagnostic signs, to our I.Q. measures, to our profiles on the Minnesota Multiphasic Personality Inventory, and to other standard predictive indexes. We can, of course, weight the signs, but we must do so according to rule. We may give one sign twice as much weight as another, just as a cook uses two cups of flour but only one of sugar. Meehl appropriately calls the procedure he advocates the 'cookbook' method.

The point is that whenever we deal with well-defined variables, possessing a known relation to a pathological type, or to success in occupation or in school, we are usually safer in following the cookbook method of combining scores according to a formula known to have a good average validity. If strictly followed the logical outcome of this procedure would be the early elimination of the clinician or practitioner as assessor or diagnostician. A computing machine could handle the data more accurately than a fallible psychologist. In coming years we shall, no doubt, increasingly encounter IBM diagnoses and IBM predictions in psychological practice. It does no good to shudder at such a lèse majesté to human dignity. It will surely come to pass. But already we can sense its limitations.

Limitations of the Cookbook

In the first place, as Meehl (1957) himself has pointed out, the cookbook is usable only under restricted circumstances. The dimensions studied must be objectively defined, reliably measured, validly related to the target of prediction (e.g. to vocational success), clearly normed for a population to which the subject belongs. Most of the dimensions we employ have not attained this level of objective perfection.

The question of weighting signs gives us special difficulty. Suppose John has a good engineering profile, but also scores high in aesthetic interests; suppose he is introverted, but has high ego-strength; and with all this suffers some physical disability — what then does the final pattern signify? Cookbook enthusiasts might say a computer could tell us. But could it? In all the world there are not enough cases of this, or of any other, personal pattern to warrant assured actuarial prediction.

Again, by keeping within a previously established dimensional frame the cookbook procedure rules out insights peculiarly relevant to the individual. True, the computer can tell whether Sam should be diagnosed as schizophrenic. But whether Sam's love for his sister and her way of dealing with him are such as to effect his recovery, the computer cannot tell. A dimensional frame is a rigid thing. It is like giving to the cook ingredients that will produce only dumplings while imagining that she has the freedom to produce a cake.

Further, the dimensions imposed on the individual are dimensions of interest to the investigator, or to the hospital, school, or firm. For this reason they may not be relevant in guiding John. The most salient features of his life — his aspirations, his sense of duty, his existential pattern, may be left untouched. In every dimensional analysis there are inevitably many 'empty cells'.

Finally, as for the discovery that clinical or morphogenic predictions are in fact poorer than cookbook predictions, I can only say, 'What a pitiful reflection on the inventiveness and sensitivity of psychologists!' The findings — which, by the way, are not necessarily the last word on the matter — prove only that we do not yet know how to maximize clinical skill through training. I suspect that our present emphasis on tests and cookbooks may actually be damaging the potential skill of young clinicians and advisers. There are studies that indicate that clinicians grow confused when they have too many data concerning an individual life, and that for this reason their predictions are better when they fall back on a mere formula (Sarbin *et al.*, 1960, pp. 262-4). But this finding, too, points chiefly to our neglect in inventing and training in sensitive morphogenic methods.

Meehl (1959) has shown that under certain circumstances a combined actuarial and clinical — a kind of 'configural' — procedure is superior in predictive power to either method used alone. This is progress indeed. But I would raise two objections: (1) the level of success achieved is still too low; (2) the diagnostic instruments employed in the first instance are too one-sided. The original instruments on which the predictions are based are nearly always of a dimensional or horizontal order (extending across people) and seldom of an intensive vertical order (within the person).

My point is that while dimensional diagnostic methods are an indispensable half of the psychologist's tools of trade, the other half of the tool box is, up to now, virtually empty. I recall that a few years before his death I was discussing this matter with the beloved psychologist, Edward Tolman. He said to me with his characteristic twinkle, employing the then-current terminology, 'I know I should be more idiographic in my research, but I just don't know how to be.' My reply now, as then, is, 'Let's learn!'

Morphogenic Methods

To start simply: it is worth asking whether we ought to seek only objective validation for our measuring instruments. Why not demand likewise, where possible, subjective validation by asking our subject what he himself thinks of the dimensional diagnosis we have made? (If the subject is a child, a psychotic, or manifestly defensive, this step, of course, has no point.) Too often we fail to consult the richest of all sources of data, namely, the subject's own self-knowledge. During the war, psychiatrists were assigned the task of screening candidates for the armed services. While they employed various dimensional tests, it is said that the best predictive question turned out to be, 'Do you feel that you are emotionally ready to enter military service?' The men themselves were often the best judges — although, of course, not infallible.

One might think that the existential outlook in psychology (now spreading at considerable speed) could logically be expected to bring a revolution in methods of psychological assessment. Its basic emphasis is upon the individual as a unique being-in-the-world whose system of meanings and value-orientations are not precisely like anyone else's. Hence an existential psychologist, be he conducting research, assessment, or therapy, would seem to need procedures tailored to each separate case. But up to now followers of this school of thought have not been as inventive as their own basic postulate requires. There is a methodological lag.

It is true that psychiatrists and clinical psychologists have long known that they should take the patient's own story as a starting point. But almost immediately they redact this story into general categories, dismembering the complex pattern of the life into standard dimensions (abilities, needs, interest inventories, and the like), and hasten to assign scores on their favourite variables. One notes too that therapists who claim to be existential in their orientation also tend to employ standard procedures in treatment. Their techniques and even their interpretations are sometimes indistinguishable from orthodox psychoanalysis (G.W. Allport, 1961a).

Our conceptual flexibility is greater than our methodologial flexibility. Let me illustrate the point by reference to the valuable and extensive bibliography of nearly 500 items prepared by Ruth Wylie (1961). Most of these items deal with empirical studies of the self-concept. (The very fact that the self in recent years has been re-admitted to good standing in psychology is proof of our conceptual flexibilty.) A close inspection, however, shows that virtually all the studies approach the self-concept only via general dimensions. We encounter such descriptions as the following: 'this test infers self-esteem from scores on an anxiety questionnaire'; or 'nine bipolar semantic differential scales are employed'; or 'self-ratings on 18 trait words on a five-point scale from which self-acceptance is inferred.' I am not objecting to these studies but point out that they are methodologically stereotyped.

But let us turn now to what at present lies available in the morphogenic half of our tool box. My inventory will be illustrative rather than exhaustive. I shall be brief in describing each method, hoping that the array as a whole will help to make clear what I mean by morphogenic method, and, best of all, may stimulate further invention.

1. Familiar is the method of matching, used with profit by both German and American investigators (see G.W. Allport, 1961b, pp. 387f. and 446f.). This method invites us to fit together any record of personal expression, however complex, with any other record. We test our skill in seeing that this case record must fit such-and-such a test profile; or that this handwriting goes with that voice. It is a good way to discover how much of a perceptible form-quality saturates separate performances. Although the method gives us no insight into causal relationships, it is, so far as it goes, a good example of a 100 per cent morphogenic procedure.

2. Another wholly morphogenic technique was devised by Baldwin (1942), who made use of a long series of personal letters written by one woman, Jenny by name. Her unique thought structure, i.e., associative complexes, was the object of interest. If she talked about women, money, or nature, with what feeling tone did she mention them? If she mentioned her son, what else did she mention in the same context? This technique, called by Baldwin 'personal structure analysis', is highly revealing, and is carried through without reference to any general or dimensional norms.

3. Somewhat similar, and wholly morphogenic, is the procedure recommended by Shapiro (1961) for psychiatrists. On the basis of a five-hour intensive interview with a patient he constructs a questionnaire which from that time on is standard for this patient but not directly relevant to any other patient. Administered over intervals of months or years, the instrument will show the course of development, including improvement or deterioration in health.

4. A somewhat more ambitious attempt, still wholly morphogenic, would be to attempt to discover the number and range of all the major structural foci a given life possesses. Many years ago in his *Experiment in Autobiography,* H. G. Wells asserted that there were only two major themes in his life: interest in world-government and in sex. Elsewhere I have explored the posssibility that a life may be understood almost completely by tracing only a few major themes or intentions. Perhaps two is too few for most lives (perhaps especially for H.G. Wells), although it is said that Tolstoy after his conversion had only

one major theme: viz., the simplification of life. More typical, I believe, would be the case of William James, who, according to his biographer, R.B. Perry (1936, Chaps. 90-91), had eight dominant trends. In some preliminary explorations with my students (G.W. Allport, 1958), I find that they regard it possible to characterize a friend adequately on the average with 7.2 essential characteristics, the range falling for the most part between 3 and 10.

What to call these central motifs I do not exactly know. They are 'essential characteristics', for the most part motivational in type although some seem to be stylistic. F.H. Allport (1937), in proposing the term 'teleonomic trends', suggests that we proceed to regard them as life-hypotheses held by the individual, and count carefully how many of his daily acts can accurately be ordered to one or more of these trends. The idea has merit, but it has not yet been systematically tried out. One question is whether we can obtain sufficiently high observer-reliability (i.e., reliable judgements of the fit of specific acts to the hypothesized trend). At present it is only one of the avenues of research needing exploration.

5. Suppose we are interested in an individual's value system. Direct questioning is, of course, useful. 'What would you rather have than anything else in the world?' 'What experiences give you a feeling of completeness, of fully functioning, or of personal identity?' 'What,' in Maslow's terms 'are your peak experiences of life?' Elsewhere I have argued strongly for the use of such direct questions as these, for in important matters we should grant our client the right to be believed. Projective methods should never be used without direct methods, for we cannot interpret the results of projective testing unless we know whether they confirm or contradict the subject's own self-image (see G. W. Allport, 1960, Chap. 6).

But how can we grow more precise in this type of work, benefiting from lessons learned from objective dimensional procedures? One such technique is the 'self-anchoring scale', devised by Kilpatrick and Cantril (1960). It consists of a simple diagram of a ladder, having 10 rungs. The subject is asked first to describe in his own terms the 'very best or ideal way of life' that he can imagine. Then he is told that rung 10 at the top of the ladder represents this ideal. Similarly he is asked to describe the 'worst possible way of life' for himself. This he is told is the bottom of the ladder. Now he is asked to point to the rung on the ladder where he thinks he stands today — somewhere between the bottom and top rungs. He can also be asked, 'Where on this scale were you two years ago? Five years ago? Where do you think you will be five years hence?'

This device has considerable value in personal counselling. It is also used by the authors to study rising or falling morale in different countries, e.g., in those having undergone recent revolution as compared with those living in a static condition. In this case, a curious thing happens; a completely morphogenic instrument is adapted for use as a tool for nomothetic research.

Ordinarily, of course, the situation is reversed: it is a nomothetic mould that is forced upon the individual.

All these various examples suffice to show that it is possible to examine the internal and unique pattern of personal structure without any dependence whatsoever on universal or group norms. All the methods I have mentioned up to now are completely morphogenic, although they are seldom explicitly recognized as such.

Let us turn our attention to certain procedures that are highly useful for exploring individuality even though they are in part also dimensional.

6. First, there is the common dimensional instrument, the rating scale. Many years ago Conrad (1932) asked teachers to rate pupils on 231 common traits. The teachers were thus forced to make the assumption that all children did in fact possess all 231 traits in some degree. Proceeding on this assumption the teachers agreed poorly, as reflected in a median reliability coefficient of .48. After this nomothetic orgy, the same teachers were asked to star *only* those traits that they considered to be of 'central or dominating importance in the child's personality'. On this part of their task the teachers agreed almost perfectly, their judgements correlating .95. This result shows that low reliability may be due to the essential irrelevance of many of the dimensions we forcibly apply to an individual. On well-configurated prominent dispositions there is likely to be good agreement.

A related method is the simple adjective checklist. Here the rater is confronted with perhaps hundreds of common trait-names (which are, of course, common linguistic dimensions). But he is required to use only those that seem to him appropriate to the primary trends in the individual life.

Both the method of starring and the use of the checklist have the advantage of permitting us to discard irrelevant dimensions — a feature lacking in most other dimensional procedures.

7. Another halfway method is the *Role Construct Repertory Test,* devised by Kelly (1955). The method asks the subject to tell in what way two concepts are alike and how they differ from a third. The concepts might, for example, be *mother, sister, wife.* The subject could, for instance, reply that mother and sister are alike because both are comforting; and the wife different because she is demanding. Not only is the particular response revealing of his family attitudes, but over a long series of comparisons it may turn out that the subject has a characteristic cognitive style in which the polarity of comfortableness versus demandingness may recur time and time again. This method is not wholly morphogenic since it prescribes for the subject what 'significant others' he shall characterize, and in other ways limits his spontaneous choices, but it allows nonetheless for a certain amount of morphogenic discovery.

8. Certain other devices for approaching cognitive style likewise move in a desirable direction. I have in mind Broverman (1960), who employs standard tests with his subjects, but makes his interpretations entirely in terms of the

subject's tendency to do well or poorly on a given type of test relative to his own mean for all tests. By the use of such ipsative scores he is able to determine which responses are strong or weak with respect to other responses within the same individual.

If this line of thought were extended we would be moving towards a psychophysics of one person — a desirable advance indeed. We would at last know, so to speak, the relation between Bill's sensory acuity and his interests, between his cognitive style and his tempo, between his respiration and extraversion. To what extent it is necessary to start, as Broverman does, with standard dimensional measures, is a question for the future. I doubt that we can answer it *a priori*.

9. Another mixed method is the Allport-Vernon-Lindzey *Study of Values* (1960), devised to measure the relative prominence of each of the six Spranger *Lebensformen* within a particular person. The resulting profile does not tell how high or low a given person stands on the economic, theoretic, or religious value in the population at large, but only which value is relatively most, or next most, or least prominent in his own life. This type of profile is semidimensional, semimorphogenic.

10. Sometimes the Q-sort (Stephenson, 1953) is said to be an idiographic technique. Yet it, like other devices we are now considering, goes only part way. It has the merit of making use of self-report, and can be used for measuring changes in the self-concept. As ordinarily used, however, only a standard set of propositions is employed, thus creating for the subject little more than a standard rating scale. And if the subject is forced, as he often is, to produce a quasi-normal distribution among his sorts, he is further restricted. In short, the method can be rigidly dimensional. Yet it is a flexible method, and some variants are highly promising, perhaps especially when combined with inverse factor analysis.

11. For example, Nunnally (1955) studied one therapy case over a two-year period, using 60 statements selected for their unique relevance to this person (and this, I think, is a great improvement over the use of uniform lists). The patient made her sorts under many different sets of instructions on many occasions. Using an inverse factor analysis it was possible to find three fairly independent factors that comprised her total self-concept. During therapy these factors showed only a moderate change.

It strikes me as curious that out of the thousands and thousands of factor-analytic studies that smother us today, scarcely any are carried through in such a manner as to discover the internal, unique, organizational units that characterize a single life. Even inverse factor analysis does not fully achieve this goal unless the initial information employed is selected for its morphogenic relevance. A good deal of creative work still lies ahead for factor-analysis. It has potentiality, I think, for discovering the main foci of organization in a given life, but has not yet moved far enough in this direction.

Final Word

This survey of possible relevant methods is not complete but may indicate that by a deliberate shift of procedures we can bring the laggard end of our science up to a more flourishing level. To effect the shift, we shall have to restrain to some extent our present dimensional debauch.

In this chapter I have introduced the term 'morphogenic psychology', borrowed from, but not identical with the usage in, biology. It is, I think, a good term, better than 'idiographic' which so many students of personality misuse and mis-spell. I hope the concept 'morphogenic' catches on, but even more do I hope that the types of research to which I have ventured to apply the label will flourish and spread. Already we know that personality (in general) is an interesting topic for study. But only when morphogenic methods are more highly developed shall we be able to do justice to the fascinating individuality that marks the personalities of Bill, John, and Betty.

Human Inquiry
Edited by P. Reason and J. Rowan
© 1981 John Wiley & Sons Ltd.

CHAPTER SEVEN

From anxiety to method in the behavioural sciences by George Devereux: an appreciation

John Rowan
Independent Consultant, London, UK

This is a book about countertransference in social science.

'Countertransference' is a word originally used in psychotherapy to denote the analyst's unconscious reactions to the patient as a person, and especially to the latter's transference reactions to the therapist. This was at first seen as a threat to good therapy, because the therapist might relate to the patient in the same way in which she or he has related to someone in the early family set-up, projecting on to the patient good or bad points which were not really there, or not there to such an important extent. More recently, Devereux has shown that countertransference is something quite valuable in therapy, so long as it is observed and used by the therapist in a constructive way, because it can be an important source of insight into what is going on within the patient.

Countertransference in social science (very close to what Madison calls 'reintegration' and to what the co-counselling people call 'restimulation') means that research situations stir up anxieties and other feelings at various levels within the researcher, some of which may have much more to do with the researcher's own problems than with anything going on out there in the world. As Weston La Barre notes in the Preface to the book, this raises the alarming possibility that a great deal of social science, as at present practised, may be a species of autobiography. And so long as researchers ignore the unconscious, and pretend that they can be totally objective, this will continue to be the case.

The kind of way this can operate in practice is well described by Devereux in his example of two-stage theory-building:

(1) The first stage consists in the formulation of a theory which accounts adequately for the *less* anxiety-arousing portion of the facts. This segmental theory then usually serves to discourage inquiry into the other — *more* anxiety-arousing — portion of the facts.

(2) At the second stage this segmental theory is systematically elaborated, in order to create the illusion that it is complete, thereby further discouraging attempts to face the disturbing aspects of the facts which one professes to have explained.

What I particularly like about this book is the number of examples which are used, so that every statement is embedded in a rich background enabling one to understand it clearly. (Since the author has thoughtfully numbered them, it is possible to say that 440 such examples are given.)

Devereux has two main ways of overcoming the problems of countertransference in social research: self-awareness and real friendship.

Self-awareness, according to Devereux, comes mostly from being psychoanalysed. My own opinion is that the same uncovering of the unconscious can be attained through other forms of therapy, such as primal integration, gestalt, co-counselling, psychodrama, etc. It can even come from non-therapy experiences, though this is much more chancy. The point is that by being aware of one's own countertransference we can turn it to advantage rather than being thrown by it. In the first approximation, both Devereux and I would say that in practice this may mean — if one is lucky — having one's own therapist, supervisor or review group, to whom one can talk about one's countertransference reactions in research.

Real friendship is also important, according to Devereux, because it gives one a way of relating to experiences which one cannot have oneself.

> I know that I understand Mohave sexuality better for having had several, much-beloved Mohave friends, than if I had had the opportunity — or the inclination — to photograph copulating Mohave couples or had indulged in participant observation, simply because friendship, quite as much as erotic love, is a creative phrasing of a real human relationship... The anthropologist can seldom find real love in the field. He can, if he is worthy of it, find friends and thereby learn all anyone can know about the epiphany, in that particular culture, of the universal Eros who is at the root of all life.

It seems clear that to use one's own subjectivity, rather than attempting to rid oneself of it, is Devereux' method.

So in studying human beings, what we have to do is to use observations, dreams, interviews and all the rest, but always to know that we ourselves are involved. 'Isn't it true, though', asks the critic, 'that this invites projection and uncontrollable subjectivity?' Devereux answers:

> The anthropomorphisation of machines and animals — erroneous as it is — has at least the excuse of constituting a (misguided) attempt at a *complete* understanding. The zoomorphisation or mechanomorphisation of man seeks, by contrast, to *segmentalise* comprehension, because of the anxieties which empathy elicits in the scientist, and therefore leads to gross distortions of reality.

If we pursue this, in the very thorough way which Devereux does, showing all the many ways in which our own *unaware* subjectivity and countertransference does get in the way of what we are trying to achieve in social science, we eventually come to the problem of the *partition* between what is inside us, and what is outside us. Where does subjectivity begin and end?

> Niels Bohr demonstrated the extent to which the experimental setup determines the locus of the partition, by analyzing a simple experiment: the exploration of an object by means of a stick. If the stick is grasped firmly, it becomes an extension of the hand; the locus of the partition is therefore at the 'other' (distal) end of the stick. If the stick is held loosely, it is perceptually not a part of the observer; the partition is therefore at 'this' (proximal) end of the stick.

These two ways of holding the stick, says Devereux, are paradigmatic of all behavioural science experimentation and observation.

> Any experiment which gives the subject no conscious choice and any way of *thinking* about behaviour which does not include, at least in principle, the notions of conscious choice and awareness correspond to rigid stick experiments. Experiments in which conscious choice is permitted and the observer is free to think about his subject's behaviour as reflecting or involving conscious ('aware') choice (as an intervening variable), correspond to a loose stick experiment.

And Devereux seems to imply that even the same experiment could be seen as a rigid-stick study by one investigator, and a loose-stick experiment by another. This is what makes it so hard to decide, on an experimental basis, between a stimulus-response theory and a fully cognitive theory.

If we have an environment of a certain temperature, and a thermometer, and an eye ready to receive that light, and a brain behind the eye, and a person behind the brain, where do we make the partition? What is the point where one says — 'And this I perceive'? This point, says Devereux, depends on the focus of interest of the observer. The biologist may place the partition at the surface of the eyeball — here is where physics turns into biology and starts to be transformed by it. An optometrist might place it at the retina, where the beam of light ceases to exist as such. A neurologist might pursue the effects of the light, now transformed into neurological, electro-chemical terms, through the pathways of the brain, into the visual cortex. And then there comes a point at which this pursuit, too, ends 'nowhere', and where we can only use psychological terms.

> In short, the psychological partition — the point/instant at which one says: 'And this I perceive' — is that at which one's real or claimed knowledge and explanations cease... The problem is therefore primarily whether this apparatus is a rigid stick, or a loose one... If it is held very rigidly, the observer begins at the surface of the thermometer — or at least at the point where light is reflected by the tip of the mercury column; if it is held very loosely, it is where electro-chemistry runs out of explanations.

All experiments in social science, says Devereux, are either rigid-stick or loose-stick in character.

> Rigid stick experiments usually yield... 'Knowledge about' types of information, whereas loose stick experiments yield 'acquaintance with' types of information. Guthrie in psychology and White in anthropology are rigid stick scientists. Freud, Tolman, Linton, Mead, Levi-Strauss and LaBarre are loose stick scientists.

He pursues the matter further by noticing that when we study something in social science we disturb it, and that the locus for the disturbance is precisely the locus of the partition. This partition is the point where we have to leave one type of explanation, and move to a different one. If we refuse to leave our existing type of explanation at a partition-boundary, we may kill off the phenomenon we are studying; but if we change our type of explanation each time we meet the disturbance which signals a partition we stay in contact with reality, and do not kill off the object of our study.

If we are to do this in any adequate way with people, says Devereux, we have to be able to research in such a way as to be able to talk about the unconscious mind. The self-aware social scientist can do this:

Like *all* of them, he studies observable behaviour and treats it as information. Like *some* of them, he scrutinises also unintentional messages and reads between the lines of behaviour. Only in one respect does he operate differently from all other behavioural scientists. He treats as a *basic* source of information phenomena emerging from the unconscious, whose very existence is denied by some other behavioural scientists.

And this means that the self-aware social scientist has the ability to exploit the partition-disturbance wherever it takes place. Yet with such an observer, the most relevant perceptions are the ones placed 'in here'; those located at least 'at' — and in a sense even 'within' — the observer's psyche. The ideal self-aware social scientist

> deliberately channels stimuli emanating from the [subject] *directly* to his own unconscious and, to a lesser extent, also to his preconscious. He will, moreover, use as his percipient apparatus — or receptor — that portion of his psyche which most other behavioural scientists seek to wall off and will first process these stimuli by means of his primary process mentation. He allows his [subject] to reach — and to reach into — him. He allows a disturbance to be created within himself and then studies this disturbance even more carefully than he studies the [subject's] utterances.

So as social scientists we understand the subject in a self-aware way only in so far as we understand the disturbances our subjects set up in us, *at the partition*. One says, 'And this I perceive' only in respect of these reverberations 'at oneself'. But it is only the fact that we *are* self-aware (which in practice usually means for Devereux psychoanalysed) which enables us to do this. Otherwise we would be overcome by anxiety stemming from our own unconcious conflicts.

And this means that the social scientist must, when doing research with people, be trained to go into a special state of consciousness, named by Freud 'free floating attention' — a state of receptive absent-mindedness which permits the subject's remarks to impinge directly upon the researcher's unconscious, without first being processed by the conscious mind. But again, this state of mind is not attainable unless the scientist in question has done a lot of work on her or his own unconscious, making it more accessible and usable, and less frightening and strange.

If Devereux is right, most social science is an elaborate avoidance of reality, under the guise of investigating it. But it is clear how this can be changed.

Human Inquiry
Edited by P. Reason and J. Rowan
© 1981 John Wiley & Sons Ltd.

CHAPTER EIGHT

The psychology of science
by Abraham Maslow: an appreciation

John Rowan
Independent Consultant, London, UK

This is not a highly unified book. It is discursive and loose in form, being based on various lectures given by Maslow at different times. It seems best, therefore, to give a series of points which Maslow makes, to suggest the range and some of the flavour of what he is saying.

(1) *Humanism vs. mechanism* Science is often seen as mechanistic and dehumanized. Maslow sees his work as about the rehumanization of science.

> I conceive this to be not a divisive effort to oppose one 'wrong' view with another 'right' view, nor to cast out anything. The conception of science in general and of psychology in general, of which this book is a sample, is *inclusive* of mechanistic science. I believe mechanistic science (which in psychology takes the form of behaviorism) to be not incorrect but rather too narrow and limited to serve as a *general* or comprehensive philosophy.

(2) *Holism vs. reductionism* If we want to do psychology, in the sense of learning about people, we have in practice to approach one person at a time. What is the state of mind in which this is best done?

> Any clinician knows that in getting to know another person it is best to keep your brain out of the way, to look and listen totally, to be completely absorbed, receptive, passive, patient and waiting

rather than eager, quick and impatient. It does not help to start measuring, questioning, calculating or testing out theories, categorizing or classifying. If your brain is too busy, you won't hear or see well. Freud's term 'free-floating attention' describes well this noninterfering, global, receptive, waiting kind of cognizing another person.

If we adopt this approach, Maslow says, we have a chance of being able to describe the person holistically rather than reductively. In other words, we can see the *whole* person, rather than some selected and split-off aspect of the person. But this depends crucially on the *relationship* between the knower and the known. We have to approach the person as a person:

> This is different from the modal way in which we approach physical objects, i.e. manipulating them, poking at them, to see what happens, taking them apart, etc. If you do this to human beings, you *won't* get to know them. They won't *want* you to know them. They won't *let* you know them.

(3)   *I-Thou vs. I-It*   If we take as the ultimate bit of knowledge what occurs in the I-Thou, interpersonal, Agapean-love relationship between two people, we have a new starting-point for psychology.

> The ultimate limit, the completion towards which this kind of interpersonal knowledge moves, is through intimacy to the mystical fusion in which two people become one in a phenomenological way that has been best described by mystics, Zen Buddhists, peak experiencers, lovers, aestheticians, etc. In this experience of fusion a knowing of the other comes about through *becoming* the other, i.e. it becomes experiential knowledge from within. . . Do you want to know? Then care!

This starting-point Maslow compares step by step and point by point with the starting-point of spectator-knowledge. He makes it clear that he sees immense value in the I-Thou approach.

> But I wish to raise the more radical question: can *all* the sciences, *all* knowledge be conceptualized as a resultant of a loving or caring interrelationship between knower and known? What would be the advantages to us of setting this epistemology alongside the one that now reigns in 'objective science'? Can we simultaneously use both? My own feeling is that we can and should use both epistemologies as the situation demands. I do not see them as contradictory but as

enriching each other... Reality seems to be a kind of alloy of the perceiver and the perceived, a sort of mutual product, a transaction.

And this leads on to a distinction between *not-caring* objectivity and *caring* objectivity. They are both trying to do justice to what is there, in the researcher and in the other, but one excludes emotion and the other includes it. Maslow seems to be suggesting that the I-Thou approach is applicable not only in psychology, but also in other fields, and that the I-It approach is applicable not only in physical science, but also in psychology. But in psychology it is the I-It approach which needs to be used sparingly and only when one really has arrived at a point where it is appropriate. The I-Thou approach in psychology needs no such special justification. And if we approach people in this way, says Maslow, we can enlarge our sense of what can be researched. We don't have to stick to the eye-blink reflex and experiments on information-processing. We can go on to study:

> ...the nature of normality, of health, of goodness, of creativeness, and love, of higher needs, beauty, curiosity, fulfilment, of heroes and the godlike in human beings, of altruism and cooperativeness, of love for the young, protection of the weak, compassion and unselfishness and humanitarianism, of greatness, of transcendent experiences, of higher values.

This is, of course, an ambitious programme, and one of the very characteristic things about Maslow, and about this book, is unquenchable optimism.

He is, however, willing to face the unpleasant and the awkward, and he writes very well about the fear of knowing.

(4) *Courage vs. fear* Most research and most knowledge, he says, comes from deficiency motivation. That is, it is based on fear, and is carried out to allay anxiety; it is basically defensive. Maslow enumerates 21 cognitive pathologies which emanate from this basic stance.

It doesn't have to be that way: research can come from growth motivation. It can be based on anxiety-free interest, and oriented towards personal fulfilment and fullest humanness. It is free to turn outward an intrinsically interesting reality. It is absorbed with the real world rather than with the researcher's own neuroses. And when it does this it is much more creative.

After saying that precision, rigour, orderliness, etc., can be neurotic, he goes on to clarify:

> *All of these same mechanisms and goals are also found in the growth-motivated scientist.* The difference is that they are not

neuroticised. They are not compulsive, rigid and uncontrollable, nor is anxiety produced when these rewards have to be postponed. They are not desperately needed, nor are they exclusively needed. It is possible for healthy scientists to enjoy not only the beauties of precision but also the pleasures of sloppiness, casualness and ambiguity. They are able to enjoy rationality and logic but are also able to be pleasantly crazy, wild or emotional. They are not afraid of hunches, intuitions or improbable ideas... This ability to be either controlled and/or uncontrolled, tight and/or loose, sensible and/or crazy, sober and/or playful seems to be characteristic not only of psychological health but also of scientific creativeness.

(5) *Science and sacralization*   Science is notorious for the way in which it seems to oppose religion — and also such emotions as reverence, mystery, wonder and awe. Maslow suggests that deficiency-oriented science has a need to desacralize as a defence.

> One can avoid feeling stunned, unworthy or ignorant before, let us say, a beautiful flower or insect or poem simply by taking it apart and feeling masterful again. So also for classifying, taxonomizing, categorizing, rubricizing in general. These, too, are ways of making awesome things mundane, secular, manageable, everyday.

The question Maslow wants to ask is — is it in the intrinsic nature of science or knowledge that it must desacralize, must strip away values in a way that Maslow calls 'countervaluing', or not? On the contrary, says Maslow:

> The psychologist knows that there are two hierarchies of esteem in science (not just one). One is the hierarchy of well organized knowledge; the other is the hierarchy of importance of the questions one chooses to work with. It is the ones who choose to work with the crucial, unresolved, human questions who have taken on their shoulders the fate of mankind.

The scientist who is committed to the work of science gets illuminations, turn-ons, peak experiences and aesthetic surprises which are highly emotional and in a sense religious.

> For my part, I think I have got more 'poetical' experiences from my own and others' researches than I have from poetry. I have got more 'religious' experiences from reading scientific journals than I have from reading 'sacred books'. The thrills of creating something beautiful come to me via my experiments, my explorations, my

theoretical work rather than from painting or composing music or dancing. Science can be a way of marrying with that which you love, with that which fascinates you and with whose mystery you would love to spend your life.... . Not only does science begin in wonder, it also ends in wonder.

(6) *Experiential knowledge vs. spectator knowledge* The world of experience can be described with two languages — a subjective (first-person) one and an objective (third-person) one. 'In his presence I feel small' is first-person, while 'He's trying to dominate me' is third-person.

> The basic coin in the realm of knowing is direct, intimate, experiential knowing. Everything else can be likened to banks and bankers, to accounting systems and checks and paper money, which are useless unless there is real wealth to exchange, to manipulate, to accumulate and to order.

But in seeing first-person experience as basic, Maslow does not wish to elevate it to universal status:

> ...experiential knowledge is *sine qua non* but not all, i.e. it is necessary but not sufficient... we avoid thereby the trap of dichotomizing experiential knowledge from and against conceptual knowledge. My thesis is that experiential knowledge is prior to verbal-conceptual knowledge but that they are hierarchically-integrated and need each other.

And he says that there are ways of checking out subjective knowledge, by comparing it with other people's subjective knowledge. This is where we should usually start:

> This is why I can think that (1) most psychological problems do and should begin with phenomenology rather than with objective, behavioural laboratory techniques, and also (2) that we must usually press on from phenomenological beginnings *toward* objective, experimental, behavioural laboratory methods. This is I think a normal and usual path — from a less reliable beginning toward a more reliable level of knowledge.

But the phenomenological approach — the use of subjective and first-person experience as a source of knowledge — requires high standards of the knower.

The injunction might read, then: make yourself into a good instrument of knowledge. Cleanse yourself as you would the lenses of your microscope. Become as fearless as you can, as honest, authentic and ego-transcending as you can.

And he notes that if this were taken seriously, the education of scientists would be very different from what it is now. One might cultivate peak experiences, or Zen Buddhism; one would explore altered states of consciousness; one would work in therapy to dispose of one's neuroses. We have to learn how to know the world by setting aside our knowledge of it.

'Self-knowledge makes better knowers.' This is something Maslow believes, but he recognizes that it is based on clinical experience rather than objective tests, and is therefore somewhat unreliable knowledge. He still wants to say, however, that knowledge which is as unreliable as this can still be extremely valuable. And knowledge which is even more unreliable than this — even wild guesses — can still be better than nothing. If science only relied on well-supported evidence there would be no science, because:

The lay picture of 'the scientist' as one who keeps his mouth shut until he is sure of his facts is quite incorrect, at least for talented, 'breakthrough' scientists. Polanyi rightly speaks of faith, connoisseurship, courage, self-confidence and boldness in gambling as intrinsic to the nature of the trail-blazing theorist or researcher, as defining characteristics, not as accidental, fortuitous or expendable.

And if we think of science only as what is well-established, we divide the world too sharply into science and non-science. If we see all knowledge, on the other hand, as a matter of degree, we let more people in. From this point of view, science is simply looking at things for yourself rather than trusting to the *a priori* or to authority of any kind.

It is this empirical attitude that I claim can and should be taught to all human beings, including young children. Look for yourself! Let's see how it works! Is that claim correct? How correct? Such as these, I believe, are the fundamental scientific questions and methods of science. And it follows that checking for yourself by going into the back yard and looking with your own eyes is more truly empirical and therefore more 'scientific' than looking up the answer in Aristotle or, for that matter, in a textbook of science.

He sees such an attitude, in fact, as almost a defining characteristic of humanness itself. A combination of reality testing and psyche testing can get one a long way. And if we add to this a transhuman or transcendental dimension, we add a layer that is often missing from scientific discussions, but which we must take into account if we are to do justice to the nature of the human person.

If we want to know more about how to do the other kind of science (the experiental kind) we can go to Taoism and learn about receptivity.

> To be able to listen — really, wholly, passively, self-effacingly listen — without presupposing, classifying, improving, controverting, evaluating, approving or disapproving, without dueling with what is being said, without rehearsing the rebuttal in advance, without free-associating to portions of what is being said so that succeeding portions are not heard at all — such listening is rare.

But if we can do it, says Maslow, these are the moments when we are closest to reality. Contemplation is something which is hard to learn, but it can be learned, and it is an essential moment in the scientific process as Maslow sees it.

But also the spectator approach is important and not to be abandoned. Abstract conceptual knowledge is necessary too.

> The attack upon abstractness dichotomized from concreteness must never be confused with an attack upon abstractness hierarchically-integrated with concreteness and experience.

The important thing in all this, says Maslow, is an appropriate humility. The researcher should be willing and eager to learn.

(7) *The comprehensive vs. the simple*   Scientific work has two directions or poles or goals: one is towards simplicity and condensation, the other towards total comprehensiveness and inclusiveness. Both of these are necessary, but we should distrust simplicity as we seek it. We should also not value simplicity and elegance to the exclusion of richness and experiential truth. We should accept the formula 'First look, and then know', but add to it 'and then look again'. We can then learn that scientific knowledge, no matter how abstract, can enrich our experience rather than impoverishing it, so long as we don't use it as a substitute for experiencing. The movement is from the comprehensive to the simple, and back again to the comprehensive, if we want to make human sense.

(8) *Suchness vs. abstraction*   There are two different kinds of meanings, which are complementary rather than mutually exclusive. Maslow calls one

'Abstractness meaning' (classifications) and the other 'Suchness meaning', having to do with the experiential realm. One tends to reduce things to some unified explanation; the other experiences something in its own right and in its own nature.

This gets us away from the tendency to call anything other than a simple unified explanation 'absurd', 'meaningless', 'ineffable', 'inexplicable', and so on; to do this is 'a failure of nerve'. By talking about 'suchness meaning' we are saying that direct experience can be studied, talked about, deepened and better understood.

There may be two kinds of scientists — the cool, who go most for abstraction and explanation, and the warm, who go for suchness and understanding. But great scientists integrate both.

(9)   *Values and value-free science*   If we say that science can tell us nothing about why, only about how; if we say that science cannot help us to choose between good and evil, we are saying that science is only an instrument, only a technology, to be used equally either by good men or by villains. But Maslow believes that science can discover the values by which people should live.

Firstly the weak instinctoid needs which he discovered and popularized can be thought of as built-in values.

> And it is these values which are found, uncovered — *re*covered, perhaps we should say — in the course of psychotherapy or self-discovery.

Secondly, science itself has a set of values. Some scientists actually confess to trying to shape the culture as they would like it to be, but almost all scientists, Maslow says, believe that science is good as an end in itself, because it creates more truth, beauty, order, lawfulness, goodness, perfection, unity and so forth. And they also believe that it is good as a means, because it lengthens life and reduces disease and pain, makes life richer and fuller, spreads information, permits mobility, reduces back-breaking labour and could (in principle) make better human beings.

> Science as a human enterprise and as a social institution has goals, ends, ethics, morals, purposes — in a word, values — as Bronowski has so conclusively and brilliantly demonstrated.

(10)   *Maturity vs. immaturity*   Science is incredibly 'masculine', in the sense of idealizing the stereotyped image of the male. Maslow sees this as a sign of immaturity, much more to do with the adolescent boy who desperately wants to be accepted as a man, rather than with the mature man, who may have many 'feminine' traits.

A certain bullfighter is reputed to have said, 'Sir, *anything* I do is masculine'. This kind of acceptance of one's own nature instead of living up to some external ideal is characteristic of the more mature male who is so sure of himself that he doesn't have to bother proving anything.

This is fine as far as it goes, but doesn't really say anything much about women, or how women can relate to science. Presumably the point would be that the mature woman would also be secure in her femaleness, and not be taken in by the masculinity bit, one way or another. And certainly the more Taoistic approach, to science which Maslow is contending for, is less hostile to women and more suitable for human beings as such.

Conclusion   Maslow is unsatisfactory in so many ways: he is repetitive; he keeps on making splits between things he likes and things he doesn't like, and then pretending to love both equally; he doesn't make an adequate distinction between primary subjectivity and realized subjectivity — and so on. But I have a strong feeling that he knows what it's all about, and I find some of his phrases and concepts extremely attractive and usable.

Human Inquiry
Edited by P. Reason and J. Rowan
© 1981 John Wiley & Sons Ltd.

CHAPTER NINE

A dialectical paradigm for research

John Rowan
Independent Consultant, London, UK

In this chapter I am trying to synthesize the old and the new paradigms of social science, and to show how different styles and traditions of social science research relate to one another. In doing so I shall use mainly three concepts — alienation, social change and the research cycle.

Alienation

By alienation I mean treating people as fragments. This is usually done by putting a person into the role of 'research subject' and then only permitting a very restricted range of behaviour to be counted. This is alienating because it is using the person for someone else's ends — the person's actions do not belong to that individual, but to the researcher and to the research plan. In the fully alienated paradigm, a person's actions are not even called actions or conduct, but are called rather 'emitted behaviours', or 'variables'. In experimental laboratory work, in experimental field research, in unobtrusive observational research, in most evaluation research and most applied research, we find alienation operating, in the four forms originally suggested by Karl Marx (1844):

(1) *Alienation from the product* The worker is related to the product of his labour as to an alien object. For on this premise

it is clear that the more the worker spends himself, the more
powerful the alien objective world becomes which he creates
over against himself, the poorer he himself — his inner world
— becomes, the less belongs to himself as his own.

For 'the worker' here we substitute the 'experimental subject' or the
'respondent'. To an important extent this also applies to the researcher, who,
like the manager, is better able to mystify his position.

> (2) *Alienation from work* This relation is the relation of the
> worker to his own activity as an alien activity not belonging to
> him; it is activity as suffering, strength as weakness, begetting
> as emasculation.

This refers in our terms to the actual process of conducting the experiment,
running the survey, pursuing the participant observations, or whatever.

> (3) *Alienation from other people* Within the relationship of
> estranged labour each man views the other in accordance with
> the standard and the position in which he finds himself as a
> worker.

This refers to the way in which researchers and the researched-upon both take
up their fixed roles, from which they must not depart.

> (4) *Alienation from self* The worker's own physical and mental
> energy, his personal life or what is life other than activity, as an
> activity which is turned against him, neither depends on nor
> belongs to him... Estranged labour turns man's species being,
> both nature and his spiritual species property, into a being alien
> to him, into a means to his individual existence. It estranges
> man's own body from him, as it does external nature and his
> spiritual essence, his *human* being.

This refers much more to the researcher than to the subject, but of course both
partake of a common culture, and this form of alienation is possibly that
which hurts most.

To Marx, these forms of alienation were objective matters. They existed
whether anyone noticed them or not. If, as a matter of empirical fact, some
workers did not experience in any conscious way these forms of alienation, it
would be necessary to use agitation and propaganda in order to awaken them
from their false consciousness. The Marxian concept of alienation, then, is one
of an objective reality brought about in the actual process of working in a

wage-labour situation — or in our case, in a research situation. But it needs to be articulated and made conscious before anyone can act on it. And in our present age of television it seems harder and harder to achieve this. Marcuse (1969) talks about 'the paralysis of the masses' and McLuhan (1964) says that:

> The principle of numbness comes into play with electric technology, as with any other. We have to numb our central nervous system when it is extended and exposed, or we will die. Thus the age of anxiety and of electric media is also the age of the unconscious and of apathy.

All this seems to apply very directly to the world of research, as comes out very clearly in the work of Jennifer Platt (1976). It is hard for researchers and subjects to see how alienated they are, because the myth says that science is so glorious that they shouldn't notice. Most experimental subjects or study respondents, etc., only do it on a temporary basis, and never rise to the level of consciousness which they would if they had to work at it every day. And most researchers are busy trying to get out of research.

> Most full-time research jobs are on short contracts, and few of those who hold them plan to stay in research indefinitely; the typical research worker, therefore, must have his next job in mind, and that will commonly be in teaching. . . . There is a paradox here: research is a high-status activity, but research jobs are not high-status jobs (Platt, 1976).

So again it is easy for researchers not to notice how alienated they are, or to ignore it so that they can go on to the next thing.

But alienated they are, and in Table 9.1 research traditions are listed in order of alienation, the most alienated at the beginning of the list, and the least at the end. This is not intended to be a comprehensive list, nor is it intended to be very precise in its ordering, but it will suffice to indicate how much is being left out of account in the standard orthodox approach to research. Each of these traditions has a substantial body of work to its credit, which is often highly regarded in its own field.

If research at the beginning of the list is alienated, as we are contending, does this mean that research at the end of the list is non-alienated, or free? Not entirely, because we live in a profoundly alienating culture, and in a way there is no escaping it. But in a relative way, we can certainly say that those at the end of the list are much less alienating than those at the start. Alienation from the product is still there to some degree — though as we shall see throughout this book, the product itself becomes less important; alienation from the work is much less of a feature, and people feel much more involved in what the

Table 9.1

Tradition	Example
1. Pure basic research	⎧ These are the four
2. Basic objective research	⎪ orthodox forms of
3. Evaluation research	⎬ research found in
4. Applied research	⎩ most textbooks.
5. Participant observation	Polsky (1969)
6. Language and class research	Labov (1972)
7. Personality and politics research	Knutson (1973)
8. Ethogenic research	Harré (1979)
9. Phenomenological research	Giorgi (1975)
10. Ethnomethodology	Turner (1974)
11. LSD research	Grof (1979)
12. Dialectical research	Esterson (1972)
13. Action research	Sanford (1970a)
14. Intervention research	Argyris (1971)
15. Personal construct research	Fransella (1972)
16. Existential research	Hampden-Turner (1976)
17. Experiential research	Heron (1974c)
18. Endogenous research	Maruyama (1978a)
19. Participatory research	Hall (1975)

research is all about; alienation from other people is broken down quite deliberately and to an important extent; and alienation from self is often entirely counteracted.

Social Change

So much for alienation, then; what about social change? If we imagine a continuum extending right down the table, from beginning to end, it turns out to be not only a continuum of alienation but also a continuum of social change.

The forms of research at the beginning involve the least social change, and indeed aim at being experimental and descriptive, and try not to change people in any way. They check hypotheses about people in as precise and unambiguous a way as possible, and they want their theories and generalizations to be just as true before and after the investigation. In other words, they are treating people as static — as if they were inanimate objects. In doing this, they mechanize things as far as possible, hitching people up to counters, timers and measurers wherever possible. A snapshot at one point in time is made into a general truth.

The forms of research at the end of the list, however, involve a great deal of social change. Research changes the world in three ways: it makes a difference to the researcher; it makes a difference to those who come to know about the research; and it makes a difference to whatever is studied. But in social research we are talking about who, rather than what, and the last of these becomes very important indeed. The later forms of research actively try to make a difference to the people being studied. They involve thinking out the need for research with the people involved, planning it with them, facilitating the process of carrying it out, and joining with them in communicating the results. They explicitly involve the researcher in the process of change, and demand that the investigator be as open to change as the 'subjects' are encouraged to be — only they are now more like co-researchers than like conventional subjects. In this book we have a number of examples of what this looks, sounds and feels like.

In terms of the Mitroff and Kilmann model mentioned in Chapter 4, it is as if the beginning of our list corresponded to Quadrant 1, while those at the end corresponded to Quadrant 4. Mitroff and Kilmann point out that these are opposites, in the sense that scientists in the first quadrant have a set of norms of scientific method, while those in the fourth quadrant have a set of counternorms which are almost the exact converse. They are also opposites in the sense that those in the first quadrant are the most 'masculine' in terms of social stereotypes, while the scientists in the fourth quadrant are the most 'feminine'. It could be seen as ironical that it is the 'feminine' end which is the strongest influence for personal and social change.

So much for social change, then; what about the research cycle?

The Research Cycle

It would obviously be convenient if we could have a more precise language for talking about these research methods, so that we could compare and contrast them more easily. The best way of doing this seems to be to consider all research as following the same basic model, but of using it quite differently. One possible model is given in Figure 9.1.

At one end of our continuum, this is seen as the standard alienated academic research project. One is working in a particular field (BEING) and finds or is given a problem. One searches the literature to find if anyone has already tackled it, and mentally combines the information to refine the problem (THINKING). One then designs a research plan and discusses it with one's supervisor or colleagues (PROJECT). One then conducts the experiment, or carries out the survey or observations (ENCOUNTER). One does one's data processing, content analysis, statistical manipulation, etc. (MAKING SENSE). And one writes the paper, or dissertation, or thesis (COMMUNICATION) and perhaps talks about it at conferences and other

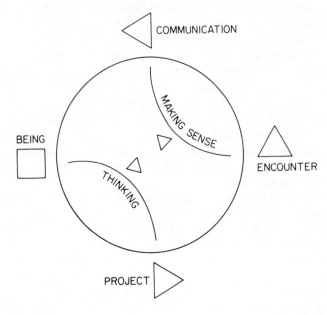

COMMUNICATION

MAKING SENSE

BEING

THINKING

ENCOUNTER

PROJECT

Figure 9.1   The cycle model

meetings, or writes an article about it, before returning to one's usual work in the field again (BEING).

At the other end of our continuum, this same cycle is seen as a dialectical process of engagement with the world. I start by resting in my own experience. But at a certain point my existing practice seems to be inadequate — I become dissatisfied. So the first negation arises; I turn *against* the old ways of doing things. A real problem has arisen. (This is not the invariable starting-point — a dialectical cycle may often start with the moment of ENCOUNTER — but it would be too confusing to cover all the possibilities at this point.)

So I move into a phase of needing new thinking. Perhaps I start by finding out what others know already — gathering information through conversations, phone calls, meetings, libraries or whatever. Ideas start churning around. THINKING in this model is not the application of a technique to inert material — it is a creative process of invention and testing. It continually asks the question — 'Will this do?' It is essentially an *inward* movement, gathering in information; but it is also a processing movement, adding and combining the new information into unfamiliar relationships, and trying it against some kind of template of what would be acceptable. The nature of this template is again dependent on the level of consciousness available. The major contradiction here is between always needing more information ('Maybe that new paper will have the answer') and feeling that there is too much information already, and it needs to be cut down. It is only when this contradiction is transcended that movement takes place to the next stage.

At a certain point I *abandon* the gathering of more and more information. Thinking is *not* enough. I have to make a definite decision as to what to aim for. What is the major contradiction? This is what we need to attack. Philosophizing any further would be sterile and useless. Some action plan has to come into being. This may require some daring, some risk-taking, some breaking of the bounds. I need to involve others at this stage in the process. PROJECT is essentially an *outward* movement. This is where I take a risk, and form an intention. It will involve some form of bridging distances — to another person, to a new field, to a different theory or whatever. I have to bring into being a thought which contradicts the present reality, and has the power to bring into being a genuinely new situation — and there may be more than one way of doing this. This may require a certain degree of assertion or even aggressiveness on my part. It essentially involves plans and decisions. The major contradiction of the formal moment itself is between the need for more and better plans and satiation with plans. 'Plans should be adequate' *versus* 'No plan can be perfect'. Again, this contradiction has to be overcome before movement can take place to the next point on the cycle.

But again, at a certain point, plans are *not* what is needed. Action itself is the thing to get into. In action I am fully present, here now. Plans are a mere distraction from the past, and can only hamper and impede. I must be ready to improvise if unexpected reactions occur. I have to be really *with* the others. ENCOUNTER is a movement of height and depth, like BEING, though it involves regular inward and outward moments. (The rhythmic nature of the cycle is now becoming more apparent.) This is where I actually meet the other. There is some action, some engagement, such that some other reality can get through to me. I may get confirmed or disconfirmed: and it appears, paradoxically, that disconfirmation is actually more valuable as a learning experience than is confirmation. An experience of unfreedom can be very stimulating to further effort. The comparison of what is expected with what is actual is potentially very revealing. The major contradiction of this moment is between the need for perseverance and assiduity, and a plethora of too much activity. 'I am just here and now' *versus* 'I am not just here and now'. This is the place for test, for experiment, for comparison. It is also a place for involvement, for commitment, for spontaneity — to the extent that I am not genuinely open to experience, to that extent I am not genuinely encountering reality, and hence not likely to learn.

This goes on until I get to the point of feeling that action is *not* enough. I must withdraw and find out what it *means*. How can I understand what I have been through? And what the others have been through? Perhaps there is more than one message, more than one way of seeing it. What does it *all* mean?

What are the contradictions, and can they be resolved? MAKING SENSE in this model involves both analysis and contemplation, and we have gone into the whole question of how experience turns into meaning and knowledge in Chapter 10. The contradiction here is between reducing the data to an understandable simplicity, and adding more and more connections to the data to make them more understandable in that way, expanding them until they say everything.

But at a certain point, after I have been immersed in this for some time, I begin to get dissatisfied. Analysis is *not* enough. I must start telling people what it means and how I have understood what we have been through. What have we actually accomplished or achieved? Can I explain it to someone else? Can others learn from our mistakes and false starts? From our successes? I or others may write papers, give lectures, go to conferences, go on the radio, on television, in the popular press, or wherever, either individually or collectively. COMMUNICATION is again an *outward* movement. This is the stage where we have digested what has happened, and made it part of our new accommodation to reality. Our mental structures become richer and more complex. Our consciousness expands. I communicate with myself about what it all meant for me. I may communicate with others who were not involved with me in it. I may communicate with others who were not involved. The major contradiction of this moment is between the need to get data more finely processed and accurately and clearly expressed, and awareness of the impossibility of communication to anyone outside the experience. The main thing is to understand what we have been through.

At a certain point, however, I do *not* want to turn into a communicator, I want to get back to some real work. Now that I have learnt what I have learnt, I can go back to my field and continue to practise, only now on a higher level. BEING is neither inward nor outward, but represents a dimension of height and depth. It is here that I am a full three-dimensional human being most truly and most fully. Existence, perception, identity are all involved here. The question of will is also involved in any movement from this point. The major contradiction here is between cultivation of the everyday and dissatisfaction with it. 'Everything is (now) all right as it is' *versus* 'Everything is not all right as it is'. Implied in any movement from this point is a negation of one's existing practice — one turns away from the old ways of doing things. This is essentially a resting place, a place of contentment. It always hurts to leave it. It always feels good to come back to it. It can represent one's daily work in the field. One only leaves it under some form of pressure. I am who I am here.

These are the six moments in the process, and it is important to notice that the sequence can start anywhere. Often the starting point is an ENCOUNTER; sometimes it may be a piece of THINKING or MAKING SENSE; BEING is a good place to start. I have used symbols (arrows and a square) instead of numbers precisely because different people need to start at different points.

(It is interesting to note that people can get hooked on just one of these moments: the academic may get hooked on THINKING; the executive may get hooked on PROJECT; the residential social worker may get hooked on ENCOUNTER; the introspective may get hooked on MAKING SENSE; the journalist may get hooked on COMMUNICATION; the hermit may get hooked on BEING. It is quite common for people coming into the Realised Level (see Chapter 10) for the first time to rush back and forth between BEING and ENCOUNTER, as if that were the whole.)

Research Diagrams

We have outlined now two extreme ways of using and thinking about the selfsame research cycle. The first way reduces it to a predictable trot round well-known landmarks, and often seems to turn the circle into a straight line, leading from gaining-the-grant to delivering-the-report.

The amount of energy involved and released in these two ways of using the cycle are quite different. The former way of using the cycle is low-energy; the latter, high-energy. The former way in uninvolving ('My record is still perfect. I have never actually seen a Great Books discussion, despite several years of almost full-time work on this project'). The latter is deeply involving, often being on some topic which is of personal significance to the researcher, and to the co-researchers, or subjects.

Having gone this far, we can now adopt one or two simple conventions for diagramming different research styles. If we use a dotted line to represent alienation (in the sense described above), we can show pure basic research as in Figure 9.2. The circle represents the researcher going round the whole cycle. The line represents the subject meeting the researcher at one point only — the point of ENCOUNTER. What results is an alienated encounter, where there is a meeting of role to role, rather than of person to person.

Figure 9.2   Pure basic research

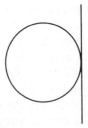

Figure 9.3   Existential research

The next diagram represents existential research, such as that which is reported in my 'T Poems' (Rowan, 1976b) — see Figure 9.3. Here again the researcher meets the subjects at one point only — ENCOUNTER — but this time both researcher and subjects are involved, non-alienated and authentic.

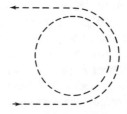

Figure 9.4   Action research

If we then use a dashed line to represent a situation where the researcher (and/or the subject) may or may not be alienated, depending on circumstances, we can represent action research, intervention research and personal construct research as in Figure 9.4. Here the researcher meets the subject at three points on the cycle: PROJECT, ENCOUNTER and COMMUNICATION. (MAKING SENSE requires, like THINKING, a period of withdrawal, whether it be carried out by the researcher alone, or by the co-researchers as well. It is only the results of this process of making sense which can be shared.) Already the value of such a diagram can be seen, in that it shows how three quite separate and distinct research traditions have all followed the same structural form, quite unknown to each other.

And finally, Figure 9.5 shows how we can represent experiential research, endogenous research and participatory research. All three of these have in common a commitment to full engagement on the part of the researcher, and a refusal to let the subjects hide behind a role. These are the most change-oriented of all the methods, because they set up a context of mutual trust, within which support and confrontation can take place.

One of the most striking things about research done in this way is the

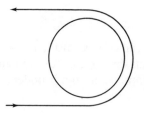

Figure 9.5 Participatory research

amount of energy released. This is why it seems fitting to call it a high-energy type of research. What is more, energy seems to be released as each point on the cycle is left behind. It seems that the point is not just left behind, it is *contradicted* in a more or less negative way. This seems to be to do with the much higher degree of involvement and commitment required of the investigator. The researcher is in touch at several levels, not just the one level favoured at the mechanistic end of the continuum.

We can now represent any given research tradition in terms of the cycle model, and therefore become much more easily aware of what has been done and what is possible, and what choices we really have. It also enables us to look at our own particular single research project and to question it. In particular, it enables us to look at the possible questions we can ask at each of the six points on the cycle.

Types of Question

There seem to be, in practice, six main types of question which researchers ask.

Positivist-efficiency

These are the Campbell and Stanley (1966) type of questions about threats to validity and so forth. They are all about tightening up and tidying up research designs so that they give the maximum of hard data.

Alienation-authenticity

These are all about the people involved in research as persons. Does the research turn the subject into an object and the researcher into a being from Mars? (Or a would-be being from Mars). Is the researcher hiding behind a role, and are the subjects being forced into fixed roles? How much deep personal commitment is there?

Political-patriarchal

These are all about the social context of the research. Whose interests does it serve? What social relations does it take for granted? What are the economics of it? What patterns of oppression does it underwrite or subvert?

Dialectical

These questions are all about the philosophical assumptions of the research. Does it assume that there is one right answer? Does it assume that the relationships are linear? Does it have room for change and transformation? Is it looking for the major contradiction? What does it take for granted? What ground is it standing on?

Legitimacy

These are questions about how the researcher is situated in the whole set-up within which she or he is operating. Is a proper research job possible? There are some very tricky questions here, because research and consultancy interventions often have to operate within existing structures which may sometimes be quite hostile.

Relevance

These are questions about how much it all matters, to the researcher or to anyone else. Who really cares? Are the findings going to be any real use to anybody? Or are the findings isolated and separated from the real world? Could anybody ever act on them?

The cycle model makes it easier to touch the reality of these questions, and to take in the fact that they can be asked at each one of the six moments in the process. What I am trying to urge is that all six of these types of question are legitimate and proper concerns for different types of social researcher. The kinds of specific question which might be asked are suggested in the Tables. Rosen's contribution in the present volume shows how they are used in practice.

This is by no means an exhaustive list of the questions which could be asked. Maslow might well suggest that people at each level of the hierarchy of needs might each have their own questions; Walford (1979) might suggest that each of his seven major ideologies might have different questions to ask; Southgate and Randall in this volume (Chapter 5) might say that each of their four types might have its own questions. But the cycle model enables us to be properly suspicious when a positivist comes along and says — 'Mine are the *only* questions to attend to' — or when a politico says — 'Mine are.' To stick to one set of questions is perfectly possible, and may even be a defensible personal choice, but it cannot be convincing as a total answer to what research is all about. If research is to be genuine human inquiry about things that matter, instead of something much more limited, we have to be aware of all the questions which can be asked, even if we are not asking them ourselves.

Multiple Cycles

The final point I would like to make is that the cycle model makes it easier to grasp the desirability of multiple cycles. Rather than trusting to the 'one big bang' type of research project, we design a number of interlocking cycles which spread a net over the phenomenon we are studying.

This gives us a new way of seeing pilot work. Instead of wanting to get rid of the pilot work as soon as possible, and get on to the real thing, we start being very interested in different kinds of pilot work, and how they can throw light on one another. We start to call them *early cycles* instead of 'pilot work', and to write them up properly, and learn from them as much as possible.

In this way we make the early cycles more available to inspection, which is highly desirable. For it is in the early stages that we reveal our presuppositions most fully. Ideas which do not appear in the early cycles are quite unlikely to get inserted later. If we are to be more involved with our research and more personally committed to it, we need to be more explicit about our prejudices and assumptions and beliefs as we go into a piece of research. To the extent that we avoid this we shall be guilty of evasion of important issues — and more importantly, we lay ourselves open to self-deception. George Devereux (see Chapter 7 in this volume) has pointed out how much social research is just unaware autobiography.

Further than that, multiple cycles give us more choices and more flexibility. We can either use them sequentially, to go deeper into a phenomenon, thus turning the cycle into a spiral or helix; or we can use them concurrently, approaching the same phenomenon from a number of different angles, and in effect triangulating it or 'knitting a pattern' of cycles. By making each cycle fully rigorous in its own terms, we can achieve a recursive validity of a cumulative nature — yielding a deeper and more extensive truth than that given by a linear approach. (We have discussed this kind of thought more fully in Chapter 10.)

A Language

My hope is that these ideas will not just be seen as a set of insights, more or less useful or stimulating, but that they can form part of a language of research, enabling people from perhaps quite different backgrounds to communicate better about research, both with lay people and between themselves. Such a language would make it easier to appreciate what we are doing ourselves, as well as to describe it to others. It would make better self-monitoring possible, whatever one's criteria or orientation. And it would open the way to wider horizons of research. With its help, we can survey the whole field of social research and relate the old to the new paradigm.

Table 9.2   Point   [ ]   : BEING

Efficiency questions

   Is E familiar with the field and its literature?
   Is E actually involved with the relevant data?
   Has E got appropriate qualifications for dealing with the relevant matters?
   Does E have dependable work habits?
   Is E intelligent enough and intellectually tough enough?

Authenticity questions

   Is E aware of her own motives?
   Is E questioning her involvement with the field?
   Does E work in a self-punishing way?

Alienation questions

   What relationships with others does E set up by her way of being?
   Can E listen to others?

Political questions

   Is E aware of the social implications of her daily practice?
   Is E aware of the sources of the money which supports her?
   Is E aware of the social pressures which influence her actions?

Patriarchy questions

   Is E sexist? racist? classist? ageist?
   Does E conduct a great deal of her life in terms of domination and submission?
      Competition and acclaim? Struggle for recognition?
   Is E aware of the patriarchal patterns which surround her?

Dialectical questions

   Does E look for the contradictions underlying daily experience?
   Does E take responsibility for her own life?
   Does E perceive the world in terms of conflicts and their resolution?
   Does E see the paradox of rhythm and the rhythm of paradox?

Legitimacy questions

   Is a client involved? If so, is there honesty or deception or lack of communication
      between E and the client?
   Who provides the problem? Who defines what the problem is? Who owns the
      problem? Who legitimates the problem?
   Who is the client? And who is the real client?

Relevance questions

   Am I choosing a problem that is relevant to my life? my career? a client? ordinary
      people? questioning patriarchy? the advancement of science? a class of problems?
      my unconscious?
   What am I really trying to do?

Table 9.3   Point   ◿ : THINKING

Efficiency questions

Can E marshal and correlate information in such a way as to bring it to focus on a
   problem?
Does E define and break down the problem into specific researchable questions?
Does E use creative imagination to think of interesting and usable hypotheses?
Can E discriminate between more and less central or crucial hypotheses to test?
Can E use the library in an efficient way to gather existing data?
Has E got the stamina to pursue what she wants in the abstracts and reprints?

Authenticity questions

Does E believe that she can be value-free?
Does E separate research from the rest of her life?
Does E have something to gain or lose from the solution of the research problem, in
   a direct practical personal way?

Alienation questions

Does E consult with others on a strict role basis?
Does E home in on a specific question early, and spend the rest of the time defending
   that selection?
If E disagrees with others on a point, does she call for a vote?
Does E consult authorities to gain new knowledge or insight, or to back up what is
   being done already?

Political questions

Does E check on the political commitment of sources of information?
Is E aware of the social implications of certain lines of inquiry?
Does E refuse to be politically isolated in her work?

Patriarchal questions

Does E take patriarchy for granted?
Does E draw attention to patriarchal patterns when she discovers them?

Dialectical questions

Is E consistently adopting a reflexive approach — applying her concepts to herself?
Is E looking for the reality beneath the appearances?
Is E looking for the major contradiction underlying her problem? As opposed to
   minor contradictions which may be easier to approach?
Is E questioning or reinterpreting positivist research findings?

Legitimacy questions

Is information being fed in from an interested party?
Is there pressure not to study certain problems?
Is certain information refused or 'not available'?
Are certain lines of thought discouraged?

Relevance questions

Am I looking for the data about how my problem can work out in practice?
How application has taken place?

Table 9.4 Point : PROJECT

Efficiency questions

Is a proper accounting procedure set up to exhaust the alternative possibilities?
Is a proper experimental design set up to ensure that alternative hypotheses are eliminated?
Is the questioning procedure open where it needs to be open, and closed where it needs to be closed?
Are the questions phrased in the optimal way?
Are non-reactive methods used where possible?
Have the deceptions been checked to make sure that they work as designed?

Authenticity questions

Is E investing herself fully, and risking something personal?
Is E setting up the project in the way she really wants?
Are E's resources fully engaged in the research plan?

Alienation questions

Is E relating to others solely in terms of roles and rules?
Is the research plan fixed and rigid, or flexible and abandonable?

Political questions

What are the political implications of the research design?
Is the social context being taken into account?

Patriarchy questions

Does the set-up take patriarchy for granted?
Does the research design reinforce patterns of domination in any way?

Dialectical questions

Does the project *negate* what was there before?
Does the project aim at a new state of affairs, which does *not* exist now, but which will exist then?
Is the research planned to allow for the maximum of serendipity — lucky findings which were not anticipated?
Is E's own response built in to the research plan?

Legitimacy questions

Is pressure being put on to have a particular type of project?
Are limitations being imposed on who can be seen?
Are certain questions not being permitted?
Is access restricted?

Relevance questions

Have I found the principal contradiction?
Could the results of this plan in principle be relevant to the client? the underdog? my career? social problems? the class struggle? humanity?
Will it make a difference to my life? Will it bring world peace?
Will it matter a damn to anyone?

Table 9.5 Point  : ENCOUNTER

Efficiency questions

Is experimental control being kept in the way intended?
Is the questioning procedure being carried out in a uniform manner?
Is the correct sample being contacted?
Is E retaining her objectivity?
Is the deception working?

Authenticity questions

Is E open to her own feelings and body reactions?
Is E prepared to express feelings in a genuine way?
Is E prepared to follow the experience wherever it leads? Improvise?

Alienation questions

Has a trusting relationship been built up?
Is E open to S?
Is S determining the situation as much as E?
Are roles actively being broken down?

Political questions

Is the social context being taken into account?
Is the encounter such as to raise S's power of self-determination?
Is S's real back-home situation being taken into account?

Patriarchy questions

Are control patterns actively being broken down?
Is the assumption being made that everyone is heterosexual?

Dialectical questions

Is conflict being encouraged and worked through?
Is E fully engaged with and committed to the process?
Is there an appreciation of the way in which quantity can transform into quality?

Legitimacy questions

Are restrictions placed on the actual interviews, observations of experiments?
Is the research stopped before completion?
Are people suddenly changing the way they interact?

Relevance questions

Is this work turning out in practice to be relevant to the subjects/respondents/
co-researchers? How does it actually affect them?
Am I doing any good? Any harm?

Table 9.6 Point ⬦ : MAKING SENSE

Efficiency questions

Does E have knowledge of software systems?
Can E recombine data in illuminating ways?
Has E an adequate knowledge of content analysis?
Are the most powerful statistical methods being used to maximize the information
  which can be extracted from the data?

Authenticity questions

Is E genuinely open to her own experience gained in the encounter?
Is E eager to get the results clear for her own sake, and for her own illumination?
Can E go into the appropriate state of consciousness to let the data make new
  patterns?

Alienation questions

Is S involved with the examination and processing of the results?
Do colleagues involved in the data processing genuinely listen to one another?
Is S encouraged to make alternative sense of what has occurred?

Political questions

What political interests are taken for granted in the categories being used?
Are any invidious analyses being made?
Is E being separated from S by interested parties?
Are there any political assumptions hidden in the statistics?

Patriarchy questions

Does the analysis make sexist, racist, classist or ageist assumptions?
Does the process involve contemplation as well as analysis?
Is there emotional support for E during the process? How about S?

Dialectical questions

Is there an assumption that just one answer is being sought?
Does the analysis bring out contradictions in a conscious way?
Are the possibilities exploited of dialogue between E and S?
Is the risk being taken of destroying all that emerged from the encounter?

Legitimacy questions

Is pressure being put on to analyse in a certain way?
Is it compulsory to use certain machinery or certain methods?
Are certain analyses discouraged?

Relevance questions

Am I analysing for relevance, or for show?
Is my analysis relevant to the people who took part?

Table 9.7   Point    : COMMUNICATION

Efficiency questions

Are the results written up in proper scientific form?
Would the appropriate professional journal publish them?
Are the results analysed in an objective way, which any outside observer could check?

Authenticity questions

Can E make the results part of her own process of living?
Can E risk herself to say she is disappointed, upset, frustrated?
Can E own up to the fact that it is *her* truth she is sharing, not necessarily *the* truth?

Alienation questions

Can S make the results part of her own process of living?
Is S involved in the communication of the results?
Has S contributed all that she really wants to the final outcome?

Political questions

Is the social effect of the information taken into account when passing it on?
If any information can be extracted, is it passed on to those who could make best
    use of it?

Patriarchy questions

If information is passed on, is it done in such a way as not to put down those who
    receive it?
Is the information elaborated into curlicues of abstraction?

Dialectical questions

Does E appreciate that communication is a two-way process?
Does E make sure to set up a real relationship with people before attempting to
    communicate with them — and while communicating with them?
Does E assume that communication has to be done through words?
Does E appreciate the importance of readiness in communication?
Does E appreciate the importance of resistance in communication, and how it can
    be used to establish a relationship?

Legitimacy questions

Is pressure being put on to publish only in a certain way? to omit relevant material?
    to destroy all or some of the report?
Is there censorship or falsification of the final report?

Relevance questions

Will publication help others? my career? the political struggle?
Will publication change the world?
Will my work take social science forward?
How will this research be seen by those whose opinions I respect most?
Will all this help my self-actualization?

Human Inquiry
Edited by P. Reason and J. Rowan
© 1981 John Wiley & Sons Ltd.

CHAPTER TEN

On making sense

John Rowan
Independent Consultant, London, UK
and Peter Reason
*Centre for the Study of Organizational Change and
Development, University of Bath, UK*

Much of the argument presented in this book is that a true human inquiry needs to be based firmly in the experience of those it purports to understand, to involve a collaboration between 'researcher' and 'subjects' so that they may work together as co-researchers, and to be intimately involved in the lives and praxis of these co-researchers. But as we have thought about and tried to practise research along these lines, we have had to keep returning to the question of ways of thinking and states of consciousness: we keep on hitting the idea that in order to do new paradigm research we need some changed way of looking at the world and interpreting it. In this chapter we attempt to deal with questions like: How are we to *think?* What is the logic (are the logics) of the inquiry process? How are we to move from theory and ideas to our encounter with our subject, and back again? But we find that before we can begin to answer these questions we have to consider the changes in states or levels of *consciousness* that may be involved in new paradigm research.

These questions are important at every stage of the research cycle, but our concern for them is particularly at the stages of Thinking and Making Sense (see Chapter 9), since it seems that it is at these stages that our ways of approaching the world can most easily interfere with the research process. These are of course enormous questions, the kind that are never finally answered. In this chapter we set out the direction our thinking has taken, and indicate the kind of answer we are choosing (for as we argue here, truth can be seen as a matter of choice and will). But these are questions it is important for all researchers to ask and ask again, so that they may find their own answers.

One of the most pervasive influences on ways of thinking in Western culture is what Mitroff and Kilmann (see Chapter 4) call the logic of the Analytical Scientist. This logic is based on two principles of Aristotelean logic — the Law of Contradiction, which states that no proposition can be both true and false at the same time; and the Law of the Excluded Middle — which holds that every proposition is either true or false. In traditional ways of doing science, this logic is coupled with a deterministic view of causality derived from Hume and Mill, leading to a view of inquiry which emphasizes precision and exactitude, causal laws and a hierarchical theory. The language of orthodox science is the language of the experiment and it derives from this underlying philosophy. But as Mitroff and Kilmann point out, this logic is not the only one available to us; there is a whole range of alternatives. And as Bateson has argued persuasively, 'The most important task today is, perhaps, to learn to think in the new way' (1972, p. 462): if we don't learn to think clearly and appropriately, in a way that suits our subject matter and our approach, we run the risk of simply doing analytical science badly. A lot of qualitative research is like this.

But to be stuck with these ways of thinking implies to be stuck with a particular state of consciousness. Just as our ways of thinking are dominated by a quasi-Aristotelean logic, so our state of consciousness is dominated by a so-called 'ordinary' consciousness (we might call it a mythical objective consciousness (Roszak, 1969), or 'straight' consciousness (Weil, 1972)), which is actually *extra*ordinary in its limitedness. It is increasingly clear that there are many different ways of being in this world, many levels of awareness about alternative 'spaces' that we may occupy either permanently or temporarily, but the trouble is that we have few clear or shared ways of identifying these or of talking about them.

Once we allow ourselves to see that there are alternatives to traditional ways of thinking and being in that world, we may permit ourselves to search for, explore, and practise them. This is enormously difficult, since the principles of traditional logic are entwined with ordinary states of consciousness so that our 'mindscape' (Maruyama, 1979) seems to represent the only possible world view. And sometimes trying to think in non-traditional ways, dialectically for example, feels rather like being a small child trying to wield Grandfather's sword. But we need to learn, because it is clear that as we engage in inquiry within the new paradigm, traditional logics and ordinary levels of consciousness are no longer appropriate; they either break down or severely limit our capacity to understand. We will first explore the changes in consciousness which we believe are needed for good new paradigm research, and then move on to explore alternative ways of thinking which may be found to be more appropriate.

The Hegel Levels

Here the Hegelian position seems very helpful in enabling us to understand what is going on. Hegel (1971) says (see Rowan, 1979) that there are three levels of consciousness available to people in everyday life. There is what Rowan rechristened as the Primary level, the Social level and the Realized level.

At the Primary level, which is where we all start, we are one-sidedly subjective, and jump to conclusions in a way that suits our own wishes. This is the stage of what we have called elsewhere 'naive inquiry' and of what Bem (1970) has called 'psycho-logic'. It is rational, in the sense that it wants to make sense of the world, but it does so in this very narrow, personal, and limited way. This is a very rich level, full of important material which we ignore at our peril — and it is at this level that we communicate best with other people, including children — but it is basically weak and subject to mental distress of various kinds. We are very much at the mercy of our feelings and at the mercy of more dominant people. And because at a certain stage in our development we see it as childish and immature, we contradict it, deny it, and push it under and away. We would rather have more control and not hurt so much and so easily. So, in what very often seems to be a quite traumatic way, we split ourselves into an outer personality which is fit to face the world and meet everyone's demands, and an inner self which is secret and private.

So we jump over into the Social level, and become one-sidedly objective. Now we are interested in the facts — what is true and false, what is real and what is illusion, what can be proved and disproved. We discover and use to the full scientific law and mathematics and formal logic. This works fine with natural objects, but when we apply it to human beings, it produces the social relation of master and slave — we want to use and control people just as we learned to use and control things. And we do this to ourselves too: we separate ourselves into a masterful social part, which is willing to play all the parts which society demands, and a submerged primitive part, which is pushed down into a slave position, and only allowed to emerge in very limited and conditional ways. So our attachment to objectivity is compulsive rather than freely chosen. This is the level of consciousness of the traditional scientific orthodoxy. And it is reinforced all the time by a patriarchal culture which sees top-down relations as the right basic structure for society, and an economic system which finds it very convenient to turn people into things or variables. But there is an inner contradiction still operating here which will not let things stay this way.

Our control becomes an over-control which starts to prevent any further development. We need to break out of the tight structure we have built up around ourselves.

So we jump over into the Realized level, which can be loosely and inadequately described as objectively subjective. At this level we refuse to go on suppressing our primary subjective experience, and we find ways of going down into it and rescuing material from it, which is then raised to conscious awareness. Because this material is brought up through the Social level, it is better-informed and educated, much stronger and less vulnerable. In the process, it changes. At the Primary level, feelings swept over us and overwhelmed us; at the Realized level, we are able to choose and to own our feelings. At the Primary level, we were at the mercy of symbolic forms, in our unchosen dreams and daydreams; at the Realized level we are now able deliberately to use images and symbols in creative ways for our research purposes. At the Primary level, intuition was an occasional flash of insight, often accurate but quite unbiddable; at the Realized level it is our main way of thinking, enabling us continually to see the wood as well as the trees. And because we now see the world as *our* world, rather than *the* world, we can see clearly through our own eyes. Being rational, we see at this stage, is doing justice to the whole — to all that is out there in the world and to all that is in here, inside ourselves.

This is a brief and hurried thumbnail sketch, and those who want more must look at the references given, but we can now see much more clearly how the new thinking develops out of the old, and why it should be in such opposition to the old. We have to oppose it to get into the Realized level — there is no other way.

Once we do this, we have clarified a very important issue. It seems that new paradigm research requires at least two separate and distinct changes in consciousness, one permanent and one temporary.

Ideology

The first of these is ideological in nature. By this we mean to say that it is a question of outlook or world-view. It is a change which can be expressed in several different, but we think parallel ways (see Table 10.1). The essence of this move seems to be that it takes us from the magistrate's position to the legislator's position; from playing a part in someone else's movie to writing one's own movie; from taking society for granted to looking over the four walls of one's social milieu. This actual experience, of moving from one to the other, often seems to take place as *disconfirmation* of some kind — a shake-up which can be extremely hurtful or relatively benign. Before the change, one is a functionary, more or less adequate or creditable; after it, one is a creator of one's life and one's world.

The examination we have just made of the Hegel levels makes it easier to see that we get into each level by negating the previous one. But this particular

Table 10.1

From	To	Reference
Social level	Realized level	Rowan (1979)
Relatedness	Growth	Alderfer (1972)
Conformist	Conscientious	Loevinger *et al.* (1970)
Law and order	Social contract	Kohlberg (1973)
Other-esteem	Self-esteem	Maslow (1970)
Consciousness II	Consciousness III	Reich (1972)
Personal	Transpersonal	Green and Green (1971)
Eidostatic	Eidodynamic	Walford (1979)

negation is a particularly difficult one, because so many of the institutions of our society (family, school, work, leisure, etc.) function so as to reinforce the norms of the Social level. Thus we have to deny many layers of social 'conditioning' (experiences of reward and punishment) in order to move wholly into the Realized level. The same is true of moving from Alderfer's Relatedness level to his Growth level, from Loevinger's Conformist level to her Conscientious level, and so forth.

Tables 10.2 and 10.3 show a speculative attempt Rowan made a few years ago to spell out what implications this might have for the (five, as he had it then) moments in the research cycle (compare Chapter 9). In Table 10.2 the change of which we are speaking is that between Relatedness and Growth; in Table 10.3 it is between the three static ideologies and the four dynamic ones. It can be seen that this change is a fundamental one, affecting both the most fundamental assumptions of intellectual life and the most fundamental identifications of emotional life.

In terms of the left-right brain distinction which Ornstein (1977) has brought out into the open, moving into this growth-dynamic ideological position entails getting much more access to and use of right-brain functioning. As explained in the section on Hegel above, this is because entry into the Realized level entails much more contact with one's own subjectivity, and in fact a whole new way of understanding and handling subjectivity. It is very often the experience of disconfirmation of our rigid social identity, mentioned earlier, which puts us in touch with our own subjectivity, and forces us to recognize that social roles cannot give us everything we need. So we are forced to use the despised and rejected right-brain functioning, and make some kind of synthesis of our two halves.

So this ideological position seems to involve a reconciliation or synthesis of two warring tendencies — left and right, male and female, yin and yang, intellect and emotions, sensation and intuition — and the assertion of a personal wholeness of some kind.

Table 10.2

		BEING ▢	THINKING ▽	PROJECT △	ENCOUNTER ◁	COMMUNICATION ▽
Existence	Safety	Follow instructions of powerful others. Avoid condemnation.	Think in prescribed ways. Find out what powerful others think and follow them.	Adopt prescribed plans. Go according to precedent. Use the most powerful rulebook.	Formalize situation as much as possible. Reduce uncertainty to minimum.	Speak when spoken to. Don't volunteer information. Say as little as possible.
	Effectance	Box clever. Keep your nose clean. Watch points. Get to know the key people and the power centres.	Go for the latest thing. Be in the fashion. Spot the trends.	Use the latest equipment. Be one up on the next person. Employ the latest statistical methods.	Use ingenious methods of situational control. Favour deception. Display technical mastery.	Adapt results to make them acceptable to journals which are on the upward path. Put down the opposition. Avoid weakness.
Relatedness	Love and belongingness	Get to know peers. Be popular. Be liked. Follow the main stream.	Go for the most acceptable, most often mentioned references. Make them all agree.	Go for the most reliable, most often used designs and statistical methods. Do it like the next person does it.	Use methods which do not require any confrontation with subjects. Be nice throughout.	Communicate in ways which do not upset or offend anyone. Accentuate the positive. Be modest.
	Esteem from others	Know where you are in the structure. Perform well at all times. Keep up standards. Admire excellence.	Go for the best authorities. Discriminate carefully. Read only the prestige journals.	Go for the designs, statistics and equipment which are most highly regarded by those who really know what they are talking about.	Go for the most rigorous conditions, the ones with the greatest discriminative power. Get clean results.	Communicate results through prestige journals only. Avoid low-quality publishers. Make steady progress. Get sense of achievement.

Table 10.2 continued

	BEING ▢	THINKING ▽	PROJECT △	ENCOUNTER ◁	COMMUNICATION ▽
Growth — Self-esteem	Have long-term goals. Be aware of unintended consequences of actions. Live by own standards.	Search out really important information, no matter where from. Put information together in original ways.	Think our really relevant designs, which really do justice to the problem. Innovate if necessary. Not necessarily statistical at all.	Get engaged in such a way that real learning becomes possible. Have a personal interest in the result.	Communicate in the most relevant way to the most relevant people. You yourself decide what is relevant.
Self-actualization	Be concerned with own personal growth. Take nothing for granted. Let go of goals.	Get absorbed in new information, follow your nose, go where it leads. See information everywhere.	Think out plans for their own sake. Get absorbed in research designs as such. Maybe invent new ones.	Go into experience completely, holding nothing back. Non-manipulative. Open to others. Involved, spontaneous, committed.	Communicate to self very thoroughly, working and reworking experience. Then with others, especially those who took part. Then maybe with others again.

Speculative treatment of possible attitudes and maxims at each point on the cycle, based on David Wright's integration of Maslow, Kohlberg and Loevinger, as developed by John Rowan in *Ordinary Ecstasy* (1976a), and incorporating the nomenclature of Clay Alderfer. This treatment, though speculative, is quite researchable.

Table 10.3

	BEING	THINKING	PROJECT	ENCOUNTER	COMMUNICATION
Proto-static	Logic-tight compartments. High opinion of self.	Find agreement. Go for charisma. Spot trends. Be acceptable.	Adopt first plan which passes muster. Change it if challenged.	Do simple experiment with minimum effort.	Make the most of communication for self-aggrandizement.
Epi-static	Dualism. Believes in grand theory. Wants to be right, correct. Wants high position.	Go to best authorities. Discriminate carefully and accurately. Present unified case.	Develop good plan, and defend it. Go for grand theory.	Do experiment according to highest standards. Observe best practice. Uphold existing order.	Communicate so as to get highest prestige authorities to listen. Go for grand theory.
Para-static	Empiricism. Very professional. Believes in small-scale theories. Isolable truths concept.	Search fairly. Search for disagreements, and leave them side-by-side.	Develop tight plan with much detail. Obey statistical requirements.	Keep tight control over variables. Use full statistical logic.	Communicate quickly and efficiently to peers. Aim at small-scale theory. Contribute to existing paradigm.
Proto-dynamic	Evolution. Does not separate role as scientist from citizen role. Wants science to be applied.	Select authorities who mention change or process. Link data chronologically.	Develop plan with built-in adaptability. Allows for some two-way communication. Allows some feelings to enter.	Set up action or applied research. Use change measures. Before-and-after designs.	Communicate in ways that are widely and practically useful. Use democratic media. Real-life emphasis.
Epi-dynamic	Historical materialism. Sees self as on workers' side against capitalism.	Select authorities who are politically correct. Link data by reference to historical function.	Develop plan which takes politics into account. Aim at discovering reality under appearances.	Set up politically pointed research. Reveal class reality. Not too esoteric.	Communicate so as to have maximum political effect. Use as part of campaign.

Table 10.3   continued

	BEING □	THINKING ▽	PROJECT △	ENCOUNTER ◁	COMMUNICATION ▽
Para-dynamic	Subjectivism. Aims at self-actualization. Sees self as authentic.	Select authorities who feel right. Unify data by reference to own consciousness.	Develop plan which brings in the researcher as a person. Non-alienating relationships.	Encourage autonomy in self and other. Develop self-awareness. Self-determination.	Communicate to those who took part and encourage them to communicate to others on the same wavelength.
Meta-dynamic	Dialectical. Sees self as part of universal process of self-development through conflict.	Seek for diversity. Look for anomalies. Search for disagreements, and unify them by reference to themselves.	Initiate plan which allows for conflict and self-development.	Initiate process of change through conflict. Self-developing process.	Communication is built in to the process, not a separate thing. Poetry of research itself.

Speculative treatment of possible outlooks at each point on the cycle, based on Walsby (1947), and on the revised nomenclature of Walford (1979).

Awareness

As well as this more ideological change in consciousness, new paradigm research also seems to require something much more specific — the ability to use a particular approach to people and to data which lays aside ordinary linear thinking. Again this can be expressed in several parallel ways, as shown in Table 10.4. This particularly refers to the ENCOUNTER and to the MAKING SENSE moments in the research cycle (see Chapter 9), and it refers to the ability to 'unfocus' from the person or group or data we are studying, and to allow a kind of communion to emerge, such that we are at one and the same time in touch with our own process and with the other.

Table 10.4

From	To	Reference
Focused attention	Free-floating attention	Freud (1925)
Ordinary listening	Listening with the third ear	Reik (1948)
Clear-cut constructs	Intuitive sensing	Rogers (1968)
Scatteredness	Mindfulness	Schuster (1979)
Mystery-mastery	Consciousness	Torbert (1972)
Avoidance	Awareness	Enright (1970)

This does appear to be something which people can be trained to do, but there is something paradoxical about this. To try to learn it is to try to give-up-trying; to concentrate on it is to concentrate on non-concentrating; to grasp it is to let go. The whole trick is to suspend thinking and to stay aware of your experience in the ever-flowing present. It is hard enough to do this kind of thing when one is just meditating with no distractions, but to do it and act at the same time is doubly hard, and Torbert (1972) has an interesting account of some of the difficulties which arise in practice.

The reason why this state of consciousness is necessary is that without it we are condemned to repeat the existing social categories as if they were the limits of what could be true. Tramping round the circle of existing preconceptions takes us out of contact with reality.

There is a paradox here, too. The more categories we have, the better it works when we switch them off; but the more categories we have, the more of an expert we become, and the harder it becomes to switch off our expertness. It seems absurd to say this, but in the research cycle, the more time and effort we put into our PROJECT stage — the devising of the research design — the better it is to let go of it during the ENCOUNTER stage.

But perhaps the main point is that this is a state of consciousness which can be switched on and switched off — we can use it or put it on one side — whereas the ideology cannot. So the ideology is permanent, while this particular state of awareness is usually temporary.

There is an important distinction which needs to be made, however, which is not at all clear in most of the writers mentioned above. This is that once we leave the well-trodden paths of our ordinary consciousness — what Rowan has called the Social level of consciousness — there are two directions in which we can go. One is to go down or back, into the Primary level from which we laboriously emerged at an earlier time; the other is to go on and up, into the Realized level to which the process of self-actualization leads. However, the choice is not as simple or stark as that, since the only way to the Realized level is through re-owning and re-accepting and rescuing material from the Primary level. Difficult as the distinction may be to make, however, it is quite crucial if we are to really grasp what is necessary here. We have looked at it very briefly already.

At the Primary level, feelings are storms which sweep over us and take us over willy-nilly; at the Realized level, we take responsibility for our feelings and own them, and so they are appropriate to the situation, usable and trustworthy. At the Primary level, intuition is brilliant but chancy, incredibly right sometimes but also quite wrong sometimes; at the Realized level, intuition enables us to see the details of something, and the broad sweep of it, at one and the same time — it lets in the world, and integrates it in one action. At the Primary level, symbols affect us, and we use symbols, without knowing what we are doing — marvellous instant communication is possible in this way, but also complete misunderstandings and crossed wires; at the Realized level, we use symbols deliberately to explore the subjective world — we can trust them because we know how to interrogate them and work with them. At the Primary level, memories come up unbidden and unpredictable, and just take over as they will; at the Realized level, we can deliberately bring up those memories which are most useful, and go into them at whatever depth seems appropriate. In other words, at the Realized level, we have access to our subjective material, but we also have choices as to how to handle that material; at the Primary level we often have no choice.

In terms of our earlier discussion, then, we need to have the ideological shift to the Realized level *before* we can convincingly use the consciousness shift to the open state of awareness. If we try to go into open awareness before the ideological change has taken place, all we get is the Primary level stuff. In other words, all we are doing is opening ourselves up to our most un-thought-out prejudices and emotional reactions. Hence the problems of countertransference in therapy, which are most aggravating for the untrained therapist who has not yet made the great leap into growth consciousness. Once the leap has been made, however, countertransference becomes a great boon and a blessing, because it turns into the open awareness of one's own healthy and constructive process, then fully at the disposal of the client.

It seems that the clear philosophical analysis of this territory which Hegel (1971) gives us is extremely useful in helping us to act more adequately in our research practice.

Cleansing the Instrument

The outcome of these moves is a considerable change in our effectiveness and our efficiency as researchers. Each one of these transitions has the effect of adding to the clarity with which we can appreciate the world generally.

Of course this includes ourselves, and it is here that a difficulty emerges. As soon as we begin to open up our own subjectivity, and to get in touch with what is there, we usually discover more than we had bargained for. We discover all kinds of unfinished business, and attaining the clarity seems to mean finishing the business. This is what some of the Eastern people call 'Karma-cleaning'. We discover rigidities and fixed patterns of behaviour which have been set up as answers to the problems of living: however effective these may have been at the time, they have now turned into handcuffs or blinkers which prevent movement or awareness. We find that we need to dismantle these structures.

This is usually done through some process of therapy, counselling, personal growth work or general self-discovery, whereby these patterns are questioned in such a way that they can change. The self-image gets taken apart, and the rich realm of subjectivity which was pushed down as being too dangerous and too weak is now opened up and entered into and allowed to exist and be used and transformed. There is a feeling which then comes in, of being real instead of unreal. I have described this in detail elsewhere (Rowan, 1976a).

In years gone by, the only well-known method for carrying out this process was psychoanalysis, which was notorious for being slow and expensive. But now there is a host of different methods available (Liss, 1974; Fadiman and Frager, 1976; Greenberg, 1974, Nichols and Zax, 1977; Grof, 1979; Assagioli, 1975; Berne, 1972; Bandler and Grinder, 1979), all of which can be sampled on a short-term basis in weekend or even one-day workshops, before a decision is made as to which one is most suitable for a given person. There is even a book available (Southgate and Randall, 1978) which tells you how to do it yourself with a friend or small group.

All these methods enable us to go down into the Primary level in such a way that we can bring material up to awareness, thus enabling us to move further into the Realized level. The first noticeable effect of this, very often, is an over-valuation of emotion and a repudiation of the intellect. Hegel explains this as a concentration on passion, as a reaction to the deadness of the Social level, but also tells how this gradually weakens and turns into interest rather than passion — an interest which is selfish in the best and most rounded sense — we know what we really want and can go after it in a way which does justice to our other wants and to the wants of other people. For the first time, our will is genuinely free.

Thinking

As we begin to make these changes in consciousness and in the way we see the world, we discover how limiting are orthodox ways of thinking. We see that there are at least four conditions under which traditional logic breaks down, conditions which are fundamentally characteristic of human social situations: (a) information overload; (b) the existence of interactive, mutual causal systems; (c) the experience of contradiction; and (d) the need to find meaning. And we find there are four interrelated approaches to thinking which are broadly appropriate for each of these conditions, which are based in (a) existentialism; (b) ecological thinking; (c) dialectics; and (d) hermeneutics; but we need the shift in consciousness before we can appreciate the full significance of these approaches.

Information Overload

This is explored in an article by Hainer (1968). He argues that there are three basic types of response which recapitulate our recent intellectual history, which he terms Rationalism, Pragmatism, and Existentialism, and he relates these in terms of the amount of information with which they can cope. Rationalism:

> begins with a generalised concept. Terms are defined; assumptions are stated; a logic is implied; conclusions are presumed to be determined on the basis of the assumptions; temporal prediction is possible; and anyone competent in the calculus will obtain the same answer to a stated problem (p. 19).

Rationalism may be appropriately applied to situations where rigour is possible, and thus to closed tautological systems where all the relevant information is available and where the logic of the situation is well known: thus it may be applied to geometries, number systems, and closed sets. Beyond this the second type of response, Pragmatism, becomes appropriate:

> The method of pragmatism is that of recurrent formulation,
> deduction, test in reality, detection of difference between
> expectation and findings, and feeding back the error into the
> formulation until the difference between the new expectation and
> the latest look at reality becomes arbitrarily small (p. 21).

Pragmatism is an appropriate response in areas of inquiry where there is more
information than can be handled rationally, but where experimentation is
possible because convergence of results may be expected; thus it may be
applied to technology and to most of the physical sciences. As the amount of
information increases so that experimentation is no longer possible with any
assurance of convergence, Existentialism becomes an appropriate mode of
inquiry:

> Existentialism begins with experience, phenomena, and existence as
> these are perceived. Concepts arise out of the uniquely human
> process of perceiving, pattern (Gestalt) forming, of symbolising, of
> comparing, and of conceptualising, which are not explicitly
> conscious. Terms cannot be defined, only described; consistency
> can be assured only through repetition of experience, and
> consistency is only possible if there is little 'noise' or random
> uncertainty in the raw data supplied by the senses, if symbols can
> be used, and anxieties are within bounds (p. 24).

Hainer argues that at root all human experience appears 'complex, unique,
unrelated, uninterpretable, and uncommunicable': there is always more
information that can be handled through rationalism and pragmatism. As
Heraclitus said, 'You can't put your foot in the same river twice' (actually you
can't put your foot in the same river even once). Thus rationalism and
pragmatism as responses to what seem to be relatively limited situations can
only be based on what Hainer calls existential *meta-concepts:*

> The 'meta' emphasis warns the reader-mover that established
> methodologies and calculi are not applicable unless arguments for
> the legitimacy of their use are explicitly established as appropriate.
> 'Meta' here means freedom for me to formulate as well as I can to
> be understandable, but at the same time 'meta' highlights the
> uncertainty of generalisation, of assumption, and of limited
> information content.

All human inquiry is based on existential meta-concepts, formulated by
choice, and by commitment to those choices, in human situations where
'existence precedes essence':

The existential emotional position is characterised by emergence of alternatives, by choice and commitment, by responsibility for the choice *you made* or *you accept,* and by willingness to work for personal contribution even if all is dark, depressed and uncertain... [In] the face of overwhelming uncertainty and insecurity, the choices you make are the 'best possible choices' from your position, provided you are honest enough to change these choices when you discover they are no longer the choices you wish to make. This is a meta-conceptual, existential statement (p. 38).

Other writers have made similar points. For example Polanyi argues that we commit ourselves to certain statements, and that the participation of the knower in shaping his knowledge 'is now recognised as the true guide and master of our cognitive powers' (1959, p. 26). So the first challenge to traditional logic is that there is simply more information, and more uncertainty, than we can handle through Aristotelean logic: we can only use such a logic after we have made an explicit, and uncertain, choice to do so.

Terry Borton (1970) makes the point that in practical terms this means that the 'making sense' phase of inquiry needs contemplation as well as analysis. This contemplative mode is:

a more relaxed approach which avoids picking at one's self and allows alternatives to suggest themselves through free association and metaphor.... . Contemplation allows a more relaxed approach to the problem, where values and meanings are allowed to suggest themselves rather than be driven into a corner.

In such a state of consciousness information is processed in a different mode from rationalism or even pragmatism. Rational analysis leads to propositional knowledge; pragmatism leads to propositional or practical knowledge; existentialism allows for the contemplative mode to be used, and can lead to propositional or practical or experiential knowledge.

Ecological Thinking

If the amount of information in human systems is such that it cannot be handled through rationalism or pragmatism, this information is also linked in much more complex ways than is assumed by traditional logic: human systems do not work through logical sequences of cause and effect, they must be seen as interactive mutual causal systems in which causality is *circular*. The classic example of such a system is the thermostat-and-heater combination, in which the state of the thermostat determines or restrains the behaviour of the heater which in turn determines the state of the thermostat: the system remains in steady state within certain limits through the process of negative feedback. This kind of deviation-counteracting loop may be found in many human and biological situations — for example the maintenance of a steady body temperature. Equally important are 'deviation-amplifying' systems which increase diversity, complexity, and structure — for example the growth of a city on a homogeneous plain, where the first settlement may be fairly accidental, but because of its existence other settlements are made around it, and the spot grows into a hamlet, a village, a town, and so on (Maruyama, 1963a).

The study of such systems has been the field of cybernetics and systems theory. A system is a bounded set of units and the relationships between them (J.G. Miller, 1965), so that the behaviour of parts is constrained by the state of other parts through feedback, so that there is a *pattern* which connects the parts (Bateson, 1979). The systems view of organization and communication challenges traditional logic, replacing notions of energy with the concept of *information,* and notions of cause and effect with *patterning, feedback,* and *redundancy.* As Bateson points out:

> It follows, of course, that we must change our whole way of thinking about mental and communicational processes. The ordinary analogies of energy theory which people borrow from the hard sciences to provide a conceptual frame upon which they try to build theories about psychology and behaviour — that entire Procrustean structure — is non-sense. It is in error.

Ideas from cybernetics and systems theory have been used and borrowed by many writers; often they have been used mechanically and conservatively (Lilienfield, 1978), as if they had been captured by our traditional ways of thinking. But they do hold out great hope for our ability to think in new ways. Bateson (1972, 1979) has taken systems notions furthest in epistemological terms, suggesting as he does that 'the elementary cybernetic systems with its messages in circuit is, in fact, the simplest unit of mind' (1972, p. 459), and in his later book identifies six 'criteria of mind', arguing that 'phenomena which we call *thought, evolution, ecology, life, learning,* and the like occur only in systems which satisfy these criteria'. Bateson's writing is well worth study by anyone who would learn to think in new ways.

The consequences for research of the epistemological shift implied by systems theory are shown by Palazzoli and her colleagues in their work in family therapy:

> we must abandon the causal-mechanistic view of phenomena, which has dominated the sciences in recent times, and adopt a systemic

orientation. With this new orientation, the therapist should be able to see the members of the family as elements in a circuit of interaction. None of the members of the circuit have unidirectional power over the whole, although the behaviour of any one of the family influences the behaviour of the others. At the same time, it is epistemologically incorrect to consider the behaviour of one individual the *cause* of the behaviour of others. This is because every member influences the others, but it is in turn influenced by them. The individual acts upon the system, but is at the same time influenced by the communications he receives from it... [To] continue looking at phenomena according to the causal model is a serious impediment to the understanding of the family game (1978).

Dialectical Thinking

The third challenge to traditional logic is that the Aristotelean Law of Contradiction, while essential to discourse within the context of Hainer's Rationalism, is not really very helpful in understanding human experience, from which the experience of contradiction is inseparable. To take an example from Martin Buber (1957), we can only grasp what it means to be *in relation* with another if we first grasp that we are *distant* from them; thus human life involves:

> a twofold movement which is of such a kind that the one movement is the presupposition of the other. I propose to call the first movement 'the primal setting at a distance' and the second 'entering into relation'. That the first movement is the presupposition of the other is plain from the fact that one can enter into relation only with being which has first been set at a distance (p. 97).

So any statement about human experience (for example, 'I am in relation with you') cannot be seen as a simple uni-polar statement, and is very likely at some level and in some form to contain its polar opposite (i.e. 'I am distant from you'). Dialectical thinking is an ancient way of thinking which deals with contradiction. It goes back a long way: in the West Heraclitus was an early example, and in the East there were a number of even earlier people. The great exponent of dialectics in the modern world is of course Hegel, and we have already seen how useful some of his ideas can be.

The first characteristic of dialectical thinking is that it places all the emphasis on change. Instead of talking about static structures, it talks about process and movement. Hence it is in line with those philosophies which say, 'Let's not be deceived by what *is,* let's not pretend we can fix it and label it and turn it into a rigid thing, let's look at how it changes.' Hence it denies the Aristotelean proposition that A is A; for dialectics, A is not simply A.

But the second characteristic, which sets it apart from any philosophy which emphasizes smooth continuous change or progress, is that it states that the *way* change takes place is through conflict and opposition. Dialectical theories are always looking for *contradictions* within people or situations as the main guide to what is going on and what is likely to happen: dialectics talks a lot about opposition, and really tries hard to understand it. It does this on three main levels:

(a) *The interdependence of opposites* This is the easiest to see: opposites *demand* each other. It wouldn't make sense to talk about darkness if there were no such thing as light. I really start understanding my love at the moment I permit myself to understand my hate. In practice, each seems to need the other to make it what it is. In the yin-yang diagram (Figure 10.1), the shape of each half is defined by the contours of the other.

Figure 10.1

(b) *The interpenetration of opposites* Here one sees that opposites can be found within each other. Just because light is relative to darkness, there is some light in every darkness, and some darkness in every light. There is some hate in every love, and some love in every hate. If we look at one thing hard enough, we can always find its opposite right there. In the yin-yang diagram this is expressed by having a black spot in the innermost centre of the white area, and a white spot in the innermost centre of the black area.

(c) *The unity of opposites* So far we have been looking at relative opposites; but dialectics goes on to say that if we take an opposite to its very ultimate extreme, if we make it absolute, it actually *turns* into its opposite. Thus if we make darkness absolute, we are blind, we cannot see anything; and if we make light absolute, we are equally blind and unable to see. In psychology, the equivalent of this is to idealize something. So if we take love to its extreme and idealize it, we get morbid dependence, where our whole existence depends completely on the other person. And if we take hate to its extreme, and idealize it, we get morbid counterdependence, where our whole existence again depends completely on the other person. The symbol for this is the circle surrounding the yin-yang diagram, which expresses total unity and unbroken serenity in and through all the seeming opposition.

So the lessons of the dialectic are hard ones. It tells us that any value we have, if held to in a one-sided way, will be an illusion. We shall try to take it as excluding its opposite, but really it will include it; and if we take it to its extreme and idealize it, it will turn into its opposite. So peace and love, cosmic harmony, the pursuit of happiness, and all the rest are doomed. So, incidentally, is the notion of absolute knowledge; we will return to this in our discussion of validity in Chapter 21. The only values, the only ideas, the only concepts, the only form of existence which will be truly stable and coherent will be one in which opposition is included rather than kept out; all such notions, from the standpoint of traditional logic, will appear paradoxical and absurd.

Another way of looking at the dialectic is to see it as a movement through contradiction. My life any particular time may be seen as centring around a theme — a way of life, a set of ideas, an ideology — and I live this theme as my life for a while. But as I do this, inevitably and in time my actions draw attention to a contradictory counter-theme which was excluded yet implied by the theme. Theme and counter-theme may co-exist, more or less uncomfortably for a period, as I try to suppress, avoid, or live with the conflict. But if I am to move on, the time will come when I have to radically restructure my life, to pull together the contradictory events into a new synthesis which includes the contradiction; and I have to do this time and again as new contradictions emerge to disturb me. Levinson and his colleagues have described this progress through the 'seasons' of a man's life (1978); it applies to all human affairs, at all levels and at all times. Contradictions are never 'resolved', there is a movement between opposites as an inevitable part of the human condition:

> we can no longer talk about simple 'growth' as the basic need of the human being, for growth is always within a dialectical relationship in a dilemma which is never fully resolved (May 1967, p. 19).

If we apply this whole set of thoughts about dialectics to the research cycle we arrive at a whole different way of doing research from the traditional one, as John Rowan has shown in Chapter 9. We shall be looking for contradictions, and trying to do justice to all that is there. And at the 'making sense' phase of research, instead of trying to 'kill' our data by setting out a list of hypotheses and shooting down each one with a 'yes' or a 'no' — as if that were what human inquiry were all about — we try instead to 'keep our data alive' by allowing the contradictions to emerge, and by exploring the ways the opposites are interdependent, how they interpenetrate, and how they are also a unity.

Hermeneutics

Human experiences are also *meaningful,* both for those involved in them, and also for those who would study them systematically; the loss of meaning in life is a basic threat to a person's continued being in this world, as Frankl (1969) has so clearly shown us. Yet traditional scientific thinking says nothing about this issue of meaning — it is quite simply not accounted for, and indeed, science gained its power as an inquiry process when it ceased to try to discover the meaning of phenomena in the physical world, and started to explore phenomena empirically. But we cannot ignore the issue of meaning in a human science, and we may turn to the discipline of hermeneutics for some help in this area. Hermeneutics is an ancient discipline which was originally concerned with the interpretation of ancient religious texts; it was primarily a method for discovering the correct interpretation from several differing versions of the same text. Modern hermeneutics has been developed by Heidegger (1962) and Gadamer (1975, 1976) as a general philosophy of human understanding and interpretation. In this section we will draw out some of the major implications of this philosophy for our approach to understanding research data, drawing largely on an article by Kockelmans (1975).

The standpoint of modern hermeneutics is that interpretive method is not a special process, totally different from everyday human understanding; it is just one example of an everyday process through which persons make sense of their world. *All* understanding is hermeneutical, taking place, and to a very large extent determined by, our finite existence in time, history, and culture. The first lesson of hermeneutics is that we are historical beings, and that our understanding is an historical process. In this historical understanding we are strongly influenced by our culture and by our place within it: human experience is partly determined by cultural traditions, and is partly creative and novel, transcending the culture. Modern hermeneutics argues that we cannot ever totally transcend our historical position, there is no point in appealing to notions of a transcendental ego, for example: our viewpoint, and therefore the prejudgements that we bring to our understanding, are largely determined by culture; this is an 'ontological fact' which we have to take as our starting-point. (In Hainer's terms it is a meta-concept, existentially chosen as the starting-point for understanding.)

If we cannot transcend our historical position, and get rid of our prejudgements, the basic problem for our understanding is how to distinguish between 'legitimate' prejudgements, and those which get in the way of our understanding:

> The tradition is not to be transcended, but to be taken up in such a manner that by giving us access to our past it continually opens up new possibilities for the future (Kockelmans, 1975, p. 74).

Feminists, for example, are reinterpreting the position of women in history and in culture in the light of their present understanding of the position of women; in reinterpreting history, they give themselves new posibilities as women in the future. The fledgling 'North-South dialogue' is reinterpreting the history of the relationships between the industrialized and developing countries, and is thus opening up possibilities for a different relationship in the future (Brandt, 1980).

Once this historicity of human experience is realized, it is clear that we must ditinguish between some notion of an 'objective' understanding or interpretation which is unattainable and meaningless, and reach for an interpretation which is 'intersubjectively valid for all the people who *share the same world* at a given time in history'. Understanding can be seen as a fusion of two perspectives: that of the phenomenon itself, whether it be an ancient text, the life of an historical figure, or a current social or psychological event or process; and that of the interpreter, located in his or her own life, in a larger culture, and in an historical point in time.

Given these assumptions we can develop what Kockelmans calls 'canons' of an interpretive social science. These are not canons in the same sense as the canons of traditional logic; they do not lead automatically to a correct result. They are rather guidelines which lead toward an acceptable inter-subjective validity. Hermeneutic understanding cannot be applied, as it were, from the outside, as in the case of an 'objectivist' perspective. It is assumed that the interpreter 'knows' to some degree the phenomena he seeks to understand.

> The task of hermeneutic interpretation is to critically examine this fore-knowledge of the world and of the phenomena we encounter there, with the intention of coming to a deeper comprehension of these phenomena.... . The canons have no other function than to help us make explicit systematically what implicitly was already there before us (p. 83).

The first canon is that of the *autonomy of the object*. The meaning of that which we study must not be projected into it; it must be derived from the phenomenon itself. It is not appropriate to take theories and ideas derived from other sources, and to try to make sense of phenomena in terms of these; it is certainly not appropriate to force fit interpretations. We may want to use ideas and analogies from many situations to help our interpretation, but ultimately 'the source and criterion of the articulated meaning is and remains the phenomenon itself' (p. 84).

The second canon is that the interpretation should make the *phenomenon maximally reasonable* in human terms. This means that the complexity and historical roots of the phenomenon must be explored and articulated, the mystifications uncovered, so that the phenomenon may be understood more clearly than by those who are actually engaged in them on a day-to-day basis. Thus, for example, the work of R.D. Laing (1960) and others has reinterpreted certain aspects of madness so that they can be seen as reasonable in human terms. In the context of a co-research venture, this canon is similar to the idea of consciousness-raising: those engaged in such a venture will have a clearer and deeper understanding of their experience, having cleared away some of their false understandings and consciousness as a result of their inquiry.

The third canon is that the interpreter must achieve the *greatest possible familiarity* with the phenomenon in all its complexity and historical connectedness. Thus a good biographer gains familiarity with his subject, maybe actually visiting the places of significance in the life, gaining an intimate (and partly tacit) understanding. This canon is similar to Heron's argument (Chapter 2) that an inquiry has little validity unless it is rooted in the experiential knowledge of those actually involved; a valid interpretation involves knowing *with* as well as knowing *about*.

The interpreter must also show *the meaning of the phenomenon for his own situation*: 'no one is really interested in understanding something that is totally irrelevant for himself and for the society in which he lives' (p. 86). We are interested in something because of what it stirs up in us; because of our political commitment; because of our own personal history.

The most important canon is the *hermeneutic circle*; this deserves more exploration, and considerable reflection:

> The hermeneutic circle is essentially a very general mode of the development of all human knowledge, namely, the development through dialectic procedures. It is assumed that there cannot be any development of knowledge without some fore-knowledge. The anticipation of the global meaning of an action, a form of life, of a social institution, etc., becomes articulated through a dialectical process in which the meaning of the 'parts' or components is determined by the fore-knowledge of the 'whole', whereas our

knowledge of the 'whole' is continuously corrected and deepened
by the increase in our knowledge of the components (p. 85).

Understanding thus consists of circular and spiral relationships between whole
and parts, between what is known and what is unknown, between the
phenomenon itself and its wider context, between the knower and that which is
known. This is a dialectical process which is in theory infinite, although we
may rest, for a time, at some acceptable point of intersubjective validity.

This represents a tremendous challenge to traditional logic in which we tend
to avoid 'going round in circles' and 'reinventing the wheel'; indeed orthodox
logic expressly forbids circular argument. But the hermeneutic circle is not a
vicious circle which we need to avoid, but is an essential aspect of
understanding; what is important is not to avoid it, but to get into it the right
way. In practice, as a researcher approaches a phenomenon for study, he or
she will have some provisional conceptions of its meaning as a whole; as the
parts are examined, the meaning of some of these will come partially clear, and
this clarity can be enhanced by relating them to each other and to the whole.
But this process of comparison will usually lead to a re-evaluation of the
meaning of the whole, which in turn can lead to a new understanding of the
components. So there is a perpetual oscillation of interpretations; we have, as
it were, to leap into the circle of understanding before we can start.

Geertz (1975) illustrates this process nicely in his discussion of
anthropological understanding. He reviews his studies of the concept of
person in different societies, and concludes:

> In seeking to uncover the Javanese, Balinese, and Moroccan sense
> of self, one oscillates restlessly between the sort of exotic minutiae
> (lexical antithesis, categorical schemes, morphophonemic
> transformations) that makes even the best ethnographies a trial to
> read and the sort of sweeping characterisations ('quietism',
> 'dramatism', 'contextualism') that makes all but the most
> pedestrian of them somewhat implausible. Hopping back and forth
> between the whole conceived through the parts which actualise it and
> the parts conceived through the whole which motivates them, we
> seek to turn them, by a sort of intellectual perpetual motion, into
> explications of one another. All this is, of course, the now familiar
> trajectory of what Dilthey called the hermeneutic circle.... . (pp.
> 52, 53).

For further reading on the hermeneutic question, the reader is directed to the
original writings of Heidegger and Gadamer. There is also a useful review in
Palmer (1969), and a comparison of different approaches to the 'hermeneutic
problem' in Bauman (1978).

Truth as Will

This review of levels of consciousness and non-orthodox ways of thinking has touched briefly on a lot of ground. We have argued for a shift in ideology which places us as creators of our world rather than as actors in someone else's; we have borrowed from Hegel to point to the possibility of a synthesis of objectivity and subjectivity at a Realized level of being. From existentialism we have seen that knowledge is based in our own choices as knowers; the ideas derived from ecological thinking ask us to look for the pattern which connects, and to think in terms of information and difference; dialectics suggest that we pay particular attention to the way things change through contradiction; and hermeneutics offers a circular path towards understanding. The pattern which connects these ideas is that we should not seek knowledge as a thing we can have, but rather be involved in a *personal, circular, contradictory process* of knowing, of inquiry.

It may seem to the critic that the philosophy here is a curious mixture of Hegelianism and Existentialism, two disciplines that are notoriously at odds. Our view is that it is at the Realized level that the insights of existentialism come in: they are deep and important, but inadequate unless put into some larger framework of ideology and consciousness.

So the important and so often overlooked thing which emerges is that truth becomes much more personal. As Rosenzweig (in Friedman, 1964) says:

> Truth must be truth for some one... . 'The' truth must be converted into 'our' truth. Thus truth ceases to be what 'is' and becomes a verity that wants to be verified, realised in active life.

And of course we realize that this is always so: that what people put forward as *the* truth is always related in some very powerful way to what they *want* to be true. (And since this statement must logically apply to itself, we can only invite the reader to consider it in the light of her own experience and decide on its validity for herself).

For us, this means that we have a special responsibility to choose research topics which are healthy for us — likely to lead to our own growth — and healthy for our subjects and co-researchers too. And it makes us ask questions like: *who* got this research result? Where was the researcher coming from? What was the researcher trying to achieve? What are the consequences, both intended and unintended? And were the unintended consequences really unintended? What were all the circumstances of this discovery? We no longer see truth as something impersonal, which hangs luminously in the void, but as something attached very firmly to a person, and a time, and a place, and a system.

These are not philosophical questions only to be asked after all the events are over ('the bird of philosophy flies only after dusk') but a set of live issues to be engaged with as the process of inquiry continues. Many people know *about* the ideas we have reviewed here, but few know them deeply and fewer practise them. We need to learn how to make these ideas part of our experiential and practical knowledge, so that they can be applied during the stickiest moments of our inquiry, not just stuck up on the wall to be admired.

METHODOLOGY

Human Inquiry
Edited by P. Reason and J. Rowan
© 1981 John Wiley & Sons Ltd.

CHAPTER ELEVEN

Why educational research has been so uneducational: the case for a new model of social science based on collaborative inquiry

William R. Torbert
Royal College, Chestnut Hill, Massachusetts, USA

Why has educational research been so uneducational? Why hasn't past educational research taught us better educational practice?

Why, for example, did the original Coleman survey research on schooling present us mainly with negative findings — namely, that none of the measured differences among schools could account for differences in student performance? Why could Coleman find no evidence from his research about how to influence the main variable that did seem to make a significant difference in students' achievement — namely, a sense of control over their own destiny? (Coleman *et al.*, 1966).

Why, later, did Jencks' research on schooling again present us mainly with negative findings — namely, that differences in schooling were *not* associated with differences in later incomes? Why did Jencks' research offer neither theory nor data on the question of whether schooling *ought* to make a difference in later income or on the question of how educators could better achieve the aims of schooling? (Jencks *et al.,* 1972).

Why did Cohen and March's research on universities, find that the 42 they studied (including many of the most eminent) could best be characterized as 'organized anarchies' with no coherent sense of mission or decision-making process? Why were their main findings about educational leadership that the presidents of these universities could not control their own time sufficiently to take the time to address the question of what the purpose of the university is? (Cohens and March, 1974).

141

Do these various kinds of negative findings indicate that anything deserving to be called 'good educational practice' is at best so rare in this country as to be unnoticeable in comprehensive empirical studies? Or do all these negative findings indicate that educational research as presently practised provides us with no access to the sort of theory and data that could identify and lead us towards 'good educational practice?'

This chapter answers 'Yes' to both these last questions, and the reason is the same in both cases. The reason why neither current practice nor current research helps us to identify and move towards good educational practice is that both are based on a model of reality that emphasizes unilateral control for gaining information from, or having effects on, others. Research in businesses, government, and educational institutions shows that administrators in all fields choose, without question, behavioural strategies which seek to maximize their unilateral control over situations (Argyris 1969, 1971, 1974). Indeed, even persons who disavow unilateral control as unpalatable usually assert unilateral control in their very disavowals (Argyris, 1968b). At the same time, the current ideal of rigorous experimental research (Campbell and Stanley, 1966) directly advocates the tightest possible unilateral control by the researcher over the research setting. Moreover, like political and religious regimes of the past, the institution of science makes assumptions about the nature of reality which it does not test in any systematic way (Husserl, 1965; Kuhn, 1962).

Both in research and in organizational practice the effort at unilateral control presumes that the initial actor (whether researcher or practitioner) knows what is significant from the outset and that this knowledge is to be put to the service of controlling the situation outside the actor, in order to implement the pre-defined design as efficiently as possible. If students, subordinates, or research subjects seek to question whether there isn't something more significant at stake in the first place, the initial actor tends to redouble the effort to control the situation unilaterally. If s/he fails to do so, s/he tends to regard the effort as a failure and the situation as 'out of control'.

The reader will already have begun to appreciate that the model of unilateral control is intrinsically anti-educational and cannot, therefore, lead to good educational practice. If everyone in a given situation acts in accord with this model, then no-one is open to learning new strategies or to examining their own assumptions. Moreover, to the extent that the different actors' substantive assumptions and strategies differ at the outset, then they won't even succeed in 'teaching' one another the 'facts' of the situation, since the relevant facts will differ according to the particular assumptions and strategies of particular actors.

This fundamentally anti-educational quality of the model of unilateral control may largely escape notice so long as the participants in situations share a culture (share substantive assumptions). But in a nation of many cultures, such as the United States, in a world where different cultures must learn to live together as one planet, at a time when different cultural groups are increasingly refusing to subordinate their values, and at a time when change is occurring so fast that each new generation of schoolchildren and college students (i.e. every four years or so) represents virtually a new culture, the model of unilateral control simply doesn't work. Literacy decreases and violence increases.

On a personal scale, the anti-educational quality of the model of unilateral control reveals itself in another way. Most practitioners today, no matter how imposing their formal titles, would agree that they act under conditions that are almost exactly the reverse of pre-defined, unilaterally controlled (and hence uninterrupted) experimental conditions. Consequently, the conditions under which knowledge is gained when following the canons of rigorous experimental research are simply not generalizable to the conditions practitioners face. Practitioners are generally attempting to act well in situations which they do not fundamentally comprehend, in pursuit of purposes which are not initially fully explicit and to which their commitment is initially ambivalent, *and* they are being interrupted all the while by other claims on their attention. Of course, it is not altogether pleasant and reassuring to acknowledge the degree of uncertainty and discontinuity to which the foregoing sentence points, so practitioners, along with researchers, generally still strive to maintain the fiction that unilateral control is the only realistic way to get things done or to discover truth. But what practitioners really require is a kind of knowledge that they can apply to *their own behaviour* in the midst of ongoing events, in order to help them *inquire* more effectively with others about their common purposes, about how to produce outcomes congruent with such purposes, and about how to respond justly to interruptions.

Scientific research based on the model of unilateral control seeks to develop descriptive theories about facts external to the researchers. Such descriptive, disembodied knowledge cannot, in principle, help acting systems learn how to act better next time. This assertion can be exemplified by returning to the survey studies of education mentioned at the outset of this essay, all three of which offered significant findings about what education currently does *not* do. Had the findings been different, the studies might have described what education *does* do. But, in either event, the findings hold no logical implications or empirical clues about: (1) what education *ought* to do, (2) *how* education might do what it ought to do, or (3) *which of their aims, strategies, or behaviours educational practitioners would need to reform* in order to educate more successfully. Moreover, none of these studies provides an educational process whereby the practitioners studied might come to question their effectiveness and seek knowledge relevant to more successful education. These omissions are not peculiar to these particular studies, but rather are characteristic of all research based on the model of unilateral control.

Despite the fact that descriptive theory cannot help acting systems learn how to act better next time — no matter how defensible it may be in analytical and statistical terms — researchers such as Coleman, Jencks, and Cohen and March usually make various suggestions about what future actions their findings imply. For example, in *Inequality* Jencks suggests how to solve various educational questions throughout the book and at the end suggests that a direct redistribution of income would be a better way than increased educational opportunity to raise the income of poor persons. Such suggestions are utterly subjective and in no way substantiated by the data, given the quality of the overall structure of such studies. Although Jencks has since been able to respond quite convincingly to technical criticisms of his analytic designs and statistical practices, he has also acknowledged, in a final phrase, that his rhetoric overreaches his findings:

> The aim of the book was to show that one specific, widely-held theory about the relationship between school reform and social reform was wrong.... The evidence in *Inequality* cannot carry us much further, even though its rhetoric sometimes tries (p. 164).

That Jencks and other social scientists should yield to the temptation to suggests courses of action based on their analyses is not so surprising, for who is not at some level interested in the implications of social knowledge for more effective and more just social action? The dilemma is that what our current model of social science regards as valid social knowledge lacks the qualities necessary to help us increase the effectiveness and justice of our actions.

The model of unilateral control is not only impractical and anti-educational. It is also fundamentally unscientific. In the first place, current experimental and survey procedure may be open to dialogue and disconfirmation in theory (Bronowski, 1963; Horton, 1967), but it is not experimental and open to disconfirmation in practice. The researcher tries to learn reflectively before and after an experiment (or survey), but not actively while s/he is doing the 'study'. In the second place, even the most rigorously controlled experimental (or survey) research does not study, nor does it succeed in eliminating, influences by the researcher on the subjects (Bakan, 1967; Friedman, 1967; Rosenthal, 1966; Perry, 1966). In the third place, the unilaterally controlled research context is itself only one particular kind of social context and a politically authoritarian context at that. It should not be surprising that some of its most spectacularly well-conceived findings concern persons' responses to authoritarianism (Milgram, 1974).

To summarize these criticisms in a still more general way, one can say that the currently regnant model of social science altogether neglects to study what is actually going on, i.e. one's own action with others and the assumptions upon which that action is based. The entire attention of the unilateral control model is focused away from the actor (researcher) towards the outside world, where it is assumed, following Locke, that there are simple facts to be observed. By contrast, philosophers since Kant have helped us to see (or have they?) that we bring an implicit social-linguistic perspective (such as the Lockean perspective) to any explicit observation (Churchman, 1972; Habermas, 1971; Husserl, 1962 and 1965; Langer, 1967; Mannheim, 1936; Merleau-Ponty, 1963; Polanyi, 1958; Wittgenstein, 1953). Since the perspective influences and frames what is attended to in the first place, the results of observation cannot in any simple way criticize the original perspective, especially when, as in the case of the Lockean or unilateral control models, the perspective does not invite criticism of its assumptions.

Since the model of unilateral control upon which social science is currently based is fundamentally anti-educational, it should not surprise us to find the wide consensus today that educational research represents the doldrums of the social sciences. But whereas this evaluation of educational research commonly leads to pleas for better educational research in the current model of rigorous research, this chapter argues that a new model of social science is necessary to give us access to educational issues.

The Model of Collaborative Inquiry

By way of contrast to the model of unilateral control, the new model of social science and social organizing presented in the remainder of this chapter can be named the model of collaborative inquiry. Some features of the model of collaborative inquiry have probably already suggested themselves by implication to the reader in the course of the foregoing critique.

The model of collaborative inquiry begins from the assumption that research and action, even though analytically distinguishable, are inextricably intertwined in practice. Knowledge is always gained through action and for action (MacMurray, 1957; Polanyi, 1958). From this starting-point, to question the validity of social knowledge is to question, not how to develop a *reflective* science *about* action, but how to develop genuinely well-informed action — how to conduct an *action science*. The researcher recognizes that s/he is simultaneously practitioner in conducting research, and the practitioner recognizes that s/he is simultaneously researcher in seeking what is really going on and whether s/he is really achieving the aims at hand. All social actors, whether individuals or organizations, whether called 'students', 'teachers', 'researchers', 'administrators', 'schools', or 'businesses', engage in continuous, more-or-less flawed inquiry-in-action aimed at functioning increasingly effectively.

In order to act more effectively, the individual or organization requires valid knowledge, and not just valid knowledge about the outside world, but valid knowledge about the acting system's own purposes and valid knowledge about the quality of interplay between actor and outside world as well. Moreover, in order to act more effectively, the individual or organization requires not just empirical and theoretical knowledge, but knowledge that directly affects purposes and practices as well. On the individual scale, we would call these two additional kinds of knowledge intuitive and sensual knowledge, intuitive knowledge about what is worthy of attention in the first place and about how to direct attention, and sensual knowledge of posture and gesture at any given moment and about how to move differently.

In general, the acting system is not interested abstractly in the frequencies of relationships between external variables so much as in the experienced interaction between consciousness and external events. Obviously, this process is only observable to a participant in it. But, on the other hand, not all participants will necessarily observe this process. For to observe this interaction, the acting system must cultivate an attention 'span' which embraces the translations back and forth among intuitive purposes, theoretical strategies, behavioural methodologies, and external effects, rather than being captured by any one of those qualities at a given time. Without such attention the person or organization cannot begin to distinguish between assumptions and observations — cannot begin to learn from experience. The author's own work (Torbert, 1972, 1976a) and that of Argyris and Schon (1974) suggest that persons and organizations in contemporary society almost never develop the quality of attention necessary to test whether their purposes, strategies, and actual behaviours are congruent with one another. Thus, for all the vaunted 'rationality' of modern bureaucratic organizing and of 'economic' man, it should not surprise us that we experience the twentieth-century pre-eminently as an era of grotesque incongruities between espoused strategies and actual effects. In the current model of social science, there is no recognition whatsoever of the primacy of an interpenetrating attention for the development of valid social knowledge.

Just as the current model of social science gives no place to the development of interpenetrating attention, so also it gives no place to the development of sensual awareness and supple behaviour. Instead, the contemporary model of social science concentrates exclusively on the structural and external qualities of experience (theoretical propositions and empirical data). But an acting system requires sensual (or operational) awareness and suppleness if it is to succeed in effectively enacting new knowledge rather than in behaving either habitually or awkwardly. Without sensual or operational awareness and suppleness, new social theories cannot really be tested in action because persons will continue to behave habitually no matter what their rhetorical commitments. And indeed, a growing body of literature shows that organizational and curricular innovations in education often result in 'no differences' on outcome measures because the innovations were not really implemented in the first place (Argyris, 1965; Gross *et al.*, 1971; Lukas, 1973; Rivlin and Timpane, 1975).

Because no acting system begins with the sort of embracing, interpenetrating attention advocated here, each actor requires others' best attention and sincere responses in order to learn whether his or her own purposes, theories, actions, and effects are mutually congruent. In other words, the aspiring action scientist requires others' friendly collaboration. A second reason why *collaborative* inquiry is necessary for effective action is that the 'topology' of social situations is determined by the qualities of each actor's intuitive, theoretical, sensual, and empirical knowledge and being. Consequently, each actor can gain increasingly valid knowledge of social situations only as other actors collaborate in inquiry, disclosing their being, testing their knowledge, discovering shared purposes, and producing preferred outcomes. As the actor-researcher increasingly appreciates these motives for collaborative inquiry, s/he increasingly wishes to approach situations in everyday life as real-time, mutual learning experiments — as experiments-in-practice.

Of course it may well be that other participants in the social situation do not share this model of collaborative inquiry and are hostile to 'experiments-in-practice'. Indeed, they may interpret the actor-researcher's initiatives as just another effort at unilateral control. This interpretation may be due either to the fact that the others can imagine no other kind of initiative, or to the fact that the actor-researcher's behaviour is actually incongruent with the model of collaborative inquiry. If the actor-researcher possesses sufficient virtuosity in the practice of collaborative inquiry, s/he can inquire into the initially hostile response. Any other move — e.g. to defend collaborative inquiry in principle (thereby attempting in most cases to assert unilateral control in practice), or to yield to another's assertion of unilateral control — betrays the model of collaborative inquiry. These various possibilities show that the structure of an experiment-in-practice cannot be fully pre-defined and stable, but rather evolves over time.

The foregoing outline of the early assumptions of collaborative inquiry already allows us to list a series of distinctions between the kind of knowledge it seeks and the kind of knowledge sought under the current paradigm of social science. In experiments-in-practice:

(1) The researcher's activities are included within the field of observation and measurement, along with the study of other subjects.
(2) The structure and variables to be studied are not merely pre-defined, but rather may change through dialogue between the initiating actor-researcher and others.
(3) Interruptions are not simply viewed as irrelevant inconveniences, to be avoided or suppressed so far as possible, but rather are treated as positive shocks, symbolizing all that is not included within the researcher's

attention at the moment of interruption, inviting a more encompassing awareness of what is at stake. (Whether or not the researcher chooses a new focus of attention when interrupted is a distinct question.)

(4) Conflict between different paradigms or models of reality is anticipated, welcomed as an opportunity to test the validity of assumptions, and explicated so far as possible. Such conflict will not only be intellectual, but rather will usually have immediate emotional and practical implications as well. Thus, the aspiring action scientist is challenged from the outset to seek and offer information that is aesthetically appropriate and politically timely as well as analytically valid.

(5) The ultimate criterion of whether a given action is aesthetically appropriate, politically timely, and analytically valid is whether it yields increasingly valid data about issues increasingly significant to the effectiveness (including, of course, the issue of what constitutes effectiveness for any given acting-system; cf. Steers, 1975; Torbert, 1977, Weick, 1976) of the participating acting systems and does so in such a way as to encourage a more encompassing, interpenetrating attention by these acting systems.

(6) The interest is as much in knowledge uniquely relevant to the particular time and place of the experiment as in knowledge that is generalizable, in so far as the interest is not focused primarily on generalizing to persons and organizations outside the experiment, but rather on generalizing to the rest of the lives of the participants in the experiment. Further, the interest in generalization is not merely cognitive, but rather in ideas that vivify one's own and others' intuitive, emotional, and sensual experience — that is, in ideas that open beyond themselves to an interpenetrating attention.

(7) The primary medium of research is an attention capable of interpenetrating, of vivifying, and of apprehending simultaneously its own ongoing dynamics and the ongoing theorizing, sensing, and external event-ualizing (Torbert, 1972). Only such an attention encompasses purposes, strategies, actions, and effects. Thus, only such an attention makes it possible to judge whether effects are congruent with purposes — i.e. whether an acting system is effective. Put another way, the requisite attention interpenetrates six dimensions of human activity, three 'spatial' and three 'temporal' dimensions — gravity, levity, extension, duration (timeboundness), eternity (timelessness), and intention (timeliness). Only such an attention makes it possible to judge whether extensions are congruent with intentions — i.e. whether an acting system is effective.

(8) The secondary medium of research is symbolic, ironic, diabolic thinking and feeling capable of vivifying and apprehending the significant issues at stake, the value-assumptions in actors' behaviour, the degree of congruity or incongruity between purposes and effects, and the efficient paths for common effort (Torbert, 1976b, 1978).

(9)   The tertiary medium of research is action — movements, tones, words, and silences — sufficiently supple, attuned, and crafty to create scenes of questionable taste, to demonstrate the good taste of collaborative questioning, and to listen silently to responses. Such disciplined research action does not screen out strangeness and disconfirmation, but rather invites tests of its own and others' sincerity and effectiveness.

(10) The quaternary medium of research is the collection, analysis, and feed-back of empirical data. The interest in empirical data is not concentrated on predicting relationships between independent and dependent variables; rather, the same study will seek empirical data relating to acting systems' aims, strategies, behaviours, and effects, in order to test, and offer feedback on, the degree of congruence or incongruence across these qualities of experience.

(11) The fundamental (though of course not the only) type of empirical instrument is a record of experience more complete than the specific measures used, for such a record represents the closest empirical analogue to an embracing attention. Such records (e.g. tape-recordings of meetings, field notes, personal journals) allow participants or other interested persons to find *post hoc* clues about what else besides the defined variables and the pre-supposed explanations was going on in a given situation. Such records can also yield codable process data that can help determine whether the organizational design of the experiment was in fact open to challenge and reformation and whether such dialogue was conducive to increasingly appropriate design decisions.

(12) The relationship between the initiating actor-researcher and any other person or organization invited to engage in collaborative inquiry will tend to develop, unless terminated, through three stages of increasing investment and subtlety of focus. In the first stage, no matter how well developed the researcher's initial theory of the situation may be, and no matter how internally reliable and valid his or her empirical data-gathering instruments may be, the primary question is whether the initiating actor-researcher and the system(s) engaged will develop a shared model of reality in which continued collaborative inquiry makes sense. Only if the participating parties come to share the aim of colla-borative inquiry and the model of interactive qualities of experience will interest during a second stage shift to investigating gross incongruities among these qualities of experience. In this stage, the participating systems are actively collecting and analysing experiential-empirical data, but they will focus more on the general direction of the findings than on the precise outcomes. Only if and as the participating systems come to share the aim of collaborative inquiry and the strategy of investigating and properly digesting major incongruities may they, during a third stage, focus on obtaining precise, high-quality results in terms of aesthetic appropriateness, political timeliness, and analytic validity.

Research, as understood in the model of collaborative inquiry, is an actual experiential process occurring in a more or less distorted and incomplete fashion at any given moment. Empirical research instruments and written reports for third parties may aid the actual research process or may impede it. How a person or an organization develops a more valid experiential-empirical research process is virtually unexplored at the present time in Western science. What have heretofore usually been thought of as 'mystical' disciplines apply to the personal development of a more illuminating attention (Krishnamurti, 1969; Ouspensky, 1949; Raymond, 1971; Torbert, 1972; Trungpa, 1969, 1974). The field of organization development begins to suggest the issues in helping organizations to engage in experiential research (Argyris, 1962, 1971; French and Bell, 1973; Schein, 1969; Torbert, 1975, 1976a).

Table 11.1

| | | SCIENTIST | |
		No self-study	Self-study in action
SUBJECTS	No self-study	Present-day, unilaterally controlled, empirical social science	Educational conflict between world-views of scientists and subjects (Argyris, 1971)
	Self-study in action	Subjects would not generally submit to study. However, Castaneda (1968, 1971, 1972) is an example	Collaborative experiential-empirical inquiry (Torbert 1976a)

According to this new model of inquiry, an acting system that does not engage in experiential self-study can neither produce nor collect valid data because of the unexamined incongruities within its experience. Such a system will both deliberately and unintentionally distort data and will resist processing feedback which identifies incongruities. A primary index of the capacity of a social system to produce valid data becomes the degree to which confrontation and exploration of possible incongruities is initiated and welcomed. Whereas at present social scientists neither engage in self-study as a part of their scientific work, nor seek to encourage self-study in those whom they study, such experiential self-study (using empirical measuring instruments where appropriate) constitutes the core of social science in the new model. The difference in quality between social science at present and as practised under the model introduced here can be simply summarized as in Table 11.1. As the table indicates, the new model of social research refocuses the fundamental concern to attain valid knowledge from unilateral efforts by the researcher aimed at preventing various kinds of 'contamination' of his preconceived empirical data (cf. Campbell and Stanley, 1966) to collaborative efforts between the researcher and the personal or social system in question, aimed at encouraging kinds of attention, conversation, and data collection which reveal and test information and theories of ever-increasing significance to that system (Argyris, 1974, 1976). In short, valid social knowledge becomes possible only as fundamental changes occur in people's commitment to personal learning and in their ways of organizing socially. The practice of genuinely educational research would transform the social world in the course of studying it.

Under the new model of scientific research, valid social knowledge depends first and foremost on the development among persons of a new politics based on a shared wish to research their everyday lives together. Valid social knowledge depends secondarily on the development among persons of a new ethics based on the commitment to confront apparent incongruities in their common life. Valid social knowledge depends only tertiarily (but, of course, by no means unimportantly) on the development among persons of technical skills in discriminating the degree of trustworthiness of experiential-empirical data.

Conclusion

Obviously, a short chapter purporting to introduce a new paradigm for the social sciences raises far more questions than it can answer. A longer chapter would examine current studies that partially illustrate the paradigm of collaborative inquiry (see Chapter 29) would speculate about the changes necessary in graduate programmes in the social sciences if they are to become experiments-in-practice which encourage collaborative inquiry (see Chapters 36 and 37); would describe disciplines useful to developing a trans-conceptual, interpenetrating attention; and would dwell in much greater detail on methods of assessing validity in the context of the new paradigm (see Chapter 21).

The present chapter has sought merely to sketch the axiomatic structure of collaborative inquiry and to argue its intuitive plausibility as a means and as an end for educational research and educational practice.

Acknowledgements

I want to express my appreciation to Henry Acland, Dan Alpert, Chris Argyris, David Cohen, Ian Mitroff, Louis Pondy, Marshall Smith, Peter Vaill, and Karl Weick who, in conversations over the past four years and in responses to earlier drafts, have helped me to sharpen my sense of what territories this chapter needed to touch upon.

Human Inquiry
Edited by P. Reason and J. Rowan
© 1981 John Wiley & Sons Ltd.

CHAPTER TWELVE

Experiential research methodology

John Heron
British Postgraduate Medical Federation, University of London, UK

Experiential research is the kind of research on persons in which the subjects of the research contribute not only to the content of the research, i.e. the activity that is being researched, but also to the creative thinking that generates, manages, and draws conclusions from, the research. And the researchers, in the full model, contribute not only to the creative thinking and management, but they also participate, like the subjects, in the activity that is being researched. The rationale for this sort of research I have given in another contribution to this book (Chapter 2).

The contribution of subjects to the research propositions — hypothesis, statements on design and management, discussions on conclusions, and so on — may be strong or weak. It is strong if the subjects are fully fledged co-researchers taking an equal part in the creative thinking that generates, accompanies, and concludes the research. It is weak if they are merely consulted by the researchers about these matters for assent or dissent and, if dissent occurs, negotiated with until agreement is reached.

The contribution of the researchers to the research action may also be strong or weak. It is strong if they go thoroughly through all the prescribed stages of the action and are thus fully fledged co-subjects. It is weak if they only go through some stages and omit others, or do one or more stages incompletely.

In the traditional model, of course, the subjects make no contribution to the research propositions, i.e. they don't help to formulate the propositions; and the researchers make no contribution to the research action, i.e. they don't do what the subjects do. If we map out all the relevant possibilities, then we have the situation shown in Example 12.1.

	RESEARCHER	SUBJECT
CONTRIBUTION TO RESEARCH PROPOSITIONS	Strong	Strong Weak Zero
CONTRIBUTION TO RESEARCH ACTION	Strong Weak Zero	Strong

Example 12.1

	RESEARCHER	SUBJECT
CONTRIBUTION TO RESEARCH PROPOSITIONS	Strong	Zero
CONTRIBUTION TO RESEARCH ACTION	Zero	Strong

Example 12.2

Figure 12.1

The traditional research model

First of all a brief consideration of the traditional model, which is shown in
Example 12.2. We can also symbolise the traditional model as shown in Figure
12.1. This is the model for unilateral control by the researcher of the research
enterprise and of the subject's contribution to it. It is similar to authoritarian,
unilateral control in traditional education: staff unilaterally decide on student
objectives, on course design (interrelating topics, teaching and learning
methods, human and physical resources, time), on criteria of assessment and
on the assessment itself. And in traditional therapy: the patient, passive and

dependent, is the recipient of a therapeutic programme unilaterally designed and managed by the therapist. And also, of course, in traditional management: the autocratic manager makes decisions without consulting any of those who are directly affected by them.

Some of the features of the traditional model are as follows. R (researcher) and S (subject) are separate roles which are non-reciprocal and are in asymmetrical relation. R gives instructions to S in accordance with a hypothesis and a research design which S has not been consulted about and will not be informed about. S's intellectual queries about the research are not required or elicited. R's human relationship to S, other than the conventional protocols of polite managerial behaviour, is irrelevant to the research. Getting to know about what S does in fulfilling his instructions is more important than relating to S and getting to know S. R's commitment is to knowledge not to persons. To this end R can influence S, but not vice-versa. And so on.

The Full Experiential Research Model

Now let us consider the full-blown experiential research model (Example 12.3), (there is also an *intermediate* experiential research model in which the Researcher's contribution to research action is zero; this is not considered in detail in this chapter). In diagram form the experiential research model is shown in Figure 12.2.

	RESEARCHER	SUBJECT
CONTRIBUTION TO RESEARCH PROPOSITIONS	Strong	Strong
CONTRIBUTION TO RESEARCH ACTION	Strong	Strong

Example 12.3

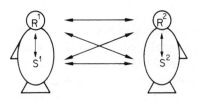

Figure 12.2

In this model each person involved is both researcher and subject. Each is involved as co-researcher, contributing to the research propositions at all stages from the working hypothesis to the research conclusions. And each is involved as co-subject, being fully involved in all stages of the research action. Each person researches the hypothesis through his own experience and action, and at the same time through the experience and action of the other. With respect to R^1, S^1, R^2, S^2, there is a reciprocal relation in all the six possible directions. Intrapsychically and interpersonally there is full reciprocity: the exchange of ideas, the mutual experiential encounter, the two-way corrective interaction between ideas and experience both within each person and between the two persons — it is all there.

There are three basic corrective feedback loops, involving the influence of ideas on experience/action, and vice-versa: one for each person and for the interaction between them (Figure 12.3). Actually there are three-times-two loops, since reciprocity requires another three with arrows going in the opposite direction. I only show one set of three here. This set shows the R^1-S^1 loop, the R^2-S^2 loop and the ideas of R^1 influencing via R^2 the actions of S^2, and the actions of S^2 via S^1 influencing the ideas of R^1. Each person goes through an action research cycle through the use of his own loop, and is his own control on a serial basis; at the same time, through his loop with the other, he can take account of corrective feedback from the other. He can also take account of comparisons between his own internal loop and the internal loop of the other. And as a dyad they go through an action research cycle, through the use of the dyadic loop (in both directions), and so together provide their own control group on a serial basis.

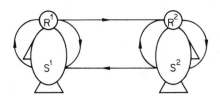

Figure 12.3

Of course there may be several dyads engaged in the same research inquiry, or one small group, or several small groups. This simply increases the range of interlooping, and of comparisons between different sorts of loops. The model is thus charged with internal checks and balances for the empirical validation of research propositions through experience and action, where this validation is always from the agents' standpoints.

The four stages of the research are as follows (see Figure 12.4):

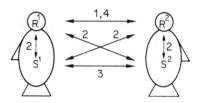

Figure 12.4

(1) The co-researchers discuss the initial research propositions, and agree on some hypothesis about persons in relation: about the basic phenomenal categories that apply and how to map them; about what persons' capacities and potentialities are, what can happen to these capacities, what can restrict them, what can liberate them; about what persons in relation can do and can become through developing these capacities, and about how they can do it and become it, what developmental procedures they can adopt.

(2) The co-researchers as co-subjects apply these mapping and/or developmental procedures, using all the corrective feedback loops, with ideas influencing action and experience, with action and experience influencing ideas, both intra- and interpersonally in the different ways indicated in Figure 12.3 and discussed above. The initial hypothesis (about both theory and procedure) may (or may not) undergo some progressive modification during this stage. In this and the following stage the co-researchers will be especially alert to how the hypothesis falls short of accounting for what they are actually doing and experiencing.

(3) The co-subjects become fully immersed in their mutual encounter and experience; they become fully open to their experiential knowledge of what is going on when applying the procedures. They encounter each other and attendant phenomena without preconception discriminating so far as possible what is actually happening, bracketing off any prejudicial influence of the ideas they started with in stage (1). They may, indeed, temporarily forget how and why they started the inquiry. This stage will, of course, be interwoven with phases of stage (2).

(4) After an appropriate period involving stages (2) and (3), the co-researchers return to consider and discuss their original research propositions, take account of modifications in them resulting from stages (2) and (3), then formulate together the final research conclusions. These conclusions may cover the following sorts of issues:

(i) Acceptance of all or some, rejection of all or some, modification of all or some of the initial research propositions as a function of the research procedure. This acceptance, rejection, modification may concern the statements about basic phenomenal categories and their mapping, about human capacities, the statements about what can restrict and what can hinder their development, the statements about what persons in relation can do to develop their capacities, the statements about the developmental procedure they can adopt to achieve this.

(ii)   Evaluative statements about the research procedure (as distinct from the mapping or developmental procedure used within the research procedure) and its impact of the research conclusions.

(iii)   Proposals for further hypotheses and/or for future modifications to the research procedure to be tried out in some future research endeavour.

Figure 12.4 above can also indicate the relations between propositional knowledge, practical knowledge, and experiential knowledge that hold within the experiential research paradigm. Propositional knowledge is knowledge of facts or truths as stated in propositions: it is entirely language-dependent. Practical knowledge is knowing how to do something as exemplified in the exercise of some special skill or proficiency. Experiential knowledge is knowing some entity by direct face-to-face encounter with her/him/it; it is direct discrimination of what is present in relation with the knower. (For further discussion of these three basic types of knowledge, see my other contribution to this book — Chapter 2).

Stages (1) and (4) are firmly within the domain of propositional knowledge: in stage (1) the co-researchers clarify and state their initial hypothesis; in stage (4) they clarify and state their research conclusions. In stage (2), two main sorts of practical knowledge, of knowing how, are involved. Firstly the co-researchers have, or have to acquire through practice, knowledge of how to work the research procedures; they need to know how to go round the various feedback loops, interrelating action/experience and ideas. Secondly, they need to know how to work the developmental procedures, the personal and interpersonal growth and change methods that constitute the practical core of the research; this sort of practical knowledge they may well have to acquire through considerable practice.

Stage (3) is the empirical bedrock of the inquiry and is firmly within the domain of experiential knowledge. The co-subjects encounter each other fully and encounter everything else that is going on within the actual realities of the research situation. This stage involves the fundamental phenomenological discrimination of persons in relation in their world. The co-subjects are open to what is going on between them, within them, between them and their environment — an openness that allows them to learn through encounter and experience, that brackets off their latent propositional knowledge, that disarms its tendency to restrict present discrimination and perception. I do not suggest that co-subjects in stage (3) can entirely disown, discard or temporarily obliterate all their latent propositional knowledge; but that, like the true poet, they can sufficiently disengage from the claims of the past language of words to be open to the present 'language' of experience, so that their future use of words may become revisionary in the most fundamental, empirical way. They are alert to the possible limitations of their hypothesis. They hold in suspension their initial theories and their view of the appropriate developmental procedures in order to discriminate what is actually going on, subsequently invoking language to symbolize this experiential discrimination, rather than crushing the experience into some preferred and pre-existent propositional mould. In diagram form these different types of knowledge can be shown as in Figure 12.5.

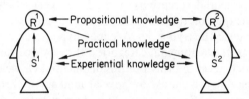

Figure 12.5

I call this research *experiential* because its empirical basis is the experiential knowledge of persons in relation in their situation, their world. And I suggest there can be no other empirical base for researching the human condition and human capacity for self-direction *from the stand point of the agent*; and that no other standpoint can have research *precedence* over the agent's standpoint (Heron, 1971).

Strictly speaking, of course, the co-researchers start off not with propositional knowledge, but with propositional belief, with hypothesis. (Propositional belief is belief that, to be distinguished from believing a person, and belief in; cf. Price, 1969). If we now put into diagram form the *relations* between the initial belief and the various forms of knowledge, we obtain figure 12.6.

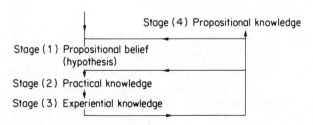

Figure 12.6

Noticing and Trying Out

There are two complementary aspects to experiential research of this sort: they are phenomenological mapping and intentional interaction (Heron, 1977a). Phenomenological mapping is simply noticing, awarely discriminating, and categorizing what is going on. It attends very fully and openly to the *phenomena,* identifying the marginal as well as the focal, the less obvious as well as the more obvious, those that tend to get screened out by our current use of language as well as those that are highlighted by our use of language.

Intentional interaction is the trying out of some developmental procedure that follows from the hypothesis about persons, about what they can do and become. So the complementarity or polarity is between noticing and trying out, between experiential receptivity and active agency. The research may focus more on one than on the other: the trying out may serve the noticing or the noticing may serve the trying out. We may hypothesise that the 'eyes' and the 'gaze' are distinct phenomenal categories, then try out various procedures in relation with each other to bring out this distinction. Or we may hypothesize that persons in relation can choose to move around at will through a variety of emotional states, positive and negative, then discriminate and notice carefully the various emotional states in order to aid the moving around them. Or the research inquiry may balance equally both the noticing and trying-out processes.

The two poles overlap when the researchers notice very carefully how they are trying something out, and then seek to categorize this accurately. They notice how they are doing something, and then formulate the 'how'. The result is a set of statements about practical knowledge. Following this analysis, there are two sorts of basic proposition in the research conclusions: statements about what the co-researchers experience and statements about what they do. These two sorts of propositions will provide the warrant for any other higher-order general and/or theoretical propositions.

Examples of Full Experiential Research

I wish now to consider a range of practical candidates for this full-blown experiential research. All of these I have been involved with over the last few years either (1) as prolegomenon only, or (2) partially and informally through various shared activities and experiences in groups and workshops, or (3) in ways that approximate more fully to the paradigm outlined here. My concept of the methodology, as clarified in this paper, has evolved gradually through many endeavours.

(1) *Phenomenological Mapping*

Here the paradigm is used to clarify and categorize what is going on for persons in relation in their research situation, to make critical distinctions between different aspects of the total experience, to characterize criteria for differentiating between phenomena, to characterize how persons can act within the research situation, and so on. All this mapping can only properly be done from *within* the experience and action. It cannot be done by a non-participant observer who simply gathers 'evidence' from others who are within the experience and action. There are many areas for phenomenological mapping. Some of them are:

(a) Elements of encounter between persons. The co-researchers explore, refine, elaborate hypothesized phenomenal categories such as: the distinction between the eyes and the gaze; the distinction between the tissues and the touch; the distinction between private experience and shared experience, that is, between private access to the contents of consciousness and shared access to the contents of consciousness; mutual gazing and all the other phenomenal categories that do justice to it; similarly with mutual touching. For a prolegomenon see Heron (1970). A further area of inquiry here is to formulate phenomenal categories that do justice to what is going on when two people speak the same language and use it to seek and find agreement.

(b) Sorts of interactions between persons, and the sorts of intrapsychic states/emotional spaces within persons. The co-researchers take on hypothetical maps about what goes on between themselves and within themselves; about the species of distorted transaction, the species of authentic transaction, the negative emotional spaces and the positive emotional spaces, sorts of need/interest/wish/want and so on (Heron, 1975a, 1977b). Pointers to this whole area come from notions such as those of transference and the defence mechanisms in classical psychoanalysis, of transactions and ego-states in transactional analysis, of patterns, states of attention, and restimulation in co-counselling theory. Research here extends to the categorizations of the whole range of phenomena that occur in groups (Heron, 1973a, 1977a).

(c) Altered states of consciousness. The co-researchers can devise and adopt procedures to explore hypothesized altered states of consciousness, and map out carefully the states, processes, and goings-on they experience. It is also important to give a careful account of the entry procedures used. Experiential research of the kind outlined in this chapter seems to me to be the paramount method for researching ASCs, ESP and the whole field of the so-called paranormal (cf. Heron, 1975b). Traditional research designs fail to get at the heart of the matter. Groups of co-researchers together need to agree to shift their state of consciousness following the relevant procedures, as co-subjects, then to monitor and discriminate the outcomes. I set up and participated in such a group which ran through three cycles of activity in 1977 (Heron, 1978a).

These are only three examples of candidates for phenomenological mapping. There are no doubt many more.

(2) *Intentional Interaction*

Here the paradigm is used to explore hypotheses about what persons can become, what they can do to develop their capacities, with presuppositions about what these capacities are and what can happen to them by way of restriction or liberation. Of course experiential research of this sort cannot be separated out entirely from phenomenological mapping, nor vice-versa, for each is more or less explicitly involved in the other. Here are *some* candidates only.

(a) Personal growth through mutual aid. Two or more persons share some hypotheses about persons, about what can and does happen to them, about what procedures they can adopt to change. They then apply these procedures in systematic interaction with each other, using this experience to review the hypotheses during the research and eventually to formulate the final research conclusions. Co-counselling theory and practice provides a ready vehicle for experiential research (Heron, 1973b, 1974a, 1977c, d). Many other growth modalities and therapies are ripe for experiential research; gestalt therapy, Reichian and neo-Reichian therapies, primal therapy, etc. Also ripe are the varieties of transpersonal development, the many meditation and related approaches, which are often in the grip of spiritual authoritarianism, dogmatic intuitionism, and appallingly exclude any spirit of discriminating inquiry. Experiential research offers a great antidote here (cf. Heron, 1975c).

(b) Peer learning community. The co-researchers are co-students who set up a course on a peer basis. They consult together and hypothesize their capacity to change in the direction of specified individual and collective objectives; they agree a programme for reaching these objectives that covers topics or areas of change, methods of change, resources for change, time allocation. They follow the programme, modifying the programme, the objectives or both as a function of action and experience. They then engage in a self- and peer-assessment procedure to see whether the original or modified objectives have been met; and in the light of the total experience, including the assessment, they evaluate and reach final conclusions about the original or modified notion of their capacity to change in the direction of the elected objectives, and about the strengths and weaknesses of the programme actually adopted. Such a community may have an initial facilitator, who ideally moves down a gradient from influential primary facilitator at the outset to influential peer at a later stage (Heron, 1974b, c, d, 1978b).

(c) Peer review audit. A group of fellow professionals — doctors, dentists, teachers, or any other — meet to co-research their capacity to monitor and improve their standards of, and performance of, professional practice. First they identify what appear to be their current standards and what they actually do in practice. Second they agree, where relevant, to commit themselves to apply what they suppose to be more desirable standards and practices. Third they devise some form of self-assessment (and if practicable reciprocal peer-assessment) which each can apply periodically to his actual professional work to assess the degree to which each is applying these more desirable standards and practices. Fourth they go back to work and apply the self-assessment schedules. Fifth, they meet after a suitable interval for a self- and peer-assessment session, each person sharing his recent self-assessment findings and being open to feedback, questions and confrontations from his peers. This may lead to a revision of the standards, the practices, the self-assessment schedules, the self- and peer-assessment session, or any combination of these. Then a further cycle is launched. After an agreed number of cycles, the group meet to evaluate the whole experience and decide whether or not, or to what degree and with what qualifications, their hypothesis about their capacity to monitor and improve their standards of and performance of professional practice has been validated (Heron, 1977b, 1979, 1981 in press).

There are many other candidates for this sort of experiential research, for example in organizational development, in work collectives using a collective contract system, in sexual interaction, in a shared life-style with spouse or living partner (Heron, 1974e), and so on. One application that comprehensively closes the gap between research and everyday living is contained in the idea of a self-generating culture in which a group of persons generate social practices and social rituals for their whole life-style together as an experiential research inquiry into their capacity for giving more meaning to, and finding more meaning in, the human condition (Heron, 1978c).

Further Features of the Full Model

(1) It is a paradigm for a state-specific science (Tart, 1972), that it is a science in which you have to shift your state of consciousness in order to do the

research, communicate it and understand communications about it. Each person involved is both co-researcher and co-subject, is both committed to inquire into an activity and committed to engage in that activity. To balance inquiry and action, discriminating critical awareness and committed active participation, conceptual grasp and experiential immersion — is itself a special state of consciousness. This special state may in its turn be the entrée to further altered states.

(2) This state-specific requirement raises the apparent paradox of experiential research: that the research *method* seems to *presuppose* a degree of personal development and self-direction which has *yet to be achieved* through the research *action*. The answer to this, I think, is that the research method is itself a way of enhancing the development of the capacities it is seeking to inquire into. The stage (2) feedback loops, processing the initial ideas through action and experience, give space for the co-researchers to improve their skill in using the method, which in turn helps them improve their skill in the developmental procedures which the research is in part about.

(3) Nevertheless, it is clear that the discipline and rigour involved in this sort of research is formidable. The rigour is essentially one of mindfulness, of inner alertness, of knowing what is and is not going on while it is and is not going on, of keeping in mind a second-order objective while fulfilling a first-order objective. It has its analogue in oriental forms of consciousness training, e.g. *satipatthana* in Buddhism (Goleman, 1972). But the ancient oriental motivation for such training is more concerned with *salvation* than it is with *inquiry*.

(4) The validation of this sort of research does not lie in numbers or statistics, but ultimately in the experiential discrimination of those who execute a common plan of action and experience in the light of some agreed hypothesis. However many persons agree in the research conclusions this is *per se* no guarantee of their validity. *Consensus gentium* is no adequate criterion of truth; it may simply represent widespread collusion to ignore crucial and relevant variables. 'What is crucial in attaining... consensual validation is the *quality* of critical awareness and discrimination in categorising and evaluating the experiential effects and referring them back to the original theory' (Heron, 1971). If in doubt about this quality in the research of others, then replicate the research including yourself as co-researcher-subject and get your own discrimination to bear upon the issues.

(5) The core of the validation process and the key to its quality is provided by the critical and corrective feedback loops, in which the theory with which the co-researchers start is continually reviewed in the light of action and *experience*. If the initial theory is stated in such a form that whatever the co-researchers do and experience has no bearing upon it,

then we are not in the domain of science. So a statement like 'Persons are always striving for a greater good whether they are aware of it or not, and whatever they do' is a non-scientific statement. If may be true but if so its validation does not rest on any kind of scientific process. The critical acumen which the co-researchers need to exercise on an *appropriately stated theory* is to be alert to whether it does justice to, whether it honours or falls short of honouring, what is actually experienced. The theory is validated to the extent, and only to the extent, that it survives this kind of alertness. The sort of knowledge that results from this process is provisional only. Its truth is relative to the critical acumen in action and experience of those who assert it. It is in principle open to revision as a function of further more extended action and experience on the part of others. There are no final truths in a science of persons any more than there are in the natural sciences (cf. Magee, 1973).

(6) But within this general account of the provisional nature of all scientific knowledge of persons, we can make a distinction between statements that are definitive and clear, even apparently apodeictic, categoric, and others that are tentative, approximate, even confused, vague. The human condition being what it is, any research paradigm that honours the human condition may well lead in practice to the emergence of ambiguity, imprecision, confusion, uncertainty, apparent contradiction and paradox — these may be present to a greater or lesser extent in the process, the product or both. Where the human condition is concerned it is better to be vaguely right than precisely wrong, better to own a fruitful confusion than mask it with irrelevant precision.

(7) The research products are both propositional and practical. There are the research conclusions: propositions about phenomenal categories, about persons and their capacities, about procedures that persons can adopt, and about norms of procedure. Then there are the skills and proficiencies of various kinds which persons involved take away both as co-researchers and as co-subjects. (Some of the products may also be presentational, i.e. pictures, paintings, sculptures, music, dance, movement — which make their own sort of statement about the human condition. For a brief discussion of presentational knowledge, see Chapter 2).

(8) Who writes up the research? Whoever does it, the writing reports the fruits of a lot of discussion among the co-researchers at the various stages. One or more persons in the research group may do the writing, send a draft to the rest for comment, on the basis of which a second draft is written and sent around for final approval. Or each person in the group may keep a research diary; one or more persons collate the diaries for the first draft, which is sent round for comments, and so on. No doubt there are numerous other ways of doing it, using video and audio recording and so on.

(9) Experiential research of this sort closes the gap between research and 'real life'. Any two or more persons, interacting in some project in everyday life, can choose to make of that project an experiential research inquiry, assuming that the social system in which the project is set gives enough room for all the manoeuvres involved. The human condition itself is one of experiential research: people meeting together and agreeing how to symbolize their experience, revising their symbolizations in the light of further experience, and so on.

(10) Many traditional social science research institutions lack the sort of research climate and culture that motivates people to do experiential research and that enables them to grasp the rationale of it. Official research on people still too often wears that bleak face that has unwittingly confused respectability with oppression. We have to do a lot to create a new climate.

Human Inquiry
Edited by P. Reason and J. Rowan
© 1981 John Wiley & Sons Ltd.

CHAPTER THIRTEEN

The Leaves of Spring
by Aaron Esterson: an appreciation

John Rowan
Independent Consultant, London, UK

In Part 2 of his book, Esterson explains a dialectical view of science which is well worth examining. He starts off by distinguishing it from natural science, by describing dialectical science as 'the study of the reciprocities of persons and groups of persons', in contrast to natural science, which he describes as 'the study of natural events'.

The reason why he wants a science of reciprocities is that he sees persons always as in relation.

> Since persons are always in relation, one cannot study persons without studying the relations they make with others.... And the method used to observe must be one that allows us to study the personal form of relating.... And so, the observer must be aware of his own pattern of response if he is to evaluate the behaviour and experience of the person he is studying... the observer, with the co-operation of the other, constitutes himself as part of the field of study, while studying the field he and the other constitute.

This brings in the whole notion of reflexivity, which we meet elsewhere in the present volume. But of course reflexivity brings its own problems with it, and it is these problems in which Esterson is particularly interested.

> Observing in this way, he requires an appropriate form of rationality. Since the field he studies is composed of himself and the other(s) by

himself and the other(s), he must be able to reflect upon, and reason about, a reciprocity that includes himself as one of the reciprocating terms. He must study from a position within the situation he is reasoning about. This requires a rationality that is dialectical in form. Such a form is not embodied in the method of natural science.

Here, then, is the completed argument. If we are to do reflexivity justice, Esterson is saying, we must recognize that it requires a new mental stance, an altered state of consciousness. (This is a point which is also made by others in the present volume.) This new mental approach has three stages or moments to it.

> First, a reciprocity between observer and the rest of the social field.... Next, a temporary nihilating withdrawal from active participation.... Third, a negation of the withdrawal and a return to the reciprocity with the rest of the social field.

It is the second stage, according to Esterson, which is crucial. It is a painful stage to go through; I am reminded at times of Maslow's 'fear of knowing'. But it is immensely important and potentially productive.

> Here the observer... relates primarily to himself, comparing and discriminating between his experience of himself and his experience of the system, between events in the system, and events in himself. Successful discrimination is followed by a change in the observer's experience of himself, reflecting an inner movement. This change may be termed self-realization.

On this account, then, research becomes a process of discovery not only of the other, but also of oneself; and of course this is the implication of reflexivity. Each time one goes round the cycle, from reciprocity to this kind of withdrawal and back to reciprocity, one comes back to the social relationship 'on a higher level' — that is, with increased insight and ability to act.

And because it is a cycle, and therefore continually re-seeing the situation in a fresh way, it is able to cope with changes in the situation — with the unexpected, with events which contradict one's expectations.

> The observer radically restructures his view of the situation, reconciling the events that contradict him in a new, more comprehensive synthesis [or]... *totalization.*

This is a process often referred to as personal growth, which Esterson sees as a creative and dialectical process. So we are not only able to deal with contradiction and unexpectedness, we are able now to see them as basic and essential to any real-life investigation. The experience of contradiction is inseparable from any real attempt to open oneself up to what is going on. For most of us, this is a painful process because we are not used to it, and our education has not prepared us for it.

It seems that three things can prepare us for it: our own experiences in counselling or therapy, where we have exposed our own internal contradictions to light, and found them illuminating and productive; our reading of dialectical philosophy, where we have become used to this method of proceeding at a conceptual level; and our historical analysis, where we are able to see history as a dialectical process including us. All this can then go into our current research stance, as Esterson now sums up:

> In the first moment the observer registers phenomenologically the situation and its contradictions, those of the rest of the system and those in which he experiences himself caught in participating. In the second, a regressive-analytic moment, he analyses both sets of issues historically, one set in terms of the history of the system, and the other in terms of his relation to it. In the third, a progressive-synthetic moment, the historical findings are, by means of a hypothesis, related synthetically to the phenomenologically observed events in a wider totalization in which he makes sense of the system and of his participation.

As we penetrate this rather tortuous language, we see that the new thing here is the emergence of the hypothesis — or in other words, some interpretation of the events being considered — some guess as to what is going on. As Esterson says, this often appears as an intuitive flash, emerging between a period of active reflection and a period of rest. At its best, this is the emergence of something quite fresh and new and unexpected, which can be a *revelation*.

> Revelation in this sense is an intervention, constitutive of a moment of the dialectic, whereby the participant makes sense of himself and his social situation.

But because the dialectical researcher is a participant *within* the social field of observation, such hypotheses or revelations are a basis for *action*. They are not merely abstract theories, they are essentially seen as practical, and as to be realized in use.

Its logic is that of social truth in action. It is a rationality requiring action, and one attained through acting. It is reasoning in, through, and for action in the field it is reasoning about; an action research.

If this is so, then it involves a peculiar responsibility on the part of the researcher. No longer able just to 'do a piece of research' which is arbitrarily chosen to fit in with academic limitations and requirements, the researcher must do something much more practically useful than that. If it is going to affect the researcher so profoundly, and quite possibly affect a social situation in some drastic manner, it presents many more problems of choice. How do I choose my research project? Esterson says:

Valid praxis requires questions relating general to specific to be part of a concrete project in respect of the particular general social situation too. This means that they should be part of an enterprise directed to resolving contradictions of that situation, in and through identifying and facilitating supersession of the relevant general principal contradiction.

What this means is that the dialectical researcher is trying to change social situations in a specific way. And that way is by identifying and working on the principal contradiction in that situation.

What is this 'principal contradiction', and how do we identify it? We are really only concerned here, Esterson says, with negatively valued contradictions — those which are causing trouble in some way. There can also be other contradictions involved in healthy growth processes, and these we may want to understand, but they do not often emerge as issues for action.

It is destructive only if the particular contradiction is no longer historically necessary, and there is a taboo on recognising either that a contradiction exists, or that it is historically redundant. That is, it is destructive if it has brought the person or group to the point where they are ready to develop beyond it, and they are forbidden to realise this. If the taboo persists, then the struggle to recognise it and the relevant contradiction, and then to transcend them both, is liable to be painful and violent. There is, in fact, a double contradiction, the original social or interpersonal contradiction, and the contradiction of the taboo itself.

We are looking, then, for something which is either non-obvious, or something which may be obvious to an external observer or to relatively uncommitted participants, but which is by no means obvious to those most intimately involved. Furthermore, the reason why it will not be obvious to them is because they actively do not want to see it. However, unless they do see it, the problems will continue.

And of course this gives us the answer to the question as to whether we have identified the principal contradiction correctly. If we have, the problem disappears; if we haven't, the problem remains. (Esterson devotes a number of pages to qualifying this general conclusion.)

However, Esterson wants to make it clear that, precisely because of the way that dialectical research is carried out, the researcher is not a wonder-worker with a magic wand. It is up to *all* the people involved to make the changes.

> Supersession of the principal contradiction can, therefore, be brought about only by the action of the group members themselves. It cannot be brought about by the scientist alone. He requires the cooperation of the relevant members of the system if his intervention is to be effective. The observer, therefore, cannot be accurately described as *causing* supersession of the principal contradiction, as if he were a natural scientist manipulating a system of things through setting in motion a mechanically determined sequence of events. He is most accurately described as *facilitating* its supersession in the system.... The role of a dialectical scientist is that of a midwife patiently easing the birth of a new existential order ready to be born.

It seems, then, as though we can sum up by saying that dialectical research is the attempt, by using a certain approach, to solve social problems. It is a form of action research which has a more than usually close involvement and engagement with the people trapped in the problem. It has a particular discipline in its approach which makes heavy demands on the *will* of the researcher. It is exemplified in Laing and Esterson's book *Sanity, Madness and the Family* and in Part 1 of *The Leaves of Spring*.

The language Esterson uses is often jargon-like, and may put some people off, but I think what he is saying is extremely important and gives us some of the essence of what new paradigm research is all about.

Human Inquiry
Edited by P. Reason and J. Rowan
© 1981 John Wiley & Sons Ltd.

CHAPTER FOURTEEN

A model for action research

Nevitt Sanford
formerly of the Wright Institute, Berkeley, California

A friend in operations research told me about doing a cost-effectiveness study of one of our great universities. In the late 1960s he and his colleagues had been seeking new funding through the US Office of Education and the Committee on Basic Research of the National Science Foundation. Enthusiastic about his work, believing he could show its usefulness to the university, my friend awaited his answer from the Committee. Finally he got the message that the funding agencies were wildly enthusiastic about the proposal but, of course, could not fund it because it was not 'basic'.

I wondered how far this rigid separation of research and action had gone. Clearly the term 'action research' is not exactly on everybody's tongue nowadays. The contrast with the 1940s and early 1950s seems to me striking. Particularly during the late 1940s there was an outpouring of reports of action research from the Research Center for Group Dynamics and the Commission on Community Interrelations. One, such as myself, who during that hopeful time was taken up with promoting psychoanalysis and personality research, could and did easily form the impression that action research was a dominant trend in social psychology.

Yet in 1957 when I spoke before the Society for the Psychological Study of Social Issues about social science and social reform, basing myself on the work of my colleagues and myself at Vassar College (Sanford, 1956), Brewster Smith said with surprise and, as I thought, with some pleasure: 'So you are really following the old Lewin model of action research.' I thought, of course, that mine was a new and improved model; but I knew it could not have existed without the work of Lewin, and was surprised to hear the latter spoken of as if it belonged to the past.

What Lewin Wrought

What was Lewin's model? I think it was well set forth in his paper 'Group decision and social change' (Lewin, 1947a). The example he used had to do with how to change people's food habits. Action research consisted in analysis, fact-finding, conceptualization, planning, execution, more fact-finding or evaluation — and then a repetition of this whole circle of activities; indeed, a spiral of such circles.

Leon Festinger told Alfred Marrow that Lewin's greatest contribution

> on the abstract level may have been the idea of studying things through changing them and seeing the effect. This theme — that in order to gain insight into a process one must create a change and then observe its variable effects and new dynamics — runs through all of Lewin's work (Marrow, 1969).

This seems very close to common sense. It is the way to solve any practical problem or to learn any skill. Yet for Lewin this kind of involvement with practical problems was a never-failing source of theoretical ideas and knowledge of fundamental social-psychological relationships.

Action research is still very much alive. It has strong advocates in high places. Martin Deutsch, in his presidential address before the Society for the Psychological Study of Social Issues, said that the need for knowledge of the effect of experiences upon development, as a basis for changes in policies and organizations, 'clearly points to an emphasis on action programs and action research as fundamental tools of the social scientist' (Deutsch, 1969).

Recent Examples of Action Research

Programmes clearly labelled action research, or which could properly be so labelled, have not been hard to find. As of 1970, for example, four major ones could be found within walking distance of the Wright Institute in Berkeley. There was Soskin and Korchin's 'after-school school', a programme for offering people of high-school age what (on theoretical grounds) they seem to need for their development but do not get in school (Soskin and Korchin, 1967). There was Peter Lenrow's 'collaborative problem-solving' with teachers and administrators of the Berkeley School System, an action research programme with some distinctive new features

(Lenrow, 1970). There was Joan and Douglas Grant's 'new careers program' which demonstrated that prison inmates can be an important source of manpower in the human-service fields (Grant and Grant, 1970). And there was the programme of Wilbur Hoff and his associates for training poor people for jobs to be defined and instituted in hospitals and clinics (Hoff, 1970). I should mention here too The Wright Institute's doctoral programme in social-clinical psychology based on knowledge of the situation and needs of graduate students and guided by a theory of individual development and organizational processes (Sanford, 1970b).

My planned systematic survey of action research programmes has not yet taken me beyond the Berkeley city limits but, even so, I receive reports from time to time of highly significant programmes in less favoured parts of the country. I recall, for example, Robert Sinnett and Angela Sachson's impeccable evaluation of their project for demonstrating that severely emotionally disturbed students can be given satisfactory care in a rehabilitation living unit in a regular university dormitory (Sinnett and Sachson, 1970).

The survey of which I speak should pay particular attention to publications in the fields of public health, social welfare, and criminology. I suspect that more action research on the Lewin model is done by specialists in these fields than by social psychologists. A great deal of work in the spirit of action research also goes under the heading of 'evaluation research', as when Donald Campbell (1969), Samuel Messick (1970), and Michael Scriven (1967) carry to a high level of sophistication the essential fact-finding feature of Lewin's model. Scriven, indeed, in distinguishing between 'formative evaluation' (which serves programme improvement) and 'summative evaluation' (appraisal of the final product), goes a long way toward filling in Lewin's cycle with precise operations. Although these three authors assume a division of labour between the evaluators and those responsible for execution, their work shows beyond question that much can be learned from studying the effects of actions.

Purity of the Mainstream

The fact remains, however, that none of this work — evaluation research, community psychology, or true action research — is in the mainstream of social psychology or social science generally. Although the great bulk of Federal funds for social science do go to applied social science, as academic social scientists never tire of pointing out (Beals, 1970), how many of these projects could qualify as action research? Very few, because nearly all of applied social science emphasizes the application to problems of what is already known, rather than the study of action as a means for advancing science.

The separation of science from practice is strongly advocated by leaders in academic social science. Thus George Miller in his Presidential Address before the American Psychological Association used a revealing Biblical image to enforce the separation:

> Many psychologists, trained in an empiricist, experimental tradition have tried to serve two masters at once. That is to say, they have tried to solve practical problems and simultaneously to collect data of scientific value on the effects of their interventions. Other fields maintain a more equitable division of labour between scientist and engineer. Scientists are responsible for the validity of the principles; engineers accept them and try to use them to solve practical problems (Miller 1969).

If the two masters are God and mammon, we do not need to ask which was being claimed for academic psychology.

What has happened to action research? I would say now that, contrary to the impression I had in the late 1940s, it never really got off the ground. By the time the Federal funding agencies were set up after World War II, action research was already condemned to a sort of orphan's role in social science, for the separation of science and practice was institutionalized by then, and has been basic to the Federal bureaucracies ever since. This truth was obscured for a time by the fact that old-timers in action research were still able to get their projects funded. Younger researchers soon discovered, however, that action research proposals *per se* received a cool reception from the funding agencies and were, indeed, likely to win for their author the reputation of being 'confused'.

Consequences of the Separation

In attempting to summarize what I suspect is a familiar story, I would say that we have separated (and then institutionalized the separation of) everything that from the point of view of action research belongs together. Analysis of the problem, conceptualization, data-gathering, planning, execution, evaluation, training — the intimate family of activities that constitutes Lewin's model — has been pretty well dispersed.

The categorical separation of research from practice has made it very difficult for a social scientist to study phenomena that cannot be experimented upon in the laboratory or social structures that can be understood only through attempts to change them. Likewise, it has laid the social sciences wide open to the charge of irrelevance, not only by students but by men of affairs. It would hardly occur to a college president to look to the social science literature for help with his problems, and as Blum and Funkhauser (1965) have shown, social scientists are among the last people state legislators would consult about the problem of drug-abuse.

Sources of the Corrupt Model

How did we get into this fix? The basic trouble is fragmentation which can be understood as an aspect of the general tendency toward specialization in modern science and scholarship. Effective social problem-solving calls for multi-disciplinary work, yet departmentalism seems everywhere on the increase.

Specialization exists within, as well as among, the disciplines, in consequence of which we have a fantastic proliferation of bitsy, disconnected, essentially unusable researches. A natural accompaniment of high levels of development in science, specialization has obviously led to intellectual and practical pay-off in the past, but the compartmentalization of social scientific activities and the scarcity of efforts to pull things together calls for explanation.

Like professional practice, social science has been adapting itself to the requirements of an advanced technological society, which demands more and more segregation of functions and the training of experts to perform them. Just as professionals in health, education, and welfare no longer deal with the whole person, but only with particular symptoms or functions, so psychologists in their research and theory-making focus more and more on part-functions without bothering to connect them with central structures in the person. Not only have we contributed to the dehumanization of our research subjects by reducing them to 'respondents' for the sake of enterprises that never yielded any benefit to them, and to the dehumanization of ourselves by encouraging self-definition in terms of narrow specialties: we have also been disseminating a most unfortunate image of man. Where social scientists see only an aggregate of meaningful 'behaviours', great masses of our people likewise are reduced to a conception of the self as fragmented and externalized: one *is* what one can present to others in a particular situation.

Another Way to Work

In contrast to the corrupt and dangerous model of social science prevalent today, I want to sketch a contemporary model for action research (or as I would prefer to say, research-action). Let us consider some of its main features in turn:

(1)   Analysis determines what kinds of questions are to be asked. These should be practical, although somewhat general and open-ended. In one of our studies the questions were how to improve teaching, how to change features of academic culture, and how to promote the development of individual faculty members. Most social science questions, in my view, should be of this general kind: how to arrange the environment, institution, or the social setting in such a way as to promote the development of all the individuals concerned.

Analysis with attention to the nature of the basic questions can save the researcher a great deal of trouble. Four or five years ago we sent to a government agency a proposal of a longitudinal study of graduate students. We were kept dangling for three years and were never funded. During this waiting period we realized that we were genuinely concerned about graduate students and that we did not need to study them in order to know that many were very unhappy or were not getting what they needed for their development. So instead of undertaking a conventional programme of research we started a new programme of graduate training in social-clinical psychology (Sanford, 1970b). Now we are really finding out what needs to be done and something about how to do it. Had we been funded we would probably still be bogged down in the analysis of data.

(2)   The aim of promoting individual development has several important implications. We must go far beyond the highly abstract formulations of Kurt Lewin, filling in his scheme with particular kinds of needs, dispositions, values, conflicts, and so forth. An approach that is concerned with individual development must be comprehensive. An interest in changing one aspect of the person or of his behaviour must take into account the implications of such change for the total person. To understand the person we must see him in his total setting. Research action is properly multi-disciplinary — and in my view only a focus on problems, ultimately problems of human development or human welfare, will bring about collaboration among the academic disciplines.

The subject is the client; reporting to him is an action. Lewin considered that his action research would favour the purpose of 'social management' as well as the self-management of groups. During World War II, and in the years shortly thereafter, it was easier than now to assume that 'management' would use social science knowledge in the interest of all concerned. For surely there was much more agreement about large national purposes then than there is now. I am not suggesting that we ought to deprive management of knowledge about the functioning of those it is appointed to manage, but the information ought to go simultaneously, if not first, to those on whose responses the report is based.

(3) Planning, or 'planning ahead', does not have such an important role in the present model as in the action research of the past. These days many people will upset plans which they have not helped to make. To arrange things in such a way that the 'natives' (students, faculty, poor people, ethnic minorities, and so on) can and do take part in the planning, should become a goal that supersedes planning from above by experts. In the case of our graduate school it would have been natural perhaps to have devoted a year to planning, preferably with the aid of a 'planning grant', before beginning any operations. Instead we decided to do it now and plan it later. It seemed to us that our graduate students would have to take part in the planning in any case, and that the experience of helping to plan a graduate programme would be of considerable educational value. This, however, puts heavy emphasis upon what Michael Scriven (1967) calls 'formative evaluation'. We institute a procedures, see how it works, and make a change if this seems necessary or wise, always in a spirit of continuous experimentation. I hope that after a decent interval there will be some 'summative evaluation', but I also hope that this would be 'formative' for the next programme in graduate education.

Who will Lead the Way?

Action research as an alternative way to work offers obvious intellectual as well as practical advantages, but seeing the advantages is one thing and being able to enjoy them is another. Who will lead the way in making the advantages widely available? Organized social science, as an elite, is part of a larger system, the political and economic establishment, which it often verbally opposes but upon which it depends for support. Like other industries, social science has been polluting its environment, not only by treating its research subjects as means rather than ends and disseminating a rather monstrous image of researchable man, but also by creating an enormous amount of waste in the form of useless information. Much of what ought to be left to decompose we now make great plans to 'retrieve'. From the developmental point of view it looks very much as if the system were designed by and for professors still in the stage of achieving a sense of competence.

We have got to make some changes. But how?

The funding of project research ought to be abandoned. It has spoiled the academic community, damaged undergraduate education almost beyond repair, given status to trivia, created an expensive bureaucracy, and corrupted thousands of investigators. This change will have to come from above, for the funding apparatus has no built-in mechanisms for self-correction.

Action Research on Academic Culture

I would not, however, put the control of social science research back into the universities if I did not have an idea as to how the academic culture might be changed, in part through action research studies of departments, colleges, professional schools, universities, state psychological associations, the American Psychological Association.

There has been much recent discussion of studying the American Psychological Association. How might this be done? Shall a task force of the central office select a national sample to whom questionnaires will be mailed, then make the data available to a committee who will use it to plan our lives? I would say not. This sort of thing might have been all right in past studies of students and other 'natives', but surely for ourselves we can arrange something more humanistic. At least we can be clients at the same time that we are subjects.

So let a few professors and students from Hayward State study a department at San Francisco State, and a group from the latter institution study a department at Berkeley, while some professors and students from Berkeley carry out a research-action at Hayward. No master plan would be needed, for those who were studied would in each case take part in the planning, contributing questions they wanted asked of others and of themselves. All that would be needed to begin would be general agreement that all hands would be interviewed.

A process of change started in this way could easily continue under its own steam. For the model that has been offered is not only designed to encourage professors to be subjects of action research, but also to arouse interest in the carrying out of action research. The particular example that I have offered — that is, of studying academic culture — is in my view the key to acceptance of action research by professors who need to be rescued from one another.

What happened in particular departments or schools could easily spread and start discussions of our identity crisis on a national scale. The widespread use of the present model would have good effects of a more general nature. By demonstrating our ability and our willingness to study ourselves we would go some way towards restoring trust in our competence to study others singly and collectively.

The study of a department or even of a profession may seem small and timid compared with consulting for national policy-making bodies or advocating policies before legislative assemblies, but how can social science be better on the national scene than it is in microcosm? If we are to build a better society, a good place to begin is with making our own department, institution, school, or association a truly human community. If it is our purpose to liberate women and other 'minorities', let us begin at home. If we are to promote human development generally, let us begin by showing that we know how to promote the development of our students.

Actually, I am not neglecting the impact of our work on the larger community. I agree with those writers such as G. Miller (1969) and Snoek (1969) who suggest that our influence on the body politic has been less through the dissemination of knowledge than through the presentation of an image of man. Of course, I take a dimmer view than do these writers of the sort of image we have been presenting. But I strongly agree that our major influence is through what we do and are. The good that we may do will derive less from the models we finally build in our own domains, than from the model we present in the building. And this, I hope, will be a model of man trying to understand and to improve himself and his society.

Human Inquiry
Edited by P. Reason and J. Rowan
© 1981 John Wiley & Sons Ltd.

CHAPTER FIFTEEN

Patterns of Discovery in the Social Sciences by Paul Diesing: an appreciation

Peter Reason
Centre for the Study of Organizational Change and Development, University of Bath, UK

In the Introduction to this book, the author identifies four dominant 'patterns of discovery' — the experimental, the survey, the participant observation, and the formal — and goes on to review in some detail the latter two. The primary interest of this book for the new paradigm researcher is in Part Two, the review of the participant observation or *holist* approach to discovery. I don't think that Diesing would regard himself as a 'new paradigm researcher' — indeed he has questioned experiential methods because of the difficulty of developing self-awareness in spite of the general human tendency to self-deception (personal communication, 1979), and his preferred role as a student of science is a participant observer. However, his book is important because it sets out at a fairly general level the holist approach to method and theory, obtained through an exploration of a wide range of researchers primarily in psychotherapy (e.g. Freud, Erikson, Rogers), anthropology (e.g. Malinowski, Radcliffe-Brown) and sociology (e.g. Gouldner, Dalton). This book is at times pedestrian (as all reviews of a field must be), but on the whole sets out the holist position with outstanding clarity.

Part Two of the book begins with an overview of the holist standpoint. Diesing argues that the holist is interested in studying a 'whole human system in its natural setting', and that students who undertake to do this, whatever their difference, share important similarities of method.

The holist standpoint includes the belief that human systems tend to develop a characteristic wholeness or integrity. They are not

> simply a loose collection of traits or wants or reflexes or variables
> of any sort...; they have a unity that manifests itself in nearly every
> part....
>
> This means that the characteristics of a part are largely determined
> by the whole to which it belongs and by its particular location in
> the whole system (pp. 137-8).

The holist goes further than arguing that wholes exist; he believes that his
account of them should 'somehow capture and express this holistic quality' (p.
138:

> By 'holistic quality' is meant not only the manifold interrelations
> among parts that appear in the original but also some of the
> unique characteristics, the distinctive qualities and patterns that
> differentiate this system from others. This is the point where many
> social scientists part company with the holists; it seems to them
> that an emphasis on uniqueness makes generalisation impossible,
> and without generalisation there can be no science (pp. 138-9).

Holism is rooted in a belief in the primacy of its subject, rather than in the
traditional canons of scientific inquiry; it starts from a 'general attitude of
respect for human beings' (p. 141), such that

> Even a scientific reduction of a person to a set of variables is in a
> way disrespectful because it mutilates integrity (p. 141).

Given this, can holism be scientific? Diesing shows how a holist approach to
inquiry that *is* scientific can be developed, an approach which has its own
method, logic, and rigour which is distinctly different from other methods. It
is this distinctive method he sets out to explain.

Having reviewed the general characteristics of the holist position, Diesing
considers the basic empirical work of the holist, the main steps in studying a
single case. He describes how the researcher prepares himself before entering a
field situation; how he enters and somehow becomes a part of the system to be
studied, either as a full member or in some particular role marginal to the
situation such as researcher, therapist, or educator; and how he discovers and
interprets themes — consistencies in the data with which he is continually
bombarded.

This is followed by an important discussion on the nature of clinical
evidence. Clearly a scientific study must produce an accurate representation of
its subject, yet notions of validity and reliability as used by experimentalists
are meaningless to the holist, implying as they do some impersonal, automatic

truth. So how is the holist to check the accuracy of data which are qualitative, fleeting, and at times frankly impressionistic? Diesing argues that he does this by pursuing the notion of *contextual validity:* he assesses the validity of a particular piece of information by comparing it with other pieces:

> Contextual validation takes two main forms. First, the validity of a piece of evidence can be assessed by comparing it with other kinds of evidence on the same point. Each kind... has its own characteristic ambiguities and shortcomings and distortions, which are unlikely to coincide with those of another kind....
>
> The second kind of contextual validation is to evaluate a source of evidence by collecting other kinds of evidence about that source... to locate the characteristic pattern of distortion in a source....
>
> The techniques of contextual validation enable the holist to use types of evidence whose independent validity might be middling to low, since the different types of error might be presumed more or less to cancel each other out (pp. 147-8).

This discussion of the meaning of validity for the holist is followed by a review of the types of data collection that may be used in the field, ranging from the relatively passive methods of observation and collecting informal statements, to the active methods of acting on an interpretation (where the researcher tests his understanding of a situation by acting within it), and challenge (where he provokes situations to see how people will deal with them). This last, Diesing argues is a 'borderline tactic belonging simultaneously to science and to action'; the new paradigm researcher, seeing inquiry as including action experiments and risk-taking in living, would wish to emphasize the active aspects of data-collection.

The information that is gathered in the field situation is used by the holist to build a model which serves both to describe and explain the system. The model is built by 'connecting themes in a network or pattern' (p. 155); the connections may be of various kinds, but they are 'discovered empirically rather than inferred logically' (p. 156); the result of this is an empirical account of the whole system. This account *explains* the system because it describes the kind of relations the various parts have for each other, so that 'the relations between that part and other parts serve to explain or interpret the meaning of that part' (p. 158). This type of explanation is called a *pattern model* of explanation:

> For the pattern model, objectivity consists essentially of this, that the pattern can be indefinitely filled in and extended: as we obtain more and more knowledge it continues to fall into place in this

pattern, and the pattern itself has a place in a larger whole (Kaplan, 1964, quoted on pp. 159-60).

This pattern model is quite different from the more familiar deductive model of explanation which is used by experimentalists. First, the deductive model involves general laws which explain some phenomena, while the pattern model involves a number of phenomena all of equal importance then explains the connections between them. Second, the deduction of unknown parts from known parts is not possible in the pattern model. Indeed, prediction is not important in the pattern model: explanation lies in demonstrating the connections of a puzzling item with other items and the whole pattern. Third, the pattern model is rarely if ever finished, and finally, the pattern is subject to change in the course of its development as new data become available.

Diesing's account of the holist approach proceeds from the level of the individual case study to the development of theory through 'controlled comparison' with similar cases (there is a chapter on different ways of doing this), and the development of typologies, which are an intermediate form of theory, midway between the pattern model of a single case and 'general theory' which aims to go beyond classification into types to more general explanatory principles. The emphasis is always on the empirical basis of this theorizing: typologies are formed and theories developed, not through logical construction, but by comparing cases and searching for new ones. The objective is always to be able to use theory to bring general knowledge to bear on a particular case. This raises the issue of the nature of general theory in holistic inquiry; Diesing reviews the general theories coming from studies of single cases, and finds four general characteristics.

First, they are holistic, to do with whole human systems:

> They deal with part-whole relations, or stages of development of a whole, or essential sub-divisions of a whole and their relations, or classifications of wholes, and so on. A holistic theory is an appropriate guide to participant observation because it continually reminds the observer that his particular, immediate observation must be understood and interpreted by reference to a larger background, and it provides a general account of the background that can illuminate the particular observed fact (p. 204).

Second, the concepts in holistic theories are empirical:

> usually complex and rich in content, and their content is close to ordinary experience with its emotive and subjective emphasis.

Diesing points out that such concepts are often regarded as vague, anthropomorphic, and scientifically useless by practitioners of other methods, but that this kind of concept is essential to the participant-observer, where

> theory and observation are closely connected, observation is closely guided and clarified by theory, and new low-level and limited hypotheses are constantly developing out of observations. This connection requires concepts that are vague and open enough to be capable of continuous modification. In a method that demands that observation range widely enough to include the whole of a human system, the concepts guiding observation must also be complex enough to lead it on rather than restrain it.... Finally, a method that requires the observer to involve himself empathically in his subject matter requires concepts that mobilise his experiences, emotions, biases and sensitivities and point to similarities between his experience and that of his subject (p. 205).

This kind of concept is quite different from those used by other methods: the experimentalist requires speculative concepts at a theoretical level, and operational concepts for observation in experiments; the formalist requires formal concepts theoretically and empirical-interpretive concepts for observation; the holist requires anthropomorphic-sensitizing concepts for theory, referring to what may be general in a number of cases, and concrete concepts, 'derived directly from the subject matter' (p. 209) for observation. Holistic concepts are also defined in a way which suits their use: the holist does not use tight operational definitions; rather, he may take a long discursive article, really an essay in theory, to define a holistic concept, which may have a core central meaning but which may also possess shades and nuances which are crucial to its subtle understanding. Holistic concepts are sometimes borrowed by those using other methods, and may become 'operationalized'; if this happens, they lose their qualities as holistic concepts.

Third, the logic of holistic theory is such that the concepts employed are related dialectically:

> Two concepts are dialectically related when the elaboration of one draws attention to the other as an opposed concept that has been implicitly denied or excluded by the first; when one discovers that the opposite concept is required (presupposed) for the validity or applicability of the first; and when one discovers that the real theoretical problem is that of the interrelation between the two concepts, and the real descriptive problem is that of determining

their interrelations in a particular case. This is known to dialecticians as the principle of the interpenetration of opposites.

Diesing discusses at length examples of dialectical and non-dialectical theories, and continues with a consideration of what accounts for the frequency of dialectical thinking among holists.

Fourth, holistic theories are concatenated rather than hierarchical: this is to say they are made up from pattern models (see above) each part of which has been independently developed, and are loosely linked to the whole, rather than deductions from a few sets of postulates. (Compare Ch. 9, p. 105).

There are thus four levels in the development of holistic theory as one moves from the specific to the general: the theme, the case model, the typology, and the general theory. General theory takes its place as the highest level of explanation in holistic method, in contrast to a theme, which is entirely empirically based. Themes are discovered from data, and are linked together in pattern models which primarily describe, but contain also a level of explanation; models are grouped into typologies, which provide a higher level of explanation, and these are explained by general theory. Thus while a theme is tested quite simply by reference to data — i.e. does a certain uniformity exist? — general theory is tested by its explanatory power:

> (1) It states the connections between the elements that make up an empirical type, that is, it gives the dynamics of the type. (2) it specifies the elements or groups of elements that are most important in a typical dynamic, distinguishing depth factors from symptoms. (3) It organises a typology into a developmental sequence or into a set of alternative solutions to a basic problem.

Thus general theory is not directly testable: it is testable indirectly by the empirical usefulness of its associated typology, which is testable by the adequacy of the case descriptions and so on. Diesing points out that questions such as 'On what specific evidence would you decide that a child did not have an Oedipus complex?', assume that holistic general theory is a universally quantified empirical generalization and may be tested as such, which is nonsense:

> The clinician does not approach each case with the question, 'Does this person have an Oedipus complex, yes or no?' What he tests is not a proposition but a type in a diachronic, development typology... a description of the Oedipal stage of development.... He tests this type by using it to guide his observations of the

oedipal aspect of a particular personality... a consistent dis-confirmation (of the type) would indicate that something is wrong with the theoretical explanation of the type....

The theory of the oedipal stage has been tested in this way in thousands of case studies. These tests... have led to many changes in the theory....

As Diesing points out through his discussion of the holist approach, there is nearly always a total misunderstanding of the nature of holist theory by those of a more positivist persuasion. If participant observation and related methods are accorded any role at all by positivists it is purely as an initial 'soft' approach to inquiry, which will later give rise to empirically (i.e. experimentally) testable hypotheses; this is quite incorrect: there is rather a whole 'rigour of softness' (our phrase), which extends from the study of an individual case right through to the development of a general theory which has a different logic from the rigour of discovery through experimentation or survey, and which is more suitable for the study of whole human situations in their natural contexts.

These methods provide information and ideas about the internal workings of human systems; as such they enable the person to work within the system, and with a creative use of passivity, a respect for and involvement with the subject matter so that the researcher may become an 'active participant in its self-development' (p. 264) as member or leader, therapist or facilitator, educator or political activist. This is for Diesing a crucial characteristic of participant observation. As well as being an approach to the development of theory from observation which fits well with new paradigm notions of rigorous subjectivity, the holist approach

exhibits the most respect for human dignity and freedom because it enables a person to work with, not on, his case, to treat him (or them) as fellow human beings rather than as things.

Human Inquiry
Edited by P. Reason and J. Rowan
© 1981 John Wiley & Sons Ltd.

CHAPTER SIXTEEN

Personal construct theory and research method

Donald Bannister
High Royds Hospital, Ilkley, Yorkshire, UK

A developed psychological theory should have clear and extended implications for research method. It should not only generate topics for research, kinds of questions to be asked: it should propose appropriate methods of inquiry, the form and logic of experiments. Most extant psychological theorizing has little to say about research method. At best it simply delineates areas of research. Thus major theoretical frameworks such as psychoanalytic theory or learning theory or any one of dozens of fashionable mini-theories point to particular phenomena which are central, in terms of the theory (transference, conditioning, information processing, short-term memory, labelling, perception of causality and so forth) but the design of research in these fields derives not from the theory, but from a mimicry of what are thought to be standard scientific procedures.

The inevitable outcome of this state of affairs has been a gross impoverishment of thought about research design in psychology. Indeed, many of our experimental ideas and practices cannot be said to be truly *psychological* at all. Standard volumes on experimental design in psychology are essentially statistical textbooks, devoid of ideas about sources of inventiveness, modes of inquiry or ways of interrogating assumptions. They merely present mathematical frames for experimental ventures and the frames they offer are so devoid of psychological implication that we have been able to fill them with the barren antics of navigationally puzzled rats or the mechanics of the standard questionnaire without the question of psychological relevance intruding. Pondering the mathematical elaboration and neatness of the

191

traditional journal paper in psychology brings to mind Wain's dictum 'a nitwit who is taught method is simply a nitwit with more power to his elbow'.

In proposing personal construct theory, Kelly (1955) integrated notions of appropriate research design into his theory, from the very beginning. He did this by creating an essentially *reflexive* theory: that is a theory which accounts for its own construction. He proposed as his model of man, 'man the scientist', thereby creating a single language and a single set of assumptions within which both 'scientist' and 'organism' are to be seen as identical and discussed in the same terms. Research is seen as simply one formalized version of ordinary human inquiry. It is an act of construing like any other and what Kelly said of construing in general, applies to research methods in particular. He spelt this out in 'The strategy of psychological research' (Kelly, 1965) and in 'Humanistic methodology and psychological research' (Kelly, 1969). This chapter is an attempt to illustrate further some of the specific implications of construct theory for research method.

The Creativity Cycle

One of the most notable omissions from papers and books on research methodology is any indication of how the psychological researcher is supposed to *think,* as distinct from how experiments are to be designed. The central issue of how questions are formulated, how we choose, fantasize about, create, uncover, and personally explore the topic of our research is almost totally neglected in literature. The novice research worker must either invent his or her modes of thought, simply copy, with minor amendments, the substance of previous papers, or rely on handy hints and tips from his or her supervisor. One dire result of this state of affairs is that the ratio of *thinking time* to *experimental time* is often ludicrously short, and the journals are full of papers which present a conventionally passable experimental design in aid of questions which were either badly formulated or simply never worth the asking.

Kelly gave the name *creativity cycle* to the form in which we often undertake changes in our construing of events, and argued that this mode of exploration applies equally to pondering a proposal of marriage, mulling over a crossword puzzle or deliberating about a piece of psychological research. He saw the creativity cycle as having three major phases: circumspection, pre-emption, and control. The circumspection phase of the cycle is that phase in which we are bound by no rules and where our mind may and should wander happily up and down every avenue and blind alley. It is the time when we fantasize, erect preposterous questions, and propose nonsensical answers: it is the phase when, no matter how institutionally formal our research requirements, we should regard humour, poetry, daydreaming, and the wildest kind of speculative argument as the legitimate tools of our trade. Circumspection is sketchily acknowledged in the literature, e.g. 'brainstorming'; but such practices are encouraged only as 'special measures'. They have neither the range nor the duration of circumspection in Kelly's meaning of the term. From circumspection there will emerge (and they should emerge and not be arbitrarily forced out of or tagged onto) *issues* and the pre-emption phase of the cycle is the phase in which we invent/choose/discover our issue of concern. We begin to see the kind of questions we want to ask. Finally, we move into the control phase of the cycle wherein we give our question an operational form; we ask it in a way that enables us to seek a specific answer by putting ourselves in relation to unfolding events. In scientific parlance we set up experimentally testable hypotheses or (at least) propose empirically explorable, if open-ended and suck-it-and-see, kinds of questions.

Key points about this creativity cycle are that it is a *cycle*. We do not go through it once, carry out our experiment and write up. The whole process is recursive. Having gained data we circumspect again in the light of the far-reaching considerations which it arouses in us, we reformulate our question (pre-empt), and move on again to prescriptive action (control). Indeed, within any larger creativity cycle there may be a number of smaller cycles of circumspection, pre-emption, and control.

Closely linked to his notion of the creativity cycle was Kelly's argument for (and pointing to) continuous tightening and loosening in our construing. Loose construing is characteristic of a circumspective phase. A loose construct (or more properly a construct used in a loose mode) is a construct which is rich and multi-predictional to the point of being 'vague' but which nevertheless retains its identity. Thus when we are drunk or whimsical or speculative or free associating or playing the part of God or leaping like a mountain goat from one ideational peak to another, we are construing loosely. Such construing is essential if we are to change or invent. But if construing is left perpetually loose then it cannot lead us into action because it does not point in any specific direction. In order to act we must tighten our construing. A construct used in a tight mode carries uni-directional predictions. When we construe tightly we get down to brass tacks, we point specifically to what we mean, we operationally define, we fill in detail, we bring our general argument to bear upon a point. Again, loosening and tightening is a cyclic process so that we are constantly moving between the two.

Bannister (1970) argues the point as follows.

It is one of the most marked and disastrous characteristics of current psychology that there has been a cleavage into loose and tight *types of psychology*. This is to say that many psychologists seem to fail to move repeatedly through the cycle but rather take up a permanent intellectual residence at one or other end of the cycle.

Thus, we have almost totally loose circumspective psychologies such as Freudian or Existential psychology. This is the kind of speculative, vague psychologizing which leads to papers of the *Unconscious aggression and overt sexual fantasies as quasi-religious substrata for international conflicts* type. At the other end of the spectrum we have the tight world of the pure learning theorist dealing in the highly defined and fragmentary and providing us with the *Short term memory for T mazes under electrically induced stress conditions in the decorticate wood louse* type of paper. Thus, psychologists tend to take up residence and spend their lives with either the vaguely significant or the specifically irrelevant rather than accept that it is a continuous movement between loose and tight construing that enables the arguments which constitute a science to elaborate. This kind of frozen positioning seems to underlie much of the tough minded *versus* tender minded argument in science and is obviously referred to by phrases concerning the problem of vitality of material *versus* precision of method.

Reflexivity

Reflexivity is at the heart of personal construct theory. At the heart of most psychological theories is a fundamental distinction between 'scientist' and 'organism'. They provide different languages for the two, they imply that the 'scientist' is *psychologically* a very different kettle of fish from the 'subject'. Thus, in learning theory terms the subject is 'being conditioned' while the experimental psychologist is 'testing hypotheses'. The analyst analyses while the patient manifests his or her psychodynamic conflicts. From a construct theory viewpoint, the difference between psychologist and subject is at best only a matter of level of abstraction: psychologists are trying to make sense out of the way in which their subjects make sense. This is a formal distinction which is easily reversed in practice. Often subjects have made better sense out of what psychologists are doing than psychologists have made out of what subjects are doing. The language of construct theory is directly and equally applicable to psychologist and subject. As a psychologist you may be hostilely inquiring into your subject's hostility, your construing may be more or less permeable or constellatory or dilated than the subject's. In investigating how varying validational fortunes influence the construing of the subject you are subjecting your own construing to varying validational fortunes.

This quality of reflexivity has many implications for research method. It implies that the questions involved in the research should have personal meaning and significance for *you*. Thus, because so-called scientific issues cannot ultimately be separated from personal issues, since as they are manifest within you, they are part of your *personal* construct system. It makes no more sense to inquire into trivial, conventional and institutionally provided issues in your work as a psychologist than it would make sense to inquire into such issues in your personal life. If a question has no seriousness for you, why should you expect other people to take seriously the answers you provide for it? This, in turn, implies that personal experience is a rich and relevant source from which to derive, and in terms of which to argue, psychological issues. Personal experience is no more a subjective, chaotic, anecdotal nonsense in relation to science than it is in relation to life.

An acceptance of the need for reflexivity is intrinsically a denial of the doctrine that scientists think and are purposive while their subjects are mechanical and determined. Curiously, psychologists are most likely to acknowledge the humanity of their subjects when they begin to fear that subjects are somehow tricking and confusing them. Hence the rush to embed 'lie scales' into questionnaires (deceiving the subject in order that the subject shall not deceive the scientist): the search for the naive subject who will be too stupid to realize the point of the experiment (a search which ultimately carries many psychologists into the land of the rat, the cat, and the wood louse): the vast maelstrom of deception experiments culminating in work such as that of Milgram (1974) where stooge subjects play-acted so as to deceive experimenters who were not really experimenters but only thought they were experimenters, for the benefit of an experimenter who was really an experimenter.

Viewed reflexively the psychological experiment is simply a formal instance of people trying to understand people and psychologists might do better to experiment conjointly *with* their subjects rather than *on* them. If we carry this argument to its logical conclusion then ultimately we may have to proceed further along the path opened up by participant research workers. Envisage a kind of democratic cooperative of people interested in a particular theme in psychology who collectively work out lines of research and then serve as both experimenters *and* subjects in a series of studies. This is the polar opposite of the practice of organizing masses of naive subjects as *objects* of study for the psychologist. Thereby, it might well provide more rewarding scientific ideas and data by changing the present *political* structure of psychological research.

Here again reflexivity points intransigently toward the need for psychologists to see their experiments as part of life and part of society, and thereby to acknowledge and make explicit its moral and political significance. If we simply carry over the assumptions of research in the natural sciences into psychology then we are saddled with the assumption (commonly set forth in textbooks) that our aim is the prediction and control of human behaviour. But are we really morally ready and willing to undertake the *control* of human behaviour? In accepting that there must be an ethic for psychological experimentation we acknowledge the common humanity of psychologist and subject, and this demands more than that we 'do no harm'. Any psychological experiment sets up a *relationship* between the experimenter and subject and that relationship is not neutral, it is for good or ill. Any psychological statement is a statement about the nature of humankind and thereby a statement about the value placed on humankind. The low value we place on the relationship between experimenter and subject is evidenced by the *level of communication* between experimenter and subject reported in the average journal paper. The convention is to present with a more or less pleasant bedside manner, issue a standard set of instructions and demand from the subject the highly restricted set of responses specified by the experimental design and hypotheses. For the subject to talk freely during and after the experiment, for the experimenter to be aware of the subject's construing of the situation, for the subjects, to offer their own hypotheses about what was happening and have the experimenter consider them: these are relatively rare phenomena in psychological research. Thereby, we have not only insulted our subjects but we have cut ourselves off from potentially valuable information about what is going on within the confines of our inquiry.

Psychological Tools

Personal construct theory has generated a number of tools of psychological inquiry, most notably grid method (Fransella and Bannister, 1977). Grid method is now accepted as a useful form of inquiry in a variety of psychological fields ranging from child development and religious belief through to group psychotherapy and architecture (see Adams-Webber, 1979; Stringer and Bannister, 1979). Yet the major significance of the method lies still in the emphasis it places on the meaning which a person attaches to his or her world. The traditional psychological experiment places a set value upon the 'stimulus', this value generally being either a consensus 'truth' or the 'truth' as predicated by a particular construct subsystem ('the line was four inches long'). Inevitably experiments of this kind can only reveal to us the discrepancy between the subject's construing and some other form of construing which has been given 'objective' status. In so far as the subject deviates from the modal answer to the questionnaire item or the 'correct' perception of the stimulus then we are moved to talk in terms of his or her abnormality, illusion, pathology, and so forth. What we are unlikely to learn is the significance of the stimulus *for* the subject and to be able to 'see the stimulus' in the context of the subject's overall way of making sense of his or her situation. As Kelly pointed out: in the standard learning experiment we are prone to say that the subject did not learn; what we fail to investigate, much less understand, is what the subject *was learning* while they were not learning what we expected them to learn.

Granted, the current vogue for phenomenological research has stressed somewhat the same point, although there is still a tendency to regard a phenomenology as something that subjects have, and not to examine the experimenters' phenomenology. Grid method and its assumptions do not imprison us in a solipsistic universe in which there are no realities but only the 'projections' of the subject. Kelly's philosophy of constructive alternativism allows us to postulate a reality, provided that we recognize that reality can only be interpreted and not directly apprehended in any absolute sense. If we construe in a confused and imperceptive way then, in terms of our future validational fortunes, we will have to suffer the penalty for such construing. Construing can be invalidated, even in its own terms.

The particular appetites of modern psychology are such that grid technique (because it generates its answers in a mathematical form) has become relatively popular, while techniques which are equally native to personal construct theory, such as self-characterization, have been virtually ignored. Self-characterization (Bannister and Fransella, 1980) is a way of directly inviting the persons to portray themselves psychologically. It involves asking the subject to offer a self-portrait (written in the third person as if by a sympathetic friend). Such a portrait can be examined for its major theme, evidence of conflict, sence of history, references to the views of others, concepts of psychological causality, and so forth. Explicitly it places the psychologist in the position of trying to make sense out of the way persons make sense of themselves. Its relative unpopularity may be due to the fact that it breaks the 'closed shop' whereby only psychologists may psychologize.

Research as Chaos or Research as Boredom

The choice corollary of personal construct theory reads: persons choose for themselves that alternative in a dichotomozed construct through which they anticipate the greatest possibility for the elaboration of their system. Kelly envisaged elaboration as having two modes: *either* extension or definition. When we *extend* our construing, we widen the range of convenience of our constructs, we take into account new elements, hitherto unexplored areas. We begin to see solutions to particular problems in ways which will inform and widen our vision. When we seek to elaborate by *defining,* then we are trying to make more precise our comprehension of some specific and delimited area, we are filling in detail, becoming more exact about what is already known rather than trying to extend the boundaries of our knowledge.

Whether research is about elaboration by extension or elaboration by definition seems to hinge on whether the constructs we use in the research are purpose-built for a particular area, or whether they are part of a larger framework. If we choose (perhaps from the literature rather than from our own ponderings) some defined, nitty gritty problem of the type 'the effect of varying levels of background illumination on the tachistoscopic perception of geometric figures' then our research is likely further to define specific variables within a highly particular situation and yield something, neat enough in itself, but offering no form of elaboration into larger questions. The literature of psychological research is replete with thousands of tiny studies of this kind which lie in an enormous intellectual heap, from which nothing can be constructed. The likely outcome of this accumulating is what Kelly referred to as death by boredom. On the other hand, if we continuously over-extend so that our research plunges on from 'religious belief and personal relationships' to 'the effect of extra-sensory perception on religious belief and personal relationships' to 'the implications of social class, body type, birth order and philosophical stance for the effect of extra-sensory perception on religious belief and personal relationships', then we may suffer what Kelly called death by chaos.

In our personal lives we can reasonably hope to avoid ultimate boredom or ultimate chaos by extending and defining in such a way that both kinds of venture are related to our personal construct system as a whole. In science we can use an overall theoretical framework to serve the same purpose. Traditionally psychology has failed to create frameworks capable of locating particular researches. The very division of psychology into a series of mini-frameworks (emotion, cognition, memory, sensory perception, social psychology, abnormal psychology, comparative psychology, physiological psychology, and so on and so forth) has segmented the discipline so that most commonly we produce masses of micro-defining researches which cannot be related or more extensive researches which ingest huge lumps of different and non-cross-translatable language systems.

The moral would seem to be that we should neither limit our researches *ad hoc* to particular situations or notions ('we did this pursuit rotor research because we had this excellent pursuit rotor' or 'there is a lot of current interest in the psychological effects of constipation'), nor should we gobble recklessly the indigestible offerings of the vast cafeteria of available concepts. We should try and choose a language (construct system, theoretical framework) in terms of which questions can generate answers which generate questions, so that the whole venture can elaborate without either disappearing into the detail of its own anal orifice or dropping off the edge of the world. The practicalities of such ventures are discussed in Bakan (1967) and Bannister (1968).

Research Freedoms

In summary, personal construct theory offers the psychological researcher certain freedoms.

The philosophy of constructive alternativism contends that no interpretation of reality is absolute and irrevocable. You may always offer an alternative construction of the confronting elements if you have the wit to devise one. This means that you do not have to spend time arguing against or disproving traditional notions but you can proceed directly to your alternative. You do not have to quote, heed, or chant the literature unless the literature truly inspires *your* argument. You do not even have to accept old interpretations when they are smuggled into the discipline disguised as 'variables'. 'Intelligence', 'age', 'sex', 'personality type' are all constructions and you do not have to heed them even though they have been reified into variables and repeatedly presented as if they *must* be taken account of. A 'variable' is simply a construct which has become so embedded in scientific thinking that it is wrongly looked on as a reality rather than an interpretation of reality. As Kelly once put it, there is not much you can do with a variable except let it sit on its own continuum.

The doctrine of reflexivity argues that you are free to choose personally relevant issues of research, to draw on and make explicit, personal experience, to enjoy the wisdom and companionship of your 'subject'. The wisdom you gain from your researching exists independently of public demonstration, though it is fine if you can publicly demonstrate it.

The contention that change — and experimentation is about changing oneself and others — involves tightening and loosening of construing, suggests (even insists) that you may be as soaring and psychotic and as specific and obsessional as you wish, so that you may explore the relationship between the two. Thus, research can be both an act of the imagination and a hard-nosed testing-out process.

The postulating of a creativity, pre-emption, control cycle gives you freedom to offer research contributions at and through any phase of the cycle. This means that you can both test specific hypotheses or prove via open-ended questions, you can contribute quantified data or thematic analysis of free-flowing material.

Finally, personal construct theory makes a demand, but one which is also an opportunity. It urges that research work be cast into the linguistic-theoretical framework, broad enough to encompass a vision of a person — this being the essential subject matter of psychology. Working within a framework gives both you and others the opportunity to elaborate outwards from the specific study.

Human Inquiry
Edited by P. Reason and J. Rowan
© 1981 John Wiley & Sons Ltd.

CHAPTER SEVENTEEN

The interviewing process re-examined*

Fred Massarik
*Graduate School of Management, University of California,
Los Angeles, USA*

While science fiction may fantasize devices that provide direct access to the brain's symbolic content and imagery, present circumstances — alas — offers no such convenience. Instead reliance must be placed on an interpersonal and interactive process, one frequently centred on the notion of the 'interview'. There is, of course, an extensive literature on this topic, revealing the vast variety of interviewing procedures proposed and utilized (e.g. Richardson *et al.*, 1965). Here, it will be purposeful to consider a typology of interviews.

The Hostile Interview

This interview is characterized by mutual hostility of interviewer and interviewee. For instance, the interviewer may seek to elicit information which the interviewee specifically seeks to withhold. The atmosphere is one of mutual distrust and antagonism. An example of this kind of interaction is an interrogation of an 'uncooperative' suspect by a detective, or a confrontation between a frustrated petitioner seeking information from a bored bureaucratic functionary. It is only the press of circumstance and the desire for specific

---

*This chapter is extracted from a longer paper (Massarik, 1979), which includes some conceptual reflections on which the interview typology and the phenomenological interview are based — Eds.

narrowly limited information that necessitates the interview in the first place. Time perspective is brief. As soon as minimum objectives are attained, or else if the quest appears useless to one or the other, the interview terminates.

The Limited Survey Interview

This interview is characterized by relative indifference or minimum trust. It is focused on a predetermined, structured, question-asking procedure by which the interviewer seeks to obtain certain information or views from the interviewee, caring little either for interview dynamics or for the interviewee as person.

The interviewee's response principally is one of minimal acquiescence, without particular commitment to interview content or to the interviewer's goals. A typical example of this type is represented by the standard 'polling' interview in the context of political and market research, often by telephone or by brief personal contact.

The Rapport Interview

This interview, while in general format resembling the limited survey interview, goes beyond the 'cut-and-dried' character of the latter, and opens the door to a more genuinely human relationship between interviewer and interviewee. This is, of course, the kind of interview situation in which rapport, as widely discussed in survey research literature, becomes a salient attribute. While the interaction is quite well-bounded, some positive inter-personal 'vibrations' are in evidence. A significant measure of mutual trust exists and, though the interview objectives are quite focused and delimited, small-talk, casual byplay and interpersonal activity not centred exclusively on interview content prevails. By way of example, one may consider the high-quality survey interview — particularly one that involves open-end questioning, cooperative information-seeking/giving interactions in formal systems such as public agencies or corporate settings, and simple short-term counselling interviews.

The Asymmetrical-Trust Interview

This interview is characterized by a substantial imbalance in trust relationships between interviewer and interviewee, typically with the interviewee more trustful of the interviewer, while the latter, though not hostile, is less concerned with issues of trust or mutual rapport. Illustrative of this genre is an interview situation as may involve a physician concerned principally with the 'medical' aspects of the case, and a patient who, with a sense of dependence, seeks the physician's views. This kind of asymmetrical relationship also may maintain in the psychotherapeutic nexus, particularly if the client seeks 'advice' from a professionally narrow or technique-focused therapist.

The Depth Interview

This interview is characterized by an intensive process on the part of the interviewer to explore thoroughly — more deeply than in the typical rapport interview — the views and dynamics of the interviewee. In this context, the level of rapport is significantly elevated; the interviewer is genuinely concerned with the interviewee as a person, going beyond search for delimited information input. In turn, the interviewee sufficiently reciprocates this feeling, valuing the interviewer's motives and seeking to respond in appropriate depth. Though still limited, the time frame is not tightly constrained, and the interviewee in turn may ask questions of the interviewer, exploring intent, seeking clarification and otherwise actively participating in the process of seeking understanding.

Illustrative of this type are skilled anthropological and clinical interviews, diagnostic interviews in consulting practice, certain 'open-end' interviews in marketing research, and such interviews as may be illustrated by the 'journalistic' inquiries of Oriana Fallaci (1977) or Studs Terkel (1974).

The Phenomenal Interview: Commitment to Empathic Search

This interview is characterized by maximal mutuality of trust, attaining a genuine and deeply experienced caring between interviewer and interviewee, and a commitment to joint search for shared understanding. Interviewer and interviewee respond to one another as total persons, ready to actively examine and disclose both remote and accessible aspects of their lives, including experiences, present responses, and imageries.

The relationship involves fundamental equality and concurring commitment to the quest at hand. The time frame is fluid, unbound by the usual constraints of a therapeutic hour, or sometimes even by considerations of night and day. Interviewer and interviewee have, within appropriate recognitions of their life constraints, free access to one another; ideas explored on one occasion may be temporarily laid aside, only to be re-examined in changed context later. There is little by way of simplistic question/answer exchange; rather free-form modes of communication and iterative opportunities for review and clarification identify the process.

Interviewer and interviewee aspire to enter, with shared commitment and mutual caring, each other's experienced 'worlds' — their existential 'Lebenswelten'. The interviewer's empathic effort to explore the interviewee's 'world' is aided by a sense of reciprocal empathy by the interviewee in which the latter acknowledges the realities of the interviewer's world. Thus, while an important emphasis remains with explication or — in the German sociological sense with 'Verstehen' — of the interviewee's world, the dynamics of the interviewer are explicitly part of the process. Unlike the conventional interview philosophy that seeks to hold constant the interviewer's impact on the interviewee — a goal of questionable feasibility — this interview style recognizes the inherent humanness of *both* participants, and indeed the genuine relevance of the total interpersonal (as well as non-human) environment within which the process occurs.

Under conditions as these, the interview result, rather than check-marks identifying responses to 'standard' questions or even typical open-end interview protocols, becomes a document revelatory of both interviewer and interviewee, chronicling the process and content of their evolving exploration. The emergent product is an *expanded protocol,* providing as possible optimally homologous replicas of what has transpired in the interviewer-interviewee interaction, showing the ups-and-downs, detours, interruptions, apparent irrelevancies, etc. with substantial fidelity. It is evident that the problems of analysis of such expanded protocols are considerable. Extending beyond the bounds of the usual 'content analysis' or 'theme analysis', improved technologies need to be devised that can reflect both richness and order, process and content, as revealed in the phenomenal interview's expanded protocol.

Examples of such phenomenal interview are rare. Much current phenomenological interviewing is rather akin to depth interviewing or to some limited forms of participant observation. Perhaps the nearest appropriate illustration is constituted by certain exceptional therapeutic relationships, as for instance those reported some years ago by Robert Lindner in *The Fifty-minute Hour* (1966). Among the most revealing in this vein is Lindner's report on the therapeutic encounter with one Kirk Allen (pseudonym), entitled 'The Jet-Propelled Couch'. The account, delightful in the telling, is best read in the original. However, we may note that the Lindner-Allen relationship involved a committed joint search for understanding centred on Allen's apparently imaginary (and presumably aberrative) extraterrestrial and intergalactic journeys — delusions of which Lindner sought to cure Allen. Eventually it is the very mutuality of the search that 'breaks the case', that 'cures' Allen? Or is the cure, too, a delusion?

It is at the end of 'The Jet-Propelled Couch' that Lindner reflects:

> but now, as I listen from my chair behind the couch, I know better. I know that my chair and the couch are separated only by a

thin line. I know that it is, after all, a happier combination of accidents that determines, finally who shall lie on that couch, and who shall sit behind it (p. 207).

In the phenomenal interview at its best, much as in the therapeutic situation described, the line between interviewer and interviewee blurs and the total vitality of the deeply probing inquiry becomes salient. Resulting data, therefore, excel in conceptual richness and human relevance.

Some Genotypic Reflections on Interview Typologies

The interview types delineated are regarded as exemplary of certain modes of inquiry now, with the possible exception of the phenomenal interview, widely extant. We may consider this typology in light of certain metaphors describing the specific relationships expressed.

(a)   In the hostile interview the interviewer is the *Enemy* and the relationship is one of combat with specific information and its consequence the prize of war.

(b)   In the limited survey interview the interviewer appears as *Automaton,* punching certain buttons, seeking to elicit mechanical response.

(c)   In the rapport interview the interviewer emerges as *Human-Being-in-a-Role,* not denying his/her humanity and acknowledging the humanity of the interviewee, while still focusing essentially on subject-matter and on specific replies.

(d)   In the asymmetrical-trust interview the interviewer is defined as *Sage,* as source of counsel and wisdom, and the interviewee as petitioner, holding the weak side of a power imbalance.

(e)   In the depth interview interviewer and interviewee, in substantial balance, meets as *Peers,* their humanities expressed in circumscribed terms, but with continuing emphasis on the specific goals of response content.

(f)   In the phenomenal interview interviewer and interviewee become *Caring Companions,* mutually committed to the enhancement of understanding, their respective humanities richly and actively revealed.

In conceptual terms, one may specify a set of dimensions that differentiate the various interview types, generally ranged along a humanistic to non-humanistic continuum; these interrelated (non-orthogonal) dimensions (listed in no particular order) may include the following:

(1)   Acceptance... Hostility.
(2)   Trust... Distrust.
(3)   Mutuality... Inequality.

(4) Psychological closeness... Psychological distance.

(5) Emphasis on total or material sector of 'life world'... Emphasis on clearly defined reply.

(6) Emphasis on shared concerns... Emphasis on interviewer's or interviewee's concerns, one to the exclusion of the other.

(7) Interview content and process determined primarily by interviewee, with facilitation by interviewer... Interview content and process determined exclusively by interviewer, with possible interference by interviewee.

(8) Unbounded time allocation... Tightly bounded time allocation.

(9) Balanced concern with both content and process... Exclusive concern with process, *or* exclusive concern with content.

(10) Intertwined spontaneous interviewer-interviewee response... Rigid role separation betwen interviewer and interviewee.

Within the humanistic framework, it must be asserted that the polarities indicated above are not value-free: with the view toward meaningful understanding of the person, and considering purpose and wholeness in human inquiry, the first-mentioned (left) polarity, above, is to be preferred. Phenomenal interviewing, while generating a unique congerie of methodological and practical problems, is intended to address head-on, not the bits and pieces of abstraction frequently found in conventional psychological research, but rather the fulness of significant human experience.

The phenomenal interview is, of course, only one element in the development of phenomenological inquiry. It does not constitute a 'hunting licence' for doing-anything-at-all in the research process. Nor does it possess intrinsic meaning outside the context of carefully conceived and disciplined research conception.

The time now seems ripe to go beyond the bland assertion to the effect that empirical phenomenology is possible. Nor is it sufficient to equate empirical phenomenology with any and all presently available unbounded or qualitative methodological modalities. Rather, next steps must take us promptly to a clear and conscientious specification of alternative strategies in *empirical phenomenological research design,* to the analytic and synthetic methods for consequent data treatment, and, most importantly, to timely means for utilization of relevant findings in enhancement of the quality of human life.

Human Inquiry
Edited by P. Reason and J. Rowan
© 1981 John Wiley & Sons Ltd.

CHAPTER EIGHTEEN

Heuristic research*

Clark Moustakas
Merrill-Palmer Institute, Detroit, USA

The impetus for writing this essay came from several sources: my own growing dissatisfaction with conventional research as a means to study significant problems, issues, and processes with reference to man and human experience; the questions of my students and colleagues; and my wish to clarify with others my own research philosophy and perspective before accepting appointments as a research consultant.

Rather than listing a series of research concepts and abstractions which would be fragmented, mechanical effort, and which I would approach unenthusiastically, I have decided to explore an actual research experience which distinguishes the discovery process from that of verification and corroboration. In this presentation, I shall outline the significant dimensions of what I am calling *heuristic research*; that is, a research approach which encourages an individual to discover, and methods which enable him to investigate further by himself.

Because of its recent significance and its impact on my own awareness and way of life, I have chosen my study of loneliness (Moustakas, 1961) to express and illustrate the nature and meaning of heuristic research.

---

*This chapter originally appeared in Bugental: *Challenges of Humanistic Psychology,* published by McGraw-Hill in 1967, and reproduced by permission.

Sources of the Study

My study of loneliness had no design or purpose, no object or end, and no hypotheses or assumptions. While I was faced with a question or problem (whether or not to agree to major heart surgery which might restore my daughter to health or result in her death) in the beginning, I was not inquiring into the nature or meaning of loneliness and its impact on the individual in modern society. However, the urgency for making this critical decision plunged me into the experience of feeling utterly alone and cut off from human companionship. The entire process of facing the terror and consequences of major heart surgery or an uncertain future and a premature death initiated my search into loneliness. At first, the search was a search into my own self, looking deeply within, trying to discover and be aware, trying to find the right way to proceed, and experiencing a sense of isolation when each path or journey ended with a question mark.

Experiences of lonely self-reflection came at unexpected moments, in the midst of a crowd of people, in response to a word or phrase in conversation. Many different kinds of situations evoked an inner process of doubt, uncertainty, and isolation. Sometimes I awakened in the night, and being overwhelmed by images and feelings and thoughts, I tried to draw from deep down within myself a single answer, a single direction, which would utilize in an integrated form all the data — my experiences with my daughter, talks with physicians, and published reports on heart surgery. The initial journey was an attempt to discover the one true way to proceed; it involved a process of self-inquiry, which was not planned but simply happened, which was not carefully sampled but occurred spontaneously at unexpected times and places. While no answer came to the problem of surgery, I became aware that at the centre of my world was a deep and pervasive feeling of loneliness. With this feeling came the tentative realization that loneliness is a capacity or source in man for new searching, awareness, and inspiration — that when the outside world ceases to have a meaning, when support and confirmation are lacking or are not adequate to assuage human suffering, when doubt and uncertainty overwhelm a person, then the individual may contemplate life from the depths of his own self and in nature. For me, this was a discovery that in a crucial and compelling crisis, in spite of comfort and sympathy from others, one can feel utterly and completely alone, that, at bottom, the experience of loneliness exists in its own right as a source of power and creativity, as a source of insight and direction, as a requirement of living no matter how much love and affirmation one receives in his work and in his relationships with others.

Thus the beginning steps of my research into loneliness (which at the time I did not know I was researching) involved not a question of the nature of loneliness, not a question of its restorative, creative, or destructive impact on the individual, but a struggle and search into another problem. Much later I realized that loneliness is often experienced by men who must make crucial decisions that will have major consequences in the lives of other men. Through inner exploration and study, I sought to find a solution which would integrate the facts into one clear pattern. The significance of inner searching for deeper awareness as a relevant step in research is cogently expressed by Polanyi (1964, pp. 10-14) in his book *Science, Faith and Society*:

> *Scientific knowing consists in discerning Gestalten that are aspects of reality.* I have here called this 'intuition'; in later writings I have described it as a tacit co-efficient of a scientific theory, by which it bears on experience, as a token of reality. Thus it foresees yet indeterminate manifestations of the experience on which it bears.
>
> Every interpretation of nature, whether scientific, non-scientific or anti-scientific, is based on some intuitive conception of the general nature of things.... But in spite of much beautiful work... we still have no clear conception of how discovery comes about. The main difficulty has been pointed out by Plato in the *Meno*. He says that to search for the solution of a problem is an absurdity. For either you know what you are looking for, and then there is no problem; or you do not know what you are looking for, and then you are not looking for anything and cannot expect to find anything.... A potential discovery may be thought to attract the mind which will reveal it — inflaming the scientist with creative desire and imparting to him intimations that guide him from clue to clue and from surmise to surmise. The testing hand, the straining eye, the ransacked brain, may all be thought to be labouring under the common spell of a potential discovery striving to emerge into actuality.

Experiences in meditation and self-searching, in intuitive and mystical reachings, and in hours and hours of silent midnight walking paved the way to a formulation of my study of loneliness, a formulation which emerged clearly during my observations of hospitalized children. In the hospital I began to see how lonely feelings impelled young children to seek a compassionate voice and a warm, friendly face; I began to see how young children separated from their parents could often be more completely involved in the struggle with loneliness than in the painful experiences connected with illness and surgery; I began to see how children separated from their parents underwent a period of protest and resistance against separation, against the mechanical actions and fixed faces and gestures of the hospital combine. I also observed a gradual deterioration of protest, rebellion, and self-assertion and, in their place, a deep sense of isolation, lonely weeping, withdrawal, depression, and numbness. In general, I witnessed a basic, pervasive feeling of dehumanization, which sought to repress lonely feelings and the whole range of human emotions that characterize the alive and growing child.

The Total Person as a Research Method

When I saw that these dimensions of loneliness were almost totally ignored, misunderstood, and misinterpreted by hospital aides, nurses, and doctors, I decided, using the hospital situation and my own intuitive awareness as a beginning, to try to understand loneliness, how it fitted into the perceptions and behaviour of hospitalized children, and the way in which it existed in myself and others. I decided to listen to the experiences of children in the hospital with objectivity and warmth, not taking notes and making records and thus objectifying, but keeping the focus of my interest on the experience of loneliness itself, on the essence of the experience through the person's rendering of it and relating of it. Objectivity, in this connection, means seeing what an experience *is* for another person, not what causes it, not why it exists, not how it can be defined and classified. It means seeing attitudes, beliefs, and feelings of the person as they exist for him at the moment he is experiencing them, perceiving them whole, as a unity. I set out to know the meaning of loneliness, not by defining and categorizing, but by experiencing it directly and through the lives of others, as a simple reality of life in the way that Moore (1903, p. 7) describes reality in *Principia Ethica*:

> My point is that 'good' is a simple notion, just as 'yellow' is a simple notion; that, just as you cannot, by any manner of means, explain to any one who does not already know it, what yellow is, so you cannot explain what good is. Definitions of the kind that I was asking for, definitions which describe the real nature of the object or notion denoted by a word, and which do not merely tell us what the word is used to mean, are only possible when the object or notion in question is something complex. You can give a definition of a horse, because a horse has many different properties and qualities, all of which you can enumerate. But when you have enumerated them all, when you have reduced a horse to his simplest terms, then you can no longer define those terms. They are simply something which you think of or percieve, and to any one who cannot think of or perceive them, you can never, by any definition, make their nature known.

Thus I set out to discover the meaning of loneliness in its simplest terms, desiring to perceive the experience of being lonely in its absolutely native state.

At the same time, I knew from my own experiences and from my conversations with hospitalized children that loneliness itself could not be communicated by words or defined in its essence, that loneliness could not be known except by persons who are open to their own senses and aware of their own experiences. I set out to discover the nature of lonely experience by intimate encounter with other persons. A quotation from Polanyi's (1958, pp. viii-6) *Personal Knowledge* may clarify this point:

> To say that the discovery of objective truth in science consists in the apprehension of a rationality which commands our respect and arouses our contemplative admiration; that such discovery, while using the experience of our senses as clues, transcends this experience by embracing the vision of a reality beyond the impression of our senses, a vision which speaks for itself in guiding us to an ever deeper understanding of reality — such an account of scientific procedure would be generally shrugged aside as out-dated Platonism: a piece of mystery-mongering unworthy of an enlightened age. Yet it is precisely on this conception of objectivity that I wish to insist.... Into every act of knowing there enters a passionate contribution of the person knowing what is known, and... this coefficient is no mere imperfection but a vital component of his knowledge.

Entering into the Experience

My way of studying loneliness, in its essential form, was to put myself into an open, ready state, into the lonely experiences of hospitalized children, and to let these experiences become the focus of my world. I listened. I watched. I stood by. In dialogue with the child, I tried to put into words the deep regions of his experience. Sometimes my words touched the child in the interior of his feelings, and he began to weep; sometimes the child formed words in response to my presence, and thus he began to break through his numbness and the dehumanizing impact of the hospital atmosphere and practice. At this point, loneliness became my existence. It entered into every facet of my world — into my teaching, my interviews in therapy, my conversations with friends, my home life. Without reference to time or place or structure, somehow (more intentionally than accidentally) the theme came up. I was clearly aware that exhaustively and fully, and in careful manner, I was searching for, studying, and inquiring into the nature and impact of loneliness. I was totally involved and immersed in this search for a pattern and meaning which would reveal the various dimensions of loneliness in modern life. This was research in the sense of a close searching and inquiring into the nature of a reality of human experience. I weas certainly not studying loneliness simply as an intellectual or academic question, in a detached manner, but rather in an integrative, living form; becoming part of the lonely experiences of others; being within lonely moments in living; being involved, committed, interested, concerned, while at the same time aware of an emerging pattern and relatedness. Facts, knowledge, insights were accumulating as I listened and later recorded and studied; but, at the same time, there were intuitive visions, feelings, sensings that went beyond anything I could record or think about or know in a factual sense. At the centre of the lonely existence were ineffable, indescribable feelings and experiences, a presence which I felt in a unified and essential way. I had gone 'wide open', at moments ceasing to be a separate individual, but wholly related to the other person, leaving something behind of my own intuitive vision and comprehension while, at the same time, taking something away — very much in the manner that Steinbeck and Ricketts (1941) approached their study of the *Sea of Cortez:*

> Let's see what we see, record what we find, and not fool ourselves with conventional scientific strictures — in that lonely and un-inhabited Gulf our boat and ourselves would change it the moment we entered. By going there, we would bring a new factor to the Gulf. Let us consider that factor and not be betrayed by this myth of permanent objective reality. If it exists at all it is only available in pickled tatters or in distorted flashes. 'Let us go', we said, 'into the Sea of Cortez, realizing that we become forever a part of it; that our rubber boots slogging through a flat of eelgrass, that the rocks we turn over in a tide pool, make us truly and permanently a factor in the ecology of the region. We shall take something away from it, but we shall leave something too.' And if we seem a small factor in a huge pattern, nevertheless it is of relative importance. We take a tiny colony of soft corals from a rock in a little water world. And that isn't terribly important to the tide pool. Fifty miles away the Japanese shrimp boats are dredging with overlapping scoops, bringing up tons of shrimps, rapidly destroying the ecological balance of the whole region. That isn't very important in the world. And six thousand miles away the great bombs are falling on London and the stars are not moved thereby. None of it is important or all of it is.

Thus I entered into a formal study of loneliness, taking into it my own growing awareness, the discovery of myself as a lonely person, my experiences in the hospital, and my many moments, conversations, dialogues, and discussions with other persons — children in school settings who spoke freely and openly and wrote themes expressing their lonely experiences; parents and young adults in therapy who struggled and found it painful to speak of loneliness but who, once initiated in this journey, were able to recapture and create in a living sense moments of the past and current feelings of isolation and solitude; and friends and colleagues who could reveal the intimate depth of lonely experiences. I steeped myself in a world of loneliness, letting my life take root and unfold in it, letting its dimensions and meanings and forms evolve its own timetable and dynamics.

The Use of the Literature

The study was culminated in my readings of published reports on loneliness and lonely experiences. But this was a point near the end, not at the beginning, where it might have acted to predispose and predetermine and colour my own growing awareness. I began to study volumes of biography and autobiography of individuals who dramatically exemplified lonely lives. Among other persons, those who captured my interest were Emily Dickinson, Abraham Lincoln, Woodrow Wilson, Benedict Arnold, and Ned Langford. I also followed the lonely experiences of Herman Buhl in his journey to the highest peak of the Himalayas, Admiral Byrd alone on an advanced base in Antarctica, Saint-Exupéry lost in the desert, and other persons involved in extreme situations of isolation. I studied the autobiographical volumes of Hiss and Chambers, as well as many political analyses of their confrontation and its implications, including the numerous volumes of the House Unamerican Activities Committee and the ten volumes of the trial transcript, to see more fully the lonely consequences of infamy and mass public rejection. I discovered additional nuances of the meaning of loneliness form the studies of Frieda Fromm-Reichmann of the loneliness of mental patients, Margaret Wood's *Paths of Loneliness,* Eithne Tabor's *Songs of a Psychotic,* Karl Menninger's *Love against Hate,* David Riesman's *Lonely Crowd,* Erich Fromm's *Escape from Freedom,* Thomas Wolfe's *Hills Beyond,* Sullivan's *Interpersonal Theory of Psychiatry,* and the numerous articles and reports appearing in newspapers and journals, accounts which could be understood both as attempts to escape and overcome loneliness and as evolutions of deeper sensitivity and awareness which enabled unique and creative expressions of loneliness in poetry, music, literature, and other art forms.

When a pattern began to emerge with reference to the nature and function of loneliness in individual experience and in modern living, the formal study came to an end. At this point the framework and detail, the clarification of loneliness, had been formed; it was possible to differentiate and refine its meaning, to expand and illustrate its nature and relevance in human experience. Thus what started as a hospital study of loneliness became an extended research into the phenomenon of loneliness. The conditions and factors which initiated and characterized the study were as follows: (1) a crisis which created a question or problem; (2) a search of self in solitude, from which emerged a recognition of the significance of loneliness both as a creative urging and as a frightening and disturbing experience; (3) an expanding awareness through being open to lonely life and lonely experiences, through watching, listening, and feeling, and through conversation, dialogue, and discussion; (4) a steeping of myself in the deeper regions of loneliness, so that it became the ingredient of my being, the centre of my world; (5) an intuitive grasping of the patterns of loneliness, of related aspects and different associations, until an integrated vision and awareness emerged; (6) further clarification, delineation, and refinement through studies of lonely lives, lonely experiences, and published reports on loneliness; and (7) creation of a form, a manuscript, in which to project and express the various forms, themes, and values of loneliness and in which to present its creative powers, as well as the anxiety which it arouses in discontent, restlessness, and boredom, and the strategies used in attempting to overcome and escape loneliness.

Human Validation

Since the publication of *Loneliness,* I have received approximately five hundred letters which verify and validate my portrayal of loneliness in modern life — its nature, its beauty, and its terror. My correspondents confirmed the meaning and essence of loneliness which had emerged from my research; each of these persons portrayed the uniqueness of lonely experience and its powers in drawing upon untouched capacities and resources, in evolving new creations, and in expanding awareness, sensitivity, and compassion, as well as the extreme pain, grief, despair, and impotency which often accompany the urge to discover, to answer the challenges and problems of living, to face genuinely and authentically separation, illness, and death. I have selected five letters as illustrations of response and confirmation:

> **1**   Today I read your book, *Loneliness.* It was one of those rare experiences that seem to come 'just in time.' Somehow I wanted you to know that I appreciated your sharing with me the 'feelings and insights' expressed in this book — for you see it is not just a book but a kind of communication not often experienced.
>
>   The greatest value I received from sharing this communication was that when circumstances of life seem to be taking from us our right to be then we must re-affirm our faith in our own being and refuse to be pushed aimlessly along. Thank you for giving some impetus to this re-affirmation.

2   Having just completed your book *Loneliness,* I must thank you for such an articulate and sensitive presentation of basic truths relating to human suffering. Since the sudden and premature death of my husband in September, 1959, and the agonizing period following it when, primarily motivated by the two babies I had been left to rear alone, I struggled to retain sanity, I have had a deep interest in loneliness, its causes, its effects. Your book clarified a number of matters for me.

3   I read your beautifully written book of *Loneliness* and was very impressed with its truthfulness. I do believe, however, that the subject matter has been expounded many times by many writers and authors, but because of the lack of a formal education I never realized that anyone could possibly see me in these dimensions. I think I know the meaning of this subject as well as, if not better, than most. I need no formal education for this. I have lived, associated myself with, become drawn toward the lonely, and know readily those who are. P.S. I am a janitor. I also work in a print shop. Please forgive the informality.

4   I read those parts which I felt a need to read from *Loneliness* during Christmas vacation. I was deeply affected by the experiences I was able to share. I picked the book up again and read and was surprised at the wonderment of being able to experience as though never before these same journeys through loneliness.

I felt that my very feelings were caught up and understood by the author — that a friendly someone could write what I had felt, but hadn't been able to express in words.

I gained something from this reading, partly that I don't have to feel that being lonely is wasteful — that I don't have to be busy every minute, to be a complete person. Before I was afraid to be lonely, afraid I was just wasting precious time and afraid that I wasn't adequate enough within myself.

For someone who usually rambles endlessly on when affected by something I can't really think of anything else to say, perhaps later, right now I'm still experiencing it.

5   Not long ago I talked to a group of people with considerable feeling in my presentation, pointing their attention to the need to be individual and independent centers for living, each man in his own. I had been able to suggest that this was an avenue also to deepest companionship and significant social value. After my lecture, I noticed that the group disbanded quickly and individuals went off by themselves, not even coming up to me as they usually do. My first impulse was to feel that my lecture had fallen flat. Later I learned that the opposite was the case with several of the group, at least. People are hungry to be their own authorities in basic life matters and, spurred by my own expression in these matters, they wanted it all the more, meaning they had to leave me to *my* own, too.

I need not tell you that I think you are doing just the right thing in forming your experience as you are doing. The vacuum of 'being', if not filled with the substance of life-realized in depth (as you are doing), will gain so much power that our people will collapse inwardly in the clutter of their own psychic debris.

The loneliness each man feels is his hunger for life itself, not only life in his being, but life in the being of creation, past, present and future. Your book allows the reader to recognize his own vacuum which is the first step to appreciation of its filling. Had you left your own vacuum uncomposed in expression, you would have left others with nothing (a disparate emptiness); composing it, you gave others not only a chance of recognizing their own, but also a way of composing a view of one's emptiness as one visualizes the cup in a ring, inviting the placement of the pearl of great price. It is the yearning that makes fulfillment possible in the most elemental ranges. It is death present within life, without which there could not be life.

Conclusion

While the subject of the research was loneliness, I have tried to portray the research process itself from its initial steps to its final phases. I now believe in such a process of searching and studying, of being open to significant dimensions of experience in which comprehension and compassion mingle; in which intellect, emotion, and spirit are integrated; in which intuition, spontaneity, and self-exploration are seen as components of unified experience; in which both discovery and creation are reflections of creative research into human ventures, human processes, and human experiences. In conclusion, I quote several passages which I believe are relevant to this study of heuristic research. Some of the effects of such an approach [selected from an essay by Rogers (1964, pp. 20-2)] are as follows:

In the first place it would tend to do away with the fear of creative subjective speculation. As I talk with graduate students in the behavioral sciences this fear is a very deep one. It cuts them off from any significant discovery. They would be shocked by the writings of a Kepler in his mystical and fanciful searching for likenesses and patterns in nature. They do not recognize that it is out of such fanciful thinking that true science emerges....

A second effect would be to place a stress on disciplined commitment, disciplined *personal* commitment, not methodology. It would be a very healthy emphasis in the behavioral sciences if we could recognize that it is the dedicated, personal search of a disciplined, open-minded individual which discovers and creates new knowledge. No refinement of laboratory or statistical method can do this....

Another effect would be that it would permit a free rein to phenomenological thinking in behavioral science, our effort to understand man and perhaps even the animals from the inside. It would recognize that no type of hypothesis has any special virtue in science save only in its relationship to a meaningful pattern which exists in the universe....

Another and more general effect would be that if the picture of science I have tried to suggest gains some general acceptance in our field then it would give a new dignity to the science of man and to the scientist who commits himself to that field. It would keep the scientist as a human being in the picture at all times, and we would recognize that science is but the lengthened shadow of dedicated human beings.

Human Inquiry
Edited by P. Reason and J. Rowan
© 1981 John Wiley & Sons Ltd.

CHAPTER NINETEEN

Illuminative evaluation

Malcolm Parlett
Education Development Centre, Newton, Massachusetts, USA

Illuminative evaluation (Parlett and Hamilton, 1972) has been fashioned and articulated in the course of studying small-scale educational programmes. One short description reads as follows:

> The basic emphasis of this approach is on interpreting, in each study, a variety of educational practices, participants' experiences, institutional procedures, and management problems in ways that are recognisable and useful to those for whom the study is made. The illuminative evaluator contributes to decision-making by providing information, comment, and analysis designed to increase knowledge and understanding of the programme under review. Illuminative evaluation is characterised by a flexible methodology that capitalises on available resources and opportunities, and draws upon different techniques to fit the total circumstances of each study (Parlett and Dearden, 1977).

The practice of illuminative evaluation is not now confined to the education field (Feuerstein, 1978), nor have studies on the national scale proved impossible to handle on the approach (Jamieson *et al.,* 1977). Yet its main field of application remains within education and it is particularly suited to intensive studies of small to intermediate-size programmes.

The approach has evolved over time. Its tenets, methods, and operating styles derive from cumulative practice and from reflecting, after each study, on what happened, went wrong, and went right (Parlett, 1975).

The chances of evaluation studies being judged successful are not high. This applies whatever the approach used. The poor record is not surprising. There is a natural resistance of individuals and organizations to being investigated; many issues addressed are politically sensitive; and there are difficulties in obtaining accurate and meaningful data under research conditions usually short of ideal. The evaluator has done well if the report is seen as useful for decision-making, is accepted as accurate, and is regarded as a stimulating commentary. Most evaluations — including a number of our own — fall short of total success.

Social scientists usually find, if they stray into evaluation, that there are extra challenges over and above the usual questions facing researchers. For example, there is often beginning suspicion on the part of those studied; often those who want a study made do not agree on what kind of evaluation they want; disputes arise over what areas should and should not be gone into; outcomes that people do not like are challenged; complaints are made afterwards that the claims of this or that sub-group have not been adequately represented. Many are the evaluators whose fingers have been burned, or at least singed, in finding their way through these difficulties.

Illuminative evaluation, sensibly conducted, seems to obviate many of the difficulties. This is not surprising; pragmatic considerations have weighed heavily in designing the approach — there seems little point in proposing strategies that do not work in practice. Numerous questions to do with the management of studies, the roles of the evaluator, and the purpose and philosophy of the approach have had to be considered carefully.

Obviously, then, illuminative evaluation is not merely a change from quantitative to qualitative methods, or from statistical treatment to narrative reporting. One can discern, in 1980, increasing enthusiasm in the USA for ethnographic techniques in evaluation. Often, however, there is no corresponding shift in the wider thinking of the evaluators. One suspects their studies will be no more successful than before. What is at issue is that evaluation methods cannot be viewed in isolation (Hastings, 1969).

This chapter explains why not. Illuminative evaluation is examined here as a system, and is viewed from four vantage points: (i) *the definition of problems studies;* (ii) *its methodology;* (iii) *the underlying conceptual framework;* (iv) *the values embodied in the approach.*

Definition of the Problems Studied

In an illuminative evaluation, the general areas to be explored begin to be defined at the first stage — *the negotiation.* At this point the evaluator has extended contact with those commissioning the study (along with others such as participants in the programme) and tries to establish what questions and problems are of most concern, and how the study can address them to best effect. Since many a good intention is jeopardized by trivial misunderstandings, numerous (well over 20) questions of a practical nature are also dealt with at this stage (e.g. What kind of report? Who will see the draft? What in-house facilities are available? How is the study to be introduced to organisation members?).

Illuminative evaluations are not pre-ordinate, designed in advance, with a set of fixed questions or tests to be made. They are far more exploratory in nature, with the problems-to-be-studied being identified through *intensive familiarisation* with the issues and character of the programme being studied. Only by appraising the full organizational, human, and political complexity of a setting or group of settings can the evaluator fully comprehend the nature of questions on people's minds and what he or she can accomplish by various investigative probes.

The approach has as much in common with *consulting* as it has with research. Yet, unlike much consulting, the outsider is not aiming to proffer prescriptions, recommendations, or judgements as such. Rather, by appropriate study and reporting, he or she is trying to increase communal awareness and bring local as well as wider-scale policy questions into sharper focus. The evaluation provides, within a single analysis, information and comment (including many different persons' 'evaluations') that can serve to promote discussions among those concerned with decisions concerning the system studied.

Oftentimes, a study will bring an issue (such as 'low staff morale') to the foreground of attention, that has hitherto been only part of the 'background' of a setting, known about at some level but effectively disregarded.

By drawing attention to staff morale, pulling together a variety of individual interpretations about why it is low, documenting how widespread it is, and showing how it has wider consequences, the evaluation study can have a profound effect on discussions of policy and practice. Our conviction is that the conventional definitions of the evaluator's role are self-defeating and that an over-concentration on 'impacts' and 'testing outcomes against intentions' can lead to the evaluator having his or her report promptly shelved.

To sum up, the subjects addressed in each study relate closely to concerns expressed: there are no fixed evaluation procedures and the exact purposes of each study are unique to that setting and to the particular policy discussions into which the report will be fed.

The Methodology

Evaluation is thus conceived in broad terms — to mean the study of an organization or curriculum in such a way that contributes to decision-making and review of policy. Such studies will often include review of the purported merits, problems, advantages, and negative side-effects of the programme's present policies but only as part of a more extended organizational analysis.

From the foregoing it is obvious that studies have to be *custom-built* — the initial strategies being chosen in accord with the complicated *contract* or *agreement* that emerges from negotiation. Moreover, each study has to be open-ended enough for the evaluator to home in on critical emerging issues.

Problems identified and discussed at the negotiation stage may correspond to those finally addressed, but not invariably so. The exact areas discussed at the reporting stage are those judged by the evaluator to be significant issues — in the light of what has been found out: significant to the participants themselves (e.g. a common difficulty but not one publicly admitted); or significant for explaining certain phenomena (e.g. trivial-seeming procedures that alienate substantial numbers of people); or significant by virtue of being central to the concerns of one or more *critical audiences* for the study (e.g. the cost implications of proposed changes in the programme).

The flexibility called for in a custom-built design requires an extended range and a choice of techniques to be used. They are chosen to fit the questions, opportunities, and restrictions that a particular investigation poses: problems dictating methods rather than methods dictating problems (Laurillard, 1978; Dearden, 1979). There has to be an assessment in each study of what methods will best serve investigative needs, with due regard to the time and other resources they consume; and also what will be responded to enthusiastically by those contributing information. Illuminative evaluations rely extensively on interviews and observing in the field, along with analyses of documents collected and short questionnaires often open-ended in structure. In addition, the study of stored records (e.g. admissions data, test scores, costs, numbers of students pursuing different options) often forms an integral part of an in-depth programmatic investigation.

Using different techniques in parallel also provides for *internal checks*. Each method has limitations and there is often an advantage in combining techniques and triangulating on issues from different directions methodologically.

Given the kind of study outlined, the *investigative design* obviously changes in the course of the inquiry in the light of the *expanding knowledge base*. Right from the beginning, the evaluator is formulating particular *thematic lines of inquiry*. This occurs in the following way. Each observational period, discussion, or interview is scrutinized as a data record: *major points* are noted (e.g. a repeated phenomenon, a contradiction between two opinions given, a succinct expression of a widespread attitude) and are grouped according to content. A cluster of major points may be identified as a tentative theme that in turn helps to organize other information being gathered. The delicate balance to achieve is when one identifies themes early enough to serve as effective organizing principles while avoiding getting 'locked into' a structured argument that prevents subsequent new information from being examined openly because it contradicts expectations.

This danger is partly avoided if the arrangement of themes is seen as tentative and one that undergoes *successive transformation* as new data are sought, analysed, and integrated with earlier material. Ultimately, of course, this 'open structure' will evolve into the more permanent chapter structure and argument of the final report.

A practical difficulty in any research relying heavily on field work is that a mass of information is collected, with the potential for massive overload. The *heuristic design* outlined here is such that modifications in the study can be made as emerging themes dictate leads to be followed up — with a switching of investigative resources to ensure that critical questions receive maximum research attention. Without such *progressive focusing* on selected phenomena there would be wastage of investigatory time and the likelihood of an irrelevant and rambling report. One cannot report everything — the selections about what to include are best made in the field while there is still time to gather missing data and check for accuracy.

Underlying Conceptual Framework

Embodied in any investigative approach are characteristic *working assumptions* or theories that may or may not be spelled out or even known about consciously, but which affect how studies are made. Several major assumptions underpin illuminative evaluation.

One obvious one is that a system (such as an academic department in a university) cannot be understood if viewed in isolation from its *wider contexts*: the academic institution of which it is part, the discipline or specialist intellectual community of which the department is a 'branch office', its geographical position on the campus, etc. Similarly, individual activities (e.g. courses) within the department need to be seen in their context: how they fare often becomes understandable when considered alongside the general philosophy, practices, ethos, rules, norms, and constraints of the department and the types of students it attracts and caters for.

In order to obtain this broad picture of systems within contexts, one needs to probe beyond 'surface' or local features and be working in an appropriately inductive mode. Often one cannot know beforehand what constitute the formative pressures upon a system from outside, nor what activities within the system are supported or undermined — although one can be sure there will be some.

A second tenet or requirement is to discover the *individual biography* of settings being examined. Each is unique in identifiable ways. The sense of an organizational unit (such as a programme) being *singular* is of the utmost phenomenological import to its members. The experiences of individuals, vivid and 'subjective' as they are, are closely tied to the intimate, familiar nature of their programme — its history, personalities, and prospects. Illuminative evaluation places considerable emphasis on discovering what people view as the defining qualities of their setting and on conveying a programme's essential character in any evaluation report. Failure to capture a *recognizable reality* may lead to a report being rejected out of hand, whatever its other merits.

The next point is that individuals are inevitably caught up in the *informal thinking* of their programme or setting, much of which they take for granted. As insiders who have become habituated to their environment, they no longer realize how much such thinking governs what transpires in the organization. Studies have to be organized so that such pervasive influences are discerned and studied in detail. This means that there can be no exclusive reliance on what people say but attention also to what is done in practice. Again, multiple methods are shown to be necessary.

A fourth assumption — without going into the philosophical arguments — is that there is no one absolute and agreed upon 'reality' that has an objective 'truth'. Rather, there are numerous different perspectives, many of which — in uncontentious realms — enjoy consensual validity, but others which are not shared at all widely. The investigator, in an illuminative evaluation, is therefore at pains to consult widely, teasing apart the different outlooks and — from a position of the *neutral outsider* — not endorsing any one viewpoint, outlook or set of beliefs to the exclusion of others.

The Values Embodied in the Approach

We move here into questions of the values held by evaluators, for the respect for different outlooks is based on the conviction that those in, say, an educational programme (the different teachers, the outside supervisors or advisers, the students) have not only insights that are worth knowing about, but also have a right to be heard. Each participant in an enterprise is a theory-builder, explainer, advocate, observer, rapporteur, informant; each has a unique perspective, vantage point, and 'stance'. Unthinkingly to include some points of view and not to take others into account has profound consequences for a study. An evaluation is vastly richer for there being broad participation with different value positions and outlooks given scope and opportunity to be expressed.

The evaluator assumes the position of being an orchestrator of opinions, an arranger of data, a summarizer of what is commonly held, a collector of suggestions for changes, a sharpener of policy alternatives. Illuminative evaluators do not act as judges and juries but, in general, confine themselves to summing up arguments for and against different interpretations, policies, and possible decisions.

A commitment to acknowledging multiple perspectives not only preserves the integrity and independence of the study but also signals to participants that they are not being 'used' as mere data points but have a significant place in the evaluation effort. In turn the chances are enhanced that the evaluators will gain acceptance and be trusted with people's genuine opinions as well as their active cooperation. Both the quality of the findings and the ultimate acceptability of the report depend on people viewing the study as fair, detached, honest, broad-based, and plain-speaking.

The evaluator needs to have negotiated a *consistent role* that goes with the general value stance he or she is adopting. It is partly for this reason that in many illuminative evaluations the report does not end up with emphatic, judgemental conclusions as this would not be congruent with the priorities expressed above. Usually, too, an 'open' report is negotiated as an essential condition for agreeing to undertake the study.

In pursuing evaluation studies, one needs to remember that all investigations of persons by other persons involve intervention to some extent in their personal and professional worlds: there is almost inevitably some invasion of privacy and some manipulation in order to carry out the study at all. Evaluators need a strong sense of professional responsibility. One can attempt to formulate codes of practice for practising evaluators but there are difficulties in so doing: ultimately there is no substitute for an acute awareness of others' rights (including the right to say no); the absolute requirement to preserve confidences; and the overriding rule not to 'investigate others in ways we would not ourselves like to be investigated' (Jamieson *et al.,* 1977).

Illuminative evaluation, pursued ineptly or with lack of attention to ethics or to politesse, can undoubtedly backfire and create a severe nuisance rather than a sense of benefit. Choice in who should undertake a study needs to be approached with care.

The discussion above, of the four vantage points, constitutes a briefly selective overview of illuminative evaluation. Noteworthy is that each component or basic characteristic tends to support other parts of the whole system: for example, the problems agreed to in the negotiation have to be possible to study in accord with the values of the evaluator; the commitment to examining wider contexts requires a holistic outlook; the need to be responsive to questions, uncertainties, and points of view of different parties requires a design that can be changed in the course of study; the mass of data emerging requires interim analyses of themes; and the articulation of this whole approach with the stated needs and requirements of those commissioning studies requires extended negotiation.

To sum up, illuminative evaluation clearly falls within the 'new paradigm' as generally understood (Hamilton *et al.*, 1977). As is implied in the idea of a paradigm change, much more is entailed than a simple shift in methodological preference. What has resulted is a complete re-thinking of the whole purposes and rationale of 'evaluation', the very assumptions of which are usually based on ideas of experimental design, formalized criteria, and statistical comparison. The illuminative approach, as it has developed over nearly a decade, embraces a whole set of still unusual features — assumptions, procedures, role definitions, and investigative purposes that are nevertheless congruent with a commitment to naturalistic methodology and a holistic perspective on human affairs.

Human Inquiry
Edited by P. Reason and J. Rowan
© 1981 John Wiley & Sons Ltd.

CHAPTER TWENTY

Endogenous research: rationale*

Magoroh Maruyama
*Department of Administrative Sciences, University of Southern
Illinois at Carbondale, USA*

In this chapter the term epistemology is used in the sense of the underlying structure of reasoning of an individual or of members of a culture, which may not necessarily be made explicit or verbalized, but which manifests itself in various aspects of the life of the individual or the member of the culture. Since the structure of reasoning may vary from individual to individual, or from culture to culture, we speak of epistemologies for the purpose of this chapter.

Some of the aspects of life in which the epistemologies are manifest are:

(1) Logical structure of verbal discourse
    Examples: Aristotelean deductive logic;
                Chinese logic of complementarity (Chang, 1938);
                Nominalism *vs.* universalism;
                Mandenka logic of heterogeneity (Camara, 1975).
(2) Concept of time
    Examples: Balinese time as cyclic;
                Western time as unidirectional flow;
                Japanese time as ephemerality.

*This chapter consists of selected portions of a much longer article entitled 'Endogenous research and polyocular anthropology' (Maruyama, 1978a). Further extracts may be found in Chapter 23 of this volume — Eds.

(3) Structure of universe

Examples: Hierarchical universe of Aristotle;

Categorizational universe of Linne;

Competitive universe of Darwin,

Navajo's mutualism between man, nature, spirits, animals, and ghosts;

Symbiotic universe.

(4) Religion

Examples: Christian and Mohammedan monotheism with one god as creator, prime mover, omniscient, omnipotent, and 'perfect';

Early Greek anthropomorphic polytheism;

Chinese religion as events and processes without god figure;

Navajo religion as technical, aesthetic, and pragmatic practice to maintain harmony with nature, spirits, animals, and ghosts.

(5) Social organization

Examples: American 'democracy' by assimilation and by majority rule over minorities (domination by quantity);

Non-hierarchical societies of Navajos and Eskimos;

Vertical mutualism of Japan (Maruyama, 1972).

(6) Scientific paradigms

Examples: Unidirectional cause-effect models;

Mutual causal models (von Foerster, 1949-53; Wiener, 1948; Milsum, 1968; Buckley, 1968; Maruyama, 1963a; Waddington, 1968-71; Riedl, 1976);

Random models and homogenization (Shannon and Weaver, 1949);

Differentiation-amplification models and heterogenization (Maruyama, 1978b).

Several Ways to Conceptualize Polyocularity

Since there are many epistemologies, as defined above, future anthropology must restructure itself with the recognition that not only the objects of research but also the researchers themselves may come from many epistemologies. This creates polyocular anthropology which incorporates different perspectives obtained with the use of different epistemologies. But the concept of polyocularity again varies from epistemology to epistemology.

Persons with a quantitative epistemology may see polyocularity as additive combinations of segmentary perspectives, such as the construction of a map from successive aerial photos. Some persons with still another version of quantitative epistemology may see polyocularity as successive enveloping of high-magnification pictures (microscopic pictures) by high-condensation pictures (telescopic pictures). In fact, persons with natural science background tend to use this scale concept of perspective.

On the other hand, persons with a non-quantitative epistemology may see polyocularity as synthesis of several overlays on the same map or as synthesis of different photos of the same object taken with different colour filters.

Furthermore, persons with a competitive epistemology may regard differences in perspectives as a conflict which must be resolved with a compromise, while persons with a complementary epistemology may view the differences in perspectives as non-contradictory and enriching useful information.

There are not only differences but also metadifferences between epistemologies. For example, a heterogeneistic epistemology can accommodate other epistemologies, while a homogeneistic epistemology must reject others. This is a metadifference. A heterogeneistic epistemology can become a meta-epistemology which includes other epistemologies as well as itself. But a homogeneistic epistemology cannot.

Steps Towards Polyocular Anthropology

There are several steps to be taken to attain polyocular anthropology:

(1) *Endogenous research* Each culture is studied by its insiders using endogenous epistemology, methodology, research design, and with endogenously relevant focus.

(2) *Binocular vision* Research by insiders and by outsiders can be juxtaposed to produce binocular vision, just as left- and right-eye vision combined produce three-dimensional perception not because the two eyes see different sides, but because the differences between the two images enable the brain to compute the invisible dimension.

(3) *Polyocular anthropology* A culture can be studied by research teams from several outside cultures. The results can be compared in order to produce an exogenous polyocular vision. If the culture is heterogeneous, it can also be studied by research teams from several inside subcultures. This will produce an endogenous polyocular vision. The subcultures may not be separate and self-contained entities, but may be interpenetrating; for example, the female and male subcultures. In most cultures females and males are not entirely separated. In fact, the pattern of the interaction between females and males characterizes these subcultures. Much of what the females do or think is a

result of their interaction with the males, and vice-versa. In this sense, the female and male visions are like the overlays discussed above, not segmentary fields of vision. Likewise, endogenous polyocular vision should be understood in the sense of overlays, *not* in the sense of a collection of mutually exclusive segmentary fields of vision. When an endogenous and an exogenous polyocular vision are combined, as in the *binocular vision,* we attain a polyocular anthropology.

Endogenous Research

The purpose of this chapter is to discuss endogenous research, which is the first step towards polyocular anthropology.

As defined above, endogenous research is conceptualized, designed, and conducted by researchers who are insiders of the culture, using their own epistemology and their own structure of relevance.

Though endogenous persons have been often used as data-collectors or information sources by outside researchers, the work of endogenous persons as conceptualizers, selectors of the focus of relevance, theory-makers, methodology-makers, hypothesis-makers, research designers, and data analysts is relatively new in white anthropologists' literature. This is largely due to the fact that only the works done in the academic format were recognized as acceptable research.

Only in a small number of cases were efforts made to conduct research in the endogenous format. For example, Worth (1967) and Worth and Adair (1972) had Navajos take films of their own life and edit them themselves, in order to study whether there were structural differences between the films the Navajos made and a film a white anthropologist would make. Robert McKnight is currently conducting a literature survey of endogenous research recorded in the past. [An example of the authors' own involvement in endogenous research projects may be found in Chapter 1 — Eds.]

Both Adair and I found that the *less* educated or trained the endogenous researchers were by academic standards, the more insightful and interesting their products turned out to be. The endogenous researchers in the projects turned out to be superior to the academic researchers in three other aspects in addition to the epistemological considerations: (1) philosophy regarding communication; (2) relevance dissonance; (3) criticality dissonance.

Philosophy Regarding Communication

In addition to the epistemological differences between cultures, there are other considerations which, if not taken into account, distort research. One of them is the cultural differences in the philosophy regarding communication. I first became aware of this consideration while I was studying interpersonal communication behaviour in Scandinavia (Maruyama, 1961; 1963b). In Sweden the main purpose of usual interpersonal communication is transmission of facts. In Denmark, on the other hand, the main purpose of usual interpersonal communication is perpetuation of a familiar atmosphere and a comfortable equilibrium of affect. The Swedes strive for factual interest and objective accuracy, while the Danes cultivate the art of not hurting one's own and others' feelings.

There, the most enjoyable type of communication takes place when a small number of persons gather frequently at the same place, eating the same pastry, sharing the same gossip. Repetition of the familiar is the key to the Danish 'cosiness' (*hygge*). Such communication is not focused on transmission of facts. It is oriented towards perpetuation of comfortable equilibrium.

A foreigner often makes the inevitable mistake in Denmark. With all good intentions he tries to win Danes' friendship by showing factual interests in Denmark, being inquisitive about Danish culture, and eager to explain his own culture and his point of view. An ordinary Dane may tolerate him for a while, but eventually will withdraw.

There are many other cultural differences in philosophy regarding communication. A research method imported from outside into a culture may encounter resistance to communication or produce purposefully phony responses.

Relevance Dissonance

In the white middle-class environment data-collection is generally accepted as a tool for direct or indirect improvement of the life of people from whom the data are collected. The purpose of data-collection as perceived by the people coincides with the researcher's purpose. The convergence of purposes between the community members and the researcher as perceived by the community people is called *relevance resonance*. In the white middle-class environment there usually is relevance resonance because the researcher usually is from the white middle-class, and shares the goals and the purposes with the community people, and the community people perceive him to be so.

This is not the case in some other cultures. For example, in most of the Native Americans' (American Indians') perception, the purpose of too many anthropological researches is to benefit the academic community or the museum, to satisfy the researcher's curiosity or vocational ambition, to contribute to the researcher's reputation and promotion, or simply to produce salaries for the researchers. In fact, some anthropologists regard Native Americans mainly from the point of view of these people's utility for academic theories. Some other anthropologists satisfy their drive for territoriality and possessiveness by selecting a tribe and calling it 'my tribe'. Still others become self-appointed spokesmen 'for' tribe members, while not allowing them to speak for themselves. Such persons erroneously assume that tribe members are not intelligent enough to do so. There are also less pretentious do-gooders who satisfy their own psychological needs with a delusion that they are doing some good for the tribe. In any case, Native Americans see researchers as leading an extravagant life (by Native standards), made possible by a research salary. In this sense the researchers are exploiters and parasites unless they prove otherwise by producing practical results congruent with the endogenous goals of the tribe.

The discrepancy of goals between the community people and the researcher as perceived by the community is called *relevance dissonance.* When relevance dissonance exists, the research project is useful to the community people only as a means for hustle. The community people may counter-exploit the project, or may simply give phony information to keep the researcher happy and busy with himself. Oppressed people are very skilled and sophisticated in the art of survival. Often the researcher is convinced that his research is useful for the community people, who actually can contrive ways to make him believe so.

The phenomena of relevance resonance and dissonance were revealed clearly in the prison project (see Chapter 23). Let me discuss this briefly.

Prison inmates often perceive the purposes of the academic researcher as: testing an academic hypothesis; proving and perpetuating a theory; producing publications as a tool for recognition, reputation, and promotion; gaining prestige of having worked with 'criminals'; or simply earning a living from a research salary.

On the other hand, most of the inmates feel that research should be undertaken for the following purposes:

(1) To make the public aware of the living and working conditions, physical and mental treatment, and some inadequate or arbitrary procedures in the prison which often fall far below what the public is led to believe.
(2) To make the society see, from an inside perspective, the environmental conditions that produce crimes, and from which most of the inmates came.
(3) If the inmate is suffering under specific injustice or abusive practice, to open a channel for rectifying the injustice.
(4) To improve through public pressure the often substandard vocational and education programmes in prison.
(5) To express their feelings and opinions which they think are entitled to be heard by the public.
(6) To have an opportunity to be considered as a human being, to be listened to and respected by the interviewer, and to talk on a person-to-person basis with the interviewer.

(7) To solve the inmate's psychological problems if the interviewer is a professional.

(8) Through the interviewer, to obtain contacts for or means for self-improvement, such as books, legal service, counselling, discussion groups, etc. (The means available within the prison are often very limited. Some prisons even discourage or deny such means.)

(9) To prevent young people in the society from becoming criminals.

Lack of relevance resonance produces phony information from the interviewee. The inmate detects the lack of relevance resonance in several ways: (1) noticing an instrumentalizing attitude in the interviewer; (2) giving reaction tests to the interviewer; and (3) observing the interviewer's action before and after the interview.

(1) *Instrumentalizing attitude* of the interviewer manifests itself in one or several of the following ways:

(a) using pre-set tests or pre-set questions which do not accommodate what the inmate really wants to communicate;

(b) considering the inmate as a response machine without allowing inter-change or independent contribution:

(c) considering the inmate as a statistical or clinical object;

(d) relying heavily on 'official records' of the inmate, attributing more validity to official records than to the inmate himself;

(e) building his knowledge on books and theories, even though he is unacquainted with real situations;

(f) posing himself as an 'expert' while discrediting the inmate's experience and insight as 'unscientific';

(g) being distrustful of the inmate;

(h) being insensitive to, unresponsive to, or unaware of the inmate's feelings;

(i) lacking interest in, or desire to know, the inmate's point of view and concern;

(j) being evasive in expressing his own points of view, attitudes, feelings, and goals;

(k) being aloof;

(l) having a patronizing or condescending attitude;

(m) being naive regarding the way the prison operates;

(n) being apathetic or lacking a cause, involvement, and commitment.

(2) The reaction test consists in (a) *value test* and (b) *click-in test*. In the value test, the inmate drops hints and observes the reaction of the interviewer in order to detect the interviewer's value orientation. In the click-in test, the inmate mentions some topic casually to see whether the interviewer catches its

relevance and picks up the topic or remains unaffected by the topic. Examples of such topics are: police harassment, court-appointed attorneys, school-teachers, store-owners, genocide.

(3) The *action observation* method consists in seeing whether the interviewer puts in action what he promises or advocates; how promptly and energetically he does so; and how skilful he is in manoeuvring through the obstacles.

When members of a culture perceive relevance dissonance with a researcher, they may feel exploited and may attempt counter-exploitation without letting him realize it. They can even nourish a delusion of his 'relevance' to them in order to exploit him, to keep him happy at a safe distance, or to enjoy making him look foolish in their eyes without permitting him to be aware of it.

Endogenous researchers can set up research with purposes that are relevant to the members of the culture, and therefore relevance resonance can easily be obtained.

It is not impossible for a researcher from outside to attain relevance resonance with the members of the culture *if* he makes his purposes converge with theirs. But even this process can be facilitated greatly with help from endogenous researchers.

Criticality Dissonance

Life in some cultures involves several types of dangers, of which the researcher may be unaware. The community people, who are *aware* that the researcher is *unaware* of the dangers, fear that the researcher may unsuspectingly let the data leak out to what the researcher assumes to be a safe place. In such cases the community people give phony data to the researcher for the purpose of self-protection, not necessarily for the purpose of deception. Such distortion of data due to data-giver's awareness of the data-collector's unawareness of the dangers is called distortion due to *criticality dissonance.*

The dangers that community members fear may come either (1) from persons connected with the authority system imposed from outside; or (2) from members of the community.

In both cases, the existence of the primary danger sources can be used as a leverage by those who manipulate the fear of the primary danger sources. These manipulators are the secondary danger sources. The term secondary does *not* mean less dangerous. In fact, the secondary danger sources may be as deadly or deadlier than the primary danger sources. Then there are those who manipulate the fear of the secondary danger sources. These are tertiary danger sources. To be more specific:

Primary danger sources: livestock reduction agents, money-collectors, thieves, policemen, prison guards, etc.

Secondary danger sources: snitches (finks, informers) who give real or purposefully fictitious informaiton to the primary danger sources for the purpose of having the primary danger sources strike the informer's rivals or for the purpose of being rewarded by the primary danger sources.

Tertiary danger sources: counterspies, snitch-killers, false-jacketers (those who label an innocent man as a snitch in order to have him killed by snitch-killers).

Fourth level danger sources: the false-jacketed (who must retaliate and kill the man whom he believes to be his false-jacketer), detectors of false-jacketers, etc.

As in the case of relevance dissonance, the phenomenon of criticality dissonance can be illustrated most vividly by using the prison project as an example.

Criticality Dissonance in Prison Culture

(1) *Danger from other inmates.* The prison life is characterized by extreme scarcity of things and occasions which fulfil basic human needs. These needs range from material ones, such as cigarettes and toothpaste, physical needs of sex, to emotional needs, such as expression of manhood, proof of one's own worth to himself, recognition by others, autonomy, and privacy. Therefore, a conflict over one pack of cigarettes, one small insult, or inadvertent physical contact may lead to physical fights and murder, as we will see in the list of 'Interpersonal and Individual Factors', (see Chapter 23).

(2) *Danger from prison guards.* There are two forms of danger from prison guards: harassment and abuse. Harassment is hostile behaviour within legal limits or with a legal pretext on the part of the guards. Abuse is illegal hostile behaviour on the part of the guards, such as physical assault or denial of medical care.

Let us emphasize that there are individual differences among prison guards. Some are calm. Others have tempers. Some are fair. Others are sadistic. Some are respected by inmates. Others are despised. Not all guards practise harassment or abuse. But what is relevant in the inmate life is that there are harassments and abuses which become the source of a realistic fear.

Harassment and abuse have three functions: message, harm, and provocation. The message is: 'I hate you. I am doing this to you because I hate you. You hate me but you cannot do anything to me.' The harm may be physical or otherwise: beating, shooting, suspension of a privilege, denial of a legal right, destruction of personal belongings, inconveniences, etc. Provocation has the purpose of inciting a hostile attitude in inmates to rationalize the guard's abuse which follows the provocation.

The direct harm may be negligible as compared to the message it intends to communicate and to the provocation it intends to create. The message and the provocation, much more than harm, create resentment and tension. Outsiders tend to see only the direct harm without realizing the message, the provocation, and the resulting tension. This is why the outsiders are unaware of or unappreciative of the fear and the indignation in the prison inmates.

(3) *Information to be hidden from other inmates*
(a) *Number of cigarettes one possesses.* Cigarettes function as money in the prisons. If it is known that an inmate has many of them, he may be pressured to repay his debts, to make loans to someone, or to engage in wheeling and dealing as a partner. Or if it becomes known that his supply is depleted, his bluffing and bargaining power decreases.
(b) *Amount of other items in possession.* To prevent theft, this information should be kept secret.
(c) *Amount of debts.* If this is known, one may become the victim of loan sharks, or someone may offer financial help or physical protection from debt collectors in exchange for a homosexual act.
(d) *Amount of gambling gain.* If this becomes known, one may be pressured into repaying debts.
(e) *Payment to protector.* If it is known that an inmate is paying someone for physical protection from an enemy, others may challenge the protector to take his business away.
(f) *Plot against other inmates.* Plots for physical attack or for financial or sexual exploitation.

(4) *Spies for other inmates.* A spy for other inmates, when discovered, is likely to be challenged to a physical fight.

(5) *Information to be hidden from the guards.* There are reasonable as well as unreasonable regulations. The inmate may violate regulations for good or bad purposes. Inmates protect one another from punishment, harassment, and abuse. Inmate ethics require that an inmate would rather suffer a false accusation by guards than disclose another's hidden facts.

(6) *Snitches.* Spies for the prison authority are called snitches. Snitching is the most despised and resented act among inmates. If a snitch is discovered, he may be killed or pressured into paying a large portion of his monthly allowance for several years to the person to whom he snitched. Sometimes a guard may spread a false rumour that an inmate is a snitch in order to get the inmate attacked by other inmates. Or the guards may set several inmates against one another by telling each of them that the others have snitched on him.

(7) *Informers against guards and prison authority.* Inmates who expose to outsiders the harassment, abuses, and other irregularities practised in the prison are retaliated against by the guards and the prison authority. They may be punished or subjected to greater harassments and abuses. Their release may be postponed for several years. The prison authority tightly controls the information channels to the outside. Letters from inmates are censored. Visitors, as well as the inmates who talk with the visitors, are registered. Thus the prison authority has several means to identify the inmates who have informed against prison authority. Therefore visitors who receive information from the inmates cannot publicly use it against prison authority for fear of retaliation. This renders the use of such information ineffective.

(8) *Research participants suspected as snitches.* Inmates have good reasons to suspect that research findings can fall into the wrong hands. The researchers and the organizers or sponsors of research may make their best efforts to keep the data confidential. But they may be unaware of all the dangers of information-giving and all the complex channels of information leakage and may unwittingly pass information to someone who may snitch or slip. An inmate has no reason to give any information to anyone unless there is a very worthwhile cause for which he is willing to risk the danger which may result from the information-giving, and unless there is evidence (promise is not enough) of absolute confidentiality.

(9) *Administrative harassment.* If the prison authority suspects that research is producing information that the prison authority wants to hide, the project may be administratively harassed or terminated, and the inmate researchers and the interviewees may be transferred to units or jobs which make them incapable of participation in further research activities. If individual guards fear the research project, they may harass and abuse the inmate researchers and the interviewees.

Aside from the leakage of hidden facts, there are some other considerations that cause the prison staff to resist research. A prison, like many other institutions, has a well-established tradition and a subtly maintained equilibrium among its mutually opposing components. For example, the prison schoolteacher may disagree with the guards on the treatment of inmates, but both sides sustain a workable relationship buffered by elaborate routines. A new project of any type may upset the tradition and the equilibrium. Especially a research project using inmates as researchers may cause anxiety among the prison staff for the following reasons:

(a) Research activities may upset daily routines. For example, (1) permitting inmates to go to a privilege area where the interview is held creates unwanted traffic; (2) taking them away from their daily assignments creates a shortage of manpower; (3) issuing passes to interviewees creates extra paperwork.

(b) The administrative policy to permit the presence of a new type of project may alter the balance of power between conflicting factions within the prison.

(c) Use of inmates as researchers may upset the traditional 'place' (status) of inmates.

(d) Those who regard certain parts of the prison as their personal territory may feel their psychological security threatened by the trespassing research project.

(e) Those staff members whose self-image is built on 'knowing the inmates' better than anybody else may feel their self-image challenged by the research project.

(f) Those who are supposed to know the inmates but do not may fear that their ignorance or incompetence may be revealed by the project.

If the anxiety level becomes sufficiently high, the prison staff can harass the project or create inconvenience and difficulties to disable the project. If the anxiety level is kept to the minimum, the project may obtain the full cooperation of the prison staff. Our teams decided that the less conspicuous the project, the less anxiety it would create among the staff. We behaved as if ours was not a new type of project; we also took special care not to violate any rules or offend the prison staff. In the dining room I avoided sitting with white-collar staff members who tended to ask me questions about the project.

Human Inquiry
Edited by P. Reason and J. Rowan
© 1981 John Wiley & Sons Ltd.

CHAPTER TWENTY-ONE

Issues of validity in new paradigm research

Peter Reason
*Centre for the Study of Organizational Change and
Development, University of Bath, UK*
and John Rowan
Independent Consultant, London, UK

The issue of validity is of critical importance for inquiry within any research paradigm; certainly, writings on traditional research method lay considerable emphasis on the issue, and devote much space to considerations of threats to validity and to ways of countering these threats. In new paradigm research, considerations of the issue have been scattered. In this chapter we are drawing from a number of sources to put together a coherent statement about the principles and practices which lead towards more valid inquiry within the new research paradigm.

In orthodox research a first approach to validity relates to measurement: a valid measure is one which 'measures what it purports to measure'. This validity may be 'definitional', in that the measure itself plays a major part in defining the term to be measured, or the validity may be based on 'empirical connections' with other measures and indications. Usually, of course, validity rests on some combination of these two. The essential notion of a valid measure is that it is reaching out for some 'true measure' which is in the end unattainable: validity is always relative, sufficient for some purpose. Possible errors in measurement are twofold: first, there is always a limit to the discriminations that an instrument may make; and second, the measuring instrument may be 'inaccurate' in that repeated measures do not yield identical results. (The reader is referred to Kaplan, 1964, for a fuller discussion of these issues).

A second traditional approach to validity relates to experimentation (Campbell and Stanley, 1966). The questions here are about internal validity

239

('Did in fact the experimental treatments make a difference in this specific experimental instance?'); and about external validity ('To what populations, settings, treatment variables, and measurement variables can this effect be generalized?'). In their important discussion of experimental and quasi-experimental designs, Campbell and Stanley identify eight threats to internal validity, a further four to external validity, and then demonstrate a whole range of research designs which may meet these threats.

Another way of looking at validity is to think about the different *sorts* of validity in which we may be interested. We have already referred to the distinction between external and internal validity. We can also refer to *face* validity — whether it 'looks right' to the reasonably discriminating observer; to *convergent* validity — whether a number of measures which purport to measure the same thing all point in the same direction, or whether a number of different viewpoints yield a similar picture; and in contrast to *discriminant* validity — which is about whether measures that are supposed to measure different things actually do come up with a difference. Then we can move to more complex questions such as *construct* validity, which involves defining and measuring an unobservable abstract or theoretical notion through its associated observables, and whether these observables can be construed in terms of more than one construct. Finally, as we move away from experimental studies towards field studies, we have notions of *contextual* validity, which is about how any particular piece of data fits in with the whole picture (Diesing, Chapter 15).

Obviously this is a very brief review of validity in traditional research. Hopefully it is sufficient to show that it is an important and rather interesting notion, one that should not be ignored by new paradigm researchers, and that there are a lot of ideas that we can borrow and develop. But it is important to note that most of these ideas about validity are based on the kind of traditional logic which we have shown to be inadequate for human inquiry in the PHILOSOPHY section of this book. If we want to develop an idea of validity in new paradigm research we must base it on an interactive, dialectical logic. In addition, from a new paradigm perspective these traditional notions of validity are all about *methods* and not much about *people*: they do not seem to have much to do with questions like, 'How will I know, and how will *we* know?' We have learned from hermeneutics that method in itself does not lead to knowledge (Kockelmans, 1975; Gadamer, 1975), and we are clear that inquiry is a particularly human process. As Rogers (1961) points out:

> scientific methodology needs to be seen for what it truly is, 'a way of preventing me from deceiving myself in regard to my creatively formed subjective hunches which have developed out of the relationship between me and my material'.

So what about validity in new paradigm research?

We have to start by looking at our notion of *truth*: the whole point about research, about checking our ideas somehow against 'reality', is to get nearer to some notion of truth, to somehow get it right. An important criterion of the truth of a set of propositions is that they are coherent with our experience of 'reality'. And we have to develop some notion of reality which gets away from the subject-object split — reality as either all out there, objective and therefore discoverable, or all in my mind, subjective and ineffable. Schwartz and Ogilvy (1979) argue that we can move away from notions of objectivity and subjectivity, by developing the notion of *perspective*. This defines 'a personal view from some distance' and 'suggests neither the universality of objectivity nor the personal bias of subjectivity' (p. 53). And as Bateson puts it (in Brockman, 1977):

> The word 'objective' becomes, of course, quite quietly obsolete; and at the same time the word 'subjective', which normally confines 'you' within your skin, disappears as well. It is, I think, the debunking of the objective that is the important change. The world is no longer 'out there' in quite the same way that it used to seem to be....
>
> I have to use the information that that which I see, the images, or that which I feel as pain, the prick of a pin, or the ache of a tired muscle — for these too are images created in their respective modes — that all this is neither objective truth nor is it hallucination. There is a combining or marriage between an objectivity that is *passive* to the outside world and a creative subjectivity, neither pure solipsism nor its opposite.
>
> Consider for a moment the phrase, *the opposite of solipsism*. In solipsism, you are ultimately isolated and alone, isolated by the premise 'I make it all up'. But at the other extreme, the opposite of solipsism, you would cease to exist, becoming nothing but a metaphoric feather blown by the winds of external 'reality'.... Somewhere between these two is a region where you are partly blown by the winds of reality and partly an artist creating a composite out of inner and outer events (p. 245).

So we have to learn to think dialectically, to view reality as a process, always emerging through a self-contradictory development, always becoming; reality is neither subject nor object, it is both wholly independent of me and wholly dependent on me. This means that any notion of validity must concern itself both with the knower and with what is to be known: valid knowledge is a matter of *relationship*. And of course this validity may sometimes be enhanced if we can say we know, rather than simply I know: we can move towards an intersubjectively valid knowledge which is beyond the limitations of one knower.

We also have to move away from the idea that there is *one* truth, that there is some simple continuum between 'error' and 'truth'. Certainly there are many ways of being 'wrong' (ignorance, illusion, collusion, delusion, hallucination, lies...) and also as many ways of being 'right'. Certainly this is the argument which Maruyama develops in his case for polyocular anthropology (Chapter 20) and in his discussion of 'heterogenistics' (1978b). Traditional research, based on a 'homogenistic' epistemology, is based in:

> Belief in the existence of one truth. If people are informed, they will agree.... Objectivity exists independent of the perceiver. Quantitative measurement is basic to knowledge (p. 78).

In contrast to this, knowledge within a heterogenistic epistemology is:

> Polyocular: binocular vision enables us to see three-dimensionally, because the *differential* between two images enables the brain to compute the invisible dimension. Cross-subjective analysis enriches our understanding (p. 78).

Maruyama points out that heterogenistic processes which increase differentiation may be found in all sorts of biological and social processes: they *increase* complexity, diversity, and structure, *increase* the amount of information available, and have enormous survival value for ecological systems. In terms of research, accepting, allowing, encouraging, and celebrating heterogenistic viewpoints will lead to an increase in our understanding. Bateson (1979) similarly points out that an increment of knowledge may result from multiple versions of the world (see also Mitroff on alternative inquiry systems, Chapter 3).

The primary strength of new paradigm research, its fundamental claim to being a valid process, lies in its emphasis on personal encounter with experience and encounter with persons. As Heron has shown earlier (Chapter 2) in this book, a research process which does not rest on experiential knowledge is not research about persons but hangs in a predicative void (see also Gendlin, 1962). Experiential research involves the joint encounter of co-researchers, and Torbert's notion of an action science is similarly based on a collaborative encounter among one's own experience, others' experience, and the outside world. The basis of new paradigm research is an encounter with experiential knowledge: these are the data whose validity we are considering.

Questions about the validity of these data are threefold. The first issue is descriptive: can I/we discriminate what is actually there? Can we notice, can we map the phenomena we experience? Here we have parallels with the earlier notion of validity in measurement: what are the limits to what we can discriminate? And there is a second aspect to this question, which is can I/we discriminate what might be there? What are the possibilities for human experience and action? This seems to be a question of great importance, but one which is not included in traditional approaches to validity. A dialectical view of truth as becoming must include the notion that there are always emerging possibilities which are not yet included. This can be called possibilia mapping (Heron, 1977a), or *catalytic* validity.

A second question for validity in new paradigm research is not about description but about trying out. If we engage in intentional interaction (Heron) or in action science (Torbert), if we make self-directed changes in the way we conduct our lives, how can we be sure that the changes we make bring about the outcomes we observe? Here we have obvious parallels with the notion of internal validity in experimental studies, which Campbell and Stanley seek to reinforce through their experimental and quasi-experimental designs. Although we must ask these questions in less deterministic ways, we must make sure we are not kidding ourselves.

The third question for validity is about meaning, about the understanding and interpretation of phenomena: we often want to go beyond a simple description of what we see to develop an *explanation* which will help account for the things we see (see Harré, Chapter 1 in this volume). When we do this, we must remember above all that 'the map is not the territory', that our explanation of a thing is not the thing itself. As we have learned from hermeneutics, the only criterion for the 'rightness' of an interpretation is *inter-subjective* — that is to say that it is right for a group of people who share a similar world (see Chapter 10). But it is also important to realize that when considering the validity of an interpretation we are not solely concerned about being right, as Torbert points out in Chapter 29. He writes:

> By positing the broad notions of analytical, political, and onto-logical validity, I mean to remind us that we are always confronted with three simultaneous dilemmas: (1) whether we are right given our way of framing the situation; (2) whether we ought or ought not to allow ourselves to be 'interrupted' by other claims to our attention in the environment; and (3) whether our way of framing the situation is in fact fruitful and meaningful. Balance among these dilemmas sharpens the questions and counters 'onesidedness' (personal communication, 1980).

In other words we need to consider not only 'is it right?', but also 'is it useful?' and 'is it illuminating?'.

What, then, are the threats to validity in new paradigm research? One broad answer to this is that the validity of our inquiry is threatened if we do not have the issues sharply delineated; and so a part of the function of this chapter is to begin to map out the questions. Another answer is that validity is threatened when the dialectical process of emerging truth gets 'stuck'. The basic way in which this happens (and this is true for all forms of inquiry), is that we cease to pay attention to that part which we create: we block the dialectic by working one-sidedly. Paradoxically, such one-sidedness occurs in both 'subjectivism' and 'objectivism'. In the former we look only inwards, so all we can learn about is our preconceptions; in the latter we look only outwards at the phenomena we are trying to understand, and in doing so we forget the part that we play as knowers, and we are unable to see that which we are unawarely contributing. So we must move continually round the hermeneutic circle from what we know to what we do not know. And as Rowan points out, this kind of soft rigour is only fully possible at the Realized level of consciousness.

To get a bit more specific, there are two main ways in which the validity of inquiry may be threatened: through unaware projection, and through consensus collusion. As we have reviewed elsewhere (Chapter 7) Devereux has pointed out that every time we do research we stir up our own unconscious material, and that this produces a disturbance that can be seen as counter-transference — the researcher projects his own internal problems onto the world he is supposedly studying. Similarly with consensus collusion, a whole group of researchers or co-researchers may band together in defence of their anxieties and

> sustain a tacit norm to the effect that certain areas of experience, ranges of human potentiality, behavioral possibilities, shall be overlooked so that the adequacy of the theory is not called experientially into question (Heron, 1971, p. 15).

These seem to us to be quite massive threats to the validity of an approach which rests primarily on a collaborative encounter with experience. At the same time, if we look at all the different approaches to new paradigm research, we can find many ways of countering these threats and strengthening the validity of our work. But these ways are not methodological: we cannot offer the equivalent of validation through the 'multi-trait-multi-method matrix' (Campbell and Fiske, 1959). Rather, validity in new paradigm research lies in the skills and sensitivities of the researcher, in how he or she uses herself as a knower, as an inquirer. Validity is more personal and interpersonal, rather than methodological. The following processes can be seen as heuristic guides which, if used skilfully, may be used to increase the validity of an inquiry.

(1) *Valid research rests above all on high-quality awareness on the part of the co-researchers*

The need for high-quality awareness has been emphasized by Heron (Chapter 2 in this volume) who says that 'the discipline and rigour involved in this sort of research is formidable', as well as by Torbert, whose initial axiom for an action science is 'that a person must undergo a to-him unimaginable scale of self-development before he becomes capable of relationally valid action' (1976a, p. 167). This high-quality awareness is state-specific in Tart's terms (1972) by which is meant that certain aspects of human experience (and not necessarily esoteric ones) can only be experienced within specific states of consciousness, and that therefore the researcher must develop high-quality, discriminating awareness, within that state of consciousness. Obvious examples of this would be with research into altered states of consciousness, where clearly one has to be 'competent' within a particular state before being able to inquire into it; and with therapeutic disciplines such as co-counselling, which can only be understood from the perspective of the balance of attention between the present adult and the distressed child. A less obvious example would be research into the female situation, which can only be well done from a perspective clearly aware of the mystifications surrounding the role and nature of women (see Helen Callaway's contribution to this volume — Chapter 39). One cannot understand any psychological state without the capacity to experience it, nor any social situation unless one can get into the 'world-taken-for-granted' perspective of those involved; yet at the same time as 'getting into' the experience, the researcher needs to be able to maintain a perspective on it. This high-quality awareness can be attained through training and practice, through learning to attend simultaneously to a variety of levels of personal experience (see Chapter 37). Nevertheless, this is a formidable requirement:

> We were at the 8,000-foot level in the *Nilgiris* (blue mountains) of South India when my eighty-four-year old hiking companion, stopping to allow me to catch my breath, told me about *Ashtaavadhaana.* We had been hiking together regularly these mornings, and our conversation was of bits and snatches of modern sociological thought from me and healthy chunks of Sanskrit language, philosophy, and cultural history from him. *Ashtaavadhaana,* he said, was a word representing the normal, perhaps minimally required, level of awareness, alertness, or intelligent attention for the beginning scholar in the Sanskrit tradition. It means, literally, 'the capability of being aware of eight things simultaneously'. In olden times, he told me, a test

based upon this word would be devised for the candidate to schooling in Sanskrit philosophy.... [My] instructor continued, 'There is another Sanskrit word, *Sataavadhaana*. It means 'the capability of being aware of one hundred things simultaneously'. For this, too, there is a test...' (Boughey, 1978).

(2) *Such high-quality awareness can only be maintained if the co-researchers engage in some systematic method of personal and interpersonal development*

This kind of high-quality awareness can only be maintained, and the problems of countertransference managed, if the co-researchers engage in some form of personal and interpersonal maintenance and development. It seems to us that the researcher must *actively* explore the stirrings of his or her own unconscious while engaged in research, and that it is essential that she or he is practised and competent in a discipline for doing this. Our own preferred discipline is co-counselling (Jackins, 1965, Heron, 1973b); on a number of occasions we have discovered, through counselling, that an important yet troublesome piece of work seemed to be acting as the focus for some favourite personal rigid patterns of reaction, and it helps to be able to discharge some of the associated distress and arrive at a new clarity. But co-counselling is not the only answer; there are many disciplines to self-awareness (see Chapters 10 and 37).

This argument for personal awareness will, no doubt, raise a lot of objections; certainly it has been at the heart of many vigorous debates with colleagues who have read earlier drafts of this section. One objection is that we are being elitist, claiming that only certain people are 'pure' enough to do research; this is followed by arguing that such purity is unattainable anyway. A second objection is to the effect that, 'I really know myself well enough, I know my bias as a researcher, without going to all these lengths'. And a third objection is that every researcher brings to the research her own biases, her own rigidities of character structure, and that these contribute to her own perspective on research and are to be valued.

We do not accept these objections (although we are curious about the amount of energy which seems to be behind them; as one of our critics implied, maybe he didn't *want* to take up our suggestions, maybe he didn't *want* to be disturbed). We are simply repeating the ancient injunction 'Know thyself' which has been repeated (and repeatedly ignored) through the ages. We cannot study human processes except as aware human beings, and for this we require a 'way' to self-knowledge, a process of self-inquiry, which is systematic and which is powerful enough to reach into unconscious processes, since that is where the disturbances are likely to lie (see Schumacher, 1977, for an interesting review of these issues).

(3) *Valid research cannot be conducted alone*

For very similar reasons to those explored above, there is always a need in research for colleagues, peers, mentors, 'friends willing to act as enemies' (Torbert, 1976a) who can challenge and shock one out of habitual ways of thinking and experiencing. Torbert argues:

> That a conversation with lifetime friends (each of whom may be pursuing different disciplines to self-discovery) is potentially the most embracing system for illuminating one's conscious lopsidedness (personal communication, 1980).

To do research one needs both people who will offer support and people who will challenge and confront; it helps if these relationships are clearly negotiated. Consensus collusion in collaborative research can be countered by inviting some of the co-researchers to take 'devil's advocate' roles, so that confronting, challenging, disagreeing, picking holes, and so on is built in to the inquiry process.

(4) *The validity of research is much enhanced by the systematic use of feedback loops, and by going round the research cycle several times*

Our fourth point towards valid inquiry is about *cycles* of research, which can be illustrated contrasting the use of interviews in research and in journalism. Once we start to do research which does not conform to the general requirements of experimental method, we run the risk of being accused of being mere journalists; indeed, we run the risk of *being* mere journalists. Journalists are often called researchers: they have to plan an investigation, interview people, ask pertinent questions, perhaps uncover new facts or reach surprising conclusions, check facts from more than one source, communicate the results effectively, and so forth. How is this different from the kinds of research at the non-alienating end of the spectrum which we are concerned about in this book?

This is an important question, because many people begin their research, as do some journalists, by doing unstructured interviews; but it seems that they then either rush off into some kind of quantitative analysis of, or taking off from, these interviews and ignore them when writing their final reports, or else they treat the interviews as the research, without *re*-searching at all.

So what exactly is the difference between a researcher like Madison (see Chapter 27) and a journalist like, for example, Gail Sheehy (1976). They both do interviews: Madison did all his own interviews, Sheehy did quite a number, but mainly used other people's. They both produce theories: maybe Sheehy's is not as interesting as Madison's, but that is a matter of judgement. They both check the same area from different directions: Madison does it by getting written and spoken data, by asking peers about peers, and by following the same individual for several years; Sheehy does it by comparing accounts of different investigators. And they publish differently, but this is an accidental difference. So what is the difference between research and journalism?

The first and foremost difference is that Madison went round the research cycle more times. Over and over again he interviewed, theorized, fed back his theories to the next lot of students, interviewed more (observed, read diaries, gave tests, etc.), theorized, fed back, tried out, interviewed.... Over and over again he checked his impressions, his tentative conclusions, his concepts, his categories, refining and clarifying and deepening and differentiating them. When he finally wrote his book it was with a sense of having reached a reasonably stable point in the process. Sheehy, on the other hand, did what amounted to just one round (or at most two or three); she did not make the same number of opportunities to check her data. A journalistic inquiry tends to relatively impressionistic.

Another difference is that journalists tend not to feed back to their subjects the conclusions they are coming to; certainly Sheehy did not involve her subjects in the same kind of depth as did Madison, and certainly journalists have a reputation for being extremely unwilling to share their findings, or to show one the transcribed or edited interview. And so are some researchers, fearful of 'contaminating' their data with the experience of their subject. But one of the most characteristic things about good research at the non-alienating end of the spectrum is that it goes back to the subjects with the tentative results, and refines them in the light of the subjects' reactions.

We can now say something about research proper, and about how to turn interviews into research. We need to make the first and most open-ended part of the research subject to a rigour and stringency which should apply to the whole project. This is a rigour of softness, of discovery, of turning things over. Instead of an 'unstructured' approach, which simply leaves the way open for all the cultural expectations to get in the way of finding anything out, there needs to be an approach which deliberately opens up the area, and gives explicit permission to explore usually *unacknowledged* realities. Madison did not just ask people about their present experience — his notion of the child-self enabled him to open up and probe into the relevance of previous family experience upon present reality.

Then, instead of a 'hit and run' approach which sucks the subject dry and leaves her by the wayside, there needs to be an involvement with the person which enables a process of correction of impressions to take place. This should not exclude the possibility of the interviewee doing some theorizing and some checking too. As Sims shows in Chapter 32, under the right conditions 'interviewees' can quite easily turn themselves into co-researchers.

Finally, instead of a single cycle of data collection, there need to be multiple cycles, where the theory, concepts, and categories are progressively extended and refined, differentiated and integrated, reaching towards a theoretical saturation. This is a rigour of clarity, accuracy, and precision. There are at least three ways of re-cycling like this: if one is interested in causal, empirical connections between phenomena, it is useful to start with 'soft' and relatively qualitative cycles, and move towards 'hard', quantitative cycles; if one is interested in descriptive research, one can start with crude and obvious categories and cycle towards ever more subtle distinctions; and if one is interested in discovering meaning, in explaining what is going on, one can start from initial interpretations and move towards deeper insights. In this way we can turn so-called qualitative research (which is so often mere journalism) into research proper. Examples of recycling can be found in the chapters by Torbert, Esterson, Eldon, Brown, Madison, and Sims.

(5) *Valid research involves a subtle interplay between different forms of knowing*

This point has already been made by Heron in Chapter 2, where he differentiates between experiential knowledge, practical knowledge, presentational knowledge, and propositional knowledge. His criticism of much orthodox research is that it is propositional knowledge disconnected from the experiential knowledge of those it purports to represent. Similarly Torbert (1976a) argues for some equivalent of practical knowledge in his statement about the value of an action science 'useful to the actor at the moment of action rather than to a disembodied thinker at the moment of reflection'. While all four forms of knowledge can have a validity in their own right, it seems that if our knowing rests on just *one* of these, this is a relatively 'thin' form of knowledge, while if our knowing rests on all four it is much 'thicker' and thus more substantial. Thus one can imagine knowing which is a 'laminate' of several 'layers' as more valid than 'single sheet' knowing.

(6) *Contradiction can be used systematically*

This needs little explanation: the co-researchers can attempt actively and consciously to deny, contradict, disprove, the data which are available and the propositions about that data which he has developed. This is close to the conventional notion of falsification, and is part of the effective use of collaborators.

(7) *Convergent and contextual validity can be used to enhance the validity of any particular piece of data*

We have already argued for multiple viewpoints in research, and these lead us to the notions of convergent and contextual validation, drawn from traditional research, and to notions of polyocularity (Maruyama, Chapter 20 in this volume). The researcher can use a number of different methods, a number of different perspectives, and compare the views. Similarly, the value of evidence from different sources can be compared and assessed. Or a research team may be formed containing a range of co-researchers with different backgrounds and perspectives.

(8) *The research can be replicated in some form*

Finally, if you doubt another's research you can sometimes go and do it yourself. Of course, if you come to different conclusions, this does not mean that one of you is right and the other wrong: the two pieces of research will probably build on each other and contribute to a binocular vision.

So there seem to be a number of ways in managing the validity issue in new paradigm research: we have argued for cultivating high-quality awareness, for engaging in some discipline for personal and interpersonal maintenance and development, for going round the research cycle several times, for using contradiction, for multiple viewpoints, and for some form of replication. None of this seems particularly easy; but then if it did we would not need a concept of *re*-search. New paradigm research rests on valid foundations because it has an adequate conception of human experience and action. We have shown that this opens up massive threats to validity. And finally we have shown that if we think in terms of the validity of knowledge in process, which is tied up with a particular knower, there is an awful lot we can do to increase the validity of our inquiry.

EXAMPLES

Human Inquiry
Edited by P. Reason and J. Rowan
© 1981 John Wiley & Sons Ltd.

CHAPTER TWENTY-TWO

Sharing the research work: participative research and its role demands

Max Elden
Institute for Industrial Social Research, Technical University of Norway, Trondheim, Norway

The idea of research 'subjects' participating actively in the research concerning them seems foreign to the scientific enterprise. In work research, however, around the problem of actively involving workers in studying and changing their own workplaces, social science research can contribute more if it is participatory. What is 'participatory research?' How does it differ from other kinds of social science research? What kind of researcher role does it require?

It is not accidental that my experience in participative research has occurred in Norway as a work researcher. Much of the social science-based work research in Norway the last two decades has been quite practical and action-oriented, and in recent years increasingly participative (Elden, 1979b). This has contributed to and been reinforced by Norway's unique and in some ways revolutionary quality work life (QWL) law passed in 1977. It regulates not only physical aspects of health and safety but also psychological and social aspects. One of its most striking provisions entitles employees to initiate and participate in efforts to improve their own workplaces (Gustavsen, 1977; Gustavsen and Hunnius, 1980). Both this law and Norwegian work research are aimed at improving and democratizing working life. The case I analyse is one of several projects in Norway aimed at realizing these political values.

How much participatory research contributes to democratizing working life is a question I take up briefly in the conclusion. My *main* purpose, however, in this chapter is to describe and analyse one case of participatory research with particular emphasis on the new role of the participatory researcher. At present little is actually known about this type of research. I am aware of only a handful of comparable cases. With the accumulation of more empirical experience we will also be better able to identify limiting conditions. I can only speculate on some of these in the conclusion.

I have chosen this particular case because it was my first experience in participative research. I made a lot of mistakes and had no guidelines in my new role as participatory researcher. I knew only that neither my experience as an academic social researcher (political science) nor as an applied behavioural scientist (planned organization change) alone would be sufficient. These roles were based on a certain distance from research subjects and a relatively high degree of unilateral control over the research process. Participatory research, I was to discover, made quite different role demands on the researcher.

A Participatory Research Project Gets Off the Ground

The organization we worked with was one of Norway's largest commercial banks with some 2000 employees in 60 or so branches. In 1974 the bank was in the final stages of designing a new 'on-line' system (OLS) of computer terminals to be installed in all its branches within two years. The bank was interested in assessing the effects of its first installations so that undesirable consequences could be minimized in subsequent installations.

They were interested in some employee participation in the implementation process. Although the OLS technology was obviously already a finished package, there were still at least four implementation tasks to be completed in each branch:

(a) How many terminals were needed?
(b) Where should they be located?
(c) Who would man them?
(d) When should they be trained?

Normally these tasks would be completed by the bank's organization and methods division. In this case, however, making these decisions was delegated to each branch bank.

Not much as far as participation and democratic decision-making goes, perhaps, but it was at least an opportunity to participate where before there was none. We hoped it would be enough at least for a jumping-off point. Initially this was only our expectation, not the bank's. Our strategy was to 'piggyback' participative research onto this technological change. Even this quite modest opportunity to participate in implementing the computer system and analysing its consequences could lead to participation in more deep-going organizational analysis and change in the branches.

In the beginning, the bank apparently expected me to function as an observer of sorts, although some kind of questionnaire might be used before and after the OLS installation. One of the research project's key supporters at a high level in the bank met with us at the end of 1974 to clarify my role. He was important to us since he was responsible for both the OLS installation and for the bank's organization and methods division. He was concerned that our project should not interfere with the computer service bureau's complex, nationwide implementation plan. 'Everything must go according to this plan. Your project must not interfere. You should be *observers*. You should *not try to influence* people to do things differently', he emphasized.

This conflict surfaced in February 1975 in the first pilot installation site when the local task force was formed. Actually, there was not much left to decide. They were a small unit located adjacent to the OLS team's offices and the team was literally in daily contact with them as the date for installation approached.

When I met with the task force I tried to interest them in suggesting topics for research. I even left them copies of short research studies we had done in other branches of the bank. But as the time of installation approached without any response from them I finally called a meeting. It was brief and not very encouraging. They had not considered the matter and had no ideas or suggestions. 'We don't have time for everything. There is a new computer coming in here you know', said one of them, perhaps a bit sharply. Nevertheless I pushed blindly ahead and railroaded through a short questionnaire which would produce data they could analyse themselves.

I later learned that the group resented my pushing them to participate, especially since I was claiming that they should decide for themselves. One of them said the meeting with me was like being in a classroom with a domineering teacher who demanded the 'right' answers. Apparently in my haste to press on with participatory research I was not too democratic: my actions belied my intentions.

The result was that when I returned the following week with a draft of the questionnaire the branch manager politely requested that I drop the research. I left immediately and never returned. It shook me up. I was kicked out of my first attempt at participatory research. It was a complete failure. Little participation and no research. Ironically, the only evidence of participation was that the people said 'no' to the research.

'Well, everything's gone bust', I said to myself. I expected the bank to drop the whole project. Fortunately they did not.

In reviewing the experience the critical problem seemed to be the existence of two conflicting models of participation in the same branch at the same time. In addition, it was felt that more time and better preparation were needed if we were to test seriously the proposition that people could participate in more than the implementation of new technology. The bank was willing to try again given better conditions at the second pilot installation.

At the same time, for reasons of his own, the OD manager quit. The new OD man and I developed a close working relationship. He enthusiastically supported our rather open-ended research design and was instrumental in helping launch our next attempt, in May at the second pilot site. This branch was to receive the new technology in July.

We now had much more lead time and no conflict over the scope of people's participation. It was quite open-ended. I was determined not to try to define too much in advance so as to help avoid the 'pusher' role I had unwittingly played in the first pilot project.

I guess I was pretty vague. During one of the planning meetings at headquarters in preparation for the second pilot project, one of my colleagues at the bank, possibly cueing from my long hair, beard, and informal attire, characterized the whole affair as a 'hippie happening'. He was only half-kidding. But at the very least, after 9 months and a rather straightforward failure *some* people were beginning to see that we were not going to play a traditional 'expert' role. This new, 'non-expert' role was developed with the people at the branch where the second pilot study occurred.

They were already finished with the four assigned implementation questions by the time we got there in May 1975. The group that had answered these questions was *drawn entirely from management*. We (me, the OD staff man, and a representative from the board of the bank's union) met with this group augmented by two of the local bank union's representatives. Initially the group was interested in a study of the consequences of the new technology for their organization but clearly expected me — the expert — to conduct the research and make recommendations. They expected an 'expert-in-charge-of-change'.

During the course of the meeting I repeatedly stressed that what the research would aim at, and whether indeed there would be any research at all, was entirely up to them. The OD staff man and the central union representative echoed the same theme so often that when one of the group answered a colleague's question with the refrain 'it all depends on you' everyone had a good laugh.

As I had done in the first pilot study, I presented our prior research work as illustrations of some of what could be done. In contrast to the first project, however, this meeting was unhurried, dealt entirely with the question of doing research, and lasted several hours. In addition, the OD man and I were clearly supporting the same model of change. The meeting ended with agreement that they would consider things and let us know within a week or two if they wished to proceed.

In fact, the next meeting was almost a month later and on our initiative. People, we learned later, were confused or at least unclear after our first meeting. They expected people from headquarters to come with assignments or at least specific suggestions. Their initial attitude was, in effect, 'What do you want us to do exactly?' At the same time our question was 'What do you want to do?' By waiting several extra weeks we lost some time, but we underlined our reluctance to play the role of expert producer of change. They also had a better chance to get their premises together so as to create their own point of departure. But finally, we felt it necessary to take the initiative in setting up the second meeting. We were not going to direct the process but we were not going to be completely 'non-directive' either.

At the second meeting the committee members fairly quickly identified six main themes for the research (only two of which came from the material I had left with them) and established a three-man subcommittee (including me) to do the research. This subcommittee presented its report in writing to each employee some four months later. Shortly thereafter, in mid-October, a general meeting of all employees was held concerning the report. The meeting lsted some five hours and led to the election of an employee task force to implement changes in the organization along the lines outlined in the report.

Thus the participatory research phase led naturally to a process of employee-managed organization change. We have successfully piggybacked on the introduction of technological change. I describe elsewhere the practical, democratizing changes instituted by the employee task force during the following years (Elden 1979a) so these will not be discussed further here.

The main point is that the bank evaluated the participatory self-study phase as highly successful. The man who earlier had warned us not to interfere described the project as the bank's 'most successful effort so far because the people are doing it themselves'. He also mentioned that while we researchers seemed to have an unusual way of working it did, in fact, work. In a later phase of the project he collaborated actively in series of participative design workshops the first of which brought together labour-management redesign teams from four branch banks including our first 'success'. The bank's OD staff, under his direction, then took over this approach to participatory change and held workshops for most of the branches outside of Oslo. The project also became the subject of a television documentary on work democracy.

In short, by all accounts we have one successful case of participatory research. We also have another case where the participatory research approach completely failed. One big difference between these two cases is the role I played as researcher. Before examining this role let us describe the participatory approach to research in comparison to other types.

A Participatory Approach to Research

In any research design one makes at least four critical decisions:

(a) What is the research problem? (PROBLEM DEFINITION)
(b) How is the problem to be studied? What methods will provide the necessary data? (METHODS CHOICE)

(c) What do the data mean? (DATA ANALYSIS)
(d) How can the findings be used? Who learns from the results of the
      research (USE OF FINDINGS)

Research is participatory when those directly affected by it influence each of
these four decisions and help carry them out. Since I am concerned about
workplaces I will define 'participants' as employees. For participation to be
meaningful and consequential I assume it must involve more than merely being
consulted but not necessarily as much as exercising control. It means here
having enough involvement and influence to impact on the decision *and* in
carrying it out. For our purpose we can dichotomize active influence: either
you have it or you do not. Taking the four decisions together with different
combinations of having influence or not produces a matrix of 12 logically
possible combinations (Table 22.1). Analysis of these categories results in four
types of research design (designated A, B, C, and D). There are two obviously
'pure' types (A and D). Type A is common among basic or academic
researchers concerned primarily with developing general or 'context-free'
knowledge (Susman and Evered, 1978).

   Type D, addressed to the problem of producing local theory (context-
bounded knowledge) in the service of employee-managed change, is much less
common. Type C, perhaps most common in combinations 8 and 9, is widely
used in a variety of problem areas. Since I am concerned about QWL
improvement I limit this category to organization change research — especially
as exemplified by the survey-feedback approach to organization development.

Table 22.1   Participant's influence in different types of research

Types of research	Problem definition	Methods selection	Data analysis	Findings
		Participant influence in decisions concerning:		
A 1	0	0	0	0
B 2	1	0	0	0
3	1	1	0	0
4	1	1	1	0
5	0	1	1	0
6	1	0	1	0
C 7	0	1	1	1
8	1	0	0	1
9	0	0	0	1
10	0	0	1	1
11	1	0	1	1
D 12	1	1	1	1

0 = no influence, 1 = influence

It could also be called 'applied research' as where an applied behavioural scientist uses his expertise to find answers to what he and/or his client(s) define as a problem. The fourth group, Type B, is a residual category of logically possible but empirically improbable combinations. There is little need to involve those affected by the research in designing and implementing it if they are excluded from using the results.

One thing that should be clear from Table 22.1 is that different research designs serve different purposes even though they can focus on the same topic. For example, in pursuing my interests in work democracy I have also used a general knowledge design (Elden, 1980). The cutting difference is the immediate goal of the research. Where the goal is to develop change capacity so that workers can solve their own problems and keep on solving them (self-maintained learning) the general knowledge research design seems to be of limited utility. As Gustavsen, one of the architects of the 1977 Norwegian QWL law, argues:

> It will never be possible to make a 'cook book' to implement... [the law]. On the way toward concrete solutions there is a lot left to be done after one has abstracted all the general knowledge that research has produced. This gap can only partially be filled by more general knowledge. For the most part it must be filled by the employees themselves — with the help of their experience and insight *in* their own situation (Gustavsen, 1980, my translation).

As we have seen, initiating local participatory processes to fill the knowledge gap is easier said than done. Let us look more closely at what actually happened in the participatory research phase of the bank project.

Participation in step 1, PROBLEM DEFINITION, turned out to be crucial. I had suggested an analysis of task and cooperative relations and of attitudes towards the new computer system. Labour-management repesentatives wanted more. Management wanted a candid assessment from the employees about the good and bad sides of their total work situation. The employee's representatives supported this but in addition wanted people's evaluation of the job rotation system and the possibilities of participating. It turned out that their topics, rather than mine alone, produced the most change-relevant findings. Participation from the beginning paid off in the end.

The research subcommittee completed step 2, METHODS CHOICE, in short order, choosing a methodology and drafting the specific questions to be asked. Given the confidential nature of the data, I alone interviewed everyone individually and provided anonymous protocols for my two colleagues on the research subcommittee.

Step 3, DATA ANALYSIS, also turned out to be critical and, in retrospect, perhaps for me the most difficult. It began in late summer 1975, and lasted over two months of what was fairly continuous and demanding work. The three of us started with a shared set of raw data. In the very beginning we did not even have any categories. 'What does it all mean?' we asked ourselves. We began to create a framework in which we could analyse the data.

It soon became apparent that we did not go about this in the same way. I tended to have a few, quite general, abstract categories; the employees had many more which were more concrete. Interestingly enough my abstract categories tended not to hold water when we got down to concrete excerpts from the interviews. Initially, for example, I did a rough content analysis of problems mentioned under what I saw as the main categories such as the rotation system (including covering absences, deciding who is trained in what when, and scheduling days-off and vacations), lack of opportunity to participate and take responsibility, social distance, and centralization.

In retrospect, I was probably categorizing and labelling problems that I saw as analytically discrete in the same way I had as an organization development consultant (for example in preparing materials for feedback to a group undergoing team-building). My two colleagues in the research subcommittee did not sort out pieces from the different interviews the same way I did. They pointed out, for example, that a complaint about the rotation system was tied to problems of not being able to participate because personnel decision-making was centralized in the top of the organization. In which of my categories should a comment on rotation decision-making be placed: participation, centralization of decision-making, development? The more I understood things from their point of view, the less meaning my own categories had. It was a bit unnerving to find my categories gradually evaporating. I started with five abstract, general categories. We ended up with 21 fairly concrete and useful ones. They were especially useful as the basis for our local theory.

In a series of meetings with the subcommittee during the following weeks we analysed the data in our 21 categories and *through the give and take of a dialogue,* mapped their interrelationships to produce a simple but comprehensive explanation of the data (local theory).

This is where I drew on my social science training. I analysed patterns in the data and suggested how things seemed to hang together. Everything was thoroughly debated. One of my biggest problems was the abstract level and conceptual orientation of my social science language. For example, I started out calling the variable that was to prove to be the core of the local theory 'interpersonal mismatch at the customer interface'. After a lot of dialogue we worked out the much more concrete and informative title of 'periodically there are not enough staff in relation to the workload'.

Subsequently, in step 5, USE OF FINDINGS, everyone received a personal copy of the report. After the five hour general meeting in which *all* employees participated actively it was accepted with only a few superficial modifications and served as an important reference document in the change programme.

The project demonstrated that employees possess special expertise concerning their own work situation and its possible improvement. Participatory research facilitated the gathering together and systematizing of isolated, individualized understandings into what I have called 'local theory'. Hall (1975, p. 29) concludes that this

> is perhaps the fundamental principle of participatory research and its point of most radical departure from both orthodox research approaches and such improvements as grounded theory. The research process should be based on a system of discussion, investigation and analysis in which the researched are as much a part of the process as the researcher. Theories are neither developed beforehand to be tested nor drawn by the researcher from his or her involvement with reality. Reality is described by the process through which a community develops its own theories and solutions about itself.

Although grounded in a specific context, our local theory seems also to have more general applicability judging from the reactions of researchers and banks here and in other countries. This more general applicability may also be in part due to the language of the final report. It was written and rewritten by different members of the subcommittee so that the final draft was in everyday language. Neither this nor its grounding in a specific context seems to have reduced its scientific value.

Researcher Role in Participative Research

In participatory research compared to other types of research the researcher is more dependent on those from whom data come, has less unilateral control over the research process, and has more pressure to work from other people's definition of the situation. A more systematic comparison of the effects and role demands of the different types of research is presented in Table 22.2. No one of these types, of course, is intrinsically right or wrong. The question is useful for what? Regardless of what one is aiming at, researcher role must be consistent with the research goal. This was the problem, for example, in the first pilot study where the goal was participation but I played an 'expert' instead of a 'co-learner' role. I was inappropriately pressuring people to participate instead of sharing control over the research process (which might have helped me see more of what was happening). I felt caught between the old roles I knew and a new one I did not know. Herbst (1976, p. 10) neatly expresses the problem I experienced:

A necessary condition for the development of an organizational learning process is that the locus of initiative is developed and lies within the organization itself. It is here, where the external change agent has a major responsibility. If his main concern is that of demonstrating his competence as an expert he will, without necessarily being aware of this, achieve the opposite and block the development of a change process. Adopting a technocratic role, or perhaps more correctly a sociocratic role himself, his aims will be contradicted by his practice. If on the other hand he adopts an ostensive non-directive role, this will not be very helpful either. The problem for the external change agent is to enter into a relationship where joint learning becomes possible. His task may or perhaps should not be the actual implementation of any new system, but that of contributing to the discovery and development of appropriate starting conditions for a process which can go on its own way.

I have described just such a process in the participatory research phase of the second pilot study which has since gone 'on its own way'. In contrast to the first pilot study I was in dialogue with the employees on their terms — a 'discussion partner' as one of them put it. I think he meant that we learned together by sharing in building a common framework. It was neither imposed nor imported. We grew it ourselves. My role, in short, was that of a *co-producer of learning* (see Table 22.2).

This is significantly different from being seen as a 'catalyst' or a 'teacher' or a 'therapist' as I was, among other things, called by my OD clients. For them I was a *producer of learning*. That was my business. I produced their learning. That's what I got paid for. I did not get paid for learning myself (in the sense of developing a new shared theory of the situation from the ground up) but for training or instructing. I was the man with the instantly relevant framework (such as a 'team-building' lab., an inter-personal competence building workshop, a managerial grid exercise, or 'open systems planning') that they were to learn in order to solve their problems. Progress was how quickly they learned my framework.

As an expert-in-charge-of-change I was not expected to develop a new framework (as would a basic researcher) but to solve local problems (as an applied researcher). As a participative researcher I needed *both* to develop a new framework *and* to solve problems.

At first I found it difficult to engage in any depth with the data and the employees without my framework: the kind of applied organization change research I was familiar with usually rested on an unarticulated framework which itself was never questioned. We tested hypotheses within a framework but not the framework itself. In other words, a participative researcher, like a

Table 22.2   Some correlates of different types of workplace research

	Type of research (from Table 22.1)		
	Type A (basic research)	Type C (applied research)	Type D (participative research)
Research goal	Abstract general knowledge (context-free knowledge)	Solutions to workplace problems (context-bound knowledge)	Local theory — actionable and generalizable (context-bound knowledge)
Who learns from the research in the first instance?	The social science community (usually but not exclusively other researchers)	The client (usually but not exclusively management)	Participants (usually but not exclusively workers and researchers)
Likelihood that those who supply the data will use the results	VERY LOW	LOW	HIGH
Relation between researcher and researchee(s)	Theoretician ↓ Object	Expert ↓ ↑ Client	Colleague ↓ ↑ Colleague
Researcher role	Producer of distant learning	Producer of organizational change	Co-producer of learning

basic researcher, must be open to deep (i.e. initially framework-less) learning himself: he cannot assume that his framework will dominate or remain unchanged.

But if the role of the participative researcher builds in some way on that of basic researcher it also builds on the applied researcher. Both applied and participative researchers need to build trust and a shared definition of reality with the people in the organization. In trying to develop local, actionable theory I had to make my contribution as a researcher meaningful to them in their world on their terms. So I was dependent on them in a close working relationship over which I felt little control. Compared to my experience as a basic or applied researcher the risks of failure were bigger, I had much less control, but I felt just as responsible.

I had lost my 'managerial prerogatives' in the research process. I felt like a foreman whose functions are taken over by a self-managed work group. The employees participated in so many of my functions that at times I felt like a research assistant. They were so autonomous in managing their own change process that I felt irrelevant. I was, in short, no longer the 'expert-in-charge-of-change'.

On Not Being in Charge of Change — Some Reflections

If I were to summarize what I learned regarding my role in this project it would be my acting as a co-producer of learning. I did not process them through my framework nor were they research objects.

We collaborated in creating a common framework that pulled together the otherwise unarticulated individual theories of different people into a new, shared understanding.

My role in part drew from the roles of basic researcher (e.g. eliciting underlying patterns in data, developing new knowledge) and applied researcher (e.g. building trust, working collaboratvely), but in part it was entirely new because I had little of the control over the research process that one has in these other roles. My new role was in addition composed of something else than just pieces of these two other roles.

This something else seems to resemble the role of the local community organizer (cf. Kahn, 1970) or Freire's facilitator of consciousness raising (Freire, 1970). In both of these approaches, as in the bank project, the initial steps are to understanding people in a particular context on their own terms, systematically elicit data on problems, and through a process of exchange with the people involved in their language boil these down to a local theory (Freire's 'generative themes') and an action plan that the people themselves carry forward.

A recent account of an attempt to apply Freire's approach with the Aymare Indians on the Peruvian high plateau (Reed, 1975) describes development stages and change agent roles strikingly similar to what I have described in the Norwegian bank project. Reed and his partner began with an initial participant-observation phase, experienced failure, gradually, while feeling their way, built up trust, and finally began a collaborative search with the Indians for new, more actionable knowledge within the context of their world. The collaborative search and dialogue that occurred in small, informal 'study sessions' with groups of villagers high in the Andes is not unlike the participative research process in a bank in Norway(!):

> Our main role during this initial stage was to draw out the participants, to listen to the way they perceived things. Then taking their disparate interpretations and ideas, Lucho and I tried to organize the ideas on a coherent, comprehensive manner. The reformulated, organized explanations then served the reflection group as the basis for a continuous discussion about a given subject (Reed, 1975, p. 4).

Consistent with what I experienced in the bank project Reed further observes that they did not undertake this 'to impose any preconceived programme designed to drive the community towards a specific action. In reality we had no prepackaged actions or answers to impose' (Reed, 1975, p. 5).

Thus a final implication is that participative research strategies rule out — or at least raise a serious question about — a role based on large scale, prepackaged standardized surveys. In addition to Reed, both Taylor (1979), in a thought-provoking paper, and Hall (1975, ˙ especially p. 30) have independently arrived at a similar conclusion (each after having demonstrated considerable professional competence in doing large-scale survey research). Hall argues for a quite different model of social science research by using an analogy to the field of medicine:

> Social science research often appears to produce a situation in which a medical doctor tries to diagnose a patient's symptoms from around the corner and out of sight. The social scientist uses his 'instruments' to measure the response of the patient as though they were a kind of long stethoscope. The focus of the researcher has been on developing a better and better stethoscope for going around corners and into houses when the real need is for the researcher to walk around the corner, into the house and begin talking with the people who live there (Hall, 1975, p. 30).

To deal with the methodological and philosophy of science questions raised here is beyond the scope of this paper. I have already noted that the kind of social science training I had prior to the experience of participatory action research was not too helpful and the experience itself raises questions — not only in my mind but in that of other researchers who also have done both participative and survey research — about the scientific utility of standardized, prepackaged surveys in participation action research.

It seems that sustained experience in participative research may well lesson one's belief not only in a particular prepackaged framework but also in the whole idea of prepackaging. I should make clear that I am opposed to prepackaged inquiry rather than the idea of packing (i.e. structure) in inquiry. I am *not* opposed to the use of structured interviews or questionnaires *per se*. Indeed I made use of the former in the research reported here and Hoel and Hvinden (1976) use the latter in their 'dialogue-based' approach to participative research. Scientific inquiry would be indeed impossible without some form for ordering and structuring data.

I argue only that if the people in a particular organizational setting are to learn from and use the research, then it should be in their language and deal with concrete issues they see as important. This is more likely if they participate in planning and carrying out the research work. This is quite different from workers discussing computer print-outs of their group's responses to a prepackaged standardized survey. I object to a change-oriented social science that would attempt to increase the control of people over their own lives but at the same time uses alienating methods.

The alternative we have explored in participatory research, however, is no panacea. As I learned in getting booted out of the first pilot study, participative research takes time. I had a few weeks in the first pilot study and over six months in the second. It also requires that people have the will and resources to participate. They did in the second case but not on the first.

All this means that participatory research has up to now been very expensive and limited to small groups (there were only 25 employees in the branch bank). Is it so custom-made that, like psychoanalysis, it benefits only a privileged few? Recently, we have had some success with participative research within a national trade union on the local level (Levin, 1980) but in this project less than a half dozen workers out of a total workforce of over 1000 have been active. We are at present planning workshops with another national union which are intended to reach many more workers. We need more evidence.

Whether or not participative research facilitates deep political change is another question we cannot answer here. We note, however, that participative research in the workplace at least initially depends on the good will of those in power. Management at least must sanction a very open-ended start-up which, if successful, might lead to a change process not subject to unilateral management control. One could question how realistic it is to expect an existing power structure to allow itself to be fundamentally transformed. Regardless of one's answer to this question it is clear that participative research in working life will have little democratizing impact if it is seen as the one and only strategy.

Finally, to the extent social scientists would democratize work they may also be called on to democratize the research work itself. A participatory, action-relevant social science would aim at both the production of new, directly applicable knowledge and at helping people learn to do their own social science. 'We need not more highly trained and sophisticated researchers operating with ever more esoteric techniques, but whole neighbourhoods, communities, and nations of 'researchers' ' (Hall, 1975, p. 30). The bank project has not yet trained many employees to be social science researchers, but such a process seems to have begun if only in a small way, and this process may in the long run be the most important product.

Note: What I have written here has benefited from extensive discussions with colleagues at the Institute for Social Research in Industry, Trondheim, Norway, especially from a substantial written critique by Børre Nylehn and suggestions from Knut Veium.

Human Inquiry
Edited by P. Reason and J. Rowan
© 1981 John Wiley & Sons Ltd.

CHAPTER TWENTY-THREE

Endogenous research: the prison project*

Magoroh Maruyama
Department of Administrative Sciences, University of Southern Illinois at Carbondale, USA

In the endogenous research, *how* the team is formed, as well as *how* the team members related to one another and to other members of the community, is extremely crucial. There were several crises in the project from which we have learned a great deal, and which contributed to later sophistication of endogenous methodology. They are described in depth in Maruyama (1975). At its formation in November 1965, the team was not a cohesive unit. The members were not well acquainted and distrusted one another. They had divergent goals, mostly self-centred. They did not know me, and they had to test me out. During the initial month the meetings looked like an encounter group or a group therapy session. Then gradually the team members started realizing that it was their own project, to be run in their way with freedoms they had been unable to exercise in the prison. They decided that if they did anything at all, it had to be meaningful to society and, especially, meaningful to themselves. Because they had been accustomed to prison life which was for the most part meaningless, the participants found that the project created a new challenge and inspiration for them. By the second month a feeling of dedication, commitment, and group solidarity had grown. One member dropped out.

*This chapter consists of selected portions of a much longer article entitled 'Endogenous research and polyocular anthropology' (Maruyama, 1978a). Further extracts may be found in Chapter 20 of this volume — Eds.

The first crisis came when a psychologist visited the team. He belonged to the prison project in a nominal capacity, though he was active on another project outside the prison. His name had been put on the project proposal mainly to facilitate its acceptance by the funding agency because of his reputation in his field. He lived 3000 miles away from where the project was conducted and was mainly an absentee member of the project. He visited the prison teams occasionally during vacations — Christmas, Easter, and summer. His first visit was during Christmas vacation, when the team had just established group solidarity. He lectured down to the team members as to what they should do and how they should do it. When the team members politely and indirectly tried to suggest their ideas and their point of view, he rejected them as being unscientific. After his departure some team members said that they wanted to quit. But after some more encounter-group type meetings they decided to stick together and give it a try. The team decided not to follow closely the ideas dictated by the psychologist.

Next, one month was spent working out conceptualizations, focus of research, and a list of factors to be researched. As mentioned earlier, I needed only to function as a catalyst using the Socratic dialogue technique. At no point did I need to supply the team with sociological or psychological theories. The team produced highly sophisticated conceptualizations of their own.

After the completion of the factor list the team devised an interview format, and conducted test interviews with other inmates to improve the format and their skills. The final format was in the form of discussion sessions rather than a question-and-answer interview, allowing as much time as the interviewee cared to spend. The interviewee was to be treated as the guest at the discussion sessions. When the data were tabulated at the end of the project, it turned out that the median length of the interviews was two days, the longest interview being seven full days.

In April the team started the interviews. First the team had to prove, by its performance, to the inmate population that it was not a snitch organization and that the interview was meaningful to the interviewees themselves. At the beginning, there was much suspicion and reluctance on the part of the interviewees. But as the interviewees went back to their friends and told them of their experiences with the team, word spread through the inmate population that the project was not only safe but was genuinely interesting and meaningful. Many inmates wanted to be interviewed. The team first completed the interviews of those who appeared on the official records of violence during the previous two years. Then the team interviewed those who were known in the inmate population for their violent tendencies, as well as those volunteers who met the criteria of violence. The waiting list of volunteers grew long. Eventually it became a prestige symbol for inmates in the yard to come up to the team members and talk on a buddy-buddy level as we crossed the yard. Some interviewees came with confidential notes they had especially prepared for the interview, and burned them up at the end of the interview session. In some instances the interviewees volunteered extremely dangerous information detrimental to themselves. The team thought it wise to erase such information from the tape after the interview, even though the interviewees had enough confidence in the team to let it be kept on tape. These indications, together with the quality and the quantity of the output of the team, were a proof of the success of the project.

There was another major crisis when a team member secretly false-jacketed another member as having been regarded as a snitch by some inmates in the past. This almost tore the team apart. But the members' dedication to the project was strong, and the painful wounds healed quickly. Then, during the peak of the team's production, some members became resentful of slow workers in the team. This was also resolved peacefully. Each of the occasional visits by the psychologist created some tension and resentment. But the team evolved a technique to deal with him, giving him what he wanted while carrying out their own project undisturbed. The team members took utmost care not to break any regulations and not to offend any guards. As a result, the guards were for the most part co-operative. Two team members' cells were shaken down by guards, but it became evident that it was not done to harass the project. The team completed its tasks at the end of August.

Successes of the prison project can be attributed to the following:

(1) allowing enough time (one month) for encounter-group type meetings to develop group solidarity and sense of dedication at the beginning;
(2) permitting endogenous researchers to design the project which was therefore meaningful to them;
(3) allowing enough time (three months) for conceptualization, selection of focus, research design, and test runs;
(4) allowing enough time (up to seven full days) for each interviewee to express freely his experiences and his point of view in a seminar atmosphere in which the interviewee was a guest, and studying the topic in depth;
(5) taking every precaution to prevent leakage of confidential information;
(6) allowing enough time (a few months) for the inmate population to gain confidence in the project.

Ability of Endogenous Researchers to Conceptualize

One of the resistances the endogenous research encounters is the professional researchers' scepticism regarding the untrained endogenous researchers' ability. Worth (1967) and Worth and Adair (1972) chose Navajos with a minimum degree of 'Americanization' or formal education in their endogenous film project. In my prison projects the average formal education level of the endogenous researchers was sixth-grade. Adair, Worth, and I found that the less contaminated the endogenous researchers by academic training, the more insightful their products are, and that the untrained researchers can be highly articulate and capable of research.

The prison project was conducted in two large state prisons. A team of endogenous researchers was formed in each of the two prisons. The overall objective of the project was to study interpersonal physical violence (fights) in the prison culture, with as little contamination as possible from academic theories and methodologies. The details of the research were left to be developed by the inmate researchers. Each team had the task of:

(1) selecting the focus and conceptualizing the dimensions and the factors to be studied;
(2) making a preliminary list of possible categories for each dimension or factor, and defining categories;
(3) making preliminary data-collection to see if these dimensions, factors, and categories were relevant and adequate, and adding new ones or eliminating unnecessary ones;
(4) when dimensions, factors, and categories had been stabilized, designing an interview format, procedure, and interactional details to interview inmates known to be violent in order to analyse specific incidents;
(5) developing a method to code the data;
(6) trying out test interviews and modifying and improving interview format, procedure, and method;
(7) conducting interviews;
(8) coding the data;
(9) analysing the data.

Let me first reproduce here a part of the list of the factors and their categories formulated before the interview was designed. The two teams in the two prisons produced two different lists. All three members of the team in Prison A had only some grammar-school education and very little reading in psychology or sociology, while two of the six members of the team in Prison B had some high-school education, and another had had some exposure to lay psychology. Let us therefore take the list made by the team in Prison A. The list consists of the following 18 dimensions or factors to be looked into, each of which are further subdivided into numerous categories:

(1) interpersonal and individual factors leading to violence;
(2) signals given prior to acts of violence;
(3) how the signals were perceived;
(4) reactions to such signals;

(5) reasons for such reactions;

(6) expected gains from the violent act;

(7) degree to which the aggressor saw violence as the only alternative;

(8) degree of communication skills;

(9) involvement of others;

(10) significance of spectators;

(11) effectiveness of others in preventing violence;

(12) extent of intended injury;

(13) feelings before, at the moment, and after violence, and present feelings about the incident;

(14) how would you react to the same situation now;

(15) subject's principles regarding violence;

(16) sequential patterns leading to violence;

(17) fashions of violence in different prisons;

(18) social climate which may vary between prisons as well as within a prison over time.

[*In the original article only coding categories for the first item – interpersonal and individual factors leading to violence – were reproduced. We have reduced this still further and have selected 13 out of the original 64 categories as examples – Eds.*]

Coding Categories for Interpersonal and Individual Factors (Alphabetical)

Accumulated hostility from different sources
  Definition: Several seemingly insignificant incidents occur with an individual, causing a build-up of anger or frustration.
  Example: X didn't get that visit from his wife yesterday, his teeth have been bothering him lately, a staff member searched him this morning, and now Y bumps into him accidentally burning him on the hand with his cigarette. This is too much for X so he attacks Y.

Collector
  Definition: One who collects debts for others on a percentage basis.
  Example: Z loans Y one carton for two weeks at 100 per cent interest rate (repay double the amount of loan). After two weeks Y is unable to repay. Z raises the interest rate to 200 per cent and hires X to collect for 50 per cent. Y is still unable to pay, or refuses to. X stabs Y.

Demonstrate not a fool
  Definition: When a person indicates that others cannot run over him.
  Example: Y makes fool of X by getting him to gamble on an event that has already happened and Y knows the result. X finds out and beats Y.

False jacket
  Definition: Untrue, derogatory labels.
  Example: Y tells Z that X is a homosexual. When X finds out, he stabs Y.

Fear of being informed on
  Definition: A person is seen by another doing an illegal act and is afraid he will tell authorities.
  Example: Z sees X stab Y. X is afraid that Z will snitch on him, so X stabs Z.

Grudge
  Definition: A fight that has been either postponed, or going on for a long time, and which finally comes to a serious violence incident.
  Example: X and Y have been fighting each other since they were kids. They fought each other in another prison in another state. They fought each other on separate sides in a couple of gang fights outside. Yesterday Y hits X in the head with a sharp tin can. Five minutes later X sneaked up on Y while Y was busy eating chow and beat him severely about the head with a lead pipe.

Hopeless outlook on life (Don't give a damn)
  Definition: An inmate (possibly a lifer) decides there is nothing to care about since he already is in as deep as he can possibly get (life sentence).
  Example: X, figuring he has nothing to lose anyway, beats the hell out of Y because Y seemed to be looking at him all the time.

Insult
  Definition: One person degrades another justly or unjustly.
  Example: Y tells X, 'You are a bum, always were a bum, and you will always be a bum.' X stabs Y.

No motive
  Definition: A violent act is committed without apparent cause.
  Example: When questioned by custody as to why he stabbed Y, X said he didn't have any reason.

Protection
  Definition: One pays someone to prevent being jumped on.
  Example: W is paying Y four cartons a month for protection. X tells W, 'I can protect you for two cartons a month'. W stops paying Y and begins paying X. X and Y fight.

Rumours

Definition: Rumours among inmates which grow into a fact.

Example: Clique S hears that Clique T is arming itself to fight Clique S. Clique S arms itself. When both cliques meet next time, they are ready.

Self-defence

Definition: Forced to fight in order to survive.

Example: Y has been telling X he is going to kill him soon. In the morning Y hit X in the mouth and told him that tomorrow he will kill X for sure. X puts some food trays around his belly and under his shirt for protection, and arms himself. Next day Y challenges X and the fight is on. X kills Y.

Wants to stay in prison

Definition: Infractions committed to avoid release.

Example: X is scheduled to be released in two weeks. X begins a fight with Y in order to get locked up in isolation and lose his date.

Ability of Endogenous Researchers to Record, Code, and Analyse the Data

The total output of the two prison teams exceeded 1200 single-spaced typed pages. In addition to recording the 18 dimensions or factors for 241 incidents, the endogenous researchers also recorded the following five items for each of the 42 interviewees:

(1) interviewee's overall pattern of violence;
(2) variations in certain incidents from his overall pattern;
(3) interviewee's philosophy of life and outlook on society;
(4) description of the interviewee during the interview;
(5) appearances and personal impressions.

Here are some examples from the output:

Examples from Coded Diagrams
Subject 36, Incident 8 (see Figure 23.1)

Background: subject had acquired a sizable bank roll (cigarettes) and had gone into 'two for three' business, i.e. loaning out two cartons for the repayment of three cartons at the end of a two-week period, in other words, 50 per cent interest. Z and W were both in similar but separate business as subject, and they worked along with the subject in the gym department.

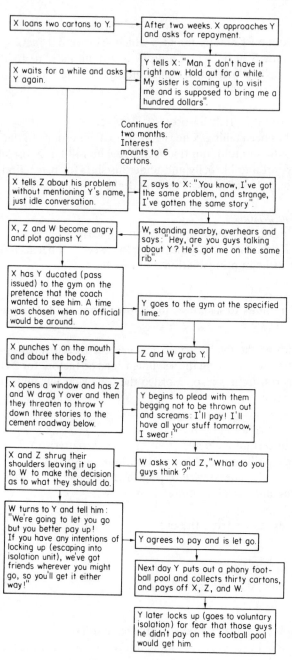

Figure 23.1

Examples from 'Principles'
Subject 36

(1) *What would I fight for?* 'As long as I have to die some day I would much rather die for a reason other than simply old age. It seems like a stupid senseless waste, you know, to die of old age. Since I'm going to die anyway, I would much rather die for something I believe in. Whether it was for a pack of cigarettes, or Mom's apple pie, or God and country, you know, I don't think it would be so much patriotism, or so much the value of the cigarettes, or anything else... I would be giving myself a reason for dying. Otherwise, I'm just going to die of old age, of cancer or something. I would just hate to die for nothing, you know, growing old. I would much rather die defending my pack of cigarettes'.

When asked what would motivate him into getting himself into a hassle, he answered: 'I guess false pride, possession, and beliefs. I've spent so many of my years in institutions where you don't really have anything.... . Everything belongs to the State. Ah, what little things you have, such as cigarettes, or your canteen, or your word, ah, these are the things I would probably go down the river for' (i.e., to get killed).

(2) *What would other people fight for?* 'Basically the same things I would fight for... Pride, possession, and beliefs. If he believes something is right, he'll fight for it. In direct proportion to the degree in which he believes in it, will he respond to a threat to it.'

Examples from 'Patterns'
Subject 42

(1) *Common patterns.* Subject states that his opponents in Incidents 1, 2, 3, and 5 were bully-type persons who had agitated him by their ways. He claims that such people make him very angry. In every incident except 6, he says that the hostility built up before he decided to do something about it. He says further that in most encounters he can take a great deal of agitation until he feels that it must be stopped, then he becomes extremely angry and fights. In Incident 1 a homosexual was involved indirectly, and again in Incident 5 another homosexual was indirectly involved. The subject says that he does not like aggressive homosexuals, and their presence may have provoked him or made him angrier than he might otherwise have been. In almost every fight there is an absence of any thought to use weapons (Incident 4 is an exception). He says that he was taught to fight fair, no weapons, no kicks, etc., and he follows this closely. The significance of these feelings come back strongly in 5 and 6, where he precipitates 6 as a result of the unfair fighting against him in 5.

(2) *Variations*. In all incidents except 4 and 6, the subject's only intention was to get someone off his back. There was no intended damage. In 4, however, the intention was to kill. In 6, he seriously intended to hospitalize the victim if at all possible. In 1 and 2 it seems important to him that his opponents were bigger than he was. In 3 the subject discloses that his opponent was very small, and that this is at least partially responsible for his not wanting to hurt the man. In other incidents there is no indication that size was important, but the subject does state with some emphasis that there is no win in fighting a small man, and he also makes much of the fact that his opponents in 1 and 2 were bigger than he. (His own height is 6 feet 3 inches.)

Example from 'Philosophy of Life and Outlook on Society'
Subject 41

(1), (2), (3) (See Maruyama, 1978a)

(4) *What would you do when you get out?* 'When I get out I'll try to make it, really try.' (The subject was paroled the day after the interview was completed.) 'My problem is to try to get along with people. In general they are phony.' 'I'll work, and I'd like to go into a business with my brother.' 'Piss on a marriage.' 'I'd like to help kids, train them in sports.'

(5) *What can society do to reduce violence?* 'If society wants to reduce violence they should begin in the home.' 'Show kids affection.' 'Someone has to really like them for what they are.'

(6) *What would you teach your children about fighting?* 'I'd teach my kids to never pick on someone weaker, or that couldn't defend himself.'

Description of the Interviewee During the Interview

The endogenous researchers in Prison B checked the following 15 points on each interviewee.

(1) Was S (interviewee) nervous or relaxed at the beginning of the interview.
(2) Did he later become relaxed? How soon?
(3) Did he speak spontaneously and continuously?
(4) Were there moments when S was hesitant or evasive?
(5) Did S try to impress the interviewers?
(6) Was S repetitious or did he seem to dwell on a certain idea?

(7) Was S interested in the interview? Did he seem to be preoccupied with something?

(8) Did his narration seem to be prefabricated?

(9) Did S tend to be abstract or did he relate concrete details? Did he illustrate his narration with hand movements, facial expressions, etc.? Was his narration vivid or dramatic?

(10) Did he show much insight into himself?

(11) Did he seem to gain insight during the interview?

(12) Did he seem to have a pet theory about himself or to parrot his psychiatrist's theory on him? (If he has a psychiatrist in the prison.)

(13) Did S's attitude change markedly during the interview?

(14) Were there moments when S seemed to want to get out of the interview or take a break, possibly with the pretext of going to the rest room or to the water fountain?

(15) Was there anything special about this s?

Validity Check and Reliability

The inmate researchers devised several methods of validity check and reliability check and carried them out. These methods are discussed elsewhere (Maruyama, 1969).

The numerous excerpts in the preceding pages indicate that persons without college or high-school education can be very articulate and sophisticated in their ability to conceptualize and design a research and to record, code, and analyse the data.

The next question is whether the data obtained show any different insights as compared to the data obtained by social scientists from outside. The answer is affirmative. The insights gained are numerous. They are discussed in detail elsewhere (Maruyama, 1968, 1969). The insights gained are on two levels: conceptual and factual. Examples are given below in a summary form.

Examples of Conceptual Insights

Some of the relations between categories made by inmate researchers make little sense as static classifications, but hold together if put into situational context of the prison culture. For example, 'associations' is listed as a subcategory of 'harm-avoidance'. Social scientists would rather put 'associations' under acceptance. As has become clear in the data, the primary motivation in joining a group in the prison or in the ghetto is often to avoid being attacked by the same group. This is one of the significant epistemological differences between the middle class and the ghetto or the prison. 'Harm-avoidance', in turn, is listed as one of the major components of prestige. This is logical in a culture in which the ability to avoid physical attack is very important.

Another example is 'defensive' which is listed as one of the subcategories of 'anxiety'. Other subcategories of 'anxiety' are: 'depression', 'emotional instability', and 'suicidal tendencies'. 'Defensive' seems to be out of place. But the data substantiate the connection: many individuals are unable to relate to others without defensiveness, and this inability frequently is a source of loneliness and its resulting anxiety.

Examples of Factual Insights

One of the findings is that there are many diverse types of philosophy of life and outlook on society among the violent individuals. I had expected that there would be some general philosophy of life and outlook on society with a smaller number of variations which would characterize violent individuals, but the number of diverse types found was much greater than anticipated. The diverse types found in the data are not amenable to neat categorization, but I have tentatively put them into the following groupings:

(1) Subjects learned violence or exploitation in childhood in ghettos for self-defence *against* their peers. The middle-class theory that a child learns to fight in order to be accepted by peers is incorrect in these cases. For example, a boy who sold narcotics to his peers in order to keep his girl friend, whom peers tried to steal from him with their money. Society is seen as individual against individual.

(2) The individual obtains protection by being subordinate to someone he fears and dislikes. Group formation by fear of insiders (*not* by fear of outsiders as the middle-class theory would interpret).

(3) Life centres around personal loyalty and individual efforts, buddy ties.

(4) Traumatic experiences with, or poor relations with, parents are the most influential factor in the subject's world-view.

(5) Life is dominated by a strong feeling of guilt.

(6) No guilt is felt about violence. While some subjects enjoy violence others consider violence as the only ability they have without enjoying it.

(7) Subjects fight for or in a clique or a group of individual friends.

(8) Life goal is to get married and raise a family. No bitterness is felt towards society.

(9) All of life is haphazard.

(10) No incentive: the individual is happier in prison than outside.

(11) The *main* factor in violence stems from homosexual relations.

(12) Phony throughout the interview.

(13) The *main* factor in violence is vocal hallucination (hearing voices).
(14), (15), (16) Three individuals with three unique types of philosophy of life and outlook on society.

Of the 16 types, the first two were far more frequent than the rest. Furthermore, these two types indicate the inadequacy of the theoretical models of violence and exploitation based on middle-class conceptualization. Two new models emerged as more adequate:

Dog-eat-dog model
(1) Each individual must defend himself *against* others in the 'peer' group.
(2) For each individual, other individuals are his enemies.
(3) He would rather get away from other individuals, but there is no way out.
(4) He fights for his defence, not for offence or for pleasure.
(5) He tries to avoid the situations in which he has to fight.
(6) He does not care whether he is liked by others. He would rather be feared.
(7) The 'group' is not formed by mutual attraction of its members. It is an aggregate *in spite of* its members.

In-or-be-killed model
(1) If the individual does not belong to the group, he is killed by the group.
(2) The members do not have to like one another.
(3) The members cooperate nevertheless, in order to produce collective power to fight individuals outside the group.

Another example of new insight is that the leader-follower model is inapplicable to most of the cases. In the incidents in which more than one individual cooperated, non-hierarchical partner relationship (whichever person gets attacked is helped by the other) and division-of-labour relationship (mostly in planned offence or defence) were prevalent.

Another insight gained is that in most of the fights (174 out of the total 241) the subjects fought alone without involving their friends.

Criteria for the Selection of Endogenous Researchers

Now that we have discussed the operational successes and failures of our past projects and pointed out for future projects several conditions for success, let me end this article with a list of criteria for the selection of future endogenous researchers.

(1) Formal education is not required.
(2) Because relevance resonance between the members of the culture and the

4

project is most crucial, the most important criterion for the selection of endogenous researchers is the sameness of his own goals with those of the people in the culture. He must have a strong identification with the people, especially the grass roots. Preferably he himself is a grass roots member. He must not be an armchair philosopher or a hermit. He must not be an Uncle Tom. He must not be a do-gooder. He must not be one of those who alienate themselves from their own culture and identify themselves with an outside culture. He may be bicultural, provided his identification is with his own culture. Monocultural, less 'contaminated' persons, are preferable if available. Relevance resonance also requires some degree of experiential, existential, and commitment resonance. The endogenous researcher therefore must have lived in the grass roots, and must have shared experiences, feelings, interests, goals, and purposes with the grass roots people, and must prove in action his commitment towards the goals of his people.

(3) He must be industrious and must have the ability for dedication to what he undertakes.

(4) He must be perceptive and must have the ability to relate to persons of all categories in his culture.

(5) Certain skills, such as typing and driving, increase the efficiency of the work, and the team should include some persons who can type, drive, operate tape-recorders, etc.

I must make here a special mention of the danger in delegating to someone the task of selecting and supervising the team members. I think anyone contemplating starting an endogenous research team should: (a) initially familiarize himself directly with different segments of the very bottom without going through intermediaries, get to know several individuals of each segment personally, and select team members from various segments. This will take several weeks. (b) Build the team from the bottom up, not from the top down; i.e. there should first be members who then elect the coordinator if needed, *not* first the coordinator who then selects the members. Both (a) and (b) are important in: (1) reducing the unfair factional representation and favouritism in the selection of team members; (2) insuring equality, democracy, and mutuality among the team members; and (3) reducing the manipulation and the leverage the intermediary may exercise against the team members or against you, or both.

Conclusion

I hope that this chapter, together with the earlier extract in Chapter 20, has sufficiently pointed out the rationale for endogenous research as the first step towards polyocular anthropology, and illustrated the capacity and contribution of endogenous researchers in my past projects. I hope it also has demonstrated the procedural and operational problems, successes, and failures we experienced, in such a way as to be useful to those who plan further explorations in endogenous research.

Human Inquiry
Edited by P. Reason and J. Rowan
© 1981 John Wiley & Sons Ltd.

CHAPTER TWENTY-FOUR

Culture and development in the Bagamoyo District of Tanzania

Marja-Liisa Swantz
Department of Sociology, University of Helsinki, Finland

> Development brings freedom, provided it is development *of people*
> (Julius Nyerere, 1973)

Tanzania's development policy emphasizes that the people's development means their participation in the decision-making, planning, and implementation processes. People develop when they become aware of their potential resources and capacity to influence their own lives and the lives of their community. This also has consequences in shaping the research policies in the country. People can be encouraged themselves to investigate how their needs could be satisfied and their life improved. Development research has the same immediate aim, which means that in this search the development researcher can join the people. Starting from the problems that the community faces, the researchers and the people themselves can cooperate to analyse the situation and to work together for the common good.

In response to an obvious need for an innovative research approach, the Ministry of National Culture and Youth, through its Department of Research

[Marja-Liisa Swantz and her colleagues will be writing about their work in Tanzania over the next few years. Jipemoyo, Development and Culture Research, Vol I is available (Swantz and Jerman, 1977); Jipemoyo II and III will be forthcoming. A list of publications is available at the project office: Bagamoyo Project Institute of Development Studies, University of Helsinki, Helsinki, Finland. The project address in Tanzania is: Jipemoyo, Ministry of National Culture and Youth, PO Box 4284, Dar es Salaam, Tanzania. — Eds.]

and Planning, initiated a research project in cooperation with the Academy of Finland, the aim of which was, together with the people of Western Bagamoyo District, to study the process of change in their villages. In the Bagamoyo Research Project, which later was named Jipemoyo, 'take heart', Tanzanian and Finnish researchers worked together over a period of four years, with 'Culture and social change in the restructuring of Tanzanian rural areas' as their general theme (Swantz and Jerman, 1977).

Summary of the Contextual Factors

The geographical area of the project covered the divisions Msoga, Msata, and Miono in West Bagamoyo District. The population of the area is over 27,000 and is composed of four main ethnic units, the Doe, Kwere, and Zigua, who are sedentary agriculturalists, and their neighbours, pastoralist Parakuyo-Maasai. The latter numbered 2882 in the previous countrywide census. They are considered by the farming population to be later immigrants to the area, and conflicts between the two sectors over land and cattle are frequent, while at the same time there is a degree of interdependence between them.

In the farming villages, more than three-quarters identify themselves as Muslims. The pastoralists have maintained their traditional mode of culture, although a number of them are Christian, and a handful of the latter have been to school. Among the farmers only recent years have brought general education, especially thrust forward since the implementation of the Universal Primary Education Act in 1978.

Long-distance trade routes from old coastal towns of Bagamoyo and Sadani went through or skirted the area, bringing it into contact with outsiders, and around it grew sisal plantations drawing seasonal labour from the villages. The climate is hot and humid, rainfall irregular, and the groundwater saline − in large areas unsuitable for human consumption. Surface and river waters have formed the main source of domestic water, often at great distance. In recent years, several villages have been provided with piped water. Since 1972 the total population has been brought to live in concentrated village areas. The moving operation caused some problems: delay in promised services, longer distances to walk to the fields, border problems between the cultivators and cattle-keepers, and grazing problems for the latter. Cultural differences between these two groups have also come into focus, resulting in some discriminatory practices.

The villages are led by popularly elected village governments, and the villagers contend for the posts of local Party Chairpersons and committee members. Several of them have learned to read and write through the adult literacy programmes, including pastoralist village leaders and, during the research project, women among them. In all important committees two places are reserved for women representatives.

Government officers and extension staff live in the larger administrative villages and their presence makes social stratification to be felt more clearly on the village level.

Identification of Research Problems

Before launching on the Bagamoyo project three other studies had been conducted in the District in which the participatory approach had been used in an experimental way (Swantz 1974, 1975a, 1975b; Swantz and Rudengreen, 1976).In them some of the problems on which the Jipemoyo research later focused had been initially identified. Parakuyo elders had been involved in this through discussions on the question of education, and through a self-study of village skills.

On the basis of background information that these studies provided, and of the initial contact with the villagers and their leaders, the focus in the new project was first on the problems the people had initially expressed. Further issues were then specified in a participatory research process with the villagers when the Jipemoyo researchers were living in the villages and took part in ordinary activities in the course of daily life.

After starting the work it became obvious that the total task had to be done in the context of people's acute problems such as unsatisfactory water supplies, livestock development, village crafts versus imported commodities, women's integration in village development, and effect of changes on nutrition, as well as difficulties faced in adjusting other needs to the demands of education.

In concrete terms, we were communicating from the start with the craftsmen whose constant complaint was lack of tools, failed promises by the field officers, and lack of material. Both Parakuyo and Kwere missed their normal supply of beads. The reasons for not engaging in potmaking or mat- and basket-weaving were lack of either time, strength, or water. With the country's policy of developing small industries in villages the obvious question arose how the crafts could be made a viable part of village production.

The water problem was constantly present for the researchers as well as for the villagers, although the former could transport their drinking water from town in large containers when they had a car available. The same services were used by the wealthier villagers. Thus the fulfilment of an elementary basic need became one of the points at which economic differentiation was manifested.

During the research the pastoralist women became activated and thus a problem which a researcher formulated to herself from the start became actual also for the women themselves, after they had started to learn reading and took part in a seminar about their own educational questions. When at the beginning of the project research the men's concerted statement about girls' education was that they would never agree to send their girls to school, in a year's time some of the women were already expressing their demand that they and their daughters be given education. It became obvious that people's daily difficulties were part of contradictions which would need problematization and theoretization.

There was clearly a dialectical unity between theory and practice. The solution of practical problems would have only temporary effect had the task not been set also in theoretical terms for the guidance of policies and strategies. Thus the theoretical goals were set in relation to the solution of people's practical problems. Participatory research was adopted as the common approach.

It was possible to solve a problem of an individual smiths' or carpenters' cooperative workshop by drawing the attention of an appropriate government official to a specific need for tools or materials, just as it was possible to exert influence so that needed supplies became available for pastoralist women's beadcraft. But no lasting solution could be affected without a policy which would permit imports of supplies needed for craftsmen's work or a sound policy concerning the interrelationship between the farm equipment or furniture manufacturing plants, the machine-equipped small production units in the city, and the village craft production, all operating under the same Ministry.

For making a policy which would make these three levels of production support each other, instead of working in competition, information was needed about the ways that distribution and marketing operated in practice, the way in which the different levels undercut one another, what obstacles there were for the advancement of the work of the village craftsmen/women in practice, etc.

The perpetual dearth of tools in villages raised the problem to yet another level. Partly it pointed to the incapability and unwillingness of the functional officers to fulfil their duties towards the villages and thus led to the theoretical issue of stratification or class analysis. Beyond that there was an acute problem: should the villagers be encouraged to be self-reliant and make most of the tools with which they could manage to produce, at least enough for their own needs, or should at this time foreign tools be imported in an effort to accelerate the development of productive forces? Examples of both were available. The solution on the national level required also an analysis on the village level.

It is obvious that the theoretical base adopted influences the policy recommendations, but no concrete support can be given to a theory unless concrete case-material and people's own thinking on such issues are incorporated. What happens when a school workshop unit starts from scrap-iron both to learn skills and to make all necessary tools? Does it lead to village industry, and if not why not? What happens should a machine workshop be introduced into a village of craftsmen? Who makes use of it? Does it lead to the development of village industry, which is based on the traditional crafts?

A mode of cooperation, still continuing today, is exercised in ritual preparations. *'Kama huna kitu ndugu watakusaidia, debe saba, gunia moja, debe mbili, upike pombe, ujamaa wa kindugu'.* 'If you do not have a thing your relatives help you, seven tin canisters, one sack, two canisters (of maize and millet) for brewing beer, *ujamaa,* i.e. socialism, familyhood of kinship'. The manifestations of *'ujamaa wa kindugu',* are many on the village level, and even appear in towns. The theoretical question which arises immediately is: in what way can the new *ujamaa* be built on the old one, or can it at all be taken as the base? Should the kin-based *ujamaa* be encouraged, or should it rather be destroyed? In either case, what is development? What is outcome? What is the theory? Both views were represented in later theoretical elaborations. The interrelatedness of the different levels of analysis became obvious and again confirmed the point that research should be built on larger units and on more interaction between theory and practice and different disciplines, not to mention the cooperation and participation of the people from all the levels.

The Jipemoyo research project was designed principally to study the local manifestations of culture in relation to the social, political, and economic changes taking place in the country. It grew out of an assumption that people's own cultural wealth could and should be utilized as the source of creative action and planning for their own advancement and development. The research was intended to discover ways and means whereby the people's own resources could be released for their development and the theoretical base worked for it to guide the action. There was a further initial hypothesis that the sources of development could be discovered only by the people themselves, but that in this search some probing and stimulation by outsiders would be helpful.

The assumptions made at the start were roughly in line with the socialist theory guiding the policy in Tanzania, as interpreted by those planning the research, and it was considered to be in accordance with the policy of the Ministry of National Culture and Youth at the time of making the plans. This did not prevent us from being critical both of policies and their application during the research process.

National interests were in the forefront also in setting another aim: recording and documenting cultural material which would disappear in the rapid process of change. In accordance with the principle of people's participation the documenting of cultural material had to be done in such a way that it, too, would benefit the people's own development process.

Initially the project research could be designed only by stating the general problems and potential research tasks, and describing the participatory approach which was planned to be applied. The nature of the task which was to be defined in a concrete context and arise from actual people's problems required scope for changes in plans and methods of research and action.

The project aims stated in the initial research plan served as the starting point:

(1) To analyse the role of culture in the process of change:
    (a) as a factor deterring change;
    (b) as a motivational and creative element in the process of change.
(2) To participate in the process of development and socialist construction, and to experiment in methods of development research which incorporate people from all levels in the process of research and create in them awareness of their own resources.
(3) To collect, document, and study cultural material which disappears in the midst of change. To organize a system of collection, systematization and archiving cultural data, oral tradition, and music.
(4) To assist in training Tanzanian and Finnish scholars in participatory research methods, in techniques of collecting cultural material, and in analysing the data.
(5) To create models of field training for cultural officers, officers working in village situations (agricultural, veterinary, health officers), and students in preparation for such tasks.

Participatory research approach has enabled the people in the area to become active components in the research. The incorporation of the people was to serve the development of the communities concerned but also to give the research a base in people's own categories of understanding and in their interpretation of their cultural forms. It was also to offer the people an opportunity for self-articulation both in cultural practice and in formulating an action base for the village communities in question.

Participatory approach has required first of all participatory presence with the people with whom the research is carried out. Ordinary discussions, participation in village events; sharing the work at hand; sitting around in front of houses, on the fields, or in bars and shopfronts; all are opportunities of mutual sharing.

One of the important ways of gaining fuller participation by all the parties concerned has been *village seminars* in which officers and leaders from all levels have been invited to meet with groups of villagers, e.g. one-day seminar for craftsmen and women, another two-day seminar for the pastoralists, a three-week training seminar for cultural officers, another two-week one for women officers, and a further village leadership seminar of two weeks in villages organized by the district. In an open encounter villagers have been able to express themselves freely. All the deliberations have been taped so that their dynamics can thus be analysed later. Reports of these encounters have been distributed to all the participants. As a result new avenues have been opened both for action and continued communication. The sense of participation by the pastoralists was enhanced by their offer to treat the officers as their guests and to provide meat and milk for feeding them.

A dialectical method has been used in the study of music whereby the techniques of instrument-building and use, as well as dancing and ritual procedures, have been worked out through a continuing mutual feedback process and interaction between the researcher and the music specialists.

The researchers have participated in formal and informal *village meetings* and committees as well as in meetings with District and Regional officers, and have made visits to parastatals, ministries, and numerous other offices.

Supplementary methods and instruments were chosen following a principle that they were in harmony with the basic approach of subject participation. The total research situation had created an atmosphere of cooperation which then allowed, for example, the use of some surveys, in the making of which members of the village community from different levels cooperated.

Whatever the theoretical preferences of the individual researchers would have been in practice, research proceeded from concrete to abstract, from practical participation to the analysis of the observed and studied material, while the theoretical starting points were also made explicit. The problem of theory and practice and their dialectical relationship was continually reflected in meetings between the researchers and associates to give fresh perspective to the task.

Since the research was designed as a local participatory study there has been an inevitable conflict between the time used for the theoretical task and background reading and the designed participation, close first-hand documentation, and analysis of the changing village societies. The task was to formulate a general theory as well as to study the local situation, and tension between these two aspects has been felt both by individual researchers and in the common struggle for a balanced emphasis in the research work.

The theoretical task has had at least the following components:

(1) historical analysis of the development of the West Bagamoyo societies;
(2) an analysis of the present-day socio-economic situation in Tanzania in general and in the Western Bagamoyo District in particular, with the aim of finding a general framework for application in the study of culture;
(3) formulating the theoretical basis for study of culture in the Tanzanian political situation which is applicable to the whole country and relates to the concrete data of the local societies in West Bagamoyo.

At the same time as some team members concentrated in formulation of an adequate theoretical framework the participatory village work continued in the context of practical undertakings, making it possible to let the concrete material influence the theory-building in relation to the following problem areas which have formed the focus of the individual research tasks:

(1) Development of music culture in Miono area and the role of music in the development process. A case study of a specific *selo-ngoma* tradition, and preparing a teaching guide of it for secondary schools. Developing a small-scale drum-making industry (Philip Donner and Juma Nasoro).

(2) The historical development of village crafts in West Bagamoyo, the role they have played in the social and economic life of the society and the decline of crafts under colonialism. The attempt to revive the crafts as the basis for small-scale village industries on socialist principles (B. K. S. Kiyenze).

(3) The historical development of the pastoralists in Western Bagamoyo District and their relationship to the national livestock industry in the context of planning a pastoral village development project together with the pastoralists (K. Mustafa, P. Rigby, A. Hurskainen, J. R. Wanga, and M. Matwi).

(4) Developing a documentation system for all types of cultural material using the Jipemoyo archives as its basis. Developing systematization based on problem-oriented collection of material (U. Vuorela and J. Shashinhale).

(5) Women in food production, distribution, and family nutrition. Replacement of subsistence production by commodity production and exchange. The changing food-culture and techniques of food production and their effect on woman's workload and role in village development. Woman's social roles in relation to the historical development of the area. Effects of *ujamaa* development on women's position (U. Vuorela, M-L. Swantz, D. Bryceson, E. Kiwale, and M. Mbilinyi).

(6) Ethnic identification and national consciousness in relation to the socio-economic structure, political organization, and ideology in Western Bagamoyo District (H. Jerman).

(7) The physical changes in village resettlement and their effects on the social and economic life of the villages (Taimi Sitari).

The Bagamoyo project has demonstrated that culture cannot be separated into a category of its own and then relegated to one corner of national life.

In retrospect, whichever theoretical framework the respective team members have applied they all have witnessed the strength that the endogenous mode of culture has within several sectors of the society. It has become evident that creative change can take place within these groups only if their contribution in it is taken seriously and their own mode of life integrated into the new plans. This has been the case especially with the pastoralists. Their mode of life differs greatly from the general pattern of an agriculturalist peasant society which tends to serve as the mode to which rural people in general are fitted. The nature of conflicts and their causes has required a cultural and social analysis, through which the people themselves — as well as the leaders — have become aware of the contradictory aspects in the necessary and (even to the people themselves, desirable) change. At the same time, ways have been found for a creative use of people's skills in cattle-keeping, of their crafts, or their music heritage.

Practical Results of Jipemoyo

The time allocated for research has been long enough both to make mistakes and to correct at least some of them. In the Ministry of Culture participatory research has been adopted as one of the major approaches to culture research and the model is being tried out in varying forms, for example in nutrition research, education, and in the evaluation of primary health services.

The major problem has been to effect lasting changes in the villages. The emphasis has been on the institutionalizing of the changes and on giving them some permanent organizational form to the extent that it has been possible. Particularly the channels of action for the villagers had to be cleared in such a way that there was no continuing dependency on intermediary agencies. The pastoralists who felt they had a little say in the local decision-making organs have become aware of their right to influence decisions concerning themselves in such a way that one can hope they will not again allow themselves to be by-passed.

The project has attempted at all points to work through the existing institutions and official channels in order to minimize the temporary effect of its work. The work has been taken over by the Ministry of Culture in such a way that its continuity and benefits for the country have been secured.

The participatory research approach, which has been widened to participatory evaluation and participatory training and is suggested for use in planning, is readily adopted by Tanzanian agencies in charge of development planning and implementation, as it is also by the Ministry of National Culture and Youth. It is much harder to convince the academically trained social scientists of its 'objectivity, reliability and validity'. In the minds of we who have had to struggle through both the practical and theoretical difficulties of the approach there is no doubt but that this will open a fruitful road for research; but it will require time and practical experience for maturing. There is no point in trying to fit the participatory approach into a formula that is not suitable for it; it is bound to develop into a critique of traditional methods of social sciences.

Human Inquiry
Edited by P. Reason and J. Rowan
© 1981 John Wiley & Sons Ltd.

CHAPTER TWENTY-FIVE

Dialogue as inquiry and intervention

Rajesh Tandon
Public Enterprises Centre for Continuing Education,
New Delhi, India

The notion of inquiry as intervention in social systems has emerged only recently in the respectable academic circles. Action research has been the forerunner of such an approach to integrate inquiry and intervention (Lewin, 1947b). However, there is beginning to emerge some consensus among the action researchers (L. D. Brown, 1972) and participatory researchers (Hall, 1975; Tandon, 1979) that inquiry can be conceptualized and practised as an intervention process. Some illustrations of such a perspective have also appeared in recent years (Brown and Tandon, 1978). Dialogue as inquiry and intervention was first described by Freire (1970) and it has since been used by Freire himself and his colleagues. Dialogue presents a potent method of integrating inquiry and intervention, and it can contribute to the intermingled processes of knowing and changing.

This chapter presents a case from the two-year field work by the author where dialogue was used as inquiry and intervention simultaneously. Small and marginal farmers in a region of Western India were the participants in this effort. The next section presents an account of this inquiry.

Inquiry with Marginal Farmers

Pre-encounter

A non-governmental voluntary agency operated in an area that is primarily agricultural and economically backward. The bulk of the population is tribal and owns small (less than ten acres) plots of land. Less than 2 per cent of the cultivated land is irrigated. Of the 230 villages in the area, only two have electricity. Since the area is hilly, only small (less than one acre) plots of land are available for cultivation. As of 1971, only about 14 per cent of the population was literate.

The agency started a programme for poor, marginal farmers in 1975. The agency identified one poor farmer each from 25 contiguous villages to act as 'peer group leaders' in their villages. These farmers were given training in techniques of modern agriculture, cooperative societies, and rural engineering. These peer group leaders were then asked to disseminate this new information and ideas among their peers in their villages. The peer group leaders were young, literate, and cultivated small (less than five acres) plots of land.

The peer group leaders were asked to organize their peers in the villages not only to disseminate the newly acquired knowledge but also to act as instruments of socio-economic and political change in the villages. The field staff of the agency maintained regular contact with the peer group leaders and organized their monthly meetings. Every peer group leader was asked to maintain a journal of his daily peer group activities and these were periodically checked by the agency staff.

Two years after the start of the programme, the author was approached by the agency to assist them in further strengthening the peer groups. The agency staff felt that despite their training efforts, peer groups were still not organized enough to take initiatives in their common interests. The author agreed to involve himself with these peer group leaders with a view to understanding the dynamics of rural situations in India and developing insights into the processes of rural change. He agreed to enter into a dialogue with these 25 peer group leaders during one of their next monthly meetings.

During the initial discussions with the agency staff, it became clear that the training provided by the agency had essentially been a cognitive input. Most of the knowledge and ideas had flowed from the agency staff to the peer group leaders. The latter had been passive recipients of these inputs. The author decided to join the next regular monthly meeting which would be a three-day event. It was felt that attempt could be made to engage in collaborative exploration of the peer group leaders' situation with a view to identifying what could possibly be done.

First Encounter

The meeting was organized in a village where the peer group leaders, some agency staff, and the author lived together and shared the responsibilities for preparing food and managing other living arrangements. After the initial introductions, the author clarified his role in the meeting. He emphasized that his main motivation to join them was to enter into a dialogue with them about their situation and its implications. The dialogue was carried out in several sequences during the three-day period. An illustration of the dialogue is presented here.

Author: Why have you become peer group leaders?

Participant: (After a five-minute silence). Because we want to improve our villages.

Author: Why do you want to improve your villages?

Participant: (The same one). Because villagers are poor; they do not have enough to eat.

Author: Are all villagers poor?

Participant: (Some soft murmur followed by a tentative response from another participant). No. Except for one or two families, all others are poor.

Author: Are you among those poor?

Participants: (Many spoke together). Yes.

Author: Why are you poor?

                  (This question led to a long silence. They looked at each other; a few talked among themselves very softly. The author repeated the question).

Participant: (This person was asked by several of them to answer the question). We are poor because we are illiterate, ignorant, weak and lazy.

Author: Do those who are not poor make you poor? Do you have any experiences of this?

                  (This led to a somewhat more active discussion among a few peer group leaders and several examples of personal experiences were shared. The ensuing discussion led to some tentative conclusions about what could be done. One of them was to get organized in order to have collective influence.)

Towards the end of the meeting, each peer group leader identified three village problems that they wanted to act upon after the meeting. The author and the agency staff assisted them in planning how to solve those problems. It was agreed that the author and agency staff visit them in their villages. They also suggested that the author attend their next monthly meeting which could also be of three days duration.

The author, acting on his research interests, had designed a research questionnaire in consultation with agency staff. This questionnaire was intended to assess the level of awareness and information base of peer group leaders, their perceived level of influence upon other villagers as well as the various government and public functionaries external to the village. Several demographic items were also included in it. It should be emphasized here that this questionnaire was based on traditional research assumptions, specifically relating to the nature of the phenomena and the methods of data-collection most appropriate for the same. The peer group leaders were requested to fill these questionnaires before, immediately after, and six weeks after the first meeting in which the author was involved. Again, the author was acting upon the research design learnt in the traditional research paradigm.

The first meeting left several discomforting elements. The meeting was a rather low-key event and many participants had maintained complete silence. In their conversations with agency staff, several peer group leaders mentioned their discomfort from the meeting. They had expected some tangible benefits from the author's presence, in the form of new subsidies or projects. They also had initial reservations about the author, being an urban stranger. They mentioned their reluctance to be frank in his presence.

The author himself felt fairly uncomfortable in that situation. The following excerpt from his personal notes gives a glimpse of the 'culture shock' that he experienced:

> It was during this visit that I experienced the sharp contrasts from the urban life that I was used to. It was summer then, and I was profusely sweating, only to realize that there was no electricity here. In the evening, it was suggested that we all take a bath. I was glad to hear that. When we reached the river, I started having second thoughts about taking a dip in that river. The water was dirty, but the whole village was bathing and washing clothes there. As if that was not enough, a herd of cattle walked into the river to cool themselves. The next morning, I realized that toilet facilities were an urban phenomenon and I had the option to use the open pastures anywhere. One after another, the rural context was devoid of things and facilities that I had taken for granted before. It was a disorienting and discomforting experience.

Second Encounter

The second meeting turned out to be a much more lively and exciting event. The primary focus of the meeting was to share and analyse the experiences of peer group leaders in acting on the problems they had identified in the previous meeting. The participants described in detail the methods adopting in solving those problems, the hurdles encountered from within the village as well as from utside, and the outcomes achieved. Most participants, along with the author and other agency staff, actively engaged in diagnosing the nature of difficulties encountered in, and possible remedies for taking collective actions in, the villages. To illustrate, the presentation made by one peer group leader, Babulal, is quoted below:

> When I went back from here last month, I decided to improve the attendance in primary school. About 30 children in the village do not go to school at all. I suggested this to other villagers who generally expressed their inability to spare children to go to school. These children were assisting the family in obtaining bread twice-a-day. Then I went to the primary school teacher and requested him to create some new and interesting opportunities for these children so that they can have a brighter future. The teacher expressed his anger against the villagers, calling them 'dumb'. You know, we are operating in a situation where the villagers as well as the society continue to make us poorer and weaker. I would like to take this up as a challenge for my peer group. We will increase the enrollment in the school within a month.

Towards the end of the meeting, the author presented some of his concepts about problem-solving and strategies for collective action. His sharing of ideas and experiences was better understood by the participants then. It appears that the author, as well as the participants, had begun to feel comfortable with each other. Interactions between them became easier and greater reciprocity was visible. As the author became more comfortable in that situation, the participants were able to share their hopes and fears more freely. As the participants felt more comfortable with the author, he was able to present his ideas more easily. It was clear that the second meeting had been a more effective dialogue between the author and the peer group leaders, largely because mutual trust and comfort had been established between them.

Post-encounter

Along with agency staff, the author met the peer group leaders in their villages after the second meeting. This follow-up was primarily aimed at supporting the peer group leaders and their peer groups in their new efforts. The author was also collecting detailed notes about the events taking place in the field in order to satisfy his research interests. The follow-up visits provided opportunities to observe the peer group leaders in their own villages and to understand the dynamics of rural situation more closely. The relationships established with these peer group leaders during those meetings helped the author to move and nose around the villages more easily. Extensive field notes were made during these follow-up visits.

The author became aware of the daily journals being maintained by the peer group leaders as a source of research data during these visits. He collected these journals and analysed them by coding the entries in six categories: active initiatives, planned initiatives, informed initiatives, collective initiatives, initiatives that showed influence on villagers, and initiatives that showed influence on government and public functionaries. As analysis of these coded entries showed that peer group leaders had shown significantly greater initiatives in all six categories in the two quarters after the first meeting in comparison to the eight quarters before that meeting. It appeared that the dialogue during the meetings empowered the peer group leaders and their peer groups both within and outside the village.

However, an analysis of the questionnaire responses showed a different picture. There was no change in any of the dimensions of activity or influence over the three time-periods in questionnaire data were collected. Moreover, the percentage response on questionnaires decreased over time. While all the 2! peer group leaders had filled in the questionnaire in the beginning, the completed response was about 70 per cent over the second administration and about 50 per cent over the third one.

The field notes of the author were consistent with the journal entries but incongruent with the questionnaire data. The field observations clearly indicated that dialogues in the two meetings had significant impact on the peer group leaders and their peer groups. To illustrate, the following field notes were made in the case of one peer group leader, Babulal:

> Babulal and his peers organised a meeting in the village to persuade villagers to send their children to school. After two months, eighteen new children had started going to the school. Twenty farmers used new variety of seeds for the winter sowing of wheat for the first time. The peer group had approached the Development Officer with complaints against the corrupt practices of the Panchayat (village council) head. On enquiry by an officer, these charges were established and the Panchayat head was suspended. The peer group had begun discussions about electing a new leader in the forthcoming Panchayat elections. They held several meetings within the village to evolve a consensus candidate. In the forthcoming Panchayat elections, one of the peers was overwhelmingly elected as the Panchayat head. By the end of a year after the first meeting, a strong peer group of fifteen members was operating in the village.

Implications

The above case highlights the close connection between inquiry and intervention. It indicates that the processes of understanding and changing were taking place simultaneously. Dialogue as the principal method led to both enhanced understanding and significant changes. Dialogue becomes the vehicle for critical consciousness and praxis (Freire, 1970). Action and reflection together can generate understanding and bring about changes. Therefore, dialogue acts as a method to integrate inquiry and intervention. Several implications follow from the notion of dialogue as inquiry and intervention. The case presented above highlights some of these implications.

(1) *Dialogue as inquiry and intervention has mutual impact.* The traditional paradigm emphasizes distinction of researcher and subjects. They are seen as two separate parties; and inquiry is the process of researcher's knowing about the subjects. In the traditional research paradigm, the process of inquiry does not entail any impact on the researcher, nor on the subjects. However, this is not so in dialogue as inquiry and intervention. Both the researcher and the subjects learn from each other; they also learn together from the very situation that they are a part of and are engaged in analysis of. The interests of both parties are mutually inclusive and supportive in dialogue.

The case presented here demonstrates this point clearly. The dialogues during the two meetings had significant impact on the peer group leaders. Their levels of initiatives increased significantly and they had acquired greater collective influence in their villages. They developed an understanding of the dynamics of their poverty and made attempts to counter it. As the field notes and journal entries showed, the behaviours of peer group leaders after the two meetings reflected the impact that dialogues had made on their lives.

Similarly, the researcher was influenced by those meetings. The author experienced discomfort in the village situation and had to unlearn his urban stereotypes. Understanding and inquiry became possible only afterwards. In dialogues with peer group leaders, he obtained insights into their lives and rural situation. In jointly analysing the actions of peer group leaders, he developed an understanding of processes of rural change. His emotional and cognitive orientations were first challenged by the situation and then modified by dialogues. His personal notes and experiences of the first meeting reflect these impacts on the author.

(2) The second implication relates to the concept of validity in research. Simply stated, validity implies an authentic representation of reality. Traditional research paradigm emphasizes an elaborate set of criteria for validity. The dialogue as a method of inquiry and intervention negates some of these criteria of validity. *The data-collection process that is most relevant to both parties determines its validity.* When the data-collection process is disjointed from the context and content of dialogues, it becomes invalid. This makes it imperative for the researcher to be inventive about his methods of data-collection. The challenge to innovate such methods of data-collection can

be met most successfully in a collaborative effort between the researcher and the subjects. The researcher alone cannot set the limits of validity in such a research process. Consensual validation that is relevant and meaningful to both parties can facilitate innovation in the data-collection process.

In the case presented here, a questionnaire based on traditional research paradigm was one source of data-collection. Clinical and anthropological data from the daily journals and field observations were also analysed. While the former source did not indicate any changes in the peer group leaders, the latter were more consistent with reality. The questionnaire data were invalid as they were not an integral part of the entire process. Questionnaires were designed and administered primarily for the purpose of finding out the impact of dialogues. That was exclusively the researcher's need. But the participants did not see any relevance of the questionnaire to their experiences before and after the meetings. As one farmer put it, 'Why do you want us to fill the questionnaire? If you want to know anything, just ask me.'

While the questionnaires appeared disjointed and disconnected from their experiences, emotions, and actions, the daily journals were quite the opposite. While the questionnaires appeared to be unnatural, arbitrary, and external intrusions in their lives, the journals were accepted as an integral and ongoing part of their role as peer group leaders. Therefore, using journal entries to understand their hopes and fears, actions, and reservations became a valid source of information. It was the collaboration of researcher's needs and farmers' interests that resulted in the use of codified journal entries for understanding. Journal entries as a source of valid data became mutually relevant.

(3) As argued earlier, such a process of inquiry has substantial impact on people and their lives. To the extent that there is impact on people, value-neutrality of the researcher is a myth. *Dialogue as inquiry and intervention thus becomes a political and ideological process.* The ideological and political implications have two primary aspects. First, the initiation of inquiry depends upon the acceptance of the researcher's value-positions by those who are his relevant 'clients'. In this case, the author's beliefs and motives were ascertained by agency staff and marginal farmers before inquiry could begin. It is important to note that verbal statements of value-positions are not enough; behavioural congruence with those values needs to be established with the 'clients'. It was not enough for the author to tell the agency staff that he was for the rural poor. They believed it only when they saw the author in action.

The second aspect relates to the political consequences of ideological positions of the researcher. When the researcher's values are in alliance with one class, antagonists to the researcher also exist in the same social situation.

Thus, the researcher has enemies too, and this may have repercussions on the inquiry — from subtle sabotage to physical injury to the researcher.

Dialogues in this case resulted in increased organization and empowerment of marginal farmers. As some peer groups became active in the politics of Panchayat elections, they challenged those in positions of power. There were also some instances of political and physical confrontations. The author had his own fears of physical assault, based on his being openly identified with the marginal farmers, especially during field visits. Similar fears related to possible adverse repercussions on his employment if political influence was used by those whose power positions were challenged by the marginal farmers. As the process proceeded further, such fears intensified. While nothing noteworthy happened in this regard, it is important to underscore the political nature of such inquiry so that enthusiastic researchers do not find themselves surprisingly caught unprepared in the midst of a major political conflict. At the same time, researchers need to be cautioned so that they do not unwittingly act to subvert their own value positions by supporting the wrong side.

(4)   When the processes of knowing and changing occur simultaneously, the researchers face a dilemma. If the situation under study undergoes changes by the process of study, then what is finally studied is something different from what was originally intended. *Dialogue as inquiry and intervention presents this dilemma.* The dialogue generates both understanding and change. To that extent, it contaminates the situation it purports to study.

In this case, the rural situation obtaining in the villages of peer group leaders was altered after the meetings. As peer group leaders took more initiatives and became more empowered, the village situation underwent changes. What the researcher and the farmers then understood was the changed village situation and the dynamics of change. It was then possible to understand why the earlier village situation was the way it was.

This indicates one method of studying under-organized systems. L.D. Brown (1979) describes under-organized systems as those which are characterized by lack of regulation and formal structures, unclear purposes and poorly defined boundaries. Dialogue as inquiry and intervention may be the only possible way to study such systems. Any attempt to study under-organized systems will make them more organized. Dialogue will certainly do that; therefore, it is through the process of organizing the under-organized systems that one can understand the forces that were keeping it under-organized. Dialogue as inquiry and intervention can help in that.

Human Inquiry
Edited by P. Reason and J. Rowan
© 1981 John Wiley & Sons Ltd.

CHAPTER TWENTY-SIX

Participative research in a factory

L. Dave Brown
*Public Enterprises Centre for Continuing Education, New
Delhi, India and Case Western Reserve University*
Robert E. Kaplan
*Centre for Creative Leadership, Greensboro, North Carolina,
USA*

There are a number of alternative approaches to social science inquiry presently available. 'Action research', for example, has emphasized solving specific problems while generating general knowledge (Lewin, 1946; Rapoport, 1970). 'Participatory research' emphasizes the cooperation of 'researchers' and 'subjects' in the problem-solving process (Hall, 1975). What we call participative research combines aspects of both of the above types of research. Participative research emphasizes joint investigation by researchers and subjects to produce both new understandings of organizational realities and solutions to specific problems. During the project described below, the initial diversity of interests and assumptions among the parties evolved into a mutually beneficial exchange of perspectives.

The following section describes events in a five-year organizational research and development project. The narration focuses on the processes of joint inquiry by which external researchers and organization members examined organizational 'realities' and encouraged constructive change. The next section considers some implications of the case study for participative research.

Participative Research at Northern Chemical Works

A full account of five years' work at the Northern Chemical Works is not practical here, but some aspects of the project are particularly relevant to participative research. Four such aspects will be considered here: (1) initial negotiations, (2) the Textiles Plant diagnosis, (3) works authority relations, and (4) understanding long-term change processes.

Initial Negotiations

The Northern Chemical Works is a subsidiary of a large multinational corporation. The three different plants at the Works employ about 1000 workers and managers in a complex technical installation. Deteriorating labour-management relations produced a four-month strike in 1972, and technical difficulties further reduced the performance of the Works in subsequent months. In 1973 a new Works Manager was appointed to 'turn the Works around', particularly in the sense of improving employee relations. He approached the authors for aid in diagnosing and solving employee relations problems.

Initial discussions between researcher-consultants (hereafter, 'researchers') and managers were characterized by curiosity, wariness, and some perplexity occasioned by their differences in interest, perspective, and experiences. The managers were primarily interested in solving their immediate problems, while the researchers were concerned with more abstract issues. The languages and concepts of the two were often mutually incomprehensible. The researchers were concerned about manager expectations ('We don't have any magic wand that will insure that you don't have another strike'). The managers were worried about the naiveté of the researchers, who had little experience in industrial organizations (Manager: 'Do you think open communications are always appropriate?' Researcher: 'Lord, no!' Manager (with evident relief): 'Oh.') After several meetings a six-month contract for initial exploration was negotiated. The managers thought its provisions too vague, and the researchers thought them too specific, but both were willing to experiment, given the chance to renegotiate after six months.

The initial discussions also revealed severe union-management conflict. Management spoke despairingly of the union as 'The Black Cloud' that hung over all events at the Plant. The researchers met the union executive and heard angry attacks on the corporation's 'international conspiracy' against the union. They concluded that joining forces with either union or management would be less beneficial to the organization as a whole than establishing credibility with both. They resisted the temptation to join either management, who offered financial support and initial access to the organization, or the union, with whom they felt ideological sympathy — though their resistance created some tensions with both parties. Instead the researchers arranged to work with both union and management personnel in some limited area of the Works.

Textiles Plant Diagnosis

The Textiles Plant was chosen for the initial research and problem-solving. The researchers took pains to enlist the participation of the 150 employees of the Plant. A Liaison Committee was formed consisting of representatives from all levels and functions of the Plant, and helped plan the diagnosis. After interviews with all the managers and a sample of the employees an 'empathic' questionnaire was devised using direct quotations from the interviews. After the interview and questionnaire data were analysed, the results were fed back to Plant personnel in small group meetings in which the report could be discussed and action steps identified.

As the diagnosis unfolded, difficulties emerged. Managers objected to some questionnaire items as excessively pro-union; union executives objected to other items as anti-union and threatened to prosecute the researchers for illegal influence on the workers. Two graduate student researchers employed for the summer in the Textiles Plant found themselves increasingly isolated from both management and union. Many managers found it difficult to relate to the workers' perception of management as 'unresponsive'; some cherished the notion that employee relations problems were all the result of 'crazy union officers'. Many workers were very sceptical about the diagnosis, and the lack of immediate action after the diagnosis confirmed their view of management as unresponsive. Thus, the diagnosis produced much information about Plant problems, but few steps towards their solution. It also failed to achieve the full participation of the various segments of the Plant population.

Each party had its own perspective on the experience. The researchers (particularly the graduate students) were critical of Textiles personnel, especially management. Textiles managers pointed to the researcher's unrealistic expectations and union intransigence. The workers saw the diagnosis as a management trick to gull the workers into thinking things were better. In short, the diagnostic process suffered from a general retreat from responsibility for taking action.

The Textiles diagnosis was generally perceived as unsuccessful, and the researchers eventually concentrated their efforts elsewhere. But the Textiles experience did produce important shared understandings between researchers and organisation members, especially top management. Given the polarized union-management relationship, the senior managers and the researchers decided to have the latter work exclusively with management unless the union explicitly requested their involvement. Given the fitful commitment of Works management to the researchers' efforts, the senior managers agreed to take a more active role and to encourage other managers to do so.

Understanding and Changing Authority Relations

While the researchers were occupied with the Textiles diagnosis, Works management launched a 'research-action' initiative of its own. They created a 'Support Group' which was intended to be a communication link with foremen, who themselves were the primary interface between management and workers. The Support Group, consisting of the Assistant to the Works Manager and three foremen highly respected by their peers, was charged with finding out what was on the foremen's minds and with advising the foremen in their work. The researchers had nothing to do with the formation of the Support Group, and for a time, the Support Group avoided associating itself overtly with the researchers because of the latter's reputation after the Textiles diagnosis. But eventually, shared interests in understanding and solving organizational problems gradually brought them together. The researchers had access to top management and skills not available to the Support Group; the Support Group had credibility with lower levels and full-time availability that the researchers lacked. The Support Group proved to be an important force in subsequent activities at the Works.

Another new institution was the Steering Committee, which resulted from the researchers' requests for more active engagement of senior managers in the project. This Committee included two senior managers (Works Manager and Assistant Works Manager), the Supervisor of the Support Group and the senior members of the research team. The Steering Committee undertook to plan, initiate, monitor, and follow up interventions. It provided sanction for experimental activities, a larger perspective on organizational problems, and organizationally visible commitment to problem-solving by top management.

The Steering Committee and the Support Group were instrumental in an organization-wide analysis and change programme launched to alter organizational authority relations. As the Support Group talked with foremen and managers, Plant-wide concerns emerged about general issues of authority and leadership. The Support Group summarized these concerns in a 'white paper', which integrated concepts from the researchers with personal knowledge of day-to-day life in the Works. On the basis of this paper, the Steering Committee (including the researchers) and Support Group designed a 'site change effort' to promote better understanding and improved relations among superiors and subordinates throughout the organization.

The proposed intervention had three components: (1) discussions of the white paper by work teams, aided by Support Group members, (2) workshops on interpersonal communications, staffed by the researchers and the Support Group together (for upper management) or by the Support Group alone (for lower management), and (3) discussions to clarify mutual expectations between superior-subordinate pairs with third-party facilitation (researcher or Support Group) when requested. The first component focused on organization-wide leadership issues; the second revolved around superior-subordinate relations in general; the third examined mutual expectations and leadership in specific superior-subordinate relationships. The intervention began with senior management and eventually included all management.

This design emerged from lively debates among the diverse members of the Steering Committee. The focus on leadership grew out of the Support Group's white paper; clarifying job expectations was particularly important to top management; prompting two-way communications and better relationships was emphasized by the researchers. In practice, the intervention was modified by participants at each level. The experience with senior managers influenced the design for middle managers; the experience with middle managers affected the design for foremen. All levels of management participated in the white paper discussions and in the workshops; all senior managers participated in superior-subordinate discussions, though lower-level managers sometimes chose not to do so.

Repeated interviews of a sample of managers by the Support Group revealed significant changes in perception during and after the site change effort: clarity of job expectations and perceived Plant efficiency and effectiveness improved immediately after the site change effort, and cooperation and general climate also improved over a longer term (L.D. Brown and Kaplan, 1978). The site change effort may have directly improved some superior-subordinate relations; certainly it catalysed widespread discussion and speculation about leadership and mutual expectations of different levels of management. It also highlighted new approaches (e.g., third-party facilitation) and new resources (e.g., the Support Group) for dealing with employee relations problems.

Understanding Organizational Change Processes

Over time it became clear that positive changes had taken place at Northern Chemical Works, though the direct causes of those changes were less clear. Labour relations improved dramatically; all-time Works records for safety were set; very substantial improvements in productivity and cost control were achieved; union executives and senior managers agreed that the Plant was a better place to work; corporate headquarters regarded the Works as a star rather than as a black sheep. But why? How could the changes be explained?

Initial efforts to conceptualize the forces and dynamics influencing Northern Chemical Works were largely undertaken by the researchers. They wrote diagnostic reports and professional papers (e.g., Kaplan, 1978; Glen, 1978) that examined Works problems and change processes. Although most managers were more interested in solving problems than in developing theories, some also made efforts to formulate general understandings of the situation. The Works Manager's initial assessment of the organization and the

Support Group's white paper are examples; but eventually many people became involved in the effort to develop more understanding of the processes of organizational change.

The Works Manager was particularly interested in understanding processes of change at the Works. He and the Manager of the Textiles Plant spent several days with the authors at their university for the purpose of constructing a framework to explain the changes. These discussions benefited from the different experience, information, and perspectives of both sets of participants. The researchers were familiar with research and theory about organizational change, and had consulting experience across a variety of organizations. Of the various change attempts made at the Works, they knew best the behaviour science interventions. The managers had experience in depth and over time at Northern Chemical Works and other plants. They had first-hand knowledge of the broad range of efforts, but especially those in technical, operational, and administrative areas. In the discussions the researchers contributed ideas about the role of: increased flows of information, new norms that promoted openness in dealing with conflict, and changes in organizational culture and structure that promoted cooperation and a more flexible response to human problems. The managers were particularly aware of the importance of changes in senior management personnel, alterations in production technology, and the ebb and flow of disruptive forces (markets, corporate headquarters, unions) from the external environment. Left to their own devices, each party would probably have offered an explanation that emphasized what they experienced most fully in the project and what they understood best. As it was, the discussion resulted in a framework that included factors high in the awareness of both parties. Two papers came out of the dialogue: the researchers formulated their understanding for a professional audience (L.D. Brown and Kaplan, 1978), and the managers prepared a presentation for corporate management. The resulting drafts were shared with the Support Group and the Works senior management, and their critiques were used to further enrich the framework.

Subsequently, the process of assessing organizational change was extended throughout the managerial ranks. Representatives of all levels of management and all departments met in homogeneous groups, managed jointly by the researchers and the Support Group, to evaluate changes and identify remaining problems. The resulting lists of changes and problems were presented to top management with the understanding that the information would be compiled and reported to all groups. This process engaged a broad sample of organization members in explaining past and present organization change. A variety of explanations emerged, some more pungent than others. As one ex-union executive pithily summed up previous problems: 'It was just piss-poor management. Now they've started treating us like adults, and things have gotten better.'

From the efforts to consolidate understanding of the change process, some basic insights into organizational change were derived (L.D. Brown and Kaplan, 1978). It was manifestly clear, for example, that change had proceeded along many fronts. Behavioural science intervention played a conspicuous part, but only a part, in a much larger campaign to turn the Plant site around. New technology, new faces, and new structural arrangements all were important. It was also obvious that behavioural science intervention made a difference only if it was allied closely with the organization's own efforts to change. Furthermore, given the multiple and often simultaneous streams of intervention, and given the interdependence between behavioural scientists and the organization, it was extremely difficult to sort out the separate contributions to the resulting changes. It was not possible to make uncontestable attributions of causality. A further lesson was the long time-frame involved. It took several years before the multi-faceted undertaking achieved results apparent to a majority of people in the organization; in fact, it had taken about two years before the behavioural scientists and the change effort in general had any credibility. Probably as important as expertise in organizational change was perseverance. Lastly, even after the organization reached a critical mass of support for modern management practices, tensions between the new order and the old order remained. Although people generally agreed that 'team management' and 'participative leadership' had become the rule, exceptions were not hard to find. These insights were valuable not only to the researchers in their pursuit of understanding about organizational change but also to the Works managers and Corporate managers as they contemplated continued efforts at Northern Chemical Works or new projects at other locations.

The participative inquiry project at Northern Chemical Works is now formally over. But the informal relations among the parties continue to influence both sides. This paper, for example, has been read and influenced by Works senior managers and the Support Group. Participative research, once launched, has a momentum of its own.

Some Implications

This discussion will examine five aspects of participative research in the light of the Northern Chemical Works experience: (1) participants and their diverse objectives, (2) ideological and political implications, (3) the dialectic among diverse perspectives, (4) the organization of research activity, and (5) its consequences for knowledge and action.

(1) *Participative Research Involves Diverse Parties and Objectives whose Interactions may be only Partially Predicted or Controlled.*

In some social science research, researcher and subject roles are clearly defined and stable over time; research objectives are well specified and unchanging; research design or data analysis can control events that might disrupt or invalidate the research. Participative inquiry, in contrast, involves diverse parties, multiple objectives and partial researcher control at best over the research process.

The Northern Chemical Works project involved a variety of different parties over the years. Managers and union leaders both sought better understanding of the perceptions of workers in the Textiles Plant; the Support Group investigated leadership problems across the site; the Steering Committee was interested in explaining changes at the Works and the underlying causes. These parties all brought quite different concerns and objectives to the research process, and the addition of a new party could reorient the objectives of the inquiry.

Even within a single party, objectives receive changing emphasis over time. The researchers were primarily interested in the development of knowledge about organizational change processes, and the managers were primarily interested in solving specific problems. But the researchers sometimes took active roles in solving specific problems and the managers sometimes took active roles in developing general theories.

The intermingling of diverse parties and multiple objectives makes participative research difficult to predict or control over time. Laboratory experiments may be able to precisely determine the objectives, participants, and outcomes of their research; participative inquirers may have difficulty in forecasting, let along controlling, any of the three.

Participative research departs from the dominant tendency in social science to study those problems that are amenable to being solved completely and finally. Social science has preferred 'clear problems that have unambiguously correct solutions', and has allowed its problem-solving style to dictate which problems it has studied (Sarason, 1978, p. 373). But basic social problems are intractable: they have to be 'solved' over and over again, and they are not readily subject to the researcher's control (Sarason, 1978). Participative research is a method well suited to the study of intractable social problems, like long-term organizational change.

(2) *Participative Research Requires Political Awareness and Continuing Ideological Choices*

Social science research has an ideological component and political consequences in spite of its aspirations to objectivity (Gouldner, 1970), but these issues are particularly relevant when researchers intend to influence events in politically polarized situations. The researchers at Northern Chemical Works initially hoped to work 'for the system as a whole', and remain neutral in the conflict between union and management. This hope proved naive. Both parties pressed the researchers to take sides, and the researchers were unable to span the gap effectively. The tensions between union and management in Textiles required a choice between them rather than continual efforts at ineffectual neutrality.

The researchers chose to work exclusively with management, in spite of their ideological sympathy for the union. This decision emerged from several considerations: (1) the researchers in fact felt empathy for *both* management and the union, (2) management requested and supported financially the initial diagnostic work, and (3) the researchers believed that work with management would have beneficial impacts for workers as well as managers. The decision to work with management exclusively was taken only after a good deal of discussion and soul-searching by the researchers, and they limited their work to activities they believed would benefit both parties. Such ideological choices were raised on several subsequent occasions. The researchers were invited several times sometimes subtly and sometimes directly, to help management undermine the union. Where they recognized those invitations, the research refused them. The choice to work with management may have resulted in harm to the union in spite of the researchers' care, though the long-term outcomes seemed positive for both workers and management; but neutrality was not feasible in the situation, nor could the ideological issues be solved with a single decision. Participative inquiry poses continuing political questions: Who is inquiring? On whose behalf? About which problems? With what potential outcomes? Research that may influence future action is both a threat and an opportunity to the systems in and about which it is conducted.

(3) *The Process of Participative Research Involves a Dialectic among the Perspectives of Diverse Parties*

The process of much social science, at least in reconstruction, appears to be a linear development of theory-building and data-collection. The interaction of theory and data seems carefully controlled to produce logically defensible increments of knowledge and understanding. 'Normal science' involves puzzle-solving within the constraints and assumptions of a generally accepted 'paradigm' that defines the important problems and the methodologies appropriate to their solution (Kuhn, 1962).

The process of participative research is much messier. It is a collective attempt to 'construct reality' and as such it is an elaborate social process (Berger and Luckmann, 1967; Glen, 1978). Participative research brings together parties whose inquiry objectives, research methodologies, and conceptual frameworks are very different, and the result may be misunderstanding, ambiguity, or conflict. Initial negotiations at Northern Chemical Works revealed substantial differences between researchers and managers, and early discussions were guarded. The parties to the Textiles Diagnosis — researchers, managers, workers — were so different that joint inquiry was very difficult, and ultimately the diagnosis produced contradictory explanations for events in the Plant. The site change effort, in contrast, grew from an understanding of site authority relations shared by the Support Group, the two senior managers, and the researchers. The intervention included attention to leadership issues identified by the Support Group, the lack of role clarity emphasized by managers, and the need for two-way communication emphasized by the researchers. Similarly the organizational change framework emerged from lively discussions of senior managers, the Support Group, and representatives of all management levels and departments in addition to the researchers. In these discussions the presentation of one perspective led to the clarification and discussion of others. Sometimes the discussions produced synthetic views that included multiple perspectives, such as the analysis of site leadership and the organizational change framework. In others the process produced conflicting perspectives such as the contradictory interpretations of events in Textiles. But diverse perspectives and dialectic among them was common to all the discussions.

(4) *Participative Research must be Organized to make use of the Resources of Diverse Parties*

Complex activities are often organized by procedures, norms, role definitions and other formal or informal structures that coordinate or simplify performance (Weick, 1979: L.D. Brown, 1979). Social science has developed a variety of role prescriptions (e.g. researchers must have special training), norms (e.g. researchers should be objective), and social structures (e.g. researchers are based in university departments) that influence the research process and its outcomes.

Participative research requires appropriate organization. Researcher and subject roles, for example, may be quite similar. Researchers may actively join subjects in solving concrete problems; subjects may actively join researchers in creating abstract knowledge. The unsuccessful attempt to develop shared responsibility for the Textiles diagnosis contributed to its fragmented outcomes. In the analysis of site authority relations and the development of the organization change theory, researchers and managers took quite similar roles. The culture of Northern Chemical Works did not encourage open communications and overt conflict among colleagues at the outset, but such norms did develop within the Steering Committee and the Support Group, and so permitted productive discussions of differences. Data-collection procedures evolved from the researcher-created and administered questionnaires used in Textiles to an interview process designed jointly by researchers and Support Group and administered by the latter for evaluating the site change effort. Structural innovations such as the Support Group and the Steering Committee provided internal resources for change, and forums such as the Textiles Liaison Committee or the Works-wide group discussions of organization changes offered a mechanism to promote widespread examinations of organizational issues. These structures, procedures, norms, and role definitions all supported the development of participative research.

The organization of inquiry at Northern Chemical Works developed in large part from the inquiry process itself. The institutions of the Support Group and the Steering Committee, the spreading involvement of more parties, the collaborative data-collection procedures, the norms of open discussion, the sharing of responsibility among researchers and managers, all evolved from interaction among the parties. Organizing mechanisms appropriate to participative research do not have to be reinvented from scratch for each project, but the nature of the process makes joint development of formal and informal structures highly likely.

(5) *The Outcomes of Participative Research Include Complex Perspectives on Social Realities and Potentials for Changing those Realities*

The desired outcomes of much social science research are law-like statements that describe the behaviour to be expected in specified circumstances (Susman and Evered, 1978). The organization and process of much social science activity is concerned with reducing ambiguity about those conclusions.

Participative research does not produce unambiguous or conclusive statements about behaviour. The conflictful, turbulent, and discontinuous process outlined above seldom yields clear or simple conclusions. The research activities in Textiles, for example, produced at least three different and contradictory explanations for events there. Even when the parties agreed on the general outcome of inquiry, specific emphases and interpretations may vary. Researchers and managers agreed on an overall explanation of organizational changes at the Works, but they disagreed about the importance of different aspects of that framework. The researchers attributed much importance to cultural changes; some managers believed that new personnel were at the heart of the change. The nature of the research did not permit assessing the relative causal influence of various factors, even though there was agreement that substantial change had occurred. Participative inquiry does not produce unambiguous explanations of a reality; on the contrary, it often produces *competing* explanations that reflect the *multiple* realities experienced by different parties to the inquiry.

Participative research may directly alter the reality it seeks to explain. The subjects of the inquiry share in creating new understanding, and that understanding may lead them to change their behaviour. Researchers using participative research intervene in the situation they study, which may also lead to change in that situation. The development of new understanding is difficult to separate from altered behaviour associated with it. A theory of organizational change developed in deliberations across multiple groups of Northern Chemical Works is both a description of a reality and an intervention into it. As the Works Manager wrote after reading the initial draft of this paper:

> I would suggest a sixth implication, and that would be: The participative research process produces irreversible changes in the people who are most closely involved with the program.

Conclusion

We have described the Northern Chemical Works project as an illustration of participative research in an organizational setting. Participative research, we have argued, brings together diverse parties and multiple objectives in a process whose outcomes may be only dimly foreseen and partially controlled by the parties. We have suggested that participative research places special demands on, and offers special rewards to, its practitioners. They must be aware of the political and ideological implications of their activities, particularly in politically polarized circumstances. They must be able to encourage and participate productively in a dialectical exchange among multiple perspectives of diverse parties. They must be able to jointly organize resources and activities in ways that capitalize on diversity. They must cope with the ambiguity and the multiplicity of outcomes produced. But for those who can cope with these demands, participative research offers a particularly rewarding window on social realities — a window through which the turbulence, the discontinuities, and the dynamism of social life may be seen... and touched.

Human Inquiry
Edited by P. Reason and J. Rowan
© 1981 John Wiley & Sons Ltd.

CHAPTER TWENTY-SEVEN

Personality development in college, by Peter Madison: an appreciation

John Rowan
Independent Consultant, London, UK

This is a research study and an attempt to arrive at a theory of personality development in college (Madison, 1969). It represents a development based on the theory contained in *Toward understanding human personalities* by Robert W. Leeper and Peter Madison.

The research extended from 1952 to 1968, and the data consisted mainly of repeated interviews over the four years of college, and extensive autobiographies. The subjects were mainly students enrolled in a second-year course on 'Personality in College'. The procedure used in most cases began with the collection of a detailed life history; it continued with periodic interviews throughout college, and in a few cases for as long as ten years afterwards. 'Extensive test and retest data were collected on some subjects', but these are not reported on. Descriptions of the subjects by their classmates 'were often used' to develop a picture of the student as seen by peers. Another method used was the 'college journal', a diary-like description written on a periodic basis, usually weekly, covering whatever event was most emotionally involving in the time period.

Most of the students were volunteers, but a few were part of a systematic sample from the files of the Stanford Student Development Study. The data from these two groups proved to be similar.

Obviously this approach led to a very close involvement of the subjects with the research study, and with the researcher.

Any longitudinal study on such a personal level is, by definition, action research. One influences, inevitably, while observing even

315

though such influence is unintentional. A good subject does not persist for years in such work unless the association with the investigator has meanings to him beyond his very real desire to contribute to science. Ideas gathered under such complex circumstances are bound to be biased to some extent. The student data on which this book is based, therefore, is neither objective nor unbiased. But it is highly illuminating. Once a process is revealed in a special case it becomes evident, although in a much less conspicuous form, in more everyday ones.

And Madison is not at all penitent about this — he sees real advantages in being biased, and even in searching for bigger and better sources of bias:

Although I have studied hundreds of students, some cases proved to be extraordinary in their power to illuminate what was going on. I have, therefore, concentrated more on these in searching for ideas... Obviously, the best subjects are not just everyday students.

The reason for his impenitence is that he is looking less for facts and more for illumination. And this is based on a view of science which does not want to replace 'commonsense' ideas with 'scientific' ones, or take the laboratory somehow as more real than the everyday world.

One can, instead, take everyday experience as the 'real' phenomena to which our word meanings and knowledge are to be related. In this view of social science, the psychologist's role is to take observations and ideas from everyday experience and language into controlled research settings for testing. When he finds they have some merit, he can ask whether the everyday view is comprehensive enough; he can explore its limitations, refine and extend the idea, and explore the relation of the phenomena to events with which everyday thought would not have connected it. The most important part of his work as a scientist is still ahead: he has the task and responsibility of reintroducing the modified idea to the everyday framework of observation and knowledge from which he borrowed it in the first place.

It is clear that he is committed to the idea of repeated research cycles, where we repeatedly check and recheck our theory against reality; and he must have completed a large number of such cycles in the course of his 16 years of research with college students.

So what did he find out? After all this work, what in the end did he come up with in the way of results?

What he came up with was a theory; and this theory relies heavily on two concepts, one of which applies specifically to college students more than to others, and the other of which is of much more general application.

The Child Self

The former of these concepts is the 'child self'. It is postulated that the adolescent brings in to college many ways of seeing the world that are essentially carried over from life as a child in the family. Many of these are concerned with things, such as sex, which are hard to check up on, or to get accurate feedback on, in the family. Others are concerned with roles from home or school which have been built up and taken for granted. All this gives an initial organization of experience when the student first goes to college. And what typically happens is that there is an erosion of the initial organization. This can led either to a resynthesis, or to an unresolvable crisis.

So there is a problem about the past. It has to do with the way in which expectations from the past are brought into a new and perhaps inappropriate setting. And there is one particular way in which this happens which is crucial. Which brings us to the other concept already mentioned.

Reintegration

The definition given of this latter concept is 'the unconscious mechanism by which brain-stored traces of past experiences are located and aroused by the contemporary situation and interact with incoming sense data to codetermine on-going psychological processes.'

Unravelling this somewhat jargon-ridden definition, what Madison means is that certain traumatic experiences build up in the child a resonator-like echo chamber, such that when a new experience reminds the student of such traumas, 'a relatively slight incoming stimulus (in energy terms) can quickly touch off and arouse powerful energizing systems'.

Obviously this is a similar idea to Freud's notion of 'transference', and to the co-counselling notion of 'restimulation', but Madison wants it to be much more general than just applying to therapy or counselling.

> In perception there is just enough of a framework to touch off past experiences which then fill in and complete the percept. When Robert appeared 'teasing' to Trixie [case history from text] his actual attitude, as other objective observers would have judged it,

could well have been quite ambiguous — just enough 'tease' quality
to provide a sketchy frame into which she poured this particular
quality from her store of father traces.

Madison gives many examples of such reintegrative processes going on and
being extremely important in explaining day-to-day actions and reactions. He
regards reintegration as exerting a constant pressure, sometimes very strong,
to see the world in certain ways rather than in others.

> Despite its relative fragility as a determinant of external stimulus
> forms, reintegration accounts for much of perception in living
> simply because clear, well-organized stimulus situations play a
> relatively minor role in perception... Because the stimulus world
> presents clear and strongly-organised forms only at selected points
> in the perceptual field, the reintegrative liquid is readily able to
> express its own inner forms. The observer himself is never the wiser
> — he thinks all the while that he is responding to obvious realities.

This seems to be more than just a reference to the defence mechanism of
projection — when linked with the idea of the child self it does give a great deal
of explanatory power to otherwise inexplicable events: a student devoted a
tremendous amount of energy into playing basketball — 'I put out more work
than I ever did for anything in my life' — just because of an incident where the
coach could not remember his name. His whole picture of himself was
organized around being a good athlete, and this action (or failure of action) on
the part of the coach was powerful because of this. Each success at athletics
'left in its wake another "room" in his echo-chamber resonating system. The
energising property of motives in the current situation would come from the
sympathetic resonating of these echo chambers.'

There is much else in this big book — a very good discussion of identity and
negative identity, for example — but this will be enough to indicate the
importance of what it has to offer.

It seems quite possible — although Madison does not say this — that his
course in personality actually prevented a few students from committing
suicide. It is this kind of real-life involvement which this sort of research
makes possible.

Human Inquiry
Edited by P. Reason and J. Rowan
© 1981 John Wiley & Sons Ltd.

CHAPTER TWENTY-EIGHT

An exploration in the dialectics of two-person relationships

Peter Reason
Centre for the Study of Organizational Change and Development, University of Bath, UK

This chapter is a brief account of an exploration of couple relations; it contains an outline of the theory which guided the exploration, an account of the methodology used, and a description of one relationship as discovered through the research. This is also an account of the evolution of a methodology, my first attempts to move away from positivism toward a 'new paradigm' (Reason, 1976). It is an approach to research which provides very rich qualitative data for theory-building and verification, a collaborative relationship with the other people involved, and also demonstrates how inquiry can become a way of life, taking place through risk-taking in living.

The theory for the exploration was developed from my notion that all relationships between persons involve the management of fundamental contradiction. The poles of these contradictions I saw as co-existing in dialectical relation — they are interdependent and give each other meaning; they interpenetrate so that each pole includes the other; and ultimately they are identical. I saw that the business of being in relation with another person involves a dialectical process; that is to say the inherent problems of living with other people can only be resolved for the present, temporarily and never finally. As I read and thought and observed, I came to the conclusion that the basic, inevitable contradictions around which relations between persons must be patterned could be contained in a simple definition of interpersonal life: *separate persons in relation.*

First, *separate:* an essential part of a relationship is that those involved in it remain separate persons. Maybe transcendence of the boundaries of

319

individuals is possible, but that transcendence would take us right out of the realm of interpersonal relations; my basic assumption is that the flow of experience and an individual is invisible even to the most intimate other, and that a relationship involves two people with separate flows of experience who are yet in contact. Thus one of the basic contradictions of relationship lies in the simultaneous existence of separateness and contact in a relationship. This I termed the dialectic of *Self and Other.*

Second, *relation:* a relationship is not a simple addition of two persons, it is the creation of an *interperson,* a system with dynamics of its own which evolve from the patterns of interaction and interexperience of its members. The development of an interperson involves the development of an interidentity: the interlocking, complementary identity of two persons. The dialectic is between the individual identity each person brings to the relationship, the self-concept which is formed through relationships with many significant others, and the identity given through membership in the interperson. Interperson identity will simultaneously enhance and inhibit individual identity. This I termed the dialectic of *Person and Interperson.*

Third, *persons:* one very basic paradox of existence is that human beings can be regarded and treated both as subject and as object (Reason, 1980), and thus a relationship involves persons as subject and as object simultaneously. One of the ways this is expressed is through two approaches to *influence.* This can be based in the other as object or utility; or alternatively in the other as subject, in an 'encounter' between persons, a mutual understanding and confirmation in which influence is the outcome of a confrontation with a different other. This I term the dialectic of *Subject and Object.*

Having developed this viewpoint, I started to wonder how to research my ideas. I was faced with three major methodological problems. First, the theory is concerned with *persons* and personal interaction between persons. This meant that above all the research should be based on Laing's (1960) premise:

> The science of persons is the study of human beings that begins from a relationship with the other as person and proceeds to an account of the other still as person.

> The other as person is seen by me as responsible, as capable of choice, in short, as a self-acting agent (pp. 21-2).

To treat the other as person means in addition to explore with them as subject, rather to study them as object; it means that the primary data must come from a personal interaction between those involved in the research.

Second, as well as being personal, the data required for a science of persons are often not immediately available, since they are concerned with subjective and experiential processes — in this case the experience of a personal and intimate relationship. An 'exterior' process of observation cannot grasp this, so the researcher must not only establish a personal relationship with his subject, he must actively involve the other in the process of discovery and description.

Third, my research was concerned not with separate variables which might be independently manipulated and measured, but rather with a search for a *holistic view* of relationships; I needed to find a process which would honour the whole.

When I compared these requirements with the available methodologies I found a major shortfall. Clearly experimental and quasi-experimental designs were inappropriate and some kind of qualitative method was required. I tried some interviews, but however much I tried it was always me doing the questioning rather than us jointly exploring. I thought about participant observations, but unless I were to write the whole dissertation about my own relationships, there was no way I could be a *participant* observer; just an ordinary outside observer.

It then occurred to me, quite suddenly, that I could solve my problem by standing it on its head: if I stopped regarding myself as a researcher and the couples as subjects, and started thinking of the *couples* as researchers into their own and each other's relationships and myself as a *facilitator* of the research process, then the whole problem resolved itself. This realization led to the research method I developed for this exploration, and to my subsequent involvement in working towards a new paradigm in research.

I decided to conduct my research — or our research as I now saw it — in an experiential workshop, following the tradition of laboratory education. I invited a close colleague to work with me, and together we designed a three-day workshop for couples, using my theory as a guide for the development of experiential learning activities. We regarded these experiential activities as personal and interpersonal *inquiry* activities, and we explicitly invited couples to attend the workshop as *researchers* of their own relationship. During the workshop we invited the couples to engage in activities as we as staff engaged in them ourselves: everyone was involved in a process of exploration and discovery with self and with others: there were no outsiders, no voyeurs. The only inequality was that the staff had major responsibility for facilitation, and primary ownership of the theory. The detailed design of the workshop is not of concern here, but it is worth noting in passing that the conduct of such workshops requires the development of facilitator skills which are quite different from the skills of the orthodox researcher.

To illustrate this process of inquiry an account of one of these couple relationships is presented. To write this, tape-recordings of the workshop were first completely transcribed, and a separate file of raw data assembled for each couple. I then explored each set of data with the dialectics in mind, searching for evidence of contradictions and their management. In doing this, I tried to subjectively immerse myself in the experience of that couple, to read and re-

read the transcripts, to listen to the tapes, until a holistic pattern of that relationship emerged. This pattern was then systematically checked against the data and the description written.

Carol and Susan are a Lesbian couple with a long and complex history. We invited each couple to introduce her partner, and to present a symbol of their relationship to the group.

Carol: I've known Susan for about three years, and we've had many many ups, and many many downs. We've been through a lot of personal hassles together, between the two of us and with other people involved. She's flighty; when she gets upset she's spacey, but yet she balances me, because what I don't do consistently or well, she seems to pick up on. We're *totally* different in what we like, which is sort of nice because she gets me into things I've never been involved with. She puts up with my bitching — which I'll commend anybody for. She's warm, and she's genuine — she's one of the most genuine people, consistently. She cares about me — she can get into what I'm into, and vice versa.

Susan: Carol has her BS out of college, and she has her Masters in library science. She's well educated, one of the smartest people I think I've known. She is bitchy, that's very true. She's very particular about some things, particularly about myself; she sometimes overpowers our relationship, and sometimes takes an awful lot for granted. But that happens seldom, and always seems to work itself out for some reason. She's a great strength to me — I've an awful lot of faults. Her intelligence is quite a problem between us, not a big problem but it does cause problems. But I'm learning from her the basics of life — elementary things that I haven't already learned...

Carol describes their symbol, a small statue of two women:

Carol: There were many things we could bring. One was a box of Tide, because we always used to meet at the laundromat. One was paper and pencil, because we play a lot of games... We settled on this because we thought the others were so silly. This is a statue that I got when I was living in DC... It's called 'Two Women'... and I think we decided on this because it shows the closeness, and it shows the caring and the touching, and for a long time our relationship was sort of in the shadows, and it was sort of nameless and faceless, and yet there was a feeling that was strong and real close...

On Person and Interperson

First impressions are that Carol really overpowers this relationship: she is a very lively, vocal woman, very much a central figure in the whole workshop group, while Susan stays more in the background. Carol appears to define and dominate the relationship, and Susan initially supports and complements her in that role.

Susan: ...part of my problem with Carol is because... she is very outgoing and can talk to anybody and do anything, and I just freeze. She *has* a better education than I do, and I have great difficulty being in the same group with her and other people — I kind of hide in the corner... She can deal with everybody and all situations, while I have more of a difficult time associating with everybody... I get shot down an awful lot... I can't express myself the way I should, or I think I should, or maybe I can't do it the way Carol thinks I should do it — that's probably what it is... she's very critical...

When it is pointed out that she always seems to define the relationship and to speak for Susan, Carol says:

Carol: I think I do that because I know exactly what she's going to say a lot of times, and I can get to the point quicker... I think I also do it because I don't want her to get fuddled...

Their levels of commitment to the relationship are different. Carol has just recently separated from her husband, and Susan has just moved in, more or less in Jim's place:

Carol: I want to find out what keeps us together... When I separated from my husband, all I wanted to do was live alone, and I haven't done that yet and that bothers me... I don't want to think I just sort of shifted people... I don't want her to move in in Jim's place... It's also convenient to have her around — I don't take her for granted as much as I did, but I still do... I don't want it to be convenience that I have her around. I don't want it to be habit; I don't want it to be substitution... I know what I *don't* want, but *why* do I want to be with *her?* I can see [many] hassles... if I stay with her. It's one of the happiest alternatives I've found, one of the happiest modes I've found of living, and I don't want to lose that. It's much easier living with a woman than with a man.

Compared with Carol's confusion and ambivalence, Susan is quite clear:

Susan: I could be very content and very happy in my life just doing for
              Carol.

A similar kind of difference between the two of them is that Carol is more
'polygamous' than is Susan, and tends to keep a lot of relationships going at
one time:

Susan: I'm content with a one-on-one relationship... and she's content
              with a one-on-all. She's got to have sixteen relationships going
              all at one time, while I'm very content with just a relationship
              with Carol.

Significantly, it is out of place for Susan to play Carol's game. When she does,
she reveals not only her own strength in the relationship, but also her role in
supporting Carol's gadfly behaviour:

Carol: ... she went out and picked up on somebody else. Nothing
              made me move quicker than when my primary one was out there
              playing my games... I had to sit there and say, 'Wow! I've been
              doing that to her.' But I *moved,* I mean I moved... she knew
              she would get a reaction out of me, and she got a strong one. I
              was pissed... I walked into the house and said, 'What the fuck
              do you think you are doing to me?' And I'd been doing [the same
              thing] for two and a half years! If you're non-monogamous, if
              you've got your anchor, you know, you can always come home
              to...

The initial definition of the relationship is that Carol is one-up — the strong
one, the leader, the one who is helping and supporting Susan. This is the aspect
of the relationship which is stressed and presented by Carol and Susan, and
from the initial descriptions would seem to be their own image of the
relationship. However, throughout their conversations are clues that this is an
incomplete and inaccurate definition of the relationship; for example above,
where Carol depends on Susan as a strong home base for her other romances.
At one point Carol allows, *sotto voce,* that Susan is stronger than she gives her
credit for being.

   To see Susan as one-down in the relationship becomes increasingly less
possible in the inquisitive social atmosphere of the workshop, and Susan
realizes her strength quite early on. This takes place in three phases. First, she
realizes how she puts herself down. Next, she discovers some of her own
contribution, and she contrasts Carol's 'inquisitive' attitude to life — her

restlessness and impetuosity — with her own 'genuine' attitude — more accepting and letting things be:

Susan: ...my genuine attitude towards people of taking it gradually and not jumping into something all of a sudden... [contrasts hers]. We're kind of complementing each other: I'm trying to meet more people, while she's trying to slow down and not get so involved with them so quickly... She has a lot more initiative than I do; she's a go-getter. She's the leader... I'm the follower, to a point, and then I hit my point and I stop, and then she gets down on me because I stop, and then more times than not we found out that where I stopped was better off to stop than continue on...

The third stage is that Susan discovers that she doesn't just sometimes lead by saying 'No', but that she brings some important qualities to the relationship.

Susan: I'm finding myself being able to find more things that I'm stronger at and more available to Carol than I thought I was. I was really feeling good about it because I've got all these good things [written] down. It makes me feel we are levelling off the relationship, instead of this leadership-followership thing.

Susan's strength is as the supportive, stable one in the relationship on whom Carol depends for nurturance. It is very easy *not* to see Susan's strength, because Carol is so lively, and because they both present the relationship as Susan one-down. However, once one sees past this initial presentation, it becomes easier to pick up clues, often non-verbal, as to the underlying relationship. For example, the words of a statement of Carol's may be disparaging or patronizing, but the tone will be loving. One very powerful non-verbal clue is in their posturing together: Susan is a physically much larger woman than is Carol, and Carol quite often assumes a physically dependent position, for example sitting on the floor at Susan's feet, holding onto her leg as if physically supported and protected by Susan. Generally Carol relies on Susan's knowledge of her, that Susan knows what she needs, even when she herself does not.

In this relationship it appears initially that Susan plays one-down to Carol's one-up — and as we shall see, Carol particularly needs to be one-up. There is a contradiction between this definition of the relationship and Susan's real strength, her capacity to be strong and nurturant for Carol: and there is also a contradiction between this definition of the relationship and Carol's dependence and need for support. In some ways, Susan has two identities in the relationship: explicitly as one-down; implicitly as strong, central, and nurturant. These two identities contradict each other, and her strength in the relationship is usually played down by both of them. However, as the workshop progressed, this strength grew clearer and more difficult for either of them to ignore. This contradiction of identity is central to this relationship.

On Self and Other: Openness and Closedness

It is clear that Carol and Susan know each other well. They are able to be open with each other in major parts of their relationship, and they have a contact with each other such that they *can* often speak for each other with creditable accuracy. On several occasions during the workshop, each described the same incident in their history independently, and in each case the two descriptions match well. In many relationships this might be seen as a collusive manoeuvre to present a united front; while there are areas of collusion in this relationship, there are also major areas in which the two women are simply well in contact with each other.

Given this basic openness, the areas in which they are not able to be open with each other are significant. These closed areas in the relationship are ones in which there is continuing tension, and the closedness serves to support and preserve the definition of the relationship of Susan as one-down.

First, they do not communicate about some of Carol's other relationships; Susan in particular feels this:

Susan: ... it gets very frustrating for me because I feel we should be
                able to talk about just about *anything*... there's some things I
                feel *should* be talked out and brought out and levelled off and be
                able to understand both parts. She should be able to understand
                that I'm having problems handling this particular situation ...
                to be able to understand my feelings... I get hurt very easily...
                [and] I'm not even going to bring it up, because I know all hell's
                going to break loose.

In order to understand two other areas in which they are closed with each other, it is important to be familiar with some pieces of their history which have led up to the present state of their relationship. Carol and Susan met just after Carol's marriage. At first, they were simply buddies, but their Lesbian relationship developed quickly, and they became more and more involved with each other as Carol's marriage broke up; in particular, Carol relied on Susan as a confidante during this process. It is quite unclear what contribution their relationship had to the break-up of the marriage.

Both of them agree that this subject is difficult for them to talk about; they place it in the 'closed' area of their relationship.

A related issue for Susan that does not get discussed is the future:

Susan: I think it's hard for us to talk about our future on a long range
           basis because we still are in the bind of the marriage... I'd like
           to sit down now and talk about getting a house... setting up a
           relationship in a house together. I think we have problems
           talking about that, and that stems from not knowing where it's
           going.

A further issue that adds to the complexity of this relationship is the fact that
Susan got pregnant by Carol's husband and had an abortion. For many
reasons this is a highly charged issue, but the details of the story are not
significant here. What *is* important is that Susan did not tell Carol who the
father was for a year, and Carol had never basically forgiven her for this
deceit. It is an indication of the closedness of this part of the relationship that
the following excerpts are taken from a conversation towards the end of a
whole day which they spent trying to grapple with this issue alone and
together. They are both very upset:

Carol: ...I had no idea it was going to go like this; and if I did I don't
           even know if I would have brought it up.
Susan: It's affected me because I don't even know how you're feeling
           about it. I don't know what it is about the abortion that's been
           sitting in the back of your head, which you didn't tell me...
Carol: Both of you supposedly said you loved me and you trusted me,
           yet neither one of you told me, and that really pissed me off.
           You waited a whole fucking year! Jim I can understand, you I
           don't understand yet.
Susan: I was afraid of losing you if I told you... I think our
           relationship developed over that year that I could finally tell
           you...
Carol: [Very harshly] It's ironic that you didn't. Jim did.
Trainer: You sound *very* angry.
Carol: Mm-hm. Because I'm closer with Susan than I've ever been with
           Jim. And if anybody's going to tell me, she should have done
           it...
Susan: So... it's affecting our relationship because I lied to you about
           the abortion?
Carol: You lied to me about the father. I don't necessarily keep
           grudges, but I remember, and it all adds up...
Susan: So our two years of such honesty and a complete togetherness,
           and then all of a sudden the shock of a *total lie* and covering up

has more or less sat back on our relationship. You're not really
trusting me and believing what I've been telling you of things.
Carol: Yeah...

All these areas of closedness in the relationship — Carol's other relationships,
Susan's part in the break-up of the marriage, their future together, and Carol's
feeling of resentment and mistrust, her failure to forgive the abortion affair —
all of them contradict the basic openness of this relationship. They serve to
preserve a distance between the two in a relationship which is otherwise very
close. They also preserve Susan's identity as one-down in the relationship, and
permit Carol to remain one-up and less than fully committed to the
relationship. These areas of closedness put Susan continually on the defensive,
so her major contribution goes almost unnoticed. Carol gets as far as
acknowledging this, and more generally her need to be one-up in life:

Carol: To me, you just don't let it all go, cause your gonna get fucked
            in the end. It goes back to my father and it goes back to my
            sister, and I'm not gonna get fucked by this woman... unless I
            do it back: I *still* gotta be one-up. You know it upsets me that
            you're feeling so fucking independent, cause it's equalling out
            again, it's *equalling out*... and I'm afraid of what she's gonna
            do when she really learns her true worth, which is why I put her
            down so she doesn't...

On Subject and Object

This relationship is in a process of change: at the end of the workshop Carol
and Susan see their relationship in new ways, and although this is no guarantee
of lasting change, it is a beginning. As the relationship changes, the two
women are increasingly influencing each other: this influence is not based in
exchange — you do this and I'll do that — but in an understanding for each
other, so that the total amount of influence in the relationship is increasing.

In the closing stages of the workshop, we invited the couples to explore some
exercises in influence. As they do this, Carol and Susan are concerned with two
intertwined issues: the ability of each to be herself, to retain individual
identity, and the possibility of a peaceful, comfortable relationship together.
Carol's need for space is matched by Susan's willingness to be less jealous;
Susan's desire for commitment is matched by Carol's willingness to stop
flirting around. The relationship is changing in some significant ways, not
through bargaining individual needs, but through a process of mutual
understanding and confirmation that each may be herself while they are
together.

Summary: A Contradictory Identity

The *principal contradiction* for Carol and Susan lies in their simultaneous affirmation and denial of Susan's central nurturant place in the relationship. This contradiction may be seen in terms of each of the three dialectics of relation, and there is considerable evidence of movement in each of these.

Person and interperson. This relationship initially appears to be based in dominance-submission, with Carol clearly the strong one, the leader, who brings Susan along in tow, as it were. This is how both present the relationship initially, but this definition is unstable, because it denies Susan's crucial central position. This aspect of the relationship, which emerges through the workshop, is usually played down by both. Both are caught in their initial definition of the relationship, which denies important parts of each — the parts of Susan that are strong, and the parts of Carol that are weak and dependent.

Self and other. While Carol and Susan know each other remarkably well and are very intimate, there were significant ways in which they were closed to each other — things that did not get discussed, or where it was very difficult for them to understand each other's viewpoint. These issues were in contradiction to the basic openness of the relationship, created a distance between them, and fostered doubts about the viability of the relationship. They serve to keep Susan one-down, on the defensive, and to keep Carol in control and relatively free; to an extent, this gives Susan the status of a utility to serve Carol. Carol becomes the full Self, and Susan's experience becomes secondary.

On the other hand, their basic openness with each other is in contradiction to the initial presentation of the relationship as one-up/one-down, since openness involves a symmetry in a relationship which does not fit well with the asymmetry of dominance-submission.

Subject and object. Most of the interaction of Carol and Susan during the workshop was concerned with their subjective experience of the relationship, and their interaction illustrates a process of influence through encounter, rather than as a process of exchange. There are ways, however, in which Susan's subordinate position as a utility for Carol essentially objectifies her and denies her a subjective identity.

However, the initial definition of the relationship as one-up/one-down is unstable, and two major changes occur during the workshop to make it no longer tenable. First, Susan begins to recognize the qualities she brings to the relationship, and second some of the patterns of closedness which supported the principal contradiction — particularly Carol's remaining resentment about the pregnancy-abortion episode — are made explicit. Thus, this relationship appears to be moving past its current principal contradiction.

Susan: Carol and I came with that hard statue, that now looks to us as... it was *us,* but it was also *her.* So we came up with — lucky we found it — it's a three of Spades [playing card]: Carol, me, and us. We are finding our perspective of being individuals, but we still have 'us'. [The card] was just lying there on the ground, and I said, 'Hey, that's cool, because there's you, and there's me, and there's us'.

Carol: And before it was, we think, me and us... there's three, not two and a half... The other thing I found was this [a cardboard tube]: we're not doing away with the touching of the statue, and the closeness, and us having two different things is not negating that. But this is more bendable than the statue, and it's lighter and it's not as powerful, and you can see all the way through it. It's a clear cut thing: we both have open ends... We didn't fight about what we were going to bring today, and when we came on Thursday, we had a real hassle...

Conclusions

The kind of research I have portrayed is a way of providing rich, detailed descriptions of situations, produced by people as researchers of their own lives in collaboration with other workshop members and facilitators. These descriptions have a number of particular qualities. First, they provide intimate, private data that would not be normally made available to an outsider: I suggest that it would be a rarely skilled interviewer who could uncover the complexities of a relationship as portrayed above. Second, the inquiry is 'real', and can become part of the life process of those involved; the data are not produced for a researcher, but for themselves — *they* will have to live with the consequences of their discoveries and revelations. Another way of putting this is that the data are living, the outcome of a non-alienating inquiry. Third, as the data are generated in the inquisitive social atmosphere of a research workshop, they combine a deep, inside view of the relationship with the probings and confrontations of other workshop members: we can argue that the relationship can be portrayed more fully because it has been seen from both inside and outside. These three qualities mean that the descriptions of relationship are based on very high-quality data.

We are not, however, simply producing high-quality data in this research, we are testing and building a theory of relationship. The end-product of the research (in terms of theory) is to build a 'pattern model' of each couple in which any aspect of their relationship can be explained. And then we can ask whether the theory we started off with was the most helpful in building these pattern models; we can ask whether we have, as we claimed, identified 'the inevitable contradictions around which relations between persons must be patterned'. The answer to this question must be both 'Yes' and 'No'. As the descriptions of the relationships were written and compared, it became increasingly clear that while the notion of relationships as involving fundamental contradiction was making a lot of sense, the three dialectics I had identified were not clear and separate, but rather shaded into each other. I came to see them more as 'windows' or perspectives through which the relationship might be viewed, rather than as clear dimensions. On the other hand, it became clear that a notion of a *principal contradiction,* a fundamental central issue around which all the tensions of the relationship might be seen as revolving, was a most useful idea, providing a holistic view of the relationship. Thus the theory was tested, amended, and developed.

There is, however, another aspect of this kind of research, apart from the data-gathering and theory-building, which I wish to emphasize. This research moves towards supporting values of inquiry as an approach to living, and of research as involving risk-taking in living. It offers one way of ceasing to see research as the prerogative of academics, and offers it back to people as a means of enhancing their lives and developing their capacities for self-direction.

The research described in this chapter does not go as far as it might in this direction: although I thought I was inviting the couples to be researchers of their own situation, in John Rowan's terms (Chapter 9) I only made contact with them at the point of Encounter (although that was a full and authentic meeting), and so only permitted them to be researchers for a fleeting moment in the whole research cycle. Clearly, the research would have been richer and more complete if we had jointly shared more of the stages of the research cycle — particularly the Project stage of planning and the Communication stage of working out meanings — and also had we completed more than one cycle. Yet despite these shortfalls, this research is a radical departure from traditional methodologies, and demonstrates the possibility that research might become truly experiential, a process of living inquiry.

Human Inquiry
Edited by P. Reason and J. Rowan
© 1981 John Wiley & Sons Ltd.

CHAPTER TWENTY-NINE

A collaborative inquiry into voluntary metropolitan desegregation

William R. Torbert
Boston College, Chestnut Hill, Massachusetts, USA

This chapter describes a year-long study of a pilot programme in voluntary metropolitan desegregation among elementary and middle-school classes in the Boston area during the 1975-76 school year.

The objectives and outcomes of this programme will be summarized briefly at the outset of the chapter. Then, the main body of the chapter will be devoted to focusing on the the experience of the research team itself, in order to illustrate one way in which a collaborative inquiry develops and one way in which graduate students can receive training in the research and intervention skills necessary for collaborative inquiry. An overall model of collaborative inquiry as a new paradigm for social science research is introduced in Chapter 11, and a further elaboration of research skills necessary for collaborative inquiry can be found in Chapter 37.

Setting and Programme

Boston during the 1975-76 school year was anything but a receptive social climate for educational innovation, particularly for a programme concerned with desegregation. In the nation's Bicentennial Year, when Boston might have expected attention primarily as one of the 'cradles of liberty', it instead achieved world attention again and again because of the violence that repeatedly erupted in its schools and in its streets in the first full year of court-mandated desegregation. As the year continued, James Coleman, in an

333

address to a joint session of the Massachusetts Legislature, would blame court-mandated desegregation efforts in education for 'white flight' from the nation's cities.

Meanwhile, the suburbs themselves were also jittery about the prospect of mandatory *metropolitan* desegregation. A recent court decision had ordered Detroit to engage in metropolitan desegregation because of a history of systematic efforts to reinforce segregated schooling through neighbourhood residential policies.

Amidst this ferment a small pilot programme named *Metropairways* appeared in Boston. Metropairways brought together interested teachers, from voluntarily participating urban and suburban school districts with different racial, ethnic, and socio-economic compositions, to plan joint meetings of their classes one day every two weeks or so. Metropairways was one of several pilot programmes initiated by its parent organization, the Metropolitan Planning Project (MPP). MPP had been founded in 1973, funded by the federal Emergency School Aid Act of 1972, and had spent several years doing demographic research on the Boston metropolitan area, as well as holding public meetings to plan voluntary metropolitan solutions to racial and ethnic isolation. As reported in MPP's monograph *Metro Ways to Understanding,* two of the central claims that emerged from this process were:

(1) that isolation is a problem for majority as well as minority students because both groups are consequently unprepared to function in a multi-cultural society;
(2) that no one can plan for others in an area as sensitive as desegregation, so planning and implementation must be at once voluntary and collaborative.

The voluntary, collaborative qualities of MPP's mission caused a variety of tensions. The communities consulted by MPP often expected MPP to develop concrete programmes. Consequently, MPP's attempts to include the communities in defining the programme frameworks left some with the impression that MPP lacked a coherent sense of mission. From another angle, the Federal Project Officers interpreted the term 'voluntary' in a purely formal way, as meaning School Committee votes (but no direct choice for schools, teachers, and parents) rather than court action. Also, they pressed for a plan which would integrate every school building in the metropolitan area, even after early research showed that to do this would spread minority students so thinly as to isolate them in a different sense. Still another source of tension was the rapid turnover in Executive Directors of MPP: the advent of the third Executive Director in 1975-76 marked a continuing dissipation of any sense of shared history and shared dedication to the original collaborative ideals of the programme.

Nevertheless, the Metropairways Coordinator, hired in the spring of 1975, did a remarkable job of canvassing metropolitan schools and beginning to generate potential pairings between urban and suburban teachers who expressed special interest. These groups of teachers were each to develop curricula collaboratively for their pairing, with parent meetings and school board meetings to test both grass-roots and formal approval of the process.

If citizens were concerned to maintain control of their schools and avoid desegregation, involvement in the very limited forms of voluntary desegregation represented by Metropairways was precisely the sort of action that could protect the suburbs from mandatory, court-ordered desegregation. But so great was the fear of mandatory desegregation in 1975-76 that two suburban school boards, in a series of explosive meetings, voted against the programme, at least partially on the grounds that 'outside forces' were trying to manipulate them into mandatory desegregation.

The following sections provide a close sense of the research on the programme, but the outcomes of the programme can be very briefly summarized here. Of four originally funded pairings, two were aborted by the school board votes just mentioned. A new pairing was created after the first of the negative votes, but the second decision came too late in the year to create still another new pairing. Of the three pairings that actually operated (including 201 students altogether), two were shown by the research to be extremely successful both in teaching basic skills and in encouraging cross-district interaction among students. Both of these pairings were directly influenced by feedback of early research findings, as will be described below. The third pairing experienced administrative problems, which prevented research feedback meetings, and was only sporadically successful. Feedback of early research results appeared both to validate the original findings and to increase the effectiveness of the pairings which received the feedback.

The Entry of the Research Team

Metropairways funding source required an evaluation process of each funded programme. The Metropairways Coordinator had originally met the author when both were at the Harvard Graduate School of Education. In September 1975 the Coordinator approached the author to test his interest in becoming Director of Evaluation for Metropairways. He agreed to write a research proposal, with the understanding that (1) four students in his advanced research course, 'Diagnosis of Human Systems', would serve as research assistants; and (2) the research would not consist merely of before-and-after questionnaires, but rather would include direct observation of participants' behaviour and feedback of the observations to participants during the year. The Coordinator happily accepted these proposals because she believed that she and the teachers probably had a lot to learn about how to enact successful collaboration.

The research proposal suggested that the surest way to determine whether Metropairways succeeded in reducing isolation caused by racial, ethnic, and district boundaries was to observe whether children and adults in fact interacted across these boundaries. Neither the mere fact that students were to be brought together in the same place, nor checkmarks on a later questionnaire, guaranteed such interaction. The proposal further hypothesized that teachers would not in fact succeed in planning and implementing curricula which encouraged collaborative interaction among children unless their planning itself exhibited collaborative interaction.

Some MPP staff members seemed somewhat surprised by the research team's decision to focus the research on collaboration. When asked what they took to be innovative about MPP and Metropairways, these persons listed such characteristics as pairing of classes, new curricula, and emphasis on basic skills. The problem with this response was that these characteristics were not systematically related to one another, nor did they appear innovative to the researchers. These characteristics sounded more like a list of politically expedient attributes which, in the absence of a coherent theory of educational practice, were likely to strain against one another and result in one more undistinctive project. That MPP members were surprised by the focus on collaboration suggested that the project as a whole was 'forgetting' its original mission.

Thus, the initial research proposal by the evaluation team amounted to an intervention which prompted the Coordinator and other members of the organization to question what theory of educational organizing guided their work. Through these discussions the Coordinator became enthusiastic about pursuing the implications of the collaborative thrust of the programme. She invited feedback about her own behaviour in meetings, and eventually invited the research team to join in planning three of the staff development workshops for teachers, in order to ask together what collaboration means and to what degree programme members were in fact succeeding in implementing the theory in practice. Through these discussions other members of the MPP staff also came to appreciate that focusing on collaboration did not distract attention from students' experiences in the programme, but rather provided a criterion for the programme's mission of 'reducing... isolation'.

The fact that the initial research proposal itself constituted an important intervention in the programme illustrates a paradoxical quality of successful collaboration. Whereas the notion of collaboration often conjures up an image of 'going with the crowd', resulting in bland and undistinguished outcomes, successful collaboration will not have these qualities. Successful collaboration requires the maintenance of the collaborative process itself, not compromising the principles of collaboration, despite probable pressure to do so. The person who wishes to work collaboratively tries simultaneously to model and advocate a process of self-disclosure, support of others' efforts to express themselves, and openness to confrontation. Through self-disclosure, support, and confrontation, creative ideas can enter discourse, theories can be clarified, behaviour can be examined, and conflicts managed openly (Argyris and Schon, 1974; Torbert, 1972). Thus, the commitment of the research team to collaboration did not require it to accede to every request for it to change its research design.

Initial Attempts to Define Collaboration in Behavioural Terms

All major decisions about the research were made by the research team at weekly Friday meetings. One research assistant studied the history of the programme, reviewing documents and doing retrospective interviews of school officials. The other three research assistants studied specific pairings. They were introduced to their pairs by the Coordinator at the first curriculum planning meeting of each Pairway's staff in November.

During several Friday research meetings an initial behaviour coding scheme was developed by the research team to determine the degree of collaborative inquiry at the teacher planning meetings. (This scoring procedure was later also used in observing students' behaviour.) The observer was to register: (1) who spoke to whom (to determine the amount different people participated); (2) whether each comment 'initiates decision' (e.g. proposes a new idea), 'makes decision', 'implements decision', 'agrees with or adds to', or 'explicitly disagrees' (to determine to what degree control of decision-making was shared); and (3) how inquiring each comment was.

A comment could be scored negative, neutral, or positive as to level of inquiry. A comment would be scored as negative if it claimed to speak for everyone, it it treated personal opinion as a non-negotiable fact, or if it changed the topic without testing with others whether such a change was useful. For example, 'We're wasting time; let's make a decision' would be scored as negative because it presents an opinion/evaluation as though it were a fact. By contrast, 'I feel we're wasting time; let's make a decision' would be scored as neutral. And 'This seems like a waste of time to me; I'd like to make a decision; how do others of you feel now?' would be scored as positive. A comment is scored as positive when it opens towards a continuing dialogue about unresolved problems or issues. Thus, informational questions are often scored as neutral because they do not imply continuing dialogue.

The research assistants began to use this scheme immediately to help them keep track of the inquiry level of teacher planning meetings, even though they were not altogether sure what patterns of behaviour represented high degrees or low degrees of collaborative inquiry and had not tested their inter-rater reliability with the instrument. Using the instrument helped raise questions relevant to refining it. Moreover, in the early stages of feedback to the teacher planning teams, specific examples of level of inquiry on which the research team could agree were more useful than statistical generalizations, since both the teachers and the researchers needed to learn what the categories referred to in concrete terms and what they signified theoretically. The research team's initial sense about what sorts of extreme behaviour patterns would tend to suggest low or high degree of collaborative inquiry is outlined in Table 29.1.

Table 29.1 Hypothesized characteristics of collaborative inquiry

Low collaborative inquiry	High collaborative inquiry
1. Skewed participation, with one or two members making a majority of comments; some members none at all	1. Participation more evenly balanced
2. Initiating, making, and implementing of decisions limited to few members	2. Initiating, making, and implementing of decisions widely shared
3. Given decisions initiated, made and implemented by same persons	3. Given decisions initiated, made and implemented by different persons
4. Little or no explicit disagreement, or else uninterrupted strings of explicit disagreements	4. Explicit disagreement interspersed with other kinds of comments
5. More negative inquiry scores than positive inquiry scores	5. More positive inquiry scores than negative inquiry scores

In the early stages of the research process the research team limited its feedback to programme participants to counts of who participated how much, and to examples of high or low inquiry comments, inviting participants to join in discussing what such findings signified about the collaborativeness of a given meeting. In this way, each researcher could offer potentially helpful feedback to the teacher team he or she was observing without claiming a spurious validity for counts of categories not yet fully defined. Even this limited approach had significant effects on participants, however, since the practice of giving or receiving such feedback was new to most.

The first feedback session with the Coordinator focused on her tendency to do most of the talking at an initial teacher planning meeting. The Coordinator experimented with alternative ways of conveying information to the teachers and at the very next initial meeting of a Pairway cut her participating rate by two-thirds, thereby enlarging the opportunity for teachers to begin working together.

But the feedback process was not immune to criticism. The first feedback with a curriculum planning team similarly focused on the degree to which one suburban district dominated the meeting, but in this case the participants reacted angrily to the data as not being valuable. The reaction of the curriculum planning team to the data about it served as a different kind of data about that group's receptiveness at that time to collaborative inquiry. Despite the negative reaction of the curriculum planning team, its collective behaviour became more collaborative (i.e. more balanced participation, explicit disagreement, and more positive inquiry scores) in its next session, and its members soon came to respect the research assistant.

Developing Personal Commitment to Experimenting with Collaborative Inquiry

From November through January, the research assistants and the Coordinator were all struggling to gain a clearer notion of what collaborative inquiry meant, why it was helpful, and how they could encourage it.

During the research meetings and in the 'Diagnosis of human systems' class, the author repeatedly invented structures which could challenge research team members to collaborate together and then to perform a task in public so that examples of incompetent or non-collaborative behaviour could immediately be confronted. If the team were to be effective, it was especially important that members would neither have the impetus, nor know the direction, to change their behaviour in order to become more collaborative. Moreover, research team members also had to learn how to react non-defensively to public disconfirmation, because such disconfirmation is so often what greets the researcher who first offers feedback to persons unaccustomed to hearing their own behaviour described back to them. If the researcher joins the clients in reacting defensively to disconfirmation, then the relationship is likely to disintegrate.

For example, feedback sessions were 'rehearsed' in the 'Diagnosis of human systems' class before being enacted. The research assistant who was faced with anger from the team to which she offered feedback had already practised facing a hostile group earlier that week in the research class. Consequently, she did not take the anger as personally as she might otherwise (though she had not really believed the anger would occur). She could remain balanced and non-hostile and continue to interpret what was happening, rather than having her behaviour unreflectively determined by what was happening. She later claimed that the rehearsal kept her from breaking down in tears at the team's attack.

The kind of learning experienced by the research assistants is exemplified by this report of a class session after the research assistant had on several occasions experienced feelings 'of not being seen or accepted; of confusion, conflict, anger'. The point is not that all professionals will share the particular negative feelings of this person, but that all professionals do share the dilemma of how to learn from experiences which generate negative feelings in them.

X's strong participation... really put [me] off... because I could see X's glee at the attention and power his acting out had gathered him. I had other issues I wanted to discuss and already understood the issue X brought up. Consequently, I was bored and angry and felt that I got nothing out of the time in terms of professional training.... After sharing my own experience... the next person who spoke directed his first two sentences to me, and the remainder of his sentence to X. Again, I felt cut out.... Later, ... I received feedback that my own participation was seen particularly by Y as high assertive/low inquiry.

The same day as this feedback, I experimented with some high inquiry participation. The results were striking. Others in the class immediately began to address their remarks to me. Once after my first high inquiry participation! Again upon my second high inquiry participation! Then a high assertion, low inquiry participation, and again I felt cut off and ignored. Then another high inquiry participation, and again I felt included and spoken to. During these experiments with my own participation and feelings, I confirmed the necessity of coming from my center when making a contribution. In the past I would see some point that I felt was crucial to the discussion, but off center within myself, and so it would come off as high assertion/low inquiry and also have no strength and energy behind it. In addition, a further learning occurred for me.... I realized that I did not have to speak in order to be included, and that when I feel excluded it is often my own responsibility for resisting inclusion that is available to me.

Many professionals develop interpersonal styles by chance, by imitation, or as a result of traumatic experiences, without ever having the opportunity to become aware of the consequences of that style or to experiment towards a consciously chosen and effective style. Like the research assistant quoted above, their behaviour in professional contexts will be controlled by unexamined feelings about inclusion or control or respect or affection. They may, for example, conclude, without even being aware of the possibility of inquiry into the matter, that they are being excluded from a group by others when they are in fact excluding themselves. Obviously, the creation of such self-fulfilling prophecies diminishes one's overall effectiveness in accomplishing tasks. And, if a group as a whole reinforces such self-fulfilling prophecies by not examining its own process, then the group as a whole will become increasingly ineffective, and its members will become increasingly isolated and alienated from one another. Instead of reducing racial, ethnic, and socioeconomic isolation, such a group would actually increase isolation.

Although the research team and the Coordinator were beginning to experience the benefits of collaboration inquiry, for the first two months of the project the teachers and administrators involved in the pairings experienced 'collaboration' as just a piece of unfamiliar jargon that someone else was using and imposing on them. 'I'm not concerned with collaboration', said one principal in response to the December feedback session described above. 'I'm just concerned with curriculum.' The author took this comment as a lead-in for his presentation to all the adult Metropairways participants at the January 17 Staff Development Workshop, his first opportunity to present the research design to participants. After the presentation a lively discussion ensued during which the author invited confronting comments and several participants responded by articulating their scepticism about the value of the research, while other participants reported a new interest in collaboration. Still, some were not about to be 'bought' so easily. One later said to the author, 'I assumed you would leave at 11.00 a.m. and then we'd never see you again.' In fact, however, he returned to lead two more staff development workshops in which the question of what constituted collaborative behaviour became increasingly sharpened, as programme events increasingly showed the need for new modes of behaviour if pairings were to be successful. Thus, the research team attempted to structure meetings and to behave in all interactions with participants in such a way as to encourage mutual confrontation and an increasing spirit of collaboration. Nevertheless the research team was also well aware that initially participants were not likely to have a high internal commitment to the evaluation process since they did not choose it; moreover, the focus on collaboration was probably contrary to many teachers' and administrators' initial preferences.

In other words, the research team seemed to be advocating a new definition of the situation for programme participants as much as it was documenting participants' existing definitions of the situation (thus paralleling the relationship of the research team to the MPP staff when the original proposal was written). But the researchers' advocacy was of a unique sort and not merely an attempt to superimpose their own subjective ideology on others. The researchers were advocating a principle which as best they could determine represented the central intent of the programme, and they were testing to what degree participants' behaviour was congruent with this intent. This description makes the researchers' role sound more neutral; but to advocate examining congruities and incongruities among purpose, structure, and behaviour is to advocate working together in a fundamentally different way from bureaucratic organizing (cf. Torbert 1974/5). Thus, the researchers were, in this sense, advocating a new definition of the situation for programme participants, but not a definition which the researchers wished to, or could, impose unilaterally, since the vision being advocated was one of collaborative inquiry.

The two ultimately successful Pairways did develop regular feedback cycles through which they tested to what degree their planning meetings and their curricula in fact encouraged collaborative interaction. The other three Pairways did not develop regular feedback cycles — two because they were discontinued after negative cycles by suburban school committees and the third because the teachers did not meet at all until the May 22 Staff Development Workshop, when the researcher led them through a retrospective process of conflict-airing-and-resolution.

A New Definition of the Situation

January was a month of numerous disappointments for the programme. In one week: one suburban School Committee voted against the programme; the camping trip planned for a triad of schools was postponed and nearly cancelled because suddenly, after a camp-site had long been selected, a competitive bidding requirement was belatedly imposed by the agency responsible for the fiscal management of the programme; the parent responsible for one pairing made it clear he was dropping out, thus endangering that pairing; and the first negative School Committee decision led to anxieties that another suburb too might reject the project (as it later did). Thus, every one of the four Pairways seemed endangered. Suddenly, the flavour of the programme was changed from an ordinary classroom project to a politically volatile project involving whole communities. The political emphasis was heightened over the next two months as heated parent meetings and school committee meetings in a second suburb led up to a 'no' vote by its School Committee on March 8, a decision which fuelled still further controversy and parent-organizing within that community.

For the researchers, as for the Coordinator, these events required fundamental recalibrations of effort. The original research design did not anticipate that community political processes would become so crucial to the success of the programme. Of course, the researchers could have continued with their original design, regarding the political events as 'extraneous variables' which interrupted the orderly process of the research through no fault of the researchers. But to do so would have been absurdly unresponsive and particularly ironic given the emphasis on collaboration. Instead, the researchers attended community meetings and sought interviews with school committee members.

The research team had actually begun to become somewhat concerned with wider political processes in early December when members began to notice what seemed like uncollaborative patterns of action by superintendents of several of the suburban school systems involved. It seemed as if the superintendents waited until the last possible moment, after the curriculum had been planned and all preparations completed, before bringing the programme to the attention of their school committees. It seemed as though the school committees were being presented with *fait accompli*. It seemed as though the superintendents were attempting to control their committees unilaterally, contrary to the spirit of Metropairways. Thus, whereas the general 'liberal' reaction to the 'no' votes in the two suburbs was that 'conservatives' unwilling to collaborate with Boston were responsible, the researchers wondered whether superintendents who did not approach their own school committees in a collaborative manner might not also share responsibility for the results. The researchers were unsure about this interpretation, and they were also unsure whether they should raise these issues since they initially had very little definite data on them.

The researchers initially decided to raise the whole issue of superintendent-school committee relations with the Metropairways Coordinator and to explore to what degree it was her responsibility to urge superintendents to take one approach or another to their committees. It turned out that the Coordinator had scrupulously and self-consciously left the question of how to approach the school committees up to each school district administration, conceiving this issue as one of 'home rule'. The researchers, however, recommended *advocating* an early approach both to community parents and to school committees in the future, on the grounds that an early approach would give a community longer to discuss and come to terms with the programme and would make a school committee feel less put on a spot and manipulated by forces beyond its control.

When a new suburb first indicated an interest in the programme both the research assistant who met with the paired teachers at the first curriculum meeting and the Coordinator, speaking to an assistant superintendent and the principal, advocated that early approaches be made to parents and the school committee. The suggestion was accepted, the school committee immediately gave approval to proceed with the planning phase, and a parent's meeting was held within a week of the first curriculum development meeting. Some open opposition to the programme developed, but after a full discussion of the programme's objectives, did not gain much support. After another parent meeting, the school committee approved implementation of the programme. Later in the spring the Coordinator had the choice of seeking or circumventing a vote by the Boston School Committee related to Boston's continuation in the programme. The alternative being considered by the Coordinator was to work directly through the superintendent's office with the board of community superintendents. Again, the research team urged her to seek the school committee vote, contrary to the conventional wisdom of maintaining as much unilateral control as possible. This time the programme received a unanimous vote in its favour.

Taken together, the two 'no' votes and the two later 'yes' votes form a pattern which suggests that on controversial issues early exchanges between a school district's central administration and its school committee, strong advocacy by the administration and programme director, opportunities for comprehensive community discussion, and no attempt either to hoard or to circumvent power lead to a greater sense of collaboration between school committee and administration in the immediate situation, to less fear by school committee and community of being manipulated by outside forces, and thus to greater openness within the school district to 'outside' groups in the future. The strategy of collaborative inquiry seems to hold the promise of practical effectiveness on the political, intergroup scale of events as well as on the interpersonal, small-group scale.

The Characteristic Dilemma of Social Action

During this same period, from January through March, the research team was struggling both to gain a clearer sense of what collaboration meant in each unique situation and, at the same time, to achieve final operationalization of, and reliability in scoring, the behaviour-observation categories which the team had devised in the fall. Both of these projects were complicated and illuminated, in turn, by the changing definition of the situation, described in the previous section, which led the research in new directions altogether.

Upon reflecting together (and the team devoted many moments to such reflection, including a long evening meeting on February 23, which the members entitled 'What collaboration isn't' in an effort to capture the evasiveness of the concept), the research team began to appreciate that its own current dilemma — *the attempt to operationalize what it did not yet fully understand, while being interrupted* — was the same dilemma facing Metropairways as a whole. Indeed, this dilemma seems to characterize all social action. Top-down bureaucratic organizing, empirical scientific experiments, and other attempts at unilateral control, do not really face this dilemma. Instead, these forms of social organizing concentrate only on operationalizing programmes or ideas, striving to prevent interruptions and taking basic assumptions for granted rather than investigating them. The research team came to see that, in contrast to attempts at unilateral control, collaborative inquiry is an inherently more ambiguous process because it not only seeks to achieve pre-defined results, but also seeks to remain open to relevant new insights and interruptions, which may change the very definition of the situation.

These 'philosophical' insights later came to explain the problems which the research team encountered as it attempted to develop reliability in the use of the behaviour scoring procedure. In a series of meetings the researchers listened together to tapes of teacher meetings, compared their attempts to score the conversations, and developed increasingly precise definitions for each term in the scoring procedure. Nonetheless, they concluded that the scoring procedure was ultimately of most use as a guide to keener qualitative observation of behaviour rather than as a fully definable and quantifiable system.

Using an Analytical System to Raise Political and Ontological Questions

Two examples will show why the researchers ultimately preferred to rely primarily on qualitative descriptions of behaviour rather than to rely heavily on statistical summaries. The first example was the difficulty in distinguishing between the two categories 'Initiates decision' and 'Additive comment'. The problem was that what began as additive comments often turned out, over the course of several further comments, to redefine the whole situation, so that in retrospect one would have scored the comment as initiating a decision. Or, one person would say something in a subordinate clause to which the next person would add something, leading to a decision on the matter. But who initiated the decision: the first person to mention it, or the second person who gave it prominence?

The second example was the difficulty in determining who should be credited with *making* a given decision. On some occasions the decision was explicitly consensual and it hardly seemed appropriate to credit the person who looked around the group in asking, 'Are we agreed, then, that we'll do X?' with making the decision. But the trickiest occasions were those when one person seemed to make a decision unilaterally and thus seemed clearly to deserve a check in the 'Makes decision' column. Yet the researcher present knew that this person had earlier been urged to take such an initiative by someone else, or else the researcher had seen this person counting how many others were on his side before announcing the decision. Such occasions raise the question whether single persons can ever validly be counted as making decisions even if they do make the decision explicit.

The difficulty of categorizing who initiates and who makes decisions in every instance ultimately becomes an insoluble problem if one's aim is to develop a comprehensive, analytically neat scoring system. This problem is insoluble in principle because political life is precisely not a temporal series of analytically discrete exchanges of similar value, but rather a swarm of exchanges based on attempts to intuit what is relevant and what is interruption, to intuit what others wish, and to intuit what symbols best comprehend a whole situation. Life does not work like the current hypotheticodeductive paradigm of science (and neither does science, in practice (Mitroff, 1974)). Life includes both 'political' interruption and 'ontological' questioning of premises, as well as analytical description; but the fact that social exchange cannot in principle be reduced to an analytically neat scoring system does not prevent the same scoring procedure from being very useful on many specific occasions to help participants gain insight into their own behaviour. Sometimes the problems noted above simply do not arise. For example, in a given group of four teachers, one teacher may make no comments whatsoever that would be categorized as either 'Initiates decision' or 'Additive comment', instead contributing only in terms of 'explicit agreement'. These data can be fed back to the teacher and can lead to an exploration of the teacher's sense of personal power and interpersonal style. Similarly, one person in a group may appear to make all decisions. Whether or not this appearance is ultimately true, these data can be fed back to the group for further exploration of its decision-making patterns.

Thus, from the point of view of an action research design, in which data collected on any given round of research are tested for empirical validity, political usefulness, and existential illuminatingness by feeding them back to the participants themselves, analytical validity is not the only, nor the final, criterion of truth. A political criterion of validity — does this information help me to act more effectively in given situations? — and an ontological criterion of validity — does this information help me to experience more directly my-real-situation-in-the-world? — complement the analytical criterion of validity — is this information internally consistent and externally replicable? Western science has until the present time concentrated its attention solely on developing increasingly elegant analytical tests of validity. As a result, analytical criteria of validity have become increasingly alienated from political and ontological criteria, and explicit validity testing of all three types remains relatively primitive and rare in most people's lives and in most social settings (including the conduct of social science itself). Given the limited time span of this project, the research team ultimately chose not to develop statistically acceptable levels of inter-rater reliability in the use of the behaviour-scoring procedure, but rather to use it primarily for two other purposes: (1) to raise 'political' questions during feedback and workshop sessions with participants about their decision-making patterns; and (2) to raise 'ontological' questions about the purpose and process of science through this report. Not until social science research actively takes responsibility for its political effects and its ontological implications, as well as for its analytic rigorousness, can it hope to inform our lives together in a balanced way.

Social science research which attempts to report and analyse real events can have powerful immediate 'political' effects on the persons described. The research team found that teachers and administrators read the early drafts of the final report with word-by-word attention, and the research team spent over 30 hours receiving detailed, and sometimes emotional, criticism of the various chapters on each Pairway. This process influenced the researchers to make many revisions and the participants to internalize more deeply how their behaviour affected the programme. Thus, the writing of the report itself served as an important feedback mechanism to participants and an important validity check for the research team.

Acknowledgements

This chapter is adapted from a comprehensive report of the same title co-authored, with Torbert, by Leon Berry, William Bickley, and Priscilla Wohstetter. The coordinator of the Metropairways projects was Audrey Melick. The author is very grateful to these persons for their colleagueship in the work described here, and would also like to thank Jean Bartunek for her helpful critique of this chapter.

Human Inquiry
Edited by P. Reason and J. Rowan
© 1981 John Wiley & Sons Ltd.

CHAPTER THIRTY

Doing dialogical research

Rosemary Randall
Department of Community Education, Open University, UK
and John Southgate
*Department of Applied Social Studies, Polytechnic of North
London, UK*

The work of Paulo Freire (1976) has become better known in recent years. In a piece of action research we did in 1977-78 we adapted some of his thinking to provide ourselves with a practical method that we hoped would give us a sound theoretical approach and a practice that would be genuinely liberatory for all concerned.

The aim of the project was to explore the psychodynamics of self-managed groups. In particular we were interested in the relationship between creativity and destructiveness in such groups since in our experience they seemed to offer greater and more extreme possibilities of both than more conventionally structured organizations.

The research led us in the end to reformulate Bion's theory of groups process (Bion, 1968). As we see it he describes accurately the typical experience of a destructive group. Acting to defend themselves from an unpalatable reality and reactivated unconscious anxieties group members utilize primitive defence mechanisms. The group switches randomly between three different modes which Bion calls dependency, fight-flight, and pairing. In the dependent group members seek reliable leaders and behave as if these pseudo-parental figures can 'save' the group. In the fight-flight group the group creates a leader or leaders from amongst its most paranoid members. These leaders then hold the group together in persecutory attack or flight from whoever or whatever can most immediately be perceived as the enemy. In the rather inaptly named pairing group, the major defence is idealization, usually of a cross-sex pair who it is phantasied will produce the 'baby' or new messiah who will save the group. We came to the conclusion that these modes were also functional opposites of three far more creative states. As we finally formulated it, when a group shares a common desire and has the knowledge and resources to achieve it, it will go through a creative cycle of activity. There is an initial prepatory phase of *nurturing,* followed by an *energizing* phase, a *peak* at which the 'new' in some sense is produced, and a *relaxing* phase. We called this the creative-orgasmic cycle because it is the same energetic cycle experienced in sexual relating as described by W. Reich (1961). Bion's dependency group is the 'dark shadow' of the nurturing phase; his fight-flight group the shadow of the energizing phase and his pairing group the shadow of the relaxing phase. The experience of the creative cycle in its pure and perfect form is as rare as the experience of Bion's basic assumption groups in their most extreme forms. Between these creative and destructive extremes lie a mass of varying situations, some towards one and some towards the other end of a creative-destructive continuum. We named these everyday experiences the 'Intermediate' group. This aspect of our work is written up in more detail elsewhere (Southgate and Randall, 1979; Randall *et al.,* 1980). In the rest of this chapter we want to describe one of the research interventions we made which contributed to the development of this theory.

The project was from the outset considered to be a piece of action research. In doing action research, however, we were concerned to adopt a method that could make it a truly interactive and hopefully liberating experience. Our solution was through an adaptation of the work of Paulo Freire. Freire ran literacy programmes in Brazil where he developed a radically new approach to the problems of teaching reading and writing skills, and to education generally. There are three crucial concepts in his approach.

The first is *dialogue.* Freire defines this as two-way intercommunication, a horizontal relationship between persons who are engaged on a joint, critical search. Its opposite is anti-dialogue, or cultural *invasion.* The relationship between people here is hierarchical, it involves the imposition of one person's set of values, assumptions, or knowledge onto the other. The receiver is seen as a container to be filled with necessary facts or information. It discourages a critical attitude. Invasion does not exist solely in the education field or in imperialist states but anywhere power relationships define a situation. Teachers and taught. Parents and children. Ruling class and oppressed class. In our case, researchers and researched. In Freire's view dialogue is a prerequisite for radical, liberatory education. It is a first step in consciousness-raising.

In deciding whether dialogue is possible in any given situation it is important to recognize at what level invasion exists. A teacher in a school who desires a more dialogical relationship with her pupils will not succeed if she simply looks at the way she teaches her given subjects to her pupils. She must also consider how invasion is structured into her total situation. If the education system in *itself* is an agent of cultural invasion and control, then dialogue must take account of this level. It must facilitate actions at this level to change this invasion or it will not really be dialogical. Dialogue properly used is never a neutral tool. It questions the nature of unequal relationships. For us as researchers it meant a questioning of our roles, the theories we held about groups and organizations, and our practice as we related to particular groups.

The second crucial concept of Freire's is that of *coding*. Coding relates to the way in which information is presented to the people you work with. Freire argues that by dialogue the educator can enter the cultural world of the educatee. He starts to appreciate the particular ways in which the 'educatees', or in our case the 'researched', construct their world. What concepts do they use? What is their language? How do they talk about things? How do they perceive the social relationships of which they are a part? Any teaching materials must be coded in a manner appropriate to the group. They must be capable of being decoded in such a way as to reveal something of the essential elements of the relationship of the group to its environment. In Freire's case this meant discovering key words, important in the peasant culture, and drawing pictures which not only showed the objects represented by such words but the underlying relationships of oppression or invasion that made up their experience. Learning to read and write was thus a way of taking hold of reality and acting on it. Reading and writing became not skills that the educated 'invaders' had, but tools with which the oppressed could understand and act upon their world.

Correct coding is dependent on an intermediate step — *problematizing* — the third of Freire's key concepts. In problematizing, the knowledge and theory of the educator is brought together through dialogue with the specific cultural experience of the educatee. The interaction gives rise to a particular way of presenting the situation. It is shown as a puzzle to be solved, a problem requiring and suggesting action. Freire's drawings were 'problematizations' of the peasants' experiences. In decoding them the peasants grasped reality in a new and vivid way, not seeing something that was new *per se,* but seeing something they had always known, recapitulated, presented in a way that was no longer a mystification but a clarification leading to action.

So we have three crucial elements taken from Freire's approach to education:

(1) the necessity of dialogue to establish relationships and understand the cultural context in which you are working;
(2) problematizing where it is essential that the analysis you as educator or researcher bring to the situation is adequate and that your understanding of it through dialogue is correct (this of course may require some modification of your generalized theory or analysis);
(3) coding so that you present the situation in such a way that consciousness is raised and actions follow.

To demonstrate what this approach meant for us in practice we can take as an example one of the projects we worked with — a new community centre in an inner-city area. The problem — in our terms — was how to help a group who were clearly involved in destructive processes understand their situation in such a way that they could take actions to change it. The community centre was the brainchild of a small group of professional people. They intended it to be not just a community centre, but also a settlement — a centre for social action — and they wanted it to be democratically run by the local community who they intended should control and manage it. When the centre opened, however, the people who were drawn in had diverse interests and did not necessarily share the founder's dreams. The divisions of the surrounding community were reflected in the divided and competing memberships of the various committees. We became involved, at the request of the workers employed there, at a point when the whole organization was in turmoil and they seemed to be getting a lot of the flack. Conflict existed between different sub-groups who desired to use the centre in different ways and who had different views on what self-management and local control meant. In addition the centre was hampered by an unwieldy constitution and a series of committees with ill-defined and overlapping roles and responsibilities. This exacerbated the underlying conflicts.

Dialogue in a situation where there are warring sub-groups is inevitably difficult. It is extremely easy to become identified with one sub-group. One may, anyway, feel partisan, according to one's sympathies. We were cautious in our initial discussions, talking only to those who expressed an interest in meeting us, and confining our appearances at the centre to occasions when we were specifically invited. Throughout our involvement we kept three principles in mind which guided our approach:

(1) Were we in dialogue? And if not, why? Because of some error on our part or because it was structurally impossible?
(2) How could we problematize the situations we found? What were the key puzzles?
(3) How could we code things to make them useful for those we worked with?

After a time we proposed at a general meeting that we interview everyone we could and then make a presentation about the problems the centre faced. This was agreed on. Our practice in interviewing is to listen without taking notes or tape-recording, and to write up our impressions and recollections immediately. We do not go in with set questions but aim to encourage people to talk on their own terms about their concerns. These interviews and the time we spent in the project began to give us a feel of the dynamics present in the place.

Our problem then was how to present information in a way in which people could act on it — in other words how to problematize and code. Our solution was to draw up a series of cartoons encapsulating the information and views we had gathered and presented in such a way as to draw out the major contradictions in the situation. We reproduce eight of them below. Our aim in doing this was to present complex information straightforwardly, in a form in which it could be remembered or returned to for reference and in a way which would stimulate change.

ABOUT US ---

We work for Loughborough University

Our goal is to find the problems and solutions of community and grass roots organisations so that future projects can learn from your experience - and not have to reinvent the wheel!

What we have done is to talk to as many people as possible and try to present these various views in one total set of pictures'

No cartoon represents any individual person - but is an amalgam of many--

We take lots of views - and cartoon it as one fictitious person --

n.b. the illustrator, Frances Tomlinson does not know any of you

Figure 30.1 There were 20 cartoons. This was the first one. We felt it important to state who we were, what our interest was, and the fact that people should not expect to find individuals represented in the cartoons — i.e. we were trying to look at the underlying structural problems and not at personalities

Figure 30.2 The size of the building and the demands on its resources was an underlying difficulty. The aim of this picture was to stimulate discussion of this. Sub-groups tended to see access to the building and use of it as an individual battle they had either with another sub-group or with the director. We hoped people might begin to see the underlying cause, and work on ways of solving the difficulty. The caption was a quote from one of the people we interviewed

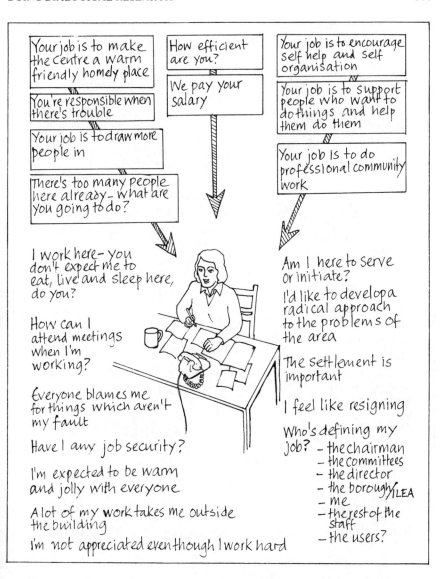

Figure 30.3 The next four cartoons are taken from a series of eight which showed some of the different sub-groups — the workers, the people who lived in the neighbourhood, the local government officials, the pensioners, the founders, the youth club members and workers, the director and the chairperson. These last two we referred to as 'the present, or any other director chairperson' because we wanted to concentrate attention on the roles and the way these fitted into the overall structure rather than on the personalities of the people who currently held them. The captions, as far as possible, were direct quotes from interviews

THE PEOPLE WHO LIVE IN THE COMMUNITY
our talents aren't used
what is a "settlement" anyway?
we would like a social centre
I'm afraid the Council will take this place over if we don't sort the problems out
staff should have given more help to the management group
there's no such thing as the "Acacia Road group"---
-- we wanted to run things in the community
the staff are shy and reserved
I'm afraid the Centre's become too much of a youth club
It seems the staff make arbitrary decisions
Is this a social centre for us?
people from my estate don't think so --
--adults have their own social groups, its the kids who need the Centre
the professional staff should sort things out
its a great place for the kids
committees aren't representative
the Centre's connected with subversives
people are new round here and they haven't got to know each other yet

Figure 30.4

catching buses and travelling is difficult at my age
everything's for young people these days
you can't rush old people - we need time to move chairs and furniture
we're only asking for 3 hours a week and our dance.
we can think of new solutions for the Centre
I'm afraid of getting mugged late at night
people don't realise we need to rest in the after-noons
we're as capable as anyone of organising our dos

Figure 30.5

Figure 30.6

Figure 30.7   This cartoon was one of a series of four all of which had the same format. The aim was to show something that was hidden to people individually — the fact that there was a lot of agreement over the nature of some of the problems. Individually people felt that something should be done about the committee structure but collectively this was never raised because people felt they were isolated in this view. This kind of process is very common in groups and is often used defensively to protect against change that is unwelcome or difficult. Although this was true of the centre we felt it was also a function of the size and unwieldy nature of the organization and that little harm could be done by confronting the problem. A number of actions did in fact follow directly on the issues that were problematized here

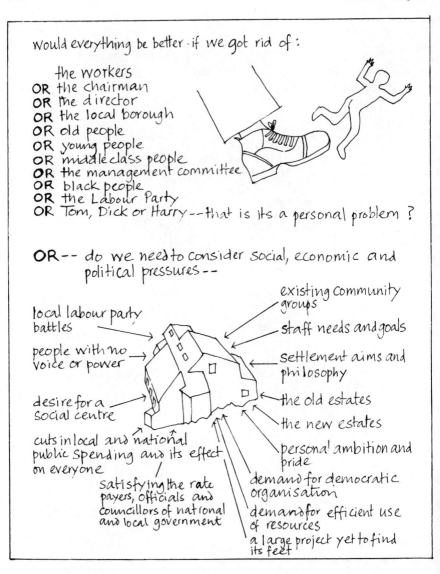

Would everything be better if we got rid of :

the workers
OR the chairman
OR the director
OR the local borough
OR old people
OR young people
OR middle class people
OR the management committee
OR black people
OR the Labour Party
OR Tom, Dick or Harry -- that is its a personal problem ?

OR -- do we need to consider social, economic and political pressures --

existing community groups

local labour party battles

staff needs and goals

people with no voice or power

settlement aims and philosophy

desire for a social centre

the old estates

the new estates

cuts in local and national public spending and its effect on everyone

personal ambition and pride

satisfying the rate payers, officials and councillors of national and local government

demand for democratic organisation

demand for efficient use of resources

a large project yet to find its feet

Figure 30.8 This was the final cartoon. It shows the contradiction between two different ways of looking at the problem. On the whole people had tended to see the problem as one of personalities. Our approach tried to accent the structure problem, our intention was to stimulate discussion of the most effective way of looking at things and taking action

Our report to the general meeting was well received. Many of the pensioners who found committee reports hard to follow congratulated us on the clear presentation. The overall effect of the intervention was to create a breathing space. Some of the problems did not seem to be so completely intractable. Meetings became less explosive. The concentration on problems as purely personal lessened. New alliances and rapprochements took place. The organization as a whole moved from being locked in a destructive process to a more intermediate one. Over the next two years a number of changes took place. One important one was that a subcommittee was set up to review the constitution and committee structure and eventually a new constitution was adopted which emphasized democratic control by those who participated directly in the centre. Lying behind these changes was the emergence of what we called the 'new culture' made up of those individuals and sub-groups whose interest in the centre was practical and continuing. The end-result was a community centre that is a modest and effective establishment. Although it doesn't reflect the dreams that were invested in it originally, either by the founders or by others involved, it is successful in other ways.

In terms of our research, we gained some added understanding of the way destructive processes operate in a large and diverse organization and some experiences in the way in which Freire's work could be used in action research to facilitate change.

Human Inquiry
Edited by P. Reason and J. Rowan
© 1981 John Wiley & Sons Ltd.

CHAPTER THIRTY-ONE

A practical example of a dialectical approach to educational research

Jack Whitehead
School of Education, University of Bath, UK

The purpose of this chapter is to present a practical example of a dialectical approach to educational research and to discuss some of the implications of this approach for the production of an educational theory which corresponds to educational practice. The example is based on my attempts to solve my practical classroom problem, 'How do I improve this process of education here?' The enquiry lasted 12 years and involved the application of four methodologies to the problem, as well as the production of seven research reports. Table 31.1 contains the title of each report, its classification in terms of Mitroff and Kilmann's (1978) analysis of methodological approaches to the social sciences and its classification in terms of the phase of the scientific inquiry. All I am meaning by the 'phase of the inquiry', is whether it follows the creative or critical episodes of scientific thinking. In the creative phase an idea is formed. It is not amenable to formal analysis in its creative formation. Once the idea is formed, however, it can be tested in the critical phase and subjected to formal analysis.

Before I describe how I solved my problem using the methodology of the particular humanist I will give my formal reasons for rejecting the methodologies of the analytical scientist (report 1), the conceptual theorist (report 3) and the conceptual humanist (report 5) as inappropriate methods for investigating my problem.

Table 31.1

Reports on my practical problem: How do I improve this process of education here?	Scientific methodology	Phase of inquiry
(1) A preliminary investigation of the process through which adolescents acquire scientific understanding	Analytic scientist	Critical
(2) Wiltshire science teachers project themselves into improving learning situations for their pupils	None	Creative
(3) An 11-14 mixed ability project in science. The report of a local curriculum development	Conceptual theorist	Critical
(4) Improving learning for 11-14-year olds in mixed ability groups	None	Creative
(5) The process of improving education within schools	Conceptual humanist	Critical
(6) The researcher's educational practice	None	Creative
(7) 'How do I improve this process of education here?'	Particular humanist	Critical

It is important to realize that the reasons given below, for the rejection of three of the four methodologies, were given in a retrospective analysis of my research. In this analysis I can give clear and precise reasons for rejecting the three methodologies. I do not, however, wish to give the false impression that the way I moved from the methodology of the analytic scientist to that of the particular humanist was by the explicit application of the reasons to my methods. As Medawar says in his paper, 'Is the scientific paper a fraud?', scientists tend to give a false impression that the development of their growth of knowledge follows a logically well-defined path when in fact intuition and guesswork play a larger part than most scientists convey in their analysis of their activities.

In the case of my own research the movement between the methodologies was characterized by an inexplicable feeling of anxiety and despair that something was fundamentally wrong with the way I was conducting my research. This sense of despair contrasted sharply with Popper's (1970) view of the satisfaction of the scientist when a cherished idea is falsified. According to Popper this satisfaction is grounded in the fact that by falsifying such ideas then one is contributing to knowledge. I can only bear witness to the fact that I experienced no such satisfaction in my knowledge that I was mistaken. I experienced despair. I overcame my despair in a decision to pursue my research in a different way. The fact that I had no clear idea where I was going in the creative phases of my research was accompanied by feelings of anxiety. The grounds of my faith that the new direction would prove fruitful are explicable only in the sense that I had a subsidiary awareness, which I could not bring into focus, that my problem was soluble. The fact that I pursued my inquiry over 12 years whilst clearly failing on three separate occasions bears witness to this inexplicable awareness that my problem was soluble and that I should 'know' the solution when it was discovered. Before describing my solution I will consider the reasons I gave for rejecting the methodologies of the analytical scientist, the conceptual theorist and the conceptual humanist.

I rejected the methodology of the analytical scientist because it assumed absolute determinism in explanations of human action. In my own explanations for my own educational practice I assumed that my actions were in part self-generated and self-explanatory and that they were not the sole outcome of a mechanical form of causality.

My reasons for rejecting the methodology of the conceptual theorist were essentially concerned with the fact that report 3 failed to fulfil the following criteria of objectivity and validity. The criterion of objectivity was based upon Popper's (1959) view that: 'The objectivity of scienfific statements lies in the fact that they can be intersubjectively tested.' Popper has generalized this idea in his view that objectivity rests in the fact that the statements can be 'subjected to the mutual rational control of critical discussion'.

The criterion of validity was developed from the work of Schutz (see Filmer *et al.*, 1973) on the concept of adequacy. This criterion can be stated:

> Each concept in the model of action must be constructed so that an act actually performed in the world in the way indicated by the construct would be understandable for the actor himself and for his fellow men in terms of commonsense schemes of interpretation.

Report 3 was tested against these two criteria by submitting my explanation in the report, for the lives of the teachers I had worked with, to the teachers and a committee constituted by the funding agency (one of whose functions was the criticism of proposed publications), for the rational control of critical discussion. The teachers and the committee rejected the explanation on the grounds that the words in my descriptions of their actions were not directly related to the words they used to describe their own immediately lived experience and that they could not see any relationship between the models I used to explain their actions and the form and content of the explanations which they gave for their own action.

Immediately the above criticisms were made I could see that they were justified. I had not generated my explanation from the data that I had gathered. I had, in fact, attempted to show how the data could fit established models of educational innovation or my own mixed-ability model. I rejected the methodology of the conceptual theorist on the grounds that the nature of the explanation generated through this methodology did not fulfil the criteria of objectivity and adequacy.

Following the rejection of the methodology of the conceptual theorist I reconstructed my explanation from the same data-base as that used for report

3. The explanation differed, however, in that it was grounded in the assumptions of a conceptual humanist. I should like it to be clear that I subjected my reconstructed explanation, based upon this methodology, to the teachers and the committee. It was accepted by both as corresponding to the actions of the teachers and thus judged to have fulfilled the criteria of objectivity and adequacy. My own rejection of the methodology was solely related to its inappropriateness as a way of investigating my problem, 'How do I improve this process of education here?' The methodology of the conceptual theorist had enabled me to answer the question, 'How do these teachers improve a process of education for their pupils?' I had not, however, answered my own question, 'How do I improve this process of education here?' What I had done up to this point in my research was to exempt myself from the question. I had assumed that I could answer this question by studying other teachers. I decided to begin a systematic exploration of my own actions in the classroom, as I attempted to solve my problem.

'How do I Improve this Process of Education Here?'

The methodology I discovered to be appropriate to the investigation of my problem was that of a particular humanist. The mode of inquiry of the particular humanist is that of the case study and the preferred logic is the logic of the individual. In the case study I video taped my own practice as I attempted to solve my problem. My claim, to have answered my question and to 'know' how I answered it, is based upon my evaluation of two video tapes which show the differences between two of my lessons. In the first lesson I was teaching the same thing to all my pupils at the same time, i.e. it was a normal class-based lesson. In this lesson I experienced a problem because I was denying my pupils the freedom to choose some of their own course of study and denying them the exercise of their responsibility for their own learning. I was also failing to distribute my professional skills in a just way. By this I mean that my pupils had different interests and abilities, and yet I was treating them as if they were the same.

I attempted to solve my problem by reorganizing my teaching method from one which relied on class teaching to one which relied on individual and small-group learning. I was assisted in this change by the system of resource management which had been developed by the Avon Resources for Learning Unit. This unit was established in 1974 to investigate the claims being made for 'independent/resource-based learning methods'. The system of resource organization developed by this unit involves the pupils in study tours. Each tour begins and ends with a consultation between teacher and pupil. The major components of the system are:

(1) Consultation — when teacher and pupil review the work already done by the pupil and plan the next piece of work.

(2) A record card — this records the work that the pupil has already done, the assessments and observations on that work, a profile of the pupil's achievements of the main objectives for the course of work and the work the pupil is about to do.

(3) A task card bank — this contains a wide selection of task cards for the varying activities and interests of the user. The task card instructs the pupils about the resources he will need and how to use them.

(4) A master plan — this shows the titles of all the task cards and a flow chart which shows suggested routes through the task cards.

(5) The resources bank.

(6) The equipment.

The relationship between the components of the system can be represented as shown in Figure 31.1.

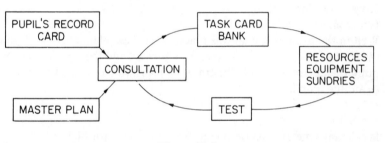

Figure 31.1

I will now describe the differences on the two video-tapes between the way I am teaching, the way the pupils are learning, and list five other differences related to my values as an educator. This description will be followed by an explanation of how I improved my practice.

The Way I am Teaching

Lesson A

I am teaching the content of my lesson plan to all the pupils at the same time. I go through my plan, demonstrating, instructing, and questioning the pupils to check that they have understood. The following extracts from the video-tape give some indication of the way I am teaching:

T. I'd like to give you some idea of how sound travels, how it gets from one place to another.

T. Turn to p. 31 of your science book.

T. Sonia please read 11.11 on the ear.

T. I'm going to give you 2 minutes to read to the bottom of the page. Then I'm going to fire questions at you very quickly to find out if you know what the outer, middle, and inner ear are for.

T. I want you to draw a diagram in your book showing the outer, middle, and inner ear and write in your own words what each one does.

Lesson B

P. Mr. Whitehead I still can't find the old and the new.

T. Do you notice any differences between the coals.

P. Yeah, they are all different shapes, some have got bigger holes some have different particles.

T. How is coal formed?

P. Is it from coke and tar?

T. Well in the beginning coal was made from these plants here — I point to the resource booklet on how coal was formed and then go on to show the pupil the diagrams which illustrate the formation of coal. I then move on to another pupil.

T. Yes Sonia

P. Is calcium a metal or a non-metal. Its a non-metal isn't it?

T. How can we find out? What would be the characteristics that would tell us?

P. Looks silvery, its heavy.

T. I've got some calcium here so should we have a look?

P. It's hard, its silvery. It's metal. Can we put some in water and see what it does?

T. Now what's happening?

P. Bubbles coming off.

T. What do you think that they are?

P. Air. Acid.

T. How would you find out?

P. Look, we've done it. pH9. Its alkaline.

In lesson A the pupils do the same thing at the same time following my instructions. I tell them what to do and they do it. In lesson B the pupils are doing different things at the same time following instructions on the task cards. Individuals are taking some responsibility for their own learning; some individuals are learning by inquiry. The pace of learning is determined by the pupils rather than determined by the rate at which the teacher presents the content.

The Way the Pupils are Learning

In lesson A the pupils are learning a pre-specified content. This form of learning has been characterized as reception learning. In lesson B the pupils are engaged in resource-based learning where the learning is organized by the master plan, task cards, and resources. They have the opportunity to experience inquiry learning. Five other differences can be as tabulated in Table 31.2.

Table 31.2

Lesson A	Lesson B
(1) No freedom for pupils to choose their topic or pace of learning (negation of the value of freedom)	Some freedom to choose their topic and pace of learning
(2) No responsibility for organizing their learning (negation of autonomy)	Some responsibility for organizing their learning
(3) No inquiry learning (negation of the imaginative episodes of scientific inquiry)	Some inquiry learning
(4) The pupils are treated the same when there are good reasons for treating them differently (negation of justice)	Pupils are treated differently for good reasons
(5) No pupil initiated activities (negation of pupil's interests)	Some pupil-initiated activities

To establish that the changes between the lessons are improvements I must apply my educational values to the changes. These values are expressed in terms of freedom, justice, consideration of interests, worthwhile activities, and personal autonomy. In lesson A I experienced the negation of my values of freedom, the imaginative episodes in scientific thinking, the consideration of my pupil's interests and the distribution of my professional skills in a just way. In lesson B I was able to give my pupils the opportunity for inquiry learning, the freedom to choose some of their topics, to consider their interests, to distribute my time in a more just way, and to encourage my pupil's autonomy. In brief the changes were improvements in the sense that they involved a movement, from the experience of the negation of my values in practice, to the experience of living my values in practice. Having described the changes in my practice I will now offer an explanation for the changes. At a later stage I will be suggesting that the form and content of this explanation has implications for educational theory because it is an explanation which corresponds to my educational practice.

The explanation for how I improved my practice has the following form and content:

(1) I experience a problem because some of my educational values are negated in my practice.
(2) I imagine a solution to my problem. This included the learning system from the Avon Resources for Learning Unit.
(3) I act in the direction of the solution.
(4) I evaluate the outcomes of my actions:
    (a) I did not know the resources well enough to switch my attention quickly enough from a pupil studying coal, to another on fossils, to another on metals, to be of much use to the pupils;
    (b) I had problems with pupils who were waiting to see me, in that a queue formed.
(5) I modified my actions and ideas in the light of my evaluations:
    (a) I familiarized myself with the contents of all the resources in greater detail than I had to begin with;
    (b) I reduced queueing by giving the pupils greater responsibility for marking their record cards and for finding their way through the master plan with the different routes.

I will now consider the implications of the form and content of the above explanation for educational theory.

The Nature of Educational Theory

The view of educational theory which has been dominant over the past 20 years is that it is constituted by the disciplines of education (Peters, 1977). This view holds that logically all questions of educational practice are hybrid questions in that they involve a crossing of value-judgements with different forms of empirical inquiry. According to Peters the first step towards answering questions of educational practice is to break down the question into its logically distinct components. Following this breaking-down the research and training carried out under the aegis of the different disciplines is then applied to the components which are then integrated in the solution of the practical problems. In this approach Peters isolates three principles which he says determine the selection and presentation of theory. These principles are: that educational theory must be presented in a differentiated way; the selection of the content must in the main be related to teacher's practical problems; and that the differentiated modes of thought about education must be presented in a way that they intimate problems at a more fundamental level in the disciplines themselves, and the forms of inquiry necessary for their solution.

I do not wish to create the impression that I believe that the disciplines of education have nothing to contribute to the production of educational theory. I am saying that the view of educational theory which is explicated in the above principles is simply mistaken. My central point is that the problem is not to present educational theory as if it were constituted by the disciplines of education; rather the problem is to encourage educators to produce educational theory on the basis of explanations for their own educational practice.

My own rejection of the disciplines approach was based in my personal knowledge that after integrating the contributions from such different forms of knowledge as the physical and social sciences into a solution to a practical problem I was still left with the problem of explaining my educational practice. In other words the explanation for my educational practice could include my ability to integrate and apply in life distinctive and articulate forms of knowledge without consisting of, or being itself, any of these forms. I have suggested that one form for educational theory could be produced from the explanations for the lives of individual educators in their educational practice.

If individual educators take the responsibility for producing educational theory there is still the problem of academic legitimation to overcome. At the present time the power to define what counts as valid knowledge rests with the proponents of the disciplines approach. Academics do not easily give up their cherished ideas, especially when these ideas have structured most of their productive life. In proposing a dialectical alternative to educational theory it is pointless attempting to gloss over the differences between the two approaches. From the dialectical perspective the disciplines approach is mistaken in its view of educational theory. It is mistaken in its view of the logic which should structure the view of education. It is mistaken in its view of rationality and its view of the methods whereby we can achieve clarity about the practical activity of education. I have explained that the disciplines approach misconceives educational theory because it is not a matter of presenting this theory as if it were constituted by the disciplines of education. It is a matter of producing educational theory from the explanations for the lives of individual educators in their educational practice. The disciplines approach is mistaken in its view that logically speaking the first step in the solution of the practical problem is to break it down into its logically distinct components. The first step in the dialectical approach, when one experiences a problem because some aspect of ones educational values are negated in ones practice, is to imagine a solution to the problem. There is some agreement between the two approaches because the view of educational theory produced through the dialectical approach does indeed intimate problems for the disciplines and for the forms of inquiry necessary for their solution. The problems are not, however, intimated through presenting educational theory as constituted by differentiated modes of thought. They are intimated in the production of educational theory itself. It is to the production of educational theory which I suggest that all educators who are seriously asking themselves questions of the form, 'How do I improve this process of education here?', should now turn to, in our productive work.

Human Inquiry
Edited by P. Reason and J. Rowan
© 1981 John Wiley & Sons Ltd.

CHAPTER THIRTY-TWO

From ethogeny to endogeny: how participants in research projects can end up doing research on their own awareness

David Sims
*Centre for the Study of Organizational Change and
Development, University of Bath, UK*

In this chapter I tell what is for me a true story about the methodology of a research project. I shall describe firstly what it was that I was trying to learn about in the research; secondly, how I set about trying to learn about it (that is, the methodology as I intended it); thirdly, how I in fact went about learning about it (that is, the methodology as it turned out); and fourthly, what kind of learning this produced.

What I Set Out to Learn About

In this project, my object was to learn about how some persons in a few Health Service teams understood the processes by which those teams came by their problems. (For a fuller description of the ideas that came out of this project, see Sims (1979), and for a fuller description of the project as a whole, including the methodology, see Sims (1978)). I had had conversations about this with a number of team members over the years, and while there is no doubt that by the time I was setting it up as a research project I was inclined to steer the conversation that way, the people I was talking to were adult human beings, independent agents with many years of experience of running conversations along the lines that suited them, and no apparent shyness or lack of skill in closing off academics on anything which they regarded as nonsense. Despite this, the topic was accepted as something that seemed to be important

373

in their worlds by plenty of team members, and about which they were happy to try to talk.

The object of my investigation was the beliefs that team members expressed about the processes of problem construction in teams. My intention was to learn something about this which would be useful to other team members in thinking about problem construction in the team they worked in. This learning would not claim to be a matter of facts or of 'true' descriptions of what 'actually' goes on, but rather one person's analytical reorganization of the beliefs of various different persons, which might serve as a heuristic or an aid to thinking for other persons.

How I Set about Learning

My object in this research was to produce a piece of grounded theory (Glaser and Strauss, 1967) about problem construction in teams. To conduct such a piece of research means collecting from the participants the categories which they use in speaking about that part of their world which the researcher is interested in learning about. An investigation which was not confined to the grounded categories of the participants in the research was highly unlikely to discover the important aspects of their team life.

The means that I chose for collecting these grounded categories was the gathering of accounts by the participants of what they understood themselves and others to be doing during the process of problem construction in teams. The justification for trusting accounts was borrowed from Harré and Secord (1972), who propound an 'anthropomorphic' model of man, in which they take one of the distinctive qualities of the human person as being awareness, and awareness as 'being capable of commenting upon action' (p. 102). Such commentaries may be given before, during, or after the action concerned. In the case of problem construction, which turned out not surprisingly to be a highly political team activity, it would clearly not have been practicable to collect the accounts of the participants at the time that they were acting. Quite apart from the fact that they would have been giving their political game away to their colleagues, 'action' in such a context is usually expressed through a verbal 'act', and is thus inconsistent with a simultaneous verbal commentary. The initial materials for analysis and discovery of grounded categories, therefore, were the anticipatory and reflective commentaries given by participants on what they expected themselves and others to do and what they believed themselves and others to have done. These accounts were mostly collected in fairly prolonged interactions between individual participants and myself — necessarily prolonged because I was interested in their accounts not as 'verbal behaviour', but rather as conveyors of meaning. This meant that it was necessary to have enough interchange between us for them to understand what meaning I had taken from the statements they made. As Psathas (1968) says:

> Any social scientist who insists that he can understand all of man's behaviour by focussing only on that part which is overt and manifested in concrete, directly observable acts is naive to say the least (p. 510).

It is with this in mind that I followed the 'imaginative, introspective, subjective' approach which Psathas advocates.

To collect accounts, however, requires that the people whose accounts you want are willing to give you the accounts that you want, and keen enough to do so that they are prepared to put in the sometimes considerable amount of effort required to articulate an account of one's actions. The most straightforward way around this problem seemed to me to be to encourage people to give accounts about things which were of such relevance and significance to themselves that their primary intention became to give those accounts, often for their own interest as well as mine. For many of the participants this then ceased to be seen as a research interview, and became a chance to tell somebody about something which was of major importance to them, and yet which they might never have talked about before. This was shown when, after about an hour and a half of animated exchange between a participant and me about what he said he was going to do or had done in various current problem constructions, he said at the end, 'Well, anyway, that was all about me, but what did you want to know?'

It is also important that the topic of accounts should matter to the participant giving an account because the collection of categories for grounded research is potentially infinite. The only way in which the researcher can really know if he has collected enough categories is if the participant either tells him that he has collected enough, or ceases to give him any new ones. In either case it has effectively been left to the participant to define the relevance or otherwise of categories to the topic, and there is not much basis for a participant to do this if he does not see the relevance of the topic for himself.

I agree with Maruyama (1974) that a 'resonance' of research interests between a researcher and his participants is essential for successful research (although the process that Maruyama describes sounds more like acceptance by the researcher of the research interests of the participants, an 'empathetic' paradigm rather than a 'negotiative' paradigm (Eden and Sims, 1979)). Thus I considered that if I was to make a good job of discovering grounded theory on problem construction in teams, I needed to be aware of the chain of causes and consequences shown in Figure 32.1. This implied that it was critically important that my research interests and those of the participants in the research should resonate; that is, that there should be a significant area for investigation which we all found exciting.

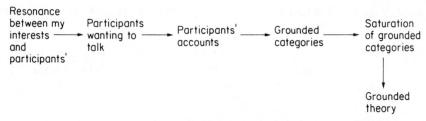

Figure 32.1   Some causes and consequences that I was aware of at
the start

How the Methodology Turned Out

When I planned this research project, I believed that it was unrealistic to hope
that it could be 'endogenous research' in the sense that Maruyama (1974) uses
the term, at least in the full sense where the researcher becomes a back-up
resource to the participants, with the latter conducting the research, defining
the terms of the inquiry, choosing the methodology, and using their own
theories of knowledge to determine what shall be held to be valid in the
research. This approach seemed unrealistic at the outset on two counts.
Firstly, I could not see any basis on which I could, at the beginning of my
relationship with them, persuade the members of the teams to which I had
access to plan, conduct, and evaluate such a programme of research upon
themselves. Secondly, I believed that endogenous research by these team
members would, paradoxically, follow a much more traditional and alienating
methodology than I would be happy with. In the event I was wrong on both
those counts — more in the questions that I was addressing than in the answers
that I was giving — and also in thinking that this was a matter in which I had a
choice.

I have explained how I came to regard resonance between my interests and
those of the participants as important. It is on the whole not very likely that
participants will spend sessions of an hour or more talking to the researcher
about something which they regard as important without that beginning to
affect the way in which they see their world. Thus for example one participant
said to me:

> and then that, there on paper, is where we are on the elderly mentally
> ill, which is, would you believe, 'yes, we know there's a problem,
> but no, we don't know what to do about it'. In fact I actually said
> it; 'The District has so far only defined the problem.' And I
> honestly wasn't thinking about you when I wrote it.

He went on to reflect that, while he might not have been thinking about me
when he wrote it, he would not have thought in that way about what was going

on before I started my research with him. What had happened here seemed to be that my interests in problem construction had resonated with interests of his, that he was seeing and thinking about his world with more emphasis on the topic of problem construction than he would otherwise have done, and that this change in awareness was, he thought, working through to the things that he said in team meetings and wrote in reports. As he and the other participants went about making sense of their situations, they explored and built up more new categories reflecting a change of awareness and a shift of attention away from other matters and towards the processes of problem construction in their teams. Sometimes the research role was taken on more self-consciously by the participants; for example one person told me just before a meeting that she was going to bring up the question of a day centre, and predicted that when she did so, Dr. So-and-so would 'immediately break in and raise another issue so as to make everyone forget what I am talking about; that's the way he does it'. In the event he did not — a circumstance which she talked about afterwards when she was trying to work out whether to revise the theories from which she had generated the wrong prediction, or whether he was just playing some other, more devious, game which she had not thought of.

As the various participants in the research started work on the investigations which stemmed from thinking about problem construction in their teams, they seemed to be using quite a variety of methodologies. Some people, like the one last mentioned, conducted almost experimental research. Some other participants had themselves been out collecting accounts, informally, from other persons about what they thought they were doing in problem construction in teams. Others again gave accounts of generalizations that they had abstracted from reflecting on the various different teams of which they were members. For example, one person talked about a team that he belonged to where the chairmanship had just passed from a physician to a surgeon:

> And that, come to think of it, will mean much shorter meetings because we won't discuss what the problem is. It's always clearer for a surgeon — 'there's the problem'. They're the incisive ones.

Others typologized the various teams in which they worked according to what they saw as the prevalent style of problem construction in those teams. One person said that they were very fed up with a particular team.

> The way I think of it now is that we could do with a much more structured use of the agenda.... The issues tend to get spread out in discussion.

While all this was going on, my role was still to go round collecting participants' accounts. The nature of those accounts, however, was not what I had anticipated when I set out. While I would start off by asking people for accounts of what they believed themselves and others to be doing with respect to the construction of particular problems, I could only pursue that line at any length with most participants at the risk of losing their interest. Resonance would only occur when I was open about my interests, which were to do with slightly more general statements about problem construction in teams, and which were not really about the particular actions of particular persons with respect to a particular problem. This then resonated with the participants' interests which were also at this more abstracted level, and they then felt free to give accounts — accounts of the progress of their own research on problem construction in teams, not of their particular actions, except in so far (as was often the case) as they used their own actions as examples of more general categories. Many statements came in a similar pattern to this one:

> I can honestly believe that we could reach a point where we couldn't think of anything else to worry about, because we may not be looking at it the right way, if too many of us are thinking too seriously about what's wrong now, what is the problem we've got at the moment that we could resolve. For example, on Monday...

— and she then went on to show how an event we had both been present at the previous Monday was an example of this.

As I collected and collated participants' accounts of their research, I was able to treat their findings as categories and to piece together from them a grounded theory of problem construction in teams. Because the categories were derived from accounts of the participants' thinking and investigating on the topic, and not only from the participants' accounts of their actions, it was closer to endogenous research (Maruyama) than to ethogenic research (Harré and Secord). I would suggest that the process of transformation that I have described is likely to take place in any research project in which the categories and concepts used by the participants are taken seriously, and which lasts over a period of time, unless that project is of no interest to the participants; if that is the case, the quality of the data needs to be questioned, because we may presume that the participants have no reason to go to the trouble of supplying good data.

This conclusion seems to me to be important, not because of its implication that more people should be flying the flag for endogenous research, but because of the difference it makes to the way that those of us who do our research in this sort of way conceive of what we are doing. Maybe those of us who adopt more holistic, ethogenic, and grounded approaches to our research are only beginning to grapple with the complexity of what it is that we are doing. From what I have said so far, for example, the reasoning behind my research project looked more like Figure 32.2 than Figure 32.1.

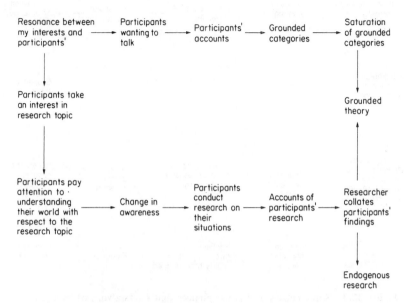

Figure 32.2   Some causes and consequences that I was aware of before the
end

How Action Research Crept In

My position at the start of this project had been that I did not want to conduct
it as action research because I had not the faintest idea in what direction I
might want to act on the organization that I was working in. Again, with
hindsight, I think I was oversimplifying. As I said in the previous section, for
the participants who became interested in the research there was a change in
awareness as they focused more on the topics, questions, and categories which
they saw as relevant to the research and less on others. By the very act of
asking questions and conducting lengthy interviews I was altering their
patterns of awareness of their situation, and thus I was acting on their realities.
This was just as much action research, albeit from a lower profile, as it would
have been if I had taken them away for a two-day seminar on problem
construction at the beginning of the research. William James said, 'Anything
is real of which we find ourselves obliged to take account in any way.' Action
research which sets off from changing other persons' awareness is no less
action research than that which sets out to change the participants' reality in
some other way; the critical quality is the attempt to understand something by
changing it (Clark, 1972). Recognizing this leads us to add a few terms to
Figure 32.2, giving us Figure 32.3.

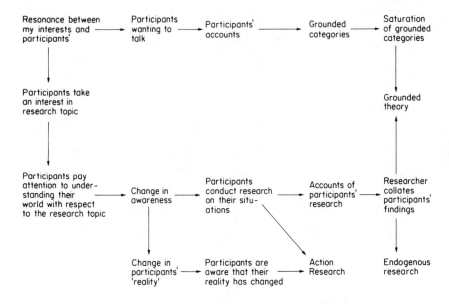

Figure 32.3   Some causes and consequences that I was aware of by the end

So what about my view that the topic was inappropriate for action research because, as yet, I did not know enough about it to know what kind of actions I might take? This too, I think, was an oversimplification; it was true that I did not know what would constitute an 'improvement' to problem construction in teams, but I felt very sure that problem construction was something that we would all do well to pay more attention to, probably at the expense of paying less attention to our abilities at getting rid of (i.e. solving) constructed problems. Because this was an action to be taken on awareness, however, I did not construe my work as action research until the participants started to talk to me about how I was affecting their awareness, and about some of the reflections on the research topic which they saw as resulting from the changed awareness.

I suspect that, as with the question of research going endogenous, research on persons or groups is practically bound to be action research, although the actions may be rendered innocuous if the research is of no interest at all to the participants. In that case again there are questions about the quality of data that can be obtained. This means that action research is practically inevitable, and that, if we wish to do research with persons without denying their everyday human qualities, the methodological choice we have is not whether or not the research we conduct should be action research, but rather whether we should acknowledge to ourselves that it is so, and be explicitly aware of more of the complexity of what we are doing. Our choice is thus not so much about the methodology as about how we shall distribute our own limited awareness within the situations that we are seeking to comprehend.

The Kind of Learning that was Produced

What can I claim to have learned about problem construction in teams by following the methodology outlined above, and what can I claim that other people could learn by reading my account of the research (Sims, 1978)? In particular, what can I claim to have learned as a result of the research becoming both endogenous research and action research that I would not have learned without these two accidents?

The outcome that I produced was a list of 95 different categories, most of which I presented with one or two supporting quotations. I organized these categories in a way that made sense to me in the light of my theoretical frameworks combined with the experience of having been immersed in that data for several months. I then organized them again, this time by connecting them into a narrative which I found I was able to do after having spent a lot of time organizing them all in the first way. I then gave these two write-ups to a number of people to read, including those of the participants who were still interested in reading it despite the fact that it was not ready until several months after I had finished work with them. My two different ways of organizing the categories were intended to convey more of the richness of meaning that I saw in the categories than would have been possible with either of them on their own.

The learning from this research obstinately resists reduction to a few neat sentences. I do not see research on social processes as being directed to the making of 'discoveries', or to making general statements about what 'really' happens. What I do think can be gained at a generalizable level, particularly where the topic being considered is relatively primitive and unexplored, is a form of knowledge that Chin (1974) describes as a 'cumulation of selectively retained tentatives'. He says:

> The implication of this position is that we do not strive for a finality of answer in applied behavioural science and, operationally, a once-and-for-all crucial experiment. We do strive for a patient and constantly alert evaluation of existing knowledge and current practices, holding on to what we have judged by explicit standards to be of 'value' and yet seeing what we are holding on to as nothing more than a set of selectively retained tentatives (p. 26).

For myself and my readers, then, I am not so much concerned with finishing up with a set of 'findings' about what really happened in the situations where I did research, but rather with developing a way of understanding a situation which can be applied to other situations. My object was to end up with a collection of 'selectively retained tentatives', which can be useful to myself and to others as a heuristic device for helping to think about other situations, and without any presumption that this collection of tentative notions will be neat, reducible to a few easily communicated propositions, internally consistent, or any of the other little luxuries that come free with many more traditional packets of research. My evidence that my research has some useful categories in it comes when people pick up those categories and use them, whether they be members of the teams in which the research was done, academics citing my papers, or people who chat with me about my research and who, when I tell them some of the categories, immediately start relating examples from their own experience to what I am saying.

This may be illustrated by considering a reasonably typical category from the 95 that were generated in the research; 'A person may accept another person's problem construction in order to get agreement on one of his own.' The notion of people doing deals with one another over what problems they shall take seriously seems to be quite widely shared; this means that this category, in the context of the examples with which I support it and the other categories to which I relate it, is one that most people who have come across this research have been able to relate to. The 'tentative' that I have selectively retained is in turn tried out by some of those who read my research, to see if it makes sense for them when they use it, and thus whether they want to retain it (at least tentatively) as part of the framework with which they understand their situations. In some cases people have told me about new ideas that they have got hold of by reading the research, but as often as not the reports are of 'bringing into focus — I mean, I think I knew it was like that, but I hadn't seen it that clearly before.' The kind of learning that comes from such grounded research, then, is an offered heuristic which may either suggest some categories which a user of the research has not thought of before, or which may make explicit some categories which he had previously only used in an implicit, intuitive way.

Because of the extent to which this was a new field, my collaborators in the research did not initially have much of a way of talking about they were doing in problem construction. This could have been very restricting given my wish not to build my understanding in academic categories, but to stay grounded in the categories of the team members who were collaborating with me in the research. It was therefore critical for the success of the research that as the participants in it thought more about problem construction, and became aware in a way they had not been before of the issues that I was paying attention to, that they were developing their own thinking and their own use of categories about the subject. As they started doing research on themselves and their own situations, and as they started trying things out on the basis of their new, developing categories, so the resulting endogenous action research started to generate more new categories; without this development my research would have been confined to the inevitably very limited categories from which the team members started, and would have ended up with a much less developed collection of heuristic categories, or 'tentatives' that might be worth retaining, to offer to its readers. For example, it seems most unlikely to me that the category, 'A solution to one person's problem may prevent the solution of another's', with the supporting material and related ideas which turn it from a trite statement of a possibility into a revealing category, could have been arrived at without a group of team members having become interested in investigating processes of problem-handling in their teams. Similarly, such categories as 'You could run out of problems', or 'A team can only address so many issues at a time', or 'You may have to go ahead with solving a past problem' only arose after a considerable amount of thinking and investigation on the part of the team members, and I do not think that they could have been reached without the research becoming endogenous action research.

In this section I have talked about the kind of learning which seemed to result from the way this research turned into endogenous action research, and I have explained why the kind of learning that arose made me glad that the research had changed. It is worth remembering, though, that I did not conduct the kind of research I did in order to get the benefits of it going endogenous, but rather that the endogeny was an unexpected bonus of the way I worked. It is not that I wanted to do endogenous research to get the kind of findings that I was after, or that I was ideologically committed to action research, but that collaborative research, conducted over a period of time, and taking it that your collaborators are not beings of a different kind from yourself, is bound to become endogenous action research.

Human Inquiry
Edited by P. Reason and J. Rowan
© 1981 John Wiley & Sons Ltd.

CHAPTER THIRTY-THREE

Mid-career change: reflections upon the development of a piece of research and the part it has played in the development of the researcher

Audrey Collin
School of Management, Leicester Polytechnic, UK

As I enter the last phase of my three-year study of mid-career change and pull together its several strands I reflect upon the changes in my life during this period and become aware of the nature of the relationship between me and my research. It has been one of increasing involvement. From the start there was a parallel between the subject of research — the *process* of change — and the way that I studied it, for I was engaged in a *learning process* as I struggled to find an appropriate methodology. My experience of life since then has accompanied the subject of my study as an insistent counterpoint and eventually I have become inextricably involved with my research. The phenomenological, holistic approach I adopted has engaged me in the work as a whole person and has drawn upon a wide range of my previous experience. The interweaving of my experiences as an individual with those as a researcher makes my final report a personal document. As well as discovering 'facts' and achieving 'results' I have through my research developed intellectually, grown in self-awareness and ultimately become, as well as researcher, the subject and consumer of my own 'findings'.

To chart the process of change I collected biographies and, to seek the origins of the process of my research, I must relate some of my life-story. In the 1950s I took a degree in English followed by a diploma in Anthropology. Entering personnel management, I acquired a basic understanding of such subjects as social psychology through evening study. After marriage and the birth of my three sons I spent the next 11 years as a family-centred, though relatively outward-looking, woman. Time passed and life changed in such a way that I decided to look for full-time employment.

385

It was difficult to break through the employability barrier and the first job was less satisfying than I had hoped. While scanning the press for another, I noticed tha the Social Science Research Council was offering Fellowships to provide post-graduate, post-experience research training. I saw an opportunity to up-date myself, to extend myself, and to broaden my job horizons: I *knew* that this was the right course for me. I chose to study 'mid-career change'; this was not only topical in 1976 — and, indeed, likely to become a 'growth area' — but, as a housewife (as I construed myself then) entering the academic world, it was of direct relevance to me. From the start, then, my research and I have been closely related and our relationship has subsequently developed in a most satisfying way.

As I now read the application for the Fellowship I recall the few weeks of urgent searching in the library, the late nights bestowed upon some of the more significant literature on the topic, and the anxious search for a methodology which would seem both impressive and realistic. While aiming at a 'scientific' approach it appears that I had some doubts about how I could implement it and wrote of the possible need for an 'anthropological' rather than a quantitative type of study.

It was difficult to settle down during the first three months of the Fellowship. I took a brief course in standard research methodology and with the apparent boundaries of my research topic as the starting-point made some forays into the literature of psychology and sociology. Lacking a basic grounding in either discipline I missed or misconstrued several significant areas at first and was influenced by the interests and enthusiasms of the people I knew.

I was forcibly struck by the difference in impact upon me of some of the works I read. Some excited me while to others I responded with indifference. It was the enthusiasm and sense of involvement with their subject-matter in Hudson (1968) and Lévi-Strauss (1973) that caught my imagination and fired my enthusiasm. I was also re-reading Bellow's novels (1959, 1965) at the time and this juxtaposition made me realize that, through their involvement, these social scientists shared with the novelist the power to convey insight into people and situations. By comparison, the objective, quantitative kind of research which I was also reading, which stripped individuals down to measurable, comparable units, left me uncertain about how I could synthesize it and apply it to the 'blooming, buzzing confusion' of life. My son had recently given me *Zen and the Art of Motorcycle Maintenance* (Pirsig, 1976) and my enjoyment of this increased my conviction that there could be vast and important areas lying outside conventional scientific thinking.

During that first vacation I felt that I should be producing a research plan and, in drafting it, found myself exploring these issues. It was through the act of writing that I came upon — or recognized — my orientation to my research. I felt a great compulsion to write. I followed my twisting thoughts through

Bellow and Hudson, Lévi-Strauss and Pirsig and gradually, hesitantly over a period of days I realized that the objective/subjective dichotomy was a viewpoint upon life rather than the essence of it and that I should seek to apprehend a wholeness which comprehended both. This approach could yield insights rather than facts and questions rather than answers. This attracted me, for facts are a matter of interpretation and answers relate only to past situations, whereas I hoped to formulate searching, probing questions to illuminate the present and the future. I wanted my research to have value and significance in the 'real world' and thus I wanted it to share some of the characteristics of creative writing, in which observation and analysis are balanced by synthesis and the recognition of a new whole.

I further discovered that I did not want to be the detached observer but to engage in a creative enterprise with the person whose experience I was studying so that we should *both* gain from it. This enabled me to take to the research task some of my personal skills and those of my original discipline so that I would be engaged in the research as a whole person.

I felt great excitement as I completed that paper. As I read it now I wonder at my naïveté then, but also remember with warmth the urgency of the quest and thrill of the discovery. It was, without doubt, an act of creation for me. It was my very own discovery and I still look back upon it as a significant point in my research and in my intellectual life.

At this stage I felt that I had conceived an idiosyncratic view of research and one likely to fall outside accepted canons. While committed to my very own 'new paradigm', I kept it to myself and, like the new convert, worried about how to react when called upon to testify to my belief.

Research, however, has its own rhythms and routines and by now I was occupied in the standard tasks of literature searches and reviews. The haphazard growth of knowledge in my subject area allowed me to clear the ground of ill- or half-conceived ideas and, in so doing, to pin-point the specific area that I should investigate empirically. I was also able to use the obvious shortcomings in the literature to justify the approach that I wanted to adopt. For example, I found that the term 'career' was ill-defined, sometimes referring to objective experience, sometimes to subjective. A new understanding became possible by adopting the holistic view and recognizing that both external happenings and internal pressures and responses interact and that the occupational is interwoven with other aspects of life. I also discerned how distorting it was to focus upon what happened to a person at one point in time — the snap-shot view — and decided that I should trace the process of change within the context of the whole life.

I was, however, still nursing my private concept of my research and in time I met others who share these views. The first encounter with such a 'kindred spirit' at a conference was heartening. I was already two years into my research when I discovered that I have never been alone, only blinkered by my own inexperience and by the conventional ways of reporting research. I eventually came upon a theoretical framework as my reading widened and deepened, as my learning increased. Now able to label this 'phenomenology', I felt greater confidence in myself. I had found a means of translating *my* discovery into acceptable academic terms and was able to declare my sense of personal involvement in my research in, for example, the draft introduction to my Ph.D. thesis.

Looking back, it seems surprising that I had not searched more thoroughly for a conceptual framework that was acceptable and appropriate. I was, however, a complete beginner and took my cues from whatever I was reading. This was obviously a wasteful method, but it undoubtedly enabled me *to learn* by making my own discoveries and judgements and this, surely, is how adults learn.

I now also see how important it had been to make a critical review of the literature and to deal with the concepts rigorously. Holistic research is not the result of woolly thinking but of an informed and clear-headed approach to the complexities of 'reality'.

How can one carry out holistic research? Can one address the whole person? We know that thought and perception are selective; the constraints of a research timetable further increase that selectivity. It is possible, though, to be aware of this selectivity and to be responsive to the cues that the individual offers; to recognize that two-way communication will be both verbal and non-verbal and will take place at cognitive and affective levels. The holistic researcher needs self-awareness, sensitivity, and responsiveness.

For my empirical study I arranged to meet men who could be construed as being in the process of change, in a new and distinct phase of life: men leaving the forces, disabled men re-training for employment, and mature students on a post-graduate course, 35 in all. The literature review had identified the issues I wanted to explore and through the 'pilot interviews' I had mapped out those which could be comfortably covered in the one to two hours available. Our encounters followed no pattern except, generally, a chronological sequence. I followed whatever paths they opened and explored whatever seemed significant in the context — for example, their first job or the events leading to the present phase.

To release me from the role of observer to that of participant I tape-recorded the session. I have thus captured on tape 35 unique encounters in which the past was recalled, the present explored, and possible futures unfolded. These encounters were unique to their particular time, place, and participants; they are as much part of me, the researcher, as they are of the 'subject'. I can draw on my memory which overlays the transcribed tape with the colour of feeling and tangible experience and can use my intuitive understanding in my analysis.

Because the tape-recording captures only one dimension, without my recall the sights and emotional warmth are already lost to the research. The transcription of the tapes, which I find I need to work from, is a brutal and irrevocable step which alters the quality of the spoken word. It lops off much of the immediacy and individuality of the original. The pauses, the inflexions, those stumbling beginnings and half-completed words become uniform symbols on the page. The imposition of punctuation reinforces this uniformity and gives the hesitant thought an orderliness it did not have when first spoken. Stage directions such as 'spoken warmly' or 'bitter laughter' offer feeble representations of the reality. Without my 'ums' and 'ahs', which take up an enormous space if reproduced, the impetus for the continuation of the story is not clear.

As well as being a personal statement by the men I met, our encounter was also the arena in which I watched played out the themes I had read of in the literature. Career 'models' and 'mentors', precipitating events, turning-points, outside influences... they appeared, sometimes alone, sometimes in new configurations, sometimes latent, at others unmistakable. There is a wealth of material here.

To recapture the original experience as far as possible and to mine the riches there I am treating the transcriptions as one might a piece of literature, respecting the words that were chosen to convey ideas and feelings. I am adopting the technique of the literary critic, examining words, images, and themes. I am thinking of reproducing parts of the text in full, with textual comments and footnotes... a latter-day *Beowulf* (Klaeber, 1950). A sample of this follows.

Meeting with Warrant Officer...

Transcript	*Comment*
I worked for my father, yes, as an apprentice.	
When you took this up — was this what you wanted to do?	
No, no, it wasn't at the time... I wanted to be a mechanic... I think my father almost forced me to go into [his trade]....	For 10 of the 35 I met the father had been a major influence in the choice of first job. Some were facilitating (arranging an apprenticeship in their own firm), others coercive: one apprenticed his son, in love with flying, as a mining engineer. National Service rescued another boy — as in this case — from his father's tyranny.
Did you enjoy it once you'd started?	

Transcript

I didn't for a year, I didn't for about a year or 18 months. Then I did. When I was on the... side of things I liked it very much...

Why did you sign on [when called to National Service]?

Well, I liked the Army, you see.

Even after a few days?

Yes — well, I had a peculiar attitude — I thought, well, it was awful and I thought it can't get any worse than this and if I can tolerate this, I'll be all right.... So I signed up.

Are you saying that by the time you reached the age of 21 you already knew that you didn't want to continue with [your trade]?

Well, I didn't want to because... I thought, well, here I am, 21, and although I'd been around a bit and what skills I've got are not to be sneezed at — it didn't amount to much, really. I was... I couldn't stand on my own two feet, you know.

Um.

When I came into the Army... for the first time in my life, I suppose, I was at the side of young men, I saw the more manly side of life, whereas, say, physical achievement stood for *something*...

Yes, yes.

Comment

This is his characteristic reaction to unpleasant events: he 'presses on' and eventually enjoys them. He disliked his first clerical job:

'It was an awfully middle-aged sort of job... most unsoldierly... nevertheless I pressed on with it for 18 months... by this time I was really getting into clerking ... and from then on I enjoyed it.'

He is enthusiastic (voice, emphasis, epithets, visual expression) about the good times:

'It was wonderful... It was terrific... I did enjoy it actually tremendously. The CO there was a terrific, a wonderful man. All the officers were terrific.'

He has never applied for a posting — that is, sought his own goals:

'I'd sooner be in the frame of mind that I go where they post me, then I'm never disappointed, really. You never know — sometimes it turns out satisfactory... I think that if you're going to be a soldier ... you might as well get into the frame of mind that you go where you're put and if you don't like it then you make it so you do like it.'

He explains his four mentions of 'soldierly' as being in this 'frame of mind'.

He hopes to be offered an extension to his Army service and, if not, to find a job as a civilian in his unit. He referred to the possibility of returning to his father's business — after an absence of 25 years. Of leaving the Army he said:

'I think it would be unusual if I wasn't anxious... if I wasn't that little bit *cautious* about it. [Sigh. Long pause]. Well, we'll see. [Very long pause.]'

Transcript

Comment

And this also appealed to me. There were no two ways about it — when I came up to 21 I was like a — almost like a middle-aged man compared with some of those who'd never been away from home. But it could also be the other way about — for instance, I couldn't play football for 90 minutes. I used to train *awfully* hard.

He uses the description 'middle-aged' three times and appears to equate it with staidness and obsolescence.
He was soon to become enthusiastically engaged in sport and in running sports teams. He is still a keen cyclist at 46.

Of the career choice and development theories, Holland's (Pietrofesa and Splete, 1975) has little to offer to account for this man's experience. Super's self-concept theory (Pietrofesa and Splete, 1975) explains the Army's attractions for him: it restored his youth, by-passed during his apprenticeship, and offers him a full, active yet comfortably secure life. Social learning theory (Pietrofesa and Splete, 1975) explains his compliance and 'soldierliness': when he sticks with the situation it turns out well.

Meeting with Major...

Transcript

Comment

Although I say the Army has a system, you've got to take advantage of the system — it's up to the individual to take advantage of the system...

The major uses 'take advantage' 16 times, 'opportunity' six times and 'lucky' or 'unlucky' nine times in about one and a half hours: he is not as repetitive in speech as this excerpt suggests. He recognizes the part that external circumstances have played in his life. When his father died, his uncles decided that he should join the Army, although he remembers how his father, pointing out to him a private school, had talked of his aspirations for his son to become a schoolmaster. He notes how, in modifying its promotion system to meet its own needs, the Army also opened unexpected pathways for him. He seems to construe the environment as tightly constraining but with intermittent chinks in it for which he has to be ever alert. He is always preparing himself for the next, unknown step.

... you start off at the bottom and you know that you hope to reach *that* point —

I'm the Fire Officer, so I've done fire training. I'm the Security Officer, so I've done security training... and then I'm given the job of Safety Officer... and I thought, "Well, I'll use this to my

Transcript   *Comment*

everyone knows this and it's nothing special.

advantage and get some safety training … another string to my bow.'''

You know full well at the top of the tree is a Warrant Officer class 1 as far as the other ranks are concerned and so, therefore, you hope that by the time you leave the Army that you're going to achieve that rank....

The 'tree' image is used by several men. It suggests an organic and relatively unpredictable view of 'career'.

You quoted your friend you didn't bother … Why do you think you bothered?

Well, I think I basically bothered because I had my uncle's example, who was a boy soldier as well and he was in the REME at the time, so I suppose I was consciously trying to achieve *his* standard.... He finished as Warrant Officer class 1.

Career 'models' are mentioned by many men: father, uncle, brother, best friend. There are also references to the 'mentor', as described by Levinson (Levinson *et al.,* 1978) and Vaillant (1977).

Self-concept theory (Pietrofesa and Splete, 1975) suggests that he has had to be on the look-out for opportunities which would enable him to achieve the identity partially defined for him by his father. Social learning theory (Pietrofesa and Splete, 1975) explains how his vigilance has successfully guided the 14-year-old recruit through the ranks to that of major. Once again, Holland's theory (Pietrofesa and Splete, 1975) offers little to the understanding of this man.

Research proves a continuing struggle as I try to find new meaning, new wholes in the parts. At the same time I am by-passing this analysis and synthesis by applying what I learned intuitively in the research to a consultancy, Mid-Life Review. This offers people the opportunity to talk through their problems, evaluate their strengths and weaknesses, and explore their possible futures. As I discuss these mid-life issues with them, I am understanding more of the meaning of my research encounters and am thus better able to analyse them. Thus, apart from, I hope, helping clients I am also continuing my research. 'Results' become 'working hypotheses' which influence actions which eventually produce further 'results'.

From the beginning my research has been partly about myself; as time has passed I have increasingly become my own subject. I have identified in the literature the issues with which I cope in *my* life. By the time I started the field work I was already identifying myself to some extent with those I studied. When my Fellowship ended my life grew even more like theirs for I was unemployed and experienced for myself the loss and doubts of which I had heard. I thus became a consumer of my research 'findings', looking to them to help me cope with what was happening.

Far from separating me from the object of my study and splitting off a 'scientific' part of me, my research approach has contributed to my sense of integrity and brought me closer to those who opened their lives to me. It will be their legacy — and mine — to others suffering the growing pains of contemporary life.

Human Inquiry
Edited by P. Reason and J. Rowan
© 1981 John Wiley & Sons Ltd.

CHAPTER THIRTY-FOUR

Making sense as a personal process

Judi Marshall
*Centre for the Study of Organizational Change and
Development, University of Bath, UK*

[Whatever methods are used to make sense of data, in the end it turns out to be a very personal and individual process. Each researcher and group of co-researchers seem to work out their own way of going about it. Since this is such a personal process, we have included a personal statement from one researcher about how she goes about making sense of the data she collects, mainly from interview data. Judi Marshall prepared the notes on which this statement was based for a postgraduate seminar at the University of Bath, and has reflected on the process for the past year. What follows is an edited transcript of her talking to us — Eds.]

What I'm trying to do with the data
It's my assumption that there is some sort of order in the data that can emerge. My job as a researcher is to be an open and receptive medium through which this order comes out. I'm trying to understand what's *there,* and to represent what's there in all its complexity and richness. Trying to portray what I've been given, what's been put into my custody in a way that *other* people will recognize because it's more human, more full of some sort of rich portrayal than just a word or a table of figures.

On getting the data
It follows on from this that it's important for me to have *been there;* I can't imagine doing an adequate analysis of data if I haven't participated in collecting it. I always tape interviews because so much happens that I'm not

able to attend to at the time, and I find that listening to it again brings all sorts of new things up. When I've got the transcripts, they are flat, written copy, so I always listen to a few tapes before I get involved in actually trying to analyse the data, to re-catch some of the flavour. And I also make notes of what people were like, the impression I got from them, and I have that in conjunction with the interview transcript so that I can conjure up that person, and still see them — the way they smoked their cigarette, or the strange combination of shirt and tie they wore that day. Something that will give me a feeling, so that I know more about what they are saying than just the 'flat' words they use. This has an added advantage that if there is a gap in the transcript I can often remember back to what they were talking about. It is important to have the full meaning because words and sentences can be very empty and stark if they don't have the full atmosphere and context in which they were said.

The early stages
When I set out to do the interviews, it's all exciting and very clear and I've got things sorted out. When I start to do the field work there's another stage of a sort of confusion about the data. Impressions seem to dominate — the particularly vocal people, the particularly unhappy people, the particularly successful cases; those I got on well with, and stayed around with a bit. These all contribute to my ideas about how the data are turning out, I have lots of impressions. But if I put these general impressions into more concrete form, usually they're *wrong* because they're skewed in all these funny directions. So at this point there is an excitement that something *is* coming out of the data, but if anyone asks me I have no idea what, and will avoid being forced into saying! And at the same time there's a kind of fear that *nothing* is going to come out of the research and that I'm going to be left with a pile of tapes and nothing to say at the end. That's part of taking risks and using a more open method, you have to learn to live with these feelings, find them exciting rather than a problem.

Structuring the data
One of the practical problems is when to reduce all these transcripts to some sort of manageable form. Sometimes when I've done long interviews and I've had some idea of the headings I've wanted to use, I've picked things out and put them under these heads. But I'm a bit unsure about this, because this seems to *rob* the individual case of its wholeness. So I have to compensate for parcelling out little bits of a person and putting them under different categories and headings, and try to appreciate the wholeness of each person as well. I'm now thinking that I could make profiles of people and compare these profiles.

It always amuses me when I read books on how to do content analysis that you have to decide on some sort of level of analysis — looking at a word, a sentence, or a section. But the units are really fairly obvious — you get chunks of meaning which come out of the data itself. If you read a side of transcript, there is something which comes out to you as, say, someone's attitude toward their job, or the feeling of powerlessness in relation to the people in the Union. These are chunks of meaning, and you don't have to look at individual sentences, or debate what level of analysis it is. Also the books say, 'Arrive at the categories you will use.' Well, I don't do that either, but let the categories build up all the time as I put things together that *go* together. I think this is partly about how much anxiety and uncertainty you're willing to tolerate for how long; I think the more you can, the better the analysis work out.

When you're doing the analysis itself, this is a good time for any insights about the data. I can usually fill several sheets a day of thoughts and flashes of inspiration which often turn out to be quite important for the structuring. Some of these have to do with the theoretical shape the material is taking, just how all the concepts and categories relate together. Often it is really this framework that directs the rest of the writing. Others are understandings of people which preserve and emphasize their wholeness, and relate them to the theoretical frameworks. For example, with my study of women managers (publications in preparation), some of them stuck out as continuously taking massive risks with their careers, and others had done well but had been very passive.

I continually build up diagrams and arrows and spaces and schemas which for me are very much part of the conceptual development. I find that some survive the analysis, but others break down in time, perhaps they don't work out because there is some sort of tension in the data that I wasn't aware of. So diagrams that *don't* work help me understand and are almost as valuable as diagrams that do work.

On the quality of attention
This sort of work is really a whole-mind activity, I can't just pick it up in half an hour and then drop it. It needs a lot of attention, I have to overcome a lot of inertia. It's difficult to get into the material and do it the way I like while thinking about other things. I've found that because it demands a lot of mental space it is best done in large chunks. I have to spend a whole day and not expect very much out of the first couple of hours, perhaps.

But then I get involved and it starts to make sense, and insights start to come from some sort of unconscious level. When analysis is going well, I really have some kind of 'broad band' attention when lots of things seem to be connecting, when I can see over horizons in all sorts of directions. Lots of things come into my consciousness which perhaps I hadn't been aware of for years, and my mind is able to make connections at all sorts of levels. My attention becomes very active. It's a feeling of being focused and quick-witted, of being independent of trying. Whilst at the beginning of analysis I plod, and have to *try* and have to *sit down* and *concentrate,* and attempt things more slowly, when things begin to tick I don't have to try and sustain this kind of attention any more, it's quite independent of trying and it's independent of any sort of surface activity. It's almost a feeling that I can direct my surface activity but I can't direct the other forms of attention, that they *come in* and start getting *involved* with what I'm doing at the surface and start speeding it up.

I often feel that there are two parts of me acting. There's a relaxed part of me that looks at the material and understands it and appreciates it for what it is; and there's this other active and directing bit which is fitting and manipulating and matching the data. It's almost as if those two have both got to be working well. If I'm not understanding things but still trying to fit them into categories, that doesn't work; or if I am understanding but the other bit is switched off, then I'm not getting anywhere.

This active attention is difficult to distract — I'll work against all odds, in a crowded room, on a train, when the television's on. It is very difficult to switch off, so I find myself going out for a drink with friends and wanting to tell them about all these people that are so real to me, they are more real than where I am. And that's the time when I need a pad beside the bed for when I wake up and everything is clear; I write things down on bits of paper all over the place.

I don't know where this attention comes from; it's almost like it has got to be ready. When I've done enough of one stage of the research I'm in a position to go onto the next bit. Sometimes I find that I try to write and it just won't work even if I persist for hours and hours this other feeling doesn't come. I can't be ready so I go off and do other things. And sometimes I do have the feeling that I am now ready, I am ready to go on.

Then toward the end of analysis there's a phase when it is quite difficult. Things start to get tough, as if I'm holding all this stuff in my head and beginning to feel overloaded. I need then to close, I'm getting tired, I want to bring things together and capture it all, it feels as if I won't be able to hold onto it much longer. That's quite a tough time. But then there's the bit toward the very end when there's a kind of feeling that I *know* what it's all about and the structure of the data. It's a feeling of relief that I know that the data is worthwhile, that I've got something meaningful, and that *I* can write it, I can put it together. It's almost like having the *essence* of things that I can always fall back on now, so it does become more solid and more understandable. That feeling gives me confidence that I can put it together.

On bias and validity

I've never worked collaboratively, or argued the toss with other people about how to interpret data. While I think there would perhaps be some value in doing this, and in looking at the data from different perspectives, I feel this might be trying to intellectualize it and bring it down. Because my feeling of *rightness* is important, my feeling that this is what I can do, it's *my* translation, what I have found and interpreted from the data. My bias is something I appreciate, it's part of me as a researcher. And while it is important for me and for others to recognize my bias, it really is what I can give as a researcher, it is my contribution, and it's coherent and it's felt and it has all these other qualities which make me value it more than a detached attempt to be objective. I work from a particular position; I appreciate other positions, and I feel that each has its own integrity and its own validity.

There's another, a dark side to this, the feeling that I've made it all up, and Help! how can I justify all this? It's this thing about *knowing,* sometimes I lose it, sometimes I look at words on a page and think, do I really remember, do I know? This is a difficulty with this approach; it is something you learn to live with.

Stages during analysis
First there's all the uncertainty at the beginning about whether I'm going to get anything, and how big a task it is going to be. And then when I start working it's all stilted and partial and nothing seems to shape up. At this stage, if it's difficult, it's worth persisting, but if it's *very* difficult perhaps it's not right, and if you really can't get anywhere, you need to stop.

Then there's this bit when 'it' takes off: there's the other layers of me taking off, and there's the material taking off in terms of shape and structure and I'm getting involved and things begin to work out. It's very exciting and I seem to be going places. That's when I'm immersed and don't want to be interrupted.

Then toward the end again it's getting tough, and it's very difficult to hold it all in my head all at once. And then there's this feeling at the end, this feeling of *knowing,* and it's very important to catch this and write it down, not looking back at the data, almost putting to one side all the work I've done, but writing it from *me* as the ultimate translator. I can go back and fill in all the details and illustrations afterwards.

When I've got it all finished, my usual reaction is not to look at it. There's a relief at having finished, usually I think I could have done more if I'd had more time, but then I know I wouldn't because I'm tired. Often there's a feeling of excitement at finishing, and then I'm often quite down for a couple of days, exhausted, and can't understand why — I really ought to feel good now I've finished. And yet I really don't want to know much about it, and I can't get into anything else.

And then there's a time when I've got to look back on it for some reason, someone prompts me and I eventually pick it up from the desk and feel absolutely surprised and in wonderment at how *good* it is. I think, 'I did that and it's good!'. That's important.

Human Inquiry
Edited by P. Reason and J. Rowan
© 1981 John Wiley & Sons Ltd.

CHAPTER THIRTY-FIVE

One researcher's self-questioning

Stephen I. Rosen
National Institute for Mental Health, UK

[This example shows how one person used the questions mentioned in John Rowan's chapter during the course of a research project.

The project was conducted in order to form the basis for an MA dissertation, and was concerned with the ideologies of social workers. It has a fairly standard design, with open-ended interviews followed by a questionnaire. This kind of research is not 'new paradigm', but asking these kinds of questions is. So this example is an interesting bridge between the old and the new, letting us hear very clearly the voice of the contradictions inherent in the traditional forms of research. It puts us in touch with the real world of the researcher, struggling with his material.

At this point, the research cycle has only five points, because MAKING SENSE had not been separated out from COMMUNICATION. And the questions were not exactly as set out in Chapter 9. But the important point is that instead of just sticking to one set of questions, which of course so often happens in research, Steve Rosen took the heroic course of trying to answer a whole range of different sorts of questions, and to ask them at every point of the research cycle (see page 98 for the basic diagram, and pages 107-112 for the revised list of questions) — Eds.]

Being

(1) *Efficiency*
My social work experience prior to this project has given me some idea of what

the voluntary sector social work field looks like. Literature dealing strictly with voluntary sector workers is scarce in terms of research, i.e. studies conducted 'with' or 'on' voluntary sector workers and their perceptions and evaluations of their work world.

In so much as I am involved with the relevant people, i.e. voluntary sector social workers, I am involved with the relevant data.

I'm not sure what qualifies an individual to 'do research'. I think an inquiring problem-solving approach to reality might be the necessary and sufficient qualification. If that is true, then I think I am qualified to deal with the subject-matter of my study.

My work habits are erratic and this fact constitutes a major impediment to getting the job done effectively.

My estimate of my intelligence and intellectual toughness rises and falls so that I can feel both equal to and incapable of the task, depending on deeper feelings about whether I have any value. Usually I feel confident that I can measure up to the intellectual demands of the task.

(2) *Authenticity*

My motives are not easy to tap and untangle and this points to conflicted feelings about what I want to do and what I think I should do. Essentially I want to earn a Masters Degree through the vehicle of a self-directed and creative study project. I also want to prove to myself that I am capable of achieving such a goal. This desire links up with a more ancient need to prove to my parents (real and imaginary) that I am capable of achieving such a goal. The motive to make a contribution both to existing knowledge and practice re the social work field is secondary if not altogether delusional, and it is probably based on what I think I ought to tell myself and others.

I am constantly questioning my involvement with the field in terms of the 'research' I am doing, the way I am doing it, and any future involvement I might have as a social work practitioner. Basically, the question I ask here is: is this field only a nice place to visit or would I like to live here?

A punitive approach to my life means a punitive approach to work and consequently, I find it difficult to reward myself for a 'good day's work'. I am overly critical of my work.

(3) *Alienation*

It is not easy to generalize about my mode of relating to others: some of my relationships are open while other relationships are closed. My general feeling about the relationships which I 'set up' is that they are defensive and distant.

I feel OK listening to others and think that I've developed a knack for it. At the same time I can see that a lot of the energy I put into listening stems from a fear of speaking. Experience tells me that the more I risk my speech, the better I hear.

(4) *Political*

The social implications of my daily practice (restricting practice in this context to my research activity) are becoming clearer as I go along. The primary implication is that so long as I attempt to do research 'on' others I will create distance and unease between myself and others. This fact reveals a central contradiction between my research style/method and my deeper needs for intimacy with others.

The financial source of my project *per se* is a USA Federal Loan Programme. While I have the freedom within the Antioch course to use the money to pursue my study objectives, I feel that 'borrowed money' exerts a pressure of time on my process.

Other social pressures or 'shoulds' are operating: on a practical level, the workers in my sample are employees within organizations and subject to a variety of constraints, especially to do with time and place. I am compelled by these same constraints to bring my research activity into accord with individual needs. This means a lot of waiting and time-wasting and sometimes means requesting permission from employers, (a) to talk with their staff and /or (b) to release individual workers in order to conduct an interview.

(5) *Patriarchy*

I consider myself an unwitting victim of the deluge of liberal rhetoric which has swept many people away in the last decade plus. It's now heresy to express or imply sentiments which cast any 'other', especially so-called 'oppressed' others, in an unfavourable light. So while my mouth espouses anti-sexist/ racist/ageist rhetoric, my heart secretly knows that I'm full of bias.

A lot (if not all) of my life is centred around these three areas: the struggle for recognition; competition and acclaim; domination and submission. Each area is fraught with ambivalence. For example, while I desperately want to be recognized, I am simultaneously afraid to win recognition. While I enjoy winning, and any acclaim which winning may yield, my fear of loss/failure dampens my competitive drive. The way this dynamic links up with domination and submission is more difficult to articulate. Simply put — I feel a need to control my environment (self and others), to get my way as much as possible. I find it difficult to 'submit' to the control of others out of a fear that my submission is equivalent to my loss. Yet, at the same time, I am aware that the form of control I usually exert is passive.

I realize I am enmeshed in patriarchial patterns both in terms of being acted upon and acting towards others in traditionally masculinist ways. Here the question is: how much of my internalized masculine imagery and external privilege am I prepared to relinquish.

(6) *Dialectical*

Identifying contradictions is much easier for me to handle than committing myself honestly to resolving them in practice.

I search around for the perfect parent into whose lap the responsibility for my life can rest. That each individual is responsible for the conduct/content of her life is still an abstraction which I'm struggling to understand and assimilate into the process of my life.

I am gradually coming to an appreciation of history (collective and individual) from a standpoint of conflict which is generated, resolved, and regenerated *ad infinitum.* This understanding of history is theoretical and 'conflicts' with a primarily undialectical and magical view of history lived out in my imagination.

I have taken the 'paradox of rhythm and the rhythm of paradox' to mean the law of contradiction — the dialectic. I can approach an understanding of dialectics mainly when I 'get inside' my own dreams.

Thinking

(1) *Efficiency*

I feel I can acquire and synthesize the information necessary to illuminate a problem.

I have defined and re-defined my original research idea into specific researchable questions.

I think I rely less on creative imagination than the authority of knowledgeable others for interesting and usable hypotheses.

I am learning to discriminate between the more or less central or crucial and *feasible* hypotheses to test.

I can use the library and research archives to gather data. My efficiency here is weak as I feel rather like a blind man in a forest.

I could use more stamina to pursue data from abstracts and reprints. Generally, most of my exploration of secondary data sources has proved to be unexciting and tangential to my research concern.

(2) *Authenticity*

The notion of value-freedom is a philosophical problem haunting my project. I have lost sympathy with 'value-freedom' as a goal worth striving for in research dealing with human beings. I am more in sympathy with the idea that value-freedom is one of the resilient illusions within social science which human research activity can well afford to shed.

I feel dominated by my project in a positive way so that I can say that my research and my life are inseparable.

What I have to gain from the solution of my research problem is the knowledge that I have pursued and effectively realized a self-directed project. Secondly, I will gain a qualification which symbolizes my achievement.

(3) *Alienation*

Sometimes I *consult* with others on a strict role basis. Sometimes I meet others in a way which permits more self and less role to emerge. Whether I do the former or latter is dependent on how safe I feel with the other I am meeting.

I do not feel overly possessive about the research questions I select and therefore I am usually open to criticism and alternative questions.

As my aim in this study is *not* to repeat or replicate my own or someone else's activity, I think I look to authorities in order to learn something afresh.

(4) *Political*

I try to check and identify the political sympathies and/or commitment of sources of information: both individuals and literature contributing to my study.

I am becoming more aware of the social implications of certain lines of inquiry. For example, it is apparent to me that strict adherence to a positivist model of research with human beings (i.e. me-them situations) can not only create distance between myself and others but also makes it more difficult to generate the knowledge I am seeking.

I think that isolation has characterized my research activity and this isolation has partly been an unforeseen consequence of my research assumptions, i.e. taking for granted that the 'researched', in spite of their lack of investment in the project, would grant the 'researcher' a congenial welcome and their cooperation.

(5) *Patriarchy*

I live, breathe, and, in short, am ruled by patriarchal assumptions and practices. I take that as a historically given but not unalterable fact.

I try to identify the ways in which I oppress and/or am oppressed by others on the grounds of sex role stereotyping. Focusing on this area requires extra vigilance, as does the struggle to avoid stereotyping in practice.

(6) *Dialectical*

The more I understand about the goals and limits of a positivist line of inquiry the more critical is my stance in relation to research findings which are based on positivist thinking.

I try not to adopt double standards in my life: the ground between this idea and action is besmirched with shadow.

It is difficult to know how 'near to reality' the reality-seeking researcher can get: a research which is after the 'reality beneath the appearance' may be as ill-fated as a research dealing with so called 'surface features' of human experience.

I think a major contradiction underlying my research problem is: while one goal of my project is to elicit personal disclosure from others about the meanings they attach to their work world, the means I am employing to elicit information may actually prevent honest self-disclosure. Here I can refer to the limitations of research thinking and practice based on 'unilateral control'.

Project

(1) *Efficiency*
I have attempted to use an accounting procedure in order to cover alternative possibilities.

As my study can be considered an experiential and descriptive study as against an 'explanatory' study, I am not utilizing an experimental design.

My questioning procedure has not been consistent throughout: sometimes I have introduced open or closed questions at inappropriate places.

My two basic methods — an interview schedule using a tape-recorder and a questionnaire — are both reactive methods.

I have not used deceptions in my research.

(2) *Authenticity*
At times I feel I am fully invested in my project — taking personal risks along the way. I also feel at times that I am copping out.

Initial satisfaction with my research design has waned. The reason for this was cited earlier (political questions: Thinking). I am finding more and more that a non-reciprocal research plan will result in a non-reciprocal encounter with others.

I am trying to fully engage my resources in the research plan. My error at this point is in over-looking my primary resource (social workers) as an input into the research design.

(3) *Alienation*
Given the fact that I am the only 'researcher' conducting research and the subjects I am meeting are 'respondents' within a sample, I can say that I am relating in terms of roles and rules.

My research plan is flexible. I would be going too far if I said that my plan is abandonable.

(4) *Political*

The research plan shows a parallel with hierarchical structures: a vertical relationship exists between myself and the subjects with power and responsibility for the form and content of the study unequally resting with me.

I have considered the social context particularly with regard to its potential to hinder or help the realization of my research task. The particular social context I have in mind here is the agency/organization whose employees comprise my data source. Things I've had to take into account are various organizational constraints and/or freedoms which would influence the interaction between myself and individual workers. One question here is: does the organization encourage or discourage its workers to participate in a study which examines workers' perceptions of their work world (i.e. agency)?

(5) *Patriarchy*

By excluding social workers from the conceptualization and design of the study but including social workers as 'sources of information', I am reinforcing patterns of domination.

(6) *Dialectical*

To the degree that my research design represents a movement towards real people and away from personal introspection and thought, I think it 'negates what was there before'. My project aims in the direction of new knowledge and action.

I do not think I consciously designed the research to manage unforeseen occurences. Yet, because my design is loose, If find it easier to pay attention to 'findings' which I accidentally meet.

I have built my own response into the research plan.

Encounter

(1) *Efficiency*

I have used no experimental controls.

The questioning procedure is being carried out in a uniform manner.

My sampling procedure is questionable on several counts. Most importantly, I am not sure whether my contacted sample represents the group I claim it represents, namely, voluntary sector *social workers.*

Taking 'objectivity' to mean viewing the world with undistorted and undistorting perception, then, at best, I try to keep check on the distortions which are accumulating.

(2) *Authenticity*

I am open to some of my feelings and body reactions; I am well-defended against other feelings and body reactions.

I am prepared to express feelings in a genuine way.

I am prepared to improvise in my research.

(3) *Alienation*

Given that my encounters with workers are brief, that we are meeting as strangers for the purpose of 'doing research', then the relationships are transient and generally characterized by a low level of trust. There are a few exceptions and this is when a 'subject' is someone with whom I have had prior contact independently of my research activity.

I try to be open with/to all the subjects I meet.

The subject (respondent) is not determining the situation as much as I am since the broad areas of inquiry have been predetermined according to the demands of my accounting scheme. Within the boundaries of the research question, the subject can determine what takes place between us as much as I can... if not more.

I try to meet the subject as person to person rather than 'researcher' to 'respondent'. I encourage the subject to respond to me from her person rather than as a 'worker' affiliated to a particular organization.

(4) *Political*

The social context is of central importance here and I try to anticipate the answers to several questions before interviews: Are we meeting at a time and place conducive to open and honest interaction between us, i.e. are we meeting in private or congested conditions? Are we pressurized by time? Will distractions of work get in the way of our meeting?

Although the parameters of the situation are predetermined (in theory and in the sense that specific areas of the worker's experience constitute my research problem and researchable questions), the subject is free to choose at any point to challenge, redirect or change the focus of our meeting. I try to remain open to these possibilities.

The subject's real 'back-home situation' is considered to the extent that it is given to me. What I mean by this is that an individual's history and extra-work life is not excluded from my inquiry.

(5) *Patriarchy*

Even though I have come to the encounter with 'my' project and my special concerns, I hope to engage in a dialogue with the subjects I meet. Sometimes I fear that the interview is 'out of control' and this usually means that control has shifted from me to the subject. My questions here are: Is there an unequal distribution of control between us now? Am I being controlled? Am I controlling? And most importantly — can I get what I need from this meeting without trespassing on the private space of the subject?

(6) *Dialectical*

Generally, I avoid conflict. I am beginning to value conflict and negativity as a means of uncovering 'cover-ups' and deceptions. An example of a conflict-generating strategy here is the question: what do you want to avoid by being/ becoming a social worker?

I try to be fully engaged and committed to the research process. At the same time I am aware that I am prone to influences identical to those which distract the subject: the uncongeniality of the time and place we inhabit; my back-home situation.

I am prone to over-valuing quantity as an end in itself. It is therefore difficult for me to appreciate the way in which quantity transforms into quality and vice versa. [Written in April 1978]

Communication

(1) *Efficiency*

The results of my study are not written up in accordance with the protocol of scientific research literature.

I doubt whether the appropriate professional journal would publish the results of my research given the absence of any standardized procedure.

The results have not been 'analysed' in an 'objective' way. The results have been 'summarized' in a 'subjective' way. Consequently, any check by an outside observer would invariably yield different results.

I have used statistics to describe, in summary fashion, the essential characteristics of the sample I am studying. I have not used statistical methods to maximize the information which can be extracted from the data.

(2) *Authenticity*

I feel that I can incorporate the results of my research into my process of living. In this connection I am thinking about the way that my interventions into social situations, whether as researcher or social worker, can lead to constructive change primarily through my openness to the other as a fellow collaborator.

Sometimes I am genuinely open to my own experience gained in the encounter. At other times I am genuinely closed to my own experience. The clincher here is whether I'm in the encounter to please myself, to please the other or to please us both.

I want to get the results of the study clear for my own sake and my own illumination at those times when I clearly recognize that this project exists primarily for my own sake and my own illumination. When I lose sight of who *owns* the project, I also forget who I am addressing.

(3) *Alienation*

At this point of communication, the subject has become an object. The course I have adopted has been to withdraw from the field to the academic environment and to write and submit my report to an academic committee — not to the people *I have studied.* Consequently, the results of the study, embodied in the thesis itself, will have little or no effect on the subjects' own processes of living.

The subjects have become strictly 'respondents' or 'informants' and have played no part in the examination and processing of the results. My data-processing has been a unilateral effort — essentially a colleagueless interior monologue.

(4) *Political*

In passing my information on I have considered the 'social effect' primarily as a passing fancy — my wish to communicate to and affect the lives of those who provided me with information about their daily labour.

I feel certain that those people who will primarily receive the information are not the people who could make best use of it. I refer here to reporting to academics in the main and only secondarily, if at all, to social work practitioners.

(5) *Patriarchy*

The information is being communicated in a way which will not put down those who receive it.

I have attempted to speak in a language which reflects my own mode of thought and feeling.

(6) *Dialectical*

The more I understand that others are not extensions of my self and servants to my own needs, the better I appreciate that communication is dialogical.

I often try to set up a real relationship with people before or while attempting to communicate with them. Often, the real relationships are set up retrospectively in the sphere of my regret-ridden imagination.

I assume that communication can emerge from sounds as well as silence, sweeping movements as well as subtle gestures, presence as well as absence.

I try to appreciate the importance of readiness in communication. In this regard I keep a close watch on my own impatience.

I am learning to develop a clearer perception of resistance in communication and understand its time and place within myself and the other. At moments when patience, empathy, vigilance, and luck converge, I can use resistance to establish contact with another person.

Here and there I am able to take risks in an encounter to say that I am disappointed, upset and frustrated.

I spend an inordinate amount of time over-ordering my speech — either ordering myself to talk or ordering around my thoughts and feelings so that they will appear 'orderly' to the other. I appreciate that an awareness of the order one is following in talking to others is necessary. What I want to avoid is speaking or being spoken to, doing or being done to in a way which creates disorder and damage in my relationships.   (Written in February 1979)

[The dissertation was duly submitted, with a rather unusual design which focused on the research process as much as the research findings. It was approved in the summer of 1979 — Eds.]

DIRECTIONS

Human Inquiry
Edited by P. Reason and J. Rowan
© 1981 John Wiley & Sons Ltd.

CHAPTER THIRTY-SIX

Implementing new paradigm research: a model for training and practice

Shulamit Reinharz
Department of Psychology, University of Michigan, USA

The purpose of this chapter is to present a model of the process by which individuals develop a commitment and ability to carry out new paradigm research. The model is both descriptive and prescriptive, for it can function as a guide for training. My own interest in this topic began several years ago as I attempted to understand my own socialization experience. Why and how had I come to hold certain views about social science research? What kind of work did I want to carry out and why? While preparing a book answering these questions (Reinharz, 1979a), I drew on published accounts by other social scientists analysing their overall professional socialization or their experience during particular research projects (Bronfenbrenner and Devereux, 1952; Bowen, 1964; Hammond, 1964; Powdermaker, 1966; Horowitz, 1969; Golde, 1970; Phillips, 1971; Vidich *et al.*, 1971; Mann, 1973, and others).

Continuing from these analyses, the model developed here is further refined by personal communications sent to me by social scientists responding to my work. More disclosure of the personal and contextual socialization of social scientists working within the dominant or alternative research paradigm is needed, so that we can more fully understand ourselves, better train newcomers, and be more responsible to society. Similarly, such an understanding will help us create a more reflexive social science (Gouldner, 1970). To serve these multiple functions, the model of socialization requires cognitive, environmental, and personality components. By way of introduction, the problem — how an individual comes to adopt a new paradigm research approach — is placed in a broader perspective.

Most people who identify themselves as social scientists (primarily sociologists and psychologists, but also anthropologists, political scientists, and economists) carry out research projects within a frame of reference based on positivist philosophy and a mathematical means of demonstrating their argument. This frame of reference is well-suited to the conditions of modern-technological-mass society. In contemporary society nearly every aspect of living is managed by centrally controlled organizations. The management system of these large bureaucracies is nearly identical with the data-collection and analysis procedures of modern social science. In fact, the line between contemporary social research and the routine functioning of such institutions is frequently hard to draw.

The emergence of positivist social research in modern society has been compared by Form (1971) with the transformation of crafts into big business. Advocates of an alternative paradigm for social research are thus suggesting getting out of step with contemporary society. Perhaps they are helping to push our current social arrangements into the post-industrial age whose dimensions are not yet known. At this moment it is unclear if the new paradigm practitioners and theorists are harbingers of a future society or if they will be remembered as a mere protest against the *status quo.*

Despite the dominance of the positivist model, there has always been a fringe of discontent and experimentation with alternative definitions of social research. Although some resources have been available to the individuals and schools which have specialized in alternative methodology, generally the resources necessary for research have been made available to those whose research thinking has fit the characteristics of modern society. Research funds, academic power, and access to publication vehicles have been scarcer for the critics. The conflict between research paradigms is therefore not merely theoretical, but also political. Paradigms do not shift overnight; and when they do, they shift people as well as ideas. In order to win the freedom and resources to conduct research in an alternative framework, the hold of the dominant paradigm on the power structure has to be loosened, and new paradigm researchers have to gain influence. In this regard a well-known educator/researcher wrote:

> Many students are now coming to me to say, 'What can you do to help us legitimate what we want to do in our dissertations, which our committee members are dismissing as sloppy research?' It appears that I have a political problem as well as a conceptual one on my hands (personal communication, E.G., 1979).

New paradigm research is a broad label used to encompass a set of assumptions which contrasts with those of the dominant paradigm. This alternative set of principles underlies a wide variety of methods which fall in the general rubric of qualitative research methodology: diffusion innovation, componential analysis, structured interview, open interview, case study, participant observation, life history, oral history, social psychiatry (see Schwartz and Jacobs, 1979). In addition to these methods, other frameworks have developed which contain explicit critiques of the dominant paradigm: ethnography, phenomenology, ethnomethodology, role-playing, experiential analysis, collaborative inquiry and more. Some methodologists view these approaches to the creation of knowledge as falling on a continuum from experimental to phenomenological. Others view the methods as discontinuous, since they operate according to mutually exclusive basic assumptions. Willems has argued that all research methods fall somewhere in a

> two-dimensional descriptive space. The first dimension... describes the degree of the investigator's influence upon, or manipulation of, the antecedent conditions of the behavior studied... the second dimension... describes the degree to which units are imposed by the investigator upon the behavior studied (1969, p. 46).

Thus, all of the alternative methods mentioned above have two characteristics in common: they minimize manipulation of the research subjects, and they try to limit *a priori* analyses or definitions of variables. In contrast with manipulation, the new paradigm researcher attempts to develop a *genuine* relation with the nominal subjects, leaving open the possibility that both will change in the process. The researcher becomes the subject's partner or student (within the model of Buber's (1937) 'I-Thou' rather than 'I-It') and describes the events using the language of the subjects rather than the language brought from outside the context of study. In this way, new paradigm research points the way towards a non-alienated, post-mass society.

A Model of Four Phases

The socialization of a new paradigm researcher can be represented by the convergence of personal attributes, traditional training, and exposure to alternative ideas within a context of sufficient support (see Figure 36.1). The socialization model can also be visualized as a set of phases, each with component parts, as suggested in Figure 36.2. In order to describe how the process unfolds, the following discussion treats the elements chronologically, although in actuality there is much movement back and forth between stages of development. The phases in the emergence of contemporary new paradigm research are the following:

(1) *immersion in the dominant paradigm* (or at least, familiarity with it) and building of commitment to research activities in general;

Figure 36.1 The socialization of new paradigm researchers: the convergence of personality, cognitive, and environmental factors

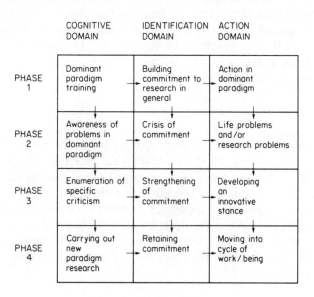

	COGNITIVE DOMAIN	IDENTIFICATION DOMAIN	ACTION DOMAIN
PHASE 1	Dominant paradigm training	Building commitment to research in general	Action in dominant paradigm
PHASE 2	Awareness of problems in dominant paradigm	Crisis of commitment	Life problems and/or research problems
PHASE 3	Enumeration of specific criticism	Strengthening of commitment	Developing an innovative stance
PHASE 4	Carrying out new paradigm research	Retaining commitment	Moving into cycle of work/being

Figure 36.2 The socialization of new paradigm researchers by phases

(2) exposure to or *awareness of problems* in the dominant paradigm, leading to conflict about methods and crisis of commitment;

(3) *resolution of conflict* in the form of enumerating specific criticisms, demystification, strengthening of commitment through receipt of support, developing an innovative stance, learning of new paradigm alternatives;

(4) *carrying out new paradigm research* within a developing model of research practice and living; retaining one's commitment through a cycle of feedback, revisions, and continuous communication with others who share one's outlook.

In brief, the process is one of learning, discovering inadequacies, rejecting what has been learned, learning an alternative, discovering inadequacies, rejecting part of it, creating an alternative form, discovering its inadequacies, rejecting part of it, etc. The process can be called dialectic, in that the forward movement is based on rejecting current conditions rather than simply building on them. Let us now look at each of these steps.

Phase 1: Immersion in the Dominant Paradigm

The ability to do research based on a new paradigm requires an understanding of that which went under the name of the old. Most research training ends here. Students are taught the dominant paradigm and its methods of experimentation, survey research, and statistical analysis, and might become aware of other research methods but not encouraged to practise them. The foundation of new paradigm thinking is a grounding in the dominant paradigm methodology plus the developing of a coherent critical analysis. Only if the new paradigm thinker is grounded will she or he be considered a critic from within, rather than a misinformed outsider.

Phase 2: Exposure to a Critical Analysis of the Dominant Paradigm

It is essential that during socialization a critical analysis develop of the dominant paradigm that is so far-reaching as to compel its rejection. How does this occur? The critical perspective can be fostered privately by force of disillusioning personal *experience* conducting research in the old paradigm. Through such dissatisfying practice, the researcher senses that something is wrong, that there is a discrepancy between promise and practice (see Phillips, 1971, Reinharz, 1979a, chap. 2). For this awareness to develop, however, there must be a willingness to learn from one's experience rather than an unwitting need to mould experience to fit previously held notions. In contrast to being experienced, the contradictions within the dominant paradigm can also be *studied* through explicit instruction (see the readings mentioned by the editors in the Foreword to this book). Sometimes the general need for a paradigm shift is recognized through personal experience, whereas the specific defects of the dominant paradigm are learned by examining literature.

In some cases a critical perspective can be acquired *within* a single training programme, whereas in other cases, students formulate their criticism because of the contradictions *among* programmes in which they participate. The development of a keen eye for paradigm assumptions is nourished by studying more than one discipline, or by practising a discipline in a multidisciplinary environment. For example, Crowle (1976) specialised both in psychological experimentation and in ethnography. The contrast between these led him to recognize the ambiguity of experiments and the service ethnography could render to reduce that ambiguity, thus transforming the nature of experiments.

The cognitive conflict leading to a critical perspective can also stem from *role conflict* between the structures of research and other activities.

> I came to research later in life, having spent time in industry, and I started from the place that I needed to integrate my experience with what I was doing in research terms. But I still had to invent my own method, since there wasn't much I could take off the peg, so to speak (sociologist, P.R., personal communication, 1979).

The critical attitude also develops from traumatic but enlightening *personal or political experiences* which shatter the individual's *status quo* (e.g. divorce, arrest, reaching a certain age, etc.)

> I turned against my professors for their objectivist views in part because of the intense subjectivist experiences I was going through as as result of the 60's milieu (sociologist, M.S., personal communication, 1979).

The new consciousness that derives from these personal changes is transferred from one domain of living to another, causing the individual to question the accepted research paradigm through a kind of 'spread process'.

In some cases the research perspective of an individual is affected by a combination of factors. Another sociologist ventured out of traditional research because he

> was simply bored with doing scholastic analyses which are descriptive and explanatory but have no discernible practical consequences. [In addition, he was] more interested in the civil rights and anti-war movements than in academic work [and] carried this interest into sociology by becoming active in the radical sociology movement

which [he] hoped would develop a sociological practice useful in
bringing about social change.... The decline of the radical movement
in American society... made [him] ready for something new. [His]
career transition was also linked to a more personal change... the
break-up of a long marriage involved considerable inner conflict
and turmoil which led [him] to undertake [many humanistically
oriented activities] (Goertzel, 1979, pp. 3-4).

These conflicts lead to disenchantment with previous practice in the
dominant paradigm and foster the insight that the challenge is not simply to
refine a method but to revise the entire paradigm. The existential crisis within
an individual researcher (or student) can thus parallel the paradigm tension in
the social sciences.

Phase 3:   Becoming Explicit about the Criticism of the Dominant Paradigm

The context of criticism has been described above without a specification of its
content. The enumeration of specific criticism is necessary in order to suggest
the dimensions of the alternative paradigm. For instance, Torbert's
contribution to this volume (Chapter 11) calls for a new paradigm based on
repudiating three assumptions of the dominant paradigm: (a) that the
researcher not influence subjects, (b) that variables be controlled, and (c) that
validity be statistically assessed. By turning these elements on their head, he
outlines an alternative called 'collaborative inquiry'. Similarly, my notion of
'experiential analysis' is grounded in a set of assumptions that are the polar
opposites of what I understand to be the assumptions of the dominant
paradigm (Reinharz, 1979a, chap. 1).
   Socialization towards the new paradigm involves an encounter with and an
internalization of a critical perspective *vis à vis* the dominant paradigm. If this
criticism cannot be articulated clearly, the alternative similarly will be unclear
and the individual's commitment to it will not have a chance to take root.
Since new paradigm research is invariably questioned by others and not itself
highly developed, clarity regarding its dimensions is crucial. By grounding
oneself in specific criticism of the dominant paradigm, the process of
demystification with the 'scientism' of the dominant paradigm can continue.
Each criticism is a crack in the edifice of belief. As the cracks accumulate there
is a psychologically perceived crumbling of the entire structure of current
research practices, and a sense that our knowledge based on current methods is
untrustworthy. Because of limitations of space, and the fuller treatment in
other parts of this book, the critical perspective is discussed only briefly here.
   In the *dominant paradigm,* the image of people is intrinsically alienated
because people are objects of research and instances of laws or patterns. They

are studied in contrived situations, or if in natural settings, then their particularity is eliminated. The trivialization of people, and their subsequent manipulation for the purpose of research designs, leads to findings which are themselves trivial and suitable for objects rather than people (Freire, 1970). For research purposes, society is typically conceived of as an aggregate of individuals, rather than as an organic, changing whole at a particular historical time. 'Being' is operationalized into the smallest number of discrete variables having unidirectional effect on one another. Positivism allows bits of movement (acts, responses) to 'stand for' theoretical constructs. Similarly, positivism assumes that two instances of the 'same' act have the 'same' meaning for the individuals involved. Behaviour is transformed to allow categorization, and ideas are reified as things which can be weighed and measured. Questions which cannot be measured are not seen as challenging the notion of measurement, but rather as not worth studying. The impact on society of such a definition of knowledge is the undermining of independent thinking and decision-making.

The instruments used in positivist methods include items shown to be vague, ambiguous, condescending, culture- and class-biased and annoying. The researcher is detached, perhaps absent, from the research setting. For example,

> 'My record is still perfect [sic]. I have never actually seen a Great
> Books discussion, despite several years of almost full-time work on
> this project' (Davis, 1964, p. 224).

Frequently, researchers deceive their subjects.

> The use of deception has become more and more extensive and it is
> now a commonplace and almost standard feature of social psycho-
> logical experiments. Deception has been turned into a game, often
> played with great skill and virtuosity (Kelman, 1968, pp. 208-9).

The by-products of deception are not only an unfair treatment of subjects, supposedly taken care of by 'debriefing', but also an undermining of the standing of social research in public opinion. Related to deception is the issue of unethical research designs causing pain, anxiety, or altered self-image. Governmental safeguards against unethical practices are still merely papering-over devices.

Most research designs are actually contaminated by response effects such as the Hawthorne effect, self-fulfilling prophecies, subject approval-seeking, and more, and by messages 'given off' by researchers, such as interaction effects of gender, race, age, personality, and other attributes. In other words, although researchers would like to think of themselves as managing the research enterprise, they are really part of and affected by macro- and micro-contexts. Sampling creates its own problems: subjects are drawn typically from a population of college sophomores, advertisement respondents, or people-who-happen-to-be-home (e.g. housewives) and are skewed in terms of certain cultures and subcultures. Researcher-subject relations are hierarchical, parallel to the hierarchical relations among research personnel, with lowly research assistants protesting their role constraints in devious ways, while seemingly collecting clean data (Roth, 1966). Even reputable researchers are hard put to substantiate their findings when asked to supply raw data (Bryant and Wortman, 1978).

Social research is likely to be politically conservative because of the social-class origins of the people who conceive and conduct it, and because funding sources protect their vested interests (see Ehrlich, 1971; Palmore, 1962). Implicit conservatism can be seen in the preponderance of studies about the underdog's plight which do not include a critical analysis of those who benefit from the underdog's position. Researchers, like social workers, live off the social problems they are supposed to ameliorate if there are no mechanisms making them accountable to those with the 'problem', and if their working conditions force them to perpetuate the problem rather than develop commitment to its resolution.

Social research is interlocked with big business, big government, and big education. Research projects are organized and designed to yield comfortable salaries and to be dependent on expensive technological equipment. Research for government (such as programme evaluation) is primarily intended to control behaviour rather than to create freedom or to improve the quality of people's lives. Research results are infrequently intended for use. Rather, they are time-bound and instantly obsolete, or they are used to justify decisions already made. Even contract research does not usually have an impact on the contracting source in the sense of compelling policy. Since the subjects of research do not usually invite research projects, they are typically not consumers of the findings.

The language of positivist research has become an obfuscated jargon which mystifies and puts-off the public, hides common sense under thick terminology, and forces social scientists to communicate primarily among themselves. Professional publication vehicles add further constraints, leading to a facade of conformity (J. Brown and Gilmartin, 1969; McCartney, 1970). Rowan (1974) has argued that the major influences on the design of a contemporary research project are its convenience, expense, proximity, dis-ruptiveness with the researcher's life-style, brevity (for quick publication), and publishability.

The overarching insight gained from these criticisms is that the scientific appearance and apparatus of contemporary social science has led to its ability to mystify and dominate our thinking of what social research can be (Polanyi,

1958). The development of an alternative paradigm involves a continuous effort to work through the blinders of mystification. In my own experience, and in the cases published by others, it appears that demystification is painful, in a way similar to cognitive dissonance. It consists of a conflict between allowing discrepant insights to lead to the development of new assumptions, or to suppress the new insights by a strengthened commitment to tradition. If the critical perspective is thoroughly internalized, then an alternative paradigm can begin to take shape.

This overview of a critique of the dominant paradigm presented a brief collection of disturbing issues. In the socialization model, the ability to enumerate specific criticisms is the cognitive element in phase 3 which also includes personality and environmental components. The various changes of this phase coalesce in a change of consciousness which is characterized by (a) the development of commitment, (b) the development of a sense of community with a supportive environment, (c) the development of dialectic thinking, and (d) tapping into and strengthening personal resources.

A nurturing personal and intellectual environment converts mere conflict into a growth-inducing process. A supportive environment allows the researcher to work through the conflicts and contradictions rather than be overwhelmed by them, because support facilitates identification with the profession or discipline. A supportive environment encourages students or researchers to communicate their criticism and to locate colleagues whose experiences resonate with theirs. The environment's function is to help the researcher maintain an adequate commitment so that the effort to innovate is a worthwhile response to the conflict. This sense of community or shared reality transcends the boundaries of the personal and professional realms.

Previously it was illustrated that individuals seek a new paradigm for research as a solution to conflicts encountered in practice (or living) and to criticisms raised in the methodological literature. It must be remembered, however, that conflict has a variety of potential outcomes. If there is sufficient detachment within a context of support, the attitude toward the problems of current research practice can be fascination rather than dismay. If there is at least a minimal identification, then the researcher can believe that his/her emerging resolution reflects a shared reality rather than being idiosyncratic. Commitment is sustained not simply by fear of career change or by virtue of obligations accrued, but because the innovator is able to metacommunicate about the problems to a community. The commitment which becomes manifest can be to a discipline, a research problem, or to the very search for an alternative paradigm. The challenge is to maintain adequate commitment to make innovation worthwhile, to sustain doubt without inviting cynicism.

In his classic essay on the various role responses to the conflict between socially desirable ends and the means available to people to achieve those ends, Merton listed ritualism, innovation, rebellion, alienation, and deviance. In other words, people respond to perceived conflict between what they want to achieve and how they are going to achieve it, by becoming dogmatic, creating, dropping out or acting out. Sedgwick suggested another response: waiting it out, claiming that some people, including himself 'grow out of being [a] psychologist' (1974, p. 36). Perhaps an example of a rebellious response is Nicolaus (1968), who tried to shake up what he perceived as the 'Establishment' of the social sciences.

New paradigm researchers choose to innovate; their response to conflict is to analyse and create an alternative. The danger is that to compensate for the risk they have taken, innovators become converts, embracing the new 'truth' while being defensive or unaware of its shortcomings, in other words, mystified anew. This can be seen when new methodological ideas are treated as so precious that they almost cannot be communicated. They then acquire the status of a secret cult or batch of private notions. If instead, the researcher has internalized a dialectic form of thinking, s/he will continuously seek and be aware of criticism of the new paradigm and its methods. For instance, does the notion of developing genuine relationships in new paradigm research lead to a skewing of studies in the direction of highly articulate, politically compatible individuals? Does the focus on individuals in natural settings lead to disregard for social and political structures and forces? Does the very development of a new paradigm confine one's vision to that which can be studied within it?

Students and others embarked on a career based on new paradigm research require an environment at least as, if not more, emotionally supportive than that available to traditional researchers. To the extent that external support is lacking (in the form of psychological confirmation or material resources), the individual has to draw on personal resources continuously. As one of my doctoral students wrote:

> Fiscally, my life is in a shambles. *Everyone* has rejected my proposals for fundings — everyone has had the same rationale, i.e. 'This is not research'. Folks don't seem to know what to do with proposals that don't specify control groups, high technology sampling methodologies, and objective outcome measures. I'm about to embark on a second go-round with a slightly less 'radical' writing stance. If I weren't so broke, I'd sort of be flattered, particularly inasmuch as the subjective success (of my research) I've enjoyed, is rooted, I'm sure, in the nontraditional nature of my approach.

Torbert's chapter on collaborative inquiry into voluntary metropolitan desegregation (Chapter 29) demonstrates the impact of a supportive, non-heirarchical research team on the ability of researchers to withstand public criticism and to tolerate the ambiguity of the concepts with which they dealt. Support counteracts the insidious obstacles of self-doubt, lack of faith, and the inability to persevere in the face of outside attack or lack of support. Can untenured faculty find enough support to take the risk to conduct unconventional research? Even the simple choice of qualitative rather than quantitative research efforts is a recognized risk in the pursuit of an academic career (McCartney, 1970). In times of economic uncertainty the numbers of people who can 'afford' to operate at the fringes of the reward structure will be particularly small. Support enables the researcher not only to respond to criticism, but to recognize the defensiveness of the critic, where it exists.

Criticism and challenge follow the new paradigm researcher at every step because even his/her vocabulary is not generally shared and his/her actions refute the assumptions underlying conventional respectable research. Becker, a phenomenological psychologist, believes that 'phenomenological research is frightening to some people... because it breaks several tacit rules of "science"' (1978, p. 5). Not all responses to external critics will convince them, but as long as one has enough personal and financial resources to carry on one's work, there is no reason to attempt to change the practice of others. Respect is harder to come by than is true for researchers who perform up to par in the conventional paradigm, because both the method and the findings are suspect to critics of new paradigm research. The person engaged in new paradigm research thus has the burden of educating everyone interested in his/her work, including the critics. This point applied not only to colleagues but to sponsors, clients, and subjects as well. There are very firm, definite ideas in the layman's mind about what constitutes research. Trying to do things otherwise with the layman as subject requires much patient, repeated explanation before 'common-sense' notions or cultural definitions of 'research' are loosened. Sponsors usually prefer scientific-sounding results as well, even if they are not understood or used. The new paradigm research must therefore remake culture, and this is nearly impossible if one feels alone.

A supportive environment builds commitment and tolerance for continued conflict. If this support contains confirmation of the researcher's experience and contribution, then the innovation will be nourished. In a description of his work with innovative communities, Trist (1979) has shown the impact on individuals of their commitment to change their environments. In turn, their commitment and success has had an impact on Trist's own sense of hope for the future and thus his ability to work in unusual ways which contribute to the 'success' of those communities. Like despair, commitment breeds environments and products which intensify themselves in continuous interaction. Here is the spontaneous response of an anthropologist whose lack of a supportive environment stifled her ability to innovate or communicate her conflicts:

> I thank you, because your paper gave me first of all the hope that I
> need not be alone. I seem to gather from it that you have a com-

munity of people who think and work like you, with whom you can indeed share your experience and thought, as a new paradigm researcher, as a person, and of course the two are not separate! Knowing that there is such a community may help me overcome the problem that I have with professional commitment to anthropology. I seem to be drifting in and out — I can neither drop out completely, nor can I truly create within it.... This going in and out is a dialectic which I do not seem to be able to resolve in a new synthesis, rather I keep going from extreme to extreme. What is the point of writing, when no one I interact with here can appreciate it? If I had a community of thought and action (a research team, a job with others who think like me, a journal or even discussion group) perhaps I would be able to overcome this lack of commitment (R.M., personal communication, 1979).

Once the support is found and this vicious cycle is disrupted, the researcher not only forges commitment to the discipline but also to the community, persons, culture or problems s/he is studying. This kind of commitment is referred to invidiously in methodological literature as 'going native', or over-rapport. By contrast, Wolff (1971) has recognized that surrendering oneself to one's research subjects opens the way to heightened commitment to one's work and personal growth.

In order to carry out new paradigm research, the basic cognitive-psychological state of a researcher becomes dialectic and rebellious, whereas the dominant paradigm has a cumulative and conservative stance. The cumulative nature of predominant social science is one of its basic characteristics, i.e. studies create conclusions which are then modified by further studies until a general 'law' is reached (even if the law applies only to the most highly specified conditions). When problems are encountered, they are eliminated by additional studies in the same vein. By dialectic thinking, on the other hand, I mean that the researcher continuously experiences and perceives conflicts within current research practice: conflict between the ideal and real (Barber and Fox, 1958; Kaplan, 1964), conflict between models of research, and conflict as characteristic of the life experience of research subjects. The dialectic perspective leads to a search for creative resolutions or syntheses in the face of conflict. The resolution is never completely fixed, but rather exists in numerous variations representing various responses depending on the severity of the conflict.

Although a supportive environment enhancing the development of commitment and the cognitive skill of dialectic thinking are ingredients in the emergence of a new paradigm researcher, some personal attributes are also important. It appears that such resarchers must know themselves well, must be grounded in multiple worlds and cultures, and must be able to express their knowledge in some communicable form. Elsewhere (Reinharz, 1979a), I have specified that these prerequisites can be acquired through numerous self-analytic therapies, deliberate involvement in a wide variety of settings, and a disciplined programme of writing. Generally, traditional paradigm researchers rely on instruments to collect data, whereas in an alternative paradigm, researchers rely much more heavily on human skills such as listening, looking, relating, thinking, feeling, acting, collaborating. In essence, the researcher's awareness is the major instrument and thus must be finely tuned. Both paradigms require that researchers have or develop enough political or entrepreneurial skill to move beyond the state of thinking about research, to actually carrying it out, and completing it in some fashion.

Within the context of personal attributes congruent with new paradigm research, it is important to note the argument that such work draws on feminine modes of thought and action as compared to the masculine mode on which science is based (Reinharz, 1979a, pp. 7-8; Bernard, 1973; Millman and Kanter, 1975). If this is true, then men might experience a threat to their masculinity in this line of research, or it might be that only androgynous types are attracted to it in the first place.

Although some of the skills and self-awareness can be acquired through training, there is a necessary foundation present in some people (and lacking in others) which enables them to operate comfortably in certain cognitive-relational-action modes rather than in others. This idea has led to the radical suggestion that training for new paradigm research is not necessary at all, particularly since the research activities of the alternative models are not esoteric.

> Whether this sort of social psychology requires any professional expertise, I am not sure. Certainly the skills would not be those of technical competence so much as of interpersonal sensitivity. There is plenty of this outside social science departments; what is lacking there are the time and facilities (tape-recorders, access to subjects) (Armistead, 1974, p. 129).

Such an argument invites a controversy as to whether new paradigm researchers are born or made. A plausible answer to this question is that people work with their strengths. This means that if a person has a philosophy and attitude-set, a cognitive style, and a behavioural style (Bedmar and Kaul, 1979) that favour a certain approach, she or he will seek it out and strengthen it to perform optimally. Elaborate training cannot compensate for basic inadequacies or incompatibilities; nor does all alternative paradigm research require elaborate training. Even the chairperson of my own department, whose mission is to train primarily traditional paradigm researchers, wrote: 'Given my druthers, I'd much rather try to select a potentially creative and effective teacher and scholar than try to create one' (Norman, 1979, p. 10).

I would argue instead that a training programme is necessary to teach the old paradigm and its criticism and to provide support for the development of new paradigm skills and practice. In the appendix to this chapter an outline of an ideal training environment is offered. It consists of elements which together constitute an optimal set of conditions. Many studies of the perceived environment of graduate programmes as they currently exist are disheartening although predictable (Sibley, 1963; Farrell *et al.,* 1967) because their motto is excellence via hierarchical evaluation and weeding out. His reading of the latter study provoked Kelman (1968) to suggest that there is a tendency to breed conservative attitudes and restricted thinking in graduate training programmes which should be countered by striving instead to train people to be imaginative. Students themselves frequently bring stifling attitudes (such as excessive instrumentalism) with them. But more often than not, these attitudes are fostered during the training programme by its reward structure.

New paradigm research demands a distinctive training environment with as much dialogue, confirmation of experience (in the sense of Laing, 1970), and sharing of responsibility, as possible. It is contradictory to expect students to adopt attitudes congruent with new paradigm research (e.g. attention to experiences *in situ,* responsiveness to subjects, study through commitment) and be themselves subjected to grossly controlling hierarchical relations 'back home'. By contrast, Argyris' 'organistically oriented research' relations could be the blueprint for relations between researchers and 'subjects' and therefore the blueprint for relations among members of the researcher's training environment. From his experience, Argyris claims that the development of suitable personal and interpersonal skills comes about from deep involvement in a suitable milieu, such as a *t*-group

> that tends to sanction minimally evaluative and attributive behavior as well as encourage maintaining cognitive inconsistency... a milieu that sanctions and rewards the expression of feelings, the helping of others, the taking of risks, and the norms of trust, concern and individuality (Argyris, 1971, p. 51).

In a study currently nearing completion, one of my own students is examining 'open communication' as the central feature of shaping such an environment (Wright, in preparation). The ideal training environment outlined in the appendix is designed to foster these attitudes within a complex of resources, models and peers, instruction, skill training, and administration.

Phase 4:   The Development of a Model for Practice and Living

I have argued that a dialectic mode of thinking is a characteristic of new paradigm research and thus is an important element in the development of the person being socialized. The student culminates the dialectic search for method by personally attempting to carry out an investigation. At this point it is necessary to have a framework on which to hang the experience of the research project. A model which has been developing in various contexts (Kolb and Fry, 1975; Fry and Kolb, 1979; Gish, 1979; and Reinharz, 1979b) is called a *learning cycle* and is useful primarily in illustrating the component phases and their pattern. The cycle is presented in terms of the researcher's cognitive set rather than the usual steps in a research sequence. The cycle can be entered at any point and a sense of psychological closure comes from a complete rotation (see Figure 36.3).

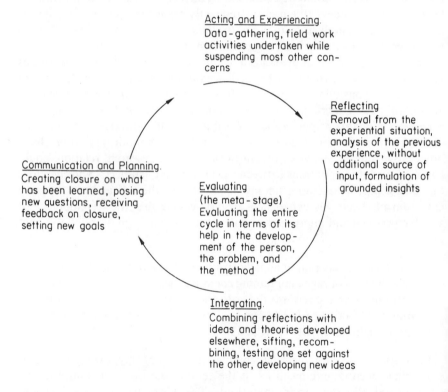

Figure 36.3 The cognitive/action or work/being cycle of new paradigm researchers

Kolb and Fry (1975) have shown that different people (and each of the various disciplines) prefer to 'remain' in various phases of the cycle, thus illustrating their strengths, or instead, their area where further development is needed. Although the two-dimensional diagram appears as a cycle, in actuality the image should be a spiral, with the propelling energy derived from critically reviewing the cycle just undergone and then moving on to a different cycle. An ideal learning environment takes into account the skills required by each stage of the research cycle and provides experiences to enhance all of them.

Rowan's 'dialectical research cycle', presented in Chapter 9 of this book, is another cyclical model developed independently. His flow of stages runs counter-clockwise, whereas the cycle presented here flows clockwise. Perhaps this indicates that the flow or order can be in either direction. Similarly we have both conceived each phase as being an existential mode which serves a purpose and then becomes out of synchrony with the passage of time and the emergence of new needs. Each phase needs an emergent one to complete its task. Somehow, the complex consciousness that represents research (or the creation of knowledge) is subsumed within the cycle. If the cycle is understood as having no beginning and no end (rather than a table with its absolute figures), then communicating about research carried out within the cyclical model will also have to develop innovative cycle-compatible forms. One form suggested by Trist (1979) is the *story,* with its power of conveying and creating experiences. Rowan's cycle and mine differ in that he conceives of evaluation (his questions of efficiency, authenticity, etc.) as occurring at every phase, whereas I suggest that evaluation might be confined to a meta-stage upon the completion of a cycle. My suggestion stems from the notion that evaluation changes the ability to carry out the phase that will follow from the dialectic needs of the current phase. Evaluation can become a block, or a diversionary force that takes one off into new cycles rather than allowing one to complete a current cycle. My point is simply that a question is useful when asked at the right time. Rowan also suggests that research 'subjects', not just researchers, have ways of being/action that are more or less fragmented, and more or less cyclical. The extent to which the researcher's activities resemble the organic integrity of a cycle will influence the subject's state, and vice-versa. The striking characteristic of new paradigm research relations with subjects is that when they both are cyclical, then the relationship lasts over a considerable period of time, and constitutes changes for both researchers and subjects. In my own work (Reinharz, 1979a) I have referred to this relationship as 'temporary affiliation' in the sense that it does not necessarily demand a lifelong commitment, nor is it limited to the brief encounter or the exchange. When persons affiliate, new social structures and ideas can arise.

When the researcher enters the evaluation phase upon completion of a cycle, she/he glances backward to see where she/he has been. At this point it is necessary to have a guideline for conducting the evaluation. Rowan offers us a long list of useful questions which can be subdivided into three categories: person, problem and method. By this I mean that each project (or cycle) is an integration of the researcher as a person, investigating a particular research question (or problem), and using a certain method. Each element needs to be reviewed before the cycle begins again, to see if there has been change and growth. The researcher who has not learned something of personal value about him/herself, has not contributed to a fuller understanding of a definable issue, and has not refined further his/her current thinking on method, has not benefited completely from the cycle she/he has undergone. If these three elements are communicated to others, it is nearly assured that their impact will be powerful and will decrease the sense of alienation. A recently completed cycle by Wolf (1979), on teenage drug-users, is an example of this tripartite approach. Nevertheless, his effort and those of others presented in this volume suggest not only how well we understand the possibilities for a new paradigm research practice, but their inherent contradictions which must be dealt with in future training. After all, each individual cycle is simply one phase in a grander cycle that includes all of our work/being throughout history.

Appendix: Constructing an Ideal Training Programme for New Paradigm Researchers

Any training programme begins with a coherent statement of purpose and some resources to carry out the purpose. The following outline contains a suggested set of resources to carry out the purpose suggested in the body of this chapter. Each element will need to be carefully defined in the light of particular circumstances and personalities. It is important to keep in mind, however, that whereas most of the elements are similar to those of conventional training programmes, the content of each element is freshly defined in the light of the nature of new paradigm research.

Resources

Time
The time-span in which students are expected to complete a programme is redefined to be very broad so that there is sufficient time to pursue time-consuming research and training; there should be a minimization of pressure to adhere to deadlines artificially set and more attention paid to when there is a psychological sense that a given training task has been completed. Short and long training units.

Money
There should be funds for support and research.

Space
There should be spaces to work along, to meet with others, perhaps field stations, an opportunity to feel ownership for the space of the programme.

Contacts
Trainers have the responsibility to assist students in gaining entry into a wide variety of situations; many of these should be outside the academic community so that students can achieve some distance and test their skills; these contacts should have an opportunity to come into the programme to report on the effect of their being studied, so that there can be a two-way dialogue.

Guidance
In addition to the models and peers listed below, there should be opportunities to meet consultants and visiting scholars; there should be consultants of both sexes, various races and ages.

Libraries
In addition to the need for scholarly literature, there should also be an internal library of field notes and transcripts of other training-programme members, so that sharing is encouraged; the library might also include technical equipment like video and tapes that have been made of training sessions, encouraging examination of visual, not only printed, materials.

Presentation and publication opportunities
Creation of alternative opportunities if needed.

Other equipment and assisting personnal
Tape-recorders, cameras, people to help transcribe, etc.

Models and Peers

Student opportunities to observe and be observed
Field experiences should include some supervision or sharing; more advanced researchers should provide others with opportunities to observe them in action, the purpose being to demystify and share as much as possible.

Informal and formal support structures
The psychological atmosphere of the training programme should be supportive rather than exclusively evaluative; this can be achieved by one-on-one advising with faculty or advanced students, support groups for specific tasks like dissertation preparation, and inclusion of spouses for some community meetings so as not to fragment the role set of the community members. (For a description of such a training community see Wright, in preparation).

Faculty commitment to students as persons
Including reading of field notes, observation in practice, participation in T-group-like discussions, interest in their personal changes.

Faculty involvement with students as researchers
Assisting them in their work, serving as a model of commitment.

Confirmation of student's experience of conflict
Faculties that are not overly defensive; the programme must also be of adequate size so that the dialectic is reflected in a community dialogue.

Information
Circulation of as much information about the programme and its members as possible among members of the programme; high value should be placed on creating and sharing information and feelings.

Instruction

Multidisciplinary, transdisciplinary
Should include *history and philosophy of social sciences* to some extent, particularly epistemology, so a vocabulary is available for discussing paradigms for social science. Can include sociology of knowledge, sociology of research, and particularly criticism of dominant paradigm. In addition to this, there must be some training in the dominant paradigm, or what Torbert calls 'instrumented research skills'. The theory or data related to a research problem which the student wishes to investigate need not be offered within the programme, but rather in an adjacent one, with the student returning to the training programme to re-examine it within the light of an alternative paradigm.

Training in models of new paradigm research

Skill Training

Personal
The purpose here is for the student to learn about himself, his/her impact on others; his/her strengths and weaknesses. This can be achieved through quasi-therapeutic *t*-groups, value-clarification sessions, assertiveness training, etc. Through these, the student will be encouraged to be self-analytic and recognize his/her characteristic ways of defining reality, identifying the critical experiences which shaped his/her life and which colour his/her perceptions,

preferences, and explanations. Such training will help students deal with areas of personal conflict, develop courage, stamina, and a high tolerance for ambiguity, marginality, and deviance. Students will learn how to self-disclose and deal with the self-disclosure of others.

Interpersonal
Listening skills, ability to relate to a wide range of people, to read their body language, to gain entry into settings and situations, to engage in 'reciprocal encounters', to share power. The student needs to learn to communicate back to others what she/he has heard, to help interviewees discover their experiencing, to work with individuals and groups as unique human beings. Becker suggested that 'the task of the researcher becomes one of creating an atmosphere of respectful receptivity to the subject's experience of the phenomena' (1978, pp. 6-7).

Linguistic
An appreciation for multiple languages (social scientific, poetic, dialects, class-based, etc.) and their nuances; facility with writing and capturing the flavour of experience in writing.

Other data-gathering skills
Memory training, observation skills, techniques to record observations, attentional skills; conduct of open-ended and structured interviews; collaborative discussions and planning; political/entrepreneurial skills to create action programmes.

Administration of Training Programme

A programme designed to train alternative paradigm researchers should attempt to create an alternative form of administration, rather than a top-down decision-making bureaucracy. Such an alternative setting would be characterized by open communication, loose role definition, a sense of community, and a high degree of participation by members. Teaching and evaluation would be conducted not only by individuals but by teams.

[This chapter was written while the author was on a research leave funded by The Josephine Nevins Keal Fellowship for 1979, University of Michigan.]

Human Inquiry
Edited by P. Reason and J. Rowan
© 1981 John Wiley & Sons Ltd.

CHAPTER THIRTY-SEVEN

Empirical, behavioural, theoretical, and attentional skills necessary for collaborative inquiry

William R. Torbert
Boston College, Chestnut Hill, Massachusetts, USA

An earlier paper (see Chapter 11 of this book) introduces a new model of social science based on three assumptions at variance with current 'normal' social science. This new model of social science assumes:

(1) that researchers are themselves active participants in the situations researched and that the researcher-situation relationship deserves to be studied;
(2) that the framework and variables of studies themselves change in the course of study; and
(3) that an important way of testing the validity and significance of social knowledge is to feed data back into the setting researched, studying how this feedback influences further action.

Together, these three assumptions provide a framework for systematically learning in settings of organized action — a framework for an 'action science', as opposed to a merely reflective science — a framework for a collaborative enquiry among all participants in the given setting, as opposed to an inquiry unilaterally defined by the self-designated researcher 'on' other respondents.

A number of studies over the past 20 years foreshadow this model of science. Five of these studies are briefly summarized below, in order to anchor the theoretical model proposed in the earlier chapter in concrete illustrations. These five examples lead to the question, what kind of graduate training is necessary for aspiring action scientists? This question receives attention in the main body of this chapter.

Five Partial Examples of Action Science

The five partial examples of action science to be summarized here derive from the disciplines of history, sociology, anthropology, and organizational behaviour. Only the fourth and fifth of these studies were originally conceived as including the researcher's own attitudes and behaviour as part of the data to be studied. In each of the first three examples, the researchers discovered only as they proceeded that their own attitudes and behaviour required study if their reports of the phenomena they encountered were to be valid.

Martin Duberman's historical study of Black Mountain College (1972) can serve as an interesting initial example of a research report which traces the mutual influence process between the researcher and the subject of research. Since Duberman was not present during the life of the college (1933-56), one might suppose that the question of mutual influence was moot; but Duberman recognizes that his way of interviewing people who were there, his views on education, and his deepest personal presuppositions may all influence what data he collects and how he analyses it. Consequntly, he provides his readers with data on how he conducted his interviews and with excerpts from his personal journal reflecting on the relationship between his experiences and those at Black Mountain. Moreover, the influence process works the other way as well: Duberman's study of the approach to teaching and writing at Black Mountain influences his own attempts to write, and his final chapter reflects his new experiments with his own writing style.

A second example of incipient collaborative inquiry is Charles Hampden-Turner's recent book, *Sane Asylum* (1976), about the Delancey Street Foundation in San Francisco, which is dedicated to the rehabilitation of criminals and drug addicts. When Hampden-Turner first visited Delancey Street on behalf of a foundation, he found an intense, unconventional educational environment. In seeking to study the organization, Hampden-Turner was challenged to participate in it himself. The book describes not only the Delancey Street Foundation as though from some neutral standpoint, but also Delancey Street's diagnosis of Hampden-Turner. In effect, this is an institution devoted to self-study in action on the part of its own members, and it challenged the visiting social scientist to join in such self-study. It seems likely that if Hampden-Turner had not been willing to do so, he could not have completed the research.

Carlos Castaneda's tetralogy (1968, 1971, 1972, 1974) about his apprenticeship to an American Indian 'sorcerer' provides another example of a conventional social scientist — this time an anthropologist out to study alien cultural practices — who is challenged by his subject to engage in self-study in action. Don Juan, Castaneda's 'informant', turns out to be a real 'man of knowledge' who teases Castaneda toward a genuine interest in developing a trained, interpenetrating attention. Over time, Castaneda carefully records his own subjective experience, his interactions with Don Juan, and Don Juan's words. After close to ten years of apprenticeship with Don Juan, new experiences force Casteneda into a fundamental re-evaluation of the world-view and theory of action he had adduced up to that time. Fortunately, his record of experience was sufficiently complete to permit him to return to his earliest meetings with Don Juan and re-evaluate their significance (as reported in the third book, *Journey to Ixtlan*).

Don Juan so choreographs experiences for Castaneda that the latter's attention gradually comes to include 'non-ordinary' states of reality which encompass and interpenetrate his ordinary thought and action. With these new experiences of attention comes increased motivation to attempt actually to listen to the ordinary jumble of thoughts and feelings which Castaneda finds in himself. His repeated, depressing discovery that he lacks sure purpose and that his thoughts and actions lack congruence reveal a need for approaching his own life in the attitude of a 'warrior', becoming 'impeccable' in ordinary thought and action (a realm Don Juan names the 'tonal'), so as not to be distracted from the play of a different realm of spiritual purposiveness (which Don Juan names the 'nagual'). Gradually, Castaneda journeys from a state of consciousness in which his ideas about himself have little correspondence with his actual moods, actions, and effects toward an attention which traces the actual transformations in his experience as they occur.

Argyris' studies of business executives (1962, 1965, 1974, 1976) provide an example of a social scientist using numerous empirical methodologies to study organizational cultures and then feeding back the results to the acting systems in an effort to encourage self-study in action and, ultimately, more effective operation. In his feedback sessions Argyris refers not only to data already collected about the system in question, but also to the quality of the interactions in the feedback session itself. To do this requires an attention to oneself and to others which simultaneously spans both espoused theories of action (what each believes in doing) and patterns of actual behaviour (what each actually does). As Argyris has become increasingly aware of how difficult it is to encourage such a quality of attention in others, Argyris has turned increasingly from short-term consulting relationships with the other acting systems to longer-term educational relationships (Argyris and Schon, 1974; Argyris, 1976).

The final example of collaborative inquiry is the author's study of his own organizing practice in *Creating a Community of Inquiry* (Torbert, 1976a). In this case, the social scientist was, from the outset, a member of the organization in question and sought to study himself in action in order to increase his effectiveness, while also encouraging other participants to engage in self-study and collaborative inquiry. Asked in 1967 to create and direct an OEC Upward Bound Program for some 70 high-school students in New Haven, the author viewed the aim of creating a genuinely educational school and the aim of conducting genuinely informative social research as mutually supportive, integratable aims. During the first year of the programme, the author was the only person who regularly pursued the integration of these two aims. He found some repeated incongruities between his espoused values and his actual behaviour (for example, he espoused working through conflict but actually feared to provoke or face it). Meanwhile, other members of the school tended to regard the data-collection (such as the taping of staff meetings) as 'Bill's research'. The author had not anticipated how unconvincing he would be, and how little interest and how much resistance others would manifest, about the ideal of collaborative inquiry.

At the end of the first year, the seven-person core staff began to find the research of interest and of direct use in diagnosing organizational problems, in developing a more articulated and a more deeply shared sense of purpose, in increasing personal effectiveness, in improving the quality of staff meetings, and in reaching specific decisions. A month largely devoted to self-study by the core staff as a group led to the development of a unique selection process for new staff members. This selection process used research and feedback as part of its decision-making process and ultimately invited applicants to participate in their own selection. At this point in the school's development, the aims of creating a genuine school and of doing significant social research seemed to be increasingly mutually supportive and integrated.

During the second year of operation, however, various political events, such as riots in the city and at the local high schools and the assassination of Martin Luther King, generated more hostile, more polarized relationships, particularly among newly hired staff members. Divisions between the revolutionary and the conventional, between black and white, and between research and action tended to be treated as absolute and unbridgeable. In the short time available, the core staff did not fully succeed in winning new staff members' allegiance to the peculiar integration of collaboration and inquiry which the core staff itself was only just beginning to recognize, value, and enact.

Thus, the author came to recognize through painful personal experience both how difficult it is in the first place to integrate research and action, no matter how much sense it may make in principle, and how difficult it is to maintain an integrative organizing design, once it is achieved, against culturally prevalent modes of organizing thought and action. This overall insight suggested the need for a theory of qualitatively distinct historical stages of organizing which would illuminate both the possibility and the difficulty of achieving more sophisticated and more effective kinds of organizing than is conventional in our culture. Although he had not been sensitive to the issue of historical stages during the conduct of the school, the author's voluminous record of experience in tapes, documents, and journals permitted him to reconstruct a theory of stages of organizing which applied not only to the overall development of the school, but also to each of five sub-cycles of its development. This theory has since proved of use in describing and intervening in other educational settings (Torbert, 1974/75) and in creating successful new settings (Torbert, 1978). Thus, one result of this episode of self-study in action was the development of a theory generalizable to the rest of the researcher's own life (and also potentially generalizable to others interested in educational organizing). A still more important but less visible result (especially in a scholarly paper like this one) was the intensification of the researcher's *practice* of inquiry from moment to moment and the concomitant relaxation of his *rhetorical espousal* of inquiry.

Implicit in the brief summaries of five studies above (and explicit in the theoretical presentation of Chapter 11) is the notion that collaborative inquiry spans four different 'territories' of human reality, and thus requires research methodologies capable of registering these four different qualities of reality. The four distinct qualities of reality are: (1) the outside world; (2) one's own behaviour; (3) one's own and other's thinking and feeling; and (4) the dynamics of human attention as it gains, loses, or changes focus and as it narrows or widens the number of qualities of which it is aware. At any given moment the attention may include all four qualities of human reality and their interaction within awareness, or it may include only one quality (e.g. the outside world; as when we are so identified with a movie we are watching that we altogether forget that we are there sitting in a theatre, feeling and interpreting what is going on).

Training in Research Methods Relevant to Collaborative Inquiry

In collaborative inquiry research methodologies which provide access to all four of these qualities of human reality are necessary, and the prospective action scientist requires training in all four types of methodology.

At present, graduate programmes in the social sciences conceive of and teach research skills primarily as skills in the development, validation, administration, and analysis of empirical research instruments, such as unobtrusive measures (Webb *et al.*, 1966), questionnaires, behaviour rating systems, interviews, and field notes. As noted in Chapter 11, different empirical research instruments offer more or less direct access to each of the four qualities of reality, and it would therefore be peculiarly inappropriate for a prospective action scientist to be trained to treat only one empirical methodology as valid.

In collaborative inquiry, empirical data are approached from a fundamentally different point of view than in conventional, reflective social science, and prospective action scientists therefore require different emphases in their training in data analysis. In terms of statistical analysis, the conventional social scientist prefers to use parametric tests to discover overall patterns and differences among sub-groups in the largest possible sample, with an interest in generalizing to a wider universe of similar situations. By contrast, the prospective action scientist often finds non-parametric statistical tests more appropriate to analysing data from small groups of people who are willing to engage in mutual self-study (see Siegel, 1956).

Moreover, in collaborative inquiry the primary interest is not in generalizing to other settings, but rather in applying knowledge to improve actors' effectiveness in the situation under study. Consequently, the prospective action scientist should develop skills in analysing data from each member's point of view. Of special interest are incongruities between a member's espoused values and actual behaviour, or incongruities between a member's description of self and other members' descriptions of that person. Such apparent incongruities can generate conversation which can lead either towards more valid research instruments or towards a more inclusive, less distorted view of their own social reality by the group engaging in the inquiry.

In searching beyond the 'central tendencies' of data to particular incongruities, it is helpful to aggregate the various frequency counts onto one master data sheet in order to be able to scan the entire complex of relationships both before and after statistical tests on relationships among particular variables. Because new variables and new hypotheses emerge in the course of study, the prospective action scientist must develop the confidence not just to 'manipulate' data through statistical tests, but also to 'play' with data in such as way as to discover unexpected patterns.

Non-Instrumented Research Skills

Although different empirical research instruments allow more or less direct access to each of the four qualities of reality (to repeat: (1) the outside world; (2) one's own behaviour; (3) thinking and feeling; (4) attention) (Torbert, 1972), *empirical research instruments register each of these qualities only as they manifest themselves in the outside world.* Moreover, there is invariably a time lapse between the collection of data, the coding and analysis of the data, and the feedback of data into the world of social action. The prospective action scientist, however, wishes to encourage a culture in which participants can study themselves while in action, recognizing their own behaviour, thought, and attentional dynamics as they occur, and also correcting incongruities as they occur. This kind of self-study-in-action requires, first and foremost, the development of a kind of attention which can continually (and perhaps, ultimately, continuously) register one's own behaviour, thought, and attentional dynamics. And self-study-in-action also requires specific kinds of behaviour and thinking conducive to discovering what is going on in social situations rather than assuming one knows to begin with. In short, in a social science which includes self-study in action, not only the quality of a researcher's empirical product is at stake, but also the quality of his or her ongoing behaviour, thinking, and attention is at stake. The question arises what kinds of behaviour, thought, and attention are conducive to disciplined research.

In one sense, this question is not new; all social scientists realize that there are behavioural skills to effective interviewing, that good theory makes the difference between an indigestible mass of data and a fruitful study, and that *how* a researcher attends to *what* problems makes the difference between a mediocre and a distinguished career.

But in many senses, the insight that valid scientific inquiry requires disciplined skills in all four 'territories' of human experience will transform the institution of social science as we now know it and, with it, the entire society. To bring the quality of ongoing behaviour, thinking, and attention into question in the training of social scientists is to become responsible for the quality of graduate programmes as action settings. From the point of view of the model of collaborative inquiry, a graduate department in the social sciences that does not study and seek to improve its own teaching and administration is, at best, a bad joke. As social scientists master the behavioural, emotional, conceptual, and attentional disciplines necessary to research their own lives with others, they can for the first time help others in this regard as well. (Of course, there is no guarantee at present that social scientists will be among the first to choose to master these disciplines.)

In Chapter 36 in this book, on training for new paradigm research, Shulamit Reinharz offers a useful list of research skills, above and beyond the design and analysis of empirical data-collection instruments, required of a researcher committed to a model of collaborative inquiry.

What would courses focusing on the development of disciplined research behaviour, thinking, and attention look like? The skills that Reinharz describes are primarily behavioural skills taught in some counselling psychology, group dynamics, organization development, and clinical research methods courses today. In such courses students can be challenged to become aware of their own behavioural patterns through others' feedback, to develop more effective inquiring behaviour, and to theorize about the very activity in which they are currently (emotionally) involved in such a way as to expose and test their own most primitive assumptions about social life (see Argyris and Schon, 1974). Beyond these courses, the prospective action scientist might well seek training in dance forms such as tai chi, judo, or the Gurdjieffian movements, all of which cultivate direct, moment-to-moment sensual awareness.

It is much harder to envision what courses in disciplined research thinking and feeling, or disciplined research attention, would look like.

Traditionally, disciplined research *thinking* has been associated with philosophical conversation, but few departments of philosophy boast such a conversation at any given time, and one searches without notable success to find a philosopher since Socrates who views everyday life as the setting for questioning conversation. What is at stake here is not the learning of social scientific or philosophical theories, not talk about theories, but *active theorizing* — an uncomfortable, disconcerting, virtually unknown process — a wondering what is going on. A brief excerpt from a memoir on Wittgenstein suggests the flavour (D.A.T.G., 1951):

> Usually at the beginning of the year Wittgenstein would warn us that we would find his lectures unsatisfactory, that he would go on talking like this for hours and hours and we would get very little out of it. ... And, if we had to work hard, Wittgenstein worked tremendously hard. He spoke without notes. Each lecture was obviously carefully prepared — its general strategy planned and numerous examples thought up. But in the lectures he thought it all through again, aloud. Members of the class would chip in briefly from time to time, though usually to make a suggestion in response to some question which was posed. At times Wittgenstein would break off, saying 'Just a minute, let me think!' and would sit for minutes on end, crouched forward on the edge of a chair, staring down at his upturned palm. Or he would exclaim with vehement sincerity: 'This is as difficult as *hell*!' (p. 26).

Related to the difficulty of pointing to, or developing, courses which exemplify and teach disciplined research thinking is the difficulty of envisioning courses that develop disciplined research feeling. Indeed, the very concept of 'disciplined research feeling' is probably unfamiliar to the reader, an apparently awkward conjunction of terms. The sense of the phrase and exercises related to developing disciplined research feeling are probably best described in contemporary literature by the leading innovative theatre directors of our time (e.g., Grotowski, 1970; Schechner, 1973). In brief, just as one can distinguish between passive thought which works with preconceived, taken-for-granted categories and active thinking which questions how to categorize, so also can one distinguish between passive feeling which works with predetermined, taken-for-granted likes or dislikes and active feeling which questions the value or significance of an occasion. Only a person who seeks the disciplines of active thinking and feeling can tolerate, or encourage, collaborative inquiry in ongoing social settings.

If activities which encourage disciplined research thinking and feeling are difficult to find in academia as presently organized, the very notion of disciplined attentional research is likely to be even more unfamiliar. The effort is to achieve a quality of attention which simply registers one's other functions (thinking, feeling, moving) and one's perceptions of the outside world. Perhaps the closest traditional discipline is Buddhist 'vipassana' type of meditation. The following brief dialogues are transcribed from group meetings wherein the participants attempt attentional research while they speak. The dialogues do not prove anything empirically. Instead, they are presented here to *illustrate* the *possibility* of attentional research.

Question: I try to observe all the functions at the same time — thought, emotion, moving, and instinctive. I attempted to separate each in an experiment while walking along the river. I am confused about what observing really is. My mind starts to grasp and think.

Response: There is no direct connection between the place that observes and words. We have very little experience bridging that gap. It's difficult to put words to it. The idea we have about observation is intellectual, but what observation tastes like... to observe an emotion is to participate in it, what is it that knows? Can I be interested in that? How can I turn toward what is observing in such a way that both the observation and thought continue? What is that movement?

Question: I had an experience at school last Monday. I felt more of a demand on my attention — how to be more here — that seemed to come back to me at two different times. I really felt that when I put more attention on myself, it expanded to the other things in the room. And it seemed for that time almost as though the children were working with more attention too, even if only for a short while. I feel it as a possibility in me, but there is so much else that forgets to have attention and is interested in other things. I guess I want to have some thread that I can call on.

Response: When you voice that wish, have you searched to see if there is some thread you can follow, that you can hold onto?

Question: It's different — at some moments I do, others it's more difficult.

Response: How does one treat those moments in all their variance? See, maybe this moment is a moment I feel I am less here — I have had an experience of knowing more than this. That memory of a deeper moment can be of use if I start to look *now*. What are the limits of my sense of being here? Am I including all of my body? Now I don't respond to that with a yes or no, but I see, with a search in myself. I find that this search brings me closer — that this is the thread, the connection I could follow. Always the remembrance of these times can be a motivation to look at this moment.

Question: I find it very hard to stop internal dialogue. As I try to collect myself when I sit in the morning, I am only able to find quiet for a brief moment... and then the internal dialogue goes on again. I realize I left it and I start again. I find it disturbing. The ability to work with the attention seems to go in patterns. There are some good weeks and some bad weeks. As I'm teaching, at home with my family, I'm not aware of this internal dialogue going on, but when I remember it and try to find quiet, it's all full of internal dialogue.

Response: And yet it's not always like that. What's the difference?

Question: I'm not sure.

Response: Are you sometimes quiet?

Question: Yes.

Response: What's the difference in you then?

Question: Then, my attention is really there.

Response: But what makes it possible for your attention to be there? Try to see. When you find yourself in internal dialogue, try to see what holds you there. What is the attraction? When you are free of it, try to see what has freed you. Anything else will just be words and explanations. It's the only way you can find out what is up to you in that situation.

Training for collaborative inquiry must somehow include four types of research skills appropriate for all four qualities of reality — skills in the design and use of empirical research instruments, behavioural skills in generating social environments conducive to inquiry, and skills in active thinking, feeling, and attending. While it is possible to design environments which introduce students to each of these types of skills separately, the ultimate aim is, of course, to use all these skills simultaneously in ongoing social settings. Because it is all too easy for beginning students to become ideologically and religiously attached to the importance of one or another of these skills, it is of special importance in training for collaborative inquiry that students engage in real-world projects with close, clinical supervision. the conflicting and confusing real-time demands of such a project emphasize the art of interweaving the four types of research skills. Chapter 29 describes a particular example of collaborative inquiry in which graduate students received research training. That chapter supplements the present chapter.

Human Inquiry
Edited by P. Reason and J. Rowan
© 1981 John Wiley & Sons Ltd.

CHAPTER THIRTY-EIGHT

The democratization of research in adult and non-formal education

Budd L. Hall
International Council for Adult Education, Toronto, Canada

Much of the recent international research in adult and non-formal education could be categorized roughly as follows:

Overviews and Surveys

Overviews and surveys have done much to stimulate an interest in non-formal education and to raise critical issues of a practical, economic, and political nature. While the work of Philip Coombs, Manzoor Ahmed, and Roy Prosser are perhaps the best known, Sheffield and Diejomaoh were the first to complie and classify the varieites of programmes and raise a number of critical issues for Africa (see Coombs and Ahmed, 1974; Sheffield and Diejomoah, 1972; Ahmed, 1975; Coombs and Prosser, 1973; Kidd, 1974). In the United States, Michigan State University (Niehoff, n.d.) and the University of Massachusetts (Gillette, 1977; Evans, 1972; Moulton, 1977) have worked on some experiences in Commonwealth nations.

Literacy

One of the important secondary effects of the UNESCO/UNDP literacy programmes, and the proliferation of national programmes which resulted, was the stimulation of research into the factors which were important to success in achieving literacy. The International Institute for Adult Literacy Methods has played the leading role in cataloguing and disseminating information about this ongoing research (Gorman, 1977; Versluys, 1977; Clason-Hook, 1977). UNESCO itself has produced an overall evaluation of their Ten-year programme which reviewed some research and evaluation (UNESCO/UNP, 1976). The International Council for Adult Education has, in cooperation with the International Development Research Centre, compiled a study of research findings from many national literacy programmes (Kidd *et al.,* in press).

Media usage and campaigns

The research and evaluation of the use of radio and television in various non-formal education settings has expanded quite rapidly in the past few years. There has been evaluation of the mass campaigns in Tanzania (Hall, 1978) and research and evaluation of similar campaigns in Botswana (Ministry of Local Government and Lands, 1977). In the UK studies are available on the effect of media in the literacy scheme. The use of television through satellites has been studied in depth in India (Dannheisser, 1975). General surveys on the use of radio in educational programmes in several commonwealth countries have been done by the specialists from the University of Manchester (see the work of M. Pilsworth and G. Weddell; also Legge 1976/77) and the International Extension College based in Cambridge, England, has studied a variety of experiences in Mauritius, Ghana, Botswana, Tanzania, and Lesotho and published broadsheets on its experiences.

Action Research

The term 'action research' has referred to several variations of activity. On one hand the term has been used by Bowers (UK) and Garforth and Warr working in Botswana. Their use suggests a concept based in Third World practice which in many ways represents the logical application of the concept of appropriate technology to the world of research and evaluation.

   Another quite different application has arisen primarily from work in Latin America and Europe and now being seen in the UK (Stringer, 1978; Holmes, 1976), Canada (Stinson, 1977) and elsewhere. This version is based on explicit political choice in which the researcher is aligned with working-class interests for structural transformation. Research is conducted with the people and is written up in a language and form which can feed directly into the ongoing struggle.

Participatory Research

The use of the term participatory research, first used in Tanzania (Hall, 1978), has spread in part through the efforts of the International Council for Adult Education which has established a network amongst persons working in the field. The term covers a variety of experiences in which those people who are experiencing a social situation identify, analyse, and act upon their problems. Examples of this approach can be found in many commonwealth nations including Tanzania, Kenya, Botswana, UK, Canada, Australia, and India (ICAE, undated).

The Trend Towards Democratization of Research

Perhaps it is best to begin with a quotation which illustrates one side of the situation:

> Here I stand, my name is Jowett
> There's no knowledge but I know it.
> I am the Master of this college
> And what I don't know isn't knowledge.
> (Attributed to Prof. B. Jowett, former Master of Balliol)

There are of course different trends which might have been identified. The trend towards democratization has been chosen for a more detailed look because of its particular importance to those whose primary concern is the means by which non-formal education can better serve the needs of the poor and exploited majority. It represents an important force for increasing the chance that research will serve those whom it is intended to serve. It should be noted that the identification of a trend does not imply that the majority of research reflects this tendency, but some positive tendencies are visible.

We are all too aware of the volumes of research in all fields, non-formal education included, which serve no purpose at all except the professional interests of the researchers. We are also aware of many cases when research is done by various institutions in order to take decisions for people who are not allowed to make decisions about their own lives. Our record as researchers is not a proud one. It is important that analysis and creativity in seeking solutions will be centred amongst those who need it most.

If research is more democratic, both in the way it is done and as regards the people with whom interaction occurs, it is likely that there will be better links between policy and practice, and between research and action. By having more involvement of those people who experience on a day-to-day basis the reality of the problem concerned, it is more likely that the research will reflect that reality. In addition much of what we know about the formation of knowledge suggests that it is only through the interaction of theory and practice that truth in the more general sense is discovered (Cornforth, 1955).

Evidence that Research is Becoming more Democratic

(1) *Shift in the Location of the Research from Metropolitan Countries to the Third World*

In terms of the volume of research, numbers of persons engaged in research, and funds expended on research, the balance is still tipped heavily towards the richer nations and the international agencies as regards the location where most research about non-formal education in Third World countries is initiated and carried out. There is, however, a quite general agreement that research really should be done by persons actually living and working in the countries where the education is taking place. The continuing delay in turning this task over completely is said often to be due to lack of appropriately trained local researchers. Through the institutional push of organizations like the Commonwealth Foundation and the Commonwealth Secretariat with their emphasis on 'TCDC' (Technical Cooperation amongst Developing Countries), the International Development Research Centre in Canada and SAREC (Swedish Research Agency in Developing Countries) in response to the political arguments in Third World countries, a growing emphasis has been placed on financial support to Third World researchers and research institutions.

(2) *Shift from Expatriate to Local Researchers*

Related to, but lagging somewhat farther behind, the question of the location of research, is the question of who actually does the work. The first stage in the democratization of research is to shift it to the place in question. The second stage is having someone from that country in control of the work. There is a general agreement and a visible tendency towards consolidating this second stage. More and more research in non-formal education is being done by the men and women in the country concerned.

(3) *Increased Involvement of Untrained Persons in Professional Roles*

The need for evaluation of results in the various literacy efforts associated with the UNESCO/UNDP literacy programme and the many national efforts which have developed at the same time have meant that many persons who did not have formal training in research or evaluation were recruited to work in research and evaluation units. In most cases it has been found that, after some experience, these untrained individuals have proven to be perfectly satisfactory. In some cases these persons have proven to be much better than their colleagues with formal qualifications, especially in terms of working with local people or explaining why a certain set of statistics have turned up.

Another way in which untrained individuals have gained experience and in a few places permanent status as researchers has been through the institution of the research assistant. It has been a common practice for years in most Third World countries for expatriate researchers to make use of local research assistants to do the actual interviewing, as the expatriates do not usually have the language necessary to actually talk with local people. As anyone will tell you who has worked either as a research assistant or with one, these people very often have a better idea about the research results than the formal researchers.

(4) *Increased Interest in Making Research Accessible to Local Decision-Makers*

While too few research results or studies have found their way into a form which allows them to be used easily by policy-makers, there are some efforts to do so. When one talks of accessibility it most often refers to the efforts to translate the reams of paper in a research report into the language and style of the upper level decision-maker — the senior civil servants in the various Ministries or busy administrators in the educational institutions.

This tendency most often takes the form of short one- or two-page summaries of longer reports, or the form of seminars or workshops where the results are shared with appropriate persons.

Another aspect of making research accessible which is not as common is increasing accessibility for the people whom research is most often written about... the exploited, the poor, the landless and underschooled.

(5) *Increased Involvement of the Poor and Exploited in the Research Process Itself*

The movements of participatory research and related approaches such as action research and militant research have emphasized the importance of involving those persons whom the research is intended to benefit in the research process itself, from the identification of the problem to the analysis and interpretation of the results.

Examples of this approach can be found in several of the non-formal education experiences including:

Botswana: evaluation of a cooperative weaving project.
Kenya: village socio-economic analysis as the basis for literacy
            programmes.
Tanzania: analysis of grain storage problems for construction of storage
            silos;
            evaluation of literacy programmes;
            analysis of music in strengthening and transforming culture.
Canada: analysis of water usage and disposal — community involvement
            and health issues in an isolated Indian community in Northern
            Ontario;
            development of curriculum for English teaching in the work-
            place;
            analysis of housing problems in a working-class residential
            neighbourhood.
England: evaluation of the effects of media in the English literacy
            campaign;
            analysis of learning needs in an urban working-class housing
            estate.
India: planning education for poor industrial workers in New Delhi;
            education of literacy programmes in Udaipur;
            development of women's clubs in Madras.

Practical Issues and Implications

The experiences which have taken place to date have allowed us to identify a
number of issues and implications of a practical nature. In some cases we have
suggested some approaches; in other cases we have pointed out continuing
difficulties.

(1) *Use of Language*

One improvement which should be reinforced is to make sure that, at the end
of any study, the materials are written up in a short and easy-to-read format
for the attention of those persons who should know about the results. This
takes a very short time to do and gives researchers practice in reading their own
studies. Another step is the organizing of a seminar or workshop with the same
persons where the results can be presented and the findings discussed. Some
ministries and institutions now require the fulfilment of these requirements as
part of the research contract.

  The question of communication of interim results to the people with whom
one works in a community in order to increase their participation in the

research process is still another challenge. Assuming that a written form is useful at all, it *is* possible to put results in a local language and a form which most people understand. It is useful to look at other forms of popular communications which are already being used as models. Photo novels, news-sheets, booklets, and brochures have all been used. A local committee can usually find an adequate way of getting the results into a usable form *if* they have been involved from the start.

(2) *Use of Alternative Research Methods*

Perhaps one of the most dramatic shifts in research is the realization that research methods need not be limited to the paper-and-pencil styles that are most common. The involvement of non-literate populations in analysis has led to the application of a wide variety of other methods for group or collective analysis. Some of the methods which are now being used include:

(a) drawings either drawn or interpreted collectively (or both);
(b) still photographs — used similarly to drawings as codifications for in-depth analysis;
(c) people's theatre — when the community itself analyses structural relation-ships and portrays them in dramatic form;
(d) song — collectively written or analysed;
(e) community meetings/dialogues;
(f) development of community self-portraits;
(g) video-tape recordings.

The focus on methodological aspects is growing rapidly. This does not of course invalidate methods which we have traditionally been using in research but it has both pushed us to re-examine our methods for collective analysis and opened up the possibility for using a large number of methods which previously would not have been considered possible.

(3) *Time Needed for Research*

While it is quite difficult to discuss this point in abstract, it is fair to say that, in general, a research process which is truly democratic will take longer than the quick one-off surveys which we are more used to. It takes time to organize meetings, to explain objectives to different groups, have discussions about interim findings, develop the analysis, and discuss subsequent action. The balance of time spent in the village, or with the people compared to time spent in an office, is altered very much. This has obvious implications for language, type of person hired to do the work, costs, and necessity of integrating the research process into other ongoing activities and actions. The counter-arguments, of course, are that an effective process is worth the time taken and that in the long run the time taken may even be less because the research process combines an educational and action phase.

(4) *Costs and Funding Patterns*

As noted above, increased time spent in a research process can have financial implications. It is true that while researchers and administrators are paid to go to meetings and carry out research, ordinary people are not. For villagers or other working people to take time out to attend meetings they must be highly motivated and quite certain that the efforts will bring some direct benefits. Some projects have begun to build in an amount of support for local participation, either directly or indirectly.

On the other hand there are possibilities of keeping costs in research down through a more democratic approach. If there are fewer professionally trained middle-class researchers involved, and more non-professionals involved, the savings can be quite appreciable. Further, if the research is incorporated into other local action programmes, the costs might be still more reduced.

(5) *Balance Between Grass Roots and Macro-Analysis*

While it is true that no-one intuitively understands the social reality of a rural village better than those who live there, there are nevertheless some facts about the control of life in those villages which are usually beyond the knowledge of those living there. If the cost of fertilizer is controlled by transnational corporations outside the village in some other country, then any analysis which involves fertilizer costs and usages will need to have some information about the ownership and price policies of the external producers and the relationship of the external producers to national or local suppliers.

The analysis of local problems must be linked to larger structural issues and the total analysis *shared* with those at the local level. In this way both the overall analysis is improved and the knowledge becomes a product which is jointly owned and produced.

(6) *Use of Class as an Analytic Tool*

Concepts of social class and the relationships of various classes to the dominant mode of production are central to the process of understanding the effects of various educational programmes and the place which varying programmes hold within the overall socio-economic structure. While this concept has not played a prominent role in non-formal education research to date, the concern which we have of the rights of the poor is making the political economic viewpoint more common. If democracy implies involving the classes which have been excluded then a class framework of analysis is useful.

More sophisticated and detailed work in the understanding of community class structures is needed. In an era when community participation is urged in every action and policy, we need to know more about the class structures within villages. We need to know more about the ways in which rich peasants maintain control and about ways to engage those in the village who are not as well off. How can non-formal education stimulate accumulation in the village? It is not enough to say simply that the community should participate in the research process. How is it possible to assure that the research process serves those who need it most?

(7) *The Blurring of the Distinction Between Research, Learning, and Action*

Participatory research, for example, is usually described as having three characteristics: it is at the same time an *approach* of social investigation, an *educational* process, and a means of taking *action*. This combination of characteristics has caused some difficulties in the academic world where reality has been divided into separate disciplines and fields of work.

When research involves a group of people in a common analysis and search for meaning it is the same thing as learning. This is not a problem in the workplace or the community where artificial separations have little meaning, but it does present some difficulties both for researchers and administrators who are trying to find where this kind of work fits into the official structure. In one case, valuable participatory research programmes have been put aside because the two administrative offices concerned could not figure out how to fund the work. The research agency said that what was being proposed was not research and so could not support the work. The educational agency said it was not education so that they could not support it either. To the people concerned it did not matter what it was called, but they still were delayed.

Conclusions

The role which research has played in the struggle for social justice has not been generally supportive. Research has more often been used to support decisions made by central authorities which were not in the interests of the majority. The process of research itself has been mystified and confused in such a way as to serve on the researchers themselves. As time has gone by the qualifications which enable persons to contribute to knowledge have risen higher and higher. More and more people have been excluded from naming their world.

The tendency towards more democratic forms of research and more democratic relationships of research to other forms of action is an important one for us to support. The belief that ordinary people have both an ability and a right to interpret their problems and be involved in solutions is a fundamental element in any development of non-formal education and the key to long-lasting solutions.

Human Inquiry
Edited by P. Reason and J. Rowan
© 1981 John Wiley & Sons Ltd.

CHAPTER THIRTY-NINE

Women's perspectives: research as re-vision

Helen Callaway
Queen Elizabeth House, Oxford, UK

> Re-vision — the act of looking back, of seeing with fresh eyes, of
> entering an old text from a new critical direction — is for us more
> than a chapter in cultural history: it is an act of survival. Until we
> can understand the assumptions in which we are drenched we
> cannot know ourselves. And this drive to self-knowledge, for
> woman, is more than a search for identity: it is part of her refusal
> of the self-destructiveness of the male-dominated society.
>
> (Adrienne Rich, 1972, p. 18)

In drawing my title from an essay by Adrienne Rich on the awakening
consciousness of women, I am taking up and continuing the poet's play on
meanings: 'revision' in the standard sense of correcting or completing the
record; then, 're-vision' as looking again, a deliberate critical act to see
through the stereotypes of our society as these are taken for granted in daily
life and deeply embedded in academic tradition; and, finally, 're-vision' in its
extended sense as the imaginative power of sighting possibilities and thus
helping to bring about what is not (or not *yet*) visible, a new ordering of
human relations.

My purpose in this chapter is to trace the development of research on
women and research by women in an attempt to show the values and projects
motivating this work and how it has led inevitably to new approaches in
methodology, theory construction, and modes of expression. Claims have
been made, and are still being made, that the women's movement holds the

most far-reaching implications for social change in our time. This is open to argument. What is clear, however, is that the research tasks women are identifying and carrying through mark a major 're-vision' of the past, of our present social constructions of the female spirit and body, and of the potentialities for creating more truly human 'life-worlds' in the future.

Women's Studies

During the past decade, research in many disciplines under the general label of 'women's studies' has proliferated on both sides of the Atlantic. Results are now coming forth in the expanded publishers' booklists on topics to do with women, the announcement by some publishers of a special series on women's studies (e.g. Tavistock, Croom Helm, Pergamon), and the establishment of new firms expressly for publications on women (Virago, Eden Press Women's Publications, etc.). Journals have appeared in sudden profusion, both of a multidisciplinary nature (including among others, *Signs, Women's Studies International Quarterly, Feminist Studies, Feminist Review*) and for special areas of interest (*Women and Literature, Women and Health, Psychology of Women Quarterly*, etc.)

This tremendous push in academic research grew out of the women's movement with its small non-hierarchical groups engaged in consciousness-raising and mutual support. The characteristic of collective enterprise still remains. It is evident in seminar groups of women formed to foster research in a particular discipline. As one example, our Oxford Women's Anthropology Seminar has been meeting regularly for over seven years now, with members presenting papers on field-work results and specific theoretical problems. It is evident also in interdisciplinary groups set up to sponsor wider efforts. Again on home grounds, the Oxford University Women's Studies Committee has been running a special lecture series each term and publishing these collections (S. Ardener, 1978; Burman, 1979; Jacobus, 1979). The Bristol Women's Studies Group has compiled and published an introduction to women's studies, *Half the Sky* (1979). The University of Kent at Canterbury now offers an M.A. in Women's Studies, the first such degree course in the United Kingdom. As a national and international link, the Women's Research and Resources Centre in London provides information services and keeps a research index for people investigating subjects of importance to women.

If cooperation in academia can be found among women involved in women's studies, there are also lively debates on many issues. As one example, the controversy continues on whether the economic class system emerging with the growth of capitalism formed the basis for the dominant-subordinate pattern of male-female relations or whether the physiological division represents the original model on which the other asymmetries are based.

Within any particular discipline, of course, female scholars are likely to represent as wide a spectrum of intellectual orientations as their male colleagues.

Even more relevant, women take quite different stands in relation to their research on women. Some use 'women's studies' and 'feminist research' as interchangeable terms. Others insist on a clear distinction. 'Women's studies' is then defined in its institutional sense as academic research and the establishment of multidisciplinary courses on what it means to be a woman in varied social and cultural contexts. This is contrasted with 'feminism' as the activist side, taking conscious political action to change women's position in society.

In summary: women researchers create collectives to work and support each other's work, to achieve within groups what we cannot do as individual women working in isolation. We build 'networks' with other similar groups for holding conferences and workshops, publishing newsletters in different subject areas, and so on. Yet at the same time we entertain diversities, contain oppositions, sometimes break apart. It is both this collective work and the expression of differences, together with discoveries of previously uninvestigated fields of data and new interpretations of familiar texts, which give research in women's studies its present vigour and reach.

The Priority of Female Experience

Dale Spender describes the new field of women's studies as it is now 'taking shape':

> Its multi-disciplinary nature challenges the arrangement of knowledge into academic disciplines; its methodology breaks down many of the traditional distinctions between theoretical and empirical and between objective and subjective. It is in the process of re-defining knowledge, knowledge gathering and making (Spender, 1978a, p. 1).

Elsewhere she articulates the emergence of a 'new paradigm', defined precisely as feminist:

> The feminist paradigm is not discipline based and as such cuts across psychology, sociology and religion (to name but a few) and integrates them within the framework of the personal experience of the female. ... Feminism involves a new way of classifying the world (Spender, 1978b, p. 259).

Such scholarship entails a strong critique of male-centred models of reality and the research which has validated traditional bodies of knowledge within the humanities and the social sciences.

In claiming the priority of female experience, women researchers are consciously attempting to shift the centre from which knowledge is generated. Linda Gordon writes:

> Social historians noticed that the factory operative was the characteristic working-class worker of the industrial period; not only did they omit female operatives, but they omitted female houseworkers — wives and domestic servants. The housewife is as much at the center of the industrial capitalist economy as the factory worker (L. Gordon, 1975, p. 563).

She makes the point: 'To put women at the center would be to turn the disciplines literally inside out.' This argument does not mean a focus exclusively on women. Rather, by looking at human experience from the point of view of women, we can understand male experience and the whole of cultural history with greater depth.

The explicit attempt to see the world from women's place in it ('re-vision') began as women started to question concepts and theories at variance with their own experience. Perhaps this has happened throughout history, but there is no cumulative record and the fragments must now be rediscovered. The next step came with the growing recognition that in much research in the social sciences women were absent altogether from the scene or 'appear as lay figures in the men's drama' (E. Ardener, 1975, p. 2). Jessie Bernard phrased it neatly in describing the development of sociology as 'a science of male society' (1973, p. 781). Her analysis goes further to locate male bias not only in the selection of data and its partial interpretations but at the deeper level, embedded in the structure of inquiry. The methodologies gaining most prestige have been those that yield 'hard' data, exhibiting what she calls the '*machismo* element in research'. Thus sociology is seen to be not only 'a science of *male* society' but also 'a *male* science of society' (Bernard, 1973, p. 784; my emphasis). These are the steps to be outlined here.

It is not surprising that before women could develop new directions evolving from female experience, we have had to take a critical stance against the dominant models of scholarship which place male at the centre and female as peripheral and which confer on males the powers to define and interpret not only themselves but females as well. This exercise, in its many phases, in its various disciplines, has turned out to be nothing less than a sustained critique of the traditions of Western culture — and beyond, of other cultures whose written texts and patterns of social action deny the autonomy of women.

Male Culture and the Obstacles to Female Autonomy

Two essays by Georg Simmel, published as long ago as 1911, are particularly instructive. Reviewing these, the sociologist Lewis A. Coser notes that had it not been for the recent women's movement these long-neglected essays would not have been recovered (Coser, 1977, p. 871).

Simmel argued that the male-dominated culture operates according to male standards and criteria and thus creates powerful obstacles for women in their attempt to gain an autonomous female identity. Civilization has been created on male terms which have then been generalized as human and considered to be objective. Although men and women may be equal on formal terms, in effect the rules of the game have been written by men and are thus rigged against women. Simmel stated:

> Man's *position of power* does not only assure his relative superiority over the woman, but it assures that his standards become generalized as generically human standards that are to govern the behavior of men and women alike (translation by Coser, 1977, p. 872; emphasis in the original).

Women are thus judged according to criteria created by men.

Simmel continued his analysis into the effects of the division of labour. Because the differentiation of labour forces men into a one-sided specialization of their faculties, they look to women to complement this with a different one-sidedness. Since women are enslaved by these requirements of the male, they are never allowed to act out their specific female qualities as determined by themselves.

In his commentary on these essays, Coser notes that Simmel's thought was rooted in Kantian moral philosophy, which holds that human beings are never to be treated as means to an end, but always as ends in themselves (Coser, 1977, p. 873). Simmel's argument thus leads to a significant insight: that in male culture it is the social and physiological destiny of women to be treated and valued as simple means, as means for the man, for the home, for the child. The problem becomes the more complex because women tend to evaluate themselves on these terms. Simmel's conclusion follows inevitably. The source of women's tragic fate is not the occasional brutality of men to women, but rather the denial by male culture of autonomous female identity.

And here we are reminded that nearly 70 years after the publication of Simmel's analysis, the popular media have taken up the same theme. In the film 'Kramer vs. Kramer', the leading female character, Mrs Kramer, states her reason for leaving the family household as the need to discover her own identity. She tells the court, hesitantly and with muted feelings, that she has always related to others, as daughter, as wife, as mother, but she did not know who she was on her own. The title of the film, the very name by which she argues her case, underlines her difficulty. In Simmel's terms, the structures of male culture had denied her autonomy. (She was, of course, awarded custody of the child, a feature which reveals the converse side of patriarchal culture, its inhibiting effects on the nurturing qualities of men.)

Without reference to Simmel's essays on this topic, another sociologist, Dorothy E. Smith, has written about 'women's exclusion from man's culture' (Smith, 1978). She argues that in the kind of society we have the work of administration, of management, of government is basically *communicative*. Organizational and political processes are *ideologically* structured forms of action — making use of images, vocabularies, concepts, abstract terms of knowledge. Further, the ways in which we think about ourselves and one another and about our society are given shape and disseminated by specialized people working in universities, in television, radio and newspapers, in advertising agencies, in book-publishing and other organizations making up the 'ideological apparatus' of the society. Her point is that women have been largely excluded from producing these forms of thought.

> It means that our experience has not been represented in the making of our culture. There is a *gap* between where we are and the means we have to express and act. It means that the concerns, interests, experiences forming 'our' culture are those of men in positions of dominance whose perspectives are built on the *silence* of women (and of others) (Smith, 1978, p. 282).

This recognition of the 'silence of women' in certain levels of discourse has come almost simultaneously in varied academic disciplines and has led to new directions in research. In Oxford anthropology, for example, the theory of 'dominant' and 'muted' groups (to be taken up later) has been examined in a number of different cultural contexts.

Feminist Critiques of 'Scientific' Models of the Female

Women began to question 'scientific' knowledge when they no longer accepted either the selection of empirical evidence ('data') or the internal coherence of a theory as the measures of objective validity, but instead matched theory against their own experience. Citing Simmel's essays, the psychoanalyst Karen Horney wrote in 1926:

> *Like all sciences and all valuations, the psychology of women has hitherto been considered only from the point of view of men.* It is

inevitable that the man's position of advantage should cause *objective validity* to be attributed to his subjective, affective relations to the woman, and according to Delius the psychology of women hitherto actually represents a deposit of the desires and disappointments of men (Horney, 1974, p. 7; my emphasis).

Horney added that a very important factor in the situation was that women have adapted themselves to the wishes of men and then feel as if this adaptation were their true nature. Because of women's unconscious compliance, and the extent to which our being, thinking, and doing conform to these masculine standards, the difficulty in shaking off these modes of thought becomes clear. Horney continues her analysis:

> Further, we observe that *men are evidently under a greater necessity to depreciate women than conversely.* The realization that the dogma of the inferiority of women had its origin in an unconscious male tendency would only dawn upon us after a doubt had arisen whether in fact this view were justified in reality (Horney, 1974, p. 12; my emphasis).

This essay represents a formidable critique of Freud's theory of the significance of penis envy in women, a topic apparently still attracting controversy in psychoanalytic circles. The point here has to do with the definitions of women created within the academic citadels of science and the apparent suppression of contrary views. Horney's essay remained buried for well over 40 years until the recent surge of interest brought it out for reprinting in a number of anthologies (Coser, 1977, p. 870). Why should this have been so? Not only was this particular article in opposition to the contemporary establishment of psychoanalytic thought, but Horney in subsequent years departed radically from Freud's emphasis on the biological determinants of the human psyche to a much greater consideration of social and cultural factors. She was disregarded by the dominant Freudian school, and through the process by which scientific knowledge filters through to wide audiences (textbooks, radio talks, mass-circulation journals, women's magazines), Freud's version of the natural inferiority of women and their unconscious envy of the male genital organ reinforced popular misogynist views (Friedan, 1963; J.B. Miller, 1974).

Gynaecological textbooks still echo Freudian views of women's sexuality based on man's experience of his body and his sexuality, and this is only one aspect of male bias generally pervading the medical literature that purports to delineate women's physiology in objective terms (Scully and Bart, 1973; Bristol Women's Studies Group, 1979, chap. 3). In recent years, much feminist research has been directed to the history of medicine and its changing definitions of the female body and psyche according to the economic and social frameworks of the time (Vicunus, 1973; Hartman and Banner, 1974; Callaway, 1978; Delamont and Duffin, 1978; Ehrenreich and English, 1979). A powerful indictment of a century of psychiatric theory and treatment of women is provided by Phyllis Chesler (1972) in her analysis of the straitjacket effects of gender stereotypes and how the social control of women leads to forms of deviance labelled and treated as 'madness'.

Women's research has thus gone beyond the 'women's liberation' problem to become threatening to traditional disciplines in more basic ways. 'Psychology constructs the female' is the theme of Naomi Weisstein's analysis (1970) of how conventional images of women become validated as scientific law. She and others (see review essays by Parlee, 1975, 1979; Vaughter, 1976) 'deconstruct' the texts that delimit female capacities by examining the characteristic male bias at the foundations of the discipline. In Helen Weinreich's words:

> It would seem that the women's movement in its broadest sense is a dangerous truth that cannot be ignored, not only because the issues it raises for psychology concern half the human race, but because so many aspects of it as a phenomenon challenge the basic assumptions of positivistic psychology (Weinreich, 1977, p. 540).

Starting then from different motivations, feminist research has undermined the positivist-empiricist tradition and moved towards a 'new paradigm' approach. Jean Baker Miller's *Toward a New Psychology of Women* (1976) might be considered the promising beginning of a new direction for understanding the psychological relations of women and men.

As a final example of (male) 'scientific' models of the female, and a particularly strong feminist response, the relatively new field of sociobiology or biosocial anthropology should not be left out. The authors of several presumably authoritative books in this field, Lionel Tiger and Robin Fox, write with typical panache:

> Women have to be in on the economy. But a basic element of the biogrammar here seems to be that they have to be in on only specially defined terms: there appears to be a tendency to define some work as female and some as male, and to maintain the distinction whatever the content and whatever the cost. This is the same principle of male-bond-female-exclusion that, in politics, so rudely circumscribed the female role. In economic matters, since females cannot be excluded totally, at least they can be segregated into some set of specific activities (Tiger and Fox, 1972, p. 144).

This particular quotation shows up what Hilary Callan (1978) considers to be a persistent tendency to confuse argument about the limits of what *is* with argument about the limits of what *can be* in living systems. She deftly analyses the levels of confusion — empirical, logical, and linguistic — that have contributed to the development of this neo-Darwinian biological determinism, whether stated in its 'strong' or 'weak' form. If the feminist critique has been particularly sharp against this biosocial approach, it has often been to deny the very possibility of a biological infrastructure to certain human relationships, thus setting the debate back to the familiar (and, at this stage, too simplistic) dichotomy of nature vs. nurture. Callan shifts the argument to more subtle and complex interrelations of the biological and the social. Her conclusion suggests a hermeneutic approach for research likely to yield new insights into the perplexing question of human sexual identity and destiny.

The 'Absence' of Women and the Process of Recovery

Another recognition of male bias came with the growing awareness of numerous areas of scholarship purporting to deal with human experience but in fact leaving women out almost totally. In 1974 I remember well the ironies so clearly apparent at the inaugural lecture in Oxford of the Harmsworth Professor of American History, C.N. Degler. He was duly ushered in with the full regalia and ceremonial of Oxford ancient academic procession, exclusively male on this occasion and preceded by the erect bronze mace (its symbolism evoking predictable comments), to give his address on the topic, 'Is there a history of women?' He noted how most of the histories of the world have been written by and about men — of wars, revolutions, diplomatic missions, the growth of nations. The histories of America (he continued) followed this pattern for the most part, relating the exploits and activities of men, as if women had played little part in the original colonial settlement or in the western movement. Providing some rather vivid illustrations from his own research, he concluded that there are indeed histories yet to be written: those bringing into the foreground the experience of women.

At that time, it seemed to many of us to be a question of addition, of extending the scope of historical work by filling in the 'absence' of women, compiling an added chapter, an appendix so to speak to the main work already done. But we soon learned that addition is only quantitative. Something different was required: a qualitative 're-vision', not only in history but in all the social sciences.

In her review of the remarkable amount of research now going on in women's history, Joan Kelly-Gadol (1976) makes the crucial point that when sex is recognized as a fundamental category for our understanding of the social order along with other classifications such as class and race, then the whole field requires a new analysis of the changing relation of the sexes through periods of historical change. As a test, she cites three periods of significant social transition usually considered as times of the advancement of civilization. In each of these cases — classical Athens, the Renaissance in Europe, and the French Revolution — a fairly regular pattern emerges of relative loss of status for women at precisely the time of this so-called progressive change.

> For women 'progress' in Athens meant concubinage and confine-
> ment of citizen wives in the gynecaeum. In Renaissance Europe it
> meant domestication of the bourgeois wife and the escalation of
> witchcraft persecution which crossed class lines. And the Revolution
> expressly excluded women from its liberty, equality, and 'fraternity'.
> Suddenly we see these ages with a new, double vision — and
> each eye sees a different picture (Kelly-Gadol, 1976, p. 811).

Her conclusion is that work in women's history has 'revitalized theory by shaking its conceptual foundations'.

Dominant and Muted Groups

In anthropology, there was no 'absence' of women at the surface detail of ethnographies, as Edwin Ardener has pointed out.

> At the level of 'observation' in fieldwork, the behaviour of women
> has, of course, like that of men, been exhaustively plotted: their
> marriages, their economic activity, their rites, and the rest (E.
> Ardener, 1975, p. 1).

He went on to say that it was at the second or 'meta' level of field work that the real imbalance has occurred, in effect 'a male world'. This has to do with indigenous world-views, the models of society, the explanatory systems that anthropologists seek from priests, other ritual specialists, elders, political figures. These informants, for a variety of reasons, are likely to be men. It is not that women do not 'utter or give tongue', but rather that anthropologists are more likely to be attuned to the public discourse of men, the language registers that are characteristically dominated and 'encoded' by males. Women in many societies are relatively 'inarticulate' at this level of discourse. Ardener went on to suggest that women's models of the world, the matters of particular concern to them (what many feminists are now calling 'the female culture') may find expression in forms other than direct expository speech, possibly through symbolic modes of art, myth, ritual, special speech registers, and so on. He adds that other groups in society may also be 'muted' in the sense that they do not form part of the dominant communication system. (In any particular society, these might include young men, children, old people, ethnic or racial minority groups, those of subordinate social classes or castes.)

These insights have been further developed in Shirley Ardener's writings:

> The implications are that a society may be dominated or over-determined by the model (or models) generated by one dominant group within the system. This dominant model may impede the free expression of alternative models of their world which subdominant groups may possess, and perhaps may even inhibit the very generation of such models. Groups dominated in this sense find it necessary to structure their world through the model (or models) of the dominant group, transforming their own models as best they can in terms of the received ones (S. Ardener, 1975, p. xii).

This theoretical approach, as she points out, offers a different and subtler way of looking at male-female interrelations from the usual approach of 'domination by men' or 'oppression of women', however appropriate this might be for any particular situation. The analysis of a 'muted' group requires sensitivity to an area that is often lacking in definition and seemingly vague, the expression in half-stated or symbolic terms of an alternative set of ideas women may have about the world and about themselves. The models of both the dominant and subdominant groups must be studied to discern the relations between them, since the models of the subdominant groups are not shaped in isolation but rather as a counterpart to the primary communications system in a society.

The distortion of women's speech to meet cultural demands is clearly illustrated in Caroline Humphrey's study (1978) of Mongolian nomadic groups (her material referring to the period before collectivization in the 1950s). Although a newly married couple had their own tent, the young bride was expected to do all the housework in the main tent of her parents-in-law. Not only was she required to rise first in the morning and go to bed last at night, and to be purposefully occupied during these hours, but she was subject to numerous strict regulations to do with her deportment and dress, in effect suppressing any evidence of her sexuality. The speech taboos were particularly complex and, in Humphrey's detailed analysis, represented the social control over a young wife who might otherwise divide the loyalty of her husband from his obligations to his father and brothers in the nomadic settlement. Her freedom for expression was allowed only after she herself became a mother-in-law, thus fully aligned to her husband's patrilineage through her sons.

The analysis of dominant and muted groups has been taken up in anthropological research (e.g. S. Ardener, 1975, 1978) and also by those engaged in social history (Delamont and Duffin, 1978) and in the analysis of language structure and use (e.g., Spender, 1980). This theory can also be seen to 'fit' with other research developed quite separately as, for example, the work of William Labov and others (Keddie, 1973) in exposing 'the myth of cultural deprivation'. Labov's work on the logic of non-standard English showed that American children of minority groups were not lacking in intellectual powers although they were labelled as 'deficient' because they were not expressing themselves in the accepted communication patterns of the dominant group.

The 'Machismo' Factor in Research

Sociology has followed traditions similar to other disciplines in its presentation of male experience and points of view taken to be general, male posing of questions and formulation of problems, male methodologies. The 'absence' of women has often been covered over in the assumption that there is a 'single society' of men and women, with male-centred generalizations made about all participants (Millman and Kanter, 1975, p. xiii). Yet men and women, even in the same physical location, may well inhabit different social worlds. Jessie Bernard writes about the 'realities' of marriage — the complex institutional web of law, religion, and custom — and how this is experienced in different ways by husbands and wives. 'Not only do men and women view a common world from different perspectives, they view different worlds as well' (Bernard, 1973, p. 782).

This development of sociology within a male universe — its methods, conceptual schemes, and theories — has resulted, in the view of Dorothy E. Smith (1974), in a certain framework of issues under such categories as industrial sociology, political sociology, social stratification, and so on. She sees this as a perspective from the top down, which takes the procedures of governing as those which order its subject-matter. Issues are not identified as they become significant in the experience of those who live them, but rather as they become relevant to administrators. Thus, mental illness, crimes, violence, work satisfaction, motivation, etc. — are all taken up within the constructs of the practice of government. She argues that those who learn sociology learn to discard the world as they experience it and substitute a way of thinking which is recognized as sociological, based on the conceptual order of government bureaucracies.

In summary, and this hardly does justice to the details and richness of her essay, Smith proposes a radical re-organization of sociology based on women's perspectives. This involves placing the sociologist where she is actually situated and making her direct experience of the everyday world the primary ground of her knowledge. This alternative sociology would aim at gaining knowledge of the social organization of the properties and events of the directly experienced world. 'The only way of knowing a socially constructed world is knowing it from within' (Smith, 1974, p. 11).

In her discussion of the sexist bias in the structure of inquiry (which I have referred to earlier), Bernard finds useful the classification proposed by David Bakan (1972) and developed by Rae Carlson (1972), the contrast between 'agency' and 'communion'.

> Agency tends to see variables, communion to see human beings. ... Agency has to do with separation, repression, conquest, and contract; communion with fusion, expression, acceptance, non-contractual cooperation. Agency operates by way of mastery and control; communion with naturalistic observation, sensitivity to qualitative patterning, and greater personal participation by the investigator (Carlson, 1972). Nothing in this polarity is fundamentally new. For almost 50 years I have watched one or another version of it in sociology (for example, statistical vs. case method, quantitative vs. qualitative, knowledge vs. understanding or *verstehen* ...) (Bernard, 1973, pp. 784-5).

What Bernard does find new and illuminating, however, is the recognition of what she calls a *'machismo'* factor in research. The specific processes involved in agentic research are identified as typically male preoccupations:

> agency is identified with a masculine principle, the Protestant ethic, a Faustian pursuit of knowledge — as with all forces toward mastery, separation, and ego enhancement (Carlson, 1972). The scientist using this approach creates his own controlled reality. He can manipulate it. He is master. He has power. He can add or subtract or combine variables. He can play with a simulated reality like an Olympian god. He can remain at a distance, safely invisible behind his shield, uninvolved. The communal approach is much humbler. It disavows control, for control spoils the results. Its value rests precisely on the absence of controls (Bernard, 1973, p. 785).

She goes on to say that until recently the 'agentic' approach has been the only one given the status of being scientific. Many women scholars (and, of course, men as well) argue that research characterized by the 'agentic', quantitative approach fails to register the most important features of the social world (e.g. Millman and Kanter, 1975, p. x). If women researchers primarily support and associate themselves with the 'communion' approach, they are arriving by a different route, as it were, to some of the basic tenets of 'new paradigm' research.

Work in Progress

Women's research in its first phase represented mainly an attack on the 'absence' of women and other forms of male bias in traditional scholarship. This was 'content-oriented' and many female researchers followed the conventional methodologies and intellectual frameworks of their disciplines, often considering this to be a necessary strategy to gain entry into and promotion within the academic world. Gradually, the engagement with problems of research itself exposed the inadequacies of accepted methodology and theory construction. As noted by so many writers across the range of disciplines in my brief survey, women's research led to the questioning of conceptual foundations, even to splitting these apart.

The principle of the priority of female experience pointed to its corollary: *ourselves as our own sources.* What does it mean to be female? We examined ourselves, our persons, not as isolated beings, but as social creations related to others within a world of socially constituted meanings and powers. Judith Okely, for example, probed the memories of her schooldays to show how 'the girls' school may be, invisibly, a preparation for dependence, while the boys' school is more visibly a preparation for independence and power' (Okely, 1978, p. 109). Her systematic analysis of her own experience provides a far more vivid (and, arguably, more 'valid') study of the structures of coercion and their manifestations in every detail of school life than, say, a questionnaire survey of girls' boarding schools. Similarly, Hilary Callan (1975) found her starting-point in her own situation within the category of 'diplomats' wives'. Personal insights illuminate her discussion of 'the premiss of dedication' which hides the deeper elements of ambiguity, paradox, and stress in the wives' situation as 'representatives' abroad. While 'participant observation' has always been a central method of anthropology, it is only fairly recently that problems of 'studying one's own people' has been confronted. Women's research makes explicit the risk of subjective involvement in the bid to gain new theoretical understanding.

The study of 'ourselves' has led inevitably to exploration of the lives of our mothers and grandmothers. The search for the hidden history of women has extended in many directions, with biographies of outstanding female figures and also of unknown women, with collections of life stories (e.g. McCrindle and Rowbotham, 1979) and with reprints of neglected historical documents such as *Maternity: Letters from Working Women* (Davies, 1978). Published first in 1915, this volume of letters tells about childbirth and abortion and death, about exhaustion and poverty and patience in working-class life at the early part of this century.

Some women scholars, particularly sociologists retaining a positivist bent, are critical of what they call the 'excessive' use of personal experience, considering this to limit women's studies to the 'anecdotal' and 'descriptive' and thus assign it to the second-rate. Along with others, I would refute this, on much the lines of 'new paradigm' ideas: that techniques of qualitative analysis have been refined to distance the writer from her material, to 'objectify' the subjective. (This process is set out elsewhere in this volume in John Rowan's analysis of a dialectical paradigm for research.) Their argument might well be set on its head: if this is the 'age of experience' in research, as some social scientists have suggested, then perhaps it is the work in women's studies which has helped to create this new emphasis and to legitimate it.

I have left until the end the question of language, at once the most problematic and pervasive, since it encodes and expresses all other dimensions of our understanding. The academic frameworks of our disciplines, the categories of our research, the distinctions and nuances even, have evolved within a male tradition of language and intellectual style. As has been pointed out so often in recent years, much of this language shows both overt and subtle forms of sexism (e.g. Miller and Swift, 1979; Spender, 1980). How then do we find the authentic forms of expression for female consciousness and experience? We are concerned not only with the discoveries and results of our research inquiry, but with the linguistic modes which shape our investigation. In the social sciences we have hardly started to think about this perplexing problem, and we must draw what we can from women writers, literary critics, linguists (e.g. Burke, 1978; Kramer *et al.,* 1978; Jacobus, 1979).

Our work is only beginning. We look ahead, anticipate, imagine. Re-vision continues.

Human Inquiry
Edited by P. Reason and J. Rowan
© 1981 John Wiley & Sons Ltd.

CHAPTER FORTY

Funding research: practice and politics

Stephen Fineman
*Centre for the Study of Organizational Change and
Development, University of Bath, UK*

Previous chapters indicate a range of challenging theories and speculations on alternative research strategies. Yet is is probably fair to say that the amount of energy devoted to actually doing research which is radically different from the traditional mainstream of activities is considerably less than the new paradigmists would desire. Maybe there is a security and cosiness in keeping close to the bosom of the established social science professions, while perhaps quietly harbouring one's doubts. Or for some, trading upon acquired idiosyncratic credits to point out how the Emperor's new clothes are perhaps a bit of a confidence trick, and *someone* ought to do something about it.

Nevertheless, for the brave (or foolhardy) researcher who does wish to *do* something, it frequently means seeking finance to make the research possible. At minimum this may concern some travelling and clerical expenses; at maximum it could include the salary of research officers or assistants. The researcher must then display his or her beliefs for a sponsor to view, dissect, and pronounce upon. This is likely to be an uncomfortable process for any researcher, but what if the declared epistemology does not meet usual expectations? What if the research is not clearly related to a single discipline, not 'neat', nicely controlled with deduced hypotheses? The purpose of this chapter is to illustrate what has indeed happened to some such applicants, and to speculate on the implications of these experiences for research funding.

473

The Research Funding Scene

In the United Kingdom the majority of funds for academic research are dispensed by Government-financed research councils. Their names echo around the university corridors, and it is believed by many academics that it is a 'good thing' to be awarded a grant by them. The application procedure is well documented in their comprehensive rational handbooks. Other major sources of sponsorship are charitable foundations which vary considerably in the amount of funds available for research. They often claim specialist interest areas, and tend to be idiosyncratic in their application procedure. Together, these bodies comprise a powerful research funding oligopoly. Competition for their attention is fierce, and most will take up references on an applicant. Proposals will usually be submitted to an independent body of experts for professional judgement on the worthiness of the intended effort.

Beyond these institutions there are Government departments and public institutions who will commission research by outside bodies, and some of these departments can be directly approached on this basis. Finally, there is some research work sponsored specifically from private industry.

Some Encounters and Experiences

Let us illustrate some of the fortunes of grant application through brief accounts of individual experiences. Each of the following short tales are drawn from discussions with researchers, all of whom made approaches to sponsors for funds to support unusual, non-traditional social research.

Encounter 1

The research represented an unorthodox blend of intervention and pure organizational research. An organization was keen to participate in the research, viewing it as very relevant to their needs. The theoretical features of the research were, nevertheless, crucial for the applicant and this was stressed in his application to the research council. Much of the intended involvement was at the idiographic and small-group level, data deriving from negotiated interventions. The applicant was well experienced in his field and had also published in more conventional applied research areas. The events in the application moved as follows:

(1) An officer of the council provided a rather hurried (he was 'a bit pressed') set of preliminary comments on a draft proposal. He suggested some text

alterations and points where emphasis should be added. Otherwise there were no special problems.

(2) Much work was spent on finalizing the application. All apparently relevant issues were thoroughly argued and referenced. Colleagues' comments were solicited and used for amending and clarifying where necessary. Supportive published and unpublished documents were added to the application.

(3) Half-way through the three-month wait for a decision, a phone call was received from one of the referees — he was known to the applicant and was perceived as a friendly supporter. Nevertheless, the referee had decided, in his wisdom, to return the application to the sponsor without comments because of the mutual association. The applicant felt gloomy — who *didn't* he know in his specific research field?

(4) After three months, the decision was made. A curt, thirteen-line letter of rejection saying '... of doubtful practical value...', '... too few major variables...', and (paradoxically) '...too big in scope...', '...lacks detail...', but '...do keep trying in this area'. The applicant felt demoralized. Was this *his* application they were referring to? Is this all one gets for all that effort — just unqualified destructive criticism?

Encounter 2

The applicant was keen to extend his already established theory and technology in action research activities into intergroup processes. The theoretical base was eclectic, and heuristically rich in ideas and application. A research council was approached:

(1) Despite plenty of advanced warning to the council's relevant officer, the initial vetting was rushed (like the previous encounter) but nevertheless encouraging in outcome.

(2) After modifications based on the feedback, the final draft was sent off. It was carefully worded to indicate the professional orientation to which it best fitted.

(3) After two months had passed, information was received that a referee required further substantial details for clarification purposes. One week was allowed for the submission of the pre-publication draft of the applicant's book, approximately six hundred pages of computer programme, plus sample data outputs. Frenetic activity resulted in meeting the requests and the applicant felt slightly hopeful — surely requesting *such* detail *must* be an expression of interest? But he also learned that the judging committee was *not* of the professional interest to which the study was aimed — a bad omen?

(4) Three months passed and the disastrous refusal was announced in a one-and-a-half page letter: 'When will your developments be tested?' (But this was explained in the action research model)... 'What is your conceptual framework?' (But detailed summaries were given, and any more would have taken a book to explain).

The applicant felt empty and absolutely put down. He was given no crumb of comfort or encouragement. He also felt unfairly dealt with as many of the criticisms seemed professionally inappropriate to his activities.

Encounter 3

Sometimes an application to a research council can have a very short life if it moves dramatically out of line within the established thinking. One researcher had spent several years in developing his ideas about interpersonal research. He had presented his work in seminars and working papers and felt ready to apply his ideas in a field setting. Many of his colleagues saw his work as an exciting development in an alternative theoretical and methodological perspective. The research council did not share this enthusiasm. Their brief response to his draft proposal was: 'This research is based upon a radical epistemological orientation. As such, we do not think that the committee will view it favourably.' This left the applicant in little doubt as to his perceived worth in the eyes of the research funding establishment.

While applications to the research councils may prove disappointing to hopeful researchers, there does seem to be some pattern to the application *procedure* which provides a little security during the lonely journey. Encounters with other funding agencies can be less predictable in procedure, and certainly no more encouraging in outcome. The following three examples will illustrate.

Encounter 4

An approach was made to a foundation which claimed to sponsor clinically relevant social research in organizations, a brief which seemed to fit precisely with the needs of the researcher. They welcomed the researcher's inquiry, and had even claimed to have heard of his work. They said that any proposal would need to be approved by their subcommittee of experts, and the researcher would be well advised to contact a particular member of this committee to seek his specialist advice.

This he did and was delighted to find that he personally knew this individual. Together they framed a proposal for the foundation — all seemed ideal.

One month passed with no acknowledgement from the foundation. The applicant phoned them and was informed that the proposal was being very favourably received, and it was about to be put to their main committee. They would keep in touch. They did not. Another call one month later determined that they were still awaiting the decision from their subcommittee of experts; but not to worry, they would soon be able to give their verdict.

The applicant was becoming less surprised that, after another two months, he had received no word from the foundation. In frustration he eventually managed to speak to the chairman of the vetting subcommittee (a medical doctor). He was informed that the subcommittee was split on the merit of the work. Apparently most of the issues thought to be important by the original member who helped the applicant were seen rather differently by the chairman and some of his other colleagues. The applicant was asked to write a supplement to the proposal to answer the queries arising, for example: 'Isn't the study a bit subjective?'; 'It's rather a specific sample, isn't it? Do you think the research design is *tight* enough?'. This supplement was duly completed and sent off. There was no acknowledgement of receipt.

After a total of six months there was still no word of a decision. As a final, weary attempt to galvanize the foundation into some form of direct action, the researcher wrote a long personal letter to the chairman of the foundation. Eventually a reply was received stating that the application had 'indeed got bogged down', and he would see what he could do. Finally, a letter was received from the foundation with their decision. They *still* had not received their subcommittee's recommendations, but in the meantime funds had been withdrawn for this kind of research! By this time the applicant was fairly exhausted, rather cynical about the whole matter, and lamented the waste of time and energy.

Encounter 5

A general inquiry for possible research funds was made to the central office of a Government department which specialized in sponsoring and devleoping training activities. Part of the applicant's research orientation was already being developed within such an applied context, so he saw them as a very appropriate potential sponsor. Furthermore, they seemed to be a body who might be less concerned with the orthodoxy of his research if it provided useful outcomes for them.

They claimed to like his research area, but would need to see that the research fitted in with the needs of one of their regional offices. If a region would *request* the research, this would then be a satisfactory base from which they could act.

Fortuitously, the researcher's existing activities were already regionally based (but unsponsored) so it was not difficult to contact the local area agent to formulate a mutually relevant proposal.

Four months passed. During this period, the application had been sent from the area agent, to a regional manager, who in turn had sent it to the officer originally contacted at the centre. This officer then returned the proposal to the regional manager saying that he was not too happy about the research design. This stimulated the regional manager to contact the applicant directly to discuss the proposal. Out of this emerged a new, but still mutually relevant, research design which was again put to the man at central office.

Several more months passed before the applicant was informed of a decision. The content of the letter stated that no-one in the central office was now interested in his research and that anyway, they had now decided that all research would be determined from the centre. The organizational wheel had creaked around twice in a period of about 12 months, leaving the applicant no further on than when he started.

Encounter 6

Our final example is another approach to a Government department — which reinforces some of the Kafkaesque atmosphere of bureaucracy suggested in the previous account.

The department specialized in issues of physical and psychological health and were known to sponsor research in the applicant's area of interest. A telephone call to a senior member of the department reinforced this belief, and he encouraged the researcher to write a brief proposal for him to consider.

After some weeks, a colleague of this person (who we shall call Dr Smith), wrote to the applicant suggesting a meeting to discuss the project. On arrival at a Victorian warren of Government offices, there was some initial flurry of concern about the whereabouts of Dr Smith, as his office was not readily traceable in the mammoth internal directory. Eventually, his second-in-charge was traced, and the researcher and he exchanged politenesses for 40 minutes, awaiting the arrival of a delayed Dr Smith. He arrived rather harrassed, and in the remaining 20 minutes of the meeting the applicant learned that he knew virtually nothing about the reason for the encounter, seemed not to have read the summary proposal which he had received, and was not too keen on research which would actually offer help of any therapeutic kind to a client. Nevertheless, he would still welcome a specific proposal for consideration and would be happy to discuss any preliminary ideas.

A letter of thanks was sent to Dr Smith soon after the meeting, shortly followed by a draft research proposal inviting his comments. No acknowledgement was received and nothing more has been heard up to the time of this account, seven months later.

Some Implications for Research and Researchers

Undoubtedly, some of the above experiences bear similarities to many researchers' attempts to gain sponsorship, for the development of ideas which they hold dear. Yet it is noteworthy in the present context that they all represent presentations of *less* conventional research to a potential sponsor and as such accrue a particular status of their own. Furthermore, they all illustrate various personal facets — costs, concerns, frustrations — of tangling with a sponsor, features which are rarely mentioned in any published formal application procedure. Let us look at each of these areas in a little more detail.

Pluralism and Politics in Research

It is no new revelation that there exists a diversity of interests between, and within, groups of researchers and sponsors (e.g. see Sjoberg, 1967; Kelman, 1968; Barnes, 1979). Yet it appears that proposing alternative, less orthodox research serves to sharpen such differences. While some writers laudably argue that scientists should present themselves as insatiably curious, and unable to define in advance the areas of knowledge which will be irrelevant to their particular inquiry (Barnes, 1979, p. 77), such statements in practice may *decrease* a researcher's chances of obtaining funds. Indeed, in many respects, open expressions of ambiguity, curiosity, and bald intellectual honesty are often quite contrary to the requirements of sponsors. For example, research councils and foundations will usually ask for *specific* aims of the research, for *specific* details of how the data are to be collected, and the nature and form of the expected results. This last aspect is perhaps most offensive to the open-minded, curious researcher. The spectre of the physical research paradigm looms pressing the researcher to distill, trim and sharpen his inquiry. The forces of conservative traditionalism add their influence to steer the researcher away from controversy towards 'safer', well-trodden routes.

The trend outline is not inconsistent with the likely values of many of the referees and vetting committees who act for the sponsoring organizations. These people themselves will probably be schooled in the more traditional forms of social inquiry, having developed a strong penchant for the nomothetic, 'the objective' and a reification of the statistically significant trend. So it is unlikely that, for example, qualitative, action-oriented, experientially related research would be viewed too sympathetically. Certainly, one finds that many of the traditional stalwarts of academia have themselves found their way on to the vetting panels and committees, and would naturally wish to defend and perpetuate research which they believe to understand well, and with which they feel most comfortable.

These political features of research funding no doubt contribute to the type of activities that researchers can, or will, undertake. It is not surprising, then, that many researchers will continue the old, well-tried genuflections, so increasing the tightness of the existing professional boundaries. The researcher who wishes to undertake activities which fall outside of such boundaries risks losing the support of his old home, and he may even become branded as a *persona non grata* in that establishment. It becomes exceedingly difficult, if not impossible, to present a research proposal which is epistemologically and methodologically so different from classical social inquiry, in a way which fits establishment values. For many researchers of the type reflected in some of our cases, their plight extends beyond simple measures of expedience. To totally reformulate a research proposal to try and make it more acceptable can destroy the very essence and spirit of that venture, as well as threaten the identity of the researcher. There is, of course, a more Machiavellian resolution. The researcher might submit a proposal which he has no intention of carrying out in its stated form. In the short term, the ends might justify the means, but in the long term, it is unlikely that he will be able to repeat the exercise — at least not with the same sponsor!

The Personal Experience of Research Application

While we may speculate on the political and organizational features which characterize fund applications and sponsorship, there are strong messages embedded within our case examples concerning the personal effects of involvement in a grant application.

A striking aspect of the process is that it is mainly one way. The implied logic appears to be a bald reflection of the ideology of market forces — if the product is sufficiently scarce, then the producer can call the tune. Consequently, dialogue between the researcher and the sponsor is strictly limited to terms dictated by that sponsor. For example, some sponsors will offer informal comments on draft proposals, but also point out that this is but a guiding service which puts them under no specific obligation. Fair enough, but when the researcher is anxiously seeking some indications of whether or not the proposal is along acceptable lines, *any* comments of this sort are likely to be taken very seriously. Yet in practice the views of the officer who makes such judgements seem to be a capricious indicator of final success in gaining funds. If he or she knows the relevant committees and referees well, and can make an accurate decision on the professional orientation of an application, then the advice received can be most useful. But if this officer is naive in these respects, then the feedback can be unhelpful, if not positively misleading.

In the process of considering applications, some agencies are highly structured and will inform the applicant exactly when and how a decision will be made. In others, applications can disappear into an apparent vacuum — there may be no acknowledgement of receipt, no indication of how any vetting procedure will be carried out, and no information on when a decision can finally be made. The applicant may then be pushed into a position of literally having to beg for information. Any waiting period can be an anxious one for a committed researcher; a period totally void of feedback can be exceedingly unsettling.

It is ironic that sponsors whose official banners proclaim a concern for social or individual amelioration often fail dismally to demonstrate understanding towards, or empathy with, their research customers' needs and concerns. For example, we find that much new paradigm research involves activity in natural, ongoing organizational settings, addressing particular problems or issues of members of that setting. To gain research access and credibility for such work is usually a delicate and lengthy process, and often requires a fair degree of skill and sensitivity on behalf of the researcher. In such circumstances the research relationship has usually, in effect, begun, and it is particularly difficult for the researcher to suddenly 'stop the music' while waiting some indefinite period for an independent research sponsor to make up its mind.

At the same time many independent sponsors will ask for evidence of an already established research site as an indication of the applicant's worthiness, but then simply to treat such evidence as if it were a mere incidental organizational issue. Maybe this is an appropriate response if the research population is a captive group of undergraduate psychology students attending a laboratory experiment — but it is exceedingly misplaced when the research involves managers, shop stewards, social workers or production workers in their own job settings.

The Rejection

Probably the most invidious and potentially injurious part of the research application procedure is in the handling of rejections. To give the researcher a short, summary and unconstructive refusal after putting that person through the hoops of proposal writing and re-writing, anonymous vetting, providing any required supplementary information, and then a lengthy wait, appears to be very wrong. This judgement is based on principles concerning the spirit of social research, and on the personal consequences to the researcher. Let us elaborate.

If research is to be a developmental process deriving from shared ideas and explorations, then no one researcher's beliefs and formal conceptualizations should be summarily dismissed without a detailed argument from the dismisser, *and* an opportunity for creative dialogue. Indeed, this is a feature of many thriving research communities, of lively academic journals, and of vigorous teaching settings. Each permits open exchanges of ideas and provides fertile ground for new developments. As the major research councils and foundations are so critical and powerful in the whole endeavour of research, then it seems not unreasonable to expect them to reflect this essence of reciprocity. Such an ideal is far removed from the experiences of many researchers who have failed to gain funds. Often, their feelings are that the rules of the game are that of 'blemish the applicant' rather than a dialogue on genuine research concerns. Could it be that whatever the *actual* reasons for rejection, it will nearly always be expressed in terms of the intrinsic unworthiness of the research? Some kinder sponsors are exceptions to this, and will point out how the applicant has failed because all of the worthy demands could not be satisfied. But again, the curious researcher is left frustrated as he would like to learn more of the sponsor's views in a way which will positively help him in his research and future applications.

The researcher can be profoundly personally affected by his rejections from research funding bodies. As is apparent from the cases, the process of application can try the patience and confidence of the keenest of researchers. A curt refusal may result in reflections of self-doubt and strong feelings of powelessness and inadequacy against faceless arbiters of one's fate. Is the research *really* worth anything at all? Such views can be infectious amongst colleagues who are also seeking research funds and may result in cynicism and perhaps nihilism. It may encourage some people to be far more instrumental in their research — to do research which is fundable, rather than research that they really want to do. Others might find ways of not doing *any* research at all. They may observe that the scrabble for funds is a generally unrewarding process, the chances of success being small, and even smaller if one's interest is in non-traditional ventures.

Some Hopes for the Future

There are many rays of light in new paradigm research, and this book illustrates that an unfavourable funding climate need not stifle actual work in the area. Nevertheless, this chapter does indicate that obtaining funds is no easy process. So what can be done?

At one level, we may naively hope for changes in the philosophy and practice of the key research-sponsoring organizations. Changes which lead to some open dialogue of the kind previously discussed may begin to soften the criteria and boundaries on which research applications are judged. Such moves might occur slowly as the balance of power and representation on various vetting committees shifts away from traditional entrenchment. This is likely to be a very slow, incremental process. Some positive change may emerge following sufficient publicity concerning the negative effects of the sponsors' practices — but this is a two-edged source of influence. Many sponsors will undoubtedly react defensively to such criticisms, and the shutters of 'administrative convenience' can be slammed down speedily. It is, perhaps, particularly difficult for them to admit that their current research funding policies and practice may actually be doing a disservice to the researcher and research endeavour. It could be that if there is to be a shake-up in the Governmental departments which control research funds, it is the responsible ministers who must act. Indeed, it is noteworthy that just such a move has recently occurred with the relatively disproportionate cut in the budget for social science research — an apparent reflection of Government dissatisfaction with the work being done in this area.

Without ready access to the major research sponsors it behoves the new paradigmist to seek elsewhere for his support. One small, but significant crumb of comfort here, is that there is no intrinsic reason for supposing that good social science research requires massive financing. For example, a university lecturer could, by himself, conduct an intensive, particularistic, small sample field study of theoretical and practical import, with a small supporting budget. Indeed, the overall payoff of such an activity may far exceed that of a heavily funded research team working in the traditional, large N, gross variable genre. Apart from the management problems which can attend such projects (e.g. Hyder and Sims, 1978), there is the now well-documented danger that the results are often in terms of broad generalizations which can prove singularly unhelpful to practitioners and obstinately refuse to replicate as good lawful relationship should (Herbst, 1970; Harré, 1978).

It may be that the funds to assist in the type of project that we have envisaged can be obtained directly from the organization in which the study is being carried out — especially if there is a strong practical payoff to the research. But this must be set against a research shyness, or even research neurosis, expressed in many organizations. They will typically recall the numerous researchers who have 'used' them as 'convenient research sites and subjects'. They will sigh at the questionnaires they have had to fill in with 'stupid, irrelevant questions' on them. And they will despair at the trite reports that they have received, and have never felt able to implement. It is understandable, therefore, if such an institution should resist financing, let alone participating in, social research.

Some universities have small sums of money allocated for research purposes. However, this is usually a pittance compared with the actual total need for research funds. It is indeed curious that a university lecturer is recruited to teach and do research, but it is only his teaching that is well resourced. At the same time, his career progress normally reflects his research output, not his teaching excellence. Should not such a research emphasis be better supported *within* the university system? Should not a university lecturer feel confident that, whatever his status or position, some funds will always be definitely available to enable him to do research? Should he have to spend possibly an inordinate amount of his potential research and teaching time in often futile searches for funds?

To meet these difficulties we might move to a position where Government research funds are decentralized, and are incorporated directly into the main budgets of the academic institution. There is already an administrative framework within university departments which can be used to decide on how they will spend their allocation of such money, thus there would be considerable saving alone resulting from the dismantling of the present research councils. But, more importantly, our new structure gives each academic department direct control over the funds which reflect their own areas of interest, so providing a much fairer representation of research of different orientations and epistemologies.

Human Inquiry
Edited by P. Reason and J. Rowan
© 1981 John Wiley & Sons Ltd.

Afterword

Editing this volume has been full of learnings for us. While we were fairly clear about our position when we started, the work of editing and thinking, discussing and criticizing, has greatly increased our clarity and under-standing: and discovering more and more people who share the 'new paradigm' perspective has been an exciting experience for us. Editing the book has also changed us: we have moved several steps towards a more radical view of inquiry. We obviously hope that reading the book will have a similar impact — clarifying, exciting, and radicalizing — on our readers. But while we may have become more radical, we would like to be seen as non-conformists rather than as deviants, accepting the traditional goals and purposes of inquiry while pointing to a very different way of pursuing them. So what directions do *we* see for new paradigm research?

The first thing is of course to get on with it. Our view is that much of the groundwork of defining a philosophical position and inventing broad methodologies to go with this has been accomplished, at least for the moment. We now need these to be creatively applied to research problems, so that they are used, stretched, amended, and developed in practice. We are at the stage of needing to know more about *how* to do new paradigm research, so we can amend our ideas in the light of our experience.

Our own plans for work are in this direction. John Rowan is hoping to start work on a collaborative project to explore stress in a contracting organization, and also to develop his inquiry into psychic celibacy in men. Peter Reason is planning a collaborative experiential inquiry into co-counselling, and is beginning to develop some longer-term ideas to explore the experience of interpersonal relationship. We are also engaged collaboratively with colleagues and with students, as encouragers, as guides, and as critics. And in the longer term we would like to edit another book which contains more, and more detailed and more critical, accounts of new paradigm research.

For the field to progress, we need more than this: we need to establish some degree of legitimacy and credibility for this way of inquiry, and we need to establish some political support. Hopefully, the publication of this volume will lend some legitimacy to new paradigm research activities. Beyond this, we need to build on the links between researchers which we have already, establish new ones, and actively push for the acceptability of the ideas put forward here. There is the beginnings of a useful network in the group of people who collaborated to produce this volume, and there are already other networks like the participatory research group associated with the International Council for Adult Education in Toronto. All these need to be developed.

On a smaller scale, people actually doing new paradigm research need supportive help. People doing research, in any mode, get very much caught up with it and affected by it. In the traditional research mode, this is supposed to be an intellectual matter only (although we know this is not true, and that all researchers get affected emotionally and in their bodies, as well as in their pure intellects). But in new paradigm research, it is explicitly recognized that the people involved are very much whole people, with bodies, feelings, intellects, and spiritual aspirations. And it is also recognized that when difficulties arise in research, people can suffer deep pain, or experience intense joy. As one of our graduate students said, 'I have never been so completely involved in anything before; I feel I am using all of me'.

As soon as we recognize this, it becomes obvious that research is not a solitary activity. In traditional research the only recognition of this is the 'Acknowledgements' section of books, where the lone researcher thanks his wife for putting up with his bad moods and impossible demands. But many researchers — particularly if they are women — don't have wives to perform this service of being a sponge to mop up their emotional messes. In any case, it seems oppressive to expect people to perform in this one-sided way.

So we strongly advocate that all new paradigm researchers should build for themselves a support group of some kind. This could be a team actually involved in some project together; it could be a University seminar (so long as the group was prepared to act on levels other than the usual intellectual one); it could be a special-interest group of some kind; or it could be a new paradigm research group, specifically devoted to this approach.

In practice, we have found the latter very useful. The New Paradigm Research Group was formed in London in 1977, and has met on a fortnightly basis ever since. It has been a place where people can bring research plans, problems, conceptual difficulties, awkward questions, new methods, successes, failures, into an atmosphere of understanding, acceptance, and relevant questioning. The experience of this group has been patchy. In the early days we were a small group of friends, and we quickly came to share perspectives, methods, and ways of going about our work. We needed little structure to our meetings beyond this. As we have grown bigger our process has become more complex and difficult, with problems of the relation between the 'in-group' and the 'out-group', between men and women, between the wish for critical discussion and the need for emotional support. It has at times been difficult, but never impossible, and we are learning to give both intellectual and emotional support to each other; And we have learned (or re-learned) that we ignore the process of the group at our peril.

It is perhaps impossible to pass on the practical wisdom obtained in this way — each group will have to work it out anew — but perhaps one or two hints are in order. A support group needs to:

> welcome people and make them feel at home;
> be just as interested in the person as in what that person has to say;
> devote as much attention to process as to task;
> listen without interrupting;
> spend less time rehearsing one's next contribution;
> be less competitive;
> give up the idea of being right.

All these are easier to say than to do, and they are especially difficult for people raised in the ordinary academic mould, as Silverstein (1972) points out in his moving essay on power and sex roles in academia. And this is probably the major danger for a new paradigm research group: that because it is about *research* it will get sucked into being a traditional academic seminar, when it needs to be a cross between a consciousness-raising group, a T-group, and an academic discussion.

We must recognize the implicit violence of the standard academic approach:

> We can formulate a sense of traditionalism in Inquiry by saying that traditional criticism thinks conversation as War, as analytic violence....

> War is the rule of our tradition to the extent that it hides its belligerence under the cosmetics of 'criticism' and 'dialogue'.

> Belligerent thinking stands out in its very duality — at base it is nothing but a community of Those who speak the truth and Those who speak falsely (Sandywell, 1975).

Of course, our whole culture goes along with all this and supports it. We live and research in an intensely competitive/domineering society. So when we try to do something which seems simple, like creating a nourishing social group, we are moving against the system. And because the system is so all-pervasive, it turns out to be harder than we thought. But it can be done, and it is well worth all the effort it takes and the painful confrontations that are part of the process.

Another issue for the future of new paradigm research is to establish standards of excellence, with regard both to process and to outcome. What does a research report look like? What does a dissertation contain? One thing that is quite clear is that we don't want to end up with the kind of 'dead' knowledge that is so often reported from orthodox research. And it is also clear that there are a whole range of possible outcomes from a piece of research within the new mode, including a particular valid action or set of actions; the development of particular skills and abilities, both with regard to external action and internal consciousness; a set of propositions or a theory of human action or skills; a variety of presentational forms of knowing. These outcomes might be presented in a whole variety of ways, including acute and sensitive verbal descriptions of phenomena, sets of linked general statements, selectively retained tentatives (see Chapter 32, by Sims), stories, paintings, even drama and dance. In general terms, what we want to see as an outcome of an inquiry is evidence of a valid process of coming-to-know, and some statement about what it is that became known (recognizing that not all of this will be communicable).

But how are such outcomes to be valued, and how are they to be judged? This question of standards is important in an emerging field. We advocate aiming at something which is reasonably achievable rather than impossibly perfect. Perfection usually means aiming at externally imposed standards, and raises all the problems of 'shouldism' which Perls (1972) has warned us about. We propose that standards should be based on the concept of *satisficing* (March and Simon, 1958), and of being 'good enough' (Winnicott, 1965). We argue that excellence involves pursuing a self-directed project to meet standards which *we* choose as appropriate.

In practice, this means that we should choose and clearly state the standards we wish to apply to our work — five or six is probably the most we can apply to any one project: we should state these in such a way that they can be clearly applied in practice; and we should apply them rigorously using a process such as self- and peer-assessment (Heron, 1979, 1981), in which the primary locus of assessment rests with the researchers themselves, with support and confrontation from peers and teachers. In this way the question of standards becomes a research project (research on research) in its own right, rather than being a chore added on by the requirements of external evaluation. And, of course, a special interest group is an ideal place for such an assessment to be applied.

We wish to close with two succinct statements, one theoretical and one practical. The first is the New Paradigm Research Manifesto, which was written collectively by the New Paradigm Research Group in an attempt to state clearly what we stood for. The second is a statement about how to do new paradigm research based on John Rowan's research cycle, and contains some basic practical statements about the approach. Obviously neither of these statements is the last word, but we have found that both are useful starting-off points and useful stimuli for discussion.

The New Paradigm Research Manifesto

(1) Research can never be neutral. It is always supporting or questioning social forces, both by its content and by its method. It has effects and side-effects, and these benefit or harm people.

(2) Even the most static and conventional research discovers and exposes rigidities and fixed patterns, which are thus enabled to change. This is so whether such change is intended or not.

Knowing and Participation

(3) New paradigm research involves a much closer relationship than that which is usual between the researcher and the researched: significant knowledge of persons is generated primarily through reciprocal encounter between subject and researcher, for whom research is a mutual activity involving co-ownership and shared power with respect both to the process and to the product of the research.

(4) The shared language and praxis of subject and researcher create 'the world' to be studied.

Knowing and Action

(5) We know that people have the capacity for self-awareness and for auto-nomous, self-directed action within their world, that they may develop the power to change their world. The whole thrust of new paradigm research is to produce the kind of active knowing which will preserve and enhance this capacity and this power. Thus the knowing acquired in new paradigm research is helpful to the flourishing of people and to the politics of self-determination.

(6) We see human inquiry not only as a systematic coming-to-know process but also as learning through risk-taking in living. Since theoretical and

practical knowledge are dialectically related, we seek knowledge which can be used in living, and regard knowledge separated from action as in need of special justification. That is why we more often speak of 'knowing' than of 'knowledge'.

Knowing and 'Softness'

(7) The old paradigm approach regarded certain kinds of research as 'soft' (loose-construing, qualitative, hypothesis-generating, informal, discovery-oriented aspects of research) and as fit only for preliminary pilot work. It was loose and subjective. The real research was 'hard' research, objective, tight and quantitative. The new paradigm approach says that beyond this one-sided objectivity there is a new kind of tight and rigorous synthesis of subjectivity and objectivity. It seeks to develop a new rigour of softness.

Knowing and the Holistic

(8) The intense particularity of individual situations is respected and celebrated. In studying persons and groups in situations we emphasize tacit understanding, phenomenological exactitude, including acceptance of ambiguities, contradictions and imprecision, which are uniquely valuable sources of insight and change. They need to be used to the full, even though they may be painful. This points to the need for emotional support to be built in to the research process.

(9) We are interested in generalization, not in order to make deterministic predictions, but as general statements about the power, possibilities, and limits of persons acting as agents. We are interested in describing the general patterns within which the particular may exist, and accept that often the most personal and particular is also the most general.

(10) We make every attempt to do justice to the person-in-context as a whole, and find in practice that this entails the use of multi-level, multi-disciplinary models of understanding.

Knowing and Values

(11) What we contend for most of all is awareness of what is being done to self and others, and of what follows from that — both meant and unmeant. We do not want to give up important ideas like truth and checkability, but we do want more people to recognize that these things can have human

costs when they are narrowly applied. For too long social science has treated people like things, and we are going on now to treat them like people, and like ourselves.

(12) The outcome of research is knowledge. Knowledge is power. The wrong kind of research gives the wrong kind of power. The right kind of research gives the right kind of power. Research can never be neutral.

This is the ninth draft of the Manifesto. We expect further drafts to emerge as ideas crystallize.

How To Do New Paradigm Research

(1) Honestly answer the question, what values am I holding? What questions do I have, implicitly or explicitly, as I go round the cycle? Where am I coming from? The cycle concept helps to make these matters more explicit.

(2) Develop your own supervision arrangements: negotiate relations of supportive confrontation with peers and teachers, and use these to explore your experience of inquiry. Ideally, choose a method of self-development and use it to explore yourself as a researcher.

(3) Set out the criteria you aim to pursue in your research as clearly as you can. What is the minimum with which you will be satisfied? What would be ideal? How will you assess yourself? Where necessary negotiate these criteria with supervisory and examining bodies.

(4) Resolve to go round the cycle very soft at first, and stay soft as long as possible. Refuse to consider quantification unless it seems really justified, all things considered. Think of your research as being a number of cycles, all knitting together.

(5) Turn the subjects into co-researchers. This means choosing an area of research where both you and they have real interests at stake. Don't hide behind a role, and don't set up situations where others can only play limited roles. Involve the co-researchers in the planning of the research, and in the making sense and communication, as well as in the data-gathering itself.

(6) Don't assume that you have to aim at some social action. The very fact of mutual exploration and common learning will produce action and change. One important change is that all the people involved will tend towards becoming more aware, realized, self-directing: new paradigm research enhances the development of persons in important ways.

(7) Do a diagram or two of your research, and have a good look at it in terms of what it is going to do to you, and what it is going to do to the other people involved. Is this what you want? what changes are required?

(8) A new paradigm approach means that criticisms of outside assessors need never be totally rejected. We are all the time taking the position of saying, 'What we are doing is perfectly justifiable as inquiry, and we are willing to conform to all reasonable demands'. A project which is well thought out and well negotiated, which is hard where appropriate and soft when appropriate, which is built on multiple cycles, is perfectly reasonable. In order to oppose a research project along these lines, a research committee would have to become rigid and unreasonable, and therefore open to public scorn and ridicule.

England, July 1980   Peter Reason
                                                                          John Rowan

References

Adams-Webber, J. R. (1979). *Personal Construct Theory: Concepts and Applications.* Wiley, New York.

Ahmed, M. (1975). *The Economics of Non-formal Education: Resources, Costs, and Benefits.* Praeger, New York.

Akin, G. (1975). 'The Phenomenology of Risk'. Ph.D. dissertation, University of California, Los Angeles.

Alderfer, C. P. (1972). *Existence, Relatedness, Growth.* Collier-Macmillan, New York.

Allport, F. H. (1937). Teleonomic description in the study of personality. *Char. and Pers.,* **6,** 202-14.

Allport, G. W. (1958). What units shall we employ? In G. Lindzey (ed.), *Assessment of Human Motives.* Rinehart, New York.

Allport, G. W. (1960). The trend in motivational theory. Chapter 6 in *Personality and Social Encounter.* Beacon, Boston.

Allport, G. W. (1961a). Comment. In R. May (ed.), *Existential Psychology.* Random House, New York.

Allport, G. W. (1961b). *Pattern and Growth in Personality.* Holt, Rinehart, & Winston, New York.

Allport, G. W. (1962). The general and the unique in psychological science. *Journal of Personality,* XXX, 405-22.

Allport, G. W., Vernon, P. E., and Lindzey, G. (1960). *A Study of Values.* (3rd edn.). Houghton Mifflin, Boston.

American Psychological Association (1959). Ethical standards for psychologists. *American Psychologist,* **14,** 279-82.

Ardener, E. (1975). Belief and the problem of women, In S. Ardener (ed.), *Perceiving Women,* pp.1-17.

Ardener, S. (ed.) (1975). *Perceiving Women,* Dent, London.

Ardener, S. (ed.) (1978). *Defining Females,* Croom Helm, London.

493

Argyris, C. (1962). *Interpersonal Competence and Organizational Effectiveness.* Dorsey, Homewood, Ill.

Argyris, C. (1965). *Organization and Innovation.* Irwin Co. Inc., Homewood, Ill.

Argyris, C. (1968a). Some unintended consequences of rigorous research. *Psychological Bulletin,* **70,** 185-97.

Argyris, C. (1968b). Students and businessmen: the bristling dialogue. *Think,* July-August, pp. 26-31.

Argyris, C. (1969). The incompleteness of social-psychological theory. *American Psychologist* (24), **10,** 893-908.

Argyris, C. (1971). *Intervention Theory and Method: a behavorial science view.* Addison Wesley, Reading, Mass.

Argyris, C. (1974). *Behind the Front Page.* Jossey-Bass, San Francisco.

Argyris, C. (1976). *Increasing Leadership Effectiveness.* Wiley, New York.

Argyris, C. and Schon, D. (1974). *Theory in Practice: increasing professional effectiveness.* Jossey-Bass, San Francisco.

Armistead, N. (1974). 'Introduction' in N. Armistead (ed.), *Reconstructing Social Psychology,* pp. 7-27. Penguin, Harmondsworth, Middx.

Asch, S. (1952). *Social Pscyhology.* Prentice-Hall, Englewood Cliffs, N.J.

Assagioli, R. (1975). *Psychosynthesis: a manual of principles and techniques.* Hobbs, Dorman, New York.

Avon Resources for Learning Unit. Redcross Street, Bristol, England.

Bakan, D. (1967). *On Method: toward a reconstruction of psychological investigation.* Jossey-Bass, San Francisco.

Bakan, D. (1972). Psychology can now kick the science habit. *Psychology Today* (March), pp. 26, 28, 86-8.

Baldwin, A. L. (1942). Personal structure analysis: a statistical method for investigation of the single personality. *Journal of Abnormal and Social Psychology,* **37,** 163-83.

Bannister, D. (1968). The logical requirements of research into schizophrenia. *British Journal of Psychiatry,* **114,** 181-8.

Bannister, D. (1970). *Perspectives in Personal Construct Theory.* Academic Press, London.

Bannister, D. and Fransella, F. (1980). *Inquiring Man* (2nd edn.). Penguin, Harmondsworth, Middx.

Barber, B. and Fox, R. (1958). 'The case of the floppy-eared rabbits: an instance of serendipity gained and serendipity lost'. *Am. J. Soc.,* **64,** 128-36.

Barnes, J. A. (1979). *Who Should Know What?* Penguin, Harmondsworth, Middx.

Bass, B. M. (1974). The substance and the shadow. *American Psychologist,* **29**(12), 870-886.

Bateson, G. (1972). *Steps to an Ecology of Mind.* Chandler, San Francisco.

Bateson, G. (1979). *Mind and Nature: a necessary unity.* E. P. Dutton, New York.

Bauman, Z. (1978). *Hermeneutics and Social Science: Approaches to Understanding.* Hutchinson, London.

Beals, R. L. (1970). Who will rule research? *Psychology Today,* **4,** 44-7, 75.

Becker, C. (1978). 'Phenomenology: an overview of theoretical and methodological issues'. Paper presented at the American Psychological Association meetings, Toronto.

Bedmar, R. and Kaul, T. (1979). 'Experiential Group Research: what never happened!'. *J. of Ap. Beh. Sci.,* **15,** 311-19.

Bellow, S. (1959). *Henderson the Rain King.* Weidenfeld & Nicolson, London.

Bellow, S. (1965). *Herzog.* Weidenfeld & Nicolson, London.

Bem, D. J. (1970). *Beliefs, Attitudes and Human Affairs.* Brooks/Cole, Belmont, Calif.

Benne, K. D. *et al* (eds.) (1975). *The Laboratory Method of Changing and Learning: theory and application.* Science and Behavior Books, Palo Alto, Calif.

Bennis, W. G. *et al* (eds.) (1969). *The Planning of Change* (2nd edn.). Holt, Rinehart & Winston, New York.

Berger, P. L. and Luckmann, T. (1967). *The Social Construction of Reality.* Doubleday, Garden City, New York.

Berkowitz, L. (1967). Experimental social psychology. In R. Harré (ed.), *The Sciences: their origins and methods.* Blackie, Glasgow and London.

Bernard, J. (1973). My four revolutions: An autobiographical history of the ASA, *Am. J. Soc.,* **78**, 773-91.

Berne, E. (1972). *'What Do You Say After You Say Hello?'* The psychology of human destiny. Grove Press, New York.

Bhaskar, R. (1978). *A Realist Theory of Science.* (2nd edn.). Harvester Press, Brighton.

Bion, W. R. (1968). *Experiences in Groups, and Other Papers.* Tavistock Publications, London.

Blanco, Matte (1975). *The Unconscious as Infinite Sets.* Duckworth, London.

Blum, R. and Funkhauser, Mary Lou (1965). Legislator's views on alcoholism: some dimensions relevant to making new laws. *Quarterly Journal of Studies on Alcohol,* **26**, 666-9.

Bogdan, R. and Taylor, S. J. (1975). *An introduction to qualitative research methods: a phenomenological approach.* Wiley, New York.

Borton, T. (1970). *Reach, Touch and Teach.* McGraw-Hill, New York.

Boughey, H. (1978). *The Insights of Sociology: an introduction.* Allyn & Bacon, Boston.

Bowen, E. S. (pseud.) (1964). *Return to Laughter: an autobiographical novel.* Doubleday, New York.

Bradford, L. P. *et al.* (eds.) (1964) *T-group theory and laboratory method: Innovations in re-education.* Wiley, New York.

Brandt, W. (1980). *North-South: a programme for survival.* Report of the Independent Commission on International development issues. Pan, London.

Brenner, M. (1978). Interviewing: the social phenomenology of a research instrument. In M. Brenner, P. Marsh, and M. Brenner (eds.), *The Social Contexts of Method.* Croom Helm, London.

Brentano, F. C. (1973). *Psychology from an Empirical Stand point.* Humanities Press, Atlantic Highlands, N.J.

Bristol Women's Studies Group (eds.) (1979). *Half the Sky. an introduction to women's studies.* Virago, London.

Brockman, J. (ed.) (1977). *About Bateson.* E. P. Dutton, New York.

Bronfenbrenner, U. and Devereux, E. C. (1952). Interdisciplinary Planning for team research on constructive community behavior. *Hum. Rel.,* **5**, 187-203.

Bronowski, J. (1963). *Science and Human Values.* Harper & Row, New York.

Broverman, D. M. (1960). Cognitive style and intra-individual variation in abilities. *J. Pers.,* **28**, 240-56.

Brown, J. and Gilmartin, B. (1969). Sociology today: lacunae, emphases and surfeits. *Am. Soc.,* **4**, 283-90.

Brown, L. D. (1972). Research Action. *Journal of Applied Behavioral Science,* **8**(6), 697-711.

Brown, L. D. (1979). Planned change in underorganised systems. In T. G. Cummings (ed.), *Systems Theory for Organisation Development.* Wiley, New York.

Brown, L. D. and Kaplan, R. E. (1978). 'De-organising an over-organised system'. Working Paper, Case Western Reserve University, Cleveland, Ohio.

Brown, L. D. and Tandon, R. (1978). Interviews as catalysts in a community setting. *Journal of Applied Psychology,* **63**(2), 197-205.

Brown, P. (ed.) (1973). *Radical Psychology.* Harper & Row, New York.

Bryant, F. and Wortman, P. (1978). Secondary analysis: the case for data archives. *Am. Psychol.,* **33**, 381-7.

Buber, M. (1937). *I and Thou.* (trans. R. G. Smith) T. & T. Clark, Edinburgh.

Buber, M. (1957). Distance and relation. *Psychiatry,* **20**(2), 97-104.

Buckley, W. (1968). *Modern Systems Research for the Behavioral Scientist.* Aldine, Chicago.

Burke, C. G. (1978). Report from Paris: women's writing and the women's movement. *Signs,* **3**(4), 843-55.

Burman, S. (ed.) (1979). *Fit Work for Women.* Croom Helm, London.

Callan, H. (1975). The premise of dedication: notes towards an ethnography of diplomats' wives. In S. Ardener (ed.), *Perceiving Women,* pp. 87-104. Dent, London.

Callan, H. (1978). 'Harems and overlords: biosocial models and the female'. In S. Ardener (ed.), *Defining Females,* pp. 200-219. Croom Helm, London.

Callaway, H. (1978). The most essentially female function of all: giving birth. In S. Ardener (ed.), *Defining Females,* Croom Helm, London.

Camara, S. (1975). The concept of heterogeneity and change among the Mandenka. *Technological Forecasting and Social Change,* **7**, 273-84.

Campbell, D. (1969). Reforms as experiments. *American Psychologist,* **24**, 409-29.

Campbell, D. T. and Fiske, D. W. (1959). Convergent and discriminant validation by the multitrait-multimethod matrix. *Psychological Bulletin,* **56**(2), 81-105.

Campbell, D. T. and Stanley, J. C. (1966). *Experimental and Quasi-experimental Designs for Research.* Rand McNally, Chicago.

Carlson, R. (1972). Understanding women: implications for personality theory and research, *Journal of Social Issues,* **28**(2), 17-32.

Castaneda, C. (1968). *The Teachings of Don Juan.* University of California Press.

Castaneda, C. (1971). *A Separate Reality.* Simon & Schuster, New York.

Castaneda, C. (1972). *Journey to Ixtlan.* Simon & Schuster, New York.

Castaneda, C. (1974). *Tales of Power.* Simon & Schuster, New York.

Chang, T. S. (1938). A Chinese philosopher's theory of knowledge. *Yenching Journal of Social Studies,* **1**.

Chesler, P. (1972). *Women and Madness.* Doubleday, New York.

Chin, R. (1974). Applied behavioral science and innovation, diffusion and adoption. *Viewpoint* (Bulletin, School of Education, Indiana University), **50**, 25-45.

Chomsky, N. (1975). *Reflections on Language.* Pantheon, New York.

Churchman, C. W. (1972). *The Design of Inquiring Systems.* Basic Books, New York.

Cicourel, A. V. (1968). *The Social Organization of Juvenile Justice.* Wiley, New York.

Cicourel, A. V. *et al.* (1974). *Language Use and School Performance.* Academic Press, New York.

Clark, P. A. (1972). *Action Research and Organizational Change.* Harper and Row, New York.

Clason-Hook, C. (1977). *Teaching Reading and Writing to Adults.* International Institute for Adult Literacy Methods, Teheran.

Cohen, M. D., Cohen, D., and March, J. G. (1974). *Leadership Ambiguity.* McGraw-Hill, New York.

Coleman, J. *et al.* (1966). *Equality of Educational Opportunity.* U.S. Government Printing Office, Washington DC.

Conrad, H. S. (1932). The validity of personality ratings of pre-school children. *Journal of Educ. Psychol.,* **23,** 671-80.

Coombs, P. and Ahmed, M. (1974). *Attacking Rural Poverty: how non-formal education can help.* Johns Hopkins University Press, Baltimore.

Coombs, P. and Prosser, R. (1973). *New Paths to Learning.* UNICEF, New York.

Cornforth, M. (1955). *The Theory of Knowledge.* International Publishers, New York.

Coser, L. A. (1977). Georg Simmel's neglected contributions to the sociology of women. *Signs,* **2**(4), 869-76.

Crowle, A. (1976). The deceptive language of the laboratory. In R. Harré (ed.), *Life Sentences: aspects of the social role of language,* pp. 160-74. Wiley, New York.

Daniels, A. K. (1970). The social construction of military psychiatric diagnoses. In H.P. Dreitzel (ed.), *Recent Sociology No. 2: patterns of communicative behaviour.* Collier-Macmillan, New York.

D.A.T.G./A.C.J. (1951) 'Ludwig Wittgenstein'. *The Australian Journal of Philosophy,* **24**(2), 73-80.

Dannheisser, P. (1975). The satellite instructional television experiment: the trial run. *Educational Broadcasting International,* **8**(4), (December), 155-9.

Davies, M. L. (ed.) (1978). *Maternity: letters from working women.* Virago, London.

Davis, J. (1964). 'Great books and small groups'. In P. E. Hammond (ed.), *Sociologists at Work: essays on the craft of social research,* Basic Books, New York.

Davis, M. (1971). That's interesting! Towards a phenomenology of sociology and a sociology of phenomenology. *Philosophy of Social Sciences,* **1**(4), 304-44.

Dearden, G. J. (1979). 'Student learning and teacher intervention in an undergraduate engineering laboratory'. Ph.D. Thesis, University of Surrey.

Delamont, S. and Duffin, L. (eds.) (1978). *The Nineteenth Century Woman. Her cultural and physical world.* Croom Helm, London.

Deutsch, N. (1969). Organizational and conceptual barriers to social change. *Journal of Social Issues,* **25,** 5-18.

Devereux, G. (1967). *From Anxiety to Method in the Behavioral Sciences.* Mouton, The Hague.

Diesing, P. (1972). *Patterns of Discovery in the Social Sciences.* Routledge & Kegan Paul, London.

Duberman, M. (1972). *Black Mountain: an exploration in community.* Dutton, New York.

Duval, S., Duval, V. H., and Neely, R. (1979). Self-focus, felt responsibility and helping behavior. *Journal of Personality and Social Psychology,* **37**(10), 1769-78.

Duval, S. and Wicklund, R. A. (1972). *A Theory of Objective Self-awareness,* Academic Press, New York.

Eden, C. and Sims, D. (1979). On the nature of problems in consulting practice. *Omega,* **7,** 1-9.

Ehrenreich, B. and English, D. (1979). *For Her Own Good. 150 years of the experts' advice to women.* Pluto Press, London.

Ehrlich, H. (1971). The sociology of social research: a discussion. In R. O'Toole (ed.), *The Organization, Management and Tactics of Social Research,* pp. 43-54. Schenkman, Cambridge, Mass.

Elden, M. (1979a). Bank employees begin to participate in studying and changing their organisation. In International Council for the Quality of Working Life, *Working on the Quality of Working Life: developments in Europe,* Martinus Nijhoff, The Hague.

Elden, M. (1979b). Three generations of work democracy experiments in Norway:

beyond classical socio-technical systems analysis. In C. L. Cooper and E. Mumford (eds.), *The Quality of Working Life in Western and Eastern Europe,* Greenwood Press, Westport, Conn.

Elden, M. (1980). Autonomy at work and participation in politics. In A. Cherns (ed.), *Quality of Working Life and the Kibbutz Experience,* Norwood Editions, Norwood, Pa.

Enright, J. (1970). Awareness training in the mental health professions. In J. Fagan and I. L. Shepherd (eds.), *Gestalt Therapy Now.* Science and Behaviour Books, Palo Alto, Calif.

Esterson, A. (1972). *The Leaves of Spring: a Study in the Dialectics of Madness.* Penguin, Harmondsworth, Middx.

Evans, H. (1972). *Nonformal Education.* University of Massachusetts.

Fadiman, J. and Frager, R. (1976). *Personality and Personal Growth.* Harper & Row, New York.

Fallaci, O. (1977). *Interview with History* (translation by J. Shepley). Houghton Mifflin, Boston.

Farrell, G., Markley, O., and Matulef, N. (1967). *Special Bulletin of the National Committee on Graduate Education in Psychology.* American Psychological Association, Washington, DC.

Farrell, W. (1975). *The Liberated Man.* Bantam, New York.

Feuerstein, M. T. (1978). The educative approach in evaluation: an appropriate technology for a rural health programme. *International Journal of Health Education,* **21**(1), 56-64.

Filmer, P. *et al.* (1973). *New Directions in sociological theory,* MIT Press, Cambridge, Mass.

Form, W. (1971). The sociology of social research. In R. O'Toole (ed.), *The Organization, Management and Tactics of Social Research,* pp. 3-42. Schenkman, Cambridge, Mass.

Frankl, V. E. (1969). *Man's Search for Meaning.* Beacon Press, New York.

Fransella, F. (1972). *Personal Change and Reconstruction.* Academic Press, New York.

Fransella, F. and Bannister, D. (1977). *A Manual for Repertory Grid Technique.* Academic Press, New York.

Freire, P. (1970). *Pedagogy of the Oppressed.* Herder & Herder, New York.

Freire, P. (1976). *Education: the practice of freedom.* Writers and Readers Publishing Co-operative, London.

French, W. L. and Bell, C. H. (1973). *Organization Development: behavioral science interventions for organization improvement.* Prentice-Hall, Englewood Cliffs, N.J.

Freud, S. (1925). Recommendation for physicians on the psychoanalytic method of treatment, In *Collected Papers,* vol.2. Hogarth Press, London.

Friedan, B. (1963). *The Feminine Mystique.* W. W. Norton, New York.

Friedlander, F. (1968). Researcher-subject alienation in behavioural research. In E. Glatt and M. Shelley (eds.), *The Research Society,* pp. 487-506. Gordon & Breach, New York.

Friedman, M. (ed.) (1964). *The Worlds of Existentialism: a critical reader.* Random House, New York.

Friedman, N. (1967). *The Social Nature of Psychological Research.* Basic Books, New York.

Fry, R. and Kolb, D. (1979). Experiential learning theory and learning experiences in liberal arts education. In S. Brooks and J. Althof (eds.), *New Directions for Experiential Learning,* No. 6, pp. 79-92. Jossey-Bass, San Francisco.

Gadamer, H. G. (1975). *Truth and Method.* The Seabury Press, New York.

Gadamer, H. G. (1976). *Philosophic Hermeneutics*. University of California Press.

Garfinkel, H. (1967) (in collaboration with Egon Bittner) 'Good' organizational reasons for 'bad' clinic records. In H. Garfinkel (ed.), *Studies in Ethnomethodology*, Prentice-Hall, Princetown, NJ.

Geertz, C. (1975). On the nature of anthropological understanding. *American Scientist*, **63**, (Jan.-Feb.), 47-53.

Gendlin, E. T. (1962). *Experiencing and the Creation of Meaning: a philosophical and psychological approach to the subjective*. Free Press, Glencoe, Ill.

Giddens, A. (1976). *New Rules of Sociological Method: a positive critique of interpretative sociologies*. Basic Books, New York.

Gillette, A. (1977). *Beyond the Non-formal Fashion: towards educational revolution in Tanzania*. University of Massachusetts, Center for International Education.

Giorgi, A. (1975). *Duquesne Studies in Phenomenological Psychology*, Vol. 2. Duquesne University Press.

Gish, G. (1979). The learning cycle, *Synergist*, **8**, 2-6.

Glaser, B. G. (1978). *Theoretical Sensitivity: advances in the methodology of grounded theory*. Sociology Press, Mill Valley, Calif.

Glaser, B. G. and Strauss, A. L. (1967). *The Discovery of Grounded Theory*. Aldine, Chicago.

Glen, R. H. (1978). 'Organizational Rules: a field study of social-construction processes'. Unpublished doctoral dissertation. Case Western Reserve University, Cleveland, Ohio.

Goertzel, T. (1979). 'On becoming a clinical sociologist: an experiential analysis'. Unpublished manuscript. Camden College, Rutgers University.

Golde, P. (ed.) (1970). *Women in the Field: anthropological experiences*. Aldine, Chicago.

Goleman, D. (1972). The Buddha on meditation and states of consciousness. *Journal of Transpersonal Psychology*, **4**(1).

Gordon, G. *et al.* (1974). A contingency model for the design of problem solving research programs: a perspective on diffusion research. In *Milbank Memorial Fund Quarterly*, (Spring), pp. 185-220.

Gordon, L. (1975). 'A socialist view of women's studies', *Signs*, **1**(2), 559-66.

Gorman, T. (1977). *Language and Literacy: current issues and research*. International Institute for Adult Literacy Methods. Teheran.

Gouldner, A. W. (1970). *The Coming Crisis of Western Sociology*. Basic Books, New York.

Grant, J. and Grant, J. D. (1970). Client participation and community change. In D. Adelson and B. Kalis (eds.), *Community Psychology and Mental Health: perspectives and challenges*. Chandler Publishing Co. Scranton, Penn.

Graumann, C. F. (1960). Eigenschaften als Problem der Persönlichkeits-Forschung. In P. Lersch and H. Thomas, (eds.), *Persönlichkeitsforschung und Persönlichkeitstheorie*. Hogrefe, Göttingen.

Green, E. E. and Green, A. M. (1971). On the meaning of transpersonal: some metaphysical perspectives. *Journal of Transpersonal Psychology*, No. 3.

Greenberg, I. A. (ed.) (1974). *Psychodrama: theory and therapy*. Behavioral Publications, New York.

Grof, S. (1979). *Realms of the Human Unconscious: observations from LSD research*. Condor Books, Souvenir Press, London.

Gross, N., Ciaquinta, J., and Bernstein, H. (1971). *Implementing Organizational Innovations*. Basic Books, New York.

Grotowski, J. (1970). *Towards a Poor Theatre*. Simon & Schuster, New York.

Gustavsen, B. (1977). A legislative approach to job reform in Norway. *International*

Labour Review, **115**(3) (May/June), 263-76.

Gustavsen, B. (1980). Arbeidsmiljóreform og organisasjonsforsknink (QWL reform and organisational research). *Forsknings Nytt,* **25**(3), 2-8.

Gustavsen, B. and Hunnius, G. (1980). *Improving the Quality of Working Life: the case of Norway.* Work Research Institutes, Oslo.

Habermas, J. (1971). *Knowledge and Human Interests.* Beacon, Boston, Mass.

Hainer, R. (1968). Rationalism, pragmatism, and existentialism: perceived but undiscovered multi-cultural problems. In E. Glatt and M. S. Shelly (eds.), *The Research Society,* pp. 7-50. Gordon & Breach, New York.

Hall, B. L. (1975). Participatory research: an approach for change. *Convergence, an International Journal of Adult Education,* **8**(2), 24-32.

Hall, B. L. (1978(a)). *Mtu ni Afya: Tanzania's Health Campaign,* Washington, DC. Clearinghouse on development communication.

Hall, B. L. (1978(b)). Notes of the development of the concept of participatory research in an international context. *Internatinal Journal of University Adult Education,* **17**(1).

Hamilton, D. F., Jenkins, D., King, C., MacDonald, B. and Parlett, M. R. (eds.) (1977). *Beyond the Numbers Game: a reader in educational evaluation.* Macmillan, London.

Hammond, P (ed.) (1964). *Sociologists at Work: essays on the craft of social research.* Basic Books, New York.

Hampden-Turner, C. (1970). *Radical Man: the process of psychosocial development.* Schenkman, Cambridge, Mass.

Hampden-Turner, C. (1976). *Sane Asylum.* San Francisco Book Co. San Francisco, Calif.

Harré, R. (1978). Accounts, actions and meanings: the practice of participatory psychology. In M. Brenner and P. Marsh (eds.), *The Social Contexts of Method.* Croom Helm, New York.

Harré, R. (1979). *Social Being.* Blackwell, Oxford.

Harré, R. and Secord, P. F. (1972). *The Explanation of Social Behaviour.* Blackwell, Oxford.

Hartman, M. and Banner, L. W. (eds.) (1974). *Clio's Consciousness Raised: new perspectives on the history of women.* Harper & Row, New York.

Hastings, J. T. (1969). The kith and kin of educational measures. *Journal of Educational Measurement,* **6**(3), 127-30.

Hearnshaw, L. S. (1956). *Bull. Brit. Psychol. Soc.,* **1**(36). See also G. W. H. Leytham, Psychology and the individual, in *Nature* (1961), **189**(4763), 435-8.

Heather, N. (1976). *Radical Perspectives in Psychology.* Methuen, London.

Hegel, G. W. F. (1971). *Philosophy of Mind.* Clarendon Press, Oxford.

Heidegger, M. (1962). *Being and Time.* Harper & Row, New York.

Herbst, P. G. (1970). *Behavioural Worlds: the study of single cases.* Tavistock, London.

Herbst, P. G. (1976). *Alternatives to Hierarchies.* Martinus Nijhoff, The Hague.

Heron, J. (1970). The phenomenology of social encounter: the Gaze. *Philosophy and Phenomenological Research,* **31**(2).

Heron, J. (1971). *Experience and Method: an inquiry into the concept of experiential research.* Human Potential Research Project, University of Surrey, England.

Heron, J. (1973a). *Experiential Training Techniques.* Human Potential Research Project, University of Surrey, England.

Heron, J. (1973b). *Re-evaluation Counselling: a theoretical review.* Human Potential Research Project, University of Surrey, England.

Heron, J. (1974a). *Reciprocal Counselling Manual.* Human Potential Research Project, University of Surrey, England.

Heron, J. (1974b). *The Concept of a Peer Learning Community.* Human Potential Research Project, University of Surrey, England.

Heron, J. (1974c). *Course for New Teachers in General Practice.* Human Potential Research Project, University of Surrey, England.

Heron, J. (1974d). *South West London College: inauguration of a peer learning community.* Human Potential Research Project, University of Surrey, England.

Heron J. (1974e). *Life-style analysis – the sexual domain.* Human Potential Research Project, University of Surrey, England.

Heron, J. (1975a). *Six Category Intervention Analysis.* Human Potential Research Project, University of Surrey, England.

Heron, J. (1975b). *Practical Methods of Transpersonal Psychology.* Human Potential Research Project, University of Surrey, England.

Heron, J. (1975c). *Criteria for Evaluating Growth Movements.* Human Potential Research Project, University of Surrey, England.

Heron, J. (1977a). *Dimensions of Facilitator Style.* Human Potential Research Project, University of Surrey, England.

Heron, J. (1977b). *Behaviour Analysis in Education and Training.* Human Potential Research Project, University of Surrey, England.

Heron, J. (1977c). *Catharsis in Human Development.* Human Potential Research Project, University of Surrey, England.

Heron, J. (1977d). *Co-counselling Teachers Manual.* Human Potential Research Project, University of Surrey, England.

Heron, J. (1978a). *An ASC Peer Research Group.* Human Potential Research Project, University of Surrey, England.

Heron, J. (1978b). *Facilitator Styles Course Prospectus.* Human Potential Research Project, University of Surrey, England.

Heron, J. (1978c). *Project for a Self-generating Culture.* Human Potential Research Project, University of Surrey, England.

Heron, J. (1979). *Peer Review Audit.* Human Potential Research Project, University of Surrey, England.

Heron, J. (1981, in press). Self and peer assessment for managers. In T. Boydell and M. Pedler (eds.), *Handbook of Management Self Development.* Gower Press, London.

Hillman, J. (1975). *Revisioning Psychology.* Harper & Row, New York.

Hoel, M. and Hvinden, B. (1976). Forskning som grunnlag for handling: skisse til en dialogmodell for fagforenings-forskning. (Research as a basis for action: sketch of a dialog model for trade union based research). *Sosiologi i dag,* **6,** 29-44.

Hoff, W. (1970). *New Health Careers Demonstration Project. Institute for Health Research* (mimeographed). Berkeley, California.

Holmes, J. (1976). Thoughts on research methodology. *Studies in Adult Education,* **8**(2) (October), 149-63.

Horney, K. (1974). The flight from womanhood: the masculinity complex in women as viewed by men and by women. In J. B. Miller (ed.), *Psychoanalysis and Women,* pp. 3-20. Penguin, Harmondsworth, Middx.

Horowitz, I. L. (ed.) (1969). *Sociological Self-images: a collective portrait.* Sage, Beverley Hills, Calif.

Horton, B. (1967). African traditional thought and western science. *Africa,* XXXVII.

Hudson, L. (1968). *Contrary Imaginations.* Penguin Books, Harmondsworth, Middx.

Humphrey, C. (1978). Women, taboo and the suppression of attention. In S. Ardener (ed.), *Defining Females*. Croom Helm, London.

Husserl, E. (1962). *Ideas*. Collier Books, New York.

Husserl, E. (1965). *Phenomenology and the Crisis of Philosophy*. Harper Torchbooks, New York.

Hyder, S. and Sims, D. (1978). *Hypothesis, Analysis and Paralysis: how to disable your research officer*. Centre for the Study of Organizational Change and Development, University of Bath, Working Paper No. 78/14.

ICAE (undated). International Council for Adult Education, Participatory Research Project. *Annotated Bibliography Working Paper No. 4*. Available from ICAE, 29 Prince Arthur Avenue, Toronto, Ontario, Canada.

Israel, J. and Tajfel, H. (eds.) (1972). *The Context of Social Psychology: a critical assessment*. Academic Press, New York.

Jackins, H. (1965). *The Human Side of Human Beings: the theory of re-evaluation counselling*. Rational Island Publishers, Seattle, Washington.

Jacobus, M. (ed.) (1979). *Women Writing and Writing About Women*. Croom Helm, London.

James, W. (1912). *Memories and Studies*. Longmans, Green, New York.

James, W. (1961). *Psychology: the briefer course*. G. W. Allport (ed.). Harper Torchbooks, New York.

Jamieson, M., Parlett, M. R., and Pocklington, K. (1977). *Towards Integration: a study of blind and partially sighted children in ordinary schools*. NFER Publishing Co., Windsor.

Jencks, C. *et al.* (1972). *Inequality: a reassessment of the effect of family and schooling in America*. New Basic Books, New York.

Joynson, R. B. (1974). *Psychology and Common Sense*. Routledge & Kegan Paul, London.

Jung, C. G. (1964). *Man and his Symbols*. W. H. Allen, London.

Jung, C. G. (1971). *Collected Works* (R. F. C. Hull, revised translation), vol. 6, *Psychological Types*. Princeton University Press, Princeton, NJ.

Kahn, S. (1970). *How People get Power: organizing oppressed communities for action*. McGraw-Hill, New York.

Kamin, L. J. (1974). *The Science and Politics of IQ*. Erlbaum, Potomac.

Kaplan, A. (1964). *The Conduct of Inquiry: methodology for the behavioural sciences*. Chandler, San Francisco.

Kaplan, R. E. (1978). Stages in developing a consulting relation: a case study of a long beginning. *Journal of Applied Behavioral Science*, 14(1), 43-60.

Keddie, N. (ed.) (1973). *Tinker, Tailor . . . The Myth of Cultural Deprivation*. Penguin, Harmondsworth, Middx.

Kelly, G. A. (1955). *The Psychology of Personal Constructs*, vols. 1 and 2. Norton, New York.

Kelly, G. A. (1965). The strategy of psychological research. *Bulletin of the British Psychological Society*, 18, 1-15.

Kelly, G. A. (1969). *Clinical Psychology and Personality: the selected papers of George Kelly* (ed. B. A. Maher). Wiley, New York.

Kelly-Gadol, J. (1976). The social relation of the sexes: methodological implications of women's history. *Signs*, 1(4), 809-23;

Kelman, H. C. (1968). *A time to speak: on human values and social research*. Jossey Bass, San Francisco.

Kidd, (1974). *Whilst time is burning*. IDRC, Ottawa.

Kidd, Gayfer, Srivastva, and Hall, (In press). *The world of Literacy*. IDRC, Ottawa.

Kilpatrick, F. P. and Cantril, H. (1960). Self-anchoring scale: a measure of the individual's unique reality world. *Journal of Indiv. Psychology*, **16**, 158-70.

Klaeber, F. (1950). *Beowulf* (3rd edn.). D. D. Heath, Boston.

Kluckhohn, C. M., Murray, H. A., and Scheiner, D. M. (eds.) (1953). *Personality in Nature, Society, and Culture*. Knopf, New York.

Knutson, J. K. (ed.) (1973). *Handbook of Political Psychology*. Jossey-Bass, San Francisco.

Kockelmans, J. (1975). Toward an interpretive or hermeneutic social science. *Graduate Faculty Philosophy Journal*, **5**(1), 73-96.

Koestler, A. (1964). *The Act of Creation*. Hutchinson, London.

Kohlberg, L. (1973). Continuities in child and adult moral development revisited. In P. B. Baltes and K. W. Schaie (eds.), *Life-span Developmental Psychology: personality and socialisation*. Academic Press, New York.

Kolb, D. and Fry, H. (1975). Toward an applied theory of experiential learning. In G. Cooper (ed.), *Theories of Group Processes*. Wiley, London.

Kramer, C., Thorne, B., and Henley, N. (1978). Perspectives on language and communication, *Signs*, **3**(3), 638-51.

Krishnamurti, J. (1969). *Freedom from the Known*. Gollancz, London.

Kuhn, T. (1962). *The Structure of Scientific Revolutions*. University of Chicago, Chicago, Illinois.

Labov, W. (1972). The logic of nonstandard English. In P. P. Giglioli (ed.), *Language and Social Context*. Penguin, Harmondsworth, Middx.

Laing, R. D. (1960). *The Divided Self*. Tavistock, London.

Laing, R. D. (1967). *The Politics of Experience*. Penguin, Harmondsworth, Middx.

Laing, R. D. and Esterson, A. (1964). *Sanity, Madness and the Family*. Tavistock, London.

Langer, S. (1967) *Mind: an essay on human feeling*, vol. 1. Johns Hopkins, Baltimore.

Laurillard, D. M. (1978). 'A study of the relationships between some of the cognitive and contextual factors involved in student learning'. Ph.D. thesis, University of Surrey.

Leeper, R. W. and Madison, P. (1959). *Toward understanding human personalities*. Appleton-Century-Crofts, New York.

Legge, C. D. (1976/77). *Register of Research in Progress in Adult Education*. Department of Adult Education, University of Manchester.

Lenrow, P. (1970). *Strengthening Early Education: collaboration in problem solving*. Berkeley Unified School District, Calif. (mimeographed).

Levi-Strauss, C. (1973). *Tristes Tropiques*. Jonathan Cape, London.

Levin, M. (1980). A trade union and the case of automation. Institute for Social Research in Industry, Trondheim, Norway. Forthcoming in *Human Futures*.

Levinson, D. J. with Darros, C. N., Klein, E. B., Levinson, M. H., and McKee, B. (1978). *The Seasons of a Man's Life*. Alfred Knopf, New York.

Lewin, K. (1946). Action research and minority problems. *Journal of Social Issues*, **2**, 34-46.

Lewin, K. (1947a). Group decision and social change. In T. M. Newcomb and E. L. Hartley (eds.), *Readings in Social Psychology*. Holt, Rinehart & Winston, New York.

Lewin, K. (1947b). Frontiers in group dynamics: channels of group life: social planning and action research. *Human Relations*, **1**(2), 143-53.

Lilienfield, R. (1978). *The Rise of Systems Theory — an ideological analysis*. Wiley, New York.

Lindner, R. (1966). *The Fifty-minute Hour*. Bantam, New York.

Liss, J. (1974). *Free to Feel: finding your way through the new therapies.* Praeger, New York. Wildwood House, London.

Loevinger, J. *et al.* (1970). *Measuring Ego Development* (2 vols.) Jossey-Bass, San Francisco.

Lofland, J. (1976). *Doing Social Life.* Wiley, New York.

Lukas, C. (1973). *Implementing social experiments.* Qualifying paper, Harvard Graduate School of Education, Cambridge, Mass.

MacMurray, J. (1957). *The Self as agent.* Faber, London.

Madison, P. (1969). *Personality Development in College.* Addison Wesley, Reading, Mass.

Magee, B. (1973). *Popper.* Fontana, London.

Mann, R. (1973). The identity of the group researcher. In G. S. Gibbard *et al.* (eds.), *Analysis of Groups: contributions to theory, research and practice.* Jossey Bass, San Francisco.

Mannheim, K. (1936). *Ideology and Utopia.* Kegan Paul, London.

March, J. G. and Simon, H. A. (1958). *Organizations.* Wiley, New York.

Marcuse, H. (1969). *An Essay on Liberation.* Allen Lane, London.

Marrow, A. J. (1969). *The Practical Theorist: the life and work of Kurt Lewin.* Basic Books, New York.

Maruyama, M. (1961). The multilateral mutual simultaneous causal relationships among the modes of communication, sociometric pattern and intellectual orientation in the Danish culture. *Phylon,* **22,** 41-58.

Maruyama, M. (1963a). The second cybernetics: deviation amplifying mutual causal processes. *American Scientist,* **51**(3), 250-6.

Maruyama, M. (1963b). Basic elements in misunderstandings. *Dialectica,* **17,** 78-92, 99-110.

Maruyama, M. (1966). Monopolarization, family and individuality. *Psychiatric Quaterly,* **40,** 133-49.

Maruyama, M. (1968). Trans-social rapport through prison inmates. *Annales Internationales de Criminologie,* **7,** 19-46.

Maruyama, M. (1969). Epistemology of social science research: exploration in inculture researchers. *Dialectica,* **23,** 229-80.

Maruyama, M. (1972). Symbiotization of cultural heterogeneity: scientific, epistemological and esthetic bases. *Third Symposium on Cultural Futuristics.* American Anthropological Association, Washington.

Maruyama, M. (1974). Endogenous research vs. 'experts' from outside. *Futures,* **6,** 389-394.

Maruyama, M. (1975). *Endogenous Research of Prison Culture by Prison Inmates.* University Microfilms Monograph N.LD0043.

Maruyama, M. (1978a). Endogenous research and polyocular anthropology. In R. E. Holloman and S. Arutionov (eds.), In *Perspectives on Ethnicity.* Mouton, The Hague.

Maruyama, M. (1978b). Heterogenistics and morphogenetics: toward a new concept of the scientific. *Theory and Society,* **5**(1), 75-96.

Maruyama, M. (1979). Mindscapes. *World Future Society Bulletin,* **13**(5), 13-23.

Marx, K. (1844). Alienated labour. In T. Burns (ed.), *Industrial Man.* Penguin, Harmondworth, Middx. (1969).

Maslow, A. H. (1966). *The Psychology of Science.* Harper & Row, New York.

Maslow, A. H. (1970). *Motivation and Personality* (2nd edn.). Harper & Row, New York.

Massarik, F. (1979). *The science of perceiving: foundations for an empirical phenomenology.* Graduate School of Management, University of California, Los

Angeles, available from the author. Published in French as La science du percevoir: fondements d'une phenomenologie empirique, in M. Parent and R. Marineau, (eds.), *L'intervention en psychologie*. L'Université du Quebec à Trois Rivières, Quebec.

May, R. (1967). *Psychology and the Human Dilemma*. Van Nostrand, Princeton, NJ.

McCartney, J. (1970). On being scientific; changing styles of presentation of sociological research. *Am. Sociol.* **5**, 30-5.

McCrindle, J. and Rowbotham, S. (eds.) (1979). *Dutiful Daughters. Women talk about their lives*. Penguin, Harmondsworth, Middx.

McLuhan, M. (1964). *Understanding media*. Routledge & Kegan Paul, London.

Meehl, P. E. (1954). *Clinical vs. statistical prediction: a theoretical analysis and a review of the evidence*. University of Minneapolis Press, Minneapolis.

Meehl, P. E. (1957). When shall we use our heads instead of a formula? *Journal of Counsel. Psychol.*, **4**, 268-73.

Meehl, P. E. (1959). A comparison of clinicians with five statistical methods of identifying psychotic MMPI profiles. *Journal of Counsel. Psychol.*, **6**, 102-9.

Merleau-Ponty, M. (1963). *The Structure of Behavior*. Beacon, Boston.

Messick, S. (1970). Evaluation of educational programs as research on the educational process. In F. F. Korten, S. W. Cook, and J. I. Lacey (eds.), *Psychology and Problems of Society*. American Psychological Association, Washington, DC.

Milgram, S. (1974). *Obedience to Authority: an experimental view*. Harper & Row, New York.

Mill, J. S. (1872). *A System of Logic*. (8th edn.). Longmans, Green, New York.

Miller, G. (1969). Psychology as a means of promoting human welfare *American Psychologist*, **24**, 1063-75.

Miller, G. A., Galanter, E., and Pribram, K. H. (1960). *Plans and the Structure of Behavior*. Holt, New York.

Miller, J. B. (ed.) (1974). *Psychoanalysis and Women*. Penguin, Harmondsworth, Middx.

Miller, J. B. (1976). *Toward a New Psychology of Women*. Beacon, Boston.

Miller, J. G. (1965). Living systems: basic concepts. *Behavioral Science*, **10**(3), 193-237.

Miller, C. and Swift, K. (1979). *Words and Women: new language in new times*. Penguin, Harmondsworth, Middx.

Millman, M. and Kanter, R. M. (eds.) (1975). *Another Voice: feminist perspectives on social life and social science*. Doubleday Anchor Books, Garden City, New York.

Milsum, J. H. (1968). *Positive Feedback*. Pergamon, Oxford.

Ministry of Local Government and Lands (1977). *Lefatshe La Rona — Our Land: the report on the Botswana Government's Public Consultation on its policy proposals on tribal grazing land*. Gaberone, Government Printers.

Mitroff, I. I. (1974). *The Subjective Side of Science: philosophical inquiry into the psychology of the Apollo Moon Scientists*. Elsevier, Amsterdam.

Mitroff, I. I. and Kilmann, R. H. (1978). *Methodological Approaches to Social Science: integrating divergent concepts and theories*. Jossey Bass, San Francisco.

Moore, G. E. (1903). *Principia Ethica*. Cambridge University Press (paperback edition, 1959).

Moulton, (1977). *Animation Rurale: education for rural development*. University of Massachusetts.

Moustakas, C. (1961). *Loneliness*. Prentice Hall, Englewood Cliffs, NJ.

Moustakas, C. (1967). Heuristic research. In J. Bugental (ed.), *Challenges of Humanistic Psychology*. McGraw-Hill, New York.

Nichols, M. P. and Zax, M. (1977). *Catharsis in Psychotherapy*. Gardner Press, New York.

Nicolaus, M. (1968). Remarks at the American Sociological Association Convention. *Am. Sociol,* **8**(1), 37-40.

Niehoff, R. (nd). *Report on the conference and workshop on non-formal education and the rural poor.* Michigan State University. See also The NFE Exchange of MSU Institute for International Studies in Education.

Norman, W. (1979). The administration of good teaching − II. *Memo to the Faculty,* (Center for Research on Learning and Teaching, University of Michigan), **63**, 7-10.

Nunnally, J. C. (1955). An investigation of some propositions of self-conception: the case of Miss Sun. *Journal of Abnorm. Soc. Psychol.,* **50**, 87-92.

Nyerere, J. (1973). *Freedom and Development: a selection from writings and speeches 1968-1973.* Oxford University Press, Oxford.

Okely, J. (1978). Privileged, schooled and finished: boarding education for girls. In S. Ardener (ed.), *Defining Females,* pp. 109-139. Croom Helm, London.

Ornstein, R. E. (1977). *The Psychology of Consciousness* (2nd edn.) Harcourt Brace, New York.

Ouspensky, P. (1949). *In Search of the Miraculous.* Harcourt, New York.

Palazzoli, M. S., Boscolo, M., Cecchin, G., Prata, G. (1978). *Paradox and Counter-paradox.* Aronson, New York.

Palmer, R. E. (1969). *Hermeneutics: interpretation theory in Schleiermacher, Dilthey, Heidegger and Gadamer.* Northwestern University Press, Evanston, Ill.

Palmore, E. (1962). Sociologists class origins and political ideologies. *Sociology and Social Research,* **47**, 45-50.

Parlee, M. B. (1975). Psychology. Review essay. *Signs,* **1**(1), 119-38.

Parlee, M. B. (1979). Psychology and women. Review essay, *Signs,* **5**(1), 121-33.

Parlett, M. R. (1975). *A Descriptive Analysis of a Liberal Arts College: methods and interpretation in a commissioned case study.* Paper written for 34th Annual Meeting of the Society for Applied Anthropology Amsterdam, March 1975, and reprinted in Parlett, M. R. and Dearden, G. J. (eds.) (1977).

Parlett, M. R. and Dearden, G. J. (eds.) (1977). *Introduction to Illuminative Evaluation: studies in higher education.* Pacific Soundings Press, Cardiff-by-the-Sea, Calif.

Parlett, M. R. and Hamilton, D. F. (1972). *Evaluation as Illumination: a new approach to the study of innovatory programs.* University of Edinburgh, Centre for Research in the Educational Sciences, Occasional Paper No. 9.

Perls, F. S. (1972). Four Lectures, In J. Fagan and I. L. Shepherd (eds.), *Gestalt Therapy Now: theory, techniques, applications.* Penguin, Harmondsworth, Middx.

Perry, R. B. (1936). *The thought and character of William James,* (2 vols). Little, Brown, Boston.

Perry, S. (1966). *The Human Nature of Science: researchers at work in psychiatry.* The Free Press, New York.

Peters, R. S. (1977). *Education and the Education of Teachers.* Routledge & Kegan Paul, London.

Phillips, D. L. (1971). *Knowledge from What? Theories and methods in social research.* Rand McNally, Chicago.

Piaget, J. (1953). *The Origin of Intelligence in the Child.* Routledge & Kegan Paul, London.

Pietrofesa, J. J. and Splete, H. (1975). *Career Development: theory and research.* Grune & Stratton, New York.

Pilsworth, M. and Weddell, G. (n.d.) Department of Adult Education, University of Manchester.

Pirsig, R. M. (1976). *Zen and the Art of Motorcycle Maintenance: an inquiry into values.* Corgi Books, London.

Platt, J. (1976). *The Realities of Social Research: an empirical study of British sociologists.* Sussex University Press.

Polanyi, M. (1958). *Personal Knowledge: towards a postcritical Philosophy.* Routledge & Kegan Paul, London.

Polanyi, M. (1959). *The Study of Man.* University of Chicago Press, Chicago.

Polanyi, M. (1964). *Science, Faith and Society.* University of Chicago Press, Chicago.

Polanyi, M. (1967). *The Tacit Dimension.* Routledge & Kegan Paul, London.

Polsky, N. (1969). *Hustlers, Beats and Others.* Doubleday, Anchor Books, New York.

Popper, K. (1959). *The Logic of Scientific Discovery.* Hutchinson, London.

Popper, K. (1970). Normal science and its dangers, In I. Lakatos and A. Musgrave (eds.), *Criticism and the Growth of Knowledge,* Cambridge University Press, Cambridge.

Powdermaker, H. (1966). *Stranger and Friend: the way of an anthropologist.* Norton, New York.

Price, H. H. (1969). *Belief.* Allen & Unwin, London.

Psathas, G. (1968). Ethnomethodology and phenomenology. *Social Research,* **35,** 500-520.

Randall, R., Southgate, J. and Tomlinson, F. (1980). *Co-operative and Community Group Dynamics... or your meetings needn't be so appalling.* Barefoot Books, London.

Rapoport, R. N. (1970). Three dilemmas in action research. *Human Relations,* **23,** 499-513.

Reason, P. W. (1976). 'Explorations in the dialectics of interpersonal relationship'. Ph.D. dissertation. Case Western Reserve University, Cleveland, Ohio.

Reason, P. W. (1980). Human interaction as exchange and as encounter. *Small Group Behavior,* **11**(1), 3-12.

Reed, D. (1975). Conscientization: an experience in Peru. *New Internationalist,* **16** (June 1974), reprinted in the *National Labour Institute Bulletin,* **1**(7) (July), 3-5.

Reich, C. A. (1972). *The Greening of America.* Penguin, Harmondsworth, Middx.

Reich, W. (1961). *The Function of the Orgasm.* Farrar, Strauss, & Giroux, New York.

Reid, T. (1764). *Inquiry into the Human Mind: on the principles of common sense.* Edinburgh.

Reik, T. (1948). *Listening with the Third Ear: the inner experience of a psychoanalyst.* Farrar, Strauss, & Giroux, New York.

Reinharz, S. (1979a). *On Becoming a Social Scientist: from survey research and participant observation to experiential analysis.* Jossey-Bass, San Francisco.

Reinharz, S. (1979b). Undergraduates as experiential learning facilitators, In S. Brooks and J. Althof (eds.), *New Directions for Experiential Learning,* pp. 45-64. Jossey-Bass, San Francisco.

Reymond, L. (1971). *To Live Within.* Doubleday, New York.

Rich, A. (1972). When we dead awaken: writing as re-vision. *College English,* **34**(1), 18-25.

Richardson, S. A., Dohrenwend, B. A., and Klein, D. (1965). *Interviewing: its forms and functions.* Basic Books, New York.

Richer, P. (1978). A phenomenological analysis of the perception of geometric illusions. *Journal of Phenomenological Psychology,* **8,** 123-35.

Riedl, R. (1976). *Die strategie der Genesis: naturgeschichte der realen welt.* Piper, München.

Rivlin, A. and Timpane, P. (1975). *Planned Variation in Education: should we give up or try harder?* The Brookings Institution, Washington, DC.

Rogers, C. R. (1961). *On Becoming a Person. A therapist's view of psychotherapy.* Constable, London.

Rogers, C. R. (1964). 'Some thoughts regarding the current philosophy of the behavioral sciences'. Unpublished Paper. Western Behavioral Sciences Institute, La Jolla, California.

Rogers, C. R. (1968). Some thoughts concerning the pre-suppositions of the behavioral sciences, In W. R. Coulson, and C. R. Rogers (eds.), *Man and the Science of Man.* Charles E. Merrill, Columbus, Ohio.

Rosenthal, R. (1966). *Experimenter Effects in Behavioral Research.* Appleton, New York.

Roszak, T. (1969). *The Making of a Counter Culture: reflections on the technocratic society and its useful opposition.* Doubleday Anchor, New York.

Roth, J. (1966). Hired hand research. *Am. Sociol,* **1**, 190-96.

Rowan, J. (1973). *Psychological Aspects of Society,* No. 2: *The Social Individual.* Davis-Poynter, London.

Rowan, J. (1974). Research as intervention, In N. Armistead (ed.), *Reconstructing Social Psychology.* Penguin, Harmondsworth, Middx.

Rowan, J. (1976a). *Ordinary Ecstasy: humanistic psychology in action.* Routledge & Kegan Paul, London.

Rowan, J. (1976b). *Psychological Aspects of Society,* No. 3: *The Power of the Group.* Davis-Poynter, London.

Rowan, J. (1979). Hegel and self-actualization. *European Journal of Humanistic Psychology.* **1**(4), 129-38 and 149-54.

Sandywell, B. (1975). Introduction: critical tradition, in B. Sandywell *et al., Problems of Reflexivity and Dialectics in Sociological Inquiry: language theorizing differences.* Routledge & Kegan Paul, London.

Sanford, N. (ed.). (1956). Personality development during the college years. *Journal of Social Issues,* **12**, 1-75.

Sanford, N. (1970a). Whatever happened to action research? *Journal of Social Issues,* **26**, (4).

Sanford, N. (1970b). The Wright Institute's program for training in social-clinical psychology. A contribution to the symposium 'Mental Health Training: revolution in professional training'. Norman Natulef, Chairman, Annual Convention of the American Psychological Association, Miami, Florida, 5 September.

Sarason, S. B. (1978). The nature of problem solving in social action. *American Psychologist,* **33**(4), 370-80.

Sarbin, T. R., Taft, R. and Bailey, D. E. (1960). *Clinical Inference and Cognitive Theory.* Holt, Rinehart, & Winston, New York.

Saussure, F. de (1966). *Course in General Linguistics.* McGraw-Hill, New York.

Schechner, R. (1973). *Environmental Theatre.* Hawthorne Books, New York.

Schein, E. H. (1969). *Process Consultation: its role in organization development.* Addison-Wesley, Reading, Mass.

Schumacher, E. F. (1977). *A Guide for the Perplexed.* Jonathan Cape, London.

Schuster, R. (1979). Empathy and mindfulness. *Journal of Humanistic Psychology,* **19**(1), 71-7.

Schwartz, H. and Jacobs, J. (1979). *Qualitative Sociology: a method to the madness.* Free Press, New York.

Schwartz, P. and Ogilvy, J. (1980). *The emergent paradigm: changing patterns of thought and belief.* Analytical Report No.7, Values and Lifestyles Program, SRI International, Menlo Park, Calif.

Scriven, M. (1967). The methodology of evaluation. In R. W. Tyler *et al.* (eds.), *Perspectives of Curriculum Evaluation.* (American Educational Research

Association monograph series on curriculum evaluation), Rand McNally, Chicago.

Scully, D. and Bart, P. (1973). A funny thing happened on the way to the orifice: women in gynecology textbooks. *American Journal of Sociology,* **78**, 1045-50.

Searle, J. R. (1969). *Speech Acts: an essay on the philosophy of language.* Cambridge University Press, Cambridge.

Sedgwick, P. (1974). Ideology in modern psychology. In N. Armistead (ed.), *Reconstructing Social Psychology,* pp. 29-37. Penguin, London.

Shannon, C. and Weaver, W. (1949). *Mathematical Theory of Communication.* University of Illinois, Urbana, Ill.

Shapiro, M. B. (1961). The single case in fundamental clinical psychological research. *Brit. Journal of Med. Psychol.,* **34**, 255-62.

Sheehy, G. (1976). *Passages: Predictable Crises of Adult Life.* Dutton, New York.

Sheffield, J. and Diejomoah, V. (1972). *Non-formal Education in African Development.* African-American Institute, New York.

Sibley, E. (1963). *The Education of Sociologists in the United States.* Russell Sage Foundation, New York.

Siegel, S. (1956). *Nonparametric Methods for the Behavioral Sciences.* McGraw-Hill, New York.

Silverstein, M. (1972). Development of an identity: power and sex roles in academia. *Journal of Applied Behavioral Science,* **8**(5), 536-63.

Sims, D. (1978). 'Problem construction in teams'. Ph.D. thesis, University of Bath, England.

Sims, D. (1979). A framework for understanding the definition and formulation of problems in teams. *Human Relations,* **32**, 909-21.

Sinnett, E. R. and Sachson, A. (1970). *A Rehabilitation Living Unit in a University Dormitory Setting: final report.* Kansas State University Counseling Center, Manhattan, Kansas (mimeographed, 70 pp.).

Sjoberg, G. (1967). *Ethics, Politics and Social Research.* Schenkman, Cambridge, Mass.

Smith, D. E. (1974). Women's perspective as a radical critique of sociology, *Sociological Inquiry,* **44**(1), 7-13.

Smith, D. E. (1978). A peculiar eclipsing: women's exclusion from man's culture, *Women's Studies International Quarterly,* **1**(4), 281-95.

Snoek, J. D. (1969). Editor's introduction. Selected papers. *Journal of Social Issues,* **25**, 1-3.

Soskin, W. and Korchin, S. (1967). 'Therapeutic explorations with adolescent drug users'. Unpublished manuscript. Psychology Clinic, University of California, Berkeley.

Southgate, J. and Randall, R. (1978). *The Barefoot Psychoanalyst.* The Association of Karen Horney Psychoanalytic Counsellors, London.

Southgate, J. and Randall, R. (1979). *The Psychodynamics of Self-managed Groups.* Loughborough University monograph.

Southgate, J., Randall, R., and Tomlinson, F. (1980). *Cooperative and community group dynamics* (or your meetings needn't be so appalling). Barefoot Books, London.

Spender, D. (1978a). Editorial. *Women's Studies International Quarterly,* **1**(1), 1.

Spender, D. (1978b). Notes on the organization of women's studies. *Women's Studies International Quarterly,* **1**(3), 255-75.

Spender, D. (1980). *Man-made Language.* Routledge & Kegan Paul, London.

Steers, R. M. (1975). Problems in the measurement of organizational effectiveness. *Administrative Science Quarterly,* **20**(4), 546-58.

Steinbeck, J. and Ricketts, E. F. (1941). *Sea of Cortez: a leisurely journal of travel and research*. Viking Press, New York.

Stephenson, W. (1953). *The Study of Behavior: Q-technique and its methodology*. University of Chicago Press, Chicago.

Stinson, A. (1977). *Action-Research for Community Action*. Carleton University School of Social Work, Ottawa.

Storr, A. (1976). *The Dynamics of Creation*. Penguin, Harmondsworth, Middx.

Stringer, D. (1978). 'Adult literacy in Great Britain'. A paper given to the European seminar on participatory research in the Netherlands, (available from J. de Vries, Studiecentrum NCVO, Nieuweweg 4, Amersfoort.)

Stringer, P. and Bannister, D. (eds.) (1979). *Constructs of Sociality and Individuality*. Academic Press, New York.

Sullivan, H. S. (1953). *The Interpersonal Theory of Psychiatry*. Norton & Co., New York.

Sullivan, H. S. (1964). *The Fusion of Psychiatry and Social Science*. Norton & Co., New York.

Susman, G. and Evered, R. (1978). An assessment of the scientific merits of action research. *Administrative Science Quarterly*, **23**, 582-682.

Swantz, M. L. (1974). *Youth and Development in the Coast Region of Tanzania*. Research Report No. 6 (new series). Bureau of Resource Assessment and Land Use Planning, University of Dar-es-Salaam.

Swantz, M. L. (1975a). *The Role of Participant Research in Development*. Research Report No. 15 (new series). Bureau of Resource Assessment and Land Use Planning, University of Dar-es-Salaam.

Swantz, M. L. (1975b). *Young Child Study* (Part I, ages 1-6: Part II, ages 7-15). Tanzania National Scientific Research Council/UNICEF. Dar-es-Salaam.

Swantz, M. L. and Jerman, H. (eds.) (1977). *Jipemoya, Development and Culture Research*, vol. I. Scandinavian Institute of African Studies, Uppsala.

Swantz, M. L. and Rudengreen, J. (1976). *Village Skills Survey: report on pre-pilot and pilot surveys*. Bureau of Resource Assessment and Land Use Planning, University of Dar-es-Salaam.

Sykes, G. (1962). *The Hidden Remnant*. Harper, New York.

Tandon, R. (1979). 'Participatory research: an exploratory statement'. Paper presented during National Meeting on Participatory Research, New Delhi.

Tart, C. T. (1971). *Journal of Transpersonal Psychology*, 3(2).

Tart, C. T. (1972). States of consciousness and state-specific science. *Science*, **176** (June), 1203-1210.

Taylor, J. C. (1979). Job satisfaction and quality of work life: a re-assessment. In L. Davis and J. Taylor, *Design of Jobs* (2nd edn.). Goodyear Publishing Company, Santa Monica, California.

Terkel, S. (1974). *Working: people talk about what they do all day and how they feel about what they do*. Pantheon, New York.

Tiger, L. and Fox, R. (1972). *The Imperial Animal*. Secker and Warburg, London.

Torbert, W. (1972). *Learning from Experience: toward consciousness*. Columbia University Press, Columbia.

Torbert, W. (1974/5). Pre- and post-bureaucratic stages of organization development. *Interpersonal Dynamics*.

Torbert, W. (1975). 'Organizing the unknown: the politics of higher education'. Unpublished manuscript. Harvard Graduate School of Education.

Torbert, W. (1976a). *Creating a Community of Inquiry: conflict, collaboration, transformation*. Wiley, New York.

Torbert, W. (1976b). On the possibility of revolution within the boundaries of propriety. *Humanitas,* **12**(1), 111-46.

Torbert, W. (1977). 'Organizational effectiveness: five universal criteria'. Unpublished manuscript. Tiburon, California.

Torbert, W. (1978). Educating toward shared purpose, self-direction, and quality work: the theory and practice of liberating structure. *Journal of Higher Education,* **49**(2), 109-135.

Trist, E. (1979). New directions of hope: recent innovations inter-connecting organizational, industrial, community and personal development. *Human Futures,* **2**, 175-85.

Trungpa, C. (1969). *Meditation in Action.* Shambhala, Berkeley.

Trungpa, C. (1974). *Cutting Through Spiritual Materialism.* Shambhala, Berkeley.

Turner, R. (1974). *Ethnomethodology: selected readings.* Penguin, Harmondsworth, Middx.

UNESCO/UNP (1976). *A Critical Assessment of the Experimental World Literacy Programme.* UNESCO, Paris.

Vaillant, G. (1977). *Adaptation to Life.* Little, Brown, Boston.

Vaughter, R. (1976). Psychology. Review essay. *Signs,* **2**(1), 120-46.

Versluys, J. (1977). *Research in Adult Literacy.* International Institute for Adult Literacy Methods, Teheran.

Vicunus, M. (ed.) (1973). *Suffer and Be Still. Women in the Victorian age.* Indiana University Press, Bloomington and London.

Vidich, A., Bensman, J., and Stein, M. (eds.) (1971). *Reflections on Community Studies.* Harper & Row, New York.

von Cranach, M., Foppa, K., Lepenies, W., and Ploog, D. (1980). *Human Ethology: claims and limits of a new discipline.* Cambridge University Press, Cambridge.

von Cranach, M. and Harré, R. (1980). *The Analysis of Action: recent theoretical and empirical advances.* Cambridge University Press, Cambridge.

von Foerster, H. (1949-53). *Transactions of Josiah Macy Jr. Foundation conferences on cybernetics.* Josiah Macy Jr. Foundation, New York.

Waddington, C. (ed.) (1968-71). *Towards a Theoretical Biology.* (4 vols.). Edinburgh University Press, Edinburgh.

Walford, G. (1979). *Ideologies and their Functions: a study in systematic ideology.* George Walford, The Bookshop, 186 Upper St., London, N1 1RH.

Walsby, H. (1947). *The Domain of Ideologies: a study of the origin, development and structure of ideologies.* MacLellan, Glasgow.

Webb, E., Campbell, D., Schwartz, R., and Sechrest, L. (1966). *Unobtrusive Measures: non-reactive research in the social sciences.* Rand McNally, Chicago.

Weick, K. (1976). 'On repunctuating the problem of organizational effectiveness'. Unpublished paper presented at the Workshop on Organizational Effectiveness, Carnegie-Mellon University, 28-29 June.

Weick, K. (1979). *The Social Psychology of Organizing.* Addison-Wesley, Reading, Mass.

Weil, A. (1972). *The Natural Mind: a new way of looking at drugs and the higher consciousness.* Houghton Mifflin, Boston.

Weinreich, H. (1977). What future for the female subject? Some implications of the women's movement for psychological research. *Human Relations,* **30**(6), 535-43.

Weisstein, N. (1970). 'Kinde, Kuche, Kirche' as scientific law: psychology constructs the female. In R. Morgan (ed.), *Sisterhood is Powerful: an anthology of writings from the women's liberation movement,* pp. 228-44. Random House, New York.

Wieder, D. (1974). Telling the code. In R. Turner (ed.), *Ethnomethodology.* Penguin,

Harmondsworth, Middx.

Wiener, N. (1948). *Cybernetics: control and communication in the animal and the machine.* Wiley, New York.

Willems, E. (1969). Planning a rationale for naturalistic research. In E. Willems and H. Rausch (eds.), *Naturalistic Viewpoints in Psychological Research,* pp. 44-71. Holt, Rinehart & Winston, New York.

Winnicott, D. (1965). *The Maturational Processes and the Facilitating Environment.* Hogarth Press, London.

Wittgenstein, L. (1953). *Philosophical Investigations.* Blackwell, Oxford.

Wolf, B. (1979). 'The teen-age drug use experience'. Unpublished doctoral dissertation. University of Michigan.

Wolff, K. (1971). Surrender and community study: the study of Loma. In A. Vidich, J. Bensman, and M. Stein (eds.), *Reflections on Community Studies.* Harper & Row, New York.

Worth, S. (1967). The Navajo as filmmaker: a brief report on some recent research in the cross-cultural aspects of film communication. *American Anthropologist,* **69,** 76-8.

Worth, S. and Adair, J. (1972). *Through Navajo Eyes: an exploration in film communication and anthropology.* Indiana University Press, Bloomington.

Wright, J. (in preparation). 'Open communication in a graduate training program', Doctoral dissertation. Department of Psychology, University of Michigan.

Wylie, R. (1961) *The Self-concept: a critical survey of pertinent research literature.* University of Nebraska Press, Lincoln.

Zelman, R. (1979). The mystical roots of Hegel's philosophy, *The Humanistic Psychology Institute Review,* **1**(2), 43-70.

Author Index

Acland, H., 151
Adair, 230, 269, 270
Adams-Webber, J.R., 196
Ahmed, M., 447
Akin, G., xxi
Alderfer, C.P., 117, 119
Allport, F.H., 73
Allport, G.W., xix, 63–76
APA, 63, 64, 176, 180
Ardener, E., 460, 466
Ardener, S., 458, 467, 468
Argyris, C., xvi, xvii, 96, 142, 146, 147,
   150, 151, 337, 429, 439, 443
Aristotle, Aristotelean, xviii, 88, 114,
   127, 129, 130, 228
Armistead, N., 428
Arnold, B., 213
Asch, S., 23
Assagioli, R., 124
Austin, J.L., 15

Bakan, D., xvi, xix, 191–199
Baldwin, A.L., 72
Banner, L.W., 464
Bannister, D., xvi, xix, 191–199
Barbar, B., 427
Bart, P., 463

Bartunek, J., 347
Bass, B.M., xvi
Bateson, G., 114, 128, 241, 242
Bauman, 2, 135
Beals, R.L., 175
Becker, C., 426, 435
Bedmar, R., 428
Bell, C.H., 150
Bellow, S., 386, 387
Bem, D.J., 115
Benne, K.D., xvii
Bennis, W.G., xvii
Berger, P.L., 311
Bernard, J., 428, 460, 468, 469
Berne, E., 124
Berry, L., 347
Bhaskar, R., 14
Bickley, W., 347
Bion, W.R., xvi, 349, 350
Blanco, M., 59
Blum, R., 177
Bogdan, T., 127
Bohr, N., 79
Borton, T., 127
Boughey, H., xxi, 245–6
Bowen, E.S., 415
Bowers, 448

Bradford, L.P., xvii
Brandt, W., 133
Brenner, M., 16
Brentano, F.C., 22
Bristol Women's Studies Group, 458, 463
Brockman, J., 241
Bronfenbreuner, U., 415
Bronowski, J., 144
Broverman, D.M., 74, 75
Brown, J., 423
Brown, L.D., 249, 293, 303–314
Brown, P., xvi
Bruner, J., 15
Bryant, F., 423
Bryceson, D., 290
Buber, M., 129, 417
Buckley, W., 228
Bugental, J., 207
Buhl, H., 213
Burke, C.G., 471
Burman, S., 458
Byrd, Admiral, 213

Callan, H., 465, 470
Callaway, H., xxii, 245, 457–471
Camara, S., 227
Campbell, D.T., 46, 103, 142, 150, 175, 239, 240, 243, 244
Cantril, H., 73
Carlson, R., 469
Castaneda, C., 150, 438–9
Chambers, W., 213
Chang, T.S., 227
Chester, P. 464
Chin, R., 381
Chomsky, N., 25
Churchman, C.W., 40, 50, 145
Cicourel, A.V., xxi
Clark, P.A., 379
Clason-Hook, C., 448
Clausius, 6
Cohen, D., 151
Cohen, M.D., 141, 144
Coleman, J., 141, 144
Collin, A., 385–394
Conrad, H.S., 74
Coombs, P., 447
Cornforth, M., 450
Coser, L.A., 461, 463
Crowle, A.J., 13, 420

Dalton, 183
Daniels, A.K., xxi
Dannheisser, P., 448
DATG/ACJ, 444
Darwin, C., 228, 465
Davies, M.L., 470
Davis, J., 422
Davis, M., 47
Dearden, G.J., 219, 222
Degler, C.N., 465
Delamont, S., 464, 468
Deutsch, M.N., 174
Devereux, E.C., 415
Devereux, G., xvi, 77–81, 105, 244
Dickinson, E., 213
Diejomoah, V., 447
Diesing, P., 183–189, 240
Dilthey, 65, 66, 135
Dionysus, 39
Donner, P., 290
Duberman, M., 438
Duffin, L., 464, 468
Duval, V.H., 10

Ebbinghaus, 64
Eddington, A., 11
Eden, C., 375
Ehrenreich, B., 464
Ehrlich, H., 423
Elden, M., 249, 253–266
English D., 464
Enright, J., 122
Erikson, E., 183
Eskimo, 228
Esterson, A., 50, 96, 167–171, 249
Evans, H., 447
Evered, R., 258, 313

Fadinman, J., 124
Fallaci, O., 203
Farrell, G., xxii, 429
Feuerstein, M.T., 219
Filmer, P., xvii, 365
Fineman, S., 473–484
Fiske, D.W., 244
Form, W., 416
Fox, R., 427, 464
Frager, R., 124
Frankl, V.E., 132
Fransella, F., xvi, 96, 196, 197

Freire, P., 53, 54, 264, 293, 299, 349, 350, 351, 361, 422
French, W.L., 150
Freud, S., xvi, 80, 81, 122, 183, 194, 317, 463
Friedan, B., 463
Friedlander, F., xvi
Friedman, N., 144
Fromm, E., 213
Fromm-Reichmann, F., 213
Fry, R., 430
Funkhauser, M., 177

Gadamer, H.G., 132, 135, 240
Galileo, 8
Garfinkel, H., xxi
Garforth, 448
Geertz, C., 135
Gendlin, E.T., 242
Giddens, A., xviii
Gillette, A., 447
Gilmartin, B., 423
Giorgi, A., 96
Gish, G., 430
Glaser, B.G., xx, xxi, 374
Glen, R.H., 307, 311
Goertzel, T., 421
Goffman, E., 5
Golde, P., 415
Goleman, D., 164
Goodall, J., 16
Gordon, G., 44
Gordon, L., 460
Gorman, T., 448
Gouldner, A.W., 183, 310, 415
Grant, J., 175
Grant, J.D., 175
Graumann, C.F., 66
Green, A.M., 117
Green, E.E., 117
Greenberg, I.A., 124
Grof, S., xxi, 96, 124
Gross, N., 147
Grotowski, J., 444
Gurdjieff, 443
Gustavsen, B., 253, 259
Guthrie, 80

Habermas, J., xvii, 145
Hacker, 16
Hainer, R., 125-127, 129, 133

Hall, B.L., 96, 261, 265, 266, 293, 303, 447-456
Hamilton, D.F., 219, 226
Hammond, P., 415
Hampden-Turner, C., xvii, 96, 438
Harré, R., xix, 3-17, 96, 243, 374, 378, 483
Hartman, M., 464
Hastings, J.T., 220
Hearnshaw, L.S., 66
Heather, N., xvi
Healy, G., 60
Hegel (Hegelian), G.L.F., xii, xviii, xx, 40, 115-124, 129, 136
Heidegger, M., xvii, 132, 135
Heider, 11
Heraditus, 126, 129
Herbst, P.G., 261-2, 483
Heron, J., xix, xxi, 19-35, 50, 96, 134, 153-166, 242, 243, 244, 245, 246, 249, 488
Hillman, J., 50
Hiss, A., 213
Hoel, M., 265
Hoff, W., 175
Holmes, J., 448
Horney, K., 462, 463
Horowitz, I.L., 415
Horton, B., 144
HUAC, 213
Hudson, L., 44, 386, 387
Hume, D., 8, 9, 13, 14, 114
Humphrey, C., 467
Hunnius, G., 253
Hurskainen, A., 290
Hussert, E., 142, 145
Hvinden, B., 265
Hyder, S., 483

IBM, 69
ICAE, 448, 449, 486
Israel, J., xvi

Jackins, M., 458, 471
Jacobs, J., 417
Jacobus, M., 458, 471
James, W., 65, 73, 379
Jamieson, M., 219, 225
Jencks, C., 141, 144
Jerman, 284, 290
Jowett, B., 449

Joynson, R.G., xvi
Jung, C.G., xvi, 39, 44

Kahn, S., 264
Kamin, L.J., xvi
Kanter, R.M., 428, 468, 469
Kant, E., 40, 145, 461
Kaplan, A., 186, 239, 427
Kaplan, R.E., 303-314
Kaul, T., 428
Keddie, N., 468
Kelly, G.A., xvi, 74, 192-199
Kelly, J., 465, 466
Kelman, H.C., 422, 429
Kepler, J., 8
Kidd, 447, 448
Kilmann, R.H., xix, 43-51, 97
Kilpatrick, F.P., 73
King, Martin Luther, 440
Kiwale, E., 290
Kiyenze, B.K.S., 290
Klaeber, F., 389
Kluckhohn, C.M., 67
Knutson, J.K., 96
Kockelmans, J., 132, 135, 240
Koestler, A., 59
Kohlberg, L., 117, 119
Kohler, W., 64
Kolb, D., 430
Korchin, S., 174
Kramer, C., 471
Krishnamurti, J., 150
Kuhn, T., 142, 311

Labov, W., 96, 468
La Barre, W., 77, 80
Laing, R.D., xvi, 134, 171, 320, 429
Langer, S., 145
Laurillard, D.M., 222
Legge, C.D., 448
Leibnitz, 40
Lenrow, P., 174, 175
Levin, M., 266
Levinson, D.J., 131, 393
Levinson, M.H., 131, 393
Levi-Strauss, C., 80, 386, 387
Lewin, K., xvii, 173, 174, 175, 178,
    293, 303
Lilienfeld, R., 204
Lincoln, A., 213
Lindner, R., 204

Lindzey, G., 75
Linton, 80
Liss, J., 124
Linne, 228
Locke, J., 40, 145
Loevinger, J., 117, 119
Lofland, J., xix
Luckman, T., 311
Lukas, C., 147
Lundberg, 66

Mach, E., 14
MacMurray, J., 145
Madison, P., 247, 248, 249, 315-318
Magee, B., 165
Malinowski, B., 183
Mann, R., 415
Mannheim, K., 145
March, J.G., 141, 144, 488
Marcuse, H., 95
Marrow, A.J., 174, 242, 250, 267-281,
    375, 376, 378
Marshall, J., 395-399
Maruyama, M., xviii, xix, xx, 50, 96,
    114, 128, 227-238
Marx, K., xvii, xviii, 54, 93, 94
Maslow, A.H., xvi, xviii, 44, 73, 83-91,
    104, 117, 119, 168
Massarik, F., 201-206
Matwi, M., 290
Maxwell, C., 6
May, R., 131
Mbilinyi, M., 290
McCartney, J., 423, 426
McCrindle, J., 470
McKnight, R., 230
McLuhan, M., 95
Mead, G.H., 11
Mead, M., 80
Medawar, P., 364
Meehl, P.E., 66, 69, 70
Mendel, 6
Menninger, K., 213
Merleau-Ponty, M., 145
Merrick, S., 175
Merton, 37
Milgram, S., 144, 195
Mill, J.S., 46, 65, 114
Miller, C., xxii, 471
Miller, G.A., 16, 176, 181
Miller, J.B., 463, 464

Miller, J.G., 128
Millman, M., 428, 468, 469
Milsum, J.H., 228
Ministry of Local Government and
Lands, Botswana, 448
Mitroff, I.I., xix, 37–41, 43–51, 97, 114,
151, 242, 345, 363
MMPI, 69
Mohave, 78
Moore, G.E., 210
Moulton, 447
Moustakas, C., 207–217
Murray, H.A., 67
Mustafa, K., 290

Nasoro, J., 290
Navajo, 228, 230, 269
Neely, R., 10
Newton, I., 6
Nicholaus, M., 425
Nichols, M.P., 124
Niehoff, R., 447
Norman, W., 428
Nunnally, J.C., 75
Nyerere, J., 283
Nylehn, B., 266

Ogilvy, J., 240
Okeley, J., 470
Ornstein, R.E., 28, 117
Ouspensky, P., 150

Palazzoli, M.S., 128–9
Palmer, R.E., 135
Palmore, E., 423
Parlee, M.B., 464
Parlett, M.R., 219–226
Perls, F.S., 488
Perry, R.B., 73, 144
Peters, R., 270
Phillips, D.L., 415, 419
Piaget, J., 58
Pietrofesa, J.J., 392, 394
Pilsworth, M., 448
Pirsig, R.M., 386, 387
Platt, J., 95
Polanyi, M., 26, 88, 127, 145, 209, 211,
423
Polsky, N., 96
Pondy, L., 151
Popper, K., 364, 365
Powdermaker, H., 415

Price, H.H., 159
Prosser, R., 447
Psathas, G., 375

Radcliffe-Brown, 183
Randall, R., 53–61, 105, 124, 349–361
Rapoport, R.N., 303
Reason, P., 43, 113–137, 183, 239–250,
319–331, 485–492
Reed, D., 264-5
Reich, C.A., 117
Reich, W., 162, 350
Reichenbach, 37
Reid, T., 25
Reik, T., 122
Reinharz, S., xx, 415–435, 443
Reymond, L., 150
Rich, A., 457
Richardson, S.A., 201
Richer, P., xxi
Ricketts, E.F., 212
Riedl, R., 228
Riesman, D., 213
Rigby, P., 290
Rivlin, A., 147
Rogers, C.R., xvi, 122, 183, 216-7, 240
Rosen, S., 104, 401–411
Rosenthal, R., 144
Rosenzweig, 136
Roszak, T., 114
Roth, J., 423
Rowan, J., xii, xix, xx, 37, 77, 83,
93–112, 113–137, 167, 239–250, 401,
423, 431, 471, 485–492
Rowbotham, S., 470
Rudengreen, 285

Sachson, A., 175
Saint-Exupéry, A., 213
Sandywell, B., 487
Sanford, N., xvii, 96, 173–181
Sarason, S.B., 310
Sarbin, T.R., 66, 70
Saussure, F. de, 58
Schechner, R., 444
Schein, E.H., xvii, 150
Schon, D., 146, 337, 439
Schumacher, E.F., 246
Schuster, R., 122
Schutz, 365
Schwartz, H., 417

Schwartz, P., 240
Scriven, M., 175, 179
Scully, D., 463
Searle, J.R., 15
Secord, 374, 378
Sedgwick, P., 425
Shannon, C., 228
Shapiro, M.B., 72
Sheehy, G., 247, 248
Sheffield, J., 447
Sibley, E., 429
Siegel, S., 442
Silverstein, M., 487
Sims, D., 248, 249, 373, 483, 488
Simmel, G., 461, 462
Simon, 488
Singer, 40
Sinnett, E.R., 175
Sitari, T., 290
Smith, D.E., 462, 468, 469
Smith, M., 151
Snoek, J.D., 181
Socrates, 444
Soskin, W., 174
Southgate, J., 53–61, 105, 124,
   349–361
Spender, D., 459, 468, 471
Splete, H., 392, 394
Spranger, 75
Stanley, J.C., 46, 103, 142, 150, 239,
   240, 243
Steers, R.M., 148
Steinbeck, J., 212
Stephenson, W., 75
Stinson, A., 448
Storr, A., 60
Strauss, A.L., xx, 374
Stringer, D., 448
Stringer, P., 196
Sullivan, H.S., xvi, 213
Susman, G., 258, 313
Swantz, M.L., 283–291
Swift, K., xxii, 471

Tabor, E., 213
Tajfel, H., xvi
Tandon, R., xviii, 293–301
Tart, C., 163, 245
Taylor, J.C., 265
Taylor, S.J., xix
Terkel, S., 203

Tiger, L., 464
Timpane, P., 147
Tolman, E., 71, 80
Tolstoy, L., 72
Torbert, W.R., xviii, xix, 50, 122,
   141–151, 242, 243, 245, 247, 249,
   333–347, 421, 425, 434, 437–446
Trist, E., 426, 431
Trotsky, L., 60
Trungpa, C., 150
Turner, R., 96

UNESCO, 448

Vaill, P., 151
Vaillant, G., 393
Vaughter, R., 464
Veium, K., 266
Vernon, 75
Versluys, J., 448
Vicunus, M., 464
Vidich, A., 415
Von Cranach, M., 15, 16
Von Foerster, H., 228
Vuorela, U., 290

Waddington, C., 228
Walford, G., 105, 117
Wallach, 64
Walsby, H., 121
Wanga, J.R., 290
Warr, 448
Weaver, W., 228
Webb, E., 441
Weddell, Co., 448
Weick, K., 148, 151, 312
Weil, A., 114
Weinreich, H., 464
Weisstein, N., 464
Wells, H.G., 72
White, 80
Whitehead, J., 363–372
Wicklund, R.A., 11
Wieder, D., xxi
Wiener, N., 228
Willems, E., 416
Winnicott, D., 488
Wittgenstein, L., 25, 145, 444
Wohstatter, R., 347
Wolf, B., 432

Wolfe, T., 213
Wolff, K., 427
Worth, S., 230, 269, 270
Wortman, P., 423
Wright, D., 119, 429, 433

Wylie, R., 71

Zax, M., 124
Zelman, R., xviii
Zen, 84, 88

Subject Index

Acausal, *see* Cause

Act, xi, xii, xiv, xv, xx, 4m 5m 6, 7, 12, 14, 15, 16, 17, 19, 20, 21, 22, 23, 24, 28, 29, 38, 49, 61, 73, 93, 94, 95, 99, 131, 142, 143, 144, 145, 146, 147, 148, 149, 150, 153, 154, 155, 156, 157, 158, 161, 162, 164, 165, 168, 169, 170, 171, 173, 175, 178, 185, 193, 203, 205, 223, 233, 234, 236, 237, 243, 245, 250, 253, 255, 258, 260, 264, 265, 266, 268, 271, 287, 288, 289, 291, 295, 296, 297, 298, 299, 300, 301, 305, 306, 309, 310, 311, 312, 313, 314, 318, 321, 344, 350, 352, 359, 360, 364, 365, 366, 367, 369, 370, 371, 374, 375, 378, 379, 380, 398, 407, 417, 418, 420, 421, 422, 426, 427, 428, 430, 431, 433, 435, 437, 439, 440, 441, 442, 443, 444, 449, 453, 454, 455, 457, 459, 460, 462, 464, 466, 473, 477, 478, 479, 481, 483, 486, 488, 489, 490, 491

Action, *see* Act

Action research, xvii, 53, 56, 96, 102, 120, 145, 148, 149, 150, 156, 170, 171, 173–181, 242, 243, 245, 249, 257, 265, 285, 293, 303, 306, 315, 346, 349, 350, 361, 379, 380, 381, 383, 437–446, 448, 451, 475, 476

Action science, *see* Action research

Activity, *see* Act

Actor, *see* Act

Affect, *see* Feelings

Agency, *see* Agent

Agent, 7, 13, 14, 21, 22, 23, 24, 26, 27, 33, 38, 48, 156, 159, 160, 262, 264, 320, 469, 490

Agentic, *see* Agency

Alienated, *see* Alienation

Alienation, xiv, xv, xvi, xx, 27, 33, 60, 93–96, 97, 101, 102, 103, 107–112, 222, 247, 248, 266, 280, 330, 340, 346, 376, 402, 405, 406, 408, 410, 417, 421, 424, 432

Altered state of consciousness, *see* Consciousness

Analysis, 3, 4, 5, 6, 7, 14, 16, 26, 45, 46, 47, 48, 49, 50, 51, 59, 75, 97, 100, 111, 114, 127, 144, 145, 148, 149, 160, 169, 176, 178, 194, 199, 204, 206, 213, 219, 221, 222, 223, 225, 230, 243, 247, 253, 254, 258, 259, 260, 261, 270, 273, 277, 283, 286, 287, 288, 289, 291, 296, 298, 299, 300, 306, 310, 312, 345, 346, 351, 363, 364, 365, 374, 387, 388, 395, 396, 397, 398, 399, 409, 415, 416, 417,

419, 420, 421, 423, 425, 428, 434, 438, 441, 442, 443, 449, 451, 452, 453, 454, 455, 460, 461, 463, 464, 465, 466, 467, 468, 471, 487
Analytic scheme, *see* analysis
Analytic scientist, *see* Analysis
Anthropologist, *see* Anthropology
Anthropology, xvii, 80, 135, 183, 203, 220, 227, 228, 229, 230, 231, 232, 281, 386, 416, 417, 420, 426, 427, 438, 458, 462, 464, 466, 468, 470
Anthropomorphic, 79, 187, 228, 374
Anxiety, 67, 72, 77, 78, 79, 81, 85, 86, 126, 214, 238, 244, 278, 349, 364, 397, 422, 480, 481
Applied behavioural science, *see* Applied research
Applied research, xvii, 93, 96, 120, 175, 259, 263, 264, 477
Attention, 67, 81, 122, 143, 144, 145, 146, 147, 148, 149, 150, 151, 161, 178, 187, 221, 223, 224, 225, 243, 244, 245, 286, 312, 333, 336, 340, 346, 370, 377, 380, 382, 296, 396, 398, 429, 432, 435, 437, 438, 439, 441, 442, 443, 445, 446, 452, 474, 487
Authenticity, xvii, 33, 88, 102, 103, 107–112, 121, 214, 331, 402, 404, 406, 408, 409, 431
Autonomy, 21, 24, 29, 34, 35, 46, 47, 48, 121, 134, 235, 263, 369, 460, 461, 489

Behaviour, xxiii, 4, 5, 9, 10, 15, 16, 17, 20, 21, 22, 23, 24, 25, 50, 65, 67, 77, 79, 81, 83, 87, 93, 124, 127, 128, 129, 143, 146, 147, 148, 149, 167, 177, 178, 195, 200, 216, 217, 231, 244, 299, 300, 308, 309, 313, 314, 335, 336, 337, 338, 339, 341, 344, 345, 346, 374, 375, 381, 417, 422, 423, 428, 429, 437, 438, 439, 440, 441, 442, 443, 446, 461, 466
Behaviourism, *see* Behaviour
Being, 31, 32, 71, 97, 98, 99, 100, 101, 107, 114, 118–121, 129, 147, 214, 216, 401–404, 422, 431, 463
Being in the world, *see* Being
Biology, 5, 21, 67, 76, 80, 128, 242, 463, 465

Capitalism, 60, 120, 458, 460

Care, 84, 85, 203, 204, 205
Case studies, 56, 186, 189, Chapters 22–33, 417, 469
Catalytic validity, *see* Validity
Categories, 4, 49, 71, 84, 86, 111, 122, 136, 160, 161, 164, 165, 176, 210, 228, 248, 249, 258, 259, 260, 270, 271, 277, 278, 280, 288, 290, 298, 338, 345, 346, 374, 375, 376, 377, 378, 379, 380, 381, 382, 383, 396, 397, 398, 422, 444, 447, 465, 468, 471
Categorization, *see* Categories
Causal-determinist, *see* Cause
Causal factors, *see* Cause
Causality, *see* Cause
Cause, 13, 14, 20, 21, 22, 46, 47, 48, 49, 55, 56, 57, 58, 59, 72, 114, 125, 127, 128, 129, 191, 197, 228, 249, 291, 307, 309, 310, 313, 352, 365, 375, 376, 379, 380
Change agent, *see* Agent
Circle, *see* Cycle
Co-counselling, 77, 78, 161, 162, 245, 246, 317
Coherence, 32, 131, 239, 241, 264, 399, 462
Collaboration, *see* Collaborative inquiry
Collaborative inquiry, xx, 113, 141–151, 242, 244, 247, 249, 264, 294, 300, 313, 319, 330, 333–347, 398, 409, 417, 421, 425, 428, 435, 437–446, 458, 459, 485, 486
Collusion, 164, 242, 244, 247, 326
Commitment, xvii, 12, 21, 28, 35, 37, 38, 41, 50, 86, 99, 102, 103, 105, 108, 110, 119, 126, 127, 134, 143, 146, 151, 155, 163, 164, 202, 203, 204, 205, 212, 217, 225, 226, 233, 267, 280, 305, 306, 316, 323, 328, 337, 339, 341, 383, 405, 409, 415, 417, 418, 419, 423, 424, 426, 427, 429, 431, 434
Communication, 23, 53, 68, 97, 100, 101, 102, 106, 107, 112, 115, 118–121, 123, 128, 129, 164, 196, 203, 211, 214, 230, 231, 233, 236, 247, 271, 285, 289, 304, 306, 307, 312, 326, 331, 350, 388, 401, 409–411, 419, 423, 425, 426, 428, 429, 430, 431, 432, 435, 452, 453, 462, 467, 468, 488, 491
Communion, 122, 469, 470
Conceptual humanist, *see* Humanism

Concreteness, 64, 65, 66, 89, 260, 265, 277, 285, 286, 289, 290, 312, 338, 375, 396, 437

Consciousness, xviii, xxii, 11, 12, 13, 22, 31, 81, 88, 94, 95, 98, 100, 111, 113, 114, 115–137, 146, 161, 162, 163, 164, 168, 244, 245, 264, 299, 350, 351, 397, 420, 424, 431, 439, 457, 458, 459, 471, 487, 488

Consciousness-raising, see Consciousness

Construe, see Construct

Construct, 22, 23, 24, 25, 26, 27, 28, 29, 30, 31, 32, 74, 122, 191–199, 240, 351, 365, 422, 468, 490

Constructive alternativism, see Personal construct research

Construing, see Construct

Contemplation, 89, 100, 111, 127, 211

Context, 37, 72, 102, 104, 109, 110, 129, 135, 144, 151, 189, 196, 203, 223, 225, 240, 258, 261, 262, 264, 277, 284, 290, 296, 299, 340, 351, 387, 396, 407, 408, 415, 417, 421, 423, 424, 428, 430, 459, 462, 477, 490

Context − free, see Context

Contradiction, 12, 40, 54, 59, 98, 99, 100, 103, 104, 107, 108, 109, 111, 114, 115, 125, 129–132, 136, 165, 168, 169, 170, 171, 222, 223, 229, 241, 249, 250, 262, 286, 291, 312, 313, 319, 320, 321, 326, 329, 330, 331, 401, 403, 404, 419, 420, 424, 429, 432, 490

Control, 34, 38, 46, 53, 54, 61, 68, 86, 110, 115, 118, 141, 142, 143, 154, 155, 156, 180, 186, 192, 193, 195, 254, 258, 261, 263, 264, 266, 307, 310, 311, 314, 316, 329, 337, 340, 343, 344, 350, 352, 361, 365, 403, 406, 408, 421, 423, 425, 429, 450, 454, 455, 464, 467, 469, 473

Control group, see Control

Cooperation, see Cooperative inquiry

Cooperative inquiry, 19, 24, 26, 30, 33, 48, 238, 287, 289, 307, 308, 458, 469

Co-participants, see Co-researchers

Co-researchers, 20, 22, 24, 30, 31, 50, 97, 101, 102, 110, 113, 136, 153–166, 262, 244, 245, 246, 247, 248, 249, 250, 395, 491

Co-subjects, see Co-researchers

Counternorms of science, xvi, 37, 38, 40, 41, 49, 51, 97

Countertransference, 77–81, 123, 244, 246

Creative, see Creativity

Creativity, xvi, 6, 20, 21, 22, 27, 29, 39, 44, 48, 55, 56, 59, 60, 61, 67, 75, 78, 85, 86, 98, 108, 116, 132, 136, 153, 166, 169, 189, 192, 193, 199, 208, 209, 213, 214, 216, 217, 228, 236, 237, 238, 240, 241, 287, 288, 290, 291, 297, 320, 337, 349, 350, 363, 364, 387, 402, 404, 417, 423, 425, 427, 428, 430, 431, 433, 435, 439, 441, 449, 461, 482, 485

Cycle, xvii, xix, 49, 93, 97–112, 117–121, 132, 156, 163, 168, 174, 175, 192, 193, 199, 247–249, 250, 316, 331, 341, 342, 350, 401–411, 418, 419, 427, 428, 429, 432, 489, 491, 492

Data, 17, 39, 40, 41, 44, 66, 69, 70, 71, 100, 107, 108, 111, 120, 121, 122, 126, 132, 141, 142, 144, 146, 148, 149, 150, 151, 176, 178, 180, 184, 185, 186, 188, 193, 195, 199, 205, 206, 208, 220, 222, 223, 224, 225, 230, 231, 234, 240, 242, 248, 249, 250, 255, 257, 258, 259, 260, 261, 262, 263, 264, 265, 268, 270, 277, 278, 288, 289, 296, 297, 298, 299, 300, 310, 311, 313, 315, 316, 317, 319, 320, 321, 322, 330, 331, 339, 343, 346, 365, 378, 380, 381, 395, 396, 397, 398, 399, 402, 407, 410, 416, 423, 428, 430, 434, 435, 437, 438, 439, 440, 441, 442, 443, 459, 460, 462, 474, 475, 479, 491

Deception, xiv, 109, 110, 118, 234, 406, 422

Deductive reasoning, 39, 186, 227, 345, 473

Defence mechanisms, see Defences

Defences, 85, 86, 161, 244, 278, 279, 318, 328, 329, 339, 349, 359, 402, 408, 425, 426, 434, 483

Defensive, see Defences

Democratic control, see Control

Demystification, 419, 421, 424, 433

Dependent variables, see variables

Determinism, xvi, 4, 20, 21, 22, 55, 56, 57, 58, 59, 114, 195, 243, 339, 365, 465, 490

Dialectical logic, see Dialectics

Dialectics, xviii, xix, 6, 38, 40, 46, 47, 48, 55, 56, 57, 59, 60, 93, 96, 98, 104,

107-112, 114, 121, 125, 129-132, 134, 135, 136, 165, 167, 171, 187, 188, 240, 241, 243, 244, 286, 289, 309, 311, 312, 314, 319-331, 363-372, 376, 404, 405, 407, 409, 410, 419, 424, 425, 427, 429, 430, 431, 434, 470, 471, 490

Dialogue, 23, 24, 53, 61, 111, 144, 147, 149, 211, 212, 214, 260, 263, 264, 265, 268, 293, 294, 295, 297, 298, 299, 300, 301, 308, 337, 349-361, 408, 410, 429, 433, 434, 445, 446, 453, 480, 482, 487

Diary, xviii, 149, 248, 297, 298, 299, 300, 315, 438, 440, 441

Disciplined attention, see Attention

Disciplined research feelings, see Feelings

Efficiency, see Positivist

Emotion, see Feelings

Empirical research, see Empiricism

Empiricism, xxi, 3, 14, 27, 30, 31, 32, 40, 46, 68, 88, 94, 120, 132, 142, 143, 146, 147, 149, 150, 151, 156, 159, 176, 184, 185, 186, 187, 188, 189, 193, 206, 239, 249, 254, 259, 344, 346, 370, 387, 388, 437, 439, 441, 442, 443, 445, 446, 459, 462, 464, 465

Empowering, see Power

Encounter, 26, 27, 28, 29, 30, 31, 32, 97, 98, 99, 100, 101, 102, 110, 111, 113, 118-121, 122, 156, 157, 158, 161, 211, 242, 244, 267, 268, 269, 288, 289, 293, 294, 296, 297, 320, 329, 331, 387, 388, 389, 406, 407-9, 411, 421, 424, 427, 431, 435, 474, 475, 476, 477, 478, 489

Endogenous research, xix, xx, 96, 102, 227-238, 267-281, 373, 376, 378, 379, 380, 381, 383

Enslaved, see Oppression

Epistemology, xix, 13, 27, 39, 43, 84, 128, 129, 227, 228, 229, 230, 242, 277, 434, 473, 476, 480, 484

Ethics, 40, 44, 63, 68, 91, 104, 107-112, 151, 125, 225, 237, 416, 422, 486

Ethnology, see Anthropology

Ethnography, see Anthropology

Ethnomethodology, xvii, xix, xxi, 96, 417

Ethogenic research, 16, 96, 373, 378

Evaluation research, 93, 96, 175, 179, 219-226, 291, 376, 423, 431, 433, 435, 448, 450, 451, 452

Existentialism, xvii, 70, 71, 96, 102, 125, 126, 127, 133, 136, 171, 194, 204, 211, 212, 280, 346, 421, 431

Experience, xi, xii, xv, 20, 24, 32, 33, 40, 49, 73, 78, 86, 87, 88, 89, 90, 98, 99, 100, 110, 111, 113, 116, 122, 125, 126, 129, 133, 136, 146, 149, 156, 157, 158, 161, 162, 163, 164, 165, 166, 167, 168, 169, 174, 186, 187, 195, 199, 203, 204, 206, 207, 208, 209, 210, 211, 212, 213, 214, 215, 216, 219, 224, 233, 241, 242, 243, 244, 245, 247, 248, 250, 253, 254, 255, 259, 264, 265, 268, 269, 278, 291, 295, 296, 300, 304, 305, 307, 308, 314, 316, 317, 320, 321, 329, 333, 336, 339, 340, 341, 346, 349, 350, 351, 361, 365, 369, 371, 373, 381, 382, 385, 387, 389, 401, 408, 409, 415, 419, 420, 424, 426, 427, 428, 429, 430, 431, 434, 435, 438, 439, 440, 443, 445, 447, 448, 449, 451, 452, 459, 460, 462, 463, 465, 468, 469, 470, 471, 473, 474, 479, 480, 482, 485, 486, 487, 491

Experiential analysis, see Experiential knowledge

Experiential knowledge, xvii, xx, 5, 9, 25, 26, 27, 28, 29, 30, 31, 84, 87, 89, 90, 96, 102, 127, 137, 149, 150, 151, 153-166, 183, 242, 249, 280, 320, 321, 331, 406, 417, 421, 430, 479, 485

Experiential research, see Experiential knowledge

Experiment, xi, xii, xiii, xvi, xvii, xx, 4, 6, 8, 10, 11, 12, 13, 14, 15, 16, 19, 23, 34, 39, 46, 55, 56, 66, 79, 80, 85, 86, 87, 93, 94, 96, 97, 99, 107, 108, 109, 110, 111, 112, 114, 120, 126, 142, 143, 144, 147, 148, 149, 176, 179, 183, 184, 185, 186, 187, 189, 191, 192, 193, 194, 195, 196, 197, 199, 226, 239, 240, 243, 247, 285, 288, 304, 306, 310, 321, 338, 339, 340, 344, 377, 381, 406, 407, 416, 417, 419, 420, 422, 438, 445, 481

Experimental research, see Experiment

Experimentalist, see Experiment

Exploitation, see Oppression

Fact(s), 3, 4, 5, 14, 17, 27, 32, 78, 88, 94, 104, 115, 133, 142, 143, 158, 175, 186, 209, 212, 231, 236, 237, 247, 316, 336, 350, 364, 365, 374, 387, 454

Fear, 85, 88, 168, 234, 235, 236, 278, 279, 297, 300, 301
Fear of knowing, see Fear
Feedback cycle, see Cycle
Feeling science, see Feelings; Science
Feelings, 9, 16, 37, 41, 44, 45, 49, 50, 51, 71, 72, 77, 85, 86, 87, 99, 110, 111, 115, 116, 117, 120, 121, 123, 124, 127, 148, 160, 161, 175, 186, 187, 198, 203, 208, 209, 210, 211, 212, 213, 214, 215, 216, 231, 232, 233, 235, 271, 278, 280, 299, 300, 315, 339, 340, 346, 364, 389, 396, 397, 398, 399, 410, 411, 425, 428, 429, 434, 439, 441, 442, 443, 444, 445, 446, 461, 486, 487, 490
Felt experience, see Experience
Female, xxii, xxiii, 51, 91, 97, 117, 229, 230, 245, 428, 458, 459, 460, 461, 462, 464, 466, 467, 470, 471
Feminism, xxi, xxii, xxiii, 133, 458, 459, 462, 463, 464, 465, 466
Field notes, see Diary
Financing of research, 41, 179, 403, 425, 426, 432, 450, 454, 455, 473–484
Freedom, 21, 22, 38, 125, 126, 189, 198, 199, 203, 267, 283, 329, 366, 369, 407, 416, 423, 467
Free-floating attention, see Attention
Funding of research, see Financing of research

Generalization, 24, 40, 44, 53, 56, 64, 65, 68, 96, 126, 143, 148, 184, 188, 240, 338, 365, 377, 381, 441, 442, 461, 468, 483, 490
Grid, see Repertory grid
Grounded theory, see Theory
Group therapy, see Psychotherapy

Hermeneutic Circle, see Hermeneutics
Hermeneutics, 132–135, 136, 240, 243, 244, 465
Heuristic research, xx, 207–217, 223
Holism, 47, 48, 83, 84, 183–189, 225, 226, 321, 322, 331, 378, 385, 387, 388, 490
Holistic, see Holism
Human inquiry, see Inquiry
Humanism, 45, 48, 49, 50, 51, 83, 363, 364, 365, 366
Humanistic psychology, xvi, 66, 180, 192, 205, 206, 421

Hypothesis, 19, 20, 64, 73, 96, 108, 109, 132, 153, 155, 156, 157, 158, 159, 160, 161, 162, 164, 169, 187, 189, 193, 194, 196, 199, 208, 217, 230, 232, 263, 287, 338, 345, 404, 442, 473
Hypothetical worlds, see Hypothesis

Ideology, 46, 47, 48, 49, 53, 54, 60, 61, 105, 116, 117, 122, 123, 131, 136, 290, 300, 304, 309, 310, 311, 314, 341, 383, 401, 446, 462, 480
Independent variables, see Variables
Inquiring systems see Inquiry
Inquiry, xi, xii, xiii, xiv, xvii, xviii, xix, xxii, xxiii, 19, 20, 21, 22, 23, 24, 26, 27, 31, 33, 39, 40, 41, 46, 47, 48, 49, 50, 78, 105, 108, 113, 114, 115, 126, 127, 132, 134, 136, 137, 141–151, 156, 157, 158, 160, 161, 162, 164, 166, 184, 185, 186, 189, 191, 192, 196, 203, 205, 206, 208, 211, 222, 239, 240, 242, 244, 245, 246, 247, 248, 250, 265, 293, 298, 299, 300, 301, 303, 309, 310, 311, 312, 313, 314, 319, 321, 330, 331, 337, 338, 340, 363, 364, 366, 368, 369, 370, 371, 376, 405, 408, 417, 421, 425, 437–446, 460, 469, 471, 479, 480, 485, 486, 487, 488, 489, 490, 491, 492
Intercommunication, see Communication
Interest(s), 34, 38, 47, 48, 49, 61, 66, 70, 71, 72, 75, 80, 85, 104, 105, 108, 111, 119, 125, 148, 149, 161, 167, 178, 195, 210, 212, 213, 231, 248, 259, 280, 294, 295, 297, 300, 303, 304, 306, 310, 352, 353, 361, 366, 367, 369, 374, 375, 376, 377, 378, 379, 380, 381, 383, 386, 420, 423, 426, 438, 440, 442, 445, 449, 451, 455, 462, 463, 475, 478, 479, 484, 486, 487, 488, 490, 491
Interesting, see Interest
Intersubjective, see Subjectivity
Intervening variables, see Variables
Intervention research, 96, 102, 104, 293, 298, 299, 300, 301, 336, 350, 361, 474
Intuition, xvi, 11, 37, 44, 45, 68, 86, 116, 117, 122, 123, 146, 147, 148, 151, 169, 209, 210, 212, 214, 216, 345, 364, 382, 388, 454
Intuitive judgement, see Intuition
Invasion, 53–61, 356, 351

Journal, *see* Diary

Knowledge, 3, 6, 9, 16, 19, 26, 27, 34,
  35, 38, 45, 46, 47, 48, 49, 50, 51, 55,
  60, 64, 80, 84, 85, 86, 87, 88, 89, 100,
  108, 127, 131, 133, 134, 135, 136, 137,
  142, 143, 144, 145, 146, 147, 148, 151,
  155, 165, 174, 178, 181, 185, 186, 197,
  211, 212, 217, 219, 222, 240, 241, 242,
  246, 249, 250, 259, 262, 264, 266, 294,
  303, 308, 309, 310, 311, 312, 316, 350,
  351, 364, 371, 376, 381, 387, 402, 405,
  407, 417, 421, 422, 428, 431, 434, 437,
  438, 442, 449, 450, 454, 456, 459, 460,
  462, 463, 469, 479, 488, 489, 490, 491

Language, xv, xxii, 6, 7, 9, 16, 24, 25,
  26, 27, 28, 29, 30, 31, 32, 33, 96, 97,
  106, 114, 145, 158, 159, 160, 161, 169,
  192, 194, 198, 199, 245, 260, 261, 264,
  265, 316, 351, 410, 417, 423, 435, 448,
  451, 453, 465, 466, 467, 468, 471, 489
Law(s), 3, 13, 14, 15, 17, 20, 21, 22, 65,
  114, 115, 186, 313, 421, 427, 464, 483
Law-like statements, *see* Law
Learning cycle, *see* Cycle
Legitimacy, *see* Ethics
Level of consciousness, *see* Consciousness
Liberation, 157, 162, 180, 349, 350, 464
Liberatory, *see* Liberation
Linguistics, *see* Language
Listening, 89, 107,111, 122, 204, 210,
  211, 214, 396, 402, 428, 435, 487
Lived experience, *see* Experience
Logic, xviii, 3, 4, 21, 40, 44, 46, 47, 48,
  49, 51, 59, 69, 86, 113, 114, 115, 120,
  125, 127, 128, 129, 131, 135, 143, 170,
  185, 186, 187, 189, 191, 227, 240, 364,
  360, 370, 371, 465, 468
Loose construing, *see* Construct
Love, 50, 78, 84, 85, 87, 91, 118, 130,
  131, 208

Machismo, *see* Male
Major contradiction, *see* Contradiction
Making sense, 97, 98, 100, 101, 102,
  111, 113–137 169, 196, 197, 377, 382,
  395–399, 401, 491
Male, xxi, xxii, xxiii, 41, 51, 91, 97, 117,
  229, 230, 403, 404, 428, 457–471, 485,
  487

Masculine, *see* Male
Mechanical, *see* Mechanism
Mechanism, 3, 6, 7, 14, 15, 16, 56, 57,
  60, 65, 66, 69, 79, 83, 85, 96, 103,
  128, 161, 179, 195, 205, 209, 313, 318,
  347, 349, 365, 423
Mechanistic, *see* Mechanism
Men, *see* Male
Methodology, xix, xx, xxi, 3, 10, 14, 16,
  20, 43, 45, 50, 51, 53, 54, 55, 58, 71,
  72, 146, 153, 192, 206, 217, 219, 220,
  221, 222, 226, 229, 230, 240, 244, 259,
  265, 267, 270, 311, 312, 319, 320, 321,
  331, 363, 364, 365, 366, 373, 376, 377,
  380, 381, 385, 386, 416, 417, 419, 424,
  425, 427, 439, 441, 453, 457, 459, 460,
  468, 470, 476, 480, 485
Misconstruing, *see* Construct
Model, xiv, 6, 7, 10, 14, 20, 21, 24, 26,
  33, 39, 40, 97, 98, 141, 142, 143, 144,
  145, 146, 147, 148, 149, 150, 151, 153,
  154, 155, 156, 173–181, 185, 186, 188,
  192, 228, 255, 256, 279, 288, 291, 330,
  331, 333, 365, 374, 389, 405, 415, 416,
  417, 419, 424, 427, 428, 429, 430, 431,
  433, 434, 437, 443, 453, 458, 460, 462,
  466, 467, 476, 490
Moral(s), 10, 11, 12, 13, 34, 35, 38, 91,
  195, 198, 461
Mutual self-study, *see* Action research
Mystification, 94, 245, 351, 423, 424,
  425, 456

Naive inquiry, *see* Inquiry
Natural order, *see* Nature
Natural science, *see* Science
Nature, 4, 8, 9, 21, 65, 115, 208, 209,
  228, 465
Neurosis, 41, 85, 86
New paradigm, *see* Paradigm
Non-alienating, *see* Alienation
Non-defensive, *see* Defences
Non-dialectical, *see* Dialectics
Non-linguistic, *see* Language
Non-reactive methods, *see* Unobtrusive
  measures
Norms, xvi, 21, 24, 26, 32, 33, 37, 38,
  46, 47, 48, 49, 53, 67, 72, 74, 97, 223,
  244, 312, 313

Objective science, *see* Objectivity
Objectivism, *see* Objectivity

Objectivity, xiii, xx, 40, 51, 60, 69, 71, 73, 77, 84, 85, 87, 88, 94, 110, 112, 114, 115, 116, 133, 136, 185, 196, 210, 211, 212, 241, 242, 244, 291, 310, 312, 316, 317, 365, 366, 386, 387, 399, 407, 409, 420, 425, 459, 461, 462, 463, 471, 479, 490

Observation, 3, 6, 7, 8, 9, 11, 14, 19, 20, 23, 50, 68, 73, 77, 78, 79, 80, 81, 93, 97, 110, 112, 145, 146, 147, 161, 167, 168, 169, 170, 171, 185, 186, 187, 188, 189, 209, 222, 224, 234, 240, 248, 255, 289, 298, 300, 315, 316, 317, 318, 319, 321, 335, 337, 344, 345, 366, 375, 387, 388, 409, 417, 433, 434, 435, 445, 466, 469

Observer, see Observation

Old paradigm, see Paradigm

Opposites, 5, 40, 41, 44, 46, 60, 97, 118, 129-132, 179, 187, 188, 195, 237, 241, 262, 300, 343, 350, 421, 459, 463

Opposition, see Opposites

Oppression, 53, 104, 166, 232, 350, 351, 403, 405, 449, 451, 461, 467, 486

Order, 85, 120, 204, 275, 309, 411, 431, 468

Organization, xvii, 34, 60, 67, 75, 128, 145, 146, 148, 149, 150, 151, 163, 174, 175, 220, 221, 222, 223, 224, 228, 254, 255, 256, 257, 258, 260, 262, 263, 265, 268, 291, 294, 295, 301, 303, 304, 306, 307, 308, 309, 310, 312, 313, 314, 317, 318, 336, 341, 344, 349, 351, 352, 353, 359, 360, 361, 366, 379, 381, 403, 407, 408, 416, 423, 437, 438, 439, 440, 441, 443, 450, 452, 453, 462, 469, 474, 476, 478, 479, 480, 481, 482, 483, 485

Organizational, see Organization

Paradigm, xi, xiii, xv, xvi, xix, xx, xxi, xxii, xxiii, 19, 20, 26, 30, 79, 93, 106, 113, 114, 116, 120, 122, 147, 148, 151, 158, 160, 161, 162, 163, 165, 171, 183, 185, 189, 226, 228, 239-250, 296, 299, 300, 311, 319, 321, 333, 345, 375, 387, 401, 415-435, 459, 464, 470, 471, 473, 479, 481, 482, 483, 485, 486, 487, 488, 489, 490, 491, 492

Paradox, see Dialectics

Participant observation, see Participation

Participation, xii, xvii, xix, xx, 23, 34, 50, 78, 94, 96, 102, 103, 127, 146, 147, 148, 149, 153, 164, 168, 169, 170, 183, 186, 187, 189, 195, 203, 204, 219, 220, 222, 224, 225, 253-266, 283-291, 293, 303-314, 321, 334, 335, 338, 339, 340, 341, 346, 347, 361, 373, 374, 375, 376, 377, 378, 379, 380, 381, 382, 388, 395, 417, 420, 434, 435, 437, 438, 439, 440, 442, 445, 449-456, 468, 469, 470, 483, 486, 489

Participative, see Participation

Particular humanist, see Humanism

Patriarchy, xxii, 107-112, 115, 403, 405, 407, 408, 410, 462, 469, 471

Pattern(s), 3, 6, 7, 9, 14, 15, 16, 44, 56, 57, 65, 66, 67, 68, 70, 71, 74, 104, 105, 107, 108, 109, 110, 111, 124, 126, 128, 136, 161, 167, 183, 184, 185, 186, 188, 209, 211, 212, 213, 214, 217, 229, 246, 260, 264, 273, 275, 290, 320, 322, 330, 331, 337, 338, 342, 343, 346, 378, 379, 403, 407, 421, 430, 439, 442, 443, 446, 460, 465, 466, 469, 489, 490

Pattern model, see Model

Peak experience, 73, 84, 85, 86, 88

Perception, 9, 27, 28, 29, 79, 80, 81, 100, 126, 158, 191, 196, 210, 229, 242, 264, 307, 310, 317, 318, 407, 427, 429, 434, 445

Personal, 72, 73, 74, 97, 101, 103, 105, 108, 109, 115, 117, 119, 136, 143, 149, 150, 151, 158, 162, 167, 169, 192, 194, 195, 198, 199, 202, 211, 217, 225, 235, 238, 241, 244, 245, 246, 250, 260, 278, 295, 296, 306, 315, 320, 321, 337, 339, 346, 360, 361, 369, 388, 389, 395, 406, 407, 415, 417, 418, 420, 421, 424, 425, 426, 427, 428, 429, 430, 432, 434, 435, 438, 440, 459, 470, 471, 477, 479, 480, 481, 490

Personal construct research, 74, 96, 102, 191-199

Personal journal, see Diary

Personal knowledge, see Knowledge

Personal wholeness, see Personal

Personality, 63, 65, 66, 67, 69, 74, 76, 96, 115, 173, 189, 199, 224, 315-318, 353, 355, 360, 415, 418, 422, 424, 432

Personality development, see Personality

Phenomenology, xvii, xix, xx, xxi, 31, 84, 87, 96, 158, 160-162, 169, 197,

201, 204, 206, 217, 224, 385, 388, 417, 426, 490
Pilot work, 105, 255, 256, 263, 333, 334, 388, 490
Play, 86, 377, 422, 442
Politics, 12, 13, 34, 48, 49, 54, 55, 60, 61, 96, 104, 105, 107–112, 120, 134, 142, 144, 148, 151, 179, 181, 189, 195, 202, 213, 220, 221, 243, 253, 266, 287, 289, 290, 294, 300, 301, 309, 310, 311, 314, 336, 342, 344, 345, 346, 374, 403, 405, 407, 408, 410, 416, 420, 423, 425, 428, 435, 440, 447, 448, 450, 455, 459, 462, 464, 466, 468, 473, 479, 480, 486, 490
Positivism, xii, xiv, xx, 3, 4, 5, 7, 8, 9, 13, 14, 17, 68, 103, 105, 107–112, 189, 319, 405, 416, 422, 423, 464, 471
Power, 14, 34, 35, 99, 118, 129, 192, 205, 208, 214, 236, 238, 266, 279, 301, 316, 318, 340, 344, 346, 350, 371, 407, 416, 431, 432, 435, 457, 461, 469, 470, 482, 483, 487, 489, 490, 491
Practical knowledge, see Knowledge
Precision, 39, 41, 45, 85, 86, 96, 114, 165, 194, 249
Prediction, 3, 4, 9, 20, 57, 68, 69, 70, 71, 186, 193, 195, 310, 377, 490
Presentational construing, see Presentational knowledge
Presentational knowledge, 28, 29, 30, 31, 32, 165, 249, 488
Pre-set questions, see Questionnaire
Primal integration, 78, 162
Principal contradiction, see Contradiction
Problem(s), 40, 55, 61, 66, 68, 77, 78, 79, 97, 98, 107, 108, 124, 127, 167, 171, 174, 175, 176, 177, 178, 187, 188, 197, 198, 207, 208, 209, 214, 219, 220, 221, 222, 225, 244, 253, 255, 257, 258, 259, 260, 261, 262, 263, 285, 286, 287, 290, 291, 295, 296, 297, 303, 304, 305, 306, 307, 308, 310, 311, 317, 321, 337, 345, 346, 350, 351, 352, 353, 359, 360, 361, 363, 364, 365, 366, 370, 371, 373, 374, 375, 376, 377, 378, 380, 381, 382, 383, 396, 402, 404, 408, 415, 418, 419, 423, 424, 427, 431, 434, 440, 443, 449, 454, 468, 470, 471, 481, 483, 485, 486
Problem construction, see Problem
Problem-solving, see Problem

Problematizing, 54, 286, 351, 352, 359
Project(s), 16, 97, 98, 99, 101, 102, 103, 105, 109, 118–121, 122, 166, 170, 175, 176, 179, 237, 238, 248, 253, 254, 255, 256, 257, 262, 266, 267, 268, 269, 270, 279, 280, 281, 286, 287, 291, 296, 303, 308, 331, 336, 341, 342, 346, 349, 350, 352, 353, 373, 376, 378, 401, 405, 406–7, 410, 415, 416, 422, 423, 430, 431, 446, 454, 457,, 483, 485, 486, 488, 492
Propositional construing, see Propositions
Propositional knowledge, see Knowledge
Propositions, 19, 24, 26, 27, 28, 29, 30, 31, 32, 40, 64, 114, 127, 130, 153, 154, 155, 156, 157, 158, 159, 160, 165, 188, 241, 249, 255, 382, 488
Psychiatry, 63, 71, 72, 277, 417, 464
Psychoanalysis, see Psychotherapy
Psycho-logic, see Logic
Psychological, see Psychology
Psychology, 5, 8, 10, 13, 14, 15, 16, 17, 43, 44, 55, 63, 64, 65, 66, 67, 68, 69, 70, 71, 76, 80, 83, 84, 85, 86, 87, 128, 131, 133, 173, 175, 176, 177, 178, 180, 191–199, 206, 207, 232, 233, 238, 245, 253, 268, 269, 270, 316, 385, 386, 416, 420, 421, 422, 425, 426, 427, 428, 430, 432, 433, 443, 458, 459, 462, 463, 464, 478, 481
Psychotherapy, 59, 60, 71, 78, 81, 124, 161, 173, 183, 191, 196, 203, 204, 205, 211, 213, 245, 263, 266, 267, 317, 428, 462, 463

Qualitative, xx, 114, 206, 220, 249, 321, 345, 417, 426, 465, 469, 471, 479, 490
Quantitative, 220, 249, 345, 386, 426, 465, 469, 490, 491
Questionnaire(s), xviii, 12, 33, 72, 180, 191, 195, 196, 222, 233, 255, 265, 295, 296, 298, 300, 305, 313, 335, 336, 401, 441, 470, 483

Racism, see Patriarchy
Rationality, 21, 37, 38, 49, 50, 51, 86, 115, 116, 126, 127, 146, 167, 168, 170, 211, 365, 371, 474
Real world, see Reality
Realism, 3, 4, 5, 8, 46

Reality, xxii, 4, 5, 6, 14, 28, 29, 40, 59, 79, 80, 81, 85, 88, 89, 94, 99, 100, 104, 108, 115, 120, 122, 124, 126, 142, 148, 149, 158, 166, 187, 197, 199, 204, 209, 210, 211, 212, 224, 235, 241, 248, 261, 263, 299, 300, 303, 311, 313, 314, 316, 318, 330, 349, 351, 379, 380, 381, 388, 398, 401, 406, 407, 424, 427, 434, 439, 441, 442, 449, 450, 454, 455, 460, 463, 468, 469

Reasoning, see Thinking

Receptivity, 81, 83, 84, 89, 160

Recursive validity, see Validity

Reductionism, xiv, 83, 84

Reflexivity, xx, 20, 108, 167, 168, 192, 194-6, 199, 415

Reintegration, 77, 317-8

Relevance, 104, 107-112, 119, 191, 231, 232, 233, 234, 235, 248, 279, 280, 299, 300, 303, 345, 375, 379, 478, 487

Reliability, 45, 46, 68, 69, 73, 74, 87, 118, 149, 184, 277, 291, 338, 344, 346

Religion, 86, 142, 196, 228

Reorganization, see Organization

Repertory grid, 74, 196, 197

Research action, see Action research

Rigour, xx, 46, 85, 105, 142, 143, 145, 164, 184, 189, 244, 245, 248, 249, 346, 388

Role(s), 94, 101, 102, 103, 108, 109, 110, 117, 120, 155, 184, 206, 225, 226, 253, 254, 255, 257, 261, 262, 263, 264, 265, 288, 290, 291, 294, 300, 305, 308, 310, 312, 313, 316, 317, 351, 352, 355, 377, 405, 406, 417, 420, 423, 424, 433, 435, 450, 455, 464, 487, 491

Rule(s), 24, 25, 109, 192, 223, 225, 238, 406, 426

Science(s), xii, xvi, xviii, xxiii, 4, 5, 6, 7, 8, 9, 12, 19, 20, 27, 30, 33, 37, 38, 39, 40, 41, 43, 44, 45, 46, 47, 48, 49, 50, 51, 53, 63, 64, 65, 66, 67, 68, 76, 77, 79, 80, 81, 83, 86, 87, 88, 89, 90, 91, 93, 97, 107, 112, 114, 115, 120, 126, 128, 132, 133, 141, 142, 143, 144, 145, 146, 148, 150, 151, 163, 165, 167, 168, 171, 173, 174, 175, 176, 177, 178, 179, 180, 183, 184, 185, 187, 191, 192, 193, 194, 195, 198, 199, 209, 211, 212, 216, 217, 220, 228, 229, 240, 253, 259, 260, 261, 262, 265, 266, 268, 277, 291, 303, 308, 309, 310, 311, 312, 316, 320, 333, 344, 345, 346, 363, 364, 365, 368, 369, 371, 375, 381, 386, 404, 409, 415, 416, 421, 423, 425, 426, 427, 428, 434, 435, 437, 438, 439, 441, 442, 443, 444, 460, 462, 463, 464, 465, 469, 471, 473, 479, 483

Scientific method, see Science

Scientific paradigm, see Paradigm

Scientism, see Science

Self, 10, 11, 12, 13, 64, 71, 72, 73, 75, 78, 80, 81, 112, 115, 119, 120, 121, 123, 124, 125, 127, 168, 177, 183, 189, 208, 209, 214, 216, 238, 245, 246, 247, 317, 318, 320, 321, 326, 329, 385, 388, 410, 422, 428, 442, 457, 489, 490, 491

Self-actualization, see Self

Self-contradiciton, see Contradiction

Self-determination, 21, 22, 34, 35, 49, 110, 121, 159, 164, 331, 402, 405, 488, 489, 490

Self-direction, see Self-determination

Self-knowledge, see Self

Self-study in action, see Action research

Sensation, 3, 4, 9, 37, 44, 45, 117, 126, 211, 212

Sexism, see Patriarchy

Shared power, see Power

Social change, 93, 96-97, 174, Chapters 22-33, 421, 458, 466, 489

Social-linguistic, see Language

Social science, see Science

Social scientists, see Science

Sociology, xvii, xviii, 43, 46, 47, 48, 49, 183, 245, 268, 270, 386, 416, 420, 421, 434, 438, 460, 461, 462, 468, 469, 471

Speculation, 39, 57, 60, 119, 121, 187, 192, 193, 194, 216, 254, 307, 473

Spiral, 105, 135, 174, 430

State of consciousness, see Consciousness

Statistics, xi, xiii, xiv, 13, 14, 66, 68, 69, 97, 111, 118, 119, 120, 144, 164, 191, 217, 220, 226, 233, 338, 345, 346, 409, 419, 421, 441, 442, 451, 469, 479

Structural, see Structure

Structure(s), 4, 8, 14, 15, 16, 25, 34, 43, 56, 57, 58, 60, 64, 66, 72, 74, 100, 102, 104, 115, 118, 124, 128, 129, 144, 146, 147, 176, 177, 195, 211, 222, 223,

227, 228, 230, 242, 244, 245, 248, 265, 266, 301, 308, 309, 312, 313, 339, 341, 349, 350, 352, 353, 355, 359, 360, 361, 371, 377, 396, 397, 399, 420, 421, 425, 426, 429, 431, 433, 435, 448, 453, 454, 455, 460, 462, 467, 468, 469, 481, 484, 487

Structurism, see Structure

Subject(s), xvi, xviii, 19, 20, 21, 22, 23, 26, 30, 31, 33, 34, 35, 48, 53, 64, 74, 75, 79, 81, 93, 94, 97, 101, 102, 103, 110, 111, 112, 113, 118, 136, 142, 144, 147, 150, 153, 154, 155, 156, 177, 178, 179, 180, 187, 194, 195, 196, 197, 199, 248, 253, 254, 271, 279, 289, 299, 300, 303, 310, 312, 314, 315, 316, 321, 385, 388, 407, 408, 409, 411, 417, 421, 422, 423, 426, 427, 428, 429, 431, 435, 483, 489

Subjective science, see Subjectivity

Subjectivism, see Subjectivity

Subjectivity, xiii, 37, 55, 56, 57, 59, 71, 78, 79, 87, 91, 115, 116, 117, 121, 123, 124, 136, 144, 186, 189, 195, 216, 224, 240, 241, 242, 243, 244, 320, 321, 329, 341, 365, 375, 386, 409, 420, 425, 439, 459, 463, 470, 471, 477, 490

Symbol(s), 23, 24, 26, 27, 29, 31, 32, 33, 100, 116, 123, 126, 147, 148, 154, 159, 166, 201, 268, 322, 345, 389, 405, 465, 467

Symbolizing, see Symbol

Tacit assumptions, see Tacit knowledge

Tacit knowledge, 4, 7, 21, 25, 26, 30, 134, 209, 426, 490

Tao, 26, 30, 89, 91, 117, 130

Theorist(s), see Theory

Theory, xi, xii, xix, xx, 3, 4, 5, 7, 9, 11, 13, 14, 16, 31, 39, 44, 45, 46, 47, 57, 59, 66, 77, 78, 79, 84, 87, 88, 96, 99, 113, 114, 120, 128, 130, 134, 141, 142, 143, 144, 146, 147, 148, 149, 157, 159, 160, 161, 164, 165, 169, 174, 175, 177, 183, 186, 187, 188, 189, 191, 192, 194, 196, 197, 198, 209, 223, 224, 230, 232, 233, 240, 244, 247, 248, 249, 258, 260, 261, 262, 263, 264, 268, 270, 277, 279, 286, 287, 289, 290, 291, 307, 308, 310, 311, 312, 314, 315, 316, 317, 319, 320, 321, 330, 331, 336, 337, 338, 349, 350, 351, 363, 364, 365, 366, 370, 371, 372, 374, 375, 376, 377, 378, 379, 380, 381, 388, 397, 416, 422, 430, 434, 437, 439, 440, 441, 443, 444, 450, 457, 458, 459, 460, 462, 463, 464, 466, 467, 468, 470, 473, 474, 475, 476, 483, 488, 489, 490

Theory-building, see Theory

Therapy, see Psychotherapy

Thinking, 37, 44, 45, 79, 97, 98, 99, 100, 101, 102, 108, 113, 114, 116, 118-121, 122, 125, 128, 129, 132, 136, 153, 192, 217, 224, 226, 227, 247, 249, 286, 363, 369, 376, 377, 378, 382, 397, 404-5, 410, 411, 422, 423, 425, 427, 428, 429, 432, 440, 441, 442, 443, 444, 445, 446, 463, 468, 476, 485

T'iai Chi, see Tao

Traditional logic, see Logic

Traditional mode, see Model

Training (of researchers) xviii, 288, 291, 312, 415-435, 437-446

Transcendent experience, see Peak experience

Truth(s), xiii, 27, 32, 33, 39, 40, 44, 47, 96, 105, 112, 114, 115, 120, 136, 143, 158, 164, 165, 170, 176, 185, 196, 224, 239, 241, 242, 243, 346, 374, 425, 428, 450, 464, 487, 491

Unconscious, xvi, xxi, 44, 54, 59, 61, 77, 78, 80, 81, 95, 107, 244, 246, 349, 397, 463

Unilateral control, see Control

Unobtrusive measures, 93, 109, 441

Unpredictability, see Prediction

Unscientific, see Science

Unstructured, see Structure

Validity, xxi, 33, 40, 46, 53, 65, 68, 69, 71, 103, 105, 131, 133, 134, 135, 136, 145, 146, 147, 148, 149, 150, 151, 156, 163, 164, 165, 176, 184, 185, 187, 194, 197, 214, 224, 233, 239-250, 277, 291, 299, 300, 338, 345, 346, 347, 365, 371, 376, 398, 399, 421, 438, 441, 442, 443, 460, 462, 463, 464, 470, 488

Value(s), 24, 32, 33, 41, 44, 51, 53, 64, 71, 73, 75, 84, 85, 86, 90, 91, 102, 131, 143, 148, 176, 178, 179, 196, 214, 215, 220, 224, 225, 233, 246, 249, 254,

300, 301, 331, 341, 345, 350, 369, 370, 371, 381, 387, 398, 399, 409, 434, 440, 442, 444, 457, 461, 469, 479, 480, 488, 490, 491
Value-free, 33, 46, 47, 48, 51, 90, 108, 206, 404
Variables, xiii, xiv, xvi, xxiii, 69, 71, 79, 93, 115, 146, 147, 149, 164, 184, 198, 199, 240, 321, 342, 417, 421, 422, 437, 442, 469, 483

Vested interests, *see* Interests
Vicious circle, *see* Cycle

Wholistic, *see* Holistic
Women, xxi, xxii, xxiii, 41, 91, 180, 245, 285, 286, 288, 290, 385, 397, 457–471, 487
Wonder, 86, 87

Yin/Yang, *see* Tao